COMPARATIVE CORPORATE LAW

■ ■ ■

by

Marco Ventoruzzo
Penn State Law, USA, and Bocconi University, Milan

Pierre-Henri Conac
University of Luxembourg

Gen Goto
University of Tokyo

Sebastian Mock
University of Hamburg

Mario Notari
Bocconi University, Milan

Arad Reisberg
University College London

AMERICAN CASEBOOK SERIES®

WEST
ACADEMIC
PUBLISHING

American Casebook Series is a trademark registered in the U.S. Patent and Trademark Office.

© 2015 LEG, Inc. d/b/a West Academic
    444 Cedar Street, Suite 700
    St. Paul, MN 55101
    1-877-888-1330

West, West Academic Publishing, and West Academic are trademarks of West Publishing Corporation, used under license.

Printed in the United States of America

ISBN: 978-1-62810-203-1

When I was young my teachers were the old.
I gave up fire for form till I was cold.
I suffered like a metal being cast.
I went to school to age to learn the past.
Now when I am old my teachers are the young.
What can't be molded must be cracked and sprung.
I strain at lessons fit to start a suture.
I go to school to youth to learn the future.

— Robert Frost (1874–1963)

Quand bien nous pourrions être savants du savoir d'autrui, au moins sages ne pouvons-nous être que de notre sagesse.

We can be knowledgeable with other men's knowledge, but we can't be wise with other men's wisdom.

— Michel de Montaigne (1533–1592)

井の中の蛙大海を知らず。

A frog in a well does not know the great sea.

— Japanese proverb

AUTHORS' NOTE

The Authors donate all the royalties of this book to the Equal Justice Initiative (EJI) of Montgomery, Alabama, USA.

The EJI is a private, nonprofit organization that provides legal representation to indigent defendants and prisoners who have been denied fair and just treatment in the legal system. Its attorneys litigate on behalf of condemned prisoners, juvenile offenders, people wrongly convicted or charged with violent crimes, poor people denied effective representation, and others whose trials are marked by racial bias or prosecutorial misconduct. EJI works with communities that have been marginalized by poverty and discouraged by unequal treatment. The EJI also prepares reports, newsletters, and manuals to assist advocates and policymakers in the critically important work of reforming the administration of criminal justice.

For more information, see http://www.eji.org/.

"Injustice anywhere is a threat to justice everywhere." (Martin Luther King Jr., "Letter from a Birmingham Jail")

FOREWORD

There are countless books on corporate law of practically all countries and there are many casebooks covering corporate law. But nearly all of them deal with the corporate law of specific states. More recently there are also books and occasionally casebooks on European company law. But in a globalized world corporate law is becoming today more and more international. Corporations are not only producing and selling across the borders and throughout the world, but also look for the most attractive place to incorporate. There is a clear and healthy competition of corporate legislators, not only in the United States where Delaware—for reasons which still are hotly debated—has emerged as the one which has attracted most US corporations, but more and more also in Europe. Fiat, the famous Italian automobile company, leaving Italy in 2014 is one of the most recent examples. But also for those corporations that stick to their home country like most large enterprises do—voluntarily or under pressure from their home countries—foreign corporate laws are important since these corporations are active in many other countries and are doing business not only by branches, but by subsidiaries that are incorporated under the law of their host states. Neglecting or even violating the law of other countries can have far-reaching and sometimes even devastating consequences as shown by the example of American and European investment banks that had and have to pay billions of dollars in fines. In a few instances and for specific reasons, both historical and commercial, one can find truly international corporations such as Shell that have formed organizations that are rooted in two countries, though this is complicated not only in law, but even more so in practice because of contrasting corporate cultures, and a good number of them have given up to become national corporations again.

This shows a clear need for knowing more about comparative corporate law. But need is something, intellectual and theoretical legal interest is another. Ideally both go together—for the students of corporate law, but also for their teachers. For all of them the casebook by Marco Ventoruzzo, Pierre-Henri Conac, Gen Goto, Sebastian Mock, Mario Notari, and Arad Reisberg comes at the right moment and with the best possible practical and intellectual offer.

After an important methodological note that is not to be skipped because it explains who the addressees of the book are and how the book is conceived, comparative corporate law is presented in 12 chapters. These chapters are designed in a way that all key problems of modern corporate law are dealt with, and this in a way that students will grasp the essence of corporate law and teachers will enjoy teaching the students with the help of this casebook. Chapter 1 presents the building blocks and explains the economic forces that lead to considerable convergence of the national corporate law, without neglecting the historical, economic, and, for many reasons, path-dependent circumstances that prevent full convergence and explain why many divergences remain. The "end of corporate law" that has been diagnosed by some American academics is an original theory, but has not become true in practice and will not become so in the foreseeable future. Factors that are relevant in this context are not only the existence of different legal families, a concept dear to traditional comparativists, but more so the shareholder structure in various countries, insider and outsider systems, differences in capital markets and securities regulation, more or less shareholders rights, court systems, and legal culture. Chapter 2 focuses on the choice of applicable corporate laws and regulatory competition both in the United States and in Europe with a glimpse also at Japan. It is highly relevant and interesting to see the different historical settings and possibly also historical stages in which these countries and their corporate laws are. The practical problems in the European Union have courageously been dealt with by the European Court of Justice in a number of landmark cases, while an academic controversy is raging on the consequences of regulatory competition: race to the bottom, the traditional fear, and race to the top, a more modern vision that has good points, but may be exaggerated.

The next seven chapters deal with corporate law from the "birth" to the "death" of the corporation. This is the best way to teach and learn corporate law, namely, starting with the incorporation process and, if successful, limited liability which of course must have certain limits (Chapter 3), continuing with the financing of the corporation which is most obviously the crucial point (Chapter 4), coming to organizing and running the corporation in the best possible way in a modern world, corporate governance (Chapter 5), dealing with the board and directors' duties and holding the directors responsible by way of shareholder litigation (Chapters 6 and 7), and selecting two important corporate phenomena—shareholder agreements (Chapter 8) and M & A (mergers and acquisitions, Chapter 9). Each of these chapters presents most important practical issues that at the same time are theoretically intriguing, for example:

- the relevance or possibly irrelevance of legal capital (a notorious controversy between common law and many civil law countries) and the eminently dangerous veil piercing in Chapter 3;

- financing the corporation by shares or debentures or hybrid forms of finances (with important consequences for shareholders and creditors in case of crisis and insolvency) in Chapter 4;

−   corporate governance under the one-tier and the two-tier system and
    duties and liability of directors, a highly topical issue in particular
    after the financial crisis and in the light of the dramatic abuses in
    the American and European banking industry (Chapter 5, 6, and 7);

−   voting agreements, their practical relevance and the issue whether
    they can be enforced before the courts in Chapter 8; and

−   "bringing corporations together" by the various forms of mergers and
    acquisitions, an art that has been developed by American and
    English law firms and has spread to Europe and all over the world,
    making use not only of corporate law, but more so of tax law, and
    creating problems for shareholders and creditors that have to be met
    by corporate law, in Chapter 9.

The remaining three chapters deal with takeovers and insider
trading, two of the most interesting practical and theoretical areas on the
borderline of corporate law and securities regulation (Chapters 10 and
11), and international corporate litigation and arbitrations, i.e., how
corporate law is enforced, a question that is already intriguing on a
merely national level, but much more so in the international context
(Chapter 12). The authors of the casebook must be congratulated to have
included these three chapters. Most of the national corporate law
treatises and casebooks remain purely doctrinal and stick to corporate
law in its traditional narrow sense. But modern reality is different:
corporate law and securities regulation are close neighbors and
sometimes it is a historical coincidence whether capital market problems
are dealt with in corporate law (take the European takeover directive
which originally was conceived as 13th company law directive, but
actually is dealing with the takeover market and the duties of the bidder
and target and their directors at this market) or by securities regulation
(as in the 1930sin the United States with its securities regulation that
had a global advance and impact on company and capital market law
around the world).

Practitioners have long known that corporate law is only as good as it
is enforceable by the parties and as it will be enforced by the state.
International corporate law in particular teaches the lesson that
sometimes enforcement of corporate law is more important than
substantive corporate law. The law and finance movement is aware of
this. Therefore modern corporate law theory is more and more focusing on
enforcement and deals with such important questions as mandatory law
and enforcement—enforcement by market participants, market
disciplines and "soft law" (cf. the modern enforcement mechanisms of
comply and disclose or, today, comply and explain; and as practitioners
sometimes sigh: "comply and complain") and, if these forces come to their
limits, enforcement by courts. These courts are usually state courts,

sometimes supranational and international courts, and in corporate law practice today very often arbitral tribunals.

The casebook ends with a final note that the writer of this foreword supports with his experience in teaching, practicing as a judge, and counseling lawyers and legislators in many countries: What is crucial in every career and at each stage of it is extensive learning. Without learning a bricklayer cannot do his job and a lawyer will not be able to serve his clients, but will fail sooner or later. I often told my students: much better be a good bricklayer than a bad lawyer. But what is even more important: without constant learning practicing law and in particular practicing company law in the modern world is not only dangerous, but is no fun.

PROF. DR. DR. DR. H.C. MULT.
KLAUS J. HOPT, MCJ

MAX PLANCK INSTITUTE FOR
INTERNATIONAL AND
COMPARATIVE PRIVATE LAW,
HAMBURG

Hamburg, Spring 2015

ABOUT THE AUTHORS

Marco Ventoruzzo is Full Professor of Business Law at Penn State Law School, in the U.S., and at Bocconi University Law School, in Milan, Italy. He teaches Corporate Law, Securities Regulation, Comparative Corporate Law, and International Business Transactions. Professor Ventoruzzo has been the director of the Max Planck Institute of Luxembourg, and is currently a Scientific Member of this Institution; and is a Research Associate of the European Corporate Governance Institute (ECGI). In addition to teaching in the United States and Italy, he has taught and lectured on comparative and international business law subjects at many Universities and Law Schools around the world, from Germany to India, from Spain to China, from Chile to Rwanda, from Brazil to Turkey, from Singapore to Israel. He is a managing editor of several peer-reviewed law journals, such as the *European Company and Financial Law Review*, the *Oxford Journal of Financial Regulation*, and the Italian *Rivista delle società*. His books and articles have been published in the United States, Europe, and India.

Pierre-Henri Conac is Professor of Commercial and Company Law at the University of Luxembourg. From 1999 to 2006, he was Associate Professor of Law at the University of Paris 1 (Panthéon-Sorbonne). He is also a Research Associate of the European Corporate Governance Institute (ECGI). His research areas deal principally with securities law, company law, and comparative law in these fields, especially with the United States. He has written numerous articles on corporate, securities, and comparative law, both in French and in English. He has been a member of several working groups in these areas, including the Reflection Group on the Future of EU Company Law of 2011 and the European Model Company Act (EMCA). In 2014, the European Commission appointed him as a member of its Informal Expert Group on Company Law (ICLEG). He is managing editor of the *Revue des Sociétés* (Dalloz), France's oldest corporate law review, and is a managing editor of the *European Company and Financial Law Review* (ECFR).

Gen Goto is Associate Professor of Law at the University of Tokyo, Graduate Schools for Law and Politics, in Japan (since 2010). He teaches Corporate Law, Payment Law, and Commercial Transactions. After graduating from the Faculty of Law at the University of Tokyo in 2003 (LLB), Professor Goto had been Assistant Professor at the University of Tokyo (2003–2006), and Lecturer and Associate Professor at Gakushuin University in Tokyo (2006–2010). He has also been a Researcher with the Japanese Ministry of Justice (2010–2013) and a Professional Member of the Financial System Council of the Japanese Financial Services Agency

(2011–2013). The research and contributions for this book were carried out during his stay at the East Asian Legal Studies Center of Harvard Law School as a visiting scholar (2013–2015), which was financially supported by the Postdoctoral Fellowship for Research Abroad of the Japan Society for the Promotion of Science.

Sebastian Mock is Associate Professor of Law at the University of Hamburg in Germany (since 2013). He teaches Corporate Law, Securities Regulation, Commercial and Bankruptcy Law. After studying at the Universities of Jena and Hamburg (both in Germany), Montpellier (France), and the New York University School of Law, Sebastian obtained a PhD in Law from the University of Hamburg in 2007 and finished his Habilitation in 2012. In addition to teaching in Germany Sebastian has also taught corporate and bankruptcy law in China, Russia, and Italy. His books and articles have been published in the United States and Europe.

Mario Notari is Full Professor of Corporate Law at Bocconi University of Milan and Director of the PhD. in business law at the University of Brescia. Previously he was Full Professor of Business Law at the University of Brescia. He has published extensively in Italian and European law journals and has authored or edited several books on corporate law, financial markets law, and competition law. He is a member of the boards of editors of several Italian law reviews and of several academic institutions. Legal consultant of many corporations and financial institutions, he is also member of the board of directors and/or auditors of some listed corporations.

Arad Reisberg is a Reader in Corporate and Financial Law at the Faculty of Laws, University College London (UCL) and Director, UCL Centre for Commercial Law. Between 2009 and 2012 Arad acted as the Faculty's Vice Dean (Research). He was formerly a Senior Arts Scholar (2001–2003) and a Tutor at Pembroke College Oxford and also taught law at six colleges at Oxford University (2001–2005). He has been a Visiting Lecturer at Oxford University (2005), a Lecturer at Warwick Law School (2005–2006), a Visiting Professor of Law at Brooklyn Law School (Fall Term 2012) and most recently (2014) a Visiting Professor of Law at NUS (Singapore). Arad is an Academic Member of ECGI (European Corporate Governance Institute). He is author of *Derivative Actions and Corporate Governance* (Oxford University Press, 2007), the first book to provide a detailed and theoretical explanation of the law governing derivative actions, co-editor of Pettet's *Company Law* 4th ed. (Pearson, 2012), and a contributing author to *Annotated Companies Legislation* 2nd ed. (Oxford University Press, 2012). Arad also sits on the Editorial Boards of the Journal *International Corporate Rescue* and the *Journal of Corporate Ownership and Control*.

SUMMARY OF CONTENTS

TABLE OF CONTENTS

TABLE OF CASES

The principal cases are in bold type.

---

xxvii

METHODOLOGICAL INTRODUCTION (DO NOT SKIP THIS)

This casebook has been designed to be used in different legal systems and for different courses, primarily for law students, but not only: also students of business administration, economics, political science, and international relationships can benefit from it. The book can be used in the basic course on corporations, as a complement to add a comparative and international dimension, and it can—more likely—be used in an upper-division course specifically dedicated to Comparative Corporate Law, or similar courses (Comparative Corporate Governance, Comparative Business Law, Comparative Corporate Finance, etc.).

We think and hope, however, that the book will also be useful for legal scholars, practitioners, regulators, and businesspeople more generally, in order to acquire or deepen their understanding of corporate law and of the international business context in which enterprises operate.

We followed a traditional casebook approach, and therefore the book contains numerous judicial decisions, statutory and other materials, and excerpts from scholarly contributions, often translated into English from different languages. In the light of the subject, and the fact that course participants might not be familiar with the different issues and legal systems discussed, however, we wrote fairly extensive introductions and connecting paragraphs that are helpful to frame the discussion and for at-home study. We also put a significant effort in identifying "Notes and Questions" for each case or material that can facilitate both class discussion and individual study. Obviously the instructor can decide whether to formally assign these parts of the book; our suggestion, however, is not to neglect them. We wanted this book to be the "missing link" between a traditional casebook, which often provides little background context for the cases and materials reprinted; and a manual, which offers more extensive explanations but does not include cases and materials to assign and discuss in class.

In translating foreign materials, especially court decisions, we often had to take some liberties and avoid a literal translation in order to make the documents more accessible for an international, English-speaking audience. We believe we have always, however, faithfully conveyed the substance of the materials. Notwithstanding these liberties and our best efforts, some foreign judicial opinions, statutes and contractual provision might at first sound strange, especially if you are not familiar with the style, approach and technical issues of the jurisdictions. Consider these possible initial difficulties part of the comparative experience. We have also taken some minor liberties with the editing and formatting of the other materials originally in English, especially scholarly contributions, for the sake of readability.

Our focus is primarily on the U.S., U.K., major European continental civil law systems (France, Germany, Italy) and European Union law, and Japan; but we also occasionally consider other jurisdictions in different continents (you will find references, for example, to Brazil, China, India and Spain). Any comparative analysis requires a selection of the systems considered: the ambition to cover everything is illusory and leads to superficiality. Our selection, however, takes into account a good variety of different legal families, and offers the occasion to illustrate the principles underlying the major corporate law models in the world. Naturally the discussion can and should be integrated and enriched by the instructor and the participants with additional information and insights from specific legal systems they are particularly interested in or familiar with.

We often (not always) start our analysis with the U.S. perspective. This is not to be U.S.-centric, but it is because we think that a consistent starting point is useful to organize the discussion in a coherent and effective way. In this perspective, U.S. students can learn or review some basic concepts of U.S. corporate law before dwelling in the comparative analysis (something too often forgotten or taken for granted in comparative courses in the U.S.). Non-U.S. students, on the other hand, can learn about the U.S. system and have a clear starting point to investigate the different systems considered.

We generally identify the underlying economic or substantive problems in order to discuss legal strategies followed by legislators, policy makers, and judges to regulate the phenomenon considered, and by lawyers and parties to achieve a desired result. We debate the causes and consequences of legal rules, and their interactions with economic events, sometimes also in light of empirical data and statistical evidence.

In terms of balance between general principles and more technical details, we tried to strike a reasonable compromise. We emphasize broad and profound differences among legal systems, but we also examine analytically provisions and court rulings. We believe that this combination allows developing both theoretical and practical skills. A comparative perspective, especially in a casebook, might sometimes appear less systematic than an in-depth analysis of one single system. Of course, this is only natural, and our goal is to offer food for thought in a clear framework, partially leaving to the instructor and the students the task of systematizing the ideas and information contained in this book.

As with any book, many people should be thanked for helping us with this project. In fact, if all the authors would thank everyone who, in different capacities, offered comments, ideas, and more generally taught us something, the list would be overwhelming, and we would almost certainly forget someone. We limit ourselves, therefore, to thanking all our students, colleagues, and mentors around the world whose intellectual curiosity, passion for learning, insights and criticisms inspired our research and teaching.

We want however to specifically thank Jake Niemyer for excellent research assistance and for his willingness to also help us with the less exciting administrative tasks related to the completion of the manuscript; Elizabeth Robinson and Angelo Borselli for reviewing a first draft; and (in order of appearance) Catherine A. Rogers, Matteo Erede, Joan MacLeod Heminway, Franklin A. Gevurtz and Giulio Sandrelli for offering suggestions and pointing at omissions or mistakes. Sherri Prosser, Wanda Boone, Cristina Di Siro and Monia Morello provided indispensable administrative assistance. The support and enthusiasm of our editors at West Academic Press, and in particular James Cahoy, were very important to keep us going. We also wish to express our gratitude to Laura Holle, Cathy Lundeen and Greg Olsen at West. Bocconi University, Penn State Law School and the Max Planck Institute of Luxembourg facilitated the project in different and valuable ways.

Please note that this book is a work in progress: we envision future editions, and we welcome all the observations, suggestions, and corrections that the readers might want to send our way (at marco.ventoruzzo@unibocconi.it or mxv23@psu.edu).

In the first chapter, we start by pointing out the reasons why studying Comparative Corporate Law is not only important from a cultural and pedagogical point of view, but also practically. And, we hope, it can also be challenging but interesting, and sometimes... fun!

Because, as Augustine of Hippo wrote in his Confessions, "The mind is nourished only by that which makes it rejoice."

COMPARATIVE CORPORATE LAW

CHAPTER 1

COMPARATIVE CORPORATE LAW: THE BUILDING BLOCKS

■ ■ ■

WHY STUDY COMPARATIVE CORPORATE LAW?

The question mark at the end of the title of this section should probably not be there. The reasons to learn about comparative corporate law should be self-evident, and they are both practical and theoretical.

On the one hand, there are practical reasons. "Globalization," to employ an abused term, has blurred national boundaries: international commerce, multinational corporations, cross-border transactions are growing and dominate the economy. In this scenario, most lawyers, businesspeople, economists, judges, regulators, and legislatures deal regularly with corporate activity that has an international dimension. Unfortunately, both in the U.S. and in other countries, there is still a lot of ignorance of foreign legal systems. This is partially due to the traditional "local" and "domestic" dimension of most legal professions. If on the one hand it is essential for jurists to know their own systems like the back of their hand, we can no longer afford to ignore at least the basics of corporate law in different legal systems. Of course none can be an expert in corporate law in all legal systems, and when dealing with complex transactions or litigation, local legal counsels are not only legally and ethically required, but also necessary as a matter of fact. Legal scholars, lawyers, executives, judges, policy makers, should however be able to interact intelligently with their foreign counterparties, to understand what the key issues are, and to be able to ask the important questions. The goal of this book is to offer a general framework and some specific technical insights about different corporate law systems that should help you, when facing an international problem, to understand where the "red flags" could be. We will explain and discuss specific rules and approaches in a quite technical and detailed fashion, also putting them in their economic and socio-political context, but most importantly we will try to offer a methodology, a way of looking at business problems that should enrich your ability to operate internationally. Imagine you are negotiating an international merger, litigating a case involving directors' liability in a multinational corporate group setting, sitting on the board of directors of a foreign corporation, drafting new legislation in the area of takeovers: familiarity with different legal systems can certainly make you more effective.

This book and a comparative corporate law course have however also theoretical and pedagogical goals. To study different legal systems, to understand why they regulate similar economic phenomena differently, and to question the rationale of precedents and of statutory and regulatory provisions from different jurisdictions, are unique ways to both understand better your own system, and to think "out of the box" and not take anything for granted. It expands your "mental library" of cases and rules that might be useful to think creatively or advocate more effectively. A Japanese case, for example, might offer you an idea if you are involved in regulatory reform in Mexico; a provision of the German Corporation Law might suggest to you how to frame an argument in a trial in the U.S.; an insight of a French scholar might be useful to lobby for legal reform in Singapore, and so on.

Interestingly enough, if you think about it, even in the basic course on Corporations there is almost always an element of comparative law. This is for sure the case in the United States: corporate law is regulated by the states, and only partially by the federal government, with the consequence that there are 50 different corporate law systems. Of course the differences among them are not extremely profound, also because several states follow the Model Business Corporation Act, and of course there are some particularly important jurisdictions, such as Delaware, New York, and California on which often the course focuses. But some differences exist and when you study corporate law in the U.S. (as well as with many other courses) you are, in a way, already engaging in a comparative exercise. Similarly, in the European Union, corporate law is regulated at the state level, but it has been partially harmonized through several European directives. In addition, regulatory competition and imitation determine the circulation of legal rules and models also in Europe. It is inevitable also in these systems to consider, at least occasionally, foreign law. This book expands this approach giving it an even more global dimension.

Some scholars have in fact argued that comparative corporate law should be included also in any basic corporate law course. It can be discussed if this is desirable, or if it is preferable to dedicate an upper-division course to comparative corporate law, but the reasons they offer contribute to clarify the relevance of comparative corporate law for anyone dealing professionally with business law issues, as you can gather from the following excerpt.

LAWRENCE A. CUNNINGHAM, COMPARATIVE CORPORATE
GOVERNANCE AND PEDAGOGY
34 Ga. L. Rev. 721 (2000)[1]

"Comparative corporate governance" [. . .] is the collection of mechanisms in use in selected parts of the world to regulate those in control of business organizations, with attention to the origins and durability of the differences between countries or regions. The United States is commonly compared to countries such as the United Kingdom and those in continental Europe, in Asia (chiefly Japan), and to a lesser extent Australia, Canada, Israel and South Africa.

Comparisons of these models typically emphasize their finance characteristics. In the United States and the United Kingdom, capital traditionally has been supplied by debt financing offered by banks and other financial institutions while equity financing is offered by public investors in organized stock markets and private placements (characteristics that may be changing). In Germany and other European nations capital historically has tended to be supplied by banking institutions that offer both debt and equity financing for their industrial clients. Ownership of industrial companies therefore tended to be fragmented in Anglo-Saxon countries and concentrated on the Continent.

Corporate governance regimes in these countries differed substantially as a result of this relative fragmentation or concentration, at least in the abstract. United States and United Kingdom managers were to focus on the shareholder interest according to a complex system of checks and balances intended to compel them to put shareholders first. German and other European corporations were to operate not by putting shareholders first but by commanding corporate boards and managers to operate the firm in the best interests of all its constituencies.

The traditional Japanese model is different yet again, with the system of lifetime employment and interlocking corporate ownership (*keiretsu*) contrasted to the Anglo-Saxon tradition of employment-at-will and the United States aversion to concentrations of power (which also may be waning). The list of potential comparative countries is increasing as privatization breaks out the world over, and could go on to include countries in economic and political transition such as former republics of the Soviet Union, former members of the Soviet Union's Council for Mutual Economic Assistance (COMECON), and former republics of Yugoslavia.

As these transitions go forward, new variations on governance approaches are emerging, often blending aspects of the models usually treated as polar. Those polar models may also be seen to be converging

---

[1] Footnotes omitted.

with one another as transnational corporations increasingly dominate global capital, labor and product markets. Indeed, one of the most important recent corners of corporate-law scholarship has been the question of such convergence and the challenge it seems to pose to the abstract conception of modular polarity.

[. . .]

An assessment of the benefits of introducing comparative corporate governance in the basic course calls for making at least some general assumptions about what the course is intended to accomplish. Apart from the objectives associated with most law school classes—training in case law analysis, statutory interpretation, argumentation, advocacy, analogical reasoning, critical thinking, and so on—the basic course in business organizations probably is supposed to give students a firm but broad understanding of the corporation and its organizational cognates in their legal, business, political, and social contexts.

The basic course should equip the student to function in professional settings where business law (corporate and otherwise) and business issues arise, which in turn means the course should give the student a sense of business and of the special and unusual role the business lawyer plays as business advisor rather than—or at least in addition to—that of advocate or litigator (the model associated with most typical law school subjects). Ultimately, the course is a vehicle for conveying the basics of corporate and related law by helping students understand that law from theoretical, normative, possibly political, and certainly practical perspectives.

So how, if at all, would including comparative corporate governance in the basic course advance these broad and general objectives? Unexceptionally, the basics of business organization law in the United States can best be taught by covering United States law. But part of that exercise is often at least a comparison of the ways different states deal with similar issues, or between how, say, Delaware or New York and the Revised Model Business Corporations Act (R.M.B.C.A) deal with those subjects, as well as some understanding of the relationship between state business organization law and various federal laws, particularly the securities laws. Common questions in such an inquiry are why these states have adopted different laws, whether one or the other is better, and ultimately how the variations reflect (and how the federal presence bears) on the competition among states for attracting business organizations and how that competition bears on bedrock principles like the internal affairs doctrine.

[. . .]

Introducing a comparative perspective could shed light on such questions and equip the students with a greater range of examples and alternatives to inform the kinds of argument necessary to sustain one view against the other. Understanding managers as the central actors in the course, it is always important to convey their role and their power in relationships with shareholders, markets, and government officials, which can vary substantially across 728 geographic borders. The variance from a global perspective can furnish a very powerful basis for argument. [. . .]

These sorts of questions can be elevated to a more political or perhaps geopolitical or policy level as well. There is a tendency of policymakers around the world to look elsewhere for answers when internal problems arise, whether intractable or otherwise. The United States tended to look toward Japan in the 1980s for lessons about how to recover from its economic malaise. Then Japan looked to the United States in the 1990s as the situations of these economic powers reversed. A similar back-and-forth has gone on for many years between the United Kingdom on the one hand and much of the rest of Europe on the other.

[. . .]

For the practical minded, as so many students in the basic course are (and teachers should be and mostly are), globalization must be considered in deciding whether and, if so, to what extent to introduce comparative corporate governance in the basic course. Merger activity is increasingly global in scale and scope, with 1998 marking the largest number of cross-border deals and involving the largest dollar amount of transactions ever, on the heels of the second largest year ever in 1997. Nearly one-fourth of all deals involving United States companies in 1998 also involved some cross-border element, including such mega-deals as the merger of Chrysler with Germany's Daimler and of Amoco with Britain's British Petroleum.

This increasing global activity means many more students are likely to encounter businesses organized outside the United States during the early stages of their professional careers.

[. . .]

Other benefits can accrue from introducing comparative corporate governance in special circumstances, such as where students from around the world are in the class [. . .]. This presence could further enrich classroom discussion of comparative issues. Contrariwise, it may be even more important for students at schools that are more homogenous to get exposure to the international arena through some treatment of comparative corporate governance.

[. . .]

[There is] the common problem of finding suitable materials. No corporate law casebooks I have reviewed treat comparative corporate governance as a topic. In addition, there are few cases specifically raising questions of comparative corporate governance.

* * *

We hope, with this book, to have at least partially answered this last concern of Professor Cunningham.

What exactly, however, is comparative corporate law, and how does it affect, or is affected by, lawyers, courts, legislatures, and legal scholars? The following excerpt by Klaus J. Hopt, one of the leading comparative corporate law scholars of our times, offers some interesting ideas, also from an historical perspective.

KLAUS J. HOPT, COMPARATIVE COMPANY LAW IN THE OXFORD HANDBOOK OF COMPARATIVE LAW

(Mathias Reimann & Reinhard Zimmermann, eds.), Oxford, 2006, 1161 ff[2]

Comparative company law is at once very old and very modern. It is very old because ever since companies and company laws first existed, trade has not stopped at the frontiers of countries and states. The persons concerned, practitioners as well as rule-makers, had to look beyond their own city, country, rules, and laws. This became even more true after the rise of the public company and the early company acts in the first half of the nineteenth century. Ever since, company lawmakers have profited from comparison.

But comparative company law is also very modern. Most comparative work has focused on the main areas of private law, such as contract and torts, rather than company law. While the law of business and private organizations was covered in voluminous *International Encyclopedia of Comparative Law*, and national company law books and articles occasionally also provided some comparative information, an internationally acknowledged standard treatise on comparative company law has not yet emerged. Company law and comparative company law work remained a task for professionals. The few academics who joined in this work tended also to be practitioners such as outside counsel, arbitrators, or advisers to legislators, who were less interested in theory and doctrine.

[. . .]

Looking across the Border in Company Law: Legislators, Lawyers, Academics, Judges

---

[2]   Footnotes omitted.

(a) *Legislators*

One important aim of comparative law is the mutual understanding of other people and nations. But this serves not only altruistic purposes. Comparative law has always been considered to be an enrichment of the 'stock of legal solutions' and a wealth of actual experience. Some speak of an *école de verité*, some even of real 'social science experiments'. The legislators in the nineteenth and early twentieth centuries were already demonstrating this when they prepared their company law statutes on the basis of thorough comparisons of the laws and experiences of other countries. The major company law codifications in the second half of the nineteenth century, when European countries moved away from the state concession system, testify to this. Before the German Company Act of 1937 was drafted, many preparatory comparative law opinions were commissioned from the Kaiser Wilhelm Institute in Berlin, the predecessor of today's Max Planck Institute in Hamburg. One of the most impressive opinions dealing with American and English company law was written by Walter Hallstein, who later became president of the European Commission, while he was still an assistant at the Institute in Berlin and *Referendar* (legal trainee) at the Berlin Court of Appeals, the *Kammergericht*.

In the United States, where company law is state law, the use of comparative company law by the legislator is common in so far as one state will take into account the company laws of other American states when reforming its own company law. Delaware has taken the lead since it became, and remains, the major incorporation state for American companies. The competition of state company legislators is a well-known and, until recently, largely indisputable phenomenon. Yet its interpretation as a 'race to the bottom' or a 'race to the top' is highly controversial, and the precise reasons for Delaware's leading position—be it its company law, or rather its company lawyers and specialized courts—remain disputed.

Merely learning from foreign company laws is one thing. More or less adopting them either voluntarily or under moral suasion or even pressure is another. Japan is one of many examples. China is another, although its position is different in important respects. Most recently the same can be seen in many of the Middle and Eastern European countries which, following the collapse of the Soviet Union, reformed or are reforming their company laws with the aim, sooner or later, of joining the European Union. In this context it is also important to mention the American Influence on these countries, particularly strategic ones such as Russia and certain former states of the Soviet Union, which is sometimes secured with the help of financial promises. The Japanese company law of 1893 (*Kyû-shôhô*) was based to a significant extent on a draft by the German scholar Carl Friedrich Hermann Roesler, and combined elements of the

French *Code de commerce* (mainly as to its form) and of the German *Allgemeines Deutsches Handelsgesetzbuch* of 1861 (concerning many substantive principles). The later company law of 1899 (*Shôhô*) was close to the German company law revision of 1870 in its revised form of 1884, and the revised *Shôhô* of 1938 was closely modelled on the German Stock Corporation Act of 1937. After World War II, Japanese company law reform closely followed the United States company law principles, in particular the Illinois Business Corporation Act of 1933. This was because the relevant American official of the Supreme Commander for the Allied Powers (SCAP) happened to come from Chicago. Such historical coincidences happen more often than is generally known, and this is also true in company law. Modern Japanese company law reform, some of which is being carried out at present, is based on extensive comparison of both United States' and European company laws.

Most recently there has been renewed interest in comparative company law, partly because of the emergence of European company law and partly because the corporate governance movement has sharpened the sense of competition with other countries. The German ministries of justice and finance, for example, have commissioned several comparative law studies from, amongst others, the Max Planck Institute when preparing their reform on highly controversial questions such as whether to make directors liable to investors for untrue or misleading financial statements.

(b) *Lawyers and Legal Counsel*

The role of lawyers and legal counsel in comparative law is traditionally underrated, since they do their work for their clients and enterprises on a day-to-day basis. Yet they are the real experts in both conflict of company laws and of foreign company laws. This is even more true now that the forces of globalization have also reached law firms, with the consequence that the top layer of firms in all major countries has become international either by merger or by cooperation. Occasionally some of their comparative work is published, often only in the form of practical advice, but sometimes also with fully legitimate academic claims. The creation of companies abroad and their subsequent control is common practice today. Working out the best company and tax law structures for international mergers, and forming and doing legal work for groups and tax haven operations, is a high, creative art.

Much more in the public eye is the comparative company law work of the American Law Institute, aimed at drafting uniform company laws and model codes. Notable results are the Principles of Corporate Governance: Analysis and Recommendations of 1992 (2 vols., 1994) and the Federal Securities Code of 1978 (2 vols., 1980).

(c) *Academia*

As stated above, traditionally only a few have engaged in comparative company law work. In all industrialized countries with well-developed companies there are, of course, standard company law treatises, many of them highly knowledgeable and some at the peak of traditional doctrinal wisdom. Yet, what is conspicuous about most of these leading texts is their restriction to national law and practice. This is certainly the impression for Germany, France, and the United Kingdom, but also for smaller countries where looking beyond their borders has always been more natural, such as Switzerland. Exceptions seem to prove the rule, but even they are usually confined to areas such as conflict of company laws, that is, national law, and, more recently, to European Community company law, or to the occasional use in a general text of foreign literature and comparative observations. Comparative company law work is rarely addressed in these leading texts as a prerequisite of European company law harmonization or to provide a better understanding, and to aid the development, of one's own national company law.

Of course, the state of comparative company law is different as far as more specialized monographs and articles are concerned. It is impossible here to go into detail; it would not only be futile, but also unjust to the many works which could not be mentioned. Some more general observations must suffice. First, of course, there is much comparative company law work in the context of conflict of laws and, more recently, of European company law. As to the latter, there were initially quite influential collections of texts on European company law, which included comments and some case law. Since then impressive treatises on European company law have been developed in most member states.

Second, in many countries American company law has had a considerable influence on legal literature. This is not surprising for those countries mentioned above where American company law and securities regulation was broadly followed. But similar trends can be discerned, for example, in Germany after World War II, where contacts with German émigrés were rekindled and whole generations of young academics studied in the United States and wrote their doctoral theses and their *Habilitationen* on comparative American and German company law. Some of these works happened to stand at the beginning of the development of whole new areas in their respective national laws. At a later stage there were even treatises and handbooks on American company law written by non-Americans in German and other languages, which provided much insight into its peculiarities.

Third, the influence of international networks has been important for comparative company law. Some examples of organized efforts include

International Encyclopedia of Comparative Law, the work of international institutions such as the International Faculty of Corporate Law and Securities Regulation and the International Academy of Comparative Law, or the research which was facilitated by international institutions such as the European University Institute in Florence, where comparative work on groups of companies, corporate governance, directors' liabilities, and the harmonization of companies was done and the so-called green book series was started. Other such networks resulted from private initiatives, for example between the United States, Germany, and Switzerland; Germany and Belgium, Italy and the United States, or within Scandinavia.

Fourth, the law and economics movement in the United States and abroad led to a new and increased interest in comparative company law. This will be dealt with in more detail below.

Fifth, this new interest in comparative company law was not only permanently covered by a few national company law reviews such as the German *Zeitschrift für Unternehmens-und Gesellschaftsrecht* (ZGR), the Italian *Rivista della Società*, and to a certain degree also the French *Revue des Sociétés*, but a number of new specialized law reviews appeared on the market such as the English *International and Comparative Corporate Law Journal* (ICCJ), that seemed for a while to have made way for the *Journal of Corporate Law Studies* (JCLS), the Dutch *European Business Organization Law Review* (EBOR), the German, and in the meantime internationally based, *European Company and Financial Law Review* (ECFR), and the *European Company Law* (ECL), published jointly by the Universities of Leiden, Utrecht, and Maastricht.

In view of the golden age of the elaboration of common principles of law such as the UNIDROIT Principles of International Commercial Contracts and the Principles of European Contract Law, it is astonishing that similarly successful work has not yet been undertaken in the area of company law.

(d) Courts

In nearly all countries it is the courts which have been particularly reluctant to look to comparative company law. There are some obvious exceptions. It is clear that United States' court decisions on company law do not only deal with the company law of the respective state, but also with precedents of other states of the Union. The same was and still is true, though to a much lesser degree, within the former Commonwealth. Apart from these instances, it is the courts of smaller countries such as Switzerland which are more likely to take foreign decisions into consideration. This is because the academics and lawyers in such countries are generally more open to looking to the wealth of experience in their larger neighboring states. But even then the fact that they look abroad rarely results in the actual citation of foreign company law in court decisions themselves. One reason for this may be the traditional theory in Continental Europe that judges simply 'find the law' as enacted by the legislature. This, of course, is not true, as is shown very clearly by many cases decided by the Second Senate of the German Federal Supreme Court, which is responsible for disputes in company law.

A similar observation can be made for the European Court of Justice. Ninon Colneric, the German Justice on that Court, remarked recently that comparative law plays a much higher role in the decision-making of the Court than one might assume from reading its decisions. The fact that the Court does not cite literature does not mean that it does not take legal literature into consideration. Quite the contrary is true: sometimes even special research notes on the treatment of a legal question in the member states are commissioned by the Court. Of course, the European Court of Justice is special due to its nature and jurisdiction; it needs to consider not only the law of the member state concerned in a specific case, but more broadly the acceptability of its decision in all member states.

While company law has long been the domain of national courts in the EU, this is no longer true. The European Court of Justice has rendered quite a number of important decisions in the fields of company law and accounting. For a long time, national courts were rather reluctant to refer questions concerning harmonized company law and accounting to the European Court of Justice. In the meantime, however, the relationship between the judiciaries has become more relaxed. Most recently, one of the landmark cases in company law and conflict of company laws was the *Centros* decision of the European Court. Combined with the decisions in the subsequent cases of *Überseering* and *Inspire Art*, this marked an end, at least within the European Union, to the seat theory that had been so dear to German lawyers for so long. These cases allow free incorporation in any of the EU member states, which has binding effects in all member states under the incorporation theory.

In concluding this section, it should be mentioned that, according to some observers, the real impetus toward comparative company law is provided by the forces of financial and other markets, with their scandals; the needs of these markets do not stop at national frontiers. Although true to a considerable extent, this is not the whole story. Comparative company law is conceived, practiced, and reformed by persons such as those dealt with in this section. Their actions and reactions depend on many influences, not only on market forces. Yet the observation that company law reforms, like many others, are driven by scandals (and therefore often come too late and overreact) can be verified throughout the history of company law and investor protection, and was seen most recently in the Enron scandal and the shock waves which it sent through company law in the United States and abroad.

* * *

Professor Hopt's analysis explains the relevance of comparative corporate law for legislatures, academics, lawyers, and courts. Let's however make this discussion even more concrete, especially with respect to courts. Does comparative corporate (and more general business) law have any specific relevance in court? In addition to situations in which courts are required to apply the laws of a different jurisdiction, in which obviously they are forced to understand foreign law, do courts look abroad for guidance? Do foreign precedents have some persuasive value?

In an interesting recent article, Martin Gelter and Mathias Siems (*Citations to Foreign Courts—Illegitimate and Superfluous, or Unavoidable? Evidence from Europe*, 62 AM. J. COMP. L. 35 (2014)), have conducted an empirical research on the use of foreign precedents by courts. As they note in the introduction (citations omitted):

> In the United States it is highly controversial whether courts should be allowed, or even encouraged, to refer to precedents from foreign courts. This is not a purely academic debate. The U.S. Supreme Court itself is divided on whether it is legitimate to consider foreign law in the interpretation of the U.S. Constitution, and the occasional reference to foreign sources by some judges has been the subject of congressional hearings and debates in the Blogosphere as well as in legal scholarship. Justice Kennedy has actually been called "the most dangerous man in America," inter alia, because of his endorsement of citations of foreign cases. In addition, the state of Oklahoma attracted considerable attention by explicitly prohibiting state courts from looking "to the legal precepts of other nations or cultures" specifically mentioning international law and Sharia Law; other states have passed or are debating measures with similar intentions.

> In Europe, the discussion about the desirability of cross-citations is less politically contentious. A possible explanation could be that due to E.U. law (as well as the European Convention on Human Rights) it may just be natural for national courts to consider the case law of other member states. But the European Union is not (yet) akin to a federal state. A study comparing the European Union with twenty federal states found that the former provides significantly less legal uniformity than the latter. Thus, for topics largely uninfluenced by E.U. law it may be a bit questionable if, say, an English court cited a Spanish one. Such reluctance may be related to the diversity of European countries in terms of legal traditions, languages and cultures.

Europe thus makes an interesting testing ground for assessing the frequency and desirability of cross-citations.

Considering a large number of cases decided by the Supreme Courts of different European countries between 2000 and 2007, the data they collected and studied offer important insights. Consider, for example, the following table (elaboration from Gelter & Siems (2014), 48):

citing court	cited court										total
	Austria	Belgium	England	France	Germany	Ireland	Italy	Netherlands	Spain	Switzerland	
Austria	-	0	1	4	447	0	3	0	0	21	476
Belgium	0	-	0	37	6	0	0	6	0	1	50
England	2	1	-	9	10	7	0	6	2	0	37
France	0	2	0	-	3	0	1	1	0	1	7
Germany	34	0	1	2	-	0	1	1	0	2	41
Ireland	0	1	228	2	0	-	0	2	0	0	233
Italy	0	2	0	2	3	0	-	0	0	0	7
Netherlands	2	13	5	9	54	0	1	-	0	6	90
Spain	0	1	0	1	14	0	0	0	-	0	16
Switzerland	3	0	2	11	42	0	0	1	0	-	59
total	41	20	237	77	579	7	6	16	2	31	1016

The most cited courts appear to be the ones of Germany, followed by England, even if this data is strongly inflated by the high number of citations from one single neighboring country, Ireland. The courts that seem to be more outward looking, at least in terms of citations of foreign judgments, are Austria (which not surprisingly very often cites German precedents), Ireland (but once again, looking almost exclusively at England), and the Netherlands. There are interesting paths that can be observed. For example, smaller countries, which have a relatively lower number of cases, consider foreign jurisprudence relatively often: this is the case of Switzerland, which often cites German or French precedents (also in the light of the legal, cultural, and linguistic commonalities), and Belgium, which often cites French, German, and Dutch precedents. The Italian and the French Supreme Courts are quite inward looking, by comparison.

An interesting fact also concerns the legal areas more often cited when courts look abroad. The following graphs, again an elaboration on Gelter & Siems (2014), 61–62, illustrate this point with respect to the same countries and courts considered previously from 2000 to 2007.

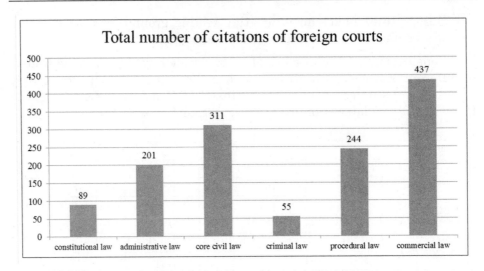

Of course, as the authors mention, these data are sometimes difficult to collect because often citations concern different fields, but it is undisputed that the greatest number of foreign citations are in the area of commercial law, which includes corporate law. This is not surprising in the light of the international nature of business activity, but it confirms the practical and theoretical importance of comparative corporate law. Interestingly enough, also in fields traditionally considered less open to the international debate, such as criminal law, administrative law, and procedural law, judges need or want to take a comparative perspective.

Gelter & Siems (2014) also offer a further breakdown of citations of foreign cases by sub-fields of law: consider for example the following data concerning the Austrian Supreme Court.

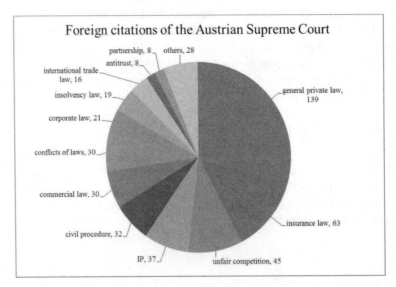

Talking about the use by courts of foreign sources, we must mention one interesting but bizzare experiment in legal history. The 1769 Portuguese *Lei da Boa Razão* prohibited the (then common) use of Roman law sources to resolve commercial disputes. This statute, however, indicated that Portuguese courts, when applicable national rules could not be identified, had to apply the laws of other "enlightened and polished Christian nations" (interestingly enough, a commentator in the XIX interpreted the reference as including all other European countries, but not Turkey). In other words, courts were obliged to engage in a comparative analysis, and apply foreign law. Contradicting the *nomen omen* adage, the statute led quickly to irrational, contradictory and arbitrary results. It was unclear which systems would be relevant, which rules should be selected, and it was obviously impracticable for Portuguese and Brazilian judges, lawyers and parties to understand and apply foreign law. This approach was abandoned both in Portugal and in Brazil, but not before several decades. None suggests replicating this bizzare experiment, but we wanted to mention it because it is very telling about the possible role of comparative law. It also confirms that, as we observed beforehand not surprisingly, smaller countries with a limited number of cases tend to be more outward looking than bigger systems. For more on the Portuguese experiment and generally on the history of corporate law reforms in Brazil *see* Mariana Pargendler, *Politics in the Origins: The Making of Corporate Law in Nineteenth-Century Brazil*, 60 AM. J. COMP. L. 805, 815 (2012).

Another interesting and more recent example of courts of one country relying or at least attentively considering decisions and scholarship of another system is offered by Israel, whose judges often take into account U.S. and specifically Delaware law. This is probably due to both the extensive cultural connections between the two jurisdictions, in light of the significant number of Israeli jurists studying and teaching in the U.S., and the economic relationships between the two countries. Whether this consideration for U.S. law is always correct and desirable is debated: for a discussion focused on how Israeli courts have used the notion of "good faith" in corporate law, *see* Itai Fiegenbaum & Jana Rabinovich, *Lost in Translation: "Good Faith" in Israeli and Delaware Corporate Law*, in Festchrift for Prof. Joseph Gross (A, Barak, Y. Zamir, D. Libai, eds., forthcoming in 2015 in Hebrew).

COMPARATIVE CORPORATE LAW AND LEGAL FAMILIES; CONVERGENCE OF CORPORATE LAW AND THE (QUESTIONABLE) SEARCH FOR THE "BEST SYSTEM"

Many of you reading this book might already be familiar with comparative law generally. You might have taken a general course on comparative law, or other courses that (often) include a comparative element, such as European Union law, International Business Transactions, and the like. Also in purely domestic law courses your instructors might have exposed you to comparative law aspects. It is nonetheless useful to say a few words on legal families, for at least three reasons: to familiarize the ones that have no background in comparative law with the field; to clarify some of the methodological perspectives shared by the authors of this book; and to discuss some specific general issues on comparative corporate law and some economic data concerning different countries. We believe this discussion will provide insights that will be useful throughout the course.

The human mind needs to organize and systematize information, even at the cost of some simplifications. In comparative law, one of the most important systematizations aggregates legal systems in different legal families based on shared features. Of course one of the basic distinctions is between common law countries (generally, the U.K., the U.S., Australia, New Zealand, and other former British colonies) and civil law countries; civil law systems are also generally divided into French civil law traditions and German civil law traditions (some comparativists distinguish a "Roman" and a "Germanic" tradition). Several other important legal families exist that cannot be easily accommodated in the common law/civil law distinction: examples are Scandinavian systems (Denmark, Finland, Norway, and Sweden), Socialist or "non-market" economies (the relevance of this group is fading for obvious reasons), and also Asian systems have distinctive features. In Africa and other parts of the world, together with the legacy of colonialism, traditional or tribal legal traditions are important, especially in certain areas such as family law. And of course non-secular legal systems also exist or co-exist with secular ones: in Arabic and Muslim countries Sharia is extremely relevant. There are also systems that, according to some scholars and practitioners, must be considered "mixed" jurisdictions that present elements of both common law and civil law, such as Louisiana in the United States and Scotland. Another fascinating example is Israel, a common law country partially based on British common law, in which however there are profound influences from civil law countries such as Germany, Ottoman law had a meaningful impact, and religious norms govern some aspects of family law. More recently U.S. law has also had a major role in shaping Israeli corporate law and securities regulation, and also on legal scholarship in these areas in light of the extensive relationships between Israeli and American law schools.

Focusing on the divide between common law and civil law, the distinctive features are often identified in the sources of the law, the model of legal education, and the approach to legal thinking. More concretely, differences often pointed out, and too well known to be here examined analytically, are the fact that in common law systems judicial precedents are particularly important and often technically binding, and that common law countries did not experience the codification of their private law in the eighteenth and nineteenth centuries; in civil law systems, on the other hand, statutory law seems to be more relevant than case law, precedents are not binding, and codification played and plays a crucial role in the development of the legal system. The role of the jury in common law systems is also often mentioned as a basic difference with civil law systems, as well as the way in which judges and justices are appointed (generally, elected in some kind of political fashion in common law, and selected through a purely technical exam in civil law countries).

We believe that these differences, which exist and are relevant, are however often overemphasized and are, in any case, fading. For example, if you are a lawyer in a civil law system and you need to research a legal issue, of course you will look at the applicable statutory provisions, but you will immediately also look at precedents and how courts interpret the law. Even if precedents are technically not binding, they have a strong persuasive authority, especially the ones of the higher courts. Keep also in mind that, differently from common law countries, in civil law ones, only a small percentage of cases are published and easily accessible in legal journals. Similarly, statutory and regulatory law is becoming more and more pervasive also in common law countries, especially in complex technical areas such as commercial law or securities regulation; and even in these systems it is often easy to distinguish a case from a precedent, therefore reducing the binding value of the precedent. The role of the jury in common law systems is also often exaggerated. In the U.S., for example, approximately 2% of litigation actually goes to trial (most is settled or dismissed before trial); and one of the most important jurisdictions for corporate law, Delaware, has a Chancery Court that decides without a jury. In addition, in many commercial contracts jury waiver provisions or arbitration clauses exclude the possibility to try the case in front of a jury. As for "legal education" and "legal reasoning," to the extent that these slippery concepts can be discussed, most lawyers and judges—and definitely the most successful ones—now study and practice not only in their home country, but also abroad, and they develop and bring with them different styles of legal thinking. As for codification, several common law systems have gone through legislative developments that resemble codification, at least in certain areas of the law, and consider in this respect the Uniform Commercial Code or the securities laws in the U.S. but also, in our area, the development of the Model Business Corporation Act.

All we want to say is that distinguishing and classifying different legal families is useful, and captures quickly and effectively some relevant differences, but one should be careful in using it too rigidly. This is also true just looking at statutory law in the very area of corporate law and financial markets regulation, and Italy is a good example: in the Italian Civil Code and in the most important statutes regulating this field, as we will see in this book, clear French and German influences can be spotted (sometimes even rules almost literally copied from foreign sources), but especially in the last few decades the influence of U.S. law, and European law inspired by British law (for example in the area of takeovers), has been profound.

Another reason of caution when dividing the world into legal families is that comparative law developed historically primarily with respect to private law. In other areas, for example constitutional laws, the usual distinctions based on private law elements do not apply. For instance, consider Central and South American systems: while their legal origins in terms of private law can be traced to civil law countries (Spain, Portugal, and to some extent Italy), in many cases the U.S. Constitution had a particularly significant influence in shaping their constitutions. In a similar vein, it is also interesting to point out that some very important differences concern procedural rules. In fact, one idea shared by many scholars and lawyers is that differences in civil procedure rules are as relevant as differences in the substantive laws to understand comparative differences. Think, for example, of the importance of discovery, class actions, contingency fees, and the absence of the loser-pays rule to explain how legal rules develop in the U.S. and the attractiveness of the U.S. as a forum for plaintiffs. Unfortunately, for historical and somehow self-evident reasons, scholars and jurists specializing in procedural law tend to be very focused on domestic law (with few notable exceptions, such as Italian scholars Michelino Taruffo and Vincenzo Varano, Professor Joachim Zekoll from Germany, and Mirjan R. Damaška at Yale Law School); procedural law courses at most law schools around the world rarely include a comparative or international perspective; and a few procedural rules are often neglected by comparativists. The result is that there is a lot of work that should be done to understand better comparative differences in the area of civil procedure. Interestingly enough, the first Max Planck Institute in law established outside of Germany, in Luxembourg, has among its research goals also comparative civil procedure, under the directorship of Professor Burkhard Hess.

To lighten up a bit our discussion, allow us a little fun quiz. Look at the following map without reading what is written below it (you would see the answer and spoil the exercise). It divides countries based on a very important legal rule, one that you should always be aware of when travelling to those countries, no matter what your business is. Can you tell the difference before looking at the answer below?

So what is the different applicable rule?

In lighter-gray countries people drive on the right side of the street, and in darker-gray countries people drive on the left side. In general, former British colonies follow the second rule, but a notable exception is the United States (by the way, the historical roots of this difference are interesting, and there are conflicting theories: we do not have space to discuss them here, but if you are curious you should look it up). This little example suggests how one should be careful in distinguishing different legal families.

Having said that, in this casebook we will focus primarily on two common law countries, the U.S. and the U.K., and on several civil law, continental European countries (in particular France, Germany, and Italy), and Japan, but occasionally we will also consider cases and materials from other jurisdictions including Asia, Latin America, and Eastern European countries. In our analysis we will often start from the U.S. perspective, and then examine comparative differences with other systems. This is not due to an "America-centric" bias, but because we believe it is useful to have a clear and consistent starting point. Focusing on the jurisdictions we mentioned, which often represent the legal origins of other systems (especially due to the colonial period), we believe, allows us to capture most of the existing variations in corporate law regimes and offers a rich enough basis to discuss specific different rules. The economic importance of some of the countries on which we focus also justifies the attention that we give them.

One basic distinction between the U.S. and the European Union in terms of sources of law must be mentioned briefly, also because we will come back to this issue in the following chapters. In the U.S., corporate law is state law, even if more recently the federal legislature has introduced some rules that affect the internal affairs of listed corporations, for example in terms of proxy access or composition of the board of directors (think of the Sarbanes-Oxley Act and the Dodd-Frank Act). In Europe, the national laws of the single member states govern corporations, but a significant effort of harmonization has been made through European directives and regulations. It is obviously impossible here to offer a crash-course on the general aspects of E.U. law, but suffice it to say that directives are enacted by the European Union and must be implemented by the single member states with a statute (and often directives present different options or a certain degree of flexibility in how to implement them), while regulations are directly and immediately applicable in all the member states. In addition, the European Court of Justice, which decides on issues concerning European law, has also played an important role in the development of European corporate law, as mentioned in the excerpt from Professor Hopt above, and as we will discuss more extensively in Chapter 2.

* * *

One interesting question is if legal systems, in the area of corporate law, are converging or diverging. The circulation of legal models and ideas might suggest greater convergence, and several scholars have argued that in this historic period the convergence is toward Anglo-Saxon corporate law models with strong protections for minority shareholders and an emphasis on the creation of wealth for shareholders (a somehow irritating formula due to its indeterminacy). The issue is however far from being clear-cut. Rather than a long theoretical discussion on the convergence vs. divergence debate, let's take a look at India and China, two jurisdictions that show significant differences from the Western legal tradition, but in some of the most recent reforms seem to have looked at Anglo-Saxon legal systems. The following excerpts offer some food for thought on this issue.

AFRA AFSHARIPOUR, CORPORATE GOVERNANCE CONVERGENCE: LESSONS FROM THE INDIAN EXPERIENCE

29 Nw. J. Int'l L. & Bus. 335 (2009)[3]

[. . .]

A vast academic inquiry has emerged, particularly at the intersection of law and economics, regarding whether globalization and increasing financial integration have led to convergence of corporate governance standards across countries. Numerous scholars have studied the differences between corporate governance structures of civil law and common law systems around the world. These scholars argue that different corporate governance regimes have been competing for dominance. Therefore, much of the corporate governance convergence debate has revolved around which of the two different models of corporate forms, the shareholder-oriented/dispersed ownership model or the stakeholder-oriented/concentrated ownership model, has triumphed or will triumph.

Most convergence theory scholars advance the primacy of the Anglo-American model of governance, arguing that this model is the "endpoint of an evolutionary development" and is "both desirable and inevitable." They contend that a global consensus of shareholder primacy is developing. These scholars further suggest that convergence to the Anglo-American model will benefit countries and companies. They assert that, given globalization and the increased interdependence of financial markets around the world, some level of uniformity and convergence would promote the global competitiveness of firms.

However, there are a number of opponents of the convergence theory. Some opponents argue that not only is there a lack of convergence toward a shareholder-oriented/dispersed ownership model, but that theories of convergence reflect U.S. economic imperialism. Other opponents, most notably Professors Roe and Bebchuk, argue that such convergence is not possible because "path dependency" creates significant obstacles to convergence. As Professor Coffee articulated, path dependence theory argues that "history matters, because it constrains the way in which institutions can change, and efficiency does not necessarily triumph."

Professors Coffee and Gilson have made important contributions to the above debates. Instead of arguing that full convergence to the Anglo-American model has occurred or will occur, Professors Gilson and Coffee classify three different levels of convergence that have been observed under various legal regimes: functional convergence, formal convergence, and convergence by contract. Functional convergence can occur when

---

[3] Footnotes omitted.

existing governance institutions are flexible enough to respond to the demands of changed circumstances without altering the institutions' formal characteristics. Formal convergence, on the other hand, occurs when an effective response requires legislative action to alter the basic structure of existing governance institutions. Convergence by contract may arise when existing governance institutions lack the flexibility to respond without formal change, and political barriers restrict the capacity for formal institutional change.

More recently, some scholars have begun to recognize a middle ground between the two opposing sides of the convergence debate. These scholars argue that corporate governance models cannot be exported merely by changes in formal laws, and that recognizing the forces of the local culture is necessary for effective corporate governance. According to Professor Pistor, "a simple convergence story does not do justice to the complexity of legal change." However, that is not to state that formal legal changes are not occurring and are not important. These scholars differentiate between de facto and de jure convergence, i.e., between adoption of similar corporate governance laws and actual corporate governance practices.

[. . .]

India was well-poised to go down the path of formal corporate governance convergence. The trajectory of India's corporate governance reform efforts was shaped by India's vast economic growth and the attempts of India's corporate elites to access new foreign and local capital. These forces placed competitive and political pressures on the Indian government to improve its formal corporate governance standards and to develop legal rules based on Anglo-American corporate governance practices. From decades of almost non-existent corporate governance, India's current regime now exhibits some of the same formal governance rules instituted in more developed economies. According to one influential scholar of the Indian economy, "India is sort of a noisier version of the U.S. system."

Despite extensive governance rules, large numbers of companies have been unable to comply with new governance standards and Indian regulators have been slow, at best, to enforce these new standards. According to a recent review of India's governance by the Asian Corporate Governance Association, Indian enforcement and implementation of Clause 49 [a provision of the listing agreement of the Indian Stock Exchange, regulating corporate governance and partially inspired to Anglo-Saxon governance rules, modified in 2005] is, at best, weak: "Most mid- and small-cap companies do not see the value of corporate governance. Most listed companies, including many large ones, take merely a box-ticking approach." A number of factors, including regulatory competition between two government institutions, an inefficient judicial system, and the sustained closed ownership structure of Indian firms, have created barriers that prevent these robust formal rules from being implemented and enforced.

India's reform efforts thus provide an interesting pattern of corporate governance convergence for they can be characterized as either formal convergence toward the Anglo-American governance practices, or as continuing persistence of the traditional weak corporate governance norms long-evident in India. Despite the initial exuberance about Clause 49 and promises of rigorous enforcement, implementation and enforcement of Clause 49 demonstrate that while formal convergence may have been achieved, complete convergence requires greater institutional changes.

What are some of the lessons we can learn from India's corporate governance experience and the ensuing enforcement and implementation process? It becomes clear that even with attentive crafting of detailed governance rules by a group of elites with a deep understanding of corporate governance standards around the world, the reform process is useless if an effective infrastructure for enforcement and implementation is not in place. Thus, the corporate governance reform process must take account of these limitations in the crafting of new standards. Convergence cannot be complete with adoption of formal rules alone; true convergence requires similarities in implementation and enforcement. In fact, introducing formal rules into a system where there is an inadequate infrastructure to support the implementation and enforcement of such rules may mean that these rules have little chance of succeeding. Moreover, even if the infrastructure is in place, as the debates between SEBI and the MCA illustrate, reform efforts are not likely to have a significant impact on the country's governance norms unless there is cohesive political support for them.

Undoubtedly the trajectory of India's corporate governance reforms and whether complete convergence to the Anglo-American model will occur will be shaped largely by local factors. India's corporate governance experience establishes that there are important political and social factors that shape the evolution of a nation's corporate governance system. These factors place such enormous pressures on countries that convergence of different national systems in a single direction is unlikely to happen in the near future, regardless of how well placed each national system is to replicate one model of governance.

CHI-WEI HUANG, WORLDWIDE CORPORATE CONVERGENCE
WITHIN A PLURALISTIC LEGAL ORDER: COMPANY LAW
AND THE INDEPENDENT DIRECTOR SYSTEM
IN CONTEMPORARY CHINA

31 HASTINGS INT'L & COMP. L. REV. 361 (2008)[4]

[. . .]

While Western capitalism is said to have its basis in the "rule of law," the developing Chinese bureaucratic capitalism, characterized as free market under central command, is based on "rule of man." Although there have been widespread arguments that the rule of law is conducive to economic growth, this assumption is challenged by China's recent prodigious economic achievements. Opponents of the theory of global convergence of corporate governance disagree that all corporate governance regimes around the globe are converging toward a single system, described above. They further disagree on the existence of a global convergence. China may be an exception since its current economic achievements apparently do not result from the certainty brought by a clear and definite legal system, but from the centrally planned commands of an autonomous government.

Is China moving toward shareholder-oriented and dispersed ownership model? Yes, convincing evidence indicates that China is indeed moving toward shareholder-oriented and dispersed ownership model regardless of how its economic developments have occurred in the past couple of decades. The establishment of the 1994 [Company Law] indicated China's determination to embrace a shareholder-oriented model. The 2006 [Company Law] amendment and the installation of legal institutions regarding independent directors affirmed that China had already started its transition to a shareholder-oriented model of corporate governance and a dispersed-ownership system. Although market participants and government regulators are still struggling with efficiency or rent protection path dependencies and other problems, there are strong indicia that China is indeed moving toward a shareholder-oriented model/dispersed-ownership corporate governance structure. Despite this progress, China's "rule of man" path-developing process has made path dependency problems much harder to overcome than other "rule of law" countries. "Chinese bureaucratic capitalism" has been using "clientelism" and "corporatism" as available options or partial substitutes for "rule of law."

"Clientelism" refers to a close-knitted society in which personal and social networks (also known as guanxi in Chinese) are highly regarded. Horizontal clientelism consists of relationships among equal interest groups. Vertical clientelism, to some extent, advocates a relationship

---

[4]   Footnotes omitted.

between superiors and subordinates such as government agencies and private entities. This phenomenon has gradually deepened the ultimate influence of the persons in power and further strengthened the power of "rent-protection" path dependency.

Corporatism has been asserted as a middle ground between Liberalism and Marxism. Liberalism promotes a state of weak government authority with strong self-regulatory private interest groups; whereas Marxism advocates a state of totalitarian or at least authoritarian with weak self-regulatory private interest groups. Corporatism is characterized by a strong central government authority with some private interest groups existing and enjoying a certain degree of autonomy. With a tradition of being a centralized, authoritarian country, the People's Republic of China survives by maintaining an accomplished hierarchical system, which can also be traced to the influence of Confucianism. This single value system has made the efficiency-driven path dependency even harder to overcome.

In China, "business is subordinate to and depends heavily on ties with the techno-bureaucracy to accomplish its (overall) goal." The strong ties of clientelism and corporatism produce an active and highly concentrated ownership structure in the newly developed shareholding system. The majority of the ownership in Chinese stock markets has traditionally been controlled by the State. Businessmen have to network, socially and professionally, in a highly concentrated ownership structure to enhance their business profits. The domestic market, which for a long time was dominated by government's discretionary black-box manipulation dealings and close-knit social network, has been challenged as China has opened their door to attract more foreign investment. China has tried to corporatize [State Owned Enterprises] to reduce the power-abusing opportunities of government officials, has stipulated numerous rules and regulations to standardize the corporatization of their [State Owned Enterprises], has amended their national company law, and has set up an independent director system in order to protect minority shareholders' rights. Nevertheless, the obstacles caused by path dependency hinder their convergence toward the worldwide corporate governance standard.

Although the Chinese government has encountered significant path [dependence] while transplanting various business laws and regulations, it firmly believes "rule of law" is the ground for economic growth. It also believes that accountability will enable China to pursue economic development without democracy. [. . .] However, an effective enforcement mechanism is needed in addition to rules and codes in order to ensure an effective legal system in practice not merely in theory. Reduction of the influence of path dependency in a "rule of man" market is China's toughest task.

NOTES AND QUESTIONS

1.   Notwithstanding the profoundly different systems and experiences considered in these two articles, they both underline a probably obvious, but often overlooked, question: one thing is the law in the books, another thing is the law in action. The formal adoption of a statutory or regulatory provision or set of provisions does not necessarily imply actual convergence. It should be considered if and how the rules are actually enforced, and in this analysis it is crucial to understand not only the role of courts and regulators, but also broader political, social, and cultural norms. In fact procedural rules and enforcement are one issue often overlooked especially by traditional comparative law, but it is clear that sometimes these aspects are as important, if not more, as substantive rules in order to fully understand how a legal system works. Think, for example, of the effect on litigation (and therefore of actual enforcement of statutory rules) of procedural devices such as the class action, discovery mechanisms, the permissibility of contingency fees agreements to compensate lawyers, or the existence of a "loser-pays" rule that puts some of the litigation expenses of the winning party on the shoulders of the losing party. These procedural rules determine profound differences among the jurisdictions that we will consider, and that you need to keep in mind.

2.   It is very difficult to determine if specific systems are converging toward one specific model, also because it means shooting a moving target. The law is alive and legal systems are not static, but continue to evolve and change. It is obviously even more difficult to determine if generally *most* systems are converging toward a core of corporate law rules. We can, however, leave this question open. You can decide what the best answer is at the end of this book. In the course of our discussion we will provide both examples of convergence and divergence among legal systems.

* * *

Some people are obsessed with rankings. Not surprisingly, even in the area of corporate law, people debate whether there is a "superior" system, at least vis-à-vis certain specific pre-defined goals.

One important and controversial attempt to "rank" both single jurisdictions and legal families has been made by four economists: Rafael La Porta, Florencio Lopez-de-Silanes, Andrei Shleifer, and Robert W. Vishny (their work became so famous that they are sometimes collectively referred to as "LLSV"). In a series of papers starting in the mid-1990s, LLSV have extensively studied the level of investors' and creditors' protection in different countries and tried to correlate it with different legal origins (in particular, English-origin, French-origin, German-origin, and Scandinavian-origin).

One article of these authors is particularly interesting in this respect: *Law and Finance*, 106 J. POL. ECONOMY 113 (1998). Their methodology is fairly straightforward, at least in theory. In a nutshell, and somehow simplifying, they identify a set of variables that indicate the level of protection of shareholders and creditors, in particular the existence of specific legal rules, and other variables including ownership structure, efficiency of the judicial system, corruption indexes, and others, and attribute a value to each of them. More specifically, for legal rules protecting shareholders or creditors they give to each country considered a value of 1 if the rule is present, and a value of 0 if it is not (they use different measures when applicable, for example they cumulate different "antidirector rights" in a single measure that ranges from 0 to 6 depending on the presence of several rules protective of shareholders). Just to give an example, they verify if a given legal system provides for pre-emptive rights in favor of existing shareholders in case of issuance of new shares and, considering this rule protective of investors, give 1 to countries that have such a rule and 0 to countries that do not have it (*see* Chapter 4 for a discussion of pre-emptive rights). They then calculate the average value for the four different legal families considered: English-origin, French-origin, German-origin, and Scandinavian-origin, and rank them.

Let's take a look at some of their results in the following graphs, which are elaborations on the data contained in the cited article for shareholders' rights (Table 2, page 1130 f.).

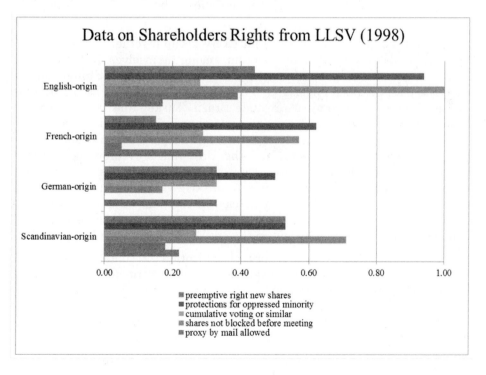

Based on these and other data, LLSV concluded that "countries whose legal rules originate in the common-law tradition tend to protect investors considerably more than the countries whose laws originate in the civil-law, and especially the French-civil-law, tradition. The German-civil-law and the Scandinavian countries take an intermediate stance toward investor protections." They also observed that "law enforcement differs a great deal around the world. German-civil-law and Scandinavian countries have the best quality of law enforcement. Law enforcement is strong in common-law countries as well, whereas it is the weakest in the French-civil-law countries" (*Id.*, at 1151). If we can make a joke, LLSV are not particularly loved in France . . .

NOTES AND QUESTIONS

1.   The work of LLSV is important and influential, and it contributed significantly to the international debate on comparative corporate law, bringing to the table a new and fresh approach; but—not surprisingly—it has attracted also a lot of criticism (*see*, e.g., Holger Spamann, *The "Antidirector Rights Index" Revisited*, 23 REVIEW OF FINANCIAL STUDIES 467 (2010)). LLSV, collectively or individually, have offered answers to some of their critics, but let's try to see the possible weaknesses of their methodology. You can both think about that yourself and then see the issues we raise below; or read them and discuss if you agree, and if there are other issues that should be considered.

2.   First of all, the countries that LLSV group together under the same legal-origin label are profoundly different among themselves: in their model, English-origin countries put together Pakistan and the United States, Malaysia and Canada, Nigeria and the United Kingdom. In addition to France, French-origin countries include Brazil, Turkey and the Philippines. German-origin countries go from Switzerland to Taiwan. You get the point. There is no need of a particularly sophisticated comparative analysis to argue that averaging together Nigeria and the U.K. raises eyebrows and evokes quite strongly the usual warning about apples and oranges. One possible answer to this objection is that their data are still valuable considering single countries, because they offer us a quick sense on the existence of certain protections for investors in one country, but even if this is the case, doubts on their classifications cast a shadow on the entire legal origins hypothesis.

3.   In addition, even the very classification of some countries has attracted specific criticism. For example Mariana Pargendler, a Brazilian scholar with broad comparative experience, has pointed out several problems in labeling Brazil as a French-civil law country in a detailed historical study (Maria Pargendler, *Politics in the Origins: The Making of Corporate Law in Nineteenth-Century Brazil*, 60 AM. J. COMP. L. 805 (2012).

4.   Lots of criticism concern the variables considered. Just to mention a few issues: first, the rules that LLSV consider represent a limited sub-set of corporate law rules, and probably the choice was also constrained by the

available data. But there are many other rules that have an impact on the level of protection for investors; think for example of rules concerning conflicts of interest of directors or of controlling shareholders, transactions with related parties, takeovers, mergers, etc.

5.   Another possible limit of LLSV's approach is that there is no consideration of how these rules are actually interpreted and applied in court. It's the problem mentioned above about legal reforms in China and India. True, LLSV include in their analysis some general measures of efficiency of the judiciary, relevance of the rule of law, and corruption, which indirectly suggest something on the ability of the courts to enforce the rights of shareholders. But the link is very tenuous. For example, the simple fact that a statute provides an appraisal or withdrawal right for minority shareholders dissenting from fundamental corporate changes (it is the variable named "protection for oppressed minority" in the graph above) does not tell us much about the actual level of protection of shareholders: are there rules that ensure a fair evaluation of the shares of the dissenting minority? How are these rules interpreted and applied? What evaluation techniques are considered acceptable in a given system? How quickly do courts adjudicate these disputes? And so on. Needless to say, this objection somehow captures a never-ending debate between a more "traditional" jurist and an economist, since the latter often needs to simplify and reduce complexity to build her models and collect data, ignoring the nuances and technicalities that the former tends to consider essential for a true and deep understanding of the law. Economists, in other words, are often accused by jurists of being too simplistic and, vice versa, jurists are accused by economists of losing themselves in minor and negligible details. A balanced approach, in our opinion, is to recognize the value of the study of LLSV (and of similar ones), but also be aware of its limits.

6.   Another quite profound critique is that the very decision that the existence of a rule is protective of investors is often questionable, or at least it is questionable which investors it protects. Consider, for example, pre-emptive rights in case of issuance of new shares. LLSV simply consider them always favorable of shareholders, giving 1 to countries that have adopted mandatory pre-emptive rights. But are we sure that this is always the case? As we will see in Chapter 4, for example, the existence of pre-emptive rights does not prevent a controlling shareholder from causing the issuance of new shares at a time when minority shareholders do not have the financial means to buy them, and therefore increase her share of control. There might be remedies against a similar conduct, but litigation might be uncertain and costly. Similarly, are we sure that a strict "one-share, one-vote" rule is always desirable for all the shareholders? Isn't it possible that, under certain circumstances, to allow more flexibility in the creation of different classes of shares might maximize the value of the corporation and be in the best interest of investors? (Also on this issue, see Chapter 4.) In other words: are we sure that LLSV's coding is always correct? Once again, in all fairness we must recognize that virtually any statistical analysis, especially when dealing

with complex variables such as legal rules, requires some kind of judgment call. It's just a matter of being aware of these possible pitfalls.

7.   In any case, one cannot avoid noting that in the 15 years following the work of LLSV, several countries have adopted the rules that would make them gain a "1" in their methodology. Just to give one example, a European directive of 2007 (2007/36/CE) on shareholders' rights has required the adoption of a "record date" system, which implies that shares are not blocked before shareholders' meetings. Institutional investors are particularly interested in this rule, because it allows them to vote without losing the ability to trade on the shares. Another example is Italy, in which an important comprehensive reform of corporate law in 2003 introduced, among many other innovations, rules more protective of investors through dissenting shareholders' appraisal rights, both expanding the grounds for appraisal, and adopting more fair evaluation criteria for the shares (Articles 2437 ff. of the Italian Civil Code). Notwithstanding all the criticism, therefore, the perspective of LLSV has had some consequences on the policy debate, and has captured some important issues that have been the object of legal reforms.

OWNERSHIP STRUCTURES OF CORPORATIONS IN DIFFERENT LEGAL SYSTEMS

One important economic data that you should keep on the back burner as you go through the materials in this casebook concerns the ownership structure of corporations, especially listed ones (in closely held corporations, by definition, the ownership structure is concentrated and there is usually one or a small group of controlling shareholders and some minority shareholders). Data on the ownership structure of listed corporations that can be compared across countries are however somehow difficult to obtain. In fact, notwithstanding extensive disclosure obligations concerning the ownership of shares in listed corporations in all developed nations and most developing ones, to precisely calculate the average stake of the controlling shareholder is fairly difficult. Different legal devices can be used to enhance, and sometimes hide, the actual voting power of shareholders, such as pyramid structures, different classes of shares, trusts, and foreign holding corporations, and shareholders' agreements. There is a general consensus, however, that the ownership structure of listed corporations in common law systems, especially the U.S. and the U.K., is more widespread than in civil law countries, even if some scholars have challenged this conclusion (*see*, e.g., an interesting study by Clifford G. Holderness, *The Myth of Diffuse Ownership in the United States*, 22 REV. FINANC. STUD. 1377 (2009), observing, "[A]lthough many believe that the United States has diffuse ownership, the evidence is to the contrary. Among a representative sample of U.S. public firms, 96% of them have block holders").

The data from an article by Professor Van der Elst of Tilburg University (Christoph Van der Elst, *Industry specificities and size of corporations: Determinants of ownership structures*, 24 INT'L REV. L. & ECON. 425 (2004)) confirm this observation:

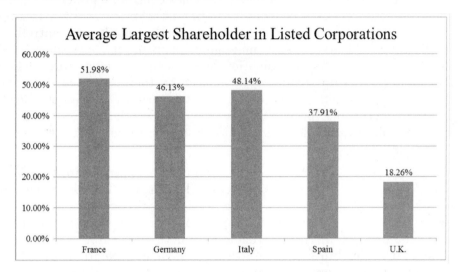

Japan has a unique ownership structure. According to empirical evidence, the percentage of listed corporations (excluding those in emerging markets) that have a controlling shareholder holding more than one-third of its shares is around 15% as of 2005. Also, controlling shareholders of Japanese listed corporations are often other listed corporations that do not have a controlling shareholder. Thus, Japanese listed corporations are rather widely held in comparison to those of continental European and other East Asian countries (for data available in English, *see*, Stijn Claessens, Simeon Djankov & Larry H.P. Lang, *The Separation of Ownership and Control in East Asian Corporations*, 58 J. FIN. ECON. 81 (2000)). Ownership structures in Japan, however, show significant differences with the U.S. or the U.K. In Japan, a substantial amount of shares of listed corporations is held by banks (this also happens in Germany), insurance companies and other non-financial corporations that have business relationships with the issuer. These shareholders usually support the management. The amount of shares held by each of these shareholders individually is not high, but the aggregate amount could be significant enough to constitute a majority in the shareholders' meeting. Cross-ownership is also very common. To make the situation more complicated, cross-shareholding in large listed corporations (especially those by banks) has declined since the late 1990s, while share ownership by foreign and domestic institutional investors has increased, as it has also happened more recently in other countries, for example, Italy. On the other hand, small and medium listed corporations still seem to keep cross-shareholding relationships. *See* Gen Goto, *Legally "Strong" Shareholders of Japan*, 3 MICHIGAN JOURNAL OF PRIVATE EQUITY AND VENTURE CAPITAL LAW, 25, 44–46 (2014).

A fascinating puzzle is whether legal rules determine or favor specific ownership structures, or on the other hand the presence of a certain ownership structure influences rulemaking. The lobbies of controlling shareholders, executives and managers, institutional investors and bankers might push for the adoption of rules that favor a more or less widespread ownership structure, depending on their interests. It is the old question of whether the economic structure influences the legal system, or vice versa: probably it is a symbiotic relationship in which economic, political, and legal institutions concur to determine the legal framework.

In any case, you want to keep in mind different ownership structures to fully understand the original effects of legal rules. For example, it is clear that when the ownership structure is more concentrated, the key agency problem concerns the relationship between controlling shareholders and minority shareholders; on the contrary, with a more widespread ownership structure, the crucial agency relationship is the one between directors and managers, on the one hand, and all shareholders, on the other.

We do not want to anticipate problems that will be considered later in this book (Chapter 10), but to further illustrate the consequences of different ownership structures consider for example a rule mandating a public tender offer on all the outstanding shares if someone acquires more than a set threshold of shares (for example, 30%, as it is provided in several European Union countries). The effects of this rule can be very different depending on the fact that the existing controlling shareholder has more or less of the triggering threshold. If he has more, the mandatory tender offer might operate as a protection against hostile bids, because in order to challenge the position of the incumbents, a bidder must be able to launch an expensive offer on *all* the outstanding shares.

But there is more. To know the stake of relevant shareholders is not enough. It is also necessary to consider who the most important shareholders are, and what their interests are. Once again, data are not easy to collect, but for a complex set of economic, legal, political, social, and historical reasons institutional investors (investment funds, pension funds, etc.) generally play a more important role in common law systems, while families often have a controlling stake in continental European countries. State ownership of large enterprises is also more common in some civil law countries (and was obviously also a dominant feature of Communist systems). Banks also play an important role, both as creditors and (sometimes also) as shareholders, in countries such as Germany,

Italy, and Japan. Also worker's ownership has attracted the attention of scholars (*see* Henry Hansmann, *When Does Worker Ownership Work? Esops, Law Firms, Codetermination and Economic Democracy*, 99 YALE L.J. 1749 (1990); more generally for a theoretical framework on different ownership structures in terms of types of relevant shareholders *see* Henry Hansmann, *Ownership of the Firm*, 4 J. LAW, ECON., AND ORG. 267 (1988)).

Different types of shareholders have an important role in the development and application of corporate rules. For example, in an insightful work, John Armour & David Skeel, Jr., *Who Writes the Rules for Hostile Takeovers, and Why?—The Peculiar Divergence of U.S. and U.K. Takeover Regulation*, in 95 GEORGETOWN L. J. 1727 (2007), argue that in the U.S. and the U.K., takeover rules developed differently largely because in the country institutional investors played a more important role and were able to successfully lobby the policy makers to introduce provisions, such as the mandatory bid rule and the board neutrality rule, intended to protect shareholders vis-à-vis directors. But also simply think of the different dynamics that can affect proxy voting or litigation when minority shareholders are institutional investors, with a relatively important stake in the corporation and the ability to use corporate information effectively, as opposed to small individual shareholders that face information asymmetries and collective actions problems.

In short, one interesting issue to keep in mind that links ownership structures with financial issues, is that—and, again, it is a simplification—there are systems that rely more on financial markets (and in particular stock exchanges) to finance the corporation, and systems that rely more on credit extended by banks ("bank-centric" systems). Anglo-Saxon systems fall in the first category; Germany, Japan, and other countries, in the latter.

Another extremely important issue to consider, with respect to ownership structure, is whether corporate groups and "pyramids" (meaning a chain of corporations in which control is exercised by the holding through a high leverage) are present and common, or free-standing corporations are more widespread. A brutal distinction indicates that in many civil law systems, from Japan to Italy, from France to Brazil, listed corporations belong to groups, and groups adopt a pyramid structure; on the other hand, "stand-alone" corporations are more common in the U.S. The distinction is very important because corporate groups raise specific problems in terms of protection of minorities and creditors, problems that will be discussed throughout this book. In addition, it could be argued that groups can offer important legal and economic advantages, but they also present unique challenges, because they create both the incentives and the opportunities to extract private benefits from investors. The existence and relevance of corporate groups is both a cause and a consequence of different legal regimes. A recent and excellent historical (but not only) analysis of the abandonment of the group structure in the U.S. is offered by E. Kandel, K. Kosenko, R. Morck, Yishay Yafeh, *The Great Pyramids of America: A Revised History of US Business Groups, Corporate Ownership and Regulation, 1930–1950*, ECGI Finance Working Paper N° 449/2015, available on *www.ssrn.com*. In the Authors' own words, as clarified in the Abstract of the paper:

"Most listed firms are freestanding in the U.S, while listed firms in other countries often belong to business groups: lasting structures in which listed firms control other listed firms. Hand-collected historical data illuminate how the present ownership structure of the United States arose: (1) Until the mid-20th century, U.S. corporate ownership was unexceptional: large pyramidal groups dominated many industries; (2) About half of these resembled groups elsewhere today in being industrially diversified and family controlled; but the others were tightly focused and had widely held apex firms; (3) U.S. business groups disappeared gradually, primarily in the 1940s, and by 1950 were largely gone; their demise took place against growing concerns that they posed a threat to competition and even to society; (4) The data link the disappearance of business groups to reforms that targeted them explicitly—the Public Utility Holding Company Act (1935) and rising inter-corporate dividend taxation (after 1935), or indirectly—enhanced investor protection (after 1934), the Investment Company Act (1940) and escalating estate taxes. Banking reforms and rejuvenated antitrust enforcement may have indirectly contributed too. These reforms, sustained in a lasting anti-big business climate, promoted the dissolution of existing groups and discouraged the formation of new ones. Thus, a multi-pronged reform agenda, sustained by a supportive political climate, created an economy of freestanding firms."

CHAPTER 2

CHOICE OF APPLICABLE CORPORATE LAWS AND REGULATORY COMPETITION

■ ■ ■

INTRODUCTION

Any time you are faced with a corporate law problem, the first question you have to ask yourself is what are the applicable laws governing the issue at hand. In essence, what you have is a choice-of-law determination, whereby you must determine which statutes and case law precedents govern the internal affairs of the corporation. This question is not only crucial from a practical point of view, but is also important, and perhaps even more interesting, from a theoretical standpoint, because it affects the way corporate law develops and influences both the legislature and the judiciary in their rulemaking activity at a substantive level.

In the United States, corporate law is largely within the competence of the states. While the federal legislature has adopted some governance rules that are applicable to publicly held corporations, the internal affairs of a corporation are for the most part subject to the laws of the state of incorporation. For obvious reasons concerning the common cultural and historical background of the states, harmonizing initiatives such as the enactment of the Model Business Corporation Act, and also a phenomenon of imitation among states, there are significant similarities among both the corporate law statutes and case law of the different states, but meaningful differences still exist.

As in the U.S., corporations in the European Union are regulated at the level of the single Member States. From a comparative perspective, however, the differences that exist among different jurisdictions within the European Union are more profound than the differences that can be found in the United States among different states. Language and cultural barriers and the path-dependency of legal systems affect, and to some extent hinder, the harmonization of European corporate law. In an effort to harmonize European corporate law, the European Union has enacted several directives and regulations. These directives and regulations cover, for example, the regulation of legal capital, financial statements, mergers and divisions, shareholders' rights, takeovers, etc.

The starting point of our analysis in this chapter is that, generally speaking, there are two choice-of-law principles that can be adopted in order to identify applicable corporate law rules. The first, typically found in the U.S. and in other common law countries, is the "incorporation principle," also referred to as the "freedom of incorporation principle." Under the "incorporation principle," the internal affairs of a corporation are governed by the laws of the state in which the corporation is incorporated, meaning the jurisdiction in which the procedure to establish the corporation as a legal entity has been perfected. Pursuant to this rule, the internal affairs of a corporation are subject to the laws of the state of incorporation even if the corporation does no business in that state, and has no meaningful contacts with the state, besides having incorporated there. The historical rationale for this rule is probably rooted in the colonial period, when England wanted to be able to regulate enterprises primarily doing business abroad, as long as they were created in England. The formal process of incorporation, in these jurisdictions, is quite simple. In order to incorporate, it is generally sufficient to file the governing documents of the corporation (charter and bylaws) with the Secretary of State or other similar office, and to pay a small fee.

The second choice-of-law principle, which prevails (or used to prevail) in continental Europe, and more generally in civil law systems, is the so-called "real seat approach." According to this rule, a corporation is subject to the laws of the state with which it has the strongest physical connection. This physical connection is known as the corporation's "real seat." The real seat of a corporation is defined in a variety of ways in different systems, for example based on where the "center of the administration" is located, which is determined by where the corporate bodies (board of directors or shareholders' meeting) meet; or alternatively, a corporation's real seat is located in the jurisdiction where most of the corporate purpose is carried on. A corporation doing business primarily in France, for instance, would have to incorporate in France and would be regulated by French law. The consequences of the real seat approach to choice-of-law can be significant. For example, using again the case of a corporation with its real seat in France, but which is formally incorporated in the U.K., a French judge might conclude that the corporation is subject to French law, and since the corporation did not properly incorporate in France, it might even be treated as a partnership, with members potentially facing unlimited liability for the obligations of the corporation; in addition, several issues concerning the internal affairs of the entity would be governed by French law, notwithstanding incorporation in the U.K.

As you can see, these two choice-of-law principles have very different effects. In a system based on the incorporation principle, corporations are free to choose the state in which they prefer to incorporate independently of where they are physically located or where they do business. In other words, they can engage in regulatory arbitrage. On the other hand, under the "real seat" approach, since the applicable law depends on physical contacts with a specific jurisdiction, it might be impossible, or inefficient, for a corporation to choose incorporation in one jurisdiction over another. This means that in countries that follow the incorporation principle, a regulatory competition can develop among states in order to attract corporations. This type of regulatory competition, however, is much rarer in systems following the real seat principle.

Why do states compete to attract corporations under the incorporation principle? Since a corporation can choose to incorporate in a certain state without carrying on any business activity there, the answer cannot simply be that a state is acting in order to attract more business activity. There are probably two major reasons why states engage in regulatory competition. One has to do with tax revenues. Because there might be state taxes or other fees that apply to corporations incorporated in a given jurisdiction, the desire for increased revenues can make it very important for a state to attract corporations. In the U.S., for example, a "franchise tax," which is based on the shares issued, must be paid in the state of incorporation (attention, this is not an income tax based on earnings!). The proceeds from these taxes can be an important percentage of the state's budget, especially in states with a smaller economy. It should be observed that in some systems, however, these kinds of taxes are not permitted, which is a potential disincentive for the development of regulatory competition. The second reason for state regulatory competition is that having a large number of corporations incorporated in a state, and therefore subject to its laws, can be very profitable for the local legal services industry. Lawyers and other legal constituencies can therefore be particularly invested in regulatory competition for incorporation.

You deserve a warning, however. The common wisdom that States, especially in the U.S., compete to attract and retain corporations, possibly with the exception of Delaware, is questioned by some scholars. In a brilliant article, Marcel Kahan of New York University and Ehud Kamar of Tel Aviv University (but at the time of the article at the University of Southern California) have argued that the existence of fierce competition among states in this area is largely an urban legend. They list several reasons to support their claim. As a side research project, find this paper and keep it in mind as you continue reading: *The Myth of State Competition in Corporate Law*, 55 STANFORD L. REV. 679 (2002).

Interestingly enough, both the incorporation and the real seat principles often have exceptions. For example, even in the U.S., where the incorporation principle prevails, there are some states that have adopted so-called "pseudo-foreign corporation statutes." These statutes mandate the application of some local state rules to corporations incorporated elsewhere, if the corporation is primarily doing business within the state.

One question we will discuss is whether these types of provisions are compatible with the U.S. Constitution. There are similar exceptions with regard to the real seat approach. In Europe, where the real seat principle is or was followed in many countries (for example, France, Germany, Italy), the principle has been eroded by the jurisprudence of the European Court of Justice, which—to put it briefly—considers it in conflict with the freedom of establishment principle set forth by the European treaties. In this chapter, we will consider these possible "exceptions" to the incorporation and real seat principles.

In the U.S., the state of Delaware is the clear "winner" in the "market for corporate charters," as the majority of the listed and the largest corporations are incorporated there. Delaware snatched the competitive advantage in incorporation originally enjoyed by the neighboring state of New Jersey. In considering the success that Delaware has had in attracting the incorporation business, one question that comes to mind is how it maintains its competitive advantage over other jurisdictions. Wouldn't it be easy for other jurisdictions to simply "copy" Delaware's corporate law statutes, therefore becoming more attractive? After all, there is no copyright on statutory materials.

The answer to this question is, obviously, that simply copying statutory materials is not sufficient to attract corporations. While Delaware's statutory rules can be copied by other jurisdictions fairly easily, one might argue that the real advantage of Delaware (and other successful states in the incorporation market) is not so much in its statutory provisions, but rather in the sophistication, specialization, and efficiency of its judiciary. Delaware courts are highly specialized in corporate law matters, partially as a consequence of the large number of important and complex cases that they decide. This level of specialization of the judges, and the extensive body of corporate law precedent, is much more difficult for another state to replicate than Delaware's statutory provisions. Another reason that might make Delaware an attractive forum for corporate litigants is the fact that the Delaware Court of Chancery is historically a court of equity, and therefore there are no jury trials.

As we have discussed, the "internal affairs" of a corporation can be regulated by either the laws of the state of incorporation or by the laws of the state where the real seat is located. The "internal affairs" of a corporation generally concern relationships among shareholders, relationships between shareholders and the corporation, relationships between the corporation and directors, the inner workings of corporate bodies, etc. It is important, however, to understand precisely what corporate actions are included in the definition of "internal affairs." For example, a bond indenture, a contract concerning the issuing of bonds to obtain financial resources, is generally not included in the definition of internal affairs (at least in the U.S.). Therefore it can happen, for example, that a Delaware corporation will issue bonds and the relationship between the corporation and the bondholders will be governed by a contract subject to New York law, rather than by Delaware law. Of course, there are always issues that fall into a "gray area," wherein it can be debated whether the issue concerns the internal affairs of a corporation or not. One example of this "gray area" is the doctrine of piercing the corporate veil (Chapter 3), which deals with the situations in which, contrary to the general rule, shareholders might be liable toward third parties for the obligations of the corporation. In this chapter we will also address this question.

Another policy question that we will address in this chapter is whether regulatory competition—famously defined by Roberta Romano as the "genius" of American corporate law—results in either a "race to the top" or a "race to the bottom." In other words, does a competitive marketplace for rules lead to the development and enforcement of more efficient rules, rules that are sufficiently protective of the different stakeholders involved with the life of the corporation, and particularly minority shareholders and creditors ("race to the top"); or does competition lead to excessive laxity in corporate law rules, brought about by state legislatures and judges, who in order to attract corporations, craft rules aimed solely at pleasing corporate decision makers such as managers and controlling shareholders who decide where to incorporate ("race to the bottom")? Does regulatory competition simply result in freedom of contract, flexibility, protections for directors and controlling shareholders against liability? Prominent scholars have argued that regulatory competition results in excessive freedom of contract and does not provide adequate protection for minority shareholders, creditors, and other stakeholders. Others advocate, however, that if a state is not protective enough of investors and other stakeholders (again, especially minority shareholders and creditors), they will not invest in a corporation incorporated locally or, at least, ask for a higher return to compensate for increased risk, therefore resulting in a higher cost of capital for the corporation. Following this view, regulatory competition produces efficient rules that strike an optimal balance between the needs of the different corporate constituencies. We will have to discuss, therefore, if the "market for rules," in corporate law, works well or is plagued by market failures. It is quite interesting, also from a methodological point of view, to look at the process of rulemaking as a "market" in which legislatures, policy makers, and courts compete.

One final caveat. The principles we discuss in this chapter concern the substantive corporate law rules applicable to a corporation. They are, as mentioned, choice-of-law rules, and must be distinguished from the issue of jurisdiction. Jurisdiction concerns the court or courts that have the power to adjudicate corporate disputes, and can follow different criteria. It is therefore possible that the courts of state X (or federal courts) have jurisdiction over a certain dispute, even if they must apply the substantive laws of state Y. This possibility further complicates our analysis, and raises also strategic procedural questions on where to litigate. While this is not the focus of this chapter (jurisdiction in the international context will be discussed in Chapter 12), it is an issue that must be taken into account and that is addressed in some of the cases presented.

FREEDOM OF INCORPORATION

As we discussed in the Introduction, under the incorporation theory, the internal affairs of a corporation are regulated by the laws of the state of incorporation. The incorporation theory provides that the laws of the state of incorporation regulate the internal affairs of a corporation, regardless of whether the corporation is in fact headquartered in that state or has business connections therein. This rule, however, which is generally followed in the U.S. as well as in other jurisdictions, is not without possible exceptions. For example, some U.S. States have adopted statutes commonly referred to as "pseudo-foreign corporations' statutes." These statutes are designed to require the application of a particular state's law when a corporation, although incorporated in a different jurisdiction, has significant connections with a particular state. In other words, these rules tend to achieve a similar legal effect as the "real seat approach." A famous example of a "pseudo-foreign corporation statute" is § 2115 of the California Corporations Code. Pursuant to this provision, when a corporation meets certain requirements that indicate that it is predominantly doing business in California, some California corporate law rules will apply. Other jurisdictions have adopted similar provisions. In the U.S. there has been a lively debate on the legitimacy of these statutes, specifically on whether they are compatible with the U.S. Constitution and/or violate the "internal affairs doctrine." The following case is an excellent example of the application of § 2115 of the California Corporations Code to a business entity incorporated in Utah, but that was doing business in California.

ROSS A. WILSON V. LOUISIANA-PACIFIC RESOURCES, INC.

Court of Appeal, First District, Division 2, California, 1982
138 Cal.App.3d 216

GRODIN, P. J.

The question presented by this appeal, one of first impression and considerable significance, is whether the State of California may constitutionally impose its law requiring cumulative voting by shareholders upon a corporation which is domiciled elsewhere, but whose contacts with California, as measured by various criteria, are greater than those with any other jurisdiction.

Section 2115 of the California Corporations Code[1] provides for the application of various provisions of that code to a foreign corporation which (on the basis of a three-factor formula including property, payroll and sales) does a majority of its business in this state, where in addition a

---

[1] Unless otherwise noted, all references are to the Corporations Code. Section 2115 provides: "(a) A foreign corporation (other than a foreign association or foreign nonprofit corporation but including a foreign parent corporation even though it does not itself transact intrastate business) is subject to this section if the average of the property factor, the payroll factor and the sales factor (as defined in Sections 25129, 25132 and 25134 of the Revenue and Taxation Code) with respect to it is more than 50 percent during its latest full income year and if more than one-half of its outstanding voting securities are held of record by persons having addresses in this state. The property factor, payroll factor and sales factor shall be those used in computing the portion of its income allocable to this state in its franchise tax return or, with respect to corporations the allocation of whose income is governed by special formulas or which are not required to file separate or any tax returns, which would have been so used if they were governed by such three-factor formula. The determination of these factors with respect to any parent corporation shall be made on a consolidated basis, including in a unitary computation (after elimination of intercompany transactions) the property, payroll and sales of the parent and all of its subsidiaries in which it owns directly or indirectly more than 50 percent of the outstanding shares entitled to vote for the election of directors, but deducting a percentage of such property, payroll and sales of any subsidiary equal to the percentage minority ownership, if any, in such subsidiary. For the purpose of this subdivision, any securities held to the knowledge of the issuer in the names of broker-dealers or nominees for broker-dealers shall not be considered outstanding. "(b) The following chapters and sections of this division shall apply to a foreign corporation subject to this section (to the exclusion of the law of the jurisdiction in which it is incorporated): "Chapter 1 (general provisions and definitions), to the extent applicable to the following provisions; "Section 301 (annual election of directors); "Section 303 (removal of directors without cause); "Section 304 (removal of directors by court proceedings); "Section 305, subdivision (c) (filling of director vacancies where less than a majority in office elected by shareholders); "Section 309 (directors' standard of care); "Section 316 (excluding paragraph (3) of subdivision (a) and paragraph (3) of subdivision (f) (liability of directors for unlawful distributions); "Section 317 (indemnification of directors, officers and others); "Sections 500 to 505, inclusive (limitations on corporate distributions in cash or property); "Section 506 (liability of shareholder who receives unlawful distribution); "Section 600, subdivisions (b) and (c) (requirement for annual shareholders' meeting and remedy if same not timely held); "Section 708, subdivisions (a), (b) and (c) (shareholder's right to cumulate votes at any election of directors); "Section 1001, subdivision (d) (limitations on sale of assets); "Section 1101 (provisions following subdivision (e)) (limitations on mergers); "Chapter 12 (commencing with Section 1200) (reorganizations); "Chapter 13 (commencing with Section 1300) (dissenters' rights); "Sections 1500 and 1501 (records and reports); "Section 1508 (action by Attorney General); "Chapter 16 (commencing with Section 1600) (rights of inspection). "(c) Subdivision (a) shall become applicable to any foreign corporation only upon the first day of the first income year of the corporation commencing on or after the 30th day after the filing by it of the report pursuant to Section 2108 showing that the tests referred to in subdivision (a) have been met or on or after the entry of a final order by a court of competent jurisdiction declaring that such tests have been met. "(d) Subdivision (a) shall cease to be applicable at the end of any income year during which a report pursuant to Section 2108 shall have been filed showing that at least one of the tests referred to in subdivision (a) is not met or a final order shall have been entered by a court of competent jurisdiction declaring that one of such tests is not met, provided that such filing or order shall be ineffective if a contrary report or order shall be made or entered before the end of such income year. "(e) This section does not apply to any corporation with outstanding securities listed on any national securities exchange certified by the Commissioner of Corporations under subdivision (o) of Section 25100, or to any corporation if all of its voting shares (other than directors' qualifying shares) are owned directly or indirectly by a corporation or corporations not subject to this section."

majority of its outstanding voting securities are held of record by persons having addresses in this state. Among the provisions are subdivisions (a), (b) and (c) of section 708,[2] which provide for cumulative voting.

Plaintiff Ross A. Wilson brought this action against Louisiana-Pacific Resources, Inc., a Utah corporation, seeking a declaratory judgment that the defendant met the tests of section 2115, and that he was therefore entitled to cumulative voting in accordance with section 708. The trial court found that in the years preceding the action, the average of the defendant's property, payroll, and sales in California as defined by the California corporations statute exceeded 50 percent, and that more than 50 percent of its shareholders entitled to vote resided in California, so that the statutory conditions had been met. It also found that except for being domiciled in Utah and having a transfer agent there, defendant had virtually no business connection with Utah, that its principal place of business has been in California since at least 1971, that its meetings of shareholders and directors are held in California, and that all of its employees and all of its bank accounts are in California. Finally, the court concluded, contrary to defendant's contentions, that there existed no constitutional obstacle to the application of the cumulative voting requirement to defendant, and that its "[c]umulative voting will be in effect a judicial addendum to defendant's articles of incorporation, and all of its shareholders are entitled to cumulative voting whether they are California residents or not." [. . .]

Discussion

The law of the State of Utah provides for straight voting in an election of directors, but permits cumulative voting if the articles of incorporation so provide. (Utah Bus. Corp. Act (1953) § 16–10–31.) Neither the articles of incorporation nor the bylaws of appellant provide for cumulative voting. Appellant contends that for California to require cumulative voting under these circumstances would violate (1) the full faith and credit clause of the United States Constitution; (2) the commerce clause of the United States Constitution; (3) the "property and vested right protections" of the United States and California

---

[2] Section 708, as relevant, provides:"(a) Every shareholder complying with subdivision (b) and entitled to vote at any election of directors may cumulate such shareholder's votes and give one candidate a number of votes equal to the number of directors to be elected multiplied by the number of votes to which the shareholder's shares are normally entitled, or distribute the shareholder's votes on the same principle among as many candidates as the shareholder thinks fit."(b) No shareholder shall be entitled to cumulate votes (i.e., cast for any candidate a number of votes greater than the number of votes which such shareholder normally is entitled to cast) unless such candidate or candidates' names have been placed in nomination prior to the voting and the shareholder has given notice at the meeting prior to the voting of the shareholder's intention to cumulate the shareholder's votes. If any one shareholder has given such notice, all shareholders may cumulate their votes for candidates in nomination. "(c) In any election of directors, the candidates receiving the highest number of affirmative votes of the shares entitled to be voted for them up to the number of directors to be elected by such shares are elected."

Constitutions; (4) the contract clauses of the United States and California Constitutions [and other issues]. We consider these contentions in turn.

I. Full Faith and Credit

(1) The full faith and credit clause of the federal Constitution (art. IV, § 1) requires that "Full Faith and Credit . . . be given in each State to the public Acts, Records, and Judicial Proceedings of every other State. . . ." Although the phrase "public Acts, Records and Judicial Proceedings" has been construed to include statutes as well as judicial decisions (e.g., *Bradford Elec. Co. v. Clapper* (1932) 286 U.S. 145 [76 L.Ed. 1026, 52 S.Ct. 571, 82 A.L.R. 696]), the Supreme Court has recognized that "[a] rigid and literal enforcement of the full faith and credit clause, without regard to the statute of the forum, would lead to the absurd result that, wherever the conflict arises, the statute of each state must be enforced in the courts of the other, but cannot be in its own. Unless by force of that clause a greater effect is thus to be given to a state statute abroad than the clause permits it to have at home, it is unavoidable that this Court determine for itself the extent to which the statute of one state may qualify or deny rights asserted under the statute of another." (*Alaska Packers Assn. v. Comm'n* (1935) 294 U.S. 532, 547 [79 L.Ed. 1044, 1052, 55 S.Ct. 518].)

Under the doctrine of *Alaska Packers, supra.*, determination as to application of conflicting statutes was to be made "by appraising the governmental interests of each jurisdiction, and turning the scale of decision according to their weight." (294 U.S. at p. 547 [79 L.Ed. at p. 1052].) In this balancing process it was presumed that "every state is entitled to enforce in its own courts its own statutes, lawfully enacted. One who challenges that right, because of the force given to a conflicting statute of another state by the full faith and credit clause, assumes the burden of showing, upon some rational basis, that of the conflicting interests involved those of the foreign state are superior to those of the forum." (*Id.*, at pp. 547–548 [79 L.Ed. at p. 1052].)

Since *Alaska Packers*, the Supreme Court has abandoned the weighing-of-interests requirement in favor of a less exacting standard corresponding to the requirements of the due process clause. (*Allstate Ins. Co. v. Hague* (1981) 449 U.S. 302, 308, fn. 10 [66 L.Ed.2d 521, 527, 101 S.Ct. 633].) In determining whether a state's choice-of-law decision exceeds federal constitutional requirements, the current rule is that "for a State's substantive law to be selected in a constitutionally permissible manner, that State must have a significant contact or significant aggregation of contacts, creating state interests, such that choice of its law is neither arbitrary nor fundamentally unfair." (*Id.*, at pp. 312–313 [66 L.Ed.2d at p. 531].)

We consider that test is met here; the criteria which a foreign corporation must meet in order to be subject to section 2115 assure the existence of significant aggregation of contacts. And the state interests created by those contacts are indeed substantial. California's present law requiring cumulative voting by shareholders continues in effect a policy which has existed in this state since the Constitution of 1879. In *Western Air Lines, Inc. v. Sobieski* (1961) 191 Cal.App.2d 399 [12 Cal.Rptr. 719], the court, observing that "[i]t would seem too evident to require protracted dissertation that the right of cumulative voting is a substantial right" (*id.*, at p. 414), held that even in the absence of express statutory mandate, the Corporations Commissioner was justified in refusing to permit the elimination of cumulative voting by a "pseudo foreign" corporation, i.e., "one with its technical domicile outside of this state but one which exercises most of its corporate vitality within this state." (*Id.*, at p. 412.) A contrary holding, the court reasoned, "would enable a foreign corporation to destroy the rights which the State of California has deemed worthy of protection by the enactment of the Corporate Securities Act." (*Id.*, at pp. 413–414.) Section 2115 incorporates the policy reflected in *Sobieski* and applies it more generally, to all pseudo-foreign corporations meeting the statutory criteria.

Utah, on the other hand, has no interests which are offended by cumulative voting; and, whatever interest it might have in maintaining a *laissez faire* policy on that score would seem to be clearly outweighed by the interests of California, in which a majority of shareholders and the corporation's business activity is located. Thus, even on the earlier analysis of *Alaska Packers*, the full faith and credit clause provides no bar to the application of California's statute. [. . .]

The "internal affairs doctrine," according to which courts traditionally looked to the law of the state of incorporation in resolving questions regarding a corporation's internal affairs (see Oldham, *California Regulates Pseudo-Foreign Corporations-Trampling Upon the Tramp?* (1977) 17 Santa Clara L.Rev. 85, 85–90); has no application here. That doctrine has never been followed blindly in California (see *Wait v. Kern River Mining etc. Co.* (1909) 157 Cal. 16, 21 [106 P. 98]; see also *Western Air Lines, Inc. v. Sobieski, supra.*, 191 Cal.App.2d 399); it is inconsistent with the "comparative impairment" approach used by this state in resolving conflict of law problems (*Offshore Rental Co. v. Continental Oil Co.* (1978) 22 Cal.3d 157, 164–165 [148 Cal.Rptr. 867, 583 P.2d 721]); and it is in any event not determinative of the constitutional issue. This is not a common choice-of-law question; the Legislature has resolved the conflicts issue by mandating application of this state's law under certain conditions. The question is whether that mandate is constitutional. (See *Allstate Ins. Co. v. Hague, supra.*, 449 U.S. at pp. 307–308 [66 L.Ed.2d at p. 527].) For the reasons we have discussed, we conclude that it is, so far as the full faith and credit clause is concerned.

II. Commerce Clause

(2) Although article I, section 8, clause 3 of the federal Constitution grants Congress power "[t]o regulate commerce . . . among the several States," Congress has not chosen to regulate the subject in litigation here nor has it undertaken to establish guidelines for regulation by the states. Appellant's commerce clause argument is based, therefore, upon the negative implications of dormant congressional authority.

The United States Supreme Court has established the standard for determining the validity of state statutes in such situations: "Where the statute regulates even-handedly to effectuate a legitimate local public interest, and its effects on interstate commerce are only incidental, it will be upheld unless the burden imposed on such commerce is clearly excessive in relation to the putative local benefits. [Citation.] If a legitimate local purpose is found, then the question becomes one of degree. And the extent of the burden that will be tolerated will of course depend on the nature of the local interest involved, and on whether it could be promoted as well with a lesser impact on interstate activities." (*Pike v. Bruce Church, Inc.* (1970) 397 U.S. 137, 142 [25 L.Ed.2d 174, 178, 90 S.Ct. 844]; see also, *Raymond Motor Transportation, Inc. v. Rice* (1978) 434 U.S. 429, 441–442 [54 L.Ed.2d 664, 675, 98 S.Ct. 787].)

We observe, initially, that the challenged statute "regulates even-handedly" within the meaning of the *Pike* guidelines; it applies to covered foreign corporations the same rules which are applied to corporations domiciled within the state. The statute thus imposes no special or distinct burden upon out-of-state interests. (See Tribe, American Constitutional Law (1978) pp. 326–327.)

The nature, strength, and duration of California's interest in the cumulative voting principle, and in the application of that principle to pseudo-foreign corporations have previously been considered in this opinion. There remain to be considered the effects of that application upon interstate activities.

One effect of section 2115 may well be to deter corporations from making their legal homes elsewhere for the purpose of avoiding California's protective corporate legislation, and thus to diminish the practice of "charter-mongering" among states (see Jennings, *The Role of the States in Corporate Regulation and Investor Protection* (1958) 23 Law & Contemp. Prob. 193, 194–196); but that, presumably, is not an effect which would offend the policies of the commerce clause; and appellant does not so contend. Rather, appellant contends that the application of cumulative voting requirements to pseudo-foreign corporations as provided by section 2115 will have the effect of causing it and other foreign corporations already operating in California to reduce their property, payroll, and sales in this state below the 50 percent level, and will deter foreign corporations contemplating the transaction of business in this state from increasing their business activities above that level.

There is no suggestion, or evidence, that section 2115 was adopted for the purpose of deterring foreign corporations from doing business in this state; nor is there any direct evidence that it has had or will have such an effect. On the contrary, what evidence there is in the record on this point consists of testimony by appellant's president that he knew of no adverse effect on appellant's business which would be caused by cumulative voting.

Appellant argues that adverse consequences are predictable from "potentially conflicting claims of shareholders as to which state [law] governs" the method of voting by shareholders, and from the "transient nature of the applicability of the California statute." [. . .]

The potential for conflict and resulting uncertainty from California's statute is substantially minimized by the nature of the criteria specified in section 2115. A corporation can do a majority of its business in only one state at a time; and it can have a majority of its shareholders resident in only one state at a time. If a corporation meets those requirements in this state, no other state is in a position to regulate the method of voting by shareholders on the basis of the same or similar criteria. It might also be said that no other state could claim as great an interest in doing so. In any event, it does not appear that any other state has attempted to do so. If California's statute were replicated in all states, no conflict would result. We conclude that the potential for conflict is, on this record, speculative and without substance.

What appellant refers to as the "transient nature" of the statute's applicability, i.e., its application from year to year based upon the prior year's activity, could conceivably be a problem for a corporation whose business activity within the state fluctuated widely, but the "worst-case" scenario-that such a corporation might find it necessary to adopt cumulative voting as a means of assuring compliance on a continuing basis-does not appear to be so burdensome as to result in a significant restraint upon commerce among the states. We are not told, for example, of any diminution of activity in this state by foreign corporations as a result of *Western Air Lines, Inc. v. Sobieski, supra.*, 191 Cal.App.2d 399. [. . .]

III. Due Process

(3) Appellant contends that section 2115 is a retrospective law which impairs property rights and destroys vested rights in violation of due process. Before 1977 the California Corporations Code did not purport to apply directly to foreign corporations, and appellant made substantial investments in California before section 2115 was enacted in 1977. Its 5,000 shareholders had a vested voting right, it argues, to insist that their

directors be elected by the straight voting procedure authorized by Utah law. This right, it asserts, was violated by section 2115.

The standard of review of economic legislation such as section 2115 is clear. Such legislative acts are clothed with a presumption of constitutionality and "... 'the burden is on one complaining of a due process violation to establish that the legislature has acted in an arbitrary and irrational way.' [Citation.]" (*Duke Power Co. v. Carolina Env. Study Group* (1978) 438 U.S. 59, 83 [57 L.Ed.2d 595, 618, 98 S.Ct. 2620].)

We discern neither arbitrariness nor irrationality in section 2115. As one comprehensive comment on the statute has pointed out, the section "attempts to insure that the social policies of California, as manifested in its corporations code, will no longer be circumvented by such [pseudo-foreign] corporations pursuant to the internal affairs doctrine." (Oldham, *California Regulates Pseudo-Foreign Corporations—Trampling Upon the Tramp?, supra,* 17 Santa Clara L.Rev. 85, 90.) Such a desire to assert control over the affairs of foreign corporations has been upheld by no less an authority than Justice Cardozo: "[W]hen countless corporations, organized on paper in neighboring states, live and move and have their being in New York, a sound public policy demands that our legislature be invested with [a] measure of control." (*German-American Coffee Co. v. Diehl* (1915) 216 N.Y. 57 [109 N.E. 875, 877].) In sum, "Section 2115 reflects a legislative judgment that California has the most significant relationship to a pseudo-foreign corporation which satisfies the section 2115 tests, and that California has the greatest interest in regulating such a corporation, since its principal place of business [is] in California and the majority of its shareholders reside in California." (Oldham, *California Regulates Pseudo-Foreign Corporations—Trampling Upon the Tramp?, supra,* 17 Santa Clara L.Rev. 85, 98, fn. omitted.) Such a judgment-in view of the significant social costs which might result if pseudo-foreign corporations could ignore the public policies of this state-is not irrational. [. . .]

IV. Contract Clause

(4) Appellant next argues that section 2115 impermissibly infringes on its corporate charter from the State of Utah in violation of the contract clause of the federal and state Constitutions. (U.S. Const., art. I, § 10, cl. 1; Cal. Const., art. I, § 9.)

The Supreme Court set forth the definitive standard for contract clause analysis in *Allied Structural Steel Co. v. Spannaus* (1978) 438 U.S. 234, 244–245 [57 L.Ed.2d 727, 736–737]: "[T]he first inquiry must be whether the state law has, in fact, operated as a substantial impairment of a contractual relationship. The severity of the impairment measures the height of the hurdle the state legislation must clear. Minimal alteration of contractual obligations may end the inquiry at its first stage. Severe impairment, on the other hand, will push the inquiry to a careful examination of the nature and purpose of the state legislation."

Here, [. . .] defendant shows only that its charter agreement has been changed to provide for cumulative voting; no showing whatever of hardship is made. This is a paradigm case of "minimal alteration" of contract (*Id.*, at p. 245 [57 L.Ed.2d at p. 737]). Section 2115's requirement of cumulative voting is "a mild one indeed, hardly burdensome . . . but nonetheless an important one to the State's interest. The Contract Clause does not forbid such a measure." (*El Paso v. Simmons* (1965) 379 U.S. 497, 516–517 [13 L.Ed.2d 446, 459, 85 S.Ct. 577].)

[The Court finally concludes that § 2115 does not violate the equal protection clause of the Fourteenth Amendment to the federal Constitution, and other minor issues]

The judgment is affirmed.

NOTES AND QUESTIONS

1.   What is cumulative voting? What advantage do you think the plaintiff sought in applying cumulative voting, as opposed to straight voting?

2.   The court discusses several quite complex constitutional law issues that you might not be very familiar with, or that you might have forgotten. Try to understand them, but keep in mind that the key point here is to understand whether California can regulate corporations that have a significant connection with the territory of the state, even if they are incorporated elsewhere.

3.   What is the test used by Section 2115 of the California Corporations Code to determine if a corporation should be subject to California law? Do you think that if other states would adopt the same test, there might be a conflict with respect to what state corporate laws would apply? Does the test create uncertainty on the applicable law from year to year?

4.   In this case, the court affirmed that Utah had no interests that were offended by cumulative voting. Do you agree with the court's reasoning? Would the ability of states like Utah to effectively compete to obtain a share of the "incorporation market" be hindered by the widespread adoption of pseudo-foreign corporation statutes?

5.   The court's decision to apply cumulative voting resulted in a stronger protection of the voting interests of minority shareholders. Would the analysis be different (for example, with respect to due process or the contract clause) if the effect of the pseudo-foreign corporation statute would result in denying the rights of the minority, such as for example the possibility to exercise appraisal rights in case of a business transaction?

6. What are the strongest political and policy arguments in favor of adopting a pseudo-foreign corporation statute? What are the potential negative consequences of adopting such a statute?

* * *

As discussed above, provisions such as § 2115 are often the exception, rather than the rule. In the following and more recent case, the Delaware Court of Chancery considered the applicability of § 2115 to a corporation incorporated in Delaware. Not surprisingly, the Court of Chancery reached the opposite conclusion of the California court in *Wilson v. Louisiana-Pacific Resources.* The court held that the internal affairs doctrine prevails, and that the laws of the state of incorporation should regulate the internal affairs of the corporation, notwithstanding the existence of a pseudo-foreign corporation statute.

EXAMEN, INC. V. VANTAGEPOINT VENTURE PARTNERS

Court of Chancery of Delaware, 2005
873 A.2d 318

LAMB, VICE CHANCELLOR.

I.

The plaintiff, a Delaware corporation, seeks a judicial declaration that a stockholder vote on a pending merger is governed by Delaware law. If the vote is governed by Delaware law, common stockholders and preferred stockholders will vote on the merger as a single class.

The defendant, a large venture capital firm that owns 83% of the corporation's preferred stock, argues that California law may control. It relies on a section of the California Corporation Code that suggests California law may apply to govern aspects of the internal affairs of the plaintiff Delaware corporation because it is headquartered in, and has other contacts with, California. If California law were to apply to determining the voting rights of the Delaware corporation's stockholders in connection with the proposed merger, the preferred stockholders would have the right to vote as a separate class, effectively giving the defendant a veto over the merger.

The defendant claims that discovery is needed to determine whether the plaintiff's contacts with California meet the statutory levels that could subject the proposed stockholder vote to California law. The plaintiff, arguing that discovery is unnecessary because Delaware law controls the voting rights of stockholders of the Delaware corporation, has moved for judgment on the pleadings. For the reasons discussed herein, the court grants the motion.

II.

A.   The Parties

The plaintiff, Examen, Inc., is a Delaware corporation that provides web-based management solutions to companies throughout the United States. It has 8,626,826 shares of common stock and 1,090,589 shares of Series A preferred stock outstanding. The preferred stock is convertible to 1,670,782 shares of common. According to its website, Examen is a privately owned corporation, headquartered in Sacramento, California with regional offices in California, Connecticut, Illinois, Massachusetts, and Texas.

The defendant, VantagePoint Venture Partners 1996, is a Delaware limited partnership that owns 83% of Examen's preferred stock. VantagePoint owns no shares of Examen's common stock. According to its website, VantagePoint "is one of the largest and most active venture firms in the world." It has offices in Manhattan and San Bruno, California.

B.   The Dispute

Examen recently entered into a merger agreement with Reed Elsevier, Inc., a Massachusetts corporation. The agreement was approved by Examen's board of directors on February 15, 2005. Immediately thereafter, Examen began preparations for a stockholder vote on the merger. Its preparations were soon complicated by VantagePoint's assertion that Examen's preferred stockholders are entitled to a separate class vote.

Examen argues that, under its charter documents and Delaware General Corporation law, all stockholders vote together as a single class. Examen maintains that the total number of voting shares is 10,297,608, which represents the common stock outstanding plus the preferred stock on a convertible basis. Examen contends that a majority vote of these shares, 5,148,805 votes, constitutes the required votes necessary to approve the merger.

C.   Procedure

In its complaint filed March 3, 2005, Examen seeks a judicial declaration that California law, including but not limited to section 2115 of the California Corporations Code ("CCC"), does not apply to the voting rights of its stockholders. Examen argues that a stockholder vote is governed by the internal affairs doctrine, which states that the internal affairs of a corporation are governed by the law of its state of incorporation. Examen comes before this court in expedited proceedings because its merger agreement with Reed Elsevier expires on April 15, 2005.

In response to Examen's complaint, VantagePoint filed an action in California Superior Court on March 8, 2005. In the California action, VantagePoint requested discovery to determine whether Examen is subject to CCC § 2115. VantagePoint argues that, if it could show that Examen is covered by section 2115, the two classes of stock would vote separately on the merger, effectively giving VantagePoint veto power.

On March 10, acting on Examen's request for an expedited hearing, this court set for March 29 a hearing on Examen's motion for judgment on the pleadings. On March 21, the California court stayed that action until this court rules.

In its answering brief, filed after the California court's ruling, VantagePoint claims there is no case or controversy between the parties. VantagePoint maintains that until it takes discovery and there is a factual inquiry into Examen's status under section 2115, this court may not hear this case. Unless Examen is found to be subject to section 2115, VantagePoint argues, there is no actual controversy between itself and Examen. This is so, the argument goes, because if Examen's contacts with California do not subject Examen to section 2115, Delaware law admittedly applies and all stockholders vote as a single class. Therefore, VantagePoint contends, until Examen's status is determined, there is no case or controversy that is properly before this court.

Alternatively, VantagePoint argues that section 2115 can be applied in conjunction with Delaware law. It argues that section 2115, like NYSE or NASD rules, gives stockholders an additional level of protection over and above Delaware law. VantagePoint maintains that this "additional protection" interpretation of section 2115 is correct despite the plain language of the statute that appears on its face to exclude the application of Delaware corporate law. In an effort to patch the obvious logical gap in its argument, VantagePoint submits that this court is free to perform judicial surgery on section 2115, excising the problematic exclusionary phrase.

In addition, VantagePoint argues that this court cannot decide the issue presented as a choice of law matter. It contends that in order to apply Delaware law to the proposed stockholder vote, this court would need to determine that section 2115 is unconstitutional. VantagePoint argues that such a determination is beyond the reach of this court's judicial power. * * *

B. Choice Of Law

[T]he court turns to VantagePoint's choice of law argument. VantagePoint claims that the issue presented is not a choice of law issue because section 2115 does not conflict with Delaware law. VantagePoint maintains that section 2115 operates only in addition to rights granted under Delaware corporate law and, further, that section 2115, like NYSE and NASD rules, is simply additive to Delaware law. This is clearly not the case. Section 2115 expressly states that it operates "to the exclusion of the law of the jurisdiction in which [the company] is incorporated." Nothing could be more clear than the statute's attempted exclusion of the laws of other jurisdictions.

Faced with the statute's clear exclusionary purpose, VantagePoint contends that section 2115's requirement that preferred stockholder vote as a separate class does not conflict with Delaware law, which permits the establishment of class voting rights. This interpretation of Delaware law is plainly wrong. Applying Delaware law to Examen's certificate of incorporation, the proposed merger must be authorized by a majority of all Examen stockholders voting together as a single class. Requiring that Examen's preferred stockholders vote as a separate class is inconsistent with this rule and in derogation of the rights of Examen's other stockholders. Simply put, in determining the vote required to authorize the merger, this court cannot enforce both Delaware and California law. Therefore, the issue the court faces is clearly one of choice of law, and the court need not determine the constitutionality of section 2115.

C. Internal Affairs Doctrine

Since the proposed stockholder vote implicates the relationship between a corporation and its stockholders, the court analyzes Examen's motion pursuant to the internal affairs doctrine. As the United States Supreme Court has said: "[n]o principle of corporation law and practice is more firmly established than a State's authority to regulate domestic corporations, including the authority to define the voting rights of shareholders." "The internal affairs doctrine is a conflict of laws principle which recognizes that only one State should have the authority to regulate a corporation's internal affairs." "[U]nder the commerce clause a state 'has no interest in regulating the internal affairs of foreign corporations.'" "Thus, . . . application of the internal affairs doctrine is mandated by constitutional principles, except in 'the rarest situations.'"

The Delaware Supreme Court defines "internal corporate affairs" as "those matters which are peculiar to the relationships among or between the corporation and its current officers, directors, and shareholders." Delaware courts have consistently followed *McDermott,* applying the internal affairs doctrine in disputes over the rights of stockholders. More specifically, this court has recently held that section 2115 does not apply to voting rights of a Delaware corporation.

This case is governed by the internal affairs doctrine. At issue here is a contested stockholder vote concerning a merger. This type of vote clearly falls within the parameters set by *McDermott.* A merger vote by stockholders plainly concerns the relationship between the corporation and the stockholders. Therefore, as a Delaware court, this court must apply Delaware law.

As the United States Supreme Court stated in *CTS Corp.,* "a corporation-except in the rarest situations-is organized under, and governed by, the law of a single jurisdiction, traditionally the corporate law of the State of its incorporation." As this court has previously determined, those rarest situations are ones in which "the law of the state of incorporation is inconsistent with a national policy on foreign or interstate commerce." There is nothing rare about the situation presented to this court by VantagePoint. Neither the vote on the proposed merger between Examen and Reed Elsevier, nor the merger itself, implicates any national policy on foreign or interstate commerce. VantagePoint makes no argument or suggestion to the contrary. Guided by the United States Supreme Court's teachings in *CTS Corp.,* this court concludes that Examen's internal affairs are governed by the law of the state of its incorporation, namely Delaware.

Instead of accepting the holdings of *Edgar* and *CTS Corp.,* VantagePoint asks the court to look to another United States Supreme Court case, *Allstate Ins. Co. v. Hague. Allstate* is, however, clearly inapposite. *Allstate* concerns an uninsured motorist lawsuit filed by a resident of one state, whose husband was killed traveling as a motorcycle passenger in another state. Nowhere in *Allstate* does the Court address the internal affairs of a corporation, which is the issue here. Furthermore, *Allstate* was decided in 1981, before both *Edgar* and *CTS Corp.* firmly established the internal affairs doctrine. Given the more recent, and apposite, United States Supreme Court cases, this court declines to apply the language of *Allstate* to the facts presented.

This decision is also not inconsistent with California law. As California courts acknowledge, "[t]he internal affairs doctrine is a conflict of laws principle which recognizes that only one state should have the authority to regulate a corporation's internal affairs ... because otherwise a corporation could be faced with conflicting demands." Additionally, the California Supreme Court acknowledges that disputes about corporate voting rights are governed by the law of the state of incorporation. Delaware is Examen's state of incorporation and thus Delaware's law should apply to Examen's corporate voting rights.

In an effort to rebut the more recent cases that support the internal affairs doctrine, VantagePoint relies on *Provident Gold Mining,* a 1916 California Supreme Court case which held that stockholders of an Arizona corporation were individually liable for the debts and liabilities of the corporation pursuant to the law of California. VantagePoint is unable to cite any more recent California Supreme Court case or one that would expand *Provident Gold Mining's* holding to encompass corporate voting rights of stockholders. The absence of recent case law is telling, especially given the landmark *Edgar* decision in 1982. Moreover, VantagePoint cannot cite one California Supreme Court case that has analyzed section 2115 or some other similar statute purporting to regulate the internal affairs of a Delaware corporation. As the Delaware Supreme Court observed in *Draper* "[t]he California cases do not reveal a clear doctrine . . . that California will, in a case like the instant case, ignore the internal affairs doctrine and apply California law, not Delaware law."

After a review of the relevant case law, this court concludes that the internal affairs doctrine controls the stockholder vote at issue. Since Examen is a Delaware corporation, Delaware law will apply to its internal affairs and all stockholders will be permitted to vote on the proposed merger as a single class.

V.

For the foregoing reasons, the motion for judgment on the pleadings is granted.

NOTES AND QUESTIONS

1. Why do you think VantagePoint wanted to apply class voting to the proposed merger?

2. The Court of Chancery relied heavily on precedents by the U.S. Supreme Court (*Edgar* and *CTS Corp.*), and especially on the arguments in favor of the internal affairs doctrine; the Court also rejected the constitutionality analysis adopted by the California court in *Wilson*. Which analysis do you find more compelling?

3. What effect would a decision by the Court of Chancery deviating from the internal affairs doctrine have had on the ability of Delaware to attract "incorporation business"? Do you think the court was influenced by political or policy concerns?

4. Are you surprised by the fact that, on a fairly similar issue, California and Delaware judges reached almost opposite conclusions? Why? What do you think might be the effect of this split in different states if, for example, a plaintiff has the option to sue either in California or in Delaware? In case of parallel proceedings in the two states, how could the disputes and their possible outcomes be coordinated?

* * *

When one examines both case law and the writings of legal scholars, the prevailing view is that, notwithstanding possible exceptions (such as § 2115 of the California Corporations Code discussed above), U.S. state jurisdictions adhere to the incorporation theory and the internal affairs doctrine. While acceptance of the internal affairs doctrine is largely a settled question in the U.S., the debate over what is included in the definition of the "internal affairs" of a corporation is less clear. As mentioned earlier, the expression "internal affairs" generally refers to disputes among shareholders concerning their corporate rights and duties, disputes concerning the distribution of powers among corporate bodies, directors' powers and liabilities, business combinations, etc. A dispute concerning a contract between a corporation and a third party, or an alleged tort committed by the corporation, however, are excluded from the definition of "internal affairs," and the choice of the law governing these conflicts will be governed by different principles applicable to contract and tort law. There are, however, some issues that fall into a gray area, for which it might be disputed whether they concern the internal affairs of the corporation—and are therefore regulated by the state of incorporation—or not. One example of a "gray area" issue is the doctrine of "piercing the corporate veil." As we will see in the next chapter, the doctrine of "piercing the corporate veil" concerns whether shareholders may be held individually liable toward corporate creditors. The following U.S. case offers some insight into the scope of the definition of "internal affairs," as well as possible exceptions to this rule.

JOHN CARBONE V. NXEGEN HOLDINGS, INC. ET AL.

Superior Court of Connecticut, Judicial District of Hartford, 2013
No. HHDCV136039761S

PECK, J.

The present case concerns a shareholder's attempt to inspect the records of the corporation in which the shareholder owns stock, as well as the records of a subsidiary limited liability company of the corporation. The plaintiff shareholder, John Carbone, commenced the present action by serving a complaint . . . on the defendant, Nxegen Holdings, Inc., on March 6, 2013. In that complaint, the plaintiff alleges the following relevant facts. The plaintiff is a shareholder of the defendant. The defendant, a corporation incorporated under Delaware law, owns the subsidiary Nxegen, LLC ("the LLC"). The defendant's principal place of business is in Middletown, Connecticut.

[The central issue concerns the application of the internal affairs doctrine and the applicability of Delaware or Connecticut laws to the inspection rights of a shareholder]

[T]he Restatement (Second) approach, applied generally by Connecticut courts, utilizes the internal affairs doctrine. Restatement (Second) Conflict of Laws § 302(1) restates the "most significant relationship test" that is the center of the entire Restatement's approach in discussing the rules for internal corporate issues: "(1) Issues involving the rights and liabilities of a corporation, other than those dealt within in § 301, are determined by the local law of the state which, with respect to the particular issue, has the most significant relationship to the occurrence and the parties under the principles stated in § 6." But, § 302(2) limits that approach by providing: *"The local law of the state of incorporation will be applied to determine such issues, except in the unusual case where, with respect to the particular issue, some other state has a more significant relationship to the occurrence and the parties,* in which event the local law of the other state will be applied." (Emphasis added.) Comment as to § 302 specifically identifies this rule as the internal affairs doctrine: "Many of the matters that fall within the scope of the rule of this Section involve the 'internal affairs' of a corporation—that is the relations inter se of the corporation, its shareholders, directors, officers or agents . . ." That same comment clarifies what type of affairs are governed by the internal affairs rule: "Matters falling within the scope of the rule of this Section and which involved primarily a corporation's relationship to its shareholders include . . . shareholder's rights to examine corporate records . . ." In light of the Restatement's clear adoption of the internal affairs doctrine, in addition to the invitation by § 33–924(c) to apply said doctrine, the court agrees with the other Connecticut courts that the internal affairs doctrine is applicable to a choice of law analysis involving corporate governance and internal shareholder dispute issues.

The internal affairs doctrine is not, however, absolute in its call for the law of the state of incorporation to be applied to internal corporate matters. Comment e to § 302 explains that the doctrine is typically applied because it "will usually be supported by those choice of law factors favoring the needs of interstate and international systems, certainty, predictability and uniformity of result, protection of the justified expectations of the parties and ease in the application of the law to be applied." But, the rule in § 302 still provides that the law of another state may be applied to an internal issue in the "unusual case" that state has a more significant relationship to "the occurrence and the parties." Comment g to § 302 discusses the possibility that the law of the state of incorporation will not be applied: "The reasons for applying the local law of the state of incorporation carry less weight when the corporation has little or no contact with this state other than the fact that it was incorporated there . . . Nevertheless, in the absence of an explicitly applicable local statute, the local law of the statute of incorporation has almost invariably been applied. This result furthers the choice-of-law factors of certainty, predictability and uniformity of result, ease in the application of the law to be applied and, at least on occasion, protection of the justified expectations of the parties . . . Nevertheless, it is in the situation where the corporation has little contact with the state of its incorporation that the local law of some other state is most likely to be applied when (1) the relevant local law rules of the other state embody an important policy of that state and (2) the matter involved does not affect

the corporation's organic structure or internal administration ..."
Comment g continues to clarify that a state other than the state of
incorporation should not apply its own law unless it has a "dominant
interest" in its application, which consequently "can only be determined
in light of the purpose sought to be achieved by the rule." The comment
identifies relevant considerations such as whether the local law is in
conformity with the incorporation state and other states in which the
corporation operates, the amount of contacts between the corporation and
the state of incorporation and whether the issue subject to the law can
only be decided by one state's law (i.e., application of the law to the issue
in one instance necessitates application of the law in all instances).

With the principles of the internal affairs doctrine firmly established,
the court now turns to the facts in the present case to determine whether
Connecticut or Delaware law should be applied. Several of the factors
that may permit application of Connecticut law are present in this case.
First, as established by the plaintiff's complaint, the defendant's principal
place of business is in Connecticut. This suggests that, at least to some
extent, the defendant's contacts with Connecticut outnumber those with
Delaware. The parties have not established, either by way of uncontested
allegations in the complaint or evidence submitted in relation to the
present motion, that the defendant engages in any business activity in
Delaware. If the defendant only operates within Connecticut, that fact
would of course weigh in favor of applying Connecticut law. As the court
is required to make every favorable presumption in favor of upholding its
own jurisdiction, the court presumes, without evidence or allegations to
the contrary, that the defendant does not engage in business activity in
Delaware.

Second, the issues in this case do not affect the defendant's "organic
structure" or "internal administration." This is a simple issue of a
shareholder's demand for inspection. It does not implicate the structure of
the board of directors, fiduciary duties owed between directors and
shareholders, the operation of the defendant's business, voting
procedures, etc. All this matter involves is determining whether, in the
specific instance at hand, the plaintiff is a shareholder of the defendant
and whether he is entitled to inspect the records he has requested. There
are no foreseeable repercussions of this litigation that would go beyond
the plaintiff's immediate request for inspection. In other words, this is not
an issue that "can only be decided by one state's law." Furthermore, the
substance of Connecticut and Delaware's inspection laws, other than the
provision pertaining to jurisdiction, is virtually identical and applying one
over the other would not be outcome determinative.

While the above factors clearly weigh in favor of permitting
application of Connecticut law, Connecticut must still have a "dominant
interest" in applying its law for the court to not apply the law of the state

of incorporation. The court holds that Connecticut does have such an interest. Both parties in this case "reside" in Connecticut. See, e.g., *Paul Dinto Elec. Contractors, Inc. v. Waterbury,* 266 Conn. at 706, 719, 835 A.2d 33 (2003) (corporation's principal place of business is the equivalent of an individual's residence). The parties should be able to avail themselves to a convenient forum for their litigation, rather than have to traverse several states to use a statute that is substantively the same as the one that can be applied in the present forum. Under its statutes, Connecticut has provided a remedy for a shareholder to seek inspection of corporate records in an expedited or otherwise efficient manner. Connecticut's interest in providing a shareholder an efficient adjudication of its inspection rights, in conjunction with the other factors discussed above, outweighs whatever Delaware's interest may be in having shareholder inspection disputes adjudicated solely in its Chancery Court. Accordingly, Connecticut law should be applied in the present matter.

NOTES AND QUESTIONS

1.   Based on this decision, are shareholders' inspection rights included in the definition of "internal affairs"? Consider the following issues and discuss if they are included in the internal affairs and, therefore, necessarily governed by the law of the state of incorporations: the right of bondholders issued by the corporation to receive an interest rate; an agreement among some shareholders to vote their shares in a specific way; whether the single shareholder of an undercapitalized closely held corporation is liable to a third party injured by a tort committed by the corporation; whether a shareholders' meeting resolution has been validly approved; whether a director who has executed a contract between the corporation and her husband breached her fiduciary duties.

2.   Did you find the court's conclusion that Connecticut had a "dominant interest" in applying its own law to be persuasive?

3.   What is a Restatement? What is its relevance as a source of law? How does the Restatement (Second) on Conflicts of Laws address choice-of-law principles in corporate law? What are the possible exceptions to the internal affairs doctrine in the approach adopted by the Restatement? In foreign jurisdictions that you might be familiar with, or in international law, are there sources analogous to Restatements in the U.S.?

* * *

As mentioned above, it is important to remember that choice of law and jurisdiction are two separate and distinct issues. Often, jurisdiction can be established (also) in a court outside of the state of incorporation, even if the internal affairs doctrine applies. In the U.S., for example, a dispute concerning the internal affairs of a Delaware corporation could be filed and adjudicated in a state court in Florida if the corporation has significant contacts with this state. Even though the Florida court must apply Delaware law, the plaintiff may still have strategic reasons to sue outside of Delaware. As an empirical matter, it is interesting to consider when, and for what reasons, it may be strategically preferable for a plaintiff to litigate outside of Delaware, even when Delaware substantive law applies. One reason might be the expectation that non-Delaware judges might interpret Delaware law in a way that is more favorable to her position; or to take advantage of procedural rules that are not available to litigants in Delaware. In addition, since in the U.S. shareholders' litigation is often attorney-driven, different and competing plaintiffs' firms might sue in different jurisdictions in the hope of retaining control of the litigation. This type of strategic litigation is known as forum shopping.

In order to avoid strategic forum shopping, some corporations have amended their articles of incorporation or bylaws to include a forum selection clause ("FSC"), providing that the courts of the state of incorporation (typically, Delaware) have exclusive jurisdiction on intra-corporate disputes. The question of whether corporations can make this option is particularly interesting because bylaws can generally be amended unilaterally (also) by the directors, without a vote of the shareholders.

In a case entitled *Galaviz v. Berg* (763 F.Supp.2d 1170, N. D. Cal., 2011), a federal court refused to enforce a forum selection clause in the bylaws. It should be noted, however, that the bylaws amendment was adopted after the alleged wrongdoing that prompted the litigation. More recently other courts, both state and federal, seem however inclined to uphold forum selection clauses, also when they are adopted as a bylaws amendment by directors. In the following recent and interesting case involving a corporation offering online education ("Aspen University"), a New York court confirmed this approach, also referring to Delaware precedents.

HEMG INC. AND PATRICK SPADA V. ASPEN UNIVERSITY, ET AL.

Supreme Court, New York
No. 650457/13, November 4, 2013

MELVIN L. SCHWEITZER, JUDGE.

[. . .]

Background

Patrick Spada (Mr. Spada) founded Aspen University, an online post-secondary education university, in October 1999. It offered one of the first series of video courses to be approved by the Department of Education (DOE) to receive Title IV funding, became one of the first online degree institutions to become accredited by the Distance Education and Training Council (DETC), and was one of the first accredited institutions to offer an online Master of Business Administration degree to students.

In May 2011, Aspen University merged with Education Growth Corporation, a start-up company controlled by Michael Matthews (Mr. Matthews), resulting in Mr. Matthews replacing Mr. Spada as CEO of Aspen University. On March 13, 2012, Mr. Matthews merged Aspen University with Aspen Group, an inactive publicly registered shell company, pursuant to which Aspen Group became a publicly traded corporation, relinquishing its status as a shell company, and the corporate parent of Aspen University, carrying out the online education business of Aspen University as Aspen Group's sole line of business (the Merger). From the date of the Merger's completion through plaintiffs' commencement of this action, Mr. Matthews, John Scheibelhoffer, Michael D'Anton, C. James Jensen, David E. Pasi, Sanford Rich, and Paul Schneier served as directors on Aspen Group's board of directors (collectively, the Board or the Director Defendants), Mr. Matthews served as Aspen Group's CEO, and David Garrity served as Aspen Group's CFO.

In order to remain eligible to receive and maintain Title IV funding, approved by the DOE, and national accreditation from the DETC, Aspen Group must submit financial statements to the Securities and Exchange Commission (SEC), DOE, and DETC, demonstrating its financial stability to continue as an educational institution. In these financial statements Aspen Group reported $2,209,960 as a collectible asset on its balance sheet. Defendants claimed those monies as a loan receivable as a consequence of unauthorized borrowings of Aspen Group funds by plaintiffs. Defendants issued a series of public statements, and filed reports and financial statements with the SEC, DOE, DETC, stating that plaintiffs had unlawfully borrowed, and failed to repay, monies from the Aspen Group. Plaintiffs allege that this loan never existed and reporting it is part of a deliberate scheme to artificially inflate Aspen Group's financial condition.

Plaintiffs brought this action on February 11, 2013 asserting 12 causes of action. Causes of action one through six are derivative actions on behalf of Aspen Group against Director Defendants for breach of fiduciary duty, waste of assets, and dilution of shareholder equity. The remaining causes of action are brought directly against Director Defendants and CFO David Garrity for, inter alia, breach of contract, breach of the implied duty of good faith and fair dealing, defamation, and defamation per se.;

Discussion

On a motion to dismiss, pursuant to CPLR 3211 (a) (7), the pleading is afforded a liberal construction. The court must "accept the facts as alleged in the complaint as true, accord plaintiffs the benefit of every possible favorable inference, and determine only whether the facts as alleged fit within any cognizable legal theory" (*Leon v. Martinez*, 84 N.Y.2d 83, 87–88, 614 N.Y.S.2d 972, 638 N.E.2d 511 (1994); *see EBC I, Inc. v Goldman Sachs & Co.*, 5 N.Y.3d 11, 19 [2005]; *Sokoloff v. Harriman Estates Dev. Corp.*, 96 N.Y.2d 409, 414 [2001]; *P. T. Bank Central Asia N. Y. Branch v. ABN AMRO Bank N. V.*, 301 A.D.2d 373, 375–6, 754 N.Y.S.2d 245 [1st Dept 2003]). The court's role is limited to ascertaining whether the complaint states a cause of action, not whether there is evidentiary support for the complaint (*Guggenheimer v. Ginzburg*, 43 N.Y.2d 268, 275 [1977]; *LoPinto v. J.W. Mays, Inc.*, 170 A.D.2d 582, 566 N.Y.S.2d 357 [2d Dept 1991]).

Derivative Claims

Aspen Group's By-Laws and Certificate of Incorporation provide that the Court of Chancery of the State of Delaware is the sole and exclusive forum for (i) any derivative action brought on behalf of the Company, and (ii) any action asserting a claim for breach of fiduciary duty owed by any director or officer of the Company to the Company or the Company's shareholders. Plaintiffs argue that the forum selection clauses are invalid because they were adopted unilaterally by the Board of Directors, without the consent or vote of the plaintiffs or other shareholders, prior to Aspen Group becoming a public company through the merger. The court finds no merit to this position as it does not contest the validity of the Certificate of Incorporation, but rather the applicability of one of its provisions due to the status of the corporation at the time of adoption. The court knows of no legal theory which supports plaintiffs' argument.

Subsequent to the filing of the instant motion to dismiss, the Delaware Court of Chancery addressed the issue of whether Delaware adopted by-laws containing a forum selection clause were valid. In *Boilermakers Local 154 Retirement Fund v. Chevron Corp.*, the plaintiffs contested the validity of a Delaware forum selection clause contained in *Chevron* and *FedEx's* by-laws. Like the plaintiffs, the plaintiffs in *Boilermakers* alleged that the forum selection clause were invalid because they were unilaterally adopted by *Chevron's* and *FedEx's* board without shareholder approval or consent. 73 A.3d 934 (Del.Ch.2013).

The *Boilermakers* court rejected this argument and held that the adoption of a forum selection clause in a corporation's by-laws is valid, provided that the corporation's certificate of incorporation gives the board the power to adopt and amend by-laws unilaterally. The court wrote:

The certificates of incorporation of Chevron and Fed-Ex authorize their boards to amend the bylaws. Thus, when investors bought stock in Chevron and FedEx, they knew (i) that consistent with 8 Del. C. § 109(b), the certificates of incorporation gave the boards the power to adopt and amend bylaws unilaterally; (ii) that 8 Del. C. § 109(b) allows bylaws to regulate the business of the corporation, the conduct of its affairs, and the rights or powers of its stockholders; and (iii) that board-adopted bylaws are binding on the stockholders. [. . .]

The plaintiffs' argument that stockholders must approve a forum selection bylaw for it to be contractually binding is an interpretation that contradicts the plain terms of the contractual framework chosen by stockholders who buy stock in Chevron and FedEx.

Here, as in *Boilermakers*, Aspen Group's Certificate of Incorporation provides that the "board of directors is expressly authorized to make, amend, alter or repeal the by-laws of the Company." Aspen Group's certificate of incorporation permitted the adoption of the Delaware forum selection clause and plaintiffs, like plaintiffs in *Boilermakers*, are bound by the forum selection clauses.

Here, all of plaintiffs' derivative claims (Counts I–IV) are subject to the forum selection clause contained in Aspen Group's By-Laws and Certificate of Incorporation, and these claims must be brought in the Court of Chancery in Delaware. Accordingly, Counts I–IV of the Amended Complaint are dismissed.

NOTES AND QUESTIONS

1. In a post on the Harvard Law School Forum on Corporate Governance and Financial Regulation, Mr. Victor Lewkow and Mr. Mitchell Lowenthal, two attorneys at Cleary Gottlieb Steen & Hamilton LLP, based on a memorandum prepared by their firm, indicate that "[w]hile many litigations bringing internal affairs claims involving Delaware companies are filed in Delaware, very frequently litigation is also brought elsewhere. Indeed, in the public M&As (Mergers and Acquisitions) context, 85% of recent proposed mergers or acquisitions of Delaware companies have faced litigation brought outside of Delaware (generally, with identical litigation also brought in Delaware)." (http://blogs.law.harvard.edu/corpgov/2014/03/29/forum-selection-clauses-in-the-foreign-court/#more–61683). Why do you think that is, and what do you think are the options of the defendants in order to litigate in Delaware?

2. Mrs. Lewkow and Lowenthal suggest that a "better course would be to include with an FSC a consent to jurisdiction and service provision for stockholders who commence the foreign litigation that would permit the defendants in the foreign case to enforce the forum selection clause in Delaware." They continue explaining that "[a] consent to jurisdiction and service provision permits defendants who are sued in a foreign court, in violation of a forum selection clause, to go to the selected forum and seek a final judgment and permanent injunction requiring the stockholder plaintiff to bring the suit in compliance with the FSC. This allows a Delaware corporation that has selected Delaware as the exclusive forum for internal

affairs claims, when faced with such a suit filed elsewhere, to bring suit in Delaware against the stockholder/plaintiff in the foreign action, and on an accelerated basis seek redress in the Delaware courts against the further prosecution of the foreign litigation. In the absence of a jurisdiction and service provision, the effectiveness of forum selection clauses will depend on how they are received in the foreign courts." Would this strategy be helpful also when a lawsuit is brought in a forum outside the United States? Discuss.

3.   In *North v. McNamara*, No. 1:13–cv–833 (S. D. Ohio Sept. 19, 2014), a federal court enforced a board-adopted forum selection clause. The board of Chemed, a Delaware corporation headquartered in Cincinnati, Ohio, adopted in August 2013 a bylaw selecting any state or federal court in Delaware as the exclusive forum for intracorporate disputes. A derivative suit was filed in federal court in Delaware, but shortly afterwards another shareholder filed a similar action in federal court in Ohio. Defendants were successful in transferring the case to the Delaware federal district court under the federal venue statute. It should be pointed out that also in this case the alleged wrongdoing occurred in 2010, while the forum selection clause ("FSC") in the bylaws was adopted in 2013: differently from *Galaviz v. Berg*, however, in this case the court showed deference to the FSC. What do you think might be the reasons to reach different conclusions depending on when the FSC has been adopted, and in particular if the FSC has been adopted before or after the facts at the basis of the claim? Is such a distinction justified?

* * *

THE REAL SEAT APPROACH AND ITS GRADUAL ABANDONMENT IN THE EUROPEAN UNION

The following is a brief summary of what could be considered the first decision (or one of the first decisions) in France addressing choice of law principles in corporate law; specifically, the court discussed whether to apply the real seat doctrine to a civil company established under French law, but whose primary business purpose was the construction of port facilities in Cadiz, Spain. The seat of the company indicated in the bylaws was in St. Etienne, France and the minutes of the board of directors were kept there. All claims against the company were subject to the French court system.

The central issue in this case was whether the company—named *Société du débarcadère de Cadix*—was a French company or a foreign company. Under French law at the time, the holder of a French company's bearer shares was subject to a French tax, not applicable to shareholders of a foreign company.

FRENCH CASS. CIV., 20 JUNE 1870

20 June 1870
Sirey

Société du débarcadère de Cadix was a civil company (société civile) established in France. The board of directors of the company met in France, and a forum selection clause in the governing documents stated that disputes among shareholders, or between the company and its shareholders, were subject to French courts. The governing documents indicated that the seat of the company was in France (so-called "*siège statutaire*"), where it had also issued and sold its shares. The shares were not listed in France. The business of the company, however, was carried on in Spain, where also its real estate assets were located.

The first degree court of St. Etienne held that the company was governed by Spanish law. The court based its holding on findings that the company's operational and profit-producing activities, as well as the company's real estate assets, were all in Spain. In essence, the court adopted a "look-through" approach. Under this approach, the court stated that the nationality of a company, and therefore its governing law, could not be derived solely from the nationality of its shareholders, its seat as indicated in the charter (*siège statutaire*), or by a forum selection clause opting for French courts.

The French Supreme Court (<u>Cour de cassation</u>) reversed, holding that because the company was established under French law, had its *siège statutaire* in France, had a board of directors who met in France, and was subject to French courts, was a French company subject to the tax duties established by the budgetary law of 23 June 1867 (art. 6 and ff.) for the sale of shares. The court, therefore, applied French law, even though the company's business operations were based in a foreign country and its shares were not listed on a French Stock Exchange (Law 23 June 1857, art. 6, 7, 9 and 10). The reference to the board of directors and the place of its meeting was clearly of special importance to the court in determining where the real seat was located.

NOTES AND QUESTIONS

1.   The original text of this old French decision (1870) adopts a language that would not be very clear to the modern reader; therefore we decided to include a summary of the case rather than the actual translation of the decision. The decision is interesting also for its historical significance, but in fact it is quite confusing. First of all, it really focuses on the scope of application of tax law, and not of corporate law rules. Second, the fact that the court emphasized the formalistic fact that the corporation was established under French law, and indicated France as its "seat," might seem not entirely in line with the modern "real seat" approach. The take-away point, however, is that the court looked at where the "brain" of the

corporation was located, *i.e.*, where the board of directors met, to determine the applicable law. The decision mandates the application of French (tax) law to businesses that are established under French law and have a meaningful connection with France. In this respect, even if the case presents peculiar aspects, it can be considered a forerunner of the real seat approach.

2. Do you think it might make sense to apply the laws of one state to the internal affairs of a corporation and the laws of a different state to tax transfers of shares or to tax income? In other words, when do you think there is a rationale to decouple corporate law and tax law?

* * *

As discussed in the Introduction, several continental European countries used to follow—and to some extent still do—the "real seat" approach. Under the "real seat" approach, the internal affairs of a corporation are regulated by the laws of the jurisdiction where it has its "real seat." "Real seat" can be defined in different ways, but the definition is primarily based on elements of "physical" contact between a corporation and a particular jurisdiction. For example, the real seat of a corporation might be the state where most of the corporate business is conducted or where the governing bodies of the corporation (especially the board of directors) meet. One consequence of the real seat approach is that corporations must incorporate according to the rules of the state where their real seat is located. If they fail to incorporate properly in the jurisdiction where the real seat is located—even if they are duly incorporated in a state in which they do not operate—there may be very serious consequences for shareholders, including denial of the benefits of limited liability and/or treatment as partners of an unincorporated business entity.

Beginning in the late 1990s, the European Court of Justice began "attacking" the real seat approach, arguing that it might be contrary to the "freedom of establishment" principle set forth by the European Treaty. The *Centros* case below opened the door toward the abolition of the real seat rule in Europe.

CENTROS LTD. v. ERHVERVS- OG SELSKABSSTYRELSEN

Judgment of the Court of 9 March 1999
Case C–212/97

Summary

It is contrary to Articles 52 and 58 of the Treaty for a Member State to refuse to register a branch of a company formed in accordance with the law of another Member State in which it has its registered office but in which it conducts no business, where the branch is intended to enable the company in question to carry on its entire business in the State in which that branch is to be created, while avoiding the need to form a company there, thus evading application of the rules governing the formation of companies which, in that State, are more restrictive as regards the paying up of a minimum share capital. Given that the right to form a company in accordance with the law of a Member State and to set up branches in other Member States is inherent in the exercise, in a single market, of the freedom of establishment guaranteed by the Treaty, the fact that a national of a Member State who wishes to set up a company chooses to form it in the Member State whose rules of company law seem to him the least restrictive and to set up branches in other Member States cannot, in itself, constitute an abuse of the right of establishment.

That interpretation does not, however, prevent the authorities of the Member State concerned from adopting any appropriate measure for preventing or penalizing fraud, either in relation to the company itself, if need be in cooperation with the Member State in which it was formed, or in relation to its members, where it has been established that they are in fact attempting, by means of the formation of a company, to evade their obligations towards private or public creditors established in the territory of the Member State concerned. * * *

THE COURT, gives the following Judgment

Grounds

By order of 3 June 1997, received at the Court on 5 June 1997 the Hojesteret referred to the Court for a preliminary ruling under Article 177 of the EC Treaty a question on the interpretation of Articles 52, 56 and 58 of the Treaty.

That question was raised in proceedings between Centros Ltd, a private limited company registered on 18 May 1992 in England and Wales, and Erhvervs- og Selskabsstyrelsen (the Trade and Companies Board, 'the Board') which comes under the Danish Department of Trade, concerning that authority's refusal to register a branch of Centros in Denmark.

It is clear from the documents in the main proceedings that Centros has never traded since its formation. Since United Kingdom law imposes no requirement on limited liability companies as to the provision for and the paying-up of a minimum share capital, Centros's share capital, which amounts to GBP 100, has been neither paid up nor made available to the company. It is divided into two shares held by Mr and Mrs Bryde, Danish nationals residing in Denmark. Mrs Bryde is the director of Centros, whose registered office is situated in the United Kingdom, at the home of a friend of Mr Bryde.

Under Danish law, Centros, as a 'private limited company', is regarded as a foreign limited liability company. The rules governing the registration of branches ('filialer') of such companies are laid down by the Anpartsselskabslov (Law on private limited companies).

In particular, Article 117 of the Law provides:

"1. Private limited companies and foreign companies having a similar legal form which are established in one Member State of the European Communities may do business in Denmark through a branch."

During the summer of 1992, Mrs Bryde requested the Board to register a branch of Centros in Denmark.

The Board refused that registration on the grounds, inter alia, that Centros, which does not trade in the United Kingdom, was in fact seeking to establish in Denmark, not a branch, but a principal establishment, by circumventing the national rules concerning, in particular, the paying-up of minimum capital fixed at DKK 200 000 by Law No 886 of 21 December 1991.

Centros brought an action before the Ostre Landsret against the refusal of the Board to effect that registration.

The Ostre Landsret upheld the arguments of the Board in a judgment of 8 September 1995, whereupon Centros appealed to the Hojesteret.

In those proceedings, Centros maintains that it satisfies the conditions imposed by the law on private limited companies relating to the registration of a branch of a foreign company. Since it was lawfully formed in the United Kingdom, it is entitled to set up a branch in Denmark pursuant to Article 52, read in conjunction with Article 58, of the Treaty.

According to Centros the fact that it has never traded since its formation in the United Kingdom has no bearing on its right to freedom of establishment. In its judgment in Case 79/85 Segers v Bedrijfsvereniging voor Bank- en Verzekeringswegen, Groothandel en Vrije Beroepen [1986] ECR 2375, the Court ruled that Articles 52 and 58 of the Treaty prohibited the competent authorities of a Member State from excluding the director of a company from a national sickness insurance scheme solely on the ground that the company had its registered office in another Member State, even though it did not conduct any business there.

The Board submits that its refusal to grant registration is not contrary to Articles 52 and 58 of the Treaty since the establishment of a branch in Denmark would seem to be a way of avoiding the national rules on the provision for and the paying-up of minimum share capital. Furthermore, its refusal to register is justified by the need to protect private or public creditors and other contracting parties and also by the need to endeavor to prevent fraudulent insolvencies.

In those circumstances, the Hojesteret has decided to stay proceedings and to refer the following question to the Court for a preliminary ruling:

"Is it compatible with Article 52 of the EC Treaty, in conjunction with Articles 56 and 58 thereof, to refuse registration of a branch of a company which has its registered office in another Member State and has been lawfully founded with company capital of GBP 100 (approximately DKK 1 000) and exists in conformity with the legislation of that Member State, where the company does not itself carry on any business but it is desired to set up the branch in order to carry on the entire business in the country in which the branch is established, and where, instead of incorporating a company in the latter Member State, that procedure must be regarded as having been employed in order to avoid paying up company capital of not less than DKK 200 000 (at present DKR 125 000)?"

By its question, the national court is in substance asking whether it is contrary to Articles 52 and 58 of the Treaty for a Member State to refuse to register a branch of a company formed in accordance with the legislation of another Member State in which it has its registered office but where it does not carry on any business when the purpose of the branch is to enable the company concerned to carry on its entire business in the State in which that branch is to be set up, while avoiding the formation of a company in that State, thus evading application of the rules governing the formation of companies which are, in that State, more restrictive so far as minimum paid-up share capital is concerned.

As a preliminary point, it should be made clear that the Board does not in any way deny that a joint stock or private limited company with its registered office in another Member State may carry on business in Denmark through a branch. It therefore agrees, as a general rule, to register in Denmark a branch of a company formed in accordance with the law of another Member State. In particular, it has added that, if Centros had conducted any business in England and Wales, the Board would have agreed to register its branch in Denmark.

According to the Danish Government, Article 52 of the Treaty is not applicable in the case in the main proceedings, since the situation is purely internal to Denmark. Mr and Mrs Bryde, Danish nationals, have formed a company in the United Kingdom which does not carry on any actual business there with the sole purpose of carrying on business in Denmark through a branch and thus avoiding application of Danish legislation on the formation of private limited companies. It considers that in such circumstances the formation by nationals of one Member State of a company in another Member State does not amount to a relevant external element in the light of Community law and, in particular, freedom of establishment.

In this respect, it should be noted that a situation in which a company formed in accordance with the law of a Member State in which it has its registered office desires to set up a branch in another Member State falls within the scope of Community law. In that regard, it is immaterial that the company was formed in the first Member State only for the purpose of establishing itself in the second, where its main, or indeed entire, business is to be conducted (see, to this effect, Segers paragraph 16).

That Mrs and Mrs Bryde formed the company Centros in the United Kingdom for the purpose of avoiding Danish legislation requiring that a minimum amount of share capital be paid up has not been denied either in the written observations or at the hearing. That does not, however, mean that the formation by that British company of a branch in Denmark is not covered by freedom of establishment for the purposes of Article 52 and 58 of the Treaty. The question of the application of those articles of the Treaty is different from the question whether or not a Member State may adopt measures in order to prevent attempts by certain of its nationals to evade domestic legislation by having recourse to the possibilities offered by the Treaty.

As to the question whether, as Mr and Mrs Bryde claim, the refusal to register in Denmark a branch of their company formed in accordance with the law of another Member State in which it has its registered office constitutes an obstacle to freedom of establishment, it must be borne in mind that that freedom, conferred by Article 52 of the Treaty on Community nationals, includes the right for them to take up and pursue activities as self-employed persons and to set up and manage undertakings under the same conditions as are laid down by the law of the Member State of establishment for its own nationals. Furthermore, under Article 58 of the Treaty, companies or firms formed in accordance with the law of a Member State and having their registered office, central administration or principal place of business within the Community, are to be treated in the same way as natural persons who are nationals of Member States.

The immediate consequence of this is that those companies are entitled to carry on their business in another Member State through an agency, branch or subsidiary. The location of their registered office, central administration or principal place of business serves as the connecting factor with the legal system of a particular State in the same way as does nationality in the case of a natural person (see, to that effect, Segers, paragraph 13, Case 270/83 Commission v France [1986] ECR 273, paragraph 18, Case C–330/91 Commerzbank [1993] ECR I–4017, paragraph 13, and Case C–264/96 ICI [1998] I–4695, paragraph 20).

Where it is the practice of a Member State, in certain circumstances, to refuse to register a branch of a company having its registered office in another Member State, the result is that companies formed in accordance with the law of that other Member State are prevented from exercising the freedom of establishment conferred on them by Articles 52 and 58 of the Treaty.

Consequently, that practice constitutes an obstacle to the exercise of the freedoms guaranteed by those provisions.

According to the Danish authorities, however, Mr and Mrs Bryde cannot rely on those provisions, since the sole purpose of the company formation which they have in mind is to circumvent the application of the national law governing formation of private limited companies and therefore constitutes abuse of the freedom of establishment. In their submission, the Kingdom of Denmark is therefore entitled to take steps to prevent such abuse by refusing to register the branch.

It is true that according to the case-law of the Court, a Member State is entitled to take measures designed to prevent certain of its nationals from attempting, under cover of the rights created by the Treaty, improperly to circumvent their national legislation or to prevent individuals from improperly or fraudulently taking advantage of provisions of Community law. [. . .]

However, although, in such circumstances, the national courts may, case by case, take account—on the basis of objective evidence—of abuse or fraudulent conduct on the part of the persons concerned in order, where appropriate, to deny them the benefit of the provisions of Community law on which they seek to rely, they must nevertheless assess such conduct in the light of the objectives pursued by those provisions. [. . .]

In the present case, the provisions of national law, application of which the parties concerned have sought to avoid, are rules governing the formation of companies and not rules concerning the carrying on of certain trades, professions or businesses. The provisions of the Treaty on freedom of establishment are intended specifically to enable companies formed in accordance with the law of a Member State and having their registered office, central administration or principal place of business within the Community, to pursue activities in other Member States through an agency, branch or subsidiary.

That being so, the fact that a national of a Member State who wishes to set up a company, chooses to form it in the Member State whose rules of company law seem to him the least restrictive and to set up branches in other Member States cannot, in itself, constitute an abuse of the right of establishment. The right to form a company in accordance with the law of a Member State and to set up branches in other Member States is inherent in the exercise, in a single market, of the freedom of establishment guaranteed by the Treaty.

In this connection, the fact that company law is not completely harmonized in the Community is of little consequence. Moreover, it is always open to the Council, on the basis of the powers conferred upon it by Article 54(3)(g) of the EC Treaty, to achieve complete harmonization.

In addition, it is clear from paragraph 16 of Segers that the fact that a company does not conduct any business in the Member State in which it has its registered office and pursues its activities only in the Member State where its branch is established, is not sufficient to prove the existence of abuse or fraudulent conduct which would entitle the latter Member State to deny that company the benefit of the provisions of Community law relating to the right of establishment.

Accordingly, the refusal of a Member State to register a branch of a company formed in accordance with the law of another Member State in which it has its registered office on the grounds that the branch is intended to enable the company to carry on all its economic activity in the host State, with the result that the secondary establishment escapes national rules on the provision for and the paying-up of a minimum capital, is incompatible with Articles 52 and 58 of the Treaty, in so far as it prevents any exercise of the right freely to set up a secondary establishment which Articles 52 and 58 are specifically intended to guarantee.

The final question to be considered is whether the national practice in question might not be justified for the reasons put forward by the Danish authorities.

Referring both to Article 56 of the Treaty and to the case-law of the Court on imperative requirements in the general interest, the Board argues that the requirement that private limited companies provide for and pay up a minimum share capital pursues a dual objective: first, to reinforce the financial soundness of those companies in order to protect public creditors against the risk of seeing the public debts owing to them become irrecoverable since, unlike private creditors, they cannot secure those debts by means of guarantees and, second, and more generally, to protect all creditors, whether public or private, by anticipating the risk of fraudulent bankruptcy due to the insolvency of companies whose initial capitalization was inadequate.

The Board adds that there is no less restrictive means of attaining this dual objective. The other way of protecting creditors, namely by introducing rules making it possible for shareholders to incur personal liability, under certain conditions, would be more restrictive than the requirement to provide for and pay up a minimum share capital.

It should be observed, first, that the reasons put forward do not fall within the ambit of Article 56 of the Treaty. Next, it should be borne in mind that, according to the Court's case-law, national measures liable to hinder or make less attractive the exercise of fundamental freedoms guaranteed by the Treaty must fulfill four conditions: they must be applied in a non-discriminatory manner; they must be justified by imperative requirements in the general interest; they must be suitable for securing the attainment of the objective which they pursue; and they must not go beyond what is necessary in order to attain it. [. . .]

Those conditions are not fulfilled in th[is] case. . . . First, the practice in question is not such as to attain the objective of protecting creditors which it purports to pursue since, if the company concerned had conducted business in the United Kingdom, its branch would have been registered in Denmark, even though Danish creditors might have been equally exposed to risk.

Since the company . . . holds itself out as a company governed by the law of England and Wales and not as a company governed by Danish law, its creditors are on notice that it is covered by laws different from those which govern the formation of private limited companies in Denmark and they can refer to certain rules of Community law which protect them, such as the Fourth Council Directive 78/660/EEC of 25 July 1978 based on Article 54(3)(g) of the Treaty on the annual accounts of certain types of companies (OJ 1978 L 222, p. 11), and the Eleventh Council Directive 89/666/EEC of 21 December 1989 concerning disclosure requirements in respect of branches opened in a Member State by certain types of company governed by the law of another State (OJ 1989 L 395, p. 36).

Second, contrary to the arguments of the Danish authorities, it is possible to adopt measures which are less restrictive, or which interfere less with fundamental freedoms, by, for example, making it possible in law for public creditors to obtain the necessary guarantees.

Lastly, the fact that a Member State may not refuse to register a branch of a company formed in accordance with the law of another Member State in which it has its registered office does not preclude that first State from adopting any appropriate measure for preventing or penalizing fraud, either in relation to the company itself, if need be in cooperation with the Member State in which it was formed, or in relation to its members, where it has been established that they are in fact attempting, by means of the formation of the company, to evade their obligations towards private or public creditors established on the territory of a Member State concerned. In any event, combating fraud cannot justify a practice of refusing to register a branch of a company, which has its registered office in another Member State.

The answer to the question referred must therefore be that it is contrary to Articles 52 and 58 of the Treaty for a Member State to refuse to register a branch of a company formed in accordance with the law of another Member State in which it has its registered office but in which it conducts no business, where the branch is intended to enable the company in question to carry on its entire business in the State in which that branch is to be created, while avoiding the need to form a company there, thus evading application of the rules governing the formation of companies which, in that State, are more restrictive as regards the paying up of a minimum share capital. That interpretation does not, however, prevent the authorities of the Member State concerned from adopting any appropriate measure for preventing or penalizing fraud, either in relation to the company itself, if need be in cooperation with the Member State in which it was formed, or in relation to its members, where it has been established that they are in fact attempting, by means of the formation of a company, to evade their obligations towards private or public creditors established in the territory of the Member State concerned. [. . .]

On those grounds,

THE COURT,

in answer to the question referred to it by the Hojesteret by order of 3 June 1997, hereby rules:

It is contrary to Articles 52 and 58 of the EC Treaty for a Member State to refuse to register a branch of a company formed in accordance with the law of another Member State in which it has its registered office but in which it conducts no business where the branch is intended to enable the company in question to carry on its entire business in the State in which that branch is to be created, while avoiding the need to form a company there, thus evading application of the rules governing the formation of companies which, in that State, are more restrictive as regards the paying up of a minimum share capital. That interpretation does not, however, prevent the authorities of the Member State concerned from adopting any appropriate measure for preventing or penalizing fraud, either in relation to the company itself, if need be in cooperation with the Member State in which it was formed, or in relation to its members, where it has been established that they are in fact attempting, by means of the formation of a company, to evade their obligations towards private or public creditors established in the territory of the Member State concerned.

NOTES AND QUESTIONS

1.   What do you think were the economic reasons why Mr. and Mrs. Bryde wanted to incorporate Centros in the U.K., even though they only intended to conduct business in Denmark?

2.   If the *Centros* decision is considered in the narrowest sense, the court did not hold that a corporation incorporated in any Member State can do business in any other Member State, but rather that the host State cannot refuse the registration of a branch of a corporation incorporated abroad. Are these two interpretations distinguishable? To the extent that *Centros* introduced freedom of incorporation in Europe, can you still distinguish the court's reasoning from the approach to freedom of incorporation adopted by U.S. courts?

3.   Fifteen years later, significant ambiguity still surrounds the *Centros* decision. While the court did in fact hold that even if a corporation is incorporated in a Member State with different rules concerning its legal capital, it can operate through a branch in another Member State, the court did, however, point out that the host State can still adopt "any appropriate measure for preventing or penalizing fraud, either in relation to the company itself, if need be in cooperation with the Member State in which it was formed, or in relation to its members, where it has been established that they are in fact attempting, by means of the formation of a company, to evade their obligations towards private or public creditors established in the territory of the Member State concerned." Is this aspect of the decision simply a "Trojan horse" permitting Member States to continue to limit freedom of incorporation?

4.   A possible research project: Is the definition of "internal affairs," regulated by the state of incorporation, the same in Europe and specifically in the U.K., and in the U.S.? What about, for example, bonds? Or shareholders' agreements?

* * *

ÜBERSEERING BV v. NORDIC CONSTRUCTION COMPANY BAUMANAGEMENT GMBH

Judgment of the Court of 5 November 2002
Case C–208/00

THE COURT, gives the following Judgment

Grounds

By order of 30 March 2000, received at the Court Registry on 25 May 2000, the Bundesgerichtshof (Federal Court of Justice) referred to the Court for a preliminary ruling under Article 234 EC two questions on the interpretation of Articles 43 EC and 48 EC.

Those questions were raised in proceedings between (i) Überseering BV ('Überseering'), a company incorporated under Netherlands law and registered on 22 August 1990 in the register of companies of Amsterdam and Haarlem, and (ii) Nordic Construction Company Baumanagement GmbH ('NCC'), a company established in the Federal Republic of Germany, concerning damages for defective work carried out in Germany by NCC on behalf of Überseering.

National Law

The Zivilprozessordnung (German Code of Civil Procedure) provides that an action brought by a party which does not have the capacity to bring legal proceedings must be dismissed as inadmissible. Under Paragraph 50(1) of the Zivilprozessordnung any person, including a company, having legal capacity has the capacity to be a party to legal proceedings: legal capacity is defined as the capacity to enjoy rights and to be the subject of obligations.

According to the settled case-law of the Bundesgerichtshof, which is approved by most German legal commentators, a company's legal capacity is determined by reference to the law applicable in the place where its actual centre of administration is established ('Sitztheorie' or company seat principle), as opposed to the 'Gründungstheorie' or incorporation principle, by virtue of which legal capacity is determined in accordance with the law of the State in which the company was incorporated. That rule also applies where a company has been validly incorporated in another State and has subsequently transferred its actual centre of administration to Germany.

Since a company's legal capacity is determined by reference to German law, it cannot enjoy rights or be the subject of obligations or be a party to legal proceedings unless it has been reincorporated in Germany in such a way as to acquire legal capacity under German law.

The Main Proceedings

In October 1990, Überseering acquired a piece of land in Düsseldorf (Germany), which it used for business purposes. By a project-management contract dated 27 November 1992, Überseering engaged NCC to refurbish a garage and a motel on the site. The contractual obligations were performed but Überseering claimed that the paint work was defective.

In December 1994 two German nationals residing in Düsseldorf acquired all the shares in Überseering.

Überseering unsuccessfully sought compensation from NCC for the defective work and in 1996 it brought an action before the Landgericht (Regional Court), Düsseldorf, on the basis of its project-management contract with NCC. It claimed the sum of DEM 1 163 657.77, plus interest, in respect of the costs incurred in remedying the alleged defects and consequential damage.

The Landgericht dismissed the action. The Oberlandesgericht (Higher Regional Court), Düsseldorf, upheld the decision to dismiss the action. It found that Überseering had transferred its actual centre of administration to Düsseldorf once its shares had been acquired by two German nationals. The Oberlandesgericht found that, as a company incorporated under Netherlands law, Überseering did not have legal capacity in Germany and, consequently, could not bring legal proceedings there.

Therefore, the Oberlandesgericht held that Überseering's action was inadmissible.

Überseering appealed to the Bundesgerichtshof against the judgment of the Oberlandesgericht.

It also appears from Überseering's observations that, in parallel with the proceedings currently pending before the Bundesgerichtshof, an action was brought against Überseering before another German court based on certain unspecified provisions of German law. As a result, it was ordered by the Landgericht Düsseldorf to pay architects' fees, apparently because it was entered on 11 September 1991 in the Düsseldorf land registry as owner of the land on which the garage and the motel refurbished by NCC were built.

The Questions Referred for a Preliminary Ruling

Although it notes that the case-law referred to at paragraphs 4 and 5 of this judgment is disputed in various respects by certain German legal commentators, the Bundesgerichtshof considers it preferable, in view of the current state of Community law and of company law within the European Union, to continue to follow that case-law for a number of reasons.

First, it is appropriate to discount any solution which entails (through taking account of different connecting factors) assessing a company's legal situation by reference to several legal systems. According to the Bundesgerichtshof, such a solution leads to legal uncertainty, since it is impossible to segregate clearly the areas of law to be governed by the various legal orders.

Second, where the connecting factor is taken to be the place of incorporation, the company's founding members are placed at an advantage, since they are able, when choosing the place of incorporation, to choose the legal system which suits them best. Therein lies the fundamental weakness of the incorporation principle, which fails to take account of the fact that a company's incorporation and activities also affect the interests of third parties and of the State in which the company has its actual centre of administration, where that is located in a State other than the one in which the company was incorporated.

Third, and by contrast, where the connecting factor is taken to be the actual centre of administration, that prevents the provisions of company law in the State in which the actual centre of administration is situated, which are intended to protect certain vital interests, from being circumvented by incorporating the company abroad. In the present case, the interests which German law is seeking to safeguard are notably those of the company's creditors: the legislation relating to 'Gesellschaften mit beschränkter Haftung (GmbH)' (limited liability companies under German law) provides such protection by detailed rules on the initial contribution and maintenance of share capital. In the case of related companies, dependent companies and their minority shareholders also need protection. In Germany, such protection is provided by rules governing groups of companies or rules providing for financial compensation and indemnification of shareholders who have been put at a disadvantage by agreements whereby one company agrees to manage another or agrees to pay its profits to another company. Finally, the rules on joint management protect the company's employees. The Bundesgerichtshof points out that not all the Member States have comparable rules.

The Bundesgerichtshof nevertheless wonders whether, on the basis that the company's actual centre of administration has been transferred to another country, the freedom of establishment guaranteed by Articles 43 EC and 48 EC does not preclude connecting the company's legal position with the law of the Member State in which its actual centre of administration is located. The answer to that question cannot, according to the Bundesgerichtshof, be clearly deduced from the case-law of the Court of Justice.

It points out, in that regard, that in Case 81/87 *The Queen v Treasury and Commissioners of Inland Revenue, ex parte Daily Mail and General Trust* [1988] ECR 5483 the Court, having stated that companies could exercise their right of establishment by setting up agencies, branches and subsidiaries, or by transferring all their shares to a new company in another Member State, held that, unlike natural persons, companies exist only by virtue of the national legal system which governs their incorporation and operation. It is also apparent from that judgment that the EC Treaty has taken account of the differences in national rules on the conflict of laws and has reserved resolution of the problems associated therewith to future legislation.

In Case C–212/97 *Centros* [1999] ECR I–1459, the Court took exception to a Danish authority's refusal to register a branch of a company validly incorporated in the United Kingdom. However, the

Bundesgerichtshof points out that the company had not transferred its seat, since, from its incorporation, its registered office had been in the United Kingdom, whilst its actual centre of administration had been in Denmark.

The Bundesgerichtshof wonders whether, in view of Centros, the Treaty provisions on freedom of establishment preclude, in a situation such as that in point in the main proceedings, application of the rules on conflict of laws in force in the Member State in which the actual centre of administration of a company validly incorporated in another Member State is situated when the consequence of those rules is the refusal to recognize the company's legal capacity and, therefore, its capacity to bring legal proceedings in the first Member State to enforce rights under a contract.

In those circumstances, the Bundesgerichtshof decided to stay proceedings and to refer the following questions to the Court for a preliminary ruling:

'1.   Are Articles 43 EC and 48 EC to be interpreted as meaning that the freedom of establishment of companies precludes the legal capacity, and capacity to be a party to legal proceedings, of a company validly incorporated under the law of one Member State from being determined according to the law of another State to which the company has moved its actual centre of administration, where, under the law of that second State, the company may no longer bring legal proceedings there in respect of claims under a contract?

2.   If the Court's answer to that question is affirmative:

Does the freedom of establishment of companies (Articles 43 EC and 48 EC) require that a company's legal capacity and capacity to be a party to legal proceedings is to be determined according to the law of the State where the company is incorporated?'

The First Question

By its first question, the national court is, essentially, asking whether, where a company formed in accordance with the legislation of a Member State ('A') in which it has its registered office is deemed, under the law of another Member State ('B'), to have moved its actual centre of administration to Member State B, Articles 43 EC and 48 EC preclude Member State B from denying the company legal capacity, and therefore the capacity to bring legal proceedings before its national courts in order to enforce rights under a contract with a company established in Member State B.

Findings of the Court

As to whether the Treaty provisions on freedom of establishment apply

In limine and contrary to the submissions of both NCC and the German, Spanish and Italian Governments, the Court must make clear that where a company which is validly incorporated in one Member State ('A') in which it has its registered office is deemed, under the law of a second Member State ('B'), to have moved its actual centre of administration to Member State B following the transfer of all its shares to nationals of that State residing there, the rules which Member State B applies to that company do not, as Community law now stands, fall outside the scope of the Community provisions on freedom of establishment.

In that regard, it is appropriate to begin by rejecting the arguments based on Article 293 EC, which were put forward by NCC and the German, Spanish and Italian Governments.

As the Advocate General maintained at point 42 of his Opinion, Article 293 EC does not constitute a reserve of legislative competence vested in the Member States. Although Article 293 EC gives Member States the opportunity to enter into negotiations with a view, inter alia, to facilitating the resolution of problems arising from the discrepancies between the various laws relating to the mutual recognition of companies and the retention of legal personality in the event of the transfer of their seat from one country to another, it does so solely 'so far as is necessary,' that is to say if the provisions of the Treaty do not enable its objectives to be attained.

More specifically, it is important to point out that, although the conventions which may be entered into pursuant to Article 293 EC may, like the harmonising directives provided for in Article 44 EC, facilitate the attainment of freedom of establishment, the exercise of that freedom can none the less not be dependent upon the adoption of such conventions.

In that regard, it must be borne in mind that, as the Court has already had occasion to point out, the freedom of establishment, conferred by Article 43 EC on Community nationals, includes the right for them to take up and pursue activities as self-employed persons and to set up and manage undertakings under the same conditions as are laid down by the law of the Member State of establishment for its own nationals. Furthermore, according to the actual wording of Article 48 EC, 'companies or firms formed in accordance with the law of a Member State and having their registered office, central administration or principal place of business within the Community shall, for the purposes of [the provisions of the Treaty concerning the right of establishment], be treated in the same way as natural persons who are nationals of Member States'.

The immediate consequence of this is that those companies or firms are entitled to carry on their business in another Member State. The location of their registered office, central administration or principal place of business constitutes the connecting factor with the legal system of a particular Member State in the same way as does nationality in the case of a natural person.

The Court's reasoning in *Centros* was founded on those premises (paragraphs 19 and 20).

A necessary precondition for the exercise of the freedom of establishment is the recognition of those companies by any Member State in which they wish to establish themselves.

Accordingly, it is not necessary for the Member States to adopt a convention on the mutual recognition of companies in order for companies meeting the conditions set out in Article 48 EC to exercise the freedom of establishment conferred on them by Articles 43 EC and 48 EC, which have been directly applicable since the transitional period came to an end. It follows that no argument that might justify limiting the full effect of those articles can be derived from the fact that no convention on the mutual recognition of companies has as yet been adopted on the basis of Article 293 EC.

Second, it is important to consider the argument based on the decision in *Daily Mail and General Trust*, which was central to the arguments put to the Court. It was cited in order, in some way, to assimilate the situation in *Daily Mail and General Trust* to the situation which under German law entails the loss of legal capacity and of the capacity to be a party to legal proceedings by a company incorporated under the law of another Member State.

It must be stressed that, unlike *Daily Mail and General Trust*, which concerned relations between a company and the Member State under whose laws it had been incorporated in a situation where the company wished to transfer its actual centre of administration to another Member State whilst retaining its legal personality in the State of incorporation, the present case concerns the recognition by one Member State of a company incorporated under the law of another Member State, such a company being denied all legal capacity in the host Member State where it takes the view that the company has moved its actual centre of administration to its territory, irrespective of whether in that regard the company actually intended to transfer its seat.

As the Netherlands and United Kingdom Governments and the Commission and the EFTA Surveillance Authority have pointed out,

Überseering never gave any indication that it intended to transfer its seat to Germany. Its legal existence was never called in question under the law of the State where it was incorporated as a result of all its shares being transferred to persons resident in Germany. In particular, the company was not subject to any winding-up measures under Netherlands law. Under Netherlands law, it did not cease to be validly incorporated.

Moreover, even if the dispute before the national court is seen as concerning a transfer of the actual centre of administration from one country to another, the interpretation of *Daily Mail and General Trust* put forward by NCC and the German, Spanish and Italian Governments is incorrect.

In that case, Daily Mail and General Trust Plc, a company formed in accordance with the law of the United Kingdom and having both its registered office and actual centre of administration there, wished to transfer its centre of administration to another Member State without losing its legal personality or ceasing to be a company incorporated under English law. This required the consent of the competent United Kingdom authorities, which they refused to give. The company initiated proceedings against the authorities before the High Court of Justice, Queen's Bench Division, seeking an order that Articles 52 and 58 of the EEC Treaty gave it the right to transfer its actual centre of administration to another Member State without prior consent and without loss of its legal personality.

Thus, unlike the case before the national court in this instance, *Daily Mail and General Trust* did not concern the way in which one Member State treats a company which is validly incorporated in another Member State and which is exercising its freedom of establishment in the first Member State.

Asked by the High Court of Justice whether the Treaty provisions on freedom of establishment conferred on a company the right to transfer its centre of management to another Member State, the Court observed, at paragraph 19 of *Daily Mail and General Trust*, that a company, which is a creature of national law, exists only by virtue of the national legislation which determines its incorporation and functioning.

At paragraph 20 of that judgment, the Court pointed out that the legislation of the Member States varies widely in regard both to the factor providing a connection to the national territory required for the incorporation of a company and to the question whether a company incorporated under the legislation of a Member State may subsequently modify that connecting factor.

The Court concluded, at paragraph 23 of the judgment, that the Treaty regarded those differences as problems which were not resolved by the Treaty rules concerning freedom of establishment but would have to be dealt with by legislation or conventions, which the Court found had not yet been done.

In so doing, the Court confined itself to holding that the question whether a company formed in accordance with the legislation of one Member State could transfer its registered office or its actual centre of administration to another Member State without losing its legal personality under the law of the Member State of incorporation and, in certain circumstances, the rules relating to that transfer were determined by the national law in accordance with which the company had been incorporated. It concluded that a Member State was able, in the case of a company incorporated under its law, to make the company's right to retain its legal personality under the law of that State subject to restrictions on the transfer of the company's actual centre of administration to a foreign country.

By contrast, the Court did not rule on the question whether where, as here, a company incorporated under the law of a Member State ('A') is found, under the law of another Member State ('B'), to have moved its actual centre of administration to Member State B, that State is entitled to refuse to recognize the legal personality which the company enjoys under the law of its State of incorporation ('A').

Thus, despite the general terms in which paragraph 23 of *Daily Mail and General Trust* is cast, the Court did not intend to recognise a Member State as having the power, vis-à-vis companies validly incorporated in other Member States and found by it to have transferred their seat to its territory, to subject those companies' effective exercise in its territory of the freedom of establishment to compliance with its domestic company law.

There are, therefore, no grounds for concluding from *Daily Mail and General Trust* that, where a company formed in accordance with the law of one Member State and with legal personality in that State exercises its freedom of establishment in another Member State, the question of recognition of its legal capacity and its capacity to be a party to legal proceedings in the Member State of establishment falls outside the scope of the Treaty provisions on freedom of establishment, even when the company is found, under the law of the Member State of establishment, to have moved its actual centre of administration to that State.

Third, the Court rejects the Spanish Government's argument that, in a situation such as that in point before the national court, Title I of the General Programme subordinates the benefit of the freedom of establishment guaranteed by the Treaty to the requirement that there be a real and continuous link with the economy of a Member State.

It is apparent from the wording of the General Programme that it requires a real and continuous link solely in a case in which the company has nothing but its registered office within the Community. That is unquestionably not the position in the case of Überseering whose registered office and actual centre of administration are within the Community. As regards the situation just described, the Court found, at paragraph 19 of Centros, that under Article 58 of the Treaty companies formed in accordance with the law of a Member State and having their registered office, central administration or principal place of business within the Community are to be treated in the same way as natural persons who are nationals of Member States.

It follows from the foregoing considerations that Überseering is entitled to rely on the principle of freedom of establishment in order to contest the refusal of German law to regard it as a legal person with the capacity to be a party to legal proceedings.

Furthermore, it must be borne in mind that as a general rule the acquisition by one or more natural persons residing in a Member State of shares in a company incorporated and established in another Member State is covered by the Treaty provisions on the free movement of capital, provided that the shareholding does not confer on those natural persons definite influence over the company's decisions and does not allow them to determine its activities. By contrast, where the acquisition involves all the shares in a company having its registered office in another Member State and the shareholding confers a definite influence over the company's decisions and allows the shareholders to determine its activities, it is the Treaty provisions on freedom of establishment which apply (see, to that effect, Case C–251/98 Baars [2000] ECR I–2787, paragraphs 21 and 22).

The Court must next consider whether the refusal by the German courts to recognise the legal capacity and capacity to be a party to legal proceedings of a company validly incorporated under the law of another Member State constitutes a restriction on freedom of establishment.

In that regard, in a situation such as that in point in the main proceedings, a company validly incorporated under the law of, and having its registered office in, a Member State other than the Federal Republic of Germany has under German law no alternative to reincorporation in Germany if it wishes to enforce before a German court its rights under a contract entered into with a company incorporated under German law.

Überseering, which is validly incorporated in the Netherlands and has its registered office there, is entitled under Articles 43 EC and 48 EC to exercise its freedom of establishment in Germany as a company incorporated under Netherlands law. It is of little significance in that regard that, after the company was formed, all its shares were acquired by German nationals residing in Germany, since that has not caused Überseering to cease to be a legal person under Netherlands law.

Indeed, its very existence is inseparable from its status as a company incorporated under Netherlands law since, as the Court has observed, a company exists only by virtue of the national legislation which determines its incorporation and functioning (see, to that effect, *Daily Mail and General Trust*, paragraph 19). The requirement of reincorporation of the same company in Germany is therefore tantamount to outright negation of freedom of establishment.

In those circumstances, the refusal by a host Member State ('B') to recognize the legal capacity of a company formed in accordance with the law of another Member State ('A') in which it has its registered office on the ground, in particular, that the company moved its actual centre of administration to Member State B following the acquisition of all its shares by nationals of that State residing there, with the result that the company cannot, in Member State B, bring legal proceedings to defend rights under a contract unless it is reincorporated under the law of Member State B, constitutes a restriction on freedom of establishment which is, in principle, incompatible with Articles 43 EC and 48 EC.

As to Whether the Restriction on Freedom of Establishment Is Justified

Finally, it is appropriate to determine whether such a restriction on freedom of establishment can be justified on the grounds advanced by the national court and by the German Government.

The German Government has argued in the alternative, should the Court find that application of the company seat principle entails a restriction on freedom of establishment that the restriction applies without discrimination, is justified by overriding requirements relating to the general interest and is proportionate to the objectives pursued.

In the German Government's submission, the lack of discrimination arises from the fact that the rules of law proceeding from the company seat principle apply not only to any foreign company which establishes itself in Germany by moving its actual centre of administration there but also to companies incorporated under German law which transfer their actual centre of administration out of Germany.

As regards the overriding requirements relating to the general interest put forward in order to justify the alleged restriction, the German Government maintains, first, that in other spheres, secondary Community law assumes that the administrative head office and the registered office are identical. Community law has thus recognised the merits, in principle, of a single registered and administrative office.

In the German Government's submission, the German rules of private international company law enhance legal certainty and creditor protection. There is no harmonisation at Community level of the rules for protecting the share capital of limited liability companies and such companies are subject in Member States other than the Federal Republic of Germany to requirements which are in some respects much less strict. The company seat principle as applied by German law ensures that a company whose principal place of business is in Germany has a fixed minimum share capital, something which is instrumental in protecting parties with whom it enters into contracts and its creditors. That also prevents distortions of competition since all companies whose principal place of business is in Germany are subject to the same legal requirements.

The German Government submits that further justification is provided by the protection of minority shareholders. In the absence of a Community standard for the protection of minority-shareholders, a Member State must be able to apply to any company whose principal place of business is within its territory the same legal requirements for the protection of minority shareholders.

Application of the company seat principle is also justified by employee protection through the joint management of undertakings on conditions determined by law. The German Government argues that the transfer to Germany of the actual centre of administration of a company incorporated under the law of another Member State could, if the company continued to be a company incorporated under that law, involve a risk of circumvention of the German provisions on joint management, which allow the employees, in certain circumstances, to be represented on the company's supervisory board. Companies in other Member States do not always have such a body.

Finally, any restriction resulting from the application of the company seat principle can be justified on fiscal grounds. The incorporation principle, to a greater extent than the company seat principle, enables companies to be created which have two places of residence and which are, as a result, subject to taxation without limits in at least two Member States. There is a risk that such companies might claim and be granted tax advantages simultaneously in several Member States. By way of example, the German Government mentions the cross-border offsetting of losses against profits between undertakings within the same group.

The Netherlands and United Kingdom Governments, the Commission and the EFTA Surveillance Authority submit that the restriction in question is not justified. They point out in particular that the aim of protecting creditors was also invoked by the Danish authorities in *Centros* to justify the refusal to register in Denmark a branch of a company which had been validly incorporated in the United Kingdom and all of whose business was to be carried on in Denmark but which did not meet the requirements of Danish law regarding the provision and paying-up of a minimum amount of share capital. They add that it is not certain that requirements associated with a minimum amount of share capital are an effective way of protecting creditors.

It is not inconceivable that overriding requirements relating to the general interest, such as the protection of the interests of creditors, minority shareholders, employees and even the taxation authorities, may, in certain circumstances and subject to certain conditions, justify restrictions on freedom of establishment.

Such objectives cannot, however, justify denying the legal capacity and, consequently, the capacity to be a party to legal proceedings of a company properly incorporated in another Member State in which it has its registered office. Such a measure is tantamount to an outright negation of the freedom of establishment conferred on companies by Articles 43 EC and 48 EC.

Accordingly, the answer to the first question must be that, where a company formed in accordance with the law of a Member State ('A') in which it has its registered office is deemed, under the law of another Member State ('B'), to have moved its actual centre of administration to Member State B, Articles 43 EC and 48 EC preclude Member State B from denying the company legal capacity and, consequently, the capacity to bring legal proceedings before its national courts for the purpose of enforcing rights under a contract with a company established in Member State B.

The second question referred to the Court

It follows from the answer to the first question referred to the Court for a preliminary ruling that, where a company formed in accordance with the law of a Member State ('A') in which it has its registered office exercises its freedom of establishment in another Member State ('B'), Articles 43 EC and 48 EC require Member State B to recognize the legal capacity and, consequently, the capacity to be a party to legal proceedings which the company enjoys under the law of its State of incorporation ('A').

On those grounds,

THE COURT,

in answer to the questions referred to it by the Bundesgerichtshof by order of 30 March 2000, hereby rules:

1.   Where a company formed in accordance with the law of a Member State ('A') in which it has its registered office is deemed, under the law of another Member State ('B'), to have moved its actual centre of administration to Member State B, Articles 43 EC and 48 EC preclude Member State B from denying the company legal capacity and, consequently, the capacity to bring legal proceedings before its national

courts for the purpose of enforcing rights under a contract with a company established in Member State B.

2.   Where a company formed in accordance with the law of a Member State ('A') in which it has its registered office exercises its freedom of establishment in another Member State ('B'), Articles 43 EC and 48 EC require Member State B to recognize the legal capacity and, consequently, the capacity to be a party to legal proceedings which the company enjoys under the law of its State of incorporation ('A').

NOTES AND QUESTIONS

1.   In *Überseering*, the corporation was incorporated in the Netherlands and conducted business there for several years before moving its real seat to Germany. Do you think the court's holding should apply even if a corporation incorporates in one Member State of the European Union and immediately transfers or establishes its real seat to another Member State?

2.   The court states in the opinion that the protection of creditors, shareholders, and employees cannot justify denying legal capacity to a foreign corporation properly incorporated in another Member State. Is this conclusion consistent with the decision in *Centros*?

3.   These decisions were followed by others that expanded or clarified the scope of freedom of establishment. Somehow simplifying, it could be said that *Centros* and its progeny limited the real seat approach. What do you think might have been the consequence of these decisions on contractual freedom in corporate law? And on the balance between mandatory and eligible rules? And on minimum legal capital?

4.   Forum shopping does not only involve newly borned or young and healthy corporations looking for the more desirable corporate regime. Like terminally ill individuals taking the decision to end their life in countries authorizing euthanasia, insolvent or distressed companies might try to "move" to jurisdictions that have more advantageous or less punitive bankruptcy laws from the perspective of the debtor; not to mention migrations of legal entities in search of a less demanding tax system. European law, however, attempts to limit forum shopping with respect to insolvency law. Federico Mucciarelli, for example, has noted in a recent and insightful analysis (*The Unavoidable Persistence of Forum Shopping in European Insolvency Law*, available on *www.ssrn.com*), that:

> "One of the goals of the EU Insolvency Regulation, confirmed by recent reform proposals of the European Parliament and the Commission, is to limit forum shopping. The real world, however, looks quite different, as forum shopping is becoming increasingly common in the EU. The reason for the increase in forum shopping cases is hidden in the mechanisms of the Insolvency Regulation. It is well known that the Member State of a debtor's centre of main interests ("COMI") is competent to govern its main insolvency

proceeding with universal effects. Additionally, companies' COMI is presumed to coincide with their registered office, unless the contrary is proven. Nowadays, however, companies can often transfer their registered office throughout the European Union. Additionally, pursuant to ECJ case law, the reference date to assess the insolvency competence is the date of filing, with the consequence that, if a company relocates its registered office abroad before the filing, the new jurisdiction becomes competent to govern its insolvency, unless creditors prove that the COMI is still in the original State."

What rationale—if any—do you think might justify stronger limitations to regulatory arbitrage and competition in insolvency law than with respect to substantive law governing the internal affairs of a solvent corporation? Why do you think that European law, at least according to Mucciarelli's analysis, does not fully prevent this phenomenon? Should the European legislature, or Member State, do something to avoid forum shopping of bankruptcy laws? If so, what, based on the few information offered by the short excerpt from Mucciarelli?

* * *

Centros and *Überseering* marked the beginning of a fundamental shift in the interpretation of the principle of freedom of establishment by the ECJ. Soon after these two decisions were issued, the number of English *"Private company limited by shares"* in other Member States of the European Union began to grow. The growth in the number of English companies occurred primarily in Member States where access to the corporate form was difficult due to administrative barriers. Response to the growing influence of English corporate law in Europe was different in each Member State.

After *Centros*, the Netherlands adopted a law allowing foreign companies to move their real seat to the Netherlands, but required them to comply with certain provisions of Dutch corporate law. The ECJ rejected this approach in the *Inspire Art* case in 2003. In *Inspire Art*, the court held that the law at issue similarly violated the freedom of establishment (30.9.2003–C–167/01, ECR 2003 I–10155). After *Inspire Art*, it became obvious that European Member States would have to compete with English corporate law. As a consequence, several States began undertaking massive reforms of their national corporate law codes in an effort to keep pace with English corporate law. These reforms focused especially on speeding up the incorporation process and modernizing rules regarding the protection of creditors, in particular reducing minimum legal capital (for a more detailed discussion, *see* Chapter 3). Hence, as a result of the decisions of the ECJ, the "incorporation market"—as it had been known in the United States— came to the European Union. To this point, however, the European Union has yet to experience a one state domination of the "incorporation market" like the U.S. has with Delaware.

While the *Centros*, *Überseering* and *Inspire Art* cases all focused on the transfer of the real seat of a corporation from the perspective of the Member state of the real seat, it was not entirely clear if limitations to the transfer of the real seat adopted by the Member State where the corporation is incorporated were admissible. These are, so to speak, limitations to "emigration" imposed by the home jurisdiction, not to "immigration" imposed by the jurisdiction of destination. The ECJ refused to recognize such a limitation as a violation of freedom of establishment in the *Cartesio* case decided in 2008 (16.12.2008–C–210/06, ECR 2008 I– 9641). The ECJ held that Art. 43, 48 EC are to be interpreted as not precluding legislation of a Member State under which a company incorporated to limit the ability of the corporation to transfer its seat to another Member State, whilst retaining its status as a company governed by the law of the Member State of incorporation. With the *Cartesio* decision, the ECJ established a confusing two-tiered approach to freedom of establishment. Under this two-tiered system, each Member State can limit the transfer of the real seat of corporations created according to its own law, yet it has to accept that corporations from other Member States move their real seat to its own territory.

Consider the following German case.

GERMAN FEDERAL COURT OF JUSTICE, 13 MARCH 2003

13 March 2003, VII ZR 370/98, BGHZ 154, 185

Facts

Plaintiff is a Dutch corporation (*Besloten Venootschnap* [BV]) founded in 1990 and which is registered in the [Dutch] companies' register in Amsterdam and Haarlem. In 1992, plaintiff asked the defendant to renovate a motel. After defendant rendered the promised services, plaintiff refused to pay the remuneration and claimed that some of the renovation work was poorly performed. After the defendant refused to fix the alleged defects, the plaintiff did it. In 1994/95 plaintiff moved its real seat from the Netherlands to Germany because the corporation's two shares were acquired by two German nationals who were mainly conducting plaintiff's business in Germany. Soon thereafter, plaintiff demanded payment of 1.163.657,77 DM from the defendant as damages. The trial regional court (Laudgericht) dismissed the suit, holding that plaintiff lacked legal capacity to bring the suit. The appellate court (Oberlaudesgericht) affirmed.

Grounds

The appellate court held that plaintiff lacked legal capacity to bring legal actions in German court. Since the legal capacity of a corporation is determined by German private international law, which follows the real seat theory of incorporation, the real seat of the corporation determines its legal capacity. This appellate court found that this is also the case when a corporation moves its real seat to Germany. The appellate court determined that application of the real seat theory does not constitute a violation of the freedom of establishment granted by the EU-treaty. [. . .]

II.

This Senate ordered a stay of the proceedings and referred the case to the European Court of Justice in a preliminary ruling under Art. 234 subs. 1a, subs. 3 EU-Treaty. The European Court held:

"1. Where a company formed in accordance with the law of a Member State ('A') in which it has its registered office is deemed, under the law of another Member State ('B'), to have moved its actual centre of administration to Member State B, Articles 43 EC and 48 EC preclude Member State B from denying the company legal capacity and, consequently, the capacity to bring legal proceedings before its national courts for the purpose of enforcing rights under a contract with a company established in Member State B.

2. Where a company formed in accordance with the law of a Member State ('A') in which it has its registered office exercises its freedom of establishment in another Member State ('B'), Articles 43 EC and 48 EC require Member State B to recognise the legal capacity and, consequently, the capacity to be a party to legal proceedings which the company enjoys under the law of its State of incorporation ('A')."

III.

The decision of the appellate court is reversed.

The action is admissible. Plaintiff has capacity to bring legal actions to German courts as a Dutch corporation.

1. Under hitherto existing German case law, a corporation's legal capacity is determined by the law of the state where the corporation has its real seat. This principle also applies when a company is founded under the law of another state and later transfers its real seat to Germany. According to this principle, the appellate court held that the plaintiff could not—after it moved its real seat to Germany—bring legal actions in German courts since it did not reincorporate according to German law (BGH, decision of March 30, 2000—VII ZR 370/98, NZG 2000, 926 with further references).

2.   The result reached by the appellate court, however, violates the freedom of establishment granted by Art. 43, 48 EU-Treaty. The European Court of Justice (ECJ), in response to the question posed by the appellate court, held that the requirement for a corporation already incorporated in another Member State, to reincorporate in Germany, denies the freedom of establishment (ECJ *supra*, Recital No. 81). The ECJ found it to be an unjustified violation of the freedom of establishment for Germany to refuse to recognize the legal capacity and the capacity to bring legal actions of a corporation already founded according to the law of another Member State, just because the corporation moved its real seat to Germany after all shares of the corporation have been transferred to German citizens (ECJ *supra*, Recital No. 82).

3.   This interpretation of Art. 43 and 48 by the ECJ is binding for this court. The interpretation requires this court to apply the law in way that it does not violate the freedom of establishment (*Forsthoff*, DB 2002, 2471, 2474).

(a).   This application could be achieved by recognizing plaintiff—after it moved its real seat to Germany—as a partnership with legal capacity and the capacity to bring legal actions under German law (BGHZ 151, 204). However, plaintiff sued defendant, not in its capacity as a German partnership, but as a Dutch corporation. Consequently, plaintiff used the freedom of establishment as guaranteed by the EU-Treaty. This means that plaintiff's legal capacity has to be determined according to Dutch law (ECJ *supra*, Recital No. 80, 95). It is not possible to force the plaintiff to use the legal form of a partnership under German law since this would have a severe impact on the liability of the members of the Dutch corporation. Such an interpretation would violate the freedom of establishment as determined by the ECJ (see *Forsthoff*, DB 2002, 2471, 2476; *Leible/Hofmann*, RIW 2002, 925, 929; *Zimmer*, BB 2003, 1, 5; *Lutter*, BB 2003, 7, 9; *Eidenmüller*, ZIP 2002, 2233, 2238; *Heidenhain*, NZG 2002, 1141, 1142; *Grosserichter*, DStR 2003, 159, 160; *Wernicke*, EuZW 2002, 758, 761; *Buck*, WuB II N. § 14 BGB 1.03).

(b).   Plaintiff must be enabled to act as a Dutch corporation even after moving its real seat to Germany. This requires that we determine the legal capacity of the plaintiff according to the law of the state where the corporation was founded. A corporation within the scope of the freedom of establishment is entitled to claim its contractual rights in every Member State, as long as it has still legal capacity according to the law of the state where it was founded. This is true even when the corporation moves its real seat to another Member State.

NOTES AND QUESTIONS

1.   Based on what you have read so far, what kind of advantages might exist, in the European Union, for corporations to incorporate in one country, but to conduct almost all of their business activity elsewhere?

2.   In this case, the German Federal Court of Justice contemplated the possibility of recognizing the corporation as a German partnership with legal capacity. What are the possible disadvantages for a business organization and its members to be treated as a partnership, besides the personal liability of the members?

3.   This case offers the occasion to research at home, and/or to discuss in class the relevance of the precedents of the European Court of Justice (ECJ) for national European courts. The German Federal Court of Justice refers and defers to the ECJ. Are the precedents of the ECJ technically binding?

* * *

TRABRENNBAHN

German Federal Court of Justice, 2008
27 October 2008, II ZR 158/06, BGHZ 178, 192

Facts

Plaintiff is a Swiss stock corporation (*Aktiengesellschaft*) with its real seat in Germany. Plaintiff has three shareholders, one of which is also the director of the corporation (*Verwaltungsrat*). In 2004, plaintiff and defendant executed a [special kind of] rental agreement for some real estate governed by German law. Defendant terminated the agreement in 2004. Plaintiff brought suit against the defendant, seeking payment for outstanding obligations, return of the real estate and compensation of legal expenses.

Grounds

The action is admissible.

The plaintiff has legal capacity and, consequently, the capacity to bring legal proceedings.

a) The appellate court held that it did not have to decide whether the plaintiff has its real seat in Germany or Switzerland because plaintiff would have legal capacity and the capacity to bring legal proceedings under German private international law in either case. The appellate court found that case law of the European Court of Justice states that corporations from either a Member State of the European Union or from the European Economic Area (EEA) have the right to transfer their real seat to another Member State. Although Switzerland is not a Member State, the court determined that Swiss corporations must be treated like corporations from a Member State because Switzerland has largely harmonized its legal system with European law. The appellate court similarly found that the principle of legal certainty mandates that the same rules for corporations in Member States of the European Union and the European Economic Area must apply to Swiss corporations. Given this line of reasoning, the appellate court did not find it necessary to decide the question of whether the incorporation theory must be applied to corporations from "third countries," those countries outside of the European Union or the European Economic Area.

b) This court does not follow the appellate court's reasoning.

We find that the incorporation theory need not apply in relationships between Switzerland and Germany.

aa) In contrast to other Member States of the European Union and the European Economic Area, there are no international treaties between Germany and Switzerland that require a Swiss corporation to be recognized in the same legal status which that corporation enjoys under the laws of its state of incorporation.

Although Switzerland is a Member of the European Free Trade Association (EFTA), it is not a Member of the European Economic Area. Therefore, neither the freedom of establishment granted in Art. 31, 24 EEA-Treaty, nor the freedom of establishment granted in Art. 43, 48 EU-Treaty, apply.

Also, the "Agreement between the European Community and its Member States, of the one part, and the Swiss Confederation, of the other, on the free movement of persons" (OJ L 114, 30.4.2002, p. 6 ff.) does not state otherwise. This agreement only establishes the right of free movement of services for citizens of the signatory states for the duration of 90 days. This does not imply a free movement for corporations (*Jung,* NZG 2008, 681, 683; dissenting *Beretta,* GPR 2006, 95, 95) since corporations can use the freedom without the transfer of real seat. Moreover, plaintiff transferred the real seat to Germany permanently, rather than temporarily.

An obligation to recognize a Swiss corporation with its real seat in Germany cannot be derived from the General Agreement on Trade in Services (GATS, Federal Gazette 1994 II, p. 1643) (*Kindler,* in: Münchener Kommentar zum BGB, 4th edition, Internationales Gesellschaftsrecht Note 471 f.; dissenting *Hoffmann,* in: Anwaltskommentar zum BGB, Anh. § 12 EGBGB Note 146 ff.). This agreement addresses only the signatory states themselves and cannot establish a private cause of action for individuals. It can also not be interpreted in this manner since this would be contrary to the international understanding of the agreement (*Lehmann,* RIW 2004, 816 ff.; *Jung,* NZG 2008, 681, 683).

Art. 6 subs. 1, Art. 14 of the European Convention on Human Rights in connection with Art. 1 subs. 1 and Art. 5 of its Protocol 1 also does not establish an obligation for Germany to recognize a Swiss corporation with real seat in Germany according to the legal status the corporation enjoys under Swiss law (*Grossfeld/Boin,* JZ 1993, 370 f.; *Ebenroth/Auer,* JZ 1993, 374 f.; dissenting *Meilike,* RIW 1992, 578; BB 1995 Beilage 9 S. 8 ff.). Although legal persons can generally enjoy fundamental rights under the convention, this protection applies only to legal persons being recognized under private international law. However, these rules of private international law are not determined by the convention but by the national legal systems.

bb) Based on the decisions of the European Court of Justice in the cases "*Centros*", "*Überseering*" and "*Inspire Art*" (ZIP 1999, 438; 2002, 2037; 2003, 1885), the Federal Court of Justice applies the incorporation theory to corporations incorporated in Member States of the European Union or in a Member State of the European Economic Area or in a state that signed an international agreement with Germany (BGHZ 154, 185; BGHZ 164, 148; BGH ZIP 2005, 805). According to these principles, the legal capacity of a corporation is determined under the law of the state of incorporation. However, the legal capacity of corporations incorporated in so called "third states," those countries which are not Member States of the European Union or the European Economic Area, nor those which have a respective international agreement with Germany, are still to be determined according to the real seat theory, under which the law of the state of the real seat determines its legal capacity (BGHZ 153, 353, 355; BayObLG DB 2003, 819; OLG Hamburg ZIP 2007, 1108; undecided by BGH, decision from December 2, 2004–III ZR 358/03 Recital No. 11).

[. . .] Although Switzerland harmonized its legal system with European law to a large extent, it is still not a Member of the European Union, nor did it ratify the Agreement on the European Economic Area. This is a deliberate decision of Switzerland against the freedom of establishment granted for the Member States of the European Economic Area, which cannot be ignored. An exemption from the general German rules of private international law for Switzerland must be denied because it would undermine the principle of legal certainty. If such an exemption was granted, courts would have to verify for every single state whether the legal system of that respective state is largely harmonized according to European standards. Therefore, because the freedom of establishment does not apply, the general rules for determining legal capacity for foreign corporations must apply to Swiss corporations.

cc) Under the German rules of private international law, the legal capacity of a corporation is determined according to the law of the state where the corporation has its real seat (BGHZ 97, 269, 271). Therefore, a Swiss stock corporation can only have legal capacity in Germany when it is registered in the [German] companies' register, which requires reincorporation in Germany. The court is not convinced that these principles should be abolished. There are certain authors in the legal literature, however, who argue that the shift from the real seat theory to the incorporation theory imposed by the case law of European Court of Justice, also requires the application of the incorporation theory to corporations from "third states." These authors refer especially to a necessary unity of the rules of private international law and the need for a competition of national company laws triggered by the incorporation theory (*Eidenmüller,* ZIP 2002, 2233, 2244; *Behrens,* in: Grosskommentar zum GmbHG, Einleitung B. Note 36; *Rehm,* in: Eidenmüller, Ausländische Kapitalgesellschaften im deutschen Recht, 2004, § 2 Note 87; *Leible/Hoffmann,* ZIP 2003, 925, 930; *Paefgen,* WM 2003, 561, 570). The dissenting authors, however, claim that the protection of creditors and minority shareholders, the prevention of an escape from German towards foreign corporate law with lower standards (*race to the bottom*) still requires the application of the real seat theory to corporations from third states and that the establishment of two different systems in the German rules of private international law has to be accepted (*Hüffer,* AktG, 7th edition, § 1 Note 32 f.; *Kindler,* in: Münchener Kommentar zum BGB, 4th edition, Internationales Gesellschaftsrecht Note 433; *Hohloch,* in: Erman, BGB, 12th edition, Anh. II Art. 37 EGBGB Note 32; *Heider,* in: Münchener Kommentar zum AktG, 2nd edition, Einl. Note 122 ff.; *Hausmann,* in Reithmann/Martiny, Internationales Vertragsrecht, 6th edition, Note 2284 b; *Wiedemann,* GesR II § 1 IV 2, 3; *Heldrich,* in: Palandt, BGB, 67th edition, Anh. zu Art. 12 EGBGB Note 9; *Bayer,* BB 2003, 2357, 2363 f.; *Ebke,* JZ 2003, 927, 929 f.; *Horn,* NJW 2004, 893, 897; *Wachter,* GmbHR 2005, 1484, 1485; *Weller,* ZGR 2006, 748, 765).

So far, the [German] legislature has not passed any regulation on this issue. Particularly, § 4a GmbHG does not govern the treatment of a foreign corporation with its real seat in Germany (*Kindler,* AG 2007, 721, 725 f.). However, the legislature has, following a recommendation of the German Council for International Private Law (see *Sonnenberger/Bauer,* RIW 2006 Beil. 1 zu Heft 4), issued a draft of a law for the private international law of corporations, associations and legal persons. This draft proposes a complete shift to the incorporation theory (Art. 10 EGBGB–E). The legislative process, however, has not been completed. Moreover, several concerns have been expressed throughout this political process. Considering these developments, this court is not willing to anticipate the will of the legislature by completely adopting the incorporation theory. Besides, there is no need for an adoption of the incorporation theory since the plaintiff is not precluded from bringing legal proceedings to German courts.

c) Although a stock corporation under Swiss law with real seat in Germany has no legal capacity as stock corporation under German law, it does have such capacity as a civil partnership or a commercial partnership under German law, neither of which requires registration in the companies' register in order to obtain legal capacity (BGHZ 151, 204; critical *Binz,* BB 2005, 2361, 2363 ff.). Since the company is doing business in Germany, it would not be acceptable to deny its legal capacity and the capacity to bring legal proceedings. One consequence of this result, however, is that in a partnership, all member are personal liable for debts. But, it is the internal business of the members of such a partnership to arrange the question of liability to third parties. These principles are—in contrast to the opinion of the appellate court—not limited to corporation from the island of Jersey or other territories in the European Union with a special status.

NOTES AND QUESTIONS

1.   What do you think are the reasons mentioned in the decision why the German Federal Court of Justice denied the application of the incorporation theory for corporations from "third countries" with a real seat in Germany? Do you think there might be any reason not mentioned in the decision that influenced the court?

2.   Why does the court differentiate between the personal liability of the members of the corporation/plaintiff in this case and not in the prior decision involving the Dutch corporation?

3.   Why does the court refer to scholarly works? What is the relevance of these sources? What are the pros and cons of citing scholars explicitly in courts' opinions?

4.   The Court considers if the European Convention on Human Rights requires to recognize a Swiss corporation (concluding that it does not). Can you explain this reference? Why could this Convention be relevant?

* * *

Notwithstanding precedents of the European Court of Justice, as well as precedents in individual Member States that abolished or mitigated the real seat approach in favor of the incorporation theory, some Member States still have statutory provisions that seemingly adopt, at least to some degree, the real seat approach. It remains up for debate whether these provisions are consistent with European law. One interesting example of these types of provisions is the following Article of the Italian statute regulating conflicts of laws. Read it carefully, and consider if it is compatible with the jurisprudence of the European Court of Justice (focus on the last sentence of Paragraph 1). Consider also the similarities and differences with Section 2115 of the California Corporations Code discussed above.

Article 25 of the Italian Private International Law Statute, Law N. 218 of 1995

1.   Corporations, associations, foundations and any other legal entity, public or private, including those without an association nature, are regulated by the law of the State in which territory the entity has been created. Italian law will apply, however, if the seat of administration is located in Italy, or if the entity's main purpose is carried on in Italy.

2.   In particular, the following issues are regulated by the law applicable to the entity:

a) its legal nature;

b) its legal name;

c) its creation, transformation and dissolution;

d) its legal capacity;

e) the appointment, powers and functioning of its governing bodies;

f) the power to act on behalf of the entity;

g) the rules concerning the acquisition and loss of the status of member or shareholder and the rights and obligations connected with such a status;

h) the liability of the obligations of the entity;

i) the consequences of the violations of the law or its articles of association.

3.   Transfers of the legal seat of the entity in a different State and mergers of entities with seats in different States produce legal effects only if accomplished pursuant to the laws of the interested States.

* * *

JAPAN'S NEW LIABILITY-BASED APPROACH

Japan has adopted a "middle ground" between the incorporation approach and the real seat approach. The default rule in Japan is freedom-of-incorporation,[1] but Japanese law also shows a "preference" for its own corporate law by providing for some pseudo-foreign corporation rules.

---

[1]   There is no provision in Japanese statutes (Cf. Act on General Rules for Application of Laws (Ho no tekiyo ni kansuru tsusoku ho, Law No.78 of 2006)) that specifically provides for this principle, but it is generally accepted that Japanese law adopts it because of the existence of pseudo-foreign corporation regulations as exceptions.

In contrast to both the U.S. and European systems, the issue of incorporation did not attract significant attention in Japan for a long period of time, presumably for two reasons: 1) Japan is not a federal state like the U.S. or part of a supranational regional union like E.U. Member States and; 2) for many years, foreign direct investment in Japan has been relatively low due to the country's geographical position.

Former Article 482 of the Japanese Commercial Code (*Sho-ho*, Law No. 48 of 1899, before amendments by Law No. 87 of 2005), which was partially inspired by Italian law, provided that the same corporate law provisions that applied to Japanese corporations should apply to a foreign corporation which had its head office in Japan or whose main purpose was to conduct business in Japan (real seat approach). Although legal scholars disagreed, courts generally interpreted this provision limiting the activity of pseudo-foreign corporations, unless they followed the incorporation procedure mandated for Japanese corporations.

In 2005, Japanese corporate law underwent a significant reform. The 2005 reform offered an opportunity for critics of the pseudo-foreign corporation rules to voice their opinion. Criticism of Article 482 ultimately led to its amendment as part of the 2005 reforms.[2] There were three primary arguments made against Article 482. First, the scope of application of this provision was unclear, thus hindering the use of offshore special purpose vehicles in structured finance transactions. Second, despite the fact that there were pseudo-foreign corporation statutes operating at the time in Japan, Article 482 was not rigorously enforced, putting its effectiveness in doubt. Third, many critics suggested to identify specific provisions that should be applied to foreign corporations as a matter of public policy, rather than requiring those corporations to comply with the entire body of Japanese corporate rules.

Based on these criticisms, Japanese policy makers briefly considered abolishing pseudo-foreign corporation rules altogether as part of the 2005 reform. Eventually, however, they settled on simply amending the rules.

Instead of mandating the application of specific provisions of Japanese law, the new pseudo-foreign corporation regulation prohibits a foreign corporation that has its head office or conducts its main business purpose in Japan from "continuously carrying out transactions in Japan" (Japanese Companies Act (*Kaisha-ho*, Law No.86 of 2005), Art.821(1)). Individuals acting in violation of this regulation (e.g., representatives or employees of the pseudo-foreign corporation in Japan) are jointly and severally liable with the foreign corporation for any liability deriving from

---

[2]   Yoshihisa Hayakawa, *Giji gaikoku gaisya (Pseudo-Foreign Corporation)*, JURISUTO 1267, 114–120 (2004).

such transactions (Japanese Companies Act 821(2))[3], and will be imposed an administrative fine of an amount equivalent to the registration and license tax for the incorporation of the corporation (Japanese Companies Act 979(2)).

NOTES AND QUESTIONS

1.   What interests does (or did) Japanese law seek to protect by enacting pseudo-foreign corporation statutes? Compare the Japanese approach to the ones existing in California and Europe. Which approach do you find more desirable and why?

2.   Do you think that the approach used to regulate the activities of foreign corporations effectively protects creditors and other stakeholders in Japan? Why yes or why not?

3.   It would be difficult to think of a pseudo-foreign corporation (i.e. a corporation that has its head office in Japan or its main purpose is to conduct business in Japan) not "continuously carrying out transactions in Japan." This concept had been originally used as the standard to regulate foreign corporations. The purpose was to make sure that financial transactions using offshore SPVs would be excluded from this regulation, since the general understanding was that issuance of securities to raise capital does not satisfy the definition of pseudo-foreign corporation just mentioned. Also, in the legislative process, the then-Minister of Justice suggested that the new regulation should be interpreted narrowly, so as to only include corporations trying to evade Japanese law. This position was expressed in response to concerns over the new regulation's potential chilling effect on foreign investment (162nd National Diet, House of Councilors, Report of the Meetings of Judicial Committee, No.26 (June 28, 2005), p.3–4). What do you think is the value, if any, of such a statement on how the rule should be interpreted? More generally, do you think that historical and extra-textual elements should be relevant to interpret a statute? Are there comparative differences concerning statutory interpretation that you are aware of?

4.   Although there was a possibility that litigation regarding pseudo-foreign corporations would increase under the new regulation, no case based on Art. 821 has been reported as of January 2014.

5.   The Japanese Companies Act also encompasses provisions regarding foreign corporations in general (i.e. not limited to pseudo-foreign corporations), which might be more important practically. In order to carry out transactions continuously in Japan, a foreign corporation must indicate its representatives in Japan, including at least one person with his or her domicile in Japan (Art. 817(1)), and register information such as the law governing its incorporation and the names and domiciles of its

---

[3]   Although there was a possibility that litigation regarding pseudo-foreign corporations would increase under the new regulation, no case on Art.821 has been reported as of January 2014.

representatives in Japan (Art. 933(2)) before it engages in business (Art. 818(1)). Individuals violating this requirement are jointly and severally liable with the foreign corporation for any obligation that has arisen from such transactions (Art. 818(2)). Also, a registered foreign corporation, which is equivalent to a Japanese stock corporation, must publish its financial statements annually (Art. 819(1)).

RACE TO THE TOP OR TO THE BOTTOM? A MORE THEORETICAL VIEW OF REGULATORY COMPETITION

As briefly mentioned in the Introduction, it is debatable whether the regulatory competition that stems from the incorporation theory leads to a "race to the top" (*i.e.*, the development of efficient rules that maximize the interests of the different stakeholders), or a "race to the bottom" (*i.e.*, a situation in which some corporate actors—typically controlling shareholders, directors, and managers—can extract private benefits through regulatory arbitrage). The following classical articles argue the two theses with respect to the U.S. "market for corporate charters." But their framework can also be relevant—with the necessary distinctions—to discuss regulatory competition in other systems and fields.

WILLIAM L. CARY, FEDERALISM AND CORPORATE LAW: REFLECTIONS UPON DELAWARE[4]
83 Yale L. J. 663 (1974)

Delaware is both the sponsor and the victim of a system contributing to the deterioration of corporation standards. This unhappy state of affairs, stemming in great part from the movement toward the least common denominator, Delaware, seems to be developing on both the legislative and judicial fronts. In the management of corporate affairs, state statutory and case law has always been supreme, with federal intrusion limited to the field of securities regulation. Perhaps now is the time to reconsider the federal role.

[. . .]

Some of the features of Delaware law demonstrating liberality have been recited in publications for practitioners. These include: greater freedom to pay dividends and make distributions; greater ease of charter amendment and less restrictions upon selling assets, mortgaging, leasing, and merging . . . freedom from mandatory cumulative voting; permission to have staggered boards of directors; lesser pre-emptive rights for shareholders; [and] clearer rights of indemnification for directors and officers. . . .

---

[4] Footnotes and paragraph numbers have been omitted.

[. . .]

A few illustrations of the legislative approach reveal the Delaware position. For example, shareholders meetings may now be dispensed with if a consent is signed by the number of votes necessary to take the intended action, thus offering a technique to avoid disclosure. Protection from this abuse is provided through the proxy rules under federal law but they do not apply to firms that are unlisted or have less than 500 shareholders and minimal assets. Under § 109 of the Delaware law any corporation may in its certificate of incorporation confer the power to amend or repeal by-law provisions upon the directors and thus possibly foreclose any initiative outside the management.

[. . .]

Judicial decisions in Delaware illustrate that the courts have undertaken to carry out the "public policy" of the state and create a "favorable climate" for management. Consciously or unconsciously, fiduciary standards and the standards of fairness generally have been relaxed. In general, the judicial decisions can best be reconciled on the basis of a desire to foster incorporation in Delaware. It is not clear, however, that the revenue thermometer should replace the chancellor's foot. This trend should be reversed.

[. . .]

Mansfield Hardwood Lumber Co. v. Johnson—A *Point of View*

Mansfield Hardwood Lumber Co. v. Johnson states the attitude of critics toward Delaware decisions. It involved the purchase of a minority interest without full disclosure and the company's subsequent liquidation for the benefit of the insiders. The first opinion of the Fifth Circuit, affirming the decision below, ordered a rescission of the stock sales and granted plaintiffs a pro rata portion of the assets realized upon liquidation. It was based upon general fiduciary principles under the law of Louisiana and upon the failure to disclose the facts concerning the asset values of the company.

Although the acts occurred in Louisiana, in view of the fact that the corporation was organized in Delaware a petition for a rehearing was filed, claiming among other things that such a fiduciary relationship did not exist in the state of incorporation and must be determined by its laws. In its second opinion the Fifth Circuit noted a number of decisions holding that "the conflict of laws rules of the forum require that court to refer to the 'law of the State of incorporation to determine the . . . relationship between corporation and stockholder. . . .' " The court said further, "Apparently Delaware imposes no fiduciary duty on the part of officers or directors or majority stockholders in buying stock from the minority or individual stockholders."

Nevertheless, it concluded that "[t]hose decisions are, however, in our opinion, either inapplicable or unsound where the only contact point with the incorporating state is the naked fact of incorporation. . . ." Applying conflicts of laws principles, it decided that "where neither the charter nor the statutory laws of the incorporating state are applicable and *all* contact points are in the forum, we believe that the laws of the forum should govern." After discussing a number of decisions in the federal courts, the court said that "most of the other cases listed . . . involve situations where the courts were seeking to impose the fiduciary rule of the state of incorporation *in order to escape the inequitable rule of the forum (generally Delaware)."* It therefore denied the petition for rehearing.

Today such an action would almost certainly be grounded on Rule 10b–5 and brought in the federal courts under the Securities Exchange Act of 1934. Thus the court would reach the same result without concerning itself with refinements of conflict of law principles.

[. . .]

Fairness between Parent and Subsidiary

The Delaware courts have tended to encourage freedom of action on the part of parent companies incorporated in that state and have indicated little concern over the fairness of dealings with subsidiaries. The consistent philosophy favors controlling shareholders and leaves fiduciary questions to the business judgment of an indentured board. The old concept that each party is "entitled to what fair arm's length bargaining would probably have yielded" has been enveloped in a new and labyrinthine rationale.

The most recent example in the Delaware Supreme Court is *Sinclair Oil Corp. v. Levien.* Sinclair totally dominated Sinclair Venezuelan Oil Company (Sinven), in which it held 97 percent of the stock. Plaintiff represented the three percent minority interest suing derivatively. At Sinclair's direction Sinven paid out over six years $108 million in dividends ($38 million in excess of earnings). Thus Sinven's activities declined; there was no opportunity for expansion despite Sinclair's company-wide policy of developing through its subsidiaries new sources of revenue.

Recognizing that by reason of Sinclair's domination, Sinclair owed Sinven a fiduciary duty, the Delaware Supreme Court nevertheless held that the transactions should be tested by the business judgment rule under which a court will not interfere unless there is a showing of gross and palpable overreaching. The chancellor in the court below had applied the intrinsic fairness test and ruled against Sinclair. The supreme court, on the other hand, reversed and said, "[T]he basic situation for the application of the [intrinsic fairness test] is the one in which the parent has received a benefit to the exclusion and at the expense of the subsidiary." Since all the stockholders received the dividends pro rata, these distributions did not represent self-dealing, an essential ingredient for invoking the intrinsic fairness test. The plaintiff, bearing the burden of proof, proved neither that business opportunities came to Sinven independently nor that Sinclair took to itself or denied opportunities to Sinven. It would have been surprising for Sinclair to generate new expansion when its whole motive was to drain the cash from Sinven.

[. . .]

The Directors' Duty of Care

Graham v. Allis-Chalmers Manufacturing Co. is an example of the low standard that Delaware shares with most other jurisdictions as to the duty of care on the part of directors. *Graham* involved a derivative action on behalf of Allis-Chalmers in connection with the much publicized price-fixing conspiracy involving electric equipment in the late 1950's. The company, together with four nondirector defendants, pleaded guilty to the indictments and as a result had been subjected not only to fines and penalties but to treble damage actions brought by purchasers of the equipment.

In this case it was impossible to establish actual knowledge on the part of any officers, but it was claimed that they should have had notice, or constructive knowledge, of what was happening. One reason why a duty might arise here is that in 1937 (19 years before the illegal action) the Federal Trade Commission had issued a cease and desist order from alleged price-fixing in connection with the sale of many of the same items. However, the point was made by the vice-chancellor that such an order was "entered at a time when none of the Allis-Chalmers directors here charged held a position of responsibility with the company."

The supreme court upheld the lower court's ruling for the defendants, finding that since the company's directors could not investigate personally all of the company's employees they were entitled to rely on summaries, reports, and corporate records. No one would expect the directors to have personal knowledge of all corporate activities. However, a student Note suggests that a state less hospitable than Delaware might have imposed upon directors the duty of installing an internal control system to prevent repeated antitrust violations.

* * *

Professor Cary was clearly very critical of the role of Delaware, and more generally regulatory competition, in the development of corporate law. In the article excerpted above, in fact, he also advocates the opportunity of the intervention of the federal legislator in order to curb the race to laxity in corporate law. Other scholars have taken an opposite perspective, arguing that freedom of incorporation leads to a more flexible regime, in which more efficient rules can be established and applied. One of the underpinnings of this reasoning is that if in one jurisdiction shareholders, creditors, or other investors do not receive sufficient protections, they will not engage in business with a corporation incorporated in that jurisdiction, or at least require a compensation for the increased risk they perceive. The consequence is that legislatures and judiciaries that are inclined to attract corporations cannot disregard the interests of other stakeholders, but will rather have to find an optimal balance between the interests of corporate insiders and other stakeholders. This is an interesting argument; it implies, however, information efficiency: stakeholders must, in other words, be well informed on the applicable corporate rules, and able to properly interpret them, a condition that can be questioned. In any case, the following article argues that the incorporation theory, and the resulting regulatory competition in the U.S., is more beneficial than harmful.

One interesting issue is to what extent, in a system based on regulatory competition among states to attract corporations, federal or international law can impose minimum standards in order to avoid "market failures." A similar role can be played by the federal government in the U.S., and by European law in the Old Continent. One author, Professor Mark Roe from Harvard Law School, has in particular argued that the policy makers in Delaware do not only face "horizontal" competition from other States, but also potential "vertical" competition from the federal legislature. Fear of federal intervention that might displace Delaware law could, in fact, operate as an incentive to Delaware policy makers to take into account the need of protection of minority shareholders, creditors, and other corporate stakeholders. The following excerpt from Mark Roe illustrates this point.

* * *

MARK J. ROE, DELAWARE'S POLITICS[5]
118 Harv. L. Rev. 2491 (2005)

The standard story is that states make corporate law, with state competition critically determining its content. This may be so, but perhaps the relationship between the states and Washington is just as determinative, because federal authorities can displace the states and often do so on big issues. Corporate law issues can always go federal or attract federal attention. The SEC is always on stand-by, and Congress takes up issues that deeply affect the economy or the opinion polls.

[. . .]

---

[5]   Footnotes omitted.

Although managers historically are often seen to have had the upper hand in Delaware, they don't fully dominate there. This is not just because of, and perhaps is in spite of, state competition. Delaware doesn't let them dominate—or they themselves choose to be moderate—because if it did, the game could move to Washington, where new players could induce new results. Hence, local interest groups compromise and local decision makers are evenhanded, even if local politics doesn't demand compromise or evenhandedness.

Sometimes, the issue is so big—generating headlines in the media and fears for the economy—that it necessarily attracts federal attention. Different coalitions can, and do, emerge at the federal level. When corporate law stays in Delaware, the state limits the range of the first decision-making stage by excluding corporate outsiders and public policymakers; sometimes managers and investors can make their deal in Delaware and then unite at the federal level to fight off other forces. Probably more often than not, their interests are sufficiently similar that both want the states and not the federal authorities to make corporate law. But sometimes Delaware loses control of the agenda, usually when the public is sufficiently motivated, because the economy is weak or because scandals dominate the media, and Congress acts. Congress ousted Delaware most recently with Sarbanes-Oxley, after the Enron and WorldCom scandals hit the headlines.

Look at what we have done here. We've reversed the conventional analytic form for Delaware, in which the making of public law governing the corporation is analogized to a market—one of competing states. We've turned that analysis inside out, into a public law perspective, with interest groups and political institutions. Instead of seeing Delaware as solely the upshot of a market of competing states, we also see it as like a federal agency—captured by its interest groups—that can only move as far as Congress allows. That range of movement is wide, but not unlimited.

By thus viewing Delaware, we have uncovered rich public choice explanations for the core nature of Delaware and American corporate law. While these public choice explanations do not let us precisely explain statute after statute or exact judicial holdings, they mark off the broad boundaries of corporate lawmaking. First, we have explained Delaware's moderation, Delaware's dominance, and the conservative, boardroom-centered nature of American corporate law via federal-state interaction, without relying solely on the state-to-state race for franchise tax revenues. Second, we have interpreted the state corporate franchise tax as not just motivating Delaware to do a good job in the abstract, but—subtly refocusing the emphasis—as excluding many players from making corporate law. Third, we've shown how Delaware's structural differences with Congress arise not merely from the presence or absence of competitors, but also from the differing interest groups and ideologies that affect each. Fourth, we've seen how the internal affairs doctrine reflects deference to some interest groups and not others. And we've seen how the Delaware-federal sequence is an agenda-setting structure.

Delaware is only a state, embedded in a federal system that has more going on than just interstate competition for charters. It has only two senators and one representative. Its law can be replaced and its acts risk reversal at the federal level by Congress, by courts, and by the SEC. When the issue is big, one of these federal institutions often acts, without paying much attention to Delaware. Each of these institutions responds, however clumsily, to its own voters and inputs, and those inputs are not identical to those that are powerful in Delaware. Delaware can usually create the initial rule, to which the federal players react, but it cannot consistently control the final results in making American corporate law.

NOTES AND QUESTIONS

1.   Compare and contrast the positions of Professors Cary and Roe concerning the effects of regulatory competition in the corporate area. What do you think are the most compelling arguments? If regulatory competition is an efficient and effective regulatory tool, wouldn't it be advisable simply not to regulate corporations at all, to allow the corporate contract (charter and bylaws) to set all the rules governing the internal affairs of the corporation, with no limitations or constraints set by statute? Could you argue that, as long as the governing documents are public, investors could evaluate the rules and the risks they pose, and decide whether to invest? In other words and more generally, if a market for rules works when states compete to attract corporations, can't it work when issuers compete to attract investors based on their governing rules?

2.   Consider the emphasis put by Professor Roe on the role of the federal government or, better, of fear of federal intervention. Do you think his thesis reinforces the argument in favor of a "race to the top" or of a "race to the bottom"? Is the U.S. federal government more or less prone than state legislatures or regulators to be influenced by business lobbies?

3.   It is not always true that corporations look for more lax rules, and therefore are attracted by jurisdictions and rules that favor flexibility and limited protection of investors. For example, lots of corporations located in certain systems, for example Brazil, Israel, but also some European and Asian countries, cross-list or dual-list in the U.S., meaning that they become listed companies exclusively or also in the U.S., often on the NYSE. Among the reasons there is certainly the desire to access the very liquid and efficient American stock exchange, but one interesting theory is the so-called "bonding hypothesis." According to this perspective, corporations list abroad exactly to subject themselves to the—generally quite rigorous—U.S. disclosure regime, something that allows them to signal to investors the quality of their governance, a high level of protection of shareholders, and more generally the

very ability to sustain the costs of compliance with the U.S. securities laws. This last idea evokes, from an evolutionary perspective, the function of the tail of the peacock. According to some naturalists, the male peacock developed a huge, colorful tail that is however clearly a handicap (it makes it harder to run from predators and to look for food) to inform females that he is so strong and genetically superior that he can "afford" to live and prosper also with that encumbering and substantially useless appendix. Similarly, cross-listed corporations indicate that they are so financially solid that the costs of compliance in the U.S. and the risk of enforcement in that country do not scare them. It should be noted, however, that foreign issuers listed in the U.S. are not subject exactly to the same regime as American issuers, but to what some have called a "watered-down" version of it. In addition, one possible side effect of this apparent race-to-the-top must be considered. In countries in which cross-listing in the U.S. is present, for example Israel, scholars have observed that corporations cross-listed in the U.S., the local stock exchange and business interests tend to oppose vigorously the adoption of rules in their home country that are more strict than the U.S. securities laws applying to foreign issuers, something that might affect the development of rigorous rules in the home jurisdiction. For a discussion of this phenomenon with respect to Israeli corporations, *see* Amir N. Licht, *David's Dilemma: A Case Study of Securities Regulation in a Small Open Market*, 2 THEO. INQ. L. 1 (2001). We must also mention that this Author (together with others), in his work, has questioned the foundations of the "bonding hypothesis." If you are interested in this problem, a recent book we strongly suggest is Lixian Liu, *International Cross-Listing of Chinese Firms*, IGI, 2014. The business perspective it offers is enriched with several legal issues.

* * *

As we mentioned in the Introduction, one might argue that the real advantage of Delaware and of other states that compete in an "incorporation market" has more to do with the role of the judiciary than with statutory law. One reason for this observation is that unlike statutory provisions, which can easily be "copied" by a competing State, the expertise, competency, efficiency, and attitudes of the judiciary cannot be replicated as easily in a different system. In addition, while it is fairly easy to copy a statute, it is not as easy to become familiar with and to effectively apply a consistent body of precedents developed over several decades.

While the judiciary may be particularly important to the "incorporation market," the judiciary and the legislature must cooperate to ensure the continued attractiveness of the jurisdiction. Even in Delaware, the courts can sometimes reach results that alienate corporate insiders, therefore threatening the advantage of the state in the "incorporation market." This exact result occurred in 1985, after the Delaware Supreme Court decided the famous case Smith v. Van Gorkom

(488 A.2d 858 (1985)). We will discuss this decision extensively in Chapter 6, but to briefly summarize, the Delaware Supreme Court affirmed the liability of the members of the board of directors of a corporation for a breach of their duty of care in approving a corporate merger. The decision sent shivers through corporate America, and many large corporations incorporated in Delaware considered reincorporating in other states to avoid the risk of directors' liability created by this precedent.

The Delaware legislature promptly stepped in to quell the fears of corporate directors. The legislature enacted § 102(b)(7) of the Delaware General Corporation Law, which provided that the articles of incorporation of a corporation can include a provision limiting the liability of outside directors. This rule was considered a reaction by the Delaware legislature to a judicial decision that could potentially derail, or hinder, Delaware's competitive edge in attracting and retaining corporations. A form of "regulatory competition" can therefore also exist between a state's legislature and the judiciary.

The provision, in relevant part, states as follows:

"(b) In addition to the matters required to be set forth in the certificate of incorporation by subsection (a) of this section, the certificate of incorporation may also contain any or all of the following matters:

[. . .]

(7) A provision eliminating or limiting the personal liability of a director to the corporation or its stockholders for monetary damages for breach of fiduciary duty as a director, provided that such provision shall not eliminate or limit the liability of a director: (i) For any breach of the director's duty of loyalty to the corporation or its stockholders; (ii) for acts or omissions not in good faith or which involve intentional misconduct or a knowing violation of law; (iii) under § 174 of this title; or (iv) for any transaction from which the director derived an improper personal benefit. No such provision shall eliminate or limit the liability of a director for any act or omission occurring prior to the date when such provision becomes effective. All references in this paragraph to a director shall also be deemed to refer to such other person or persons, if any, who, pursuant to a provision of the certificate of incorporation in accordance with § 141(a) of this title, exercise or perform any of the powers or duties otherwise conferred or imposed upon the board of directors by this title."

* * *

MARCO VENTORUZZO, "COST-BASED" AND "RULES-BASED"
REGULATORY COMPETITION: MARKETS FOR CORPORATE
CHARTERS IN THE U.S. AND IN THE E.U.[6]

3 N.Y.U. J. L. & Bus. 91 (2006)

[. . .]

Conventional wisdom holds that in Europe the degree of regulatory competition among single Member States is far lower than in the U.S. Several features of the various European systems [. . .] contribute to this situation. One of the most frequently invoked explanations is that most States in continental Europe follow the so-called "real seat" principle. Under this regime, a corporation must be incorporated in, and be subject to the laws of, the State where it has its "real seat." While the criteria for determining the "real seat" of a corporation may differ among jurisdictions, generally it includes examining the center of the administration and/or the place where most corporate affairs are performed. In this respect, the choice of where to place the real seat of the corporation is not "free," or, more precisely, does not depend exclusively on a selection of the applicable corporate laws; moving the real seat can be expensive, if not impossible. For these reasons, European corporations do not enjoy nearly as much liberty in shopping around for the most desirable corporate rules as their American counterparts. As a result, according to this view a market for corporate rules is prevented from developing in Europe.

This conventional view is being abandoned, however, in light of recent developments. Over the past several years, the European Court of Justice has issued some ground-breaking decisions in favor of corporations' freedom of movement, of which three are considered revolutionary: Centros, Uberseering and Inspire Art. A growing body of empirical evidence suggests that, largely as a consequence of the doctrines affirmed in these cases, regulatory competition in corporate law is on the rise in Europe. For instance, research by economists Becht, Mayer and Wagner reveals that "the average number of private limited companies from all Member States incorporating in the U.K. per year has increased from 3,360 firms pre-Centros to 19,860 firms post-Centros." Other authors have pointed out that several firms now offer, for a few hundred euros, on-line "incorporation" services for incorporating in the U.K.

In addition, [. . .], recent EU legal reforms such as the directive on cross-border mergers and the introduction of a European-level corporation (the Societas Europea, or SE), as well as proposed European legislation, might make it easier for a corporation to change its applicable

---

[6]   Footnotes omitted.

corporate laws. These changes have, in turn, prompted legal reforms by individual Member States to make their corporate law more attractive.

Predictably, these developments have sparked an intense debate, similar to that in the U.S., about whether an efficient market for rules is possible and desirable in Europe. Most existing analysis assumes that removal of the rules that limit the ability of the corporations to shop around for the most desirable corporate laws (epitomized by the real-seat principle), will result—to a greater or lesser extent—in increased regulatory competition. Relatively less attention is devoted to the other elements that explain the basic features of the market for charters in Europe (to the extent that one exists), and that might affect its future development.

[. . .]

II.

The U.S. "Rule-Based" and European "Cost-Based" Markets for Corporate Law

The basic distinction between corporate charters' competition in Europe and in the U.S., which is particularly evident when viewing the two markets from the demand-side, is that in the United States regulatory competition occurs primarily at the re-incorporation stage and involves, for the most part, larger or quickly growing corporations. These companies are often publicly held or about to go public; on the other hand, small, closely held U.S. corporations, especially at their start-up, usually incorporate in the state where they operate. It is only afterwards, if at all, that these smaller corporations select a different jurisdiction, most often choosing to reincorporate in Delaware.

In Europe, by contrast, the companies that shop around and incorporate in a jurisdiction with which they have no physical connection tend to be smaller, closely-held firms with few shareholders. Corporate mobility in Europe, in other words, "is for new company formation, not for established companies", and "[m]igration is driven by differences in the regulation of new company formation, but most likely not at all by more specific differences in company law." Empirical evidence strongly supports these claims, indicating how, in the last few years, there has been a steady increase in the number of smaller, closely-held corporations that operate in continental Europe and incorporate in the U.K., while the same phenomenon did not involve the reincorporation of larger, publicly held corporations.

The reasons for these different outcomes in the European and U.S. markets can be understood through examining the dynamics of regulatory competition. Economic models that describe regulatory competition in corporate law point out how managers and controlling shareholders, in deciding if and where to incorporate or reincorporate, look at different variables that represent the competitive leverages of the competing jurisdictions. While there are obvious overlaps, these variables can be roughly divided into two categories.

In the first category, which can be described as comprising the financial costs associated with the incorporation process itself, the variables include jurisdictions' franchise taxes and the other fees due upon incorporation, the costs of the legal services necessary in order to perfect the incorporation process, the length of the incorporation process and, most importantly, the necessity to subscribe and pay in a "minimum legal capital" determined by the state of incorporation.

In the second category are rules that affect more directly the internal affairs and the life of an existing and already operating corporation, particularly in respect to its corporate governance. In this context, "rules" does not refer only to statutory rules, but also to the body of precedents and case-law, and, more generally, to the existing legal infrastructure used to enforce those rules (such as expertise of the judiciary, network externalities related to the general knowledge in the financial industry of the chosen legal rules, and the like). Some of the most important rule-based variables influencing where to incorporate are rules relating to directors' liability and conflict of interest, distribution of powers between shareholders and mangers, protection of minorities, and defensive measures in case of takeover.

Even while recognizing the potential overlap and blurring at the margins of these two categories, they can be helpful in explaining differences between the markets for charters in the United States and the European Union. When smaller, private companies first incorporate, they are concerned about costs, whereas larger corporations are more concerned about the rules regulating their internal corporate governance. In the U.S., costs can be reduced by incorporating at home, whereas in Europe, given the fact that significant differences still exist among the Member States, certain incorporation costs can be reduced by picking jurisdictions with low minimum capital requirements and relatively easy and fast incorporation processes. On the other hand, larger corporations are relatively insensitive to issues such as franchise taxes, other incorporation-related costs and minimum legal capital, all of which have a minor impact on their larger budgets. Small, closely-held corporations are presumably less concerned—at least in their ex-ante evaluation— about takeover defenses, protection of minorities, or directors' liability.

Based on these observations, it becomes clear that not all competition is the same. On the demand side, there are two types of "consumers." On the one hand, there are small businesses, generally at the stage of first incorporation, that put an emphasis on the front-load costs of incorporation. On the other hand, larger corporations, which are generally reincorporating, often in light of a corporate event such as going public, are more interested in some specific substantive rules governing the internal corporate affairs. These two types of "consumers" react, in theory and in general terms, to distinctive competitive leverages and thus determine, demand-wise, two different markets that we will call "cost-based" and "rule-based." It is fair to conclude that a primarily "cost based" market is developing in Europe. Even if a rule-based market is not entirely absent in Europe, it is presently less common and less relevant than in the U.S. In the U.S., while the cost-based market has a limited scope, the rule-based market plays a significant role in shaping corporate laws.

III.

Demand-side Drivers of Regulatory Competition

What are the possible elements explaining, from the demand-side point of view, this difference between the European and the U.S. markets for corporate charters? To identify what elements corporate decision-makers consider in deciding where to incorporate or reincorporate, it is necessary to first distinguish among different types of corporations. Factors such as a corporation's size, status as publicly or privately held, general ownership structure, and stage of its life-cycle can all affect corporate decision-makers' assessments of where to incorporate or reincorporate. It is also necessary to bear in mind that, as a general rule, the decision makers dealing with the initial incorporation of a small- or medium-sized business association will be the controlling and founding shareholders themselves, often operating also as directors or managers of the corporation. In larger, publicly held and well-established corporations, those who decide where to reincorporate, or at least those who initiate the process, will be directors and managers. These decision-makers may or may not be controlling shareholders. In systems characterized by a widespread ownership structure, the two roles will tend not to overlap, however, in those systems characterized by concentrated ownership structures, even in large listed corporations, overlap is likely.

The following sections will analyze some basic distinctive features of the European and the American rule-based markets in light of the different decision-makers involved. This discussion will illuminate why the U.S. scenario is compatible with rule-based competition affecting reincorporation decisions of larger corporations while the European system is more compatible with cost-based competition affecting the first incorporation of smaller businesses.

1. Minimum Legal Capital

One of the most relevant elements shaping regulatory competition in Europe is the regulation of minimum legal capital. Extensive literature exists debating the effectiveness and efficiency of a mandatory requirement of minimum legal capital as a protective device for creditors and investors. Apart from the merits of the debate, it can hardly be doubted that shareholders—especially in the case of smaller businesses—might perceive the obligation to subscribe and pay an up-front, minimum amount of capital as a significant cost of the incorporation process.

[. . .]

In the U.S. there are no significant differences regarding minimum legal capital among the individual states. Virtually none of the states require minimum legal capital, and the rules concerning the formation of the capital of the corporation are not particularly rigorous.

In Europe the situation is markedly different. The Second Directive on legal capital, implemented by all Member States, requires the corporation to provide for minimum legal capital of 25,000 euro, which shall consist of "assets capable of economic assessment." Several States impose an even higher minimum capital requirement. The directive, however, applies only to public corporations. Therefore, with respect to closely-held, non-listed corporations, significant comparative differences exist among Member States. In contrast to the states that provide for a rather substantial amount of minimum legal capital, the United Kingdom follows the common law approach providing for a very low level of minimum legal capital, and, more generally, is quite lax in the related rules regarding formation of legal capital.

These differences create significant room for regulatory arbitrage, especially for smaller firms incorporating for the first time, as it is possible that some shareholders would prefer to incorporate in a state with lower capital requirements even if they are operating exclusively in other jurisdictions. Regulatory responses to this form of a market for rules have already been adopted in some countries, particularly in Spain and France, with the enactment of statutes significantly simplifying the incorporation of smaller firms and lowering the minimum capital requirements, at least for limited liability corporations. Also, in Italy the above mentioned 2003 reform of corporate law introduced some new rules concerning capital endowment of a limited liability corporation,) intended to render the formation of this type of corporation easier and less expensive. . . .

2. The Length and Other Costs of the Incorporation Process

Consistent with the different minimum legal capital standards, there are also a range of regulatory approaches to the incorporation process. On the one hand, common law systems such as the U.S. and the U.K. provide for a relatively simple and expedited process. In those systems, the content of the articles of incorporation, the type and severity of controls on the relevant documentation, and the related legal fees are relatively minor and not particularly cumbersome. In general terms, those systems protect investors and stakeholders through ex post litigation rather than ex ante controls on the lawfulness of the articles of incorporation.

By contrast, civil law systems are characterized by more analytical and therefore more lengthy and expensive control in the pre-incorporation phase. Depending on the system, either judges or notaries are responsible for controlling the lawfulness of the articles of incorporation, and the whole process might take up to several weeks. These systems rely more on ex ante quasi-administrative controls than ex post litigation to protect creditors.

[. . .]

In Europe, therefore, there is a meaningful regulatory difference in this respect, in particular between continental civil law systems and the U.K. Analogous differences do not exist, or exist to a lesser extent, among individual states in the U.S.; as a result, for smaller businesses deciding where to incorporate in the U.S., there is less room for regulatory arbitrage.

3.   Coordination with "Local" Laws and Rules: Securities Regulation, Stock Exchanges and Taxation

Another important element that corporations might take into account in deciding whether to (re)incorporate is the clarity of the compatibility of the applicable corporate statutes and case law with other applicable laws that might not follow the choice of law made through incorporation. It is obviously impossible in the space of this Article to analyze the multi-dimensional matrix in this area that could affect the outcome of regulatory competition. There are, however, three aspects worth mentioning: securities regulation, stock exchange rules, and tax law.

In Europe, a corporation incorporated in State X with its real seat in State Y might be subject to the securities regulations of a system different from that whose laws govern the internal corporate affairs. This might be true, in particular, if the corporation performs certain activities, such as a public offering, or is listed in a country different from either X or Y. In the U.S., securities laws might provide a disincentive for out-of-state incorporation of a business that operates solely within the boundaries of the state where it has its real seat.

[. . .]

While this deterrent effect may have a significant impact on smaller corporations, however, larger corporations already operating in different states, which are also more likely to go public and to have capital needs that require a multi-state public offering, are less likely to be affected. As a result, larger corporations do not have a similar disincentive to reincorporate in a different state.

Once this decision is taken, the existence of a single regulatory regime at the federal level is either neutral or a factor that favors reincorporation in Delaware. There are still securities laws at the state level (so-called "Blue Sky Laws") that might theoretically apply to offerings by an already listed issuer, but the most important body of regulation in the field is at the federal level. In fact, notwithstanding the possibility in principle that "state blue sky laws can come into conflict with federal securities laws," as a matter of fact, "[t]he state securities acts generally exempt securities listed on a national or qualifying regional stock exchange." The federal system is harmonized and compatible with any applicable corporate laws, independently from the state of incorporation of the issuer. In addition, the most important U.S. stock exchanges have a national dimension, and their rules and procedures are integrated with applicable corporate statutes.

A principal consequence of these features of the U.S. system is that for corporations subject to securities regulation, either because they are publicly held or because they are planning an important public offering of securities, the costs and uncertainties related to possible divergences between corporate law and securities regulation are relatively low. Reincorporation is therefore not discouraged. To the contrary, some states might offer corporate laws that better fit the specific needs of a listed corporation in light of the common securities regulation framework.

In Europe, on the other hand, every individual Member State has its own securities regulation regime, each with different regulatory authorities and local stock exchanges. These different systems, while partially harmonized, still have relevant differences. Moreover, each of them is primarily designed to apply within the given system of local corporate laws. Of course, this situation is quickly evolving and noteworthy harmonization efforts are being made, as demonstrated by the recent regulation of securities offerings and prospectuses which allows the application of the laws of the "home State" to securities offerings and the "Markets in Financial Instruments," also known by the acronym "MiFid." Securities regulators are also constantly improving their coordination. In the same vein, national stock exchanges are going through an extensive process of aggregation that is likely to ultimately lead to a few competing markets. The harmonization, however, is far from being complete, and not even close to reaching the U.S. situation, as demonstrated by the Thirteenth Directive on takeovers.

In such a scenario, it is not surprising that some corporations, at least in particular circumstances, will strive to avoid subjection to different sets of rules for securities regulation and corporate laws. This creates a certain tension for forum shopping in corporate law. If the internal affairs of a corporation are subject to the rules of State X, while the applicable securities regulation, competent authorities and stock exchange are governed by State Y, there is a risk of incongruence, uncertainties and coordination costs. All of these may combine to discourage the development of a market for reincorporation in Europe. This market for reincorporation, however, is again most relevant to larger publicly held corporations (or a corporation about to go public) than to smaller businesses not subject to securities regulations.

Finally, other compatibility problems might arise with respect to tax law, in particular the income tax. Some authors have pointed out that:

In the European market for corporate charters, double taxation is not an obstacle to corporate mobility either. The bilateral agreements between the Member States of the European Community to avoid double taxation typically follow the Model Double Taxation Convention on Income and Capital (MDTC) of the Organization for Economic Co-operation and Development (OECD). As a result, corporations have little to fear from incorporating in another Member State.

Even assuming away the possible, and even probable, coordination problems of these agreements, a similar argument presents some shortcomings. The first of these shortcomings is that avoidance of double taxation rarely is costless. At least some administrative expenses, or costs relating to dealing with different tax authorities, are probable. In addition, in several systems the earnings of the corporation, from which taxable income is derived, are determined by some corporate law rules, such as those governing financial statements. If a corporation is subject to the rules of state A in this respect, and to those of state B for taxation, some frictions and coordination problems might occur, resulting in additional expenses. This issue might, once again, influence the decision of reincorporating.

4.   The Role of the Lawyers

In theory, in both the U.S. and in Europe, lawyers are licensed to offer legal advice and litigate only in one jurisdiction. If we move from a more formalistic to a more substantive approach, however, several factors suggest that rigid state divisions are less rigorously observed in practice in the U.S. For example, given the absence of language barriers, the existence of standardized education, and the commonalities of bar admission standards across states, as well as the similarities among state corporate laws, the reincorporation in Delaware of a business association that maintains its headquarters in New York is unlikely to lead to losses of clients for New York attorneys. On the other hand, it is much more likely that a Spanish attorney or legal counsel would be unable to continue to offer the same legal services to a client corporation that becomes subject to the laws of the U.K. Consequently, and again with some intentional simplification, it would not be surprising that-in good faith and independent from possible conflicts of interest—U.S. attorneys are less resistant than their European colleagues to the idea of reincorporation in another jurisdiction.

[. . .]

Consequently, the explanation for the different features of the European and the American markets for corporate charters, from a comparative perspective, must acknowledge higher lawyer resistance to regulatory arbitrage in corporate law in the Continent. To the extent that greater resistance exists in Europe, it is likely to affect in particular larger, already established corporations considering whether to reincorporate. In such situations there are extensive and on-going relationships between the corporation and its attorneys, who are often influential lawyers in their own systems, as well as significant forces internal to the corporation that might oppose change (for instance, in-house counsel who know the law of only one system). There are, in other words, more economic agents that have made a sunk investment through time, relationships, and so on, and therefore whose personal profitability would decrease as a result of a change in the applicable corporate laws.

5.   The Cost of Difference: Degrees of Separation

[. . .]

Regulatory competition, in order to function properly, requires that the "available menus" of rules and legal institutions are "different enough" to create room for regulatory arbitrage. At the same time, however, the rules and the legal institutions should not be "so deeply different" that they cannot be compared, or can only be compared with great difficulty and costs. In other words, assuming it were possible to "rank" the depth of the differences among the competing jurisdictions, if the costs in terms of uncertainty of a change in the applicable corporate laws are excessive, they prevent the development of an effective market for rules. In other words, if the elements on which the different states compete to attract corporations cannot be clearly compared, the resulting information asymmetries might impugn the very existence of regulatory arbitrage.

This observation might have even more traction with respect to the information asymmetries suffered by creditors and investors, such as banks and bondholders. A sudden change in the applicable corporate laws might result in lower credit standards and a drop of the market price of the securities, at least in the short term, if the differences between the two systems are so broad that they impair the ability of the investors and other stakeholders to properly assess the different regulatory regimes.

In a system like the United States, it is relatively easy for corporate stakeholders to understand and assess the implications of a reincorporation. The similarities among the competing jurisdictions, combined with the absence of language barriers and the presence of cross-trained lawyers, allow for a more straightforward comparison of jurisdictions. In Europe, on the other hand, notwithstanding the growing harmonization of national corporate laws, the existing differences are still profound. These differences adversely affect the ability to properly assess the comparative advantages and disadvantages of the rules affecting the internal affairs of a corporation.

Remembering that these rules are, for the above-mentioned reasons, often more relevant (or, more precisely, perceived as more relevant) in larger, publicly held corporations, we would expect less competition for reincorporation than for first incorporation in Europe due to the greater heterogeneity of the different legal systems.

6.   The Existence of a Dominant State and Network Externalities

The very fact that a rule-based regulatory competition has not developed in Europe so far, and that, consequently, no truly dominant state has emerged, itself reduces the benefits connected to possible reincorporation in a different jurisdiction. Network externalities related to the simple fact that most corporations have chosen one particular system are however an important driver of regulatory competition. Network externalities exist when the utility of one subject depends on the number of subjects that are in a similar situation. In a market context, for instance, positive network externalities exist when consumers attach a higher value to the product chosen by the majority of the other consumers, or by some specific consumers.

Thus, when a sizable number of corporations comply with a given body of rules and doctrines, their compliance can make that body of rules and doctrines more attractive in the market for corporate charters. In fact, widespread adoption of one legal regime elevates the rules of that particular system to the state of "the standard" of the corporate world. The rules of the dominant state become accepted by the financial industry, are better understood by institutional investors and creditors, facilitate mergers and acquisitions with other corporations (more likely to be subject to similar rules), and are more familiar to managers and directors that the corporation might want to hire in the future.

These network effects are particularly alluring for larger public corporations, or for corporations that intend to grow through specific transactions and therefore consider reincorporating. The fact that a smaller, closely-held corporation is not active on national financial markets, and is relatively less likely to negotiate the issuance of securities with a major investment bank, renders network effects more crucial in the reincorporation market. For smaller, closely-held business associations whose founders have local connections with investors, clients, providers and other stakeholders, the network effects connected with the choice of where to incorporate are less important; these businesses are in fact more likely to look at the relative "costs" of incorporating in the different jurisdictions.

Despite the relative success of the U.K. in attracting some corporations, Europe cannot be considered a dominant corporate jurisdiction on the same scale as Delaware. As a result, network externalities are less important than the reincorporation market for larger, public corporations, at least if compared to the U.S. scenario. This phenomenon occurs independently from the causes of the existing lack of competition, and can be considered an inertia in the system that acts to limit the development of a market for rules.

7.   Capture of Regulators and Corporate National Identity

Regulatory capture, the phenomenon by which the members of an industry might exercise some control over their regulators and not necessarily involving illegal conduct, might also explain the existence of an active market for reincorporation in the U.S. in contrast to Europe. If we compare Europe and the U.S., it seems intuitive to conclude that in the former system a large corporation or industry association able to implement an effective lobbying effort toward the legislature and the regulatory authorities will be more effective within its own national borders than in other states. For example, a corporation founded in Italy decades ago probably has already established significant connections with local policy makers, governmental agencies, and members of the judiciary. Given that it has thus significantly invested in the country, and furthermore if its most prominent shareholders or managers are citizens of that country, the corporation will be more influential in Italy with respect to corporate lawmaking than it will be in, for example, the Netherlands.

In the United States, such relative strength of corporate influence in one state as compared to another is, on average, less dramatic. For a large publicly held corporation, it is, at least in comparison with the European situation, not so different to lobby in the state where real seat is as opposed to where the corporation is incorporated or at the federal level. Cultural, linguistic, economic, and political reasons support this claim.

[. . .]

8.   Choice of Law and Jurisdiction

If a corporation has its real seat in state A, but is incorporated in state B without any particular connection to its territory, in the event of litigation, depending on the applicable rules either the courts of state A or state B might have jurisdiction. On both sides of the Atlantic, choice of law rules and jurisdiction rules might point at different legal systems. In order to assess this issue, a brief preliminary discussion of jurisdictional rules is necessary.

In the United States, a corporation is subject to jurisdiction in any state in which it has minimum contacts and in which the exercise of the state's authority comports with notions of fair play and substantial justice. While, under this test, jurisdiction is always available in the corporation's place of incorporation and the place where it has its principal place of business, there may be several other jurisdictions where the corporation is "doing business" and thus subject to jurisdiction. The "doing business" standard allows a court to exercise jurisdiction for any cause of action, including claims relating to the internal affairs of the company. For example, a company incorporated in Delaware with its principle place of business in California but which advertises, sells substantial products, and places salespersons in Texas might be subject to jurisdiction in all three states.

To complicate things, if the case is filed in state court, it can be removed to federal court if the case is either based on a federal question, such as a suit by shareholders for securities fraud, or if there is diversity of citizenship. Citizenship of a corporation includes both where it is incorporated and where it has its principal place of business. In the previous example, the case could thus only be removed to a federal court on diversity grounds if none of the plaintiffs were from either Delaware or California.

Just because it is possible to exercise jurisdiction over the parties in a particular judicial district, however, does not necessarily imply that that is the proper venue for the lawsuit. Once jurisdiction is established, either a plaintiff or a defendant can move to transfer the case to a place where there is such proper venue. Venue is determined by looking to where all defendants reside, where the substantial part of the acts or omissions giving rise to the suit occurred, or, if neither of these is applicable, where any single defendant is subject to jurisdiction. Given that a defendant is deemed to "reside" wherever he or it is subject to personal jurisdiction, this provision is not frequently a basis for transferring a case. However, there is also a separate provision that grants courts the discretionary power to transfer a case to another federal forum in which venue is proper, based on the convenience of parties and witnesses and in the interest of justice. Under this provision, if a plaintiff sues a corporation in Texas, but the witnesses and documents are all in California, the court may transfer the case to California. These same provisions apply when the company is a large publicly held company and when there is a class action suit.

The European situation is also quite complicated, and litigation might easily occur in a state different from the one in which the corporation is incorporated and whose laws must therefore be applied. First of all, according to Article 2(1) of the Council Regulation 44/2001 of 22 December 2000 on Jurisdiction and the Recognition of Enforcement of Judgments in Civil and Commercial Matters, the general forum is in the state where the person is domiciled: "persons domiciled in a Member State shall, whatever their nationality, be sued in the courts of that Member State." As for corporations, Article 60(1) provides that the domicile is in the state where it has its: "(a) statutory seat, or (b) central administration, or (c) principal place of business." These fora are alternative, with the consequence that a corporation might easily be sued in a state different from the one where it is incorporated and the judges might be required to apply a foreign corporate statute and case law.

In addition, Article 22(2) of the Regulation provides for mandatory jurisdiction in the Member State where the corporation "has its seat," for cases raising certain issues such as "the validity of the constitution, the nullity or the dissolution of companies" and, most importantly because it is a common issue raised in corporate litigation in Europe, "the validity of the decisions of their organs." Needless to say, the seat state might differ from the state of incorporation whose laws shall be applied.

In addition, depending on the type of litigation, in particular on whether the plaintiff is bringing an action in contract (as might be the case for a bondholder suing the corporation) or in tort (e.g., when a shareholder or an investor sues the directors that caused a direct damage that is not the consequence of a damage suffered by the corporation—like under art. 2395 of the Italian Civil Code), other forums might come into play, such as "the place where the harmful event occurred or may occur" (Article 5(3) of the Regulation). Finally, at least for certain subject matters, although the law in this area is very unsettled, the parties to a suit might agree to a different jurisdiction through a forum selection clause (Article 23(1) of the Regulation).

Also, in Europe, if a corporation shops around for substantive corporate laws, jurisdiction and choice of law might not overlap. As a matter of fact, especially if the corporation has its real seat in a state different from the one where it is incorporated, they are likely to be different. A business incorporated in the U.K., for instance, and subject to U.K. corporate laws might be sued or sue in the state where its real seat is located, depending on the applicable rules on jurisdiction. The judges of the latter state would, in this case, have to apply the relevant foreign substantive rules.

The above analysis shows that in both the U.S. and Europe, it is possible that the internal affairs of the corporation may be litigated in the state of incorporation, the state of the real seat, or, in some situations, a third state. This fact demands consideration of the relative advantages and disadvantages of litigating in a forum different from the one in which the corporation has its real seat or one whose substantive laws must be applied, as well as the possible effects on regulatory competition of such forum-shopping.

[. . .]

In light of this intuitive consideration, it appears clear that with respect to this factor, regulatory competition is not likely to be as intense in Europe as in the U.S., especially for those corporations that either anticipate possible litigation or base their choice of applicable laws on the availability of a judiciary with the ability to apply the chosen rules efficiently and correctly. This acts as another factor helping to explain why in Europe there is less rule-based competition and more cost-based competition. In fact, the elements discussed above might be even less significant for a small, closely held corporation incorporating in a given state mainly to take advantage of the lower incorporation costs rather than considerations related to potential shareholders' lawsuits.

IV.

Supply-side Drivers of Regulatory Competition

The different types of regulatory competition that presently exist in the U.S. and Europe also depend on the different incentives the individual states have to enact a body of rules, as well as maintain legal institutions, that are capable of attracting corporations. In this respect, it can be observed in general terms that European States have fewer incentives to compete in the market for corporate charters than do U.S. states.

1.   Franchise Taxes

Franchise taxes similar to those levied in the U.S., which constitute one of the major incentives for "Delaware-style" regulatory competition, are not permissible in Europe. Articles 2(1) and 10 of Directive 69/335/EEC of July 17, 1969 prohibit single Member States from imposing a "tax for the mere fact of incorporation in a certain state." Additionally, some authors point out that case law interpreting these provisions also prohibits states from circumventing the principle through means such as "registration fees that exceed the real cost [of registration]."

Franchise taxes in the U.S., particularly in Delaware, act as a proxy for the capitalization of the corporation and the number of shares issued. As this variable is obviously larger for big, publicly held corporations, it is reasonable that regulatory competition in the U.S. focuses in particular on reincorporation of such established and economically larger corporations.

This difference also helps to explain why a cost-based regulatory competition prevails in Europe for incorporation of small businesses. European States are relatively less interested in attracting corporations deciding where to incorporate or reincorporate on the basis of an analytical examination of the applicable corporate laws and the overall judicial attitude toward corporations. As a result, from a fiscal point of view, these States are less dependent than Delaware on reincorporation of large corporations. Different corporate regimes in Europe are, therefore, more the consequence of different judgments of the policy makers with respect to the most efficient and desirable rules for their constituencies rather than the product of efforts to lure corporate decision-makers to a certain jurisdiction.

[. . .]

2. The Market for Legal Services and the Efficiency of the Legal System

Obviously, franchise taxes are not the only element on which regulators compete. On the one hand, the ability of a jurisdiction to attract a large number of incorporations might have a significant effect on the local market for legal services. Lawyers, institutions of legal education, and other professionals specializing in business law and related fields might greatly benefit and create a thriving network effect. The above-mentioned persons and institutions not only represent an important industry in absolute economic terms, but also are a social group particularly influential with the legislatures and policy makers.

In addition, a strong system of business law, regarded as efficient and respective of minorities' rights, is also in itself a goal of the policy makers, as it enhances the economic strength of the country and results in increased influence for its politicians, regulators, practicing lawyers and academics. It can be expected, therefore, that some form of competition, or room for regulatory arbitrage, results among the Member State almost automatically as an indirect consequence of the goals and activities of the individual legislatures.

While these elements might drive regulatory competition somewhat, they do not seem sufficient to generate a U.S.-style system focused on luring the reincorporation of listed corporations, at least in the short-run.

[. . .]

VI.

Regulatory Competition in Europe and in the U.S.: Implications of the Two Different Markets

The above analysis illustrates some of the elements accounting for the different types of regulatory competitions in corporate law occurring in the U.S. and in Europe. The features of the European market for rules in this field, to the extent that one exists, are profoundly different from the ones shaping American corporate law, and do not depend entirely on the relative lesser freedom of movement due to the adoption of the real seat principle in many European States.

The most evident effect of these differences is that the rule-based reincorporation movement that distinguishes the U.S. system, is not nearly as relevant in Europe. The type of corporate mobility that Europe is witnessing affects a different "segment" of the incorporation market, namely small or medium, and usually closely held, corporations that are in search of a less costly jurisdiction allowing a quick and inexpensive incorporation. Obviously an indirect effect of this development is that corporations that incorporate in a state that requires, for instance, a significantly lower legal capital, will also be subject to some extent to the applicable internal affairs rule provided for in the jurisdiction of incorporation. In other words, the "cost-based" regulatory competition occurring in Europe also forces a change in the most widely applied corporate laws. But the different drivers, and effects, of this type of corporate mobility should not be underestimated. This type of market for rules is not mimicking the U.S. market.

The rationale underlying the above analysis is partially but powerfully confirmed by another very interesting example, which has to date been somehow overlooked in the scholarly debate on regulatory competition in corporate law. A recent study shows that in Canada, notwithstanding some similarities with the U.S. system, in particular the existence of jurisdictions that might compete to attract corporations, little reincorporation occurs in different provinces as compared to the process in the United States. Interestingly enough, but perhaps not surprisingly, the causes of this lesser rule-based competition for reincorporation identified by the authors of the cited work, partially overlap—mutatis mutandis—with those pointed out in this study as possible explanations of the peculiar features of the European market for rules in corporate law.

[. . .]

Comparing these elements with the current U.S. situation, the following conclusions can be drawn: While greater freedom in choice of law is certainly possible as a consequence of both the jurisprudence of the European Court of Justice and recent European legislation (including, in particular, new rules on cross-border mergers), this freedom is still far from complete. Significant uncertainties still limit corporate emigration and most of the new European instruments that might increase freedom of movement (such as the SE) still pose some delicate coordination problems that limit their effectiveness;

European States, while not indifferent to their ability to attract incorporations, lack incentives similar to those of Delaware and other U.S. States driving them to attract a large share of the "charter business."

Most importantly, in Europe, several elements affect regulatory competition from the point of view of the corporation. These elements create the pre-conditions for a "cost-based" competition affecting smaller, closely held businesses deciding to incorporate for the first time. The features of European corporate laws, and other substantive areas of the law in Europe, are presently not particularly favorable for the type of "rule-based" competition that developed in the U.S., which affects larger corporations considering to reincorporate (often publicly held or about to go public). Specifically, these features include the different rules concerning minimum legal capital, the greater differences among European States as to incorporation procedures, securities regulations, lawyers' resistance, lack of a dominant state comparable to Delaware, regulators' capture, and the rules on jurisdiction.

These differences between the European and the U.S. situation are clearly evolving, and even a casual look at contemporary European legal history suggests that the sun is setting on them. They are vanishing, and probably—or one might say, hopefully—at an ever increasing rate. At certain latitudes, however, the sunset can be particularly long, and a true "rule-based" competition in Europe similar to the American one does not seem to be as visible on the horizon as several commentators have assumed.

NOTES AND QUESTIONS

1. Professor Ventoruzzo points out some comparative differences concerning "regulatory competition" in Europe and in the U.S. Even if after *Centros* and its progeny freedom of establishment has played a role in shaping European corporate law, interestingly enough the determinants and effects of regulatory competition are not as intuitive as it might appear. One intriguing example is offered by Christoph Teichmann and Ralf Knaier. In a recent article (*Die deutsche Unternehmergesellschaft als Alternative für österreichische Gründer*, in *Der Gesellschafter*, 2014, 285 ff.), the authors point out how, since 2008, it is possible to form in Germany a limited liability corporation with almost no minimum legal capital and a management center abroad. In neighboring Austria, on the other hand, the establishment of a similar type of business organization still requires (at the time of the research) a significantly higher legal capital (35,000 euro). Notwithstanding this competitive advantage of Germany, according to Teichmann and Knaier relatively few Austrian businesses—or, at least, less than it could have been expected—decided to incorporate or reincorporate in Germany. This data is even more meaningful considering the similarities between the German and the Austrian legal systems: same language, largely similar legal culture, geographical proximity . . . This study suggests that minimum legal capital

might, in fact, not be very relevant for regulatory competition. What do you think about this empirical evidence? Could an explanation be that very few businesses, as a matter of fact, can operate with less than 35,000 euro of capital? Would it be easy for corporations with a trivial amount of capital to obtain financial resources from banks and other sophisticated lenders?

2.   In an empirical research, Wolf-Georg Ringe has compared the propensity of German and Austrian corporations, especially closely held LLCs, to incorporate in the U.K. while doing business primarily in Germany and Austria (*Corporate Mobility in the European Union—a Flash in the Pan?*, in *European Company and Financial Law Review*, 2013, 230 ff.). The author observed an increased propensity to incorporate in the U.K. after the ECJ's decisions on freedom of establishment, but also noticed that in Germany the phenomenon receded in parallel with the introduction of a lower minimum legal capital. The same trend occurred in Austria, even if in the period considered no reduction of minimum legal capital was adopted in this country. The previously cited work by Teichmann and Knaier also seems to suggest that corporations doing business in Austria did not massively incorporate in Germany. The propensity of Austrian businesses to incorporate in the U.K. and its decline are interesting and puzzling. Any hypothesis?

3.   As discussed in the article, regulatory competition in Europe seems so far to affect (or have affected) primarily relatively small, closely held corporations. There are, however, some recent important examples of large multinational listed corporations engaging in forum shopping. In 2014, the Italian car manufacturer Fiat, after its merger with the American Chrysler, has moved its place of incorporation from Italy to the Netherlands, and will therefore be subject to Dutch corporate law. In addition, Fiat will have its tax residence in the U.K., since this country offers a more desirable tax regime in particular for the payment of dividends, and will be listed both in the United States (on the NYSE) and in Milan, Italy. A true example of a global corporation, to which a complex web of corporate, tax, and securities laws from different jurisdictions will apply. This anecdotal, but highly symbolic, example shows how lawyers in the future cannot really limit themselves to operate in one jurisdiction, but must somehow be able to "follow" their clients. Students might be assigned a short research on the possible motivations of Chrysler-Fiat to reincorporate. Newspaper articles easily available on the internet can offer a basis for discussion.

4.   An apt conclusion for this Chapter is to cast a doubt on almost everything we have said. As mentioned before, in fact, the idea that U.S. States compete to attract competition is questioned by some noted scholars: Marcel Kahan & Ehud Kamar, *The Myth of State Competition in Corporate Law*, 55 STANFORD L. REV. 679 (2002). Find this article, also available free of charge on *www.ssrn.com*, and consider if their arguments are convincing. Compare their analysis with the perspective adopted by Professor Ventoruzzo in explaining why regulatory competition is not particularly effective in Europe, and discuss if there are points of contact between his analysis and

the study of Kahan and Kamar. Professor Kamar, in another article, considers how regulatory competition in Europe, also in light of the still-existing limitations to reincorporation (notwithstanding *Centros* and its progeny), results in a competition for "investment" rather than for "charters." According to this perspective, legislatures and policy makers focus on the ability to attract capital and investments, which also requires more flexible corporate rules, for example with respect to minimum capital. If you are interested, *see* Ehud Kamar, *Beyond Competition for Incorporations*, 94 GEORGETOWN L.J. 1725 (2006), also available on *www.ssrn.com*.

CHAPTER 3

THE INCORPORATION PROCESS AND LIMITATIONS ON LIMITED LIABILITY

∎ ∎ ∎

INTRODUCTION

This chapter is dedicated to two separate, yet closely related issues. The first issue we discuss is differences in the incorporation process between countries. In discussing this issue, we will provide a quick comparative overview of how the incorporation process functions in different systems. The second issue we will consider is exceptions to the general rule of shareholders' limited liability. One of the distinctive features of a corporation is the fact that, normally, shareholders are not liable for the obligations of their corporation. This rule, however, has exceptions: most notably, the common law doctrine of "piercing the corporate veil" or "lifting the corporate veil." In addition to "veil piercing," there are other rules in different jurisdictions, which provide for situations where shareholders might be held liable for the debts of the corporation. These rules generally apply when there is some kind of "abuse" of the corporate structure.

One key idea linking the discussion of these two issues is the relative ease of the incorporation process in a particular country. In common law systems that follow the incorporation theory, the incorporation process is generally easy, quick, and inexpensive. In these countries, it is often sufficient to file very brief articles of incorporation with the Secretary of State or other similar office. The articles filed often contain minimal information about the corporation. The costs associated with filing are relatively low, and there are no—or very few—specific *ex ante* controls on the content of the articles of incorporation. In addition, with the exclusion of corporations in some regulated industries (such as banks), there is generally no minimum legal capital (or very low capital) required to incorporate. Thus, it is possible to incorporate with even a nominal capital of $1. The evaluation of possible contributions in kind is quite flexible, and basically left to the discretion of the directors. The entire procedure is also very fast: it is often possible to incorporate in less than 24 hours and, in some cases, even in minutes (e.g., in New Zealand).

On the other hand, traditionally, in civil law countries (and more generally under European law), the incorporation process is more complex and requires more time. In these systems there are often specific rules on the form and the content of the articles of incorporation and bylaws. Additionally, there is an *ex ante* control on the legality of the governing documents of the corporation conducted by public or quasi public officers, such as judges or a notary public. Minimum legal capital is also required for the protection of creditors, and in part for the protection of shareholders. For example, in the E.U., a minimum capital of 25,000 euros is necessary to incorporate a joint stock corporation, and in some countries, a higher sum is necessary. Furthermore, specific and more rigid rules apply to the evaluation of contributions in kind, which often require a fairness opinion by an independent expert appointed by the court. In these systems, even if the duration of the incorporation process varies, it might easily take a few weeks, and to incorporate is often more expensive than in common law systems.

In many civil law countries, however, these stringent rules have recently been at least partially relaxed, probably as a consequence of increased regulatory competition and the desire of individual legislatures to create incentives for business activities. One notable example is Japan, which abolished its minimum legal capital requirement in 2005. Japan, however, still requires articles of incorporation to be certified by a notary public and contributions in kind to be evaluated by a court-appointed expert. Despite recent changes, it is fair to say that in these systems the incorporation process is still strictly regulated.

These different approaches to incorporation are partially reflected in the rules on piercing the corporate veil. Simplifying the issue, it can be observed that in jurisdictions where it is "easier" to incorporate, courts are often more willing to pierce the corporate veil on an equitable basis when the plaintiff can establish some kind of abuse of the corporate structure. Differences still exist even within common law jurisdictions. For example, U.S. and U.K. case law differ substantially on this issue, with veil piercing being quite more common in the U.S. In fact, piercing of the corporate veil is one of the most commonly litigated issues in U.S. corporate law. In the U.K., on the other hand, piercing is less frequent. For example, a leading British case of the 1990s, *Adams v. Cape Industries plc*, held that piercing is appropriate only in case of fraud, or when the corporation is established to avoid an existing obligation. A similarly restrictive approach was followed in three subsequent cases: *Ord v. Belhaven Pubs Ltd* (1998), *Prest v. Petrodel Resources* (2013) and *VTB Capital plc v. Nutritek International* (2013). In *VTB Capital plc*, one of the judges observed: "The notion that there is no principled basis upon which it can be said that one can pierce the veil of incorporation receives some support from the fact that the precise nature, basis and meaning of the principle are all somewhat obscure, as are the precise nature of circumstances in which the principle can apply".

On the other hand, in civil law countries where incorporation is more "difficult," judges and policy makers are quite reluctant to go beyond the corporate veil. If judges decide to pierce the corporate veil, it is usually on very narrow grounds, often explicitly regulated in statutory provisions. Examples of such provisions include when a parent corporation "dominates" a subsidiary and takes inequitable advantage of its position (e.g., in Germany and in Italy), or when a single shareholder does not comply with the rules concerning the formation or the maintenance of the corporate capital. There are, however, some exceptions to this more narrow approach to shareholders' liability, and we will discuss the German concept of "*Durchgriffshaftung*," the local equivalent of "piercing the corporate veil."

In this perspective, we will also consider if minimum legal capital requirements can really be considered protective of creditors and other stakeholders, or are just an ineffective and inefficient relic of the past, as some authors have argued.

THE INCORPORATION PROCESS

The word "corporation" comes from the Latin word "*corpus*," meaning "body." The etymological origins of the word "corporation" evoke the notion that a group of people is joining forces to create a separate legal "body" in order to conduct business. In fact, however, early "corporations" were created for all sorts of purposes, often not for profit. For example, in the Middle Ages, churches and universities were organized as corporations, and it is fairly well known that the City of London—as well as other local governments in different jurisdictions—is technically a corporation (its first recorded charter dates back to the eleventh century). Different types of business organizations, with specific rules governing them, have almost always existed, but it is only since the early seventeenth century, during the colonial period, that the prototype of the modern corporation came into existence. The features of the modern corporation are four key elements: legal personality; limited liability of shareholders; a formal governance structure with specific corporate bodies (typically, a shareholders' meeting and a board of directors); and shares representing shareholders' investment that can be more or less freely transferred and traded.

It has been argued that the world's first commercial corporation originated in Sweden. The corporation, known as Stora Kopparberg, operated a copper mine and obtained a charter from the king before 1350. The progenitors of the modern corporation, however, are usually considered the British East India Company, established by Queen Elizabeth I in 1600, and the Dutch *Vereenigde Oost-Indische Compagnie*, or *VOC* ("United East India Company"), formed in 1602. These corporations were created especially to exploit the new trading routes with the colonies, and both presented some of the above-mentioned elements of the modern corporation. First of all, investors were issued certificates (shares) that could be traded. Second, they both had a governance structure that had distinctive features, but would still be recognized by a contemporary corporate person. In addition, investors (shareholders) were granted limited liability, in the sense that they were only responsible for their own contribution, and could not be held liable for the debts of the corporation. This acceptance of limited liability is particularly important because the traditional approach was that joint investors in the capital of a business enterprise should be liable for the debts of the business, with a few exceptions. It became clear, however, that the resources necessary to finance colonial enterprises were so significant that they could only be efficiently obtained by offering the shares to a fairly large number of investors that would not be directly involved in the managing of the corporation, but whose maximum loss was capped at their initial investment. In order to be able to accomplish this task, it became necessary to grant limited liability to shareholders.

These early corporations were also often given monopoly rights on the trade with some parts of the world or on some goods. For example, the British East India Company had the exclusive right to trade with all the territories east of the Cape of Good Hope (today in South Africa), therefore being able to exploit the lucrative spice and tea trades. Beyond monopoly rights, these companies also enjoyed quasi-governmental powers. In some cases, they ruled the colonies on behalf of the monarch. Pursuant to their status as "ruler" of a colonial possession, their powers even included the right (and duty) to maintain an army and wage war, or at least conduct police operations.

Limited liability, monopoly, and quasi-governmental powers were clearly seen as exceptional attributes and as a result, the granting of corporate charters was originally very limited. The British Bubble Act of 1720, for example, explicitly prohibited the creation of joint-stock companies without a royal charter. In some countries, including the United States, it was necessary that the state legislature would pass a specific statute to create a corporation.

When the industrial revolution started to gain steam, however, it became clear that limited liability could be a good, indeed a necessary, idea to foster economic prosperity and facilitate technological development. Especially in the light of the great risks associated with modern industrial activities (consider for example building and operating railroads), limited liability was necessary in order to attract the resources needed to finance the industrial revolution. At the same time, the idea that corporate charters could be granted exclusively and with discretion by the sovereign or by the legislature, started to come under criticism, both for its impracticality, and for its unfairness and allegations of corruption, nepotism and favoritism. As a result, in the nineteenth century, the first "general incorporation statutes" were enacted. Under these statutes, anybody who met certain pre-determined statutory requirements could establish a corporation and enjoy the benefits of limited liability. Among the first U.S. states to adopt this approach were Pennsylvania (1836) and Connecticut (1837), as well as New York, which enacted a general incorporation law in 1811, yet largely ignored it for over 20 years.

While the trend toward general incorporation laws spread quickly almost everywhere, different states followed different approaches. Civil law countries, for example, especially countries in continental Europe, allowed general incorporation laws, but were concerned about possible abuses of the corporate structure, and therefore considered it preferable to retain some kind of public check of the lawfulness of the incorporation process. This control was, however, taken away from the executive or legislative powers, and given to courts, perceived to be more independent and apt to perform a simple control over the legality of the incorporation, with no discretion to deny the right to incorporate. In the last few years, several countries that still required judges to control the legality of the incorporation process went one step further toward a more liberal approach, entrusting public notaries with this preliminary control (Italy, for example, took this step in 2000). In these countries, even if significantly simplified, the incorporation process is still more strictly regulated than in common law systems. There are specific and more extensive rules concerning both the form and the content of the governing documents of the corporation, either courts or notaries must control the lawfulness of the charter and bylaws, and the incorporation process can require several days, if not weeks.

On the other hand, in most common law systems, and certainly in the U.S., the incorporation process is extremely streamlined. It is sufficient to file with the Secretary of State of the chosen jurisdiction a simple form representing the charter of the corporation, pay a small fee, and often in a matter of hours the corporation is formally established, with very little *ex ante* controls. Actually, to reincorporate in Delaware, very often out-of-state corporations simply merge with and into empty-shell corporations kept in existence by lawyers and specialized agents solely for this purpose.

While some countries, such as Japan, recognize only one governing document, most countries distinguish the "articles of incorporation," also referred to as the "articles of association" or "charter," from the "bylaws." The "articles of incorporation" is basically the contract expressing the will of the parties to create a corporation, and it includes some minimum information, such as the name of the first shareholders and directors, the amount of the capital, the agent for service of process, the business purpose, and so forth. The bylaws, on the other hand, are generally a longer document, containing all the specific rules applicable to the corporation. In particular it includes governance rules on shareholders' meetings and board of directors (e.g., the procedure to call a meeting, quorum, and majority), rules concerning different classes of shares, limitations to the free transferability of the shares, and so on.

Before spending a few words on "strategic" considerations concerning the drafting of charter and bylaws, it is useful to take a look at two very simple examples of charter and bylaws (selected provisions) of a Delaware corporation, collectively known as the "governing documents" of the corporation.

State of Delaware

Certificate of Incorporation

A Stock Corporation

1.   The name of the corporation shall be . . .

2.   Its registered office in the State of Delaware is located at . . . in the city of . . . , County of . . . , Zip Code . . . and its Registered Agent at such address is . . .

3.   The purpose or purposes of the corporation shall be . . .

4.   The total number of shares and par value of stock which the corporation shall be authorized to issue is: . . .

5.   The powers, preferences and rights and the qualifications, limitations or restrictions thereof shall be determined by the board of directors.

6.   The name and address of the incorporator is as follows: . . .

7.   The Board of Directors shall have the power to adopt, amend or repeal by-laws.

8.   No director shall be personally liable to the Corporation or its stockholders for monetary damages for any breach of fiduciary duty by such director as a director. Notwithstanding the foregoing sentence, a director shall be liable to the extent provided by applicable law, (i) for breach of the director's duty of loyalty to the Corporation or its stockholders, (ii) for acts or omissions not in good faith or which involve intentional misconduct or a knowing violation of law, (iii) pursuant to Section 174 of the Delaware General Corporation Law or (iv) for any transaction from which the director derived an improper personal benefit. No amendment to or repeal of this Article Eighth shall apply to or have any effect on the liability or alleged liability of any director of the Corporation for or with respect to any acts or omissions of such director occurring prior to such amendment.

IN WITNESS WHEREOF, the undersigned, being the incorporator herein before named, has executed signed and acknowledged this certificate of incorporation this . . . day of . . .

BY: (Incorporator)

ByLaws[1]

of

"Company Name"

A Delaware Corporation

ARTICLE I—Offices

Section 1.   The registered office of this corporation shall be in the County of County, State of Delaware.

Section 2.   The corporation may also have offices at such other places both within and without the State of Delaware as the Board of Directors may from time to time determine or the business of the corporation may require.

ARTICLE II—Meetings of Stockholders

Section 1.   All annual meetings of the stockholders shall be held at the registered office of the corporation or at such other place within or without the State of Delaware as the directors shall determine. Special meetings of the stockholders may be held at such time and place within or without the State of Delaware as shall be stated in the notice of the meeting, or in a duly executed waiver of notice thereof.

Section 2.   Annual meetings of the stockholders, commencing with the year . . ., shall be held on the . . . day of . . . each year if not a legal holiday and, if a legal holiday, then on the next secular day following, or at such other time as may be set by the Board of Directors from time to time, at which the stockholders shall elect by vote a Board of Directors and transact such other business as may properly be brought before the meeting. Meetings may be held by telephonic conference call provided all stockholders are present telephonically, or have expressly declined to "attend."

Section 3.   Special meetings of the stockholders, for any purpose or purposes, unless otherwise prescribed by statute or by the Articles of Incorporation, may be called by the President or the Secretary by resolution of the Board of Directors or at the request in writing of stockholders owning a majority in amount of the entire capital stock of the corporation issued and outstanding and entitled to vote. Such request shall state the purpose of the proposed meeting.

---

[1]   Sample Bylaws available at http://fileonline.biz/UserFiles/docs/bylaws/de/

Section 4.   Notices of meetings shall be in writing and signed by the President or a Vice-President or the secretary or an Assistant Secretary or by such other person or persons as the directors shall designate. Such notices shall state the purpose or purposes for which the meeting is called and the time and the place, which maybe within or without this State, where it is to be held. A copy of such notice shall be either delivered personally to or shall be mailed, postage prepaid, to each stockholder of record entitled to vote at such meeting not less than ten nor more than sixty days before such meeting. If mailed, it shall be directed to a stockholder at his address as it appears upon the records of the corporation and upon such mailing of any such notice, the service thereof shall be complete and the time of the notice shall begin to run from the date upon which such notice is deposited in the mail for transmission to such stockholder. Personal delivery of any such notice to any officer of a corporation or association, or to any member of a partnership shall constitute delivery of such notice to such corporation, association or partnership. In the event of the transfer of stock after delivery of such notice of and prior to the holding of the meeting it shall not be necessary to deliver or mail notice of the meeting to the transferee.

Section 5.   Business transacted at any special meeting of stockholders shall be limited to the purposes stated in the notice.

Section 6.   The holders of a majority of the stock, issued and outstanding and entitled to vote thereat, present in person or represented by proxy, shall constitute a quorum at all meetings of the stockholders for the transaction of business except as otherwise provided by statute or by the Articles of Incorporation. If, however, such quorum shall not be present or represented at any meeting of the stockholders, the stockholders entitled to vote thereat, present in person or represented by proxy, shall have power to adjourn the meeting from time to time, without notice other than announcement at the meeting, until a quorum shall be present or represented. At such adjourned meeting at which a quorum shall be present or represented, any business may be transacted which might have been transacted at the meeting as originally notified.

Section 7.   When a quorum is present or represented at any meeting, the vote of the holders of a majority of the stock having voting power present in person or represented by proxy shall be sufficient to elect directors or to decide any question brought before such meeting, unless the question is one upon which by express provision of the statutes or of the Articles of Incorporation, a different vote is required in which case such express provision shall govern and control the decision of such question.

Section 8.   Each stockholder of record of the corporation shall be entitled at each meeting of stockholders to one vote for each share of stock standing in his name on the books of the corporation. Upon the demand of any stockholder, the vote for directors and the vote upon any question before the meeting shall be by ballot.

Section 9.   At any meeting of the stockholders any stockholder may be represented and vote by a proxy or proxies appointed by an instrument in writing. In the event that any such instrument in writing shall designate two or more persons to act as proxies, a majority of such persons present at the meeting, or, if only one shall be present, then that one shall have and may exercise all of the powers conferred by such written instrument upon all of the persons so designated unless the instrument shall otherwise provide. No proxy or power of attorney to vote shall be used to vote at a meeting of the stockholders unless it shall have been filed with the secretary of the meeting when required by the inspectors of election. All questions regarding the qualification of voters, the validity of proxies and the acceptance or rejection of votes shall be decided by the inspectors of election who shall be appointed by the Board of Directors, or if not so appointed, then by the presiding officer of the meeting.

Section 10.   Any action which may be taken by the vote of the stockholders at a meeting may be taken without a meeting if authorized by the written consent of stockholders holding at least a majority of the voting power, unless the provisions of the statutes or of the Articles of Incorporation require a greater proportion of voting power to authorize such action in which case such greater proportion of written consents shall be required.

ARTICLE III—Directors

Section 1.   The business of the corporation shall be managed by its Board of Directors which may exercise all such powers of the corporation and do all such lawful acts and things as are not by statute or by the Articles of Incorporation or by these Bylaws directed or required to be exercised or done by the stockholders.

Section 2.   The number of directors which shall constitute the whole board shall be three (3). The number of directors may from time to time be increased or decreased to not less than one nor more than fifteen by action of the Board of Directors. The directors shall be elected at the annual meeting of the stockholders and except as provided in Section 2 of this Article, each director elected shall hold office until his successor is elected and qualified. Directors need not be stockholders.

Section 3.   Vacancies in the Board of Directors including those caused by an increase in the number of Directors, may be filled by a majority of the remaining directors, though less than a quorum, or by a sole remaining director, and each director so elected shall hold office until his successor is elected at an annual or a special meeting of the stockholders. The holders of two-thirds of the outstanding shares of stock entitled to vote may at any time peremptorily terminate the term of office of all or any of the directors by vote at a meeting called for such purpose or by a written statement filed with the secretary or, in his absence, with any other officer. Such removal shall be effective immediately, even if successors are not elected simultaneously and the vacancies on the Board of Directors resulting therefrom shall be filled only by the stockholders. A vacancy or vacancies in the Board of Directors shall be deemed to exist in case of the death, resignation or removal of any directors, or if the authorized number of directors be increased, or if the stockholders fail at any annual or special meeting of stockholders at which any director or directors are elected to elect the full authorized number of directors to be voted for at that meeting. The stockholders may elect a director or directors at any time to fill any vacancy or vacancies not filled by the directors. If the Board of Directors accepts the resignation of a director tendered to take effect at a future time, the Board or the stockholders shall have power to elect a successor to take office when the resignation is to become effective. No reduction of the authorized number of directors shall have the effect of removing any director prior to the expiration of his term of office.

ARTICLE IV—Meetings of the Board of Directors

Section 1.   Regular meetings of the Board of Directors shall be held at any place within or without the State which has been designated from time to time by resolution of the Board or by written consent of all members of the Board. In the absence of such designation regular meetings shall be held at the registered office of the corporation. Special meetings of the Board may be held either at a place so designated or at the registered office.

Section 2.   The first meeting of each newly elected Board of Directors shall be held immediately following the adjournment of the meeting of stockholders and at the place thereof. No notice of such meeting shall be necessary to the directors in order legally to constitute the meeting, provided a quorum be present. In the event such meeting is not so held, the meeting may be held at such time and place as shall be specified in a notice given as hereinafter provided for special meetings of the Board of Directors.

Section 3.   Regular meetings of the Board of Directors may be held without call or notice at such time and at such place as shall from time to time be fixed and determined by the Board of Directors.

Section 4.   Special meetings of the board of Directors may be called by the Chairman or the President or by any Vice-President or by any two directors. Written notice of the time and place of special meetings shall be delivered personally to each director, or sent to each director by mail or by other form of written communication, charges prepaid, addressed to him at his address as it is shown upon the records or is not readily ascertainable, at the place in which the meetings of the Directors are regularly held. In case such notice is mailed or telegraphed, it shall be deposited in the United States mail or delivered to the telegraph company at least forty-eight (48) hours prior to the time of the holding of the meeting. In case such notice is delivered as above provided, it shall be so delivered at least twenty-four (24) hours prior to the time of the holding of the meeting. Such mailing, telegraphing or delivery as above provided shall be due, legal and personal notice to such director.

Section 5.   Notice of the time and place of holding an adjourned meeting need not be given to the absent directors if the time and place be fixed at the meeting adjourned.

Section 6.   The transactions of any meeting of the Board of Directors, however called and noticed or wherever held, shall be as valid as though had at a meeting duly held after regular call and notice, if a quorum be present, and if, either before or after the meeting, each of the directors not present signs a written waiver of notice, or a consent to holding such meeting, or an approval of the minutes thereof. All such waivers, consents or approvals shall be filed with the corporate records or made a part of the minutes of the meeting.

Section 7.   A majority of the authorized number of directors shall be necessary to constitute a quorum for the transaction of business, except to adjourn as hereinafter provided. Every act or decision done or made by a majority of the directors present at a meeting duly held at which a quorum is present shall be regarded as the act of the Board of Directors, unless a greater number be required by law, or by the Articles of Incorporation. Any action of a majority, although not at a regularly called meeting, and the record thereof, if assented to in writing by all of the other members of the Board shall be as valid and effective in all respects as if passed by the Board in regular meeting.

Section 8.   A quorum of the directors may adjourn any directors meeting to meet again at a stated day and hour; provided, however, that in the absence of a quorum, a majority of the directors present at any directors meeting, either regular or special, may adjourn from time to time until the time fixed for the next regular meeting of the Board.

[. . .]

ARTICLE IX—Certificates of Stock

Section 1.   Every stockholder shall be entitled to have a certificate signed by the President or a Vice-President and the Treasurer or an Assistant Treasurer, or the Secretary or an Assistant Secretary of the corporation, certifying the number of shares owned by him in the corporation. If the corporation shall be authorized to issue more than one class of stock or more than one series of any class, the designations, preferences and relative, participating, optional or other special rights of the various classes of stock or series thereof and the qualifications, limitations or restrictions of such rights, shall be set forth in full or summarized on the face or back of the certificate which the corporation shall issue to represent such stock.

Section 2.   If a certificate is signed (a) by a transfer agent other than the corporation or its employees or (b) by a registrar other than the corporation or its employees, the signatures of the officers of the corporation may be facsimiles. In case any officer who has signed or whose facsimile signature has been placed upon a certificate shall cease to be such officer before such certificate is issued, such certificate may be issued with the same effect as though the person had not ceased to be such officer. The seal of the corporation, or a facsimile thereof, may, but need not be, affixed to certificates of stock.

Section 3.   The Board of Directors may direct a new certificate or certificates to be issued in place of any certificate or certificates theretofore issued by the corporation alleged to have been lost or destroyed upon the making of an affidavit of that fact by the person claiming the certificate of stock to be lost or destroyed. When authorizing such issue of a new certificate or certificates, the Board of Directors may, in its discretion and as a condition precedent to the issuance thereof, require the owner of such lost or destroyed certificate or certificates, or his legal representative, to advertise the same in such manner as it shall require and/or give the corporation a bond in such sum as it may direct as indemnity against any claim that may be made against the corporation with respect to the certificate alleged to have been lost or destroyed.

Section 4.   Upon surrender to the corporation or the transfer agent of the corporation of a certificate for share duly endorsed or accompanied by proper evidence of succession, assignment or authority to transfer, it shall be the duty of the corporation, if it is satisfied that all provisions of the laws and regulations applicable to the corporation regarding transfer and ownership of shares have been complied with, to issue a new certificate to the person entitled thereto, cancel the old certificate and record the transaction upon its books.

Section 5.   The Board of Directors may fix in advance a date not exceeding sixty (60) days nor less than ten (10) days preceding the date of any meeting of stockholders, or the date for the payment of any dividend, or the date for the allotment of rights, or the date when any change or conversion or exchange of capital stock shall go into effect, or a date in connection with obtaining the consent of stockholders for any purpose, as a record date for the determination of the stockholders entitled to notice of and to vote at any such meeting, and any adjournment thereof, or entitled to receive payment of any such dividend, or to give such consent, and in such case, such stockholders, and only such stockholders as shall be stockholders of record on the date so fixed, shall be entitled to notice of and to vote at such meeting, or any adjournment thereof, or to receive payment of such dividend, or to receive such allotment of rights, or to exercise such rights, or to give such consent, as the case may be, notwithstanding any transfer of any stock on the books of the corporation after any such record date fixed as aforesaid.

Section 6.   The corporation shall be entitled to recognize the person registered on its books as the owner of shares to be the exclusive owner for all purposes including voting and dividends, and the corporation shall not be bound to recognize any equitable or other claim to or interest in such share or shares on the part of any other person, whether or not it shall have express or other notice thereof, except as otherwise provided by the laws of Delaware.

ARTICLE X—General Provisions

Section 1.   Dividends upon the capital stock of the corporation, subject to the provisions of the Articles of Incorporation, if any, may be declared by the Board of Directors at any regular or special meeting, pursuant to law. Dividends may be paid in cash, in property or in shares of the capital stock, subject to the provisions of the Articles of Incorporation.

Section 2.   Before payment of any dividend, there may be set aside out of any funds of the corporation available for dividends such sum or sums as the directors from time to time, in their absolute discretion, think proper as a reserve or reserves to meet contingencies, or for equalizing dividends or for repairing or maintaining any property of the corporation or for such other purpose as the directors shall think conducive to the interest of the corporation, and the directors may modify or abolish any such reserve in the manner in which it was created.

Section 3.   All checks or demands for money and notes of the corporation shall be signed by such officer or officers or such other person or persons as the Board of Directors may from time to time designate.

Section 4.   The fiscal year of the corporation shall be fixed by resolution of the Board of Directors.

Section 5.   The corporation may or may not have a corporate seal, as may from time to time be determined by resolution of the Board of Directors. If a corporate seal is adopted, it shall have inscribed thereon the name of the corporation and the words "Corporate Seal" and "Delaware." The seal may be used by causing it or a facsimile thereof to be impressed or affixed or in any manner reproduced.

[. . .]

<u>ARTICLE XII</u>—Amendments

Section 1.   The Bylaws may be amended by a majority vote of all the stock issued and outstanding and entitled to vote at any annual or special meeting of the stockholders, provided notice of intention to amend shall have been contained in the notice of the meeting.

Section 2.   The Board of Directors by a majority vote of the whole Board at any meeting may amend these bylaws, including Bylaws adopted by the stockholders, but the stockholders may from time to time specify particular provisions of the Bylaws which shall not be amended by the Board of Directors.

APPROVED AND ADOPTED this . . . day of . . . , . . .

_____
Secretary

* * *

A well-drafted corporate charter and bylaws, as any contract, can be a work of art. A bad one can be a receipt for disaster. A complex mix of different skills is necessary in drafting the governing documents of a corporation: negotiation skills, the ability to fully understand the intent of the parties, the ability to foresee problems or specific needs that might arise in the future, etc. There are some very important strategic considerations that you need to make when drafting charters and bylaws. The first one concerns which provisions should be included in the articles of incorporation and which provisions should be included in the bylaws, when there is a choice between the two. In some legal systems, for example, there might be provisions that can only be included in one of these documents in order to produce specific legal effects. An example is the provision limiting the liability of directors included in article 8 of the sample charter above that, pursuant to section 102(b)(7) of the Delaware General Corporation Law, must be included in the articles of incorporation.

You should also keep in mind the rules concerning future amendments to the governing documents. Who has the authority to make the amendments and what procedural rules shall be followed? This can obviously be extremely important for your client, because she might want to be sure that a certain provision will not be changed or erased without her consent. For example, in most U.S. state jurisdictions, shareholders must approve amendments to the charter, but the directors must initiate the amendment and require the vote of the shareholders. This implies that it might be difficult to quickly obtain an amendment of the charter if the directors oppose it. On the other hand, generally both the directors and the shareholders have a concurrent power to amend the bylaws. More precisely, in some states, such as Delaware, directors have this power only if the articles of incorporation specifically grants it to them (opt-in systems); while in other states that follow the Model Business Corporation Act, directors have the power to amend the bylaws as a default rule, unless the charter provides otherwise (opt-out systems). In any case, also based on the bylaws, shareholders can sometimes indicate provisions of this documents that directors cannot amend (*see* Article XII, Section 2, of the sample bylaws above).

In other countries, especially continental European civil law countries and Japan, shareholders have a more central role with respect to amendments of the charter and bylaws. A vote at the shareholders' meeting is (almost) always necessary to approve such amendments, and often shareholders, at least if they own a minimum threshold of shares, can unilaterally call a shareholders' meeting to propose an amendment. Keeping in mind what we discussed at the end of Chapter 1 concerning ownership structures, this central role of shareholders is also a reflection of concentrated ownership.

You should also pay attention to the procedural rules applicable to amendments to the articles or bylaws. For example, if you are assisting a minority shareholder who owns 20% of the voting shares of a closely-held corporation, and there is one provision in the bylaws that is particularly important for him (for example, a right of first offer in case other shareholders intend to sell their shares), you might negotiate that this provision can only be amended with a supermajority (for example, 85%), in order to give your client a veto power over the amendment of the clause. An interesting application of this strategy will be discussed in Chapter 8 with respect to limitations to the transferability of shares.

A third element to consider is whether both the charter and the bylaws are public documents, accessible to everybody, and also if a provision included in the governing documents is enforceable toward shareholders that have not voted in favor of it, future shareholders, or third parties more generally. This depends of course on the jurisdiction. In the U.S., for example, the bylaws are not necessarily a public document, especially in closely held corporations. Bylaws' provisions might not be binding for a third party, and sometimes these provisions are only binding for shareholders that approved them. This also applies to charters in Japan. On the other hand, in other civil law countries, the governing documents are generally publicly available and, for this reason, enforceable against third parties.

Consider, for example, a right of first offer included in the bylaws providing that shareholders, before selling their shares to a third party, must offer them at the same conditions to other existing shareholders. If a shareholder violates this provision and sells the shares to a third party breaching the pre-emptive right of his fellow shareholders in the U.S., he might be liable toward the other existing shareholders, but the buyer of the shares, especially if he ignored in good faith the existence of the right of first offer, will surely become a shareholder and be able to exercise his rights as such. In some civil law countries, in which the bylaws are a public document, the fact that the provision is included in the bylaws creates a sort of unrebuttable presumption that the third-party buyer knew (or could have known) about the limitation to the free transferability of the shares. As a consequence, the third party that bought the shares can be prevented from exercising shareholders' rights (he might have a cause of action against the seller, but that's irrelevant for his position vis-à-vis the corporation).

MINIMUM LEGAL CAPITAL

As mentioned above, one important comparative distinction must be drawn between countries that require a minimum legal capital for the incorporation and operation of a corporation, and countries that have abolished this requirement. In Europe, the Second Directive (now directive 2012/30/EU), requires a public corporation to have a minimum legal capital of 25,000 euro (roughly $25,000 in March 2015). This provision applies to joint-stock corporations, for example, "public company limited by shares" in the U.K. and Ireland; "société anonyme" in France, Belgium, and Luxembourg; "Aktiengesellschaft" in Germany; "sociedad anónima" in Spain; "società per azioni" in Italy, etc. This provision, however, does not apply to other limited liability companies roughly equivalent to an LLC in the U.S., such as a "Gesellschaft mit beschränkter Haftung" or "GmbH" in Germany; or a "società a responsabilità limitata" or "s.r.l." in Italy. In many E.U. Member States, the minimum capital is even higher than the 25,000 euro threshold set by the directive. In Italy the minimum capital requirement is 50,000 euro (120,000 until 2014). It should be pointed out that systems based on minimum legal capital also provide for quite detailed rules concerning eligible contributions (often services are not admissible), as well as a quite rigid system for the evaluation of contributions in kind, payment of contributions, and rules concerning capital maintenance (with respect to distributions to shareholders, and capital loss).

The basic idea behind such a requirement is that a minimum legal capital must be maintained throughout the life of the corporation to protect creditors. In theory, a minimum capital requirement should ensure that the value of the assets exceeds the liabilities at least by the amount of the minimum capital. As a consequence, at least in theory, if all assets are sold, their value should exceed the value of the liabilities, and creditors could be satisfied. Additionally, the minimum capital also indicates a certain "seriousness" and "commitment" of shareholders to the joint enterprise.

Many legal systems, however, have completely abandoned the concept of minimum legal capital. In the U.S. there is generally no minimum capital required, and it is possible to incorporate a corporation with a very low, purely nominal, capital. In 2005, Japan followed the U.S. and abolished the minimum legal capital requirement, which before the reform was 10 million JPY for stock corporation and 3 million JPY for limited liability corporation, while preserving other rules related to legal capital such as limitation on eligible contributions, rigid evaluation of contributions in kind, and restrictions of distributions to shareholders based on the amount of legal capital.

Several scholars argue that minimum legal capital should be abolished in other jurisdictions. These scholars often observe that minimum legal capital does not protect either creditors or shareholders, and it is simply a relic of the past that causes inefficiency by setting forth complex, yet ineffective rules and increases the costs of incorporation without any real benefit. In a nutshell, one key argument is that minimum legal capital does not really protect creditors because the actual value of the assets of the corporation can easily decrease also in systems with minimum legal capital, or because unexpected liabilities (such as for a mass tort) can burn all the assets. Consider the following example: a corporation is incorporated in Spain with a capital of 200,000 euro, entirely paid in cash by the shareholders. A few days after the incorporation, the directors use the 200,000 euro in cash to purchase an asset that they believe worth roughly 200,000 euro, but that in fact is a bad investment. The actual value of the asset is 50,000 euro. In the financial statements, the asset should be valued at 50,000 euro, but also assuming that the directors are capable and willing to recognize the lower value of the assets, financial statements might not be prepared and published for several months. Creditors, therefore, might contract with the corporation mistakenly believing that its net worth is at least 200,000 euro, when in fact it is only 50,000.

Critics of minimum legal capital also point out that it does not in any way ensure an adequate capitalization of the corporation because, in fact, 25,000 euro or even a higher statutory threshold might be completely inadequate also based on the type of business (consider a corporation that builds and sells airplanes with a capital of 25,000 euro). Moreover, critics point out that minimum legal capital imposes higher costs on corporations and barriers to new and competing entrepreneurs that might want to enter the market (this last critique, however, could be partially inconsistent with the observation that the minimum legal capital required is often "trivial").

While these criticisms are not unfounded, the case can be made that minimum legal capital is not completely useless, at least if all the applicable rules are followed. For example, in most systems that follow minimum legal capital, a "recapitalize or liquidate" rule applies (*see*, for example, Article 2447 of the Italian Civil Code. In contrast, Japanese law did not have such a rule even when minimum legal capital was required). Simplifying the issue, pursuant to these provisions, directors must monitor the financial situation of the corporation and if at any time the capital is reduced below the minimum statutory threshold, they must immediately call a shareholders' meeting in order to either recapitalize the corporation with new contributions, or wind it up liquidating the assets and paying the creditors. Failure to comply with this rule can result in civil and criminal liability for the directors. In the previous example of the corporation created with a capital of 200,000 euro, therefore, as soon as the directors realize that the real value of the assets is 50,000 euro, they should activate the "recapitalize or liquidate" procedure.

Of course, critics of minimum legal capital object that these rules are of little, if any, consequence for creditors. Imagine for instance a bank that has loaned 100,000 euro to the corporation, relying on a purported capital of 200,000 euro. If the corporation is liquidated, and the proceeds from the sale of the (only) asset are just 50,000 euro, the bank, as a creditor, will not be satisfied. It should not be forgotten, however, that the recapitalize or liquidate rule might play a role as an "early red flag" that things are going south, and might be helpful, at least, in reducing the amount of potential damage to creditors, as well as put shareholders on notice that the corporation is losing money. Some authors (for example, the Italian scholar Francesco Denozza) have also argued that mandatory rules concerning the protection of creditors are desirable in terms of fairness, because they reduce the different treatment of sophisticated creditors that can fend for themselves, such as banks, and weaker creditors such as employees, or the victims of a tort that had no chance of negotiating with the corporation any specific guarantee before the accident.

The debate goes on. The following excerpt offers a basis for the discussion.

LUCA ENRIQUES AND JONATHAN R. MACEY, CREDITORS
VERSUS CAPITAL FORMATION: THE CASE AGAINST THE
EUROPEAN LEGAL CAPITAL RULES
86 Cornell L. Rev. 1165 (2001)[2]

[. . .]

The Second Directive's minimum initial capital requirement provides no meaningful protection for creditors. The amount required, euro 25,000, is trivial. It is also meaningless because it is unrelated to the debt that a company may incur and to the sorts of business activities that a company may pursue. Clearly, it makes no sense for a highly leveraged company that transports radioactive waste to have the same minimum capital requirement as a company with little leverage that designs software.

The legal capital doctrine assumes, falsely, that the fixed amount of a firm's legal capital informs current and potential creditors of the resources that a firm possesses and may not freely distribute to its shareholders. In the real world, however, creditors (and potential creditors) care neither about these resources nor about the legal capital rules that are supposed to signal these resources.

The primary reason that creditors do not give significant weight to legal capital is that as soon as a firm starts to operate, it can use its capital to purchase assets that decline in value. Because a firm may immediately begin to incur losses, either merely in the normal course of business or by entering into one of the many kinds of unfair transactions that Article 11 of the Second Directive does not cover, the initial paid-in capital is a meaningless amount. In other words, creditors willing to inform themselves about a firm's existing equity cushion must examine its entire balance sheet. Moreover, creditors must consider the current value of the firm's assets, not the value of such assets at the time of purchase. The legal capital entry on the right-hand side of a corporation's balance sheet thus provides no useful information to creditors. Even if it did, creditors could just choose to deny credit to firms without satisfactory amounts of paid-in capital.

Even assuming that creditors care about how much equity shareholders really injected into a venture at its outset, requiring an expert report on contributions in kind is of little benefit to them. First, evaluation techniques leave experts with a very wide range of discretion. This is true even when the expert must explicitly state "the methods of valuation used," as the Second Directive requires. Second, experts can never really be "independent." Even when a third party (like a judge) chooses the expert, that expert will be a professional offering her accounting and valuation services on the market. Normally, she will

---

[2]   Footnotes omitted.

derive more profits from her normal services than from her Article 9 valuation activities. Furthermore, she must constantly attract and retain clients for these normal services. Hence, she will not risk losing her current or prospective clients by acting too independently in the valuation of non-cash consideration. Because of motivating professional interests, experts will tend to approve any contribution in kind that is not so outrageously overvalued that a non-expert could surmise that the company had watered its stock.

[. . .]

The "recapitalize or liquidate" rules of individual European Union Member States are undeniably much more effective at protecting creditors than the other legal capital rules, at least so long as such rules are easily enforceable. However, because these rules penalize risk-taking, they are highly inefficient and severely retard the growth of equity markets.

First of all, from a more formalistic point of view, such rules are inconsistent with the very concept of limited liability. In a hypothetical world in which every single company abided by these rules, no company would ever become insolvent because every company would either liquidate or reorganize before that. This, in turn, would mean that there would be no operational role for limited liability.

Second, rules requiring a company to liquidate or recapitalize when the value of the company's net assets falls below some preordained minimum level create the potential for opportunistic shareholder behavior. Shareholders can, in fact, take advantage of such provisions in disputes with other shareholders.

Third, majority shareholders may use such rules in order to get rid of financially constrained minority shareholders. If the company's capital falls to zero, a shareholder who is unable or unwilling to contribute more money to the venture will lose her shareholder status.

Another reason why these rules are inappropriate is because they are based on unreliable balance-sheet data. The relevant legal inquiry is whether the value of a firm's net assets as shown on its balance sheet has fallen below the requisite statutory minimum. A company with a real economic value significantly higher than the minimum legal capital amount will nonetheless have to undergo the radical restructuring that these rules require because its balance sheet does not reflect the true economic value of its assets. In order to avoid liquidation, such a company will either have to transform itself into a private limited-liability company (thereby losing the opportunity to access outside financing) or issue more equity.

If the company in question really does face financial risks, then the cost of equity financing will be very high. Controlling shareholders may not have sufficient funds to contribute, and will face a Hobson's choice of either liquidating the company or diluting their control positions by finding other investors willing to subscribe to the new issue. Ex ante, the prospect of having to choose between contributing more funds to a company in distress and diluting one's own control will be a disincentive for people to found new companies.

Finally (needless to say), if liquidation is the only result of this rule, then creditors as well as shareholders will suffer. After all, the assets of the company will, ipso facto, devalue in liquidation.

[. . .] One interest group that benefits from the legal capital regime is incumbent management. In Europe, incumbent managers tend also to be either aligned with controlling shareholders, or as is more usually the case in continental Europe, major blockholders themselves. Management benefits from a system that limits dividend payments and share repurchases; these limitations give management more freedom to reinvest the company's profits, even when there are no available positive-net-present-value investment projects. Management will make such inefficient investments as long as the opportunity cost of capital is offset by the higher private benefits derived from controlling a larger company. The higher the legal limitations on distributions, the more opportunity this interest group has to make inefficient investments.

Two other interest groups that clearly benefit from the Second Directive's status quo are accountants (who provide the required valuation services) and lawyers (who must guide managers through the labyrinth of needlessly complicated legal capital rules). Lawyers, who play a critical role in influencing the shape of the European company law directives, and benefit from them professionally, defend European legal capital rules. They do so both because it is in their self-interest and because they often lack sophistication in finance and economics and may honestly but erroneously believe that the legal capital rules are an efficient tool for creditor protection. Furthermore, most European corporate lawyers have invested significant human capital in becoming familiar with the legal capital rules. Repealing these rules would destroy the value of that human capital.

Additionally, incumbents in the various product markets, and especially those in the most mature markets, benefit from the Second Directive's legal capital rules. This is because these rules make it more difficult for new competitors to enter the market. As legal capital rules create obstacles to capital formation, they are especially costly for start-up companies.

Finally, legal capital rules benefit banks. Banks take advantage of the fact that legal capital rules reduce the risk that their corporate borrowers will go bankrupt. More importantly, however, banks have an interest in preserving rules, like the legal capital doctrine, which negatively affect equity markets and thereby protect bank market power in the European financial markets.

NOTES AND QUESTIONS

1.   Do you find the arguments of Professors Enriques and Macey convincing?

2.   What do you think about the argument that the evaluation of contributions in kind will always be flawed because no expert can really be "independent"? Is this a sufficient reason to abolish minimum legal capital, or is it more a problem of how to ensure, protect, and enforce the independence of the experts?

3.   The authors opine that the recapitalize or liquidate rule is not only useless, but also dangerous, among other reasons, because it might give majority shareholders the occasion to liquidate the corporation and get rid of minority shareholders that do not have financial resources to subscribe new shares. Is this critique convincing? Can't a controlling shareholder, in the absence of minimum legal capital rules, decide in any case—or make directors decide—to liquidate the corporation and reincorporate without minority shareholders? Isn't it possible for a controlling shareholder, at least in some jurisdictions, to freeze out minorities through a cash-out merger?

4.   Adopting a somewhat cynical perspective, Enriques and Macey observe that minimum capital rules are advantageous for specific interest groups, such as managers (and controlling shareholders), lawyers and accountants, and banks. Do you share this view? With respect to managers, for example, the argument is that these rules help them to avoid distributions to shareholders and promote reinvestment in the corporation. Is this consistent with the argument that these rules are ineffective? Are there other and more important legal strategies that should take care of conflicts of interest of the managers?

5.   Minimum legal capital might represent a barrier to new start-ups. In fact, as was discussed in Chapter 2, since the 1990s, several closely held corporations located in countries with rigid minimum legal capital rules (for example, Germany) decided to incorporate in the U.K. also because of more flexible capital requirements. This trend was clearly a consequence of the jurisprudence of the European Court of Justice concerning freedom of establishment that we considered in the previous chapter. It is interesting to point out that one effect of European regulatory competition is that several continental countries, including Germany, France, Spain, and Italy, have recently revised the rules on minimum legal capital applicable to an LLC (as mentioned above, not covered by the Second Directive). In these Member

States, it is now possible to create an LLC with a very limited capital. And in some countries also rules governing the capital of other corporations have become less demanding. Do you think this trend confirms the inutility of minimum legal capital?

PIERCING THE CORPORATE VEIL

As we pointed out in the Introduction of this chapter, in systems where it is "easier" to incorporate, and where there is no minimum legal capital required, courts developed the equitable doctrine of piercing the corporate veil. According to this doctrine, under certain circumstances, shareholders can be held liable for the debts of the corporation when there is some kind of "abuse" of the corporate structure. On the other hand, in systems characterized by more extensive controls at the incorporation stage, and minimum legal capital, piercing is generally more difficult, and often possible only under narrowly defined statutory circumstances.

According to a famous remark by Benjamin Cardozo, piercing the veil is a doctrine "enveloped in the mist of metaphor" (*Berkey v. Third Ave. Ry. Co.*, 155 N.E. 58, 61 (N.Y. 1926)). As with many equitable doctrines developed through case law, the precise elements that allow a court to go beyond the corporate veil are confusing, and often misinterpreted or misapplied. Basically, courts, especially in the U.S., try to ascertain if two elements are met in order to justify piercing. The two elements are: (1) if there is such a unity of interest and ownership between the corporation and the individual shareholders that they no longer exist as separate entities; and (2) if the acts are treated as those of the corporation alone, equity would not be satisfied (*see*, e.g., *Laya v. Erin Homes, Inc.*, 177 W.Va. 343 (1986)). Some courts have also considered a third element: the veil should not be pierced if the creditor in contract could have conducted an investigation on the financial soundness of the corporation. If such an investigation was possible, the assumption could be that the creditor accepted the risk of undercapitalization of the corporation.

To make these elements somehow more concrete, case law indicates the following typical indicia for piercing: (a) commingling of funds between the corporation and the shareholders; (b) lack of corporate formalities; (c) gross undercapitalization of the corporation; (d) fraud. Often one single element is insufficient to pierce, especially when it comes to undercapitalization. More commonly, courts tend to look at the totality of the circumstances, something that also makes it difficult to precisely define the scope of the doctrine.

One particular version of the veil piercing doctrine in the U.S. is the so-called enterprise liability approach, or alter ego approach, according to which the veil can be pierced when a corporation is entirely dominated by one shareholder. This version of the doctrine could sometimes (but not always) be considered a particular case of commingling of funds or lack of corporate formalities. Occasionally there might also be specific statutory grounds for piercing, for example based on federal statutes, such as the Comprehensive Environmental Response, Compensation, and Liability Act of 1980 (CERCLA).

Piercing is generally used when the debtor corporation is insolvent, and therefore creditors try to reach the (hopefully) deeper pockets of shareholders. It is interesting, however, to point out that sometimes there are also strategic procedural reasons to pierce, especially in the U.S. Consider, for example, the case of a West Virginia corporation sued by West Virginia creditors for an alleged tort (this example refers to the tragic but interesting case of the "Buffalo Creek Flood"; the lawsuit following the disaster is powerfully recounted in a great book by Gerald M. Stern, one of the attorneys for the plaintiffs, a must-read for lawyers). In this situation, only a West Virginia State Court might have jurisdiction over the dispute. Imagine, however, that the plaintiffs would prefer to sue in Federal Court, for example because they are concerned that the local judiciary could be biased in favor of a corporation that invests heavily in the state, or because they might want to take advantage of federal rules of civil procedure. If the defendant corporation is the subsidiary of a New York corporation, and the plaintiffs can argue that the veil should be pierced and the holding corporation should be held liable, they might be able to assert federal diversity jurisdiction. More generally, piercing when the shareholders and the corporation are from different states or nations might affect jurisdiction and allow plaintiffs to litigate in a forum perceived as preferable for a number of easy-to-imagine tactical reasons.

It should be mentioned, finally, that the liability of a controlling shareholder could also be based on other legal theories. One good example is to argue that the controlling shareholder was the principal and the controlled corporation the agent, and therefore, according to agency law, the principal might be liable for the acts of the agent. It might however be impossible, or more difficult, to establish an agency relationship and to assert the basis for liability.

Piercing in the U.S., as we will see shortly, is far from uncommon. The two following cases, however, were decided in favor of the defendant (the corporate veil was not pierced). They are very instructive of the U.S. approach, and can be considered leading cases often used to illustrate veil piercing.

BAATZ V. ARROW BAR

Supreme Court of South Dakota
452 N.W.2d 138 (1989)

SABERS, JUSTICE.

Kenny and Peggy Baatz (Baatz), appeal from summary judgment dismissing Edmond, LaVella, and Jacquette Neuroth, as individual defendants in this action.

Facts

Kenny and Peggy were seriously injured in 1982 when Roland McBride crossed the center line of a Sioux Falls street with his automobile and struck them while they were riding on a motorcycle. McBride was uninsured at the time of the accident and apparently is judgment proof.

Baatz alleges that Arrow Bar served alcoholic beverages to McBride prior to the accident while he was already intoxicated. Baatz commenced this action in 1984, claiming that Arrow Bar's negligence in serving alcoholic beverages to McBride contributed to the injuries they sustained in the accident. Baatz supports his claim against Arrow Bar with the affidavit of Jimmy Larson. Larson says he knew McBride and observed him being served alcoholic beverages in the Arrow Bar during the afternoon prior to the accident, while McBride was intoxicated.

Edmond and LaVella Neuroth formed the Arrow Bar, Inc. in May 1980. During the next two years they contributed $50,000 to the corporation pursuant to a stock subscription agreement. The corporation purchased the Arrow Bar business in June 1980 for $155,000 with a $5,000 down payment. Edmond and LaVella executed a promissory note personally guaranteeing payment of the $150,000 balance. In 1983 the corporation obtained bank financing in the amount of $145,000 to pay off the purchase agreement. Edmond and LaVella again personally guaranteed payment of the corporate debt. Edmond is the president of the corporation, and Jacquette Neuroth serves as the manager of the business. [. . .] [T]he corporation did not maintain dram shop liability insurance at the time of the injuries to Kenny and Peggy.

In 1987 the trial court entered summary judgment in favor of Arrow Bar and the individual defendants. Baatz appealed that judgment and we reversed and remanded to the trial court for trial. *Baatz, supra.* Shortly before the trial date, Edmond, LaVella, and Jacquette moved for and obtained summary judgment dismissing them as individual defendants. Baatz appeals. We affirm.

Individual liability by piercing the corporate veil.

Baatz claims that even if Arrow Bar, Inc. is the licensee, the corporate veil should be pierced, leaving the Neuroths, as the shareholders of the corporation, individually liable. A corporation shall be considered a separate legal entity until there is *sufficient reason* to the contrary. When continued recognition of a corporation as a separate legal entity would "produce injustices and inequitable consequences," then a court has sufficient reason to pierce the corporate veil. Factors that indicate injustices and inequitable consequences and allow a court to pierce the corporate veil are:

1) fraudulent representation by corporation directors;

2) undercapitalization;

3) failure to observe corporate formalities;

4) absence of corporate records;

5) payment by the corporation of individual obligations; or

6) use of the corporation to promote fraud, injustice, or illegalities.

When the court deems it appropriate to pierce the corporate veil, the corporation and its stockholders will be treated identically.

Baatz advances several arguments to support his claim that the corporate veil of Arrow Bar, Inc. should be pierced, but fails to support them with facts, or misconstrues the facts.

First, Baatz claims that since Edmond and LaVella personally guaranteed corporate obligations, they should also be personally liable to Baatz. However, the personal guarantee of a loan is a contractual agreement and cannot be enlarged to impose tort liability. Moreover, the personal guarantee creates individual liability for a corporate obligation, the opposite of factor 5), above. As such, it supports, rather than detracts from, recognition of the corporate entity.

Baatz also argues that the corporation is simply the alter ego of the Neuroths, and, [that accordingly] the corporate veil should be pierced. Baatz' discussion of the law is adequate, but he fails to present evidence that would support a decision in his favor in accordance with that law. When an individual treats a corporation "as an instrumentality through which he [is] conducting his personal business," a court may disregard the corporate entity. Baatz fails to demonstrate how the Neuroths were transacting personal business through the corporation. In fact, the evidence indicates the Neuroths treated the corporation separately from their individual affairs.

Baatz next argues that the corporation is undercapitalized. Shareholders must equip a corporation with a reasonable amount of capital for the nature of the business involved. Baatz claims the corporation was started with only $5,000 in borrowed capital, but does not explain how that amount failed to equip the corporation with a reasonable amount of capital. In addition, Baatz fails to consider the personal guarantees to pay off the purchase contract in the amount of $150,000, and the $50,000 stock subscription agreement. There simply is no evidence that the corporation's capital in whatever amount was inadequate for the operation of the business. Normally questions relating to individual shareholder liability resulting from corporate undercapitalization should not be reached until the primary question of corporate liability is determined. Questions depending in part upon other determinations are not normally ready for summary judgment. However, simply asserting that the corporation is undercapitalized does not make it so. Without some evidence of the inadequacy of the capital, Baatz fails to present specific facts demonstrating a genuine issue of material fact.

Finally, Baatz argues that Arrow Bar, Inc. failed to observe corporate formalities because none of the business' signs or advertising indicated that the business was a corporation. Baatz cites SDCL 47–2–36 as requiring the name of any corporation to contain the word corporation, company, incorporated, or limited, or an abbreviation for such a word. In spite of Baatz' contentions, the corporation is in compliance with the statute because its corporate name—Arrow Bar, Inc.—includes the abbreviation of the word incorporated. Furthermore, the "mere failure upon occasion to follow all the forms prescribed by law for the conduct of corporate activities will not justify" disregarding the corporate entity. Even if the corporation is improperly using its name, that alone is not a sufficient reason to pierce the corporate veil. This is especially so where, as here, there is no relationship between the claimed defect and the resulting harm.

In addition, the record is void of any evidence which would support imposition of individual liability by piercing the corporate veil under any of the other factors listed above in 1), 4) or 6).

In summary, Baatz fails to present specific facts that would allow the trial court to find the existence of a genuine issue of material fact. There is no indication that any of the Neuroths personally served an alcoholic beverage to McBride on the day of the accident. Nor is there any evidence indicating that the Neuroths treated the corporation in any way that would produce the injustices and inequitable consequences necessary to justify piercing the corporate veil. In fact, the only evidence offered is otherwise. Therefore, we affirm summary judgment dismissing the Neuroths as individual defendants.

* * *

WALKOVSZKY V. CARLTON

Court of Appeals of New York
18 N.Y.2d 414 (1966)

FULD, J.

This case involves what appears to be a rather common practice in the taxicab industry of vesting the ownership of a taxi fleet in many corporations, each owning only one or two cabs.

The complaint alleges that the plaintiff was severely injured four years ago in New York City when he was run down by a taxicab owned by the defendant Seon Cab Corporation and negligently operated at the time by the defendant Marchese. The individual defendant, Carlton, is claimed to be a stockholder of 10 corporations, including Seon, each of which has but two cabs registered in its name, and it is implied that only the minimum automobile liability insurance required by law (in the amount of $10,000) is carried on any one cab. Although seemingly independent of one another, these corporations are alleged to be "operated . . . as a single entity, unit and enterprise" with regard to financing, supplies, repairs, employees and garaging, and all are named as defendants. The plaintiff asserts that he is also entitled to hold their stockholders personally liable for the damages sought because the multiple corporate structure constitutes an unlawful attempt "to defraud members of the general public" who might be injured by the cabs.

The defendant Carlton has moved to dismiss the complaint on the ground that as to him it "fails to state a cause of action".

[. . .]

The law permits the incorporation of a business for the very purpose of enabling its proprietors to escape personal liability but, manifestly, the privilege is not without its limits. Broadly speaking, the courts will disregard the corporate form, or, to use accepted terminology, "pierce the corporate veil", whenever necessary "to prevent fraud or to achieve equity".

[. . .]

In the case before us, the plaintiff has explicitly alleged that none of the corporations "had a separate existence of their own" and, as indicated above, all are named as defendants. However, it is one thing to assert that a corporation is a fragment of a larger corporate combine which actually conducts the business. It is quite another to claim that the corporation is a "dummy" for its individual stockholders who are in reality carrying on the business in their personal capacities for purely personal rather than corporate ends. Either circumstance would justify treating the corporation as an agent and piercing the corporate veil to reach the principal but a different result would follow in each case. In the first, only a larger *corporate* entity would be held financially responsible while, in the other, the stockholder would be personally liable. Either the stockholder is conducting the business in his individual capacity or he is not. If he is, he will be liable; if he is not, then, it does not matter—insofar as his personal liability is concerned—that the enterprise is actually being carried on by a larger "enterprise entity".

[. . .]

Reading the complaint in this case most favorably and liberally, we do not believe that there can be gathered from its averments the allegations required to spell out a valid cause of action against the defendant Carlton.

The individual defendant is charged with having "organized, managed, dominated and controlled" a fragmented corporate entity but there are no allegations that he was conducting business in his individual capacity. Had the taxicab fleet been owned by a single corporation, it would be readily apparent that the plaintiff would face formidable barriers in attempting to establish personal liability on the part of the corporation's stockholders. The fact that the fleet ownership has been deliberately split up among many corporations does not ease the plaintiff's burden in that respect. The corporate form may not be disregarded merely because the assets of the corporation, together with the mandatory insurance coverage of the vehicle which struck the plaintiff, are insufficient to assure him the recovery sought. If Carlton were to be held individually liable on those facts alone, the decision would apply equally to the thousands of cabs which are owned by their individual drivers who conduct their businesses through corporations organized pursuant to the Business Corporation Law and carry the minimum insurance required by the Vehicle and Traffic Law. These taxi owner-operators are entitled to form such corporations and we agree [. . .] that, if the insurance coverage required by statute "is inadequate for the protection of the public, the remedy lies not with the courts but with the Legislature." It may very well be sound policy to require that certain corporations must take out liability insurance which will afford adequate compensation to their potential tort victims. However, the responsibility for imposing conditions on the privilege of incorporation has been committed by the Constitution to the Legislature and it may not be fairly implied, from any statute, that the Legislature intended, without the slightest discussion or debate, to require of taxi corporations that they carry automobile liability insurance over and above that mandated by the Vehicle and Traffic Law.

[. . .]

This is not to say that it is impossible for the plaintiff to state a valid cause of action against the defendant Carlton. However, the simple fact is that the plaintiff has just not done so here. While the complaint alleges that the separate corporations were undercapitalized and that their assets have been intermingled, it is barren of any "sufficiently particular[ized] statements" (CPLR 3013; see 3 Weinstein-Korn-Miller, N. Y. Civ. Prac., par. 3013.01 et. seq., p. 30–142 et. seq.) that the defendant Carlton and his associates are actually doing business in their individual capacities, shuttling their personal funds in and out of the corporations "without regard to formality and to suit their immediate convenience." Such a "perversion of the privilege to do business in a corporate form" would justify imposing personal liability on the individual stockholders. Nothing of the sort has in fact been charged. [. . .]

In point of fact, the principle relied upon in the complaint to sustain the imposition of personal liability is not agency but fraud. Such a cause of action cannot withstand analysis. If it is not fraudulent for the owner-operator of a single cab corporation to take out only the minimum required liability insurance, the enterprise does not become either illicit or fraudulent merely because it consists of many such corporations. The plaintiff's injuries are the same regardless of whether the cab which strikes him is owned by a single corporation or part of a fleet with ownership fragmented among many corporations. [. . .]

In sum, then, the complaint falls short of adequately stating a cause of action against the defendant Carlton in his individual capacity.

KEATING, J. (Dissenting).

The defendant Carlton, the shareholder here sought to be held for the negligence of the driver of a taxicab, was a principal shareholder and organizer of the defendant corporation which owned the taxicab. The corporation was one of 10 organized by the defendant, each containing two cabs and each cab having the "minimum liability" insurance coverage mandated by the Vehicle and Traffic Law. The sole assets of these operating corporations are the vehicles themselves and they are apparently subject to mortgages.*

From their inception these corporations were intentionally undercapitalized for the purpose of avoiding responsibility for acts which were bound to arise as a result of the operation of a large taxi fleet having cars out on the street 24 hours a day and engaged in public transportation. And during the course of the corporations' existence all income was continually drained out of the corporations for the same purpose.

The issue presented by this action is whether the policy of this State, which affords those desiring to engage in a business enterprise the privilege of limited liability through the use of the corporate device, is so strong that it will permit that privilege to continue no matter how much it is abused, no matter how irresponsibly the corporation is operated, no matter what the cost to the public. I do not believe that it is.

Under the circumstances of this case the shareholders should all be held individually liable to this plaintiff for the injuries he suffered. At least, the matter should not be disposed of on the pleadings by a dismissal of the complaint. If a corporation is organized and carries on business without substantial capital in such a way that the corporation is likely to have no sufficient assets available to meet its debts, it is inequitable that shareholders should set up such a flimsy organization to escape personal liability. The attempt to do corporate business without providing any sufficient basis of financial responsibility to creditors is an abuse of the separate entity and will be ineffectual to exempt the shareholders from corporate debts. It is coming to be recognized as the policy of law that shareholders should in good faith put at the risk of the business unencumbered capital reasonably adequate for its prospective liabilities. If capital is illusory or trifling compared with the business to be done and the risks of loss, this is a ground for denying the separate entity privilege."

[. . .]

The defendant Carlton claims that, because the minimum amount of insurance required by the statute was obtained, the corporate veil cannot and should not be pierced despite the fact that the assets of the corporation which owned the cab were "trifling compared with the business to be done and the risks of loss" which were certain to be encountered. I do not agree.

The Legislature in requiring minimum liability insurance of $10,000, no doubt, intended to provide at least some small fund for recovery against those individuals and corporations who just did not have and were not able to raise or accumulate assets sufficient to satisfy the claims of those who were injured as a result of their negligence. It certainly could not have intended to shield those individuals who organized corporations, with the specific intent of avoiding responsibility to the public, where the operation of the corporate enterprise yielded profits sufficient to purchase additional insurance. Moreover, it is reasonable to assume that the Legislature believed that those individuals and corporations having substantial assets would take out insurance far in excess of the minimum in order to protect those assets from depletion. Given the costs of hospital care and treatment and the nature of injuries sustained in auto collisions, it would be unreasonable to assume that the Legislature believed that the minimum provided in the statute would in and of itself be sufficient to recompense "innocent victims of motor vehicle accidents . . . for the injury and financial loss inflicted upon them".

[. . .]

What I would merely hold is that a participating shareholder of a corporation vested with a public interest, organized with capital insufficient to meet liabilities which are certain to arise in the ordinary course of the corporation's business, may be held personally responsible for such liabilities. Where corporate income is not sufficient to cover the cost of insurance premiums above the statutory minimum or where initially adequate finances dwindle under the pressure of competition, bad times or extraordinary and unexpected liability, obviously the shareholder will not be held liable.

The only types of corporate enterprises that will be discouraged as a result of a decision allowing the individual shareholder to be sued will be those such as the one in question, designed solely to abuse the corporate privilege at the expense of the public interest.

NOTES AND QUESTIONS

1.   Let's start with a side issue, one not exactly centered on piercing the veil. In *Baatz*, the plaintiffs based their complaint on dram-shop liability provisions, and in particular on the rule stating that bartenders can be held liable for the damages caused by an intoxicated client, if they served him liquor when he was already clearly intoxicated. In lots of countries there are no similar provisions, and it might in fact be extremely difficult, if not impossible, to hold a bartender liable under similar circumstances. It can be interesting, especially when discussing this in a culturally diverse group, to consider the pros and cons of dram-shop liability.

2.   In *Baatz*, the Court strongly disagrees with the way in which the plaintiff considers the personal guarantees given by individual shareholders for the benefit of the corporation. For the plaintiffs, it confirms that the corporation and the shareholders are acting as one single entity, but for the Court it proves the opposite. Who do you think is right?

3.   Did you find Judge Keating's dissenting opinion in *Walkovszky* convincing? Do you think that the conclusion of the majority would allow private parties to make a mockery of justice, and use the corporate structure to avoid liability in a way that is clearly contrary to the spirit of the law?

4.   What are the possible economic consequences of easy piercing? Could it adversely affect business activity, and therefore hinder economic growth? Is there any possible inequitable consequence of piercing? Consider, for example, the position of "innocent" creditors of the shareholders that might be adversely affected as a consequence of piercing.

* * *

The doctrine of piercing the corporate veil also exists in the United Kingdom. Notwithstanding the fact that the two previous U.S. cases were decided against piercing, courts in the U.K. are less inclined to pierce than their U.S. counterparts.

The context in which the following UK case arose was a complex international transaction. The claimant/appellant, VTB Capital plc, had entered into a Facility Agreement and Interest Swap Agreement with a Russian company, Russagroprom LLC ("RAP"). RAP subsequently defaulted on its loan. As a result, VTB brought proceedings in England against several defendants on the basis of tortious claims in conspiracy and deceit. The proceedings having been served on all but one of the defendants (all of whom were located overseas), a challenge was made to the English court's jurisdiction to hear the matter. VTB then sought to amend its claim, to include breach of contract, the primary motive for which appears to have been to provide an alternative basis for establishing jurisdiction before the English courts.

The issues in this matter were considered by both the High Court (http://www.bailii.org/ew/cases/EWHC/Ch/2011/3107.html) and the Court of Appeal (http://www.bailii.org/ew/cases/EWCA/Civ/2012/808.html).

The High Court was asked to rule first on whether the permission granted to VTB to serve the claims outside the jurisdiction should be set aside; second, on whether VTB should be permitted to amend its particulars of claim; and third, on whether a worldwide freezing order should be continued or discharged. The High Court found against VTB on all three issues, holding that (i) permission to serve the claim outside the jurisdiction should be set aside; (ii) VTB should not be permitted to amend the particulars of claim, and (iii) the worldwide freezing order should be discharged on grounds of deliberate and significant non-disclosure by VTB. In particular, the point that is relevant for our analysis is that the High Court (declining to follow *Antonio Gramsci Shipping Corp v Stepanovs* [2011] EWHC 333 (Comm)), held that where a claim of wrongdoing was brought against the person controlling the company, it was inappropriate to pierce the corporate veil to allow the claimant to pursue a contractual claim against such a person.

VTB appealed to the Court of Appeal. On appeal, the Court upheld the High Court's ruling on each of the three issues. The Court of Appeal accepted the existence of the principle of piercing the corporate veil, and clarified the circumstances in which this would apply, again providing that this principle should not allow contractual claims to proceed against non-contracting parties. Let us see what the Supreme Court thinks.

VTB CAPITAL PLC v. NUTRITEK INTERNATIONAL CORP AND OTHERS

[2013] UKSC 5

On appeal from: [2012] EWCA Civ 808

[. . .] LORD NEUBERGER

[. . .] The second issue: piercing the corporate veil: the principle of piercing the veil

I turn first to consider the argument that there are no circumstances in which the court should pierce, or lift, the corporate veil. The terms "piercing" and "lifting" appear throughout the authorities, sometimes interchangeably. As Toulson J observed in *Yukong Line Ltd of Korea v Rendsburg Investments Corpn of Liberia (No 2)* [1998] 1 WLR 294, 305, "it may not matter what language is used as long as the principle is clear; but there lies the rub". Staughton LJ in *Atlas Maritime Co SA v Avalon Maritime Ltd (No 1)* [1991] 4 All ER 769, 779G, expressly separated the two, on the basis that "pierc[ing] . . . is reserve[d] for treating the rights or liabilities or activities of a company as the rights or liabilities or activities of its shareholders", whereas "lift[ing] . . . [is] to have regard to the shareholding in a company for some legal purpose". In *Ben Hashem v Al Shayif* [2008] EWHC 2380 (Fam) [2009] 1 FLR 115, a case which included a claim that a company was no more than one man's alter ego, Munby J said, at para 150, that "in this context the expressions are synonymous".

For present purposes, I shall use the phrase "piercing" in preference to "lifting". It is the more familiar expression and it is the expression which all counsel have used. It is unnecessary to decide whether, in truth, there is a difference in this context between "piercing" and "lifting" the corporate veil.

We were referred to a number of cases where courts have either granted relief on the basis of piercing the corporate veil, or where courts have proceeded on the assumption, or concluded, that there is power to do so. The only case in that connection in the House of Lords, or Supreme Court, to which we were referred, was *Woolfson v Strathclyde Regional Council* 1978 SLT 159, a case where, on the facts, the House of Lords had no difficulty in rejecting an argument that the corporate veil could be pierced. At 1978 SLT 159, 161, Lord Keith suggested that the court could only take such a course "where special circumstances exist indicating that [the involvement of the company] is a mere façade concealing the true facts".

There is obvious attraction in the proposition that the court can pierce the veil of incorporation on appropriate facts, in order to achieve a just result. However, the spirited and sustained attack mounted against the proposition by Mr Michael Lazarus, who appeared for Marshall Capital Holdings Ltd, is worthy of serious consideration. The brief discussion of the principle in *Woolfson* does not justify the contention that it was somehow affirmed or approved by the House: Lord Keith's remarks were obiter, and the power of the court to pierce the corporate veil does not appear to have been in issue in that case. The most that can be said about *Woolfson* from the perspective of VTB is that the House was prepared to assume that the power existed.

The starting point for the argument that the principle does not exist is the well known decision in *Salomon v A Salomon & Co Ltd* [1897] AC 22. There is great force in the argument that that case represented an early attempt to pierce the veil of incorporation, and it failed, pursuant to a unanimous decision of the House of Lords, not on the facts, but as a matter of principle. Thus, at 30–31, Lord Halsbury LC said that a "legally incorporated" company "must be treated like any other independent person with its rights and liabilities appropriate to itself . . ., whatever may have been the ideas or schemes of those who brought it into existence". He added that it was "impossible to say at the same time that there is a company and there is not."

The notion that there is no principled basis upon which it can be said that one can pierce the veil of incorporation receives some support from the fact that the precise nature, basis and meaning of the principle are all somewhat obscure, as are the precise nature of circumstances in which the principle can apply. Clarke J in *The Tjaskemolen* [1997] 2 Lloyd's Rep 465, 471 rightly said that "[t]he cases have not worked out what is meant by 'piercing the corporate veil'. It may not always mean the same thing" (and to the same effect, see *Palmer's Company Law*, para 2.1533). Munby J in *Ben Hashem* seems to have seen the principle as a remedial one, whereas Sir Andrew Morritt V-C in *Trustor AB v Smallbone (No 2)* [2001] 1 WLR 1177 appears to have treated the principle as triggered by the finding of a "façade".

The "façade" mentioned by Lord Keith is often regarded as something of a touchstone in the cases—e.g. per Munby J in *Ben Hashem*, para 164, and per Sir Andrew Morritt V-C in *Trustor*, para 23. Words such as "façade", and other expressions found in the cases, such as "the true facts", "sham", "mask", "cloak", "device", or "puppet" may be useful metaphors. However, such pejorative expressions are often dangerous, as they risk assisting moral indignation to triumph over legal principle, and, while they may enable the court to arrive at a result which seems fair in the case in question, they can also risk causing confusion and uncertainty in the law. The difficulty which Diplock LJ expressed in *Snook v London and West Riding Investments Ltd* [1967] 2 QB 786, 802, as to the precise meaning of "sham" in connection with contracts, may be equally applicable to an expression such as "façade".

Mr Lazarus argued that in all, or at least almost all, the cases where the principle was actually applied, it was either common ground that the principle existed (*Gilford Motor Co Ltd v Horne* [1933] Ch 935, *Re H (restraint order: realisable property)* [1996] 2 BCLC 500, and *Trustor*) and/or the result achieved by piercing the veil of incorporation could have been achieved by a less controversial route—for instance, through the law of agency (*In re Darby, Ex p Brougham* [1911] 1 KB 95, *Gilford*, and *Jones v Lipman* [1962] 1 WLR 832), through statutory interpretation (*Daimler Company Ltd v Continental Tyre and Rubber Company (Great Britain) Ltd* [1916] 2 AC 307, *Merchandise Transport Ltd v British Transport Commission* [1962] 2 QB 173, *Wood Preservation Ltd v Prior* [1969] 1 WLR 1077, and *Re A Company* [1985] BCLC 333), or on the basis that, as stated by Lord Goff in *Goss v Chilcott* [1996] AC 788, 798, money due to an individual which he directs to his company is treated as received by him (*Gencor ACP Ltd v Dalby* [2000] 2 BCLC 734, and *Trustor*).

In summary, therefore, the case for Mr Malofeev is that piercing the corporate veil is contrary to high authority, inconsistent with principle, and unnecessary to achieve justice.

I see the force of this argument, but there are points the other way. I am not convinced that all the cases where the court has pierced the veil can be explained on the basis advanced by Mr Lazarus. Further, as Mr Howard QC said, the fact is that those cases were decided on the basis of piercing the veil. More generally, it may be right for the law to permit the veil to be pierced in certain circumstances in order to defeat injustice. In addition, there are other cases, notably *Adams v Cape Industries plc* [1990] Ch 433, where the principle was held to exist (albeit that they include *obiter* observations and are anyway not binding in this court). It is also difficult to explain the first instance decision in *Kensington International Ltd v Republic of the Congo* [2005] EWHC 2684 (Comm), [2006] 2 BCLC 296 on any basis other than the principle (but I am not at all sure that the case was rightly decided—see *Continental Transfert Technique Ltd v Federal Government of Nigeria* [2009] EWHC 2898 (Comm), paras 27–29). Further, the existence of the principle is accepted by all the leading textbooks—see *Palmer op. cit*, *Gore-Browne on Companies* at paras 7[3] to 7[6], Gower and Davies on *Principles of Modern Company Law* (8th ed) at paras 8–5 to 8–14, and *Farrar's Company Law* (4th ed), pp 69–78.

In answer to the contention that the approach of the courts to the issue of piercing the veil is unprincipled, there is real force, at least on the face of it, in the fact that it cannot be invoked merely where there has been impropriety. As Munby J put it in *Ben Hashem*, paras 163–164, "it is necessary to show both control of the company by the wrongdoer(s) and impropriety, that is, (mis)use of the company by them as a device or façade to conceal their wrongdoing ... at the time of the relevant transaction(s)".

In its recent decision in *La Générale des Carrières et des Mines v F G Hemisphere Associates LLC* [2012] UKPC 27, para 24, the Judicial Committee of the Privy Council, in a judgment given by Lord Mance, was prepared to assume that the appellant was right in contending that it was open to a court in this jurisdiction to pierce the corporate veil, but it is to be noted that this was not challenged by the respondent. In para 27, reference was made to *Case concerning Barcelona Traction, Light and Power Company, Ltd* [1970] ICJ 3, in which, it was said,

> "[T]he International Court of Justice referred (para 56) to municipal law practice to lift the corporate veil ... 'for instance, to prevent the misuse of the privileges of legal personality, as in certain cases of fraud or malfeasance, to protect third persons such as a creditor or purchaser, or to prevent the evasion of legal requirements or of obligations' ".

However, at para 27, Lord Mance pointed out that *Barcelona Traction* concerned "international legal considerations, indicating that there may not always be a precise equation between factors relevant to the lifting of the corporate veil under domestic and international law."

In my view, it is unnecessary and inappropriate to resolve the issue of whether we should decide that, unless any statute relied on in the particular case expressly or impliedly provides otherwise, the court cannot pierce the veil of incorporation. It is unnecessary, because the second argument raised on behalf of Mr Malofeev, to which I shall shortly turn, persuades me that VTB cannot succeed on this issue. It is inappropriate because this is an interlocutory appeal, and it would therefore be wrong (absent special circumstances) to decide an issue of such general importance if it is unnecessary to do so.

The second issue: piercing the corporate veil: why it cannot succeed in this case

I therefore approach this question in the same way as the Court of Appeal, namely by considering whether, assuming in VTB's favour that the court can pierce the veil of incorporation on appropriate facts, the basis on which VTB seeks to pierce the veil can be justified in the present case. I do so on the basis that this issue is to be resolved by reference to English law. It seems to me, however, that there may be a choice of law question to be addressed in cases which concern the piercing of the veil of a foreign incorporated company. That question is whether the proper law governing the piercing of the corporate veil is the *lex incorporationis*, the *lex fori*, or some other law (for example, the *lex contractus*, where the issue concerns who is considered to be party to a contract entered into by the company in question). The ultimate conclusion may be that there is no room for a single choice of law rule to govern the issue: see Tham "Piercing the corporate veil: searching for appropriate choice of law rules" [2007] LMCLQ 22, 27. However, given that it has been common ground throughout these proceedings that the issue is to be resolved pursuant to English law, it is inappropriate to say more about this issue.

In so far as VTB invokes the principle of piercing the veil of incorporation, its case involves what, at best for its point of view, may be characterised as an extension to the circumstances where it has traditionally been held that the corporate veil can be pierced. It is an extension because it would lead to the person controlling the company being held liable as if he had been a co-contracting party with the company concerned to a contract where the company was a party and he was not. In other words, unlike virtually all the cases where the court has pierced the corporate veil, VTB is claiming that Mr Malofeev should be treated as if he were, or had been, a co-contracting party with RAP under the two agreements, even though neither Mr Malofeev nor any of the contracting parties (including VTB) intended Mr Malofeev to be a party.

The notion that the principle can be extended to such a case receives no support from any case save for a very recent decision of Burton J, *Antonio Gramsci Shipping Corporation v Stepanovs* [2011] EWHC 333 (Comm), [2011] 1 Lloyd's Rep 647 (which he followed in his later decision in *Alliance Bank JSC v Aquanta Corporation* [2011] EWHC 3281 (Comm) [2012] 1 Lloyd's Rep 181, which was considered by the Court of Appeal at [2012] EWCA Civ 1588). None of the other decisions relied on by VTB in this connection is, on analysis, of assistance to its case.

In *Gilford*, Mr Horne had undertaken not to compete with his former employer, and a company, in which only he and his wife were shareholders, and which he formed after leaving his employment, was enjoined from competing. He effectively broke his undertaking by trading through the company, in the same way as if it had been carrying on the competing business through his wife—as indeed had happened in *Smith v Hancock* [1894] 2 Ch 377, 385, a case relied on by the Court of Appeal in *Gilford*. Thus, the decision in *Gilford* had nothing to do with the fact that a company was involved, and therefore, as a matter of logic, the decision cannot have been based on piercing the corporate veil—a point made by Toulson J in *Yukong Line* at 308, and rightly accepted by Arnold J and the Court of Appeal in this case.

The same point (as was said in *Yukong Line*) applies to *Jones v Lipman*, which I do not find an entirely easy case. After agreeing to sell a property to a purchaser, the vendor sold the same property to a company owned by him and his wife, and the purchaser obtained an order for specific performance against the company. On the judge's reasoning, it would have equally been entitled to do so if, instead of the company, the property had been transferred to the vendor's wife. Another view of *Jones* is that the sale by the vendor to the company was treated as a sham transaction.

In both *Gencor* and *Trustor*, the court pierced the corporate veil in order to impose liability on a company, effectively owned and controlled by the wrongdoer, for money which he had misappropriated from the claimant and diverted to the company. There was no question of the wrongdoer being treated as contractually liable under a contract to which the company, rather than he, was a party. Even the doubtful decision in *Kensington* did not involve going so far as to hold that the person sheltering behind the veil was liable as if he was a contracting party under a contract entered into by the company.

The fact that there has been no case (until *Gramsci*) where the power to pierce the corporate veil has been extended in the way for which VTB contends in these proceedings does not necessarily mean that VTB's case, in so far as it is based on piercing the veil, must fail. However, given that the principle is subject to the criticisms discussed above, it seems to me that strong justification would be required before the court would be prepared to extend it. Once one subjects the proposed extension to analysis, I consider that it is plain that it cannot be sustained: far from there being a strong case for the proposed extension, there is an overwhelming case against it.

First, it is not suggested by VTB that any of the other contracting parties under the two agreements is not liable. Indeed, as mentioned above, VTB's proposed pleaded case is that Mr Malofeev is "jointly and severally liable with RAP". Even accepting that the court can pierce the corporate veil in some circumstances, the notion of such joint and several liability is inconsistent with the reasoning and decision in *Salomon*. A company should be treated as being a person by the law in the same way as a human being. The fact that a company can only act or think through humans does not call that point into question: it just means that the law of agency will always potentially be in play, but, it will, at least normally, be the company which is the principal, not an agent. On VTB's case, if the agency analogy is relevant, the company, as the contracting party, is the quasi-agent, not the quasi-principal.

Subject to some other rule (such as that of undisclosed principal), where B and C are the contracting parties and A is not, there is simply no justification for holding A responsible for B's contractual liabilities to C simply because A controls B and has made misrepresentations about B to induce C to enter into the contract. This could not be said to result in unfairness to C: the law provides redress for C against A, in the form of a cause of action in negligent or fraudulent misrepresentation.

In any event, it would be wrong to hold that Mr Malofeev should be treated as if he was a party to an agreement, in circumstances where (i) at the time the agreement was entered into, none of the actual parties to the agreement intended to contract with him, and he did not intend to contract with them, and (ii) thereafter, Mr Malofeev never conducted himself as if, or led any other party to believe, he was liable under the agreement. That that is the right approach seems to me to follow from one of the most fundamental principles on which contractual liabilities and rights are based, namely what an objective reasonable observer would believe was the effect of what the parties to the contract, or alleged contract, communicated to each other by words and actions, as assessed in their context—see e.g. *Smith v Hughes* (1871) LR 6 QB 597, 607.

In his argument, Mr Howard QC relied by analogy with the law relating to undisclosed principals. In my view, the analogy tells against VTB's argument. The existence of the undisclosed principal rule has long been regarded as an anomaly, as discussed in *Bowstead & Reynolds on Agency*, 19th ed (2010), para 8–070, and as observed by Dillon LJ in *Welsh Development Agency v Export Finance Co Ltd* [1992] BCLC 148, 173. As the Court of Appeal said in this case at para 89, it would be inappropriate to extend an anomaly—save where it would be unjust and unprincipled not to do so. To adapt what Lord Hoffmann said in *OBG Ltd v Allan* [2007] UKHL 21, [2008] AC 1, paras 103 and 106, "an anomaly created by the judges to solve a particular problem" is "an insecure base" on which to justify an extension to a principle, especially when that principle can itself be said to be anomalous.

Quite apart from this, it seems to me that the facts relied on by VTB to justify piercing the veil of incorporation in this case do not involve RAP being used as "a façade concealing the true facts". In my view, if the corporate veil is to be pierced, "the true facts" must mean that, in reality, it is the person behind the company, rather than the company, which is the relevant actor or recipient (as the case may be). Here, on VTB's case, "the true facts" relate to the control, trading performance, and value of the Dairy Companies (if one considers the specific allegations against Mr Malofeev), or to the genuineness of the nature of the underlying arrangement (which involves a transfer of assets between companies in common ownership). Neither of these features can be said to involve RAP being used as a "façade to conceal the true facts".

It was suggested, however, by Mr Howard QC that the case against Mr Malofeev involves him "abusing the corporate structure", and that that is sufficient to justify piercing the corporate veil. However, in my view, abuse of the corporate structure (whatever that expression means) adds nothing to the debate, at least in this case. It may be another way of describing use of the company as a façade to conceal the true facts (in which case it adds nothing to Lord Keith's characterisation in *Woolfson*), or it may be an additional requirement before the corporate veil will be pierced: otherwise, it seems to me that it would be an illegitimate extension of the circumstances in which the veil can be pierced.

It is true that in many civil law systems, abuse of rights is a well recognised concept, and it may be appropriate for a domestic court to apply such a principle in relation to some areas of EU law. However, it was not suggested to us that it should be applied as a new or separate ground in domestic law for treating Mr Malofeev as contractually liable to VTB, or that it would assist VTB in this case.

Accordingly, in agreement with the Court of Appeal and for substantially the same reasons, I consider that VTB's contention represents an extension to the circumstances in which the court will pierce the corporate veil, and on analysis it is an extension which is contrary to authority and contrary to principle.

The proposed extension is all the more difficult to justify given that it is not needed to enable VTB to seek redress from Mr Malofeev. It is clear that, if VTB establishes that it was induced to enter into the agreements by the fraudulent statements which he is alleged to have made, then Mr Malofeev will be liable to compensate VTB. The measure of damages may be different, but that is not a particularly attractive reason for extending the principle in a new and unprincipled way. And I am not at all attracted by the notion that the principle should be invoked simply to enable VTB to justify the proceedings being heard in this jurisdiction, if they otherwise could not be. That would be precious close to its application being permitted to pull itself up by its own bootstraps.

It follows from this analysis that I doubt that the decision in *Gramsci* can be justified, at least on the basis of piercing the corporate veil. In agreement with the Court of Appeal and Arnold J, I think that the reasoning in that case involved a misinterpretation of the basis of the decisions in *Gilford* and *Jones*. It seems to me that the conclusion in *Gramsci* was driven by an understandable desire to ensure that an individual who appears to have been the moving spirit behind a dishonourable (or worse) transaction, action, or receipt, should not be able to avoid liability by relying on the fact that the transaction, action, or receipt was effected through the medium (but not the agency) of a company. But that is not, on any view, enough to justify piercing the corporate veil for the purpose of holding the individual liable for the transaction, action, or receipt, especially where the action is entering into a contract.

For these reasons, I agree with the Court of Appeal in concluding that, assuming that there is jurisdiction to pierce the corporate veil on appropriate facts, VTB's proposed pleaded case does not give rise to arguable grounds for contending that this jurisdiction could be invoked in the present case. I would therefore refuse VTB permission to amend its pleaded case to raise such a claim.

Conclusion

I would therefore dismiss VTB's appeal on both main issues.

[. . .]

NOTES AND QUESTIONS

1. Even in the absence of specific empirical evidence, assuming that piercing is in fact more rare in the U.K. than in the U.S., can you imagine possible reasons for this divergence between two common law systems that share meaningful elements?

2. Can one of the reasons for divergence be that the U.K., as a Member State of the E.U., has implemented (at least for public companies) rules on legal capital? Can the explanation for divergence be found in procedural reasons that might create an incentive, in the U.S., to bring lawsuits based on not settled legal principles, such as for example the absence, in the latter system, of the so-called "loser-pays rule"?

3. If you could formulate a single rule that would provide the courts with guidance as to when to pierce/lift the corporate veil, what would this rule look like or what elements would it require for piercing?

4. Do you think that the use of the term "piercing" rather than "lifting" makes any difference in this context? Do you think that the use of the terminology interchangeably makes any difference? Or perhaps it reveals something about the judges' attitudes? Judge Toulson stated in *Yukong Line Ltd v Rendsburg Investments Corporation of Liberia* (No.2) [1998] 1 WLR 294, 305: "metaphor can be used to illustrate a principle; it may also be used as a substitute for analysis and may therefore obscure reasoning." To what extent do you think this statement is true with respect to how U.K. v. U.S. courts have approached this area of law?

5. An important and fairly recent British case, *Chandler v Cape plc* [2012] EWCA Civ 525, seems to open the door to the possibility of holding a parent corporation liable for the torts of a subsidiary (the litigation concerned the asbestosis developed by an employee of the subsidiary). As a research project, look up this case, and discuss if it makes piercing the veil easier in the U.K.

6. Consider for a moment the style and language of this decision. Comparing it with U.S. cases reprinted above, do you find English judges more or less clear than American ones? How would you explain your answer?

* * *

Generally speaking, in civil law countries, once the corporation has been duly incorporated it is more difficult to pierce. The doctrine is not, however, completely unknown in civil law systems. In some countries, most notably in Spain and in some Latin American systems based on Spanish law, courts have occasionally pierced the corporate veil based on an "abuse of the law." A good and recent account of veil piercing in Spain and in Latin America is offered by Dante Figueroa, *Comparative Aspects of Piercing the Corporate Veil in the United States and Latin America*, 50 DUQ. L. REV. 683 (2012).

A good example of the reluctance of civil law courts to pierce the corporate veil is offered by the following French case. It's useful, before reading the case, to summarize the facts and procedural history. A French company, SA Metaleurop, owned 99% of the shares of a subsidiary, named SAS Metaleurop. The subsidiary became insolvent and went into bankruptcy. The trustee in bankruptcy and a prosecutor sued the parent corporation arguing that the bankruptcy proceedings should be extended to it, and that it was liable for the obligations of the subsidiary, basing their complaint on commingling of funds between the two entities, the existence of extensive contractual relationships between them, and the domination of the subsidiary by the parent. The court of first instance dismissed the claim, and decided not to pierce the corporate veil, but the court of appeal reversed. The French Supreme Court, in the following decision, reverses the court of appeal and holds that the parent cannot be held liable. Depending on your legal background, you might find this decision difficult to read and understand but, as indicated in the Notes following the case, this is a comparative experience in itself (and, in addition, it is very short)!

DENIS FACQUES V. JÉRÔME THEETTEN

French Cass. Com., 2005
19 April 2005, n° 05–10.094

According to the challenged decision of the court of appeals, the SAS (*Société par actions simplifiée or simplified public limited corporation*) Metaleurop Nord (the SAS, 99% subsidiary of the SA Metaleurop (the SA)), was put into insolvency proceedings by the first degree court of Béthune, on 28 January 2003, and in liquidation on the following 10 March. Theetten and Martin were appointed as liquidators; these court-appointed administrators of the SAS requested the first degree court to extend the insolvency proceeding of the SAS to the SA. On April 11, 2003 this request was dismissed. Following an appeal of the liquidators of the SAS and of the prosecutor, the [Court of Appeal] appointed an expert to determine the degree of dependence of the SAS from the SA. [After considering the report of the expert] the liquidators of the SAS, the SAS, the works' council and the prosecutor requested to vacate the first degree court judgment of 11 April 2003 on the basis of Article L. 621–5 of the Commercial code [*article L 621–2 of the Commercial code since 2005*] and to hold that the SAS was a fictitious company. The SA argued that the relationships between the companies of the group were normal and requested to affirm the judgment. Whereas [the Court of Appeals decided], on December 16, 2004 that the assets of the SAS and SA had been commingled and ordered the extension of the insolvency proceedings to the latter; whereas, on request of the liquidators of the companies, the SA was authorized to continue its activity by application of article L. 622–10 of the Commercial code;

Considering article L. 621–5, alinea 1st, of the Commercial code;

Whereas in order to extend the insolvency proceedings from the SAS to the SA, the decision [of the Court of Appeal] notes that the management of the currency risk by the treasurer of the SA had led to an important revenue shortfall and had been covered by a contract only in April 2001; whereas the court held afterwards that the organization, within the group, of product lines did not lead to the modification of the intercompany services "chargeback" contracts, that the SAS had to pay the salaries of two employees who were exercising the functions of technical advisors and management controller for all the entities of the group, while its autonomy was limited because most decisions were taken by the employee of another company and that no agreement detailed the responsibilities and powers of these employees. Also after the abandonment of this organization, the parent company managed the treasury of the SAS, the repayment of the long term loan had been postponed for two years, the default of the first payment had not led to any particular reaction, despite the loss of value of its claims, the SA had continued to grant the SAS significant cash advances. Nothing could indicate an improvement of the financial situation of the subsidiary, and the SAS depended on very heavy investments that it could not assume alone.

Whereas [the court of appeal does not explain how], in a group of companies, treasury and currency management contracts, exchange of employees and the funds' advances by the parent company, reveal abnormal financial relations constituting a commingling of assets of the estate of the parent company with one of its subsidiaries, the court of appeals, which was not deciding the case on the basis of article L. 624–3 of the Commercial code, did not provide a legal basis for its decision.

For these reasons [. . .]

Vacates and nullifies the decision of the court of appeal [. . .]

NOTES AND QUESTIONS

1. As mentioned, depending on your background, you might have found this case difficult to read with all the "whereas" that the court uses. You also might have found that the facts are not clearly stated, and that the legal reasoning of the court is quite brief if present at all. This is, however,

something you might come across when practicing internationally. The "style" of judicial opinions varies significantly around the world, and you will sometimes have to deal with a decision written in a very different fashion to what you might be accustomed. Supreme Courts in civil law systems, for example, generally deal only with the interpretation and application of the law, and they do not carefully and clearly explain the underlying facts of a dispute. To understand the facts you must often read the decision of the lower courts, and especially the one of the court of first instance. In addition, some courts are known for rendering quite brief decisions, without too much elaboration on how they interpret the law.

2.   The take-away point of the case, however, is that transfers of funds, commingling of assets and domination might not be sufficient to hold the parent corporation liable. Do you agree with this decision? If you would have to decide on the same facts applying the principles used in the U.S., for example as explained in the two cases above, would the conclusion be different?

* * *

It should be noted, however, that French case law is not entirely averse to piercing. In the following and more recent case, the French Supreme Court decided to hold a separate legal entity liable for the obligations of another company. According to case law developed under article L. 621–2 of the Commercial code, courts can decide to pierce the corporate veil in a case of commingling of assets (*confusion de patrimoine*) or in a case of abnormal financial relations (*relations financières anormales*) or abnormal financial flows (*flux financiers anormaux*). These two last concepts are very similar to each other. Commingling of assets is mostly determined by the lack of separate accounting, making it impossible to identify the respective assets of the companies. Piercing decisions are nonetheless very rare.

STÉ ROUSSY V. ROUSSEL ÈS QUAL

French Cass. Com., 2010
26 May 2010, F–D, n° 09–66.615

Regarding the single argument

Whereas, according to the case appealed (Nîmes, 19 March 2009), on 1st October 2004, the companies *Pr Abc Billard* and *Les Belles Pierres*, MM. Hours and Naddeo established the Limited company (*société à responsabilité limitée*) Black Clover (the Black Limited), having as its purpose the management of a pub; in December 2004, the latter company signed a commercial lease with the real estate civil company (*Société civile immobilière* or *SCI*) Roussy (Roussy company) regarding a building where the pub would be located [. . .] for a monthly rent of 3,100 HT; the tenant would leave at the end of the lease to the landlord all improvements, changes or repairs without any indemnification, save to return the property in its pristine situation at its expenses; as soon as October 1st, 2004, the Black company started at its own expenses a full renovation of the building for a cost of 358,365 while, at the same time, it defaulted on the rent up to an amount of 47,201.56 when the landlord then enforced the cancellation clause in February 2006; on 20 September 2006, the Black company was put into immediate judicial liquidation, M. Roussel being appointed as liquidator; by judgment of 22 January 2008 of the court of first instance, the liquidator's claim to extend the insolvency proceeding from the Black company to the Roussy company, was dismissed. [Roussy won the trial, but the court of appeal reversed the decision and hold Roussy liable.]

Whereas the Roussy company complains that the Court of appeals decision held that abnormal financial flows existed between itself and the Black company, establishing a commingling of assets, and decided the extension of the liquidation proceedings to Roussy; whereas, according to the plea, the existence of abnormal financial flows between a company undergoing an insolvency proceeding and the one targeted by a request for extension implies a systematic abuse of the insolvent corporation; whereas the Court of appeals concluded that the assets of Roussy and the Sarl Black Clover had been commingled because the landlord waited more than one year before enforcing the cancellation clause due to non-payment of rent, which allowed it to appropriate the works done by the tenant. This observation did not justify the decision of the Court because the extension given to the tenant was justified by the start of the activity and the attribution of the works to the landlord, and therefore the decision violates Article L. 621–2 of the Commercial code.

However, having held that the Black company financed works which significantly exceeded its current and even future financial capacities from the considered commercial activity and that, since the origin, this company was in a situation of full and abnormal economic and legal dependency from the Roussy company, its landlord, this situation was necessarily known to the landlord whose senior manager, M. Naddéo, was one of the four shareholders of the Black company, the Court holds that the unusual and repeated systematic passivity of the landlord, which waited until 6th January 2006, that is more than one year, to deliver a first request for payment while a sum of 42,000 was due, indicated a collusion between the two companies, the landlord benefiting from an abnormal financial flow, to the prejudice of the creditors of the company subject to liquidation proceedings, as this was foreseeable at the origin of the commercial lease contract executed in the conditions of commingling of assets; by these facts and appreciations which characterize abnormal financial relations between the two companies, the court of appeal has legally justified its decision; the claim is not grounded.

For these reasons:

The claim is dismissed.

NOTES AND QUESTIONS

1. In its frankly not very clear explanation of the facts, the Court describes the following situation: Roussy rented some real estate to Black, but remained passive when the latter started defaulting on rent. The passivity of Roussy damaged other creditors, also because Black made some improvements to the property that Roussy could benefit from. For these reasons, Roussy was held liable for some obligations of Black, and the Court of Cassation affirmed.

2. The French Supreme Court agreed with the Court of Appeal that Roussy should be liable for the obligations of Black. This decision is quite extreme because Roussy was not even a shareholder of Black and they were two separate companies. However, one of the managers of Roussy (called Naddeo) was also a shareholder and the general manager of Black. Therefore, the companies were not unrelated and this explains why there were abnormal financial relations. In the U.S., this might be characterised as a case of "horizontal" veil piercing, whereby a "sister" corporation is held liable.

3. Can you identify the elements of "abnormal financial connections" and "domination" that justify the decision of the court? Can you point to situations in which the passivity of a creditor and/or of a controlling shareholder could be indicia of commingling and, therefore, lead to piercing?

* * *

In contrast to French courts, Japanese courts are somehow more inclined to pierce the corporate veil, especially under certain circumstances. Several veil piercing cases in recent years dealt with situations in which shareholders controlling a financially distressed corporation transferred its assets to another entity in order to protect them from the creditors. Courts have generally considered these practices illegal as an abuse of corporate personality and allowed the creditors of the transferor corporation to exercise their claims against the transferee corporation (*see for example*, Supreme Court of Japan, Oct. 26, 1973, 27 SAIKO SAIBANSHO MINJI HANREISHU 1240, Fukuoka District Court, Mar. 25, 2004, 1192 KINYU SHOJI HANREI 25). These decisions are similar to fraudulent transfer cases, and limitation of limited liability is not a problem.

In 1970s and 1980s, some Japanese lower courts started imposing liability for corporate debts on controlling shareholders based on veil piercing. These cases often dealt with small family-run enterprises. The factors often pointed out by the courts are: disregard of formal procedures required by law, commingling of assets, commingling of business, empty-shell corporation (with no employees and assets), and creditor's reliance

on controlling shareholders: in some cases, the reliance was not induced
by actions of the shareholders (for example, see Osaka High Court, Jul.
19, 1977, 871 HANREI JIHO 47). This type of veil piercing, however, is
apparently becoming rarer, at least on the basis of reported cases (keep in
mind that, in civil law jurisdictions, only a relatively small number of
cases is published and easily available in law journals). In the following
decision, a contractual creditor of the subsidiary of a listed corporation
sued the parent based on tort law, asserting that the parent violated its
duty to protect the creditors of its subsidiary. The case shows the
reluctance of Japanese courts to deny limited liability and impose liability
on a controlling shareholder or a parent corporation, although it does not
explicitly refer to veil piercing.

TOKYO DISTRICT COURT, 29 NOVEMBER 2005
29 November 2005, 1209 HANREI TAIMUZU 196

[. . .]

The plaintiff claims that the defendant should direct the [subsidiary
corporation] to pay its debt to the plaintiff in full, since the defendant has
provided funds to the [subsidiary] and made it pay its debt to its other
creditors, but not to the plaintiff. The plaintiff explains that this does not
mean that the defendant must pay the debt to the plaintiff, but means
that [the controlling entity] owes a duty of protection to the creditors [of a
controlled entity] based on the principles of good faith and fairness.

However, the parent corporation is a shareholder of its subsidiary
corporation, and as a matter of law, in relation to the creditors of the
subsidiary, it enjoys limited liability and is only liable for the amount of
its contribution (Commercial Code, Art. 200, Para. (1), and it does not owe
any other duty to make direct payments to the creditors of the subsidiary
for the debts of the subsidiary. In other words, a parent corporation has
no liability for the debts of its subsidiary, may it be a direct payment to
the creditors of the subsidiary or an indirect one through provision of
funds to the subsidiary.

[. . .]

In addition, the plaintiff asserts that it is quite natural for the
creditors of the [subsidiary corporation] to expect [. . .] full payment for
their claims, even though the [subsidiary corporation] lacks the necessary
funds, when the defendant [made the subsidiary pay some of its
creditors].

However, since a parent corporation owes no duty to the creditors of
its subsidiary regarding the payment of the debts of the subsidiary simply
because it is the parent corporation, such an unilateral reliance by the
plaintiff, which is a creditor of a subsidiary, that it would be able to

receive payment through the provision of funds by the defendant to the [subsidiary], is not protected legally and is insufficient as a basis to impose any legal duty on the parent corporation to the creditors of the subsidiary.

[. . .]

NOTES AND QUESTIONS

1.   How do you think this case fits in our discussion on veil piercing? It is clearly almost impossible to tell, but hypothetically, if the same facts would be litigated in the U.S., do you think the outcome would have been different (i.e. in favor of piercing)? In your opinion, if the controlling shareholder causes a subsidiary to repay some creditors and not others, even without a valid legal reason, should the controlling shareholder be sanctioned? Is the situation different if the subsidiary is insolvent?

2.   The Japanese Supreme Court has developed a doctrine that permits to pierce the corporate veil: (a) when the legal personality is no more than a mere formality; or (b) when the legal personality has been abused (Supreme Court of Japan, Feb. 27, 1969, 23 SAIKO SAIBANSHO MINJI HANREISHU 511 and Supreme Court of Japan, Oct. 26, 1973, *supra*). Lower courts have applied this approach to different types of cases. This case law, however, has been criticized by scholars arguing that standards such as "a mere formality" and "abuse" are too vague and obscure to be effectively and fairly applied. Is the vagueness of the basis for piercing also a problem in other jurisdictions?

3.   These critics also observed that several cases could be properly addressed applying statutory rules without recurring to the elusive notion of veil piercing. For example, fraudulent conveyance law deals with situations in which assets of a distressed corporation have been abusively transferred to another corporation in order to hide them from the creditors. Applying fraudulent conveyance rules, the remedy is usually limited to the amount of assets being transferred; the consequence of veil piercing is, on the other hand, much more severe for the shareholders, since once the veil has been pierced, the liability of the shareholder can exceed the value of the assets illegally transferred. Do you think this is an interesting argument? In other words, do you think that sometimes veil piercing can lead to outcomes that are too harsh for the shareholders?

4.   Does recent Japanese case law confirm the relationship between the complexity of the incorporation process and the ex ante controls it entails, and the willingness of the courts to pierce the corporate veil, discussed above?

5.   Even though the general trend in Japanese case law is toward a more restrictive approach to veil piercing, some decisions still hold a controlling shareholder or a parent corporation liable against a creditor of a subsidiary corporation when additional facts indicating some type of abuse are present. For example, in Tokyo District Court, Jun. 20, 2001, 1797 Hanrei Jiho 36, a parent corporation was accused of deliberately hiding the risk of a

financial transaction from the counterparty of its subsidiary. Also, in Tokyo District Court Jul. 25, 2001, 813 Rodo Hanrei 15, an employee of a subsidiary was granted a judgment for unpaid wages and retirement allowance against the parent corporation. It should be noted that the parent corporation had originally employed the employee and had been exploiting the subsidiary by imposing overly high rent for the premises it leased to the subsidiary.

6.   Keep in mind that a controlling shareholder who is also the director of a corporation, which is often the case especially in closely held corporations, can be held liable to the creditors of the corporation also in her capacity as director (Art. 429(1), Japanese Companies Act). We will discuss these issues more broadly in Chapter 6.

* * *

In some countries, even if piercing based on general (and/or judge-made) principles is rare, piercing can be based on specific statutory provisions, for example in the case of a corporation with one single shareholder if certain rules concerning contributions and disclosure are not followed, or in the case of a controlling corporation that abuses its powers to the detriment of the creditors or minority shareholders of the subsidiary. In Germany and in Italy there are rules covering this particular case in the context of corporate groups. Probably the most important and well-known example of regulation of corporate groups, with provisions concerning the liability of the parent corporation, is the German *Konzernrecht*, which has inspired also several other systems, for example Portugal and Italy.

The doctrine of piercing the corporate veil has no statutory basis in German corporate law. However, the Imperial Court of Justice, and later the Federal Court of Justice developed some judge-made rules imposing liability on shareholders especially in small, closely held corporations or LLCs (*Gesellschaft mit beschränkter Haftung, GmbH*). One approach was based on the concept of under-capitalization (*Unterkapitalisierung*), which required that the corporation was founded with a complete insufficient amount of capital not reflecting the risks for the creditors in the light of the purpose of the corporation. The other approach was based on the concept of *Vermögensvermischung* (a sort of commingling of funds), under which a shareholder loses the privilege of limited liability when he did not keep his own assets and liabilities sufficiently separated from the ones of the corporation. This doctrine was based on the idea that a shareholder must treat the corporation as a separate entity. As you can see, these doctrines were not profoundly different from the ones developed in the U.S.

Starting in the 1980s, however, the Federal Court of Justice developed a different approach based on the statutory regulation of corporate groups, adopting the concept of *qualifiziert faktischer Konzern* ("qualified de facto corporate group") which by statute is limited to stock corporations. To understand this approach, we should mention that pursuant to the German statute on corporate groups corporations can execute (usually for tax purposes) a so-called "domination contract" (*Unternehmensverträge*) enabling the dominating entity to control the controlled corporation directly (§§ 291 ff. German Stock Corporation Act). In other words, one entity accepts, by contract, to be bound by the directives of another one (it should be noted that these types of contracts are not considered enforceable in other jurisdictions, for example in Italy, basically because they take away the managerial discretion of the directors of the dominated entity). To protect the creditors of the dominated entity, §§ 302 ff. of the German Stock Corporation Act state that the dominating entity has to compensate any loss (as stated in the balance sheet) of the controlled corporation due to the agreement. Although the scope of the provisions in the German Stock Corporation Act is limited to stock corporations, the Federal Court of Justice started to apply this rule extensively, especially to LLCs, when it recognized the existence of a "de facto group." The following case illustrates this idea.

TBB

German Federal Court of Justice, 1993
29 March 1993

Facts

The wife of the defendant was the sole shareholder of the *T. Baubetreuungsgesellschaft mit beschränkter Haftung* [closely held corporation] and the defendant its sole director. The defendant also conducted several businesses in his individual capacity. In addition the defendant and his wife were shareholders and directors of several other corporations engaged in the same construction projects. The plaintiff and the *T. Baubetreuungsgesellschaft mit beschränkter Haftung* entered into a contract for construction works to be performed by the plaintiff. The plaintiff and the *T. Baubetreuungsgesellschaft mit beschränkter Haftung* were the parties of this contract. After almost all of the construction of the defendant was performed, the *T. Baubetreuungsgesellschaft mit beschränkter Haftung* was not able to pay the plaintiff due to insufficient funds. As a consequence the plaintiff claims the amount of 54.875,31 DM from the defendant directly. The court of first instance [Regional Court or Laudgericht] granted the claim. The court of appeals (Oberlandesgericht) dismissed the defendant's claims.

Grounds

[. . .]

The first instance court granted the claims of the plaintiff against the defendant according to the case law of this *Senat* under the doctrine of the so called *qualifiziert faktischer Konzern* (qualified de facto group of companies) and the application to this situation of § 303 German Stock Corporation Act [pursuant to which creditors have specific protections where there is a contract of domination]. The lower court applied these principles even if the wife of the defendant was the sole shareholder of the *T. Baubetreuungsgesellschaft mit beschränkter Haftung* because the defendant, and not his wife, was in fact in charge of the company. [. . .]

According to the facts as stated liability of the defendant pursuant to § 303 German Stock Corporation Act cannot be denied. The defendant was an indirect shareholder of the *T. Baubetreuungsgesellschaft mit beschränkter Haftung* [. . .]

a) This *Senat* follows the leading opinion among legal scholars that under certain conditions of control minority shareholders and creditors of a controlled company are endangered and need protection. This protection is necessary since in the situation of a controlled company the interest of the (controlling) shareholders and the interest of the corporation are not in accordance anymore as it is the case of an independent corporation. In fact in these cases the majority shareholder has a different interest than the corporation itself which he can pursue due to his ability to influence the affairs of the corporation. This conflict of interest was the basis for the legislator to create a specific regulation for stock corporations in corporate groups (BGHZ 69, 334, 337). This idea also prompted the *Senat* to develop a specific legal regime for LLCs since these cases often involve this kind of corporation (BGHZ 95, 330, 334 f.).

The need for the development of a specific doctrine of liability in corporate groups for LLCs is based on the fact that in the case of a corporate group the dominating corporation usually does not interfere with the affairs of the controlled corporation on a continuous and intense basis. As a consequence, it is almost impossible to determine which single intervention of the dominating corporation damaged the controlled corporation. Therefore, the usual instruments of corporate law (liability for the violation of fiduciary duties, system of stated capital) and civil law (especially tort law) are not sufficient. Despite the criticism of legal scholars this *Senat* holds on to that principle.

b) The regime of liability in corporate groups does not depend on a certain corporate form of the controlling shareholder. The danger for the minority shareholders and the creditors of a controlled corporation does not depend on the fact that the corporation is controlled by another corporation or a natural person. As a consequence, also a natural person can be a controlling entity in the context of the regulation of corporate groups (BGHZ 69, 334, 338; BGHZ 95, 330, 337; BGHZ 115, 187, 189). The ratio for a specific law of corporate groups is not to generally exclude controlling shareholders from limited liability (*Wiedemann*, ZGR 1986,

656, 671), but to deal with the specific danger determined by a conflict of interest. Therefore the privilege of limited liability for natural persons forming a corporation cannot be applied . . .

[. . .]

However, a direct claim of the creditors of the corporation requires also that the controlling shareholder interferes with the affairs of the controlled corporation in an abusive way. This is the case when the controlling shareholder exercises his rights without considering the interest of the controlled corporation and the controlled corporation cannot be compensated adequately. A single shareholder abuses his powers when the corporation is forced to act not in its own interest but in the interest of the corporate group, and as a consequence is not able to pay its debts as they come due.

The case law of this *Senat* held that a claim can be granted under these principles when the controlling shareholder had a permanent and ongoing influence on the management of the controlled company (BGHZ 95, 330, 344). Moreover it held that the controlling shareholder had the burden of proof that the losses of the controlling corporation were not related to the influence of the controlling shareholder over the management of the controlled corporation (BGHZ 107, 7, 18; BGHZ 115, 187, 194). These decisions were interpreted in a way that the liability was based on the permanent and ongoing influence on the management of the controlled company, and that the successful proof of the missing impact of the influence on the losses . . . would only reduce the amount of the liability (BGHZ 107, 7, 18). However, it was not the intention of the court to establish such a doctrine. Liability requires not only permanent and ongoing influence on the management of the controlled company by the dominating company, but also an adverse impact on the interest of the controlled corporation.

This adverse impact on the interest of the controlled corporation cannot be assumed by the mere fact of a permanent and ongoing influence on the management of the controlled company by the dominating company [. . .]: additional proof is required. Otherwise the controlling shareholder would be liable also in cases where he actually did not neglect the interest of the controlled shareholder [. . .]

* * *

Later the concept of the so called *qualifiziert faktischer Konzern* [*qualified de facto corporate group*] was abandoned by the Federal Court of Justice in favor of another concept for piercing the corporate veil. This new concept was called *Existenzvernichtungshaftung* (try pronouncing that if you are not fluent in German!) and basically states that the shareholder of a corporation is personally liable when he appropriates assets of the corporation without properly considering the interest of the creditors (BGHZ 151, 181 ff.). Whereas the Federal Court of Justice originally did not state a specific legal basis for this doctrine, it later clarified that this concept is based on tort law. The following case discusses this approach.

TRIHOTEL

German Federal Court of Justice, 2007
16 July 2007

Facts

The plaintiff (a bankruptcy trustee) claims the payment of 713. 996,51 euro from the defendant according to the concept of *Existenzvernichtungshaftung*. The debtor (a German LLC [GmbH]) was founded in 1993 with a capital of 300,000 euro and leased a hotel from the defendant who was together with his wife the only shareholders of the debtor [that leased the hotel]. Later the lease contract was terminated and the defendant entered into another lease contract for the hotel with J.-corporation which was basically owned by the mother of the defendant who was also a director of the J.-corporation. Additionally the plaintiff and the J.-corporation executed a service contract under which the plaintiff would have managed the hotel (which was leased by J.-corporation) and received as compensation for these services 40% of the revenues. Moreover the contract stated the right of J.-corporation to reduce the compensation for the plaintiff. In the following years the plaintiff incurred significant losses. As a consequence, the contract was terminated and the hotel was managed only by J.-corporation [. . .]. Later the plaintiff filed for bankruptcy.

Grounds

[. . .] This *Senat* upholds the concept of *Existenzvernichtungshaftung* (developed to compensate shortcomings of the system of stated capital [see *Röhricht*, Festschrift 50 Jahre BGH volume I, p. 83, 92 ff.; *Röhricht*, ZIP 2005, 505, 514; *Hueck/Fastrich* in Baumbach/Hueck, GmbHG 18th edition, § 13 note 18; Zöllner, Festschrift Konzen, p. 1, 13 f.; *Dauner-Lieb*, DStR 2006, 2034, 2037]), under which a shareholder can be held liable for an abusive intervention in the affairs of the corporation without adequate compensation eventually triggering the bankruptcy of the corporation without properly considering the interest of the creditors.

However, this *Senat* abolishes the idea of an independent concept being based on the concept of an abuse of the legal form and being designed as direct liability of the shareholders to the creditors. Instead this *Senat* based liability solely on an abusive impairment of the corporate assets and considers this concept as an application of § 826 of the German Civil Code (*intentional damage contrary to public policy*)[1].

According to the recent case law of this *Senat* developing the so called *Existenzvernichtungshaftung* by abolishing the concept of the *qualifiziert faktischer Konzern* (*qualified de facto corporate group*), a shareholder can be held personally liable for the liabilities of the corporation if he appropriates assets from the corporation without properly considering the interest of the creditors. If he withdraws assets from the corporation and causes it to go bankrupt, he abuses the concept of limited liability. By doing so he loses the privilege of limited liability. He can only avoid liability if he proves that the corporation would have suffered the same consequences without the abusive conduct (BGHZ 149, 10 [*Bremer Vulkan*]; BGHZ 150, 61; BGH 151, 181 [*KBV*]).

A critical analysis of this concept shows [. . .] that it is justified in order to protect creditors since the system of capital maintenance often fails in these cases.

[. . .]

The determination of the legal basis for this concept and its limitation has to consider that the sole purpose of this concept is the protection of the assets of the corporation as they are necessary to pay the debts (*Röhricht*, ZIP 2004, 514). The *Existenzvernichtungshaftung* constitutes a violation of the duty of the shareholders to consider the interest of the creditors properly during the existence of the corporation. This duty is the logical consequence of the concept of limited liability (*Zöllner*, Festschrift Konzen, p. 1, 23).

However, this concept is based solely on the violation of this duty towards the creditors as a group and not on the impairment or the violation of single claims of creditors.

In contrast to the case law of this *Senat* it is not necessary to combine such an abuse of the corporate form with a complete loss of the privilege of limited liability (BGHZ 151, 181) because this would basically mean that the shareholders would be directly liable to the creditors as it is the case in a (commercial) partnership. Such a (direct) liability would constitute a constant danger that the courts would generally apply this concept which would lead to a *de facto* abolishment of the concept of limited liability for corporations.

The abusive impairment of the corporate assets in violation of the duty of the shareholders to consider the interest of the creditors properly during the existence of the corporation does not constitute an abuse of the

---

[1]   § 826 German Civil Code states:
"A person who, in a manner contrary to public policy, intentionally inflicts damage on another person is liable to the other person to make compensation for the damage."

legal form and therefore does not have to be applied solely when the corporate form is founded or constantly abused by closing a contract with a creditor (*Zöllner*, Festschrift Konzen, p. 1, 23). As a consequence this concept can only establish a compensatory claim of the corporation itself and not for each single creditor as the corporation itself suffers directly consequences of the violation of the duty. In this regard, the concept of *Existenzvernichtungshaftung* constitutes an amendment to the system of stated capital and provides a sufficient protection for creditors in the cases where the system of stated capital usually fails. Consequently, the limits for distributions to shareholders as set by the system of stated capital are not the only limits when it comes to the transfer of assets from the corporation to shareholders. In fact also the *Existenzvernichtungshaftung* constitutes a limitation in this regard.

[. . .]

NOTES AND QUESTIONS

1.   As a curiosity, note that these German cases do not indicate the names of the parties. In some countries published cases omit, at least sometimes, the names of the parties.

2.   Let's try to summarize this somehow complex development of German law in this area. Basically, at first German courts adopted an approach that would allow piercing based on undercapitalization and commingling of funds, not profoundly different from the U.S. approach. Starting in the 1980s, however, a new approach was developed through case law. It was based on the application of a statutory provision to de facto groups. The statutory provision is §§ 302 f. of the German Stock Corporation Act, pursuant to which a corporation that has entered into a "dominating contract" with another one, can be held liable for the debts of the latter. Courts started applying this rule, regulating joint-stock corporations, also to LLCs in situations of de facto control. The first case illustrates this approach. The second and more recent case shows a different approach, holding that shareholders' liability can be based on a wrongful appropriation of corporate assets, and grounds this liability in (general) tort law. This approach is much narrower and, as the Court in the second case votes, it is basically a way to protect the assets and the capital of the controlled corporation against illegal "distributions" to shareholders. What do you think is the rationale for these rules as compared with common law concepts of piercing the corporate veil? Do you see more similarities or differences? Do these doctrines seem precisely defined by the courts?

3.   What is a "domination contract" or *Unternehmensverträge* under German law? If you do not know, you can research it before class!

4.   In the *TBB*-case the Federal Court of Justice held that liability of a shareholder for the debts of a corporation should be based on two elements: (1) a permanent and continuous influence on the management of the

controlled company by the controlling shareholder; and (2) an adverse impact on the interests of the controlled corporation. What could such an adverse impact be? Can you make some examples? Imagine that a controlled corporation suffers a damage due to the fact that it is controlled by another one, but also receives some advantages. For example, the controlling corporation forces the purchase of goods at a price above market value, but on the other hand also allows the controlled corporation to obtain a loan at a particularly low interest rate, that it would not be able to obtain otherwise. Do you think the damages should be compensated with the advantages? What about future advantages derived from the group structure not realized yet? Can they be relevant to avoid liability? (Hint: consider § 311 of the German Aktiengesetz)

5.   In the *Trihotel*-case the Federal Court of Justice bases piercing the corporate veil on general tort law. What could the consequences of this approach in the context of private international law be?

6.   In several legal systems, including Germany, Portugal, and Italy, liability of a controlling corporation can also be based on other, specific statutory provisions. For example, under Article 2497 ff. of the Italian Civil Code, a controlling corporation that exercises a dominating influence on a controlled corporation can be held liable toward the creditors and the minority shareholders of the latter if it "abuses its powers" and causes a damage to the controlled corporation. Except in fairly egregious circumstances, however, it can be difficult for creditors and minority shareholders to demonstrate the elements of this liability, not only for substantive reasons, but also for procedural ones. For example, in most civil law jurisdictions "U.S.-style discovery," i.e., obtaining from the opposite party in a litigation all the documents and information related to the lawsuit, is not allowed, and basically the plaintiff must look for evidence in other ways. Can you see why without discovery it can be particularly difficult for creditors and minority shareholders to sustain their claims in these situations?

* * *

A very interesting example of rules concerning veil piercing is offered by Chinese law, a country whose legal system is difficult to pigeonhole, but that could fairly be considered closer to the civil law tradition than to the common law tradition (even if, to be sure, some recent reforms have been inspired, at least partially, by U.S. law, as we will see below specifically on veil piercing). Before 2005, when a new corporate statute was enacted, there were no statutory provisions governing veil piercing, and courts had timidly and occasionally held shareholders, and in particular a parent corporation, liable for the debts of a controlled corporation. In those early cases, however, "piercing" was generally allowed when the rules concerning minimum legal capital were not followed (*see* Jiang Yu Wang, *Company Law in China: Regulation of Business Organizations in a Socialist Market Economy*, Edward Elgar Publishing, 2014, 80). Strictly speaking, therefore, those were not really cases of veil piercing, but rather sanctions for the violations of the rules protecting legal capital. In 2005, however, the new corporate law statute included a quite rare provision for civil law systems, which opens the door to a factual analysis not dissimilar to the doctrine of veil piercing in common law systems. This seems also to indicate the influence of common law in the regulation of corporations in China.

The new Article 20 of the Chinese Company Act states that: "Any of the shareholders of a company who abuses the independent legal person status of the company and the limited liability of the shareholders to evade the payment of the company's debts, thus seriously damaging the interests of the company's creditors, shall bear joint liabilities for the debts of the company." The provision seems therefore to require three elements: an abuse of the corporate structure, the intent to avoid the payment of debts, and a significant prejudice to creditors. It is not easy to predict how these elements will be interpreted and applied, but it definitely appears that most of the usual elements considered in piercing, such as undercapitalization, commingling of funds, and lack of corporate formalities, might be relevant in the analysis (for additional information *see* Jiang Yu Wang, *Company Law in China: Regulation of Business Organizations in a Socialist Market Economy*, Edward Elgar Publishing, 2014, 81 f.).

SOME FINAL CONSIDERATIONS ON VEIL PIERCING: EMPIRICAL EVIDENCE AND CONFLICT OF LAWS

Let's go back, for a moment, to the United States. How common is it to successfully pierce the corporate veil and under which circumstances do courts tend to pierce?

In a 1991 article, Professor Robert B. Thompson conducted an empirical analysis of about 1,600 cases on veil piercing (Robert B. Thompson, *Piercing the Corporate Veil: An Empirical Study*, 76 CORNELL L. REV. 1036 (1991)). Although subsequent studies, including an update of this first work by Thompson himself, have clarified additional details (and in some cases questioned some of the empirical results), the 1991 study still offers the occasion to discuss some important elements of veil piercing. We indicate hereinafter some elaborations based on the data presented by Professor Thompson that offer material for a classroom discussion.

In a total of over almost 1,600 cases litigated through 1985, courts found for the plaintiffs and pierced the corporate veil in roughly 40% of the situations. This data indicates that the possibility of shareholders' liability is far from negligible in the U.S. Courts are slightly more inclined to pierce when the shareholder is an individual (43% of the cases), rather than when it is another corporation (37% of the cases). This is not surprising because commingling of funds and lack of corporate formalities are much more common when the shareholder is an individual. Interestingly enough, the lower the number of shareholders, the more courts are inclined to pierce: the veil was pierced in 50% of the cases involving a corporation with one single shareholder, 46% of the cases when there were two or four shareholders, 35% of the cases when more than three shareholders were present, and never in situations involving a publicly held corporation. Can you comment on these data? Does this information make sense? Can you argue that when more shareholders are present, they can control each other, and therefore abuse such as commingling of funds is less common? Can you argue, therefore, that the presence of a multitude of shareholders indirectly protects creditors? Is it surprising to you that the veil is never pierced in listed corporations?

One of the most interesting pieces of evidence concerns a correlation between veil piercing and the underlying substantive claim. According to Thompson, courts are more inclined to pierce when the plaintiff is a creditor based on a contract, rather than when he is the victim of a tort. As observed by Thompson himself, this is quite surprising because it could be argued that creditors in contract have the opportunity to collect information on the corporation, and therefore decide whether to rely only on the financial resources of the corporation, while creditors in tort are not "voluntary" creditors. Principles of fairness might suggest that piercing should be easier for the victims of a tort. Can you elaborate on this information? What might be the reasons why contractual creditors are, on average, more successful in piercing? Could the reason be that they are often sophisticated creditors (for example, banks or providers), and also tend to be sophisticated (and wealthy) plaintiffs, with good lawyers?

Especially in an international setting, piercing the veil raises the question of which law should be applied. This question should be framed in the context of our discussion, in Chapter 2, of the applicable corporate law. Generally speaking piercing the veil deals with shareholders' liability, and should be considered part of the internal affairs of a corporation. As a consequence, the laws applicable to the corporation should also govern the issue of veil piercing. For example, in the U.S., a system based on the incorporation theory, the decision on whether to pierce the veil of a California corporation should be resolved in the light of California law. This, however, is not always the case. Some courts, especially in tort cases, apply the substantive law of the jurisdiction where the tort occurred. In other words, veil piercing is not considered part of the internal affairs of a corporation. What do you think about this question? What do you think are the pros and cons of the two different approaches, from a policy perspective?

In an international context you should also always keep in mind problems concerning the possible enforcement of a judgment. A decision in favor of piercing, obtained in a jurisdiction in which the doctrine is well-established, might be difficult to enforce against a foreign defendant who has assets in a country in which the corporate veil is rarely pierced. Veil piercing, in fact, in some systems might be regarded as such a departure from the principle of limited liability that it would be considered against public policy (for some observations on enforcement of foreign judgments, *see* Chapter 12).

CHAPTER 4

FINANCING THE CORPORATION

■ ■ ■

INTRODUCTION

This chapter discusses selected issues concerning the financial structure of the corporation. There are, of course, almost endless instruments to provide the corporation with the funds it needs to carry on its business: equity (shares), debt in the form of bonds and debentures (securities representing a loan, generally issued and distributed to a large number of investors; for the sake of brevity we will refer to these instruments as "bonds"), financial loans obtained from banks and other intermediaries and third parties, commercial loans obtained from providers, and so on. We will focus our attention on shares and bonds, but also briefly discuss one important issue concerning equitable subordination of shareholders' loans.

Needless to say, the basic distinction between shares and bonds is that shareholders are residual claimants of the corporation, and they risk losing their investment and not obtaining any dividend if the corporation is in financial distress, while bondholders generally have a contractual right to receive interest and the principal. For this reason, shareholders have more significant administrative rights, in particular voting rights to appoint and remove directors, while bondholders have limited powers to interfere with corporate decisions, and their rights are primarily protected contractually. Financial innovation has, however, somehow blurred the distinctions between these securities. For example, a corporation can issue subordinated bonds, for which the repayment of the principal is conditioned on the prior payment of other creditors, or that pay a variable interest rate based on the economic performance of the corporation. In terms of financial risk, these instruments can be more similar to shares. Conversely, shares with enhanced economic rights, such as a minimum dividend, can be issued, making the shareholders' position potentially more secure. Similarly, in terms of administrative rights, there might be shares with limited or no voting rights, and in some legal systems it is possible to issue bonds with voting rights. Additionally, bond indentures (the contracts regulating bonds) often provide covenants that significantly restrict the freedom of directors to adopt certain decisions, for example distributing dividends or seeking additional credit.

Be aware, however, that different legal rights are relevant only when there is a chance of enforcement. For example, the contractual right of a bondholder to the repayment of the principal has very little meaning or consequence, economically, if the corporation is insolvent and does not have the funds to make any payment.

In 1958, Franco Modigliani and Merton Miller, two finance scholars, published a groundbreaking paper on the financial structure of the corporation, introducing the "Capital Structure Irrelevance Principle" (the article, entitled "The Cost of Capital, Corporation Finance and the Theory of Investment" was published in 48 AMERICAN ECONOMIC REVIEW 261 (1958)). They both won the Nobel Prize for this contribution. In short, the Modigliani-Miller theorem posits that in an efficient market, in the absence of asymmetric information, agency costs, taxes, and bankruptcy costs, the value of a firm is unaffected by how it is financed (for example, the balance between shares and bonds), and its dividend policy. Of course in the real world the limit of the theorem is that the hypotheses on which it is based are totally unrealistic: taxes, bankruptcy, agency costs, and information asymmetries exist, and market efficiency is highly debatable. Consequently, the reality is that financial decisions have a profound impact on the value and profitability of the corporation.

The chapter is organized as follows. First, we will discuss classes of shares, focusing on the flexibility existing in different jurisdictions for creating categories of shares with different economic and administrative rights. We will also consider some important protections for shareholders, and specifically pre-emptive rights in case of issuing of new shares, and class voting. Second, we will concentrate on selected problems concerning bonds: different legal strategies used to protect bondholders, statutory limits to the issuance of bonds (when present), and interpretation of the bond indenture. Finally, we will illustrate the problem of equitable subordination of shareholders' loans.

THE RIGHTS OF SHAREHOLDERS AND CLASSES OF SHARES

Common shares, also sometimes called ordinary shares, are the "plain vanilla" type of securities representing an equity interest in a corporation. These shares generally grant full administrative and economic rights to the holders.

More specifically, even if there are differences among different jurisdictions, common shareholders can vote in the general shareholders' meeting on the election and removal of board members and also on the appointment and removal of the board of supervisors, in systems where this corporate body is present. They also vote on amendments to the governing documents of the corporation, and in particular on financial transactions such as mergers and issuing of new, non-authorized shares. Depending on the legal system considered, the shareholders' meeting can have broader or narrower competences. As a rough rule-of-thumb, it can be said that in civil law countries, often characterized by a more concentrated ownership structure and strong controlling shareholders, shareholders have more powers, while in common law systems, especially in listed corporations with a widespread ownership structure, the board of directors enjoys more extensive powers (remember what we mentioned in the last paragraph of Chapters 1). For example, the power to amend the bylaws can also be given to directors, and in some jurisdictions a lawsuit of the corporation against the directors for breach of their fiduciary duties must be approved by the shareholders, even if often shareholders can also bring a derivative lawsuit on behalf of the corporation (we will discuss this in Chapter 7). Of course, the actual power of a shareholder also depends on rules concerning the quorum and majority rules applicable to the resolutions of the shareholders' meeting.

The most important economic rights are the right to obtain dividends, if declared by the corporation and subject to limitations intended to protect creditors; in addition shareholders are "residual claimants" of the corporation, in the sense that they are entitled to receive what is left (if anything) after the creditors have been paid in full in case of voluntary liquidation or insolvency. Common shareholders (but also other shareholders) can also enjoy a pre-emptive right in case of issuance of new shares: the shares must be first offered to old shareholders, and only if they do not buy them, the shares can be sold to third parties. In some systems pre-emptive rights are mandatory (generally in the U.K. and in the European Union, also due to a E.U. directive), and can only be excluded under limited circumstances; while in other systems (generally in the U.S.) they are not available as a default rule, unless the governing documents grant pre-emptive rights to shareholders.

The quite broad administrative rights of common stockholders are justified, from an economic standpoint, exactly by the fact that they are residual claimants, and that they bear the risk of not receiving dividends and/or losing their investment.

In order to raise capital at better conditions, however, corporations are also allowed to create different classes or categories of shares with different economic and administrative rights. The corporation can for instance create shares with limited voting rights (for example, voting only on amendments to the governing documents) or no voting rights, but with stronger economic rights (a minimum dividend). Or, in some jurisdictions, multiple-voting shares can be issued. A peculiar type of shares worth mentioning are "tracking stock": as the name suggests, these are shares that "track" a particular division of the corporation, and pay dividends based on the economic results only of that division, not of the corporation as a whole. This might be, in theory, an interesting technique to unlock hidden value, because if there are investors only interested in one particular business of the corporation, with certain financial characteristics in terms of risk and return, they might be willing to pay relatively more for shares whose value only depends on the success of that business. A similar result could be obtained by incorporating the division as a separate corporation issuing shares, but tracking stock avoids the administrative and organizational costs of setting up a separate corporation. Even if they have been used by some large multi-divisional corporations, such as Coca Cola, tracking shares have not been particularly successful because they raise delicate accounting problems in precisely identifying the result of the tracked division (think, for example, to the allocation of common fixed costs), and because they might raise conflicts of interests (directors and controlling shareholders might want to favor one division over another one).

The creation of different classes of shares raises issues because it can alter the proportionality between investment and administrative and economic rights, and in terms of equal treatment and protections of the holders of the different shares. The following are the relevant statutory provisions regulating the creation of different classes of shares under New York and Italian law. Compare and contrast them.

New York Business Corporation Law § 501—Authorized Shares

(a) Every corporation shall have power to create and issue the number of shares stated in its certificate of incorporation. Such shares may be all of one class or may be divided into two or more classes. Each class shall consist of either shares with par value or shares without par value, having such designation and such relative voting, dividend, liquidation and other rights, preferences and limitations, consistent with this chapter, as shall be stated in the certificate of incorporation. The certificate of incorporation may deny, limit or otherwise define the voting rights and may limit or otherwise define the dividend or liquidation rights of shares of any class, but no such denial, limitation or definition of voting rights shall be effective unless at the time one or more classes of outstanding shares or bonds, singly or in the aggregate, are entitled to full voting rights, and no such limitation or definition of dividend or liquidation rights shall be effective unless at the time one or more classes of outstanding shares, singly or in the aggregate, are entitled to unlimited dividend and liquidation rights. (b) If the shares are divided into two or more classes, the shares of each class shall be designated to distinguish them from the shares of all other classes. Shares which are entitled to preference in the distribution of dividends or assets shall not be designated as common shares. Shares which are not entitled to preference in the distribution of dividends or assets shall be common shares, even if identified by a class or other designation, and shall not be designated as preferred shares.

Italian Civil Code Article 2351—Voting Rights

1.　Each share grants the right to vote.

2.　With the exception of provisions in separate statutes, the bylaws can allow the issuance of shares without voting rights, with voting rights limited to specific decisions, with voting rights conditioned upon specific events not merely depending on the will of a party. The amount of limited voting shares cannot exceed half of the capital.

3.　The bylaws can provide for limitations to the voting rights of a single shareholder independently from the amount of shares owned, or scaling voting rights.

4.　In the absence of special provisions, the bylaws can allow the issuance of multiple-voting shares also with respect to specific decisions or conditioned upon specific events not merely depending on the will of a party. Each multiple-voting share can attribute a maximum of three votes.

NOTES AND QUESTIONS

1.　A cursory review of these provisions suggests that the New York provision (quite representative of similar rules in other states) is more flexible in allowing the creation of different classes of shares than its Italian corresponding rule. In the U.S., however, additional limitations are provided, for example, by stock exchange rules for listed corporations, as we will discuss below.

2.　Let's focus on the somehow more restrictive Italian provision. The law provides that limited voting shares cannot exceed half of the capital. Similar restrictions are present in other states: in France nonvoting shares cannot exceed 25% of the capital in public limited liability companies, in Japan 50%. What do you think is the rationale of these rules? Hint: does it depends on the risk of entrenchment of controlling shareholders? And/or on the desirability of a certain proportionality between financial investment and administrative powers? In order to discuss where the limit should be set, consider the example of Brazil. In Brazil, until 2001, publicly held corporations could issue non-voting shares up to 2/3 of the capital. In 2001 a new statute limited the threshold to 1/2 (even if with some exceptions for existing corporations). What is interesting to note, however, is that empirical studies show that also under the more liberal regime, the average corporation would have 53% of its capital composed by voting shares, and only 47% by non-voting shares (*see* É. Gorga, *Direito Societário Atual*, Elsevier, 2013, 146 f.). This seems to indicate that even when legally permissible, to issue more than half of the shares without voting rights is not desirable. Can you offer a possible explanation for this? Do you think this empirical evidence tells us something cynical about the adoption, by the legislature, of a 50% cap to limited voting shares?

3.   Why do you think a shareholder could be interested in buying limited voting shares? Note that under Italian law, when issuing limited voting shares, no additional economic right is mandated by law, but it is possible that the corporation can attach augmented economic rights to limited voting shares. Can you imagine investors not interested in participating in the governance of the corporation, but interested in enhanced economic protections? In a listed corporation, in case of a hostile takeover, would limited voting shares appreciate as full voting shares? Why?

4.   Can you imagine a situation in which it could be interesting to issue shares that vote only if certain conditions are met, for example if the economic and financial situation of the corporation deteriorates? Which investors might be interested in a similar financial instrument?

5.   Paragraph 3 of Article 2351 of the Italian Civil Code contains a peculiar provision. Voting caps might work as follows: independently from the number of shares you own, the maximum number of voting rights that each shareholder can exercise are capped at 10% of the outstanding shares. This provision would include an element of "democracy" in the shareholders' meeting, in the sense that the voting power of each shareholder is not entirely proportional to her investment. Scaling voting rights means that, for example, up to 20% of the shares each shareholder has one vote per share, from 20% to 40% only one vote per two shares, and over 40% only one vote per three shares. What is the goal of these provisions?

6.   An interesting provision is Paragraph 4 of Article 2351 of the Italian Civil Code, regulating multiple-voting shares. Until 2014, multiple-voting shares were prohibited under Italian law. The principle has however been called into question, also in order to create an incentive for going public. After the 2014 amendments, somehow simplifying, closely held corporations can issue multiple-voting shares (up to three votes per shares). Listed corporations, pursuant to Articles 127-quinquies and 127-sexies of the Consolidated Law on Financial Markets, cannot issue multiple-voting shares. They can, however, issue "loyalty shares" similar to the ones available in France: these are shares whose owner obtains double voting rights if they are held continuously for a two-year period by the same shareholder. The goal, clearly, is to favor long-term investors. On the other hand, somehow similarly to the U.S., corporations that have issued multiple-voting shares *before* going public can keep them also after they are listed. Can you explain why these provisions might push more corporations to go public? (For more on multiple-voting shares, see M. Ventoruzzo, *The Disappearing Taboo of Multiple Voting*

Shares: Regulatory Responses to the Migration of Chrysler-Fiat, ECGI Law
Working Paper No. 288/2015, available on *www.ssrn.com*).

7. Empirical evidence on the desirability of multiple-voting shares,
and more generally dual-class structures, is mixed and not entirely
conclusive. Several studies seem to suggest that dual-class structures reduce
the value of the corporation, reduce possible returns for shareholders (also in
the long-term), increase the cost of capital, and foster conflicts of interests
and the ability of controlling shareholders and managers to extract private
benefits from the corporation. Other contributions, however, appear to
contradict the argument that diversions from one-share, one-vote are
damaging for investors. Some scholars have, for example, found positive
abnormal returns for corporations that have adopted dual-class structures.
Corporations in certain industries and with certain features seem to
gravitate more toward the use of multiple-voting shares, especially in the
U.S., than others. Those are news and media corporations, high-tech
corporations, and fashion corporations. There are two possible explanations.
One is that often corporations in these industries, for self-evident reasons,
are founded and develop under the leadership of charismatic and skilled
entrepreneurs (think of Larry Paige and Sergey Brin for Google, which went
public in 2004 with multiple-voting shares), who do not want to lose control
by going public, and therefore use multiple-voting shares. Investors, on the
other hand, might want, or at least accept, that the founders remain in
control in the light of their technical, creative or managerial abilities. The
other possible reason for the use of multiple-voting shares in these industries
is that in these sectors the "private benefits of control" that controlling
shareholders want to exploit might be particularly significant, and here
consider the political and social influence of news and media corporations.

* * *

Since the beginning of the twentieth-century, U.S.-listed corporations
issued limited voting shares or nonvoting shares that allowed some
shareholders, holding full voting shares, to retain control of the
corporation even with a minority stake. Pundits and public opinion were
strongly against this practice, but at first most U.S. stock exchanges
allowed it. In 1926, however, the New York Stock Exchange (NYSE)
refused to list nonvoting shares issued by Fox Theaters Corporation. In
the following decades, possibly also as a reaction to the climate following
the Great Depression, the New York Stock Exchange confirmed and
expanded its policy in favor of the "one share, one vote" principle. Other
financial markets competing with the NYSE to attract issuers, such as
Nasdaq or Amex had, however, a more liberal approach with respect to
limited voting shares and dual class stock, and in the 1980s the NYSE
started to reconsider its policy. The NYSE was, in particular, worried that
some large corporations (for example, General Motors) would delist from
the NYSE and trade their shares on a different exchange. In 1986,

therefore, the NYSE submitted to the SEC an amendment to its listing rules that would allow listing dual class stock.

In retrospect, this episode can be seen as an interesting example of regulatory competition not among states (as we have discussed in Chapter 2), but among stock exchanges: it's up to you to decide whether this was a race to the top or to the bottom.

The SEC did not remain idle. Concerned that dual class shares could result in an inefficient separation between ownership and control, it enacted Rule 19c–4 in 1988. Even if the rule did not rigidly adopt the one share, one vote principle, it significantly restricted the ability of listed corporations to issue shares with different and disproportionate voting rights or to change the voting rights of outstanding shares.

The rule was short-lived. The Business Roundtable, an association of executives of large corporations, challenged it in court. The following case is the decision of the D.C. Court of Appeals in this matter.

THE BUSINESS ROUNDTABLE V. SECURITIES AND EXCHANGE COMMISSION

United States Court of Appeals, District of Columbia Circuit
905 F.2d 406 (1990)

STEPHEN F. WILLIAMS, CIRCUIT JUDGE:

In 1984 General Motors announced a plan to issue a second class of common stock with one-half vote per share. The proposal collided with a longstanding rule of the New York Stock Exchange that required listed companies to provide one vote per share of common stock. The NYSE balked at enforcement, and after two years filed a proposal with the Securities and Exchange Commission to relax its own rule. The SEC did not approve the rule change but responded with one of its own. On July 7, 1988, it adopted Rule 19c–4, barring national securities exchanges and national securities associations, together known as self-regulatory organizations (SROs), from listing stock of a corporation that takes any corporate action "with the effect of nullifying, restricting or disparately reducing the per share voting rights of [existing common stockholders]." . . . The rule prohibits such "disenfranchisement" even where approved by a shareholder vote conducted on one share/one vote principles. Because the rule directly controls the substantive allocation of powers among classes of shareholders, we find it in excess of the Commission's authority under § 19 of the Securities Exchange Act of 1934, as amended (the "Exchange Act"), 15 U.S.C. § 78s (1988). Neither the wisdom of the requirement, nor of its being imposed at the federal level, is here in question.

[. . .]

On the matter before us, the SEC's authority, the academic commentary has been far more mixed, perhaps leaning to the negative. See Dent, 54 Geo.Wash.L.Rev. at 726–37 (Commission lacks authority); Comment, Rule 19c–4: The SEC Goes Too Far in Adopting a One Share, One Vote Rule, 83 Nw. U. L. Rev. 1057 (1989) (same); Richard A. Booth, The Problem With Federal Tender Offer Law, 77 Cal. L. Rev. 707, 760 n. 154 (1989) (Commission's authority is "questionable" because the rule does not further a purpose of the Exchange Act). Even proponents of the merits of the Rule generally concede that Commission's authority is uncertain. See Seligman, 54 Geo. Wash. L. Rev. at 714–19 (arguing the Exchange Act "probably empowers the SEC" to adopt such a rule, but conceding that the interpretation of the relevant statutory sections "is not free from doubt" and that a narrow reading of the key § 14 is "arguable"). At the very least, proponents concede the Commission's exercise of this authority is "unprecedented regulation of corporate governance." Roberta S. Karmel, Qualitative Standards for "Qualified Securities": SEC Regulation of Voting Rights, 36 Cath. U. L.Rev. 809, 831 (1987).

In conducting our review, we assume that we owe the Commission deference under Chevron U.S.A. Inc. v. NRDC, 467 U.S. 837, 104 S.Ct. 2778, 81 L.Ed.2d 694 (1984), even though the case might be characterized as involving a limit on the SEC's jurisdiction.

What then are the "purposes" of the Exchange Act? The Commission supports Rule 19c–4 as advancing the purposes of a variety of sections, see Final Rule, 53 Fed.Reg. at 26,390/1, but we first take its strongest— § 14's grant of power to regulate the proxy process. The Commission finds a purpose "to ensure fair shareholder suffrage." See Final Rule, 53 Fed.Reg. at 26,391/2. Indeed, it points to the House Report's declarations that "[f]air corporate suffrage is an important right," H.R.Rep. No. 1383, 73d Cong., 2d Sess. 13 (1934) ("1934 House Report"), and that "use of the exchanges should involve a corresponding duty of according to shareholders fair suffrage," id. at 14. The formulation is true in the sense that Congress's decision can be located under that broad umbrella.

But unless the legislative purpose is defined by reference to the means Congress selected, it can be framed at any level of generality—to improve the operation of capital markets, for instance. In fact, although § 14(a) broadly bars use of the mails (and other means) "to solicit . . . any proxy" in contravention of Commission rules and regulations, it is not seriously disputed that Congress's central concern was with disclosure. See J.I. Case Co. v. Borak, 377 U.S. 426, 431, 84 S.Ct. 1555, 1559, 12 L.Ed.2d 423 (1964) ("The purpose of § 14(a) is to prevent management or others from obtaining authorization for corporate action by means of deceptive or inadequate disclosure in proxy solicitation."); see also Santa Fe Industries, Inc. v. Green, 430 U.S. 462, 477–78, 97 S.Ct. 1292, 1302–04, 51 L.Ed.2d 480 (1977) (emphasizing Exchange Act's philosophy of full disclosure and dismissing the fairness of the terms of the transaction as "at most a tangential concern of the statute" once full and fair disclosure has occurred).

While the House Report indeed speaks of fair corporate suffrage, it also plainly identifies Congress's target—the solicitation of proxies by well informed insiders "without fairly informing the stockholders of the purposes for which the proxies are to be used." 1934 House Report at 14. The Senate Report contains no vague language about "corporate suffrage," but rather explains the purpose of the proxy protections as ensuring that stockholders have "adequate knowledge" about the "financial condition of the corporation . . . [and] the major questions of policy, which are decided at stockholders' meetings." S.Rep. No. 792, 73d Cong., 2d Sess. 12 (1934) ("1934 Senate Report"). Finally, both reports agree on the power that the proxy sections gave the Commission—"power to control the conditions under which proxies may be solicited." 1934 House Report at 14. See also 1934 Senate Report at 12 (similar language).

That proxy regulation bears almost exclusively on disclosure stems as a matter of necessity from the nature of proxies. Proxy solicitations are, after all, only communications with potential absentee voters. The goal of federal proxy regulation was to improve those communications and thereby to enable proxy voters to control the corporation as effectively as they might have by attending a shareholder meeting. Id. See also S.Rep. No. 1455, 73d Cong., 2d Sess. 74 (1934); Sheldon E. Bernstein and Henry G. Fischer, The Regulation of the Solicitation of Proxies: Some Reflections on Corporate Democracy, 7 U. Chi. L. Rev. 226, 227–28 (1940).

We do not mean to be taken as saying that disclosure is necessarily the sole subject of § 14. See Louis Loss, Fundamentals of Securities Regulation 452–53 (1988) (asserting that § 14 is not limited to ensuring disclosure), quoted in Final Rule, 53 Fed.Reg. at 26,391 n. 163; Karmel, 36 Cath. U.L.Rev. at 824 (similar). But see also Dent, 54 Geo. Wash. L. Rev. at 733–34 (§ 14 is primarily if not exclusively directed at disclosure); Comment, 83 Nw. U. L. Rev. at 1071 (similar). For example, the Commission's Rule 14a–4(b)(2) requires a proxy to provide some mechanism for a security holder to withhold authority to vote for each nominee individually. See 17 CFR § 240.14a–4(b)(2). It thus bars a kind of electoral tying arrangement, and may be supportable as a control over management's power to set the voting agenda, or, slightly more broadly, voting procedures. See generally, Dennis C. Mueller, Public Choice 38–58 (1979) (noting that difficulties inherent to majority voting, such as logrolling and cycling (in which different outcomes can be produced as coalitions reshape on successive votes), can increase the power of the agenda setter and lead to results that decrease the welfare of the voting community). But while Rule 14a–4(b)(2) may lie in a murky area between substance and procedure, Rule 19c–4 much more directly interferes with the substance of what the shareholders may enact. It prohibits certain reallocations of voting power and certain capital structures, even if approved by a shareholder vote subject to full disclosure and the most exacting procedural rules. See Voting Rights Listing Standards; Disenfranchisement Rule, 52 Fed.Reg. 23,665, 23,672/1 (1987) ("Proposed Rule"); Final Rule, 53 Fed.Reg. at 26,385/1–2.

[. . .]

At least one Commissioner [stated that] "[s]ection 19(c) does not provide the Commission carte blanche to adopt federal corporate governance standards through the back door by mandating uniform listing standards." Final Rule, 53 Fed.Reg. at 26,395/1 (Grundfest, Comm'r, concurring). See also Seligman, 54 Geo. Wash. L. Rev. at 715 (§ 19(c) "does not appear to authorize the SEC to amend SRO rules for the purpose of establishing a comprehensive federal corporation act (covering such matters as the number of directors or how many shall be outsiders)"). We read the Act as reflecting a clear congressional determination not to make any such broad delegation of power to the Commission.

[. . .]

The petition for review is granted and Rule 19c–4 is vacated.

NOTES AND QUESTIONS

1.　The Court argues that the SEC does not have the power, under the Federal Securities Laws, to regulate corporate governance issues such as the one addressed by Rule 19c–4. One possible source of this power that the Court discusses is the regulation of proxy voting, but the Court seems to conclude that the power of the Commission to regulate proxy voting is generally limited to disclosure or procedural issues. The Court appears skeptical of the development of a federal corporate law, especially in the absence of explicit Congressional intent. How do you think this position of the Court relates to the phenomenon of regulatory competition among States in corporate law? As you consider this issue, the excerpt from the article by Mark Roe included in Chapter 2 might be particularly helpful.

2.　The SEC lost a battle, but probably not the war. Also through its powers of "moral suasion," it convinced the stock exchanges to introduce limitations to dual-class recapitalizations just a few months after this decision. Currently, therefore, while a corporation can adopt dual-class shares structure before it goes public, once it is listed there are limitations to "dual class recapitalizations" and to the possibility to diverge from the one share, one vote principle.

3.　You have probably noticed that the opinion of the Court contains references to scholarly works. In some systems, courts are more reluctant to cite (and sometimes formally prohibited from citing) legal scholars. What do you think of these different approaches? What might be the rationale for avoiding citations to law review articles and scholarly books?

4.   The Canadian experience is worth mentioning, also in light of the ties that link the U.S. and Canada. Dual-class structures are used in Canada. According to a 2006 paper, approximately 6.5% of the roughly 1,450 corporations listed on the Toronto Stock Exchange; the leverage allowed by superior-voting shares in these companies is also quite significant: the median controlling shareholder has 4.83 more votes than the equity owned (in other words, for example, with 10% of the capital it is possible to control almost 50% of the votes). It should be noted that in 1987 the Toronto Stock Exchange provided that tender offers aimed at acquiring control should be extended at the same conditions also to shares with inferior voting rights, a sort of coattail provision (coattail provisions, generally, mandate that in case of takeover holders of restricted-voting shares can convert their shares into full-voting ones). One of the consequences of this approach is that superior-voting shares are traded at a fairly limited premium over inferior-voting ones. Can you explain the rationale of this rule, its effects on market prices, and discuss if it is desirable? Should a similar rule always be enacted when shares with disproportionate voting rights can be issued by listed corporations? What are the pros and cons of coattail provisions in this area? (For further information on the Canadian case, and some interesting data, *see* Yvan Allaire, *Dual-Class Shares in Canada: Some Modest Proposals* (2006), available on *www.ssrn.com*).

5.   Based on the arguments used in *Business Roundtable v. SEC*, above, do you think the S.E.C. in the U.S. could mandate a coattail provision similar to the one required in 1987 by the Toronto Stock Exchange (see point 4 above)? Why yes or why not?

6.   Some argue that multiple voting shares should be allowed at the IPO stage, when investors are fully informed about the voting structure of the corporation and can freely decide whether to invest, but should not be permitted after the corporation has been listed. It has also been suggested that there should be a mandatory "sunset" provision, meaning a rule that eliminates superior-voting rights after a certain period, for example three years from the listing. What do you think of a similar proposal? If you were the legislature of a country, or the head of the regulatory agency in charge of financial markets, would you consider adopting a similar rule (assuming you have the power to do so)?

* * *

We have seen above that the Italian legislature provides for several limitations to the issuing of different classes of shares, even if it has recently abolished the pre-existing absolute prohibition of multiple-voting shares. But what is the situation in Europe and other systems more generally with respect to listed corporations? In several countries multiple-voting shares, with some limitations, are allowed, in others they are not. Also with respect to nonvoting shares the situation varies from jurisdiction to jurisdiction. The following table and graphs, taken from a Report on the Proportionality Principle in the European Union commissioned by the European Commission to Sherman & Sterling, ISS, and ECGI published in 2007,[1] illustrate the situation. (Note: with respect to Italy, the table has been updated because, as mentioned above, in 2014 multiple-voting shares have been made available.)

Availability of different classes of shares

country	multiple-voting shares	nonvoting shares
Belgium	NO	NO
Germany	NO	NO
Denmark	YES	NO
Finland	YES	YES
France	YES	YES
Greece	NO	NO
Ireland	YES	YES
Italy	YES	YES
Luxembourg	NO	NO
The Netherlands	YES	NO
Poland	NO	NO
Sweden	YES	NO
Spain	NO	NO
United Kingdom	YES	YES
Australia	NO	YES
Japan	YES	YES
USA	YES	YES

---

[1] Available at http://ec.europa.eu/internal_market/company/docs/shareholders/study/final_report_en.pdf

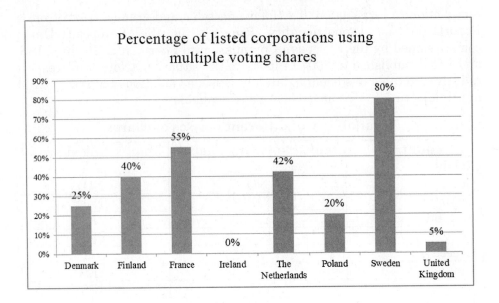

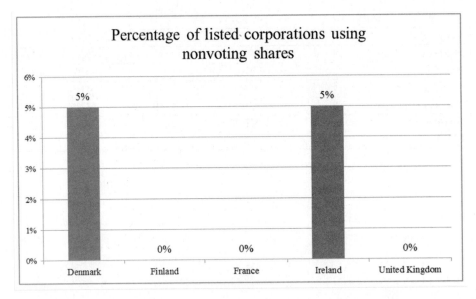

Multiple-voting shares, or more precisely "loyalty shares," are particularly common among French listed corporations (Art. L. 225–123 and L. 225–124 of the French Commercial code). The French case is indeed quite peculiar and interesting.

Until 1930, multiple-voting shares were allowed in all public limited companies, listed or non-listed, without limitation on the number of votes per share. This led to grave abuses and a 1930 law prohibited issuing new multiple-voting shares, but the previously issued ones were not suppressed. In 1933, as a compromise, another law allowed only double-voting shares and all previously issued multiple-voting shares were cancelled. This regime was slightly modified in 1966 and turned into the default rule in 2004 for listed companies.

The French situation is interesting because of the peculiar type of multiple-voting shares used, called "loyalty shares." Double-voting rights are entrusted only to a nominative shareholder if the shares have been fully paid and held for a minimum period of two years. For listed companies, the securities regulator is hostile to vesting periods longer than four years. Therefore, double-voting rights are not attached to the shares themselves but rather to the shareholder. Any share that is sold, transferred, or converted into a bearer share loses its double-voting rights. However, a transfer on succession or on the partition of property jointly owned by spouses, or a gift *inter vivos* to a spouse or a relative entitled to inherit the donor's estate shall neither cause the right to be lost, nor interrupt the holding period. If the shareholder is a company and merges or splits, the double vote is kept unless there is a contrary provision in the articles of incorporation of the issuing corporation. If the company which has issued the shares merges or is split, double-voting rights are also preserved unless the charter provides differently. The reason is that there is no substantial change, but only a formal one, and another reason is not to hinder value-maximizing and desirable business transactions for the fear of losing votes.

The rationale for loyalty shares, clearly enough, is to enhance the power of long-term shareholders and a stable control.

Since 2014, with the so-called Loi Florange, the French legislature has made "loyalty shares" the default rule for listed companies. Listed companies that do not want to have double-voting shares, or wish a different vesting period, will have to introduce this in the governing documents with a two-thirds majority in the extraordinary shareholders' meeting. In practice, most listed French companies already had double-voting shares in their articles of association so that the 2014 legislative amendment was mostly symbolic. This reform is designed to reward long-term shareholders and, allegedly, to allow listed companies to focus on a long-term perspective by reducing the influence of investors (often Anglo-American ones) accused of being subject to short termism. Double-voting shares can also interfere with a takeover, but here the "breakthrough" rule contained in the Takeovers directive should be considered, as we will discuss in the chapter on takeovers. The Loi Florange, more generally, was a controversial statute (some provisions have also been challenged in court) quite explicitly aimed at protecting French listed corporations from hostile acquisitions, especially from foreign buyers.

In non-listed corporations or in corporations whose shares are not listed on a regulated market, double-voting shares may be established by the bylaws with the vote of two-thirds of the shareholders. Double-voting shares are, however, less common in non-listed corporations because in these corporations a family has often absolute control, sometimes through a shareholders' agreement, and therefore similar controlling enhancing devices are less desirable.

* * *

In Japan, multiple-voting shares are not explicitly permitted by the Companies Act, but it is possible to achieve a similar result by differentiating the number of shares representing one "share unit" for different class of shares. As a default rule, each share is assigned one vote under Japanese law (Japanese Companies Act Art. 308(1)). By a charter provision, however, corporations can designate a number of shares necessary to constitute a "share unit" for each class of shares (Japanese Companies Act Art. 188). In this case, one voting right is assigned to each share unit, and shares that are not sufficient to constitute one share unit are not entitled to vote (Japanese Companies Act Art. 308(1)). In practice, however, such an arrangement has been rarely used, at least until now. The first IPO using this device, by a high-tech venture corporation, took place in March 2014.

* * *

In Germany, on the other hand, listed corporations were originally allowed to issue multiple-voting shares. However, already in the reform of the stock corporation law of 1937 the legislature took a more restrictive position towards multiple-voting rights by generally prohibiting them except in case a special permission was given by the responsible government authority (obviously, in that period of German history, the government tried to control the economy quite strictly). As a rationale, the legislature gave the following official reasoning:

Official Statement on the Law on Stock Corporations
(*Gesetz über Aktiengesellschaften und Kommanditgesellschaft auf Aktien*) of January 30, 1937

Deutscher Reichsanzeiger und Preußischer Staatsanzeiger 1937, No. 28 of February 2, 1937

§ 12 subs. 2 generally forbids the issuance of multiple voting rights. This prohibition is based on the concept that every share can grant only the same rights to every shareholder and that every voting privilege for a single shareholder or a group of shareholders has to be considered as economically unjustified and dangerous. However, practical experience showed that multiple voting shares can be necessary. As a consequence this draft allows the issuance of multiple-voting shares with the permission of the Ministry of Economic Affairs, the Ministry of Justice and other ministries if the issuance is in the best interest of the stock corporation or of general economic development (§ 12 subs. 2 sent. 2). By this regulation, an abuse of multiple-voting rights can be prevented but the issuance is still possible in cases where the best interest of the stock corporation or the general economic development requires the issuing.

* * *

This concept was later confirmed in the general reform of the stock corporation law in 1965, which however further limited the possibility to grant an exception only in the presence of a general economic interest for issuing multiple-voting rights. Finally, in 1998 the German legislature completely abolished multiple-voting rights with a new statute, the *Gesetz zur Kontrolle und Transparenz im Unternehmensbereich* ("KonTraG"), the Law on Control and Transparency in Business, introducing a strict proportionality principle. In contrast to earlier reforms the German legislature explained the rationale focusing on the function of capital markets.

Official Statement on the Law on Control and Transparency in Business (*Gesetz zur Kontrolle und Transparenz im Unternehmensbereich*) (BT-Drucks. 13/9712, p. 12 f.)

Multiple-voting rights were always controversial in German stock corporation law. They contradict the general principle that the voting power in a stock corporation should be based on the number of shares being issued. The granting of an influence without a corresponding number of shares does not comply with the expectations of the capital market and weakens the control of the stock corporation by its owners. Nevertheless, this is different in the case of the issuance of preferred stock without voting rights (*stimmrechtslose Vorzugsaktie*) since this kind of share is explicitly defined by the stock corporation law and is usually priced at a lower level on capital markets. The prohibition of multiple-voting rights also strengthens the concept of standardization of shares as a form of investment.

The reform of the stock corporation law in 1965 already limited the issuance of multiple-voting stocks. With its (third amendment of the) proposal for a Fifth Directive based on Article 54 (3) (g) of the EEC Treaty concerning the structure of public limited companies and the powers and obligations of their organs (OJ EC C 321 of 12.12.1991) the European Commission also proposed an unconditional prohibition of multiple-voting rights. Consequently, the permission to allow the issuance of multiple-voting rights should be abolished under German law.

* * *

In the U.K., it is possible to issue shares which have an enhanced voting rights. These can produce the situation where a management group can entrench itself so that although an outsider owns more than

51% of the market value of the company's shares he or she nevertheless has no control over the company. A good illustration of this was the long-running saga of the attempt by Trust House Forte to take over the Savoy Hotel. In this case, the takeover battle began in the 1950s and ended in the late 1980s when Trust House Forte finally abandoned its attempt, probably one of the longest battles for control of a corporation in history.[2] We will discuss this in Chapter 10.

* * *

Scholarly opinions on the desirability of the one-share, one-vote rule differ. Some academics have argued that, at least under certain conditions, the principle could be desirable and maximize the value of the corporation, other scholars think differently (*see*, for an overview of the literature, G. Ferrarini, *One Share—One Vote, A European Rule?*, ECGI Law Working Paper No. 58/2006, available on www.ssrn.com). One argument often raised against dual-class structures is that they might hinder the market for corporate control making hostile takeovers more difficult. In this respect, at least in Europe, one should however consider the so-called "break-through rule" contained in Article 11 of the Takeover Directive (2004/25/EC) that basically provides that, in the case of a tender offer, both limitations on the voting rights and multiple-voting rights do not apply in the shareholders' meeting that must decide on the adoption of defensive measures against the bidder. We will discuss takeovers regulation in Chapter 10, but can you anticipate the rationale of this rule?

CLASS VOTING AND PRE-EMPTIVE RIGHTS

Two important protections of shareholders are class voting, when different categories of shares are issued, and pre-emptive rights in case of issuance of new shares. After our discussion of classes of shares, let's start with the first issue.

Holders of different classes of shares often have the right to vote on corporate events (for example a merger) that might adversely affect their position. Depending on the jurisdiction, this protection might apply also to shareholders that normally do not enjoy the right to vote. A first question is whether holders of a particular class of shares vote together with all the other shareholders in the general meeting, or are entitled to a separate vote only of the holders of the class considered. The option between the two approaches can have a profound effect because the majority of the common stockholders and of the holders of different classes of shares might be different and have different interests. Consider, for example, a situation in which a corporation has issued 100 common shares and 50 limited voting preferred shares. Shareholder A

---

[2]   The story is outlined in *Re Savoy Hotel Ltd* [1981] 3 WLR 441.

has a majority of the common shares (80), but not of limited voting preferred shares, and vice versa shareholder B has a majority of the preferred shares (40), but not of the common shares. If in order to approve a merger all shareholders vote together as a single class, shareholder A will be able to impose the merger on the other investors (she holds 80 shares over 150). On the contrary, if the merger needs to be approved by two separate meetings in which shareholders vote as separate classes, shareholder B has a veto power on the transaction.

Go back and read again, in this perspective, the case *Examen v. Vantagepoint* in Chapter 2. Do you see more clearly now why the plaintiff wanted Delaware law to apply, and have all shareholders voting on the merger as a single class, while the defendant wanted California law to apply, and vote as a separate class?

Japanese law allows corporations to assign veto powers to classes of shares by making class voting necessary for certain types of actions (Japanese Companies Act Art. 108(1)(viii), Art .323). Even when there is no such arrangement, the law mandates class voting on several important actions, when the contemplated action is likely to cause a detriment to the holder of any class of shares (Japanese Companies Act Art. 322(1)). Examples include the creation of a new class of shares, modification of the rights of shareholders, increase of the authorized shares, mergers, etc., but not the issuance of shares to a particular third party. The charter can however eliminate these protections (Japanese Companies Act Art. 322(2)(3)). In this case, class shareholders are in some cases protected by appraisal rights (Japanese Companies Act Art. 116(1)(iii)).

In several European civil law jurisdictions, when common shareholders can take a decision that adversely affects the rights of a category of shares, holders of the affected category must approve the resolution as a separate class. This protection, however, only applies when the *rights* of the class are affected, not when there is a simple prejudice as a matter of fact (*see*, for example, Article 2376 of the Italian Civil Code). We will discuss this distinction below, with a case involving also pre-emptive rights.

Before getting there, however, let's discuss pre-emptive rights. The following excerpt from a law review article compares the regulation of this important protection of shareholders in Europe and in the U.S.

MARCO VENTORUZZO, ISSUING NEW SHARES AND PREEMPTIVE RIGHTS: A COMPARATIVE ANALYSIS[3]

12 Richmond J. Global L. & Bus. 517 (2013)

Introduction

[. . .] One fundamental area in which [European and U.S. corporate laws] diverge concerns how they regulate the issuing of new shares, in particular preemptive rights—a problem rarely addressed by comparative corporate law scholars. [. . .]

The issuing of new shares by a corporation is often a recipe for litigation. In fact, when new shares are issued and not offered to existing shareholders, shareholders may suffer two types of damages. On the one hand, shareholders' voting power within the corporation is diluted. On the other hand, the value of their investment can be reduced if the selling price is lower than the actual value of the shares.

Consider the following scenario. Corporation XYZ, worth four million dollars, has 1,000 shares outstanding. Shareholder A owns 25% of the shares (250 shares). A controls one-fourth of the voting power, and the value of her investment is one million dollars. If the corporation issues 1,000 new shares and sells them to a third party, A's voting power is reduced to 12.5% (250 shares over 2,000 outstanding). Depending on the price at which the new shares are offered, the value of A's investment could also be jeopardized. If XYZ sells the new shares at $4,000 each (the value before the new issue), no damage is caused. In fact, A will still own 12.5% of a corporation worth eight million dollars, which equals one million dollars. If, however, XYZ sells the shares at a "discount," the value of A's investment will be proportionally reduced. If, for example, the new 1,000 shares are sold for $3,000 each, the value of A's stake in the corporation will decrease to $875,000 (12.5% x $7,000,000).

Of course the law could dramatically curb this risk by providing that all existing shareholders always have a mandatory preemptive right to buy newly issued shares. Similar protections, however, would be detrimental to the corporation. It is essential that directors retain a certain degree of flexibility in designing the financial structure of the corporation. Granting preemptive rights to shareholders is time-consuming because the shares must be first offered to existing stockholders and might hinder the ability of the corporation to quickly obtain fresh financial resources when market conditions are favorable. The law must therefore strike a delicate balance between the protection of existing shareholders, on the one hand, and the ability of the corporation to pursue its optimal financial structure, on the other.

---

[3]   Footnotes omitted.

There are three basic sets of rules that contribute to strike such a balance: rules concerning the allocation of powers between directors and shareholders to decide on the issuing of new shares, preemptive rights in case new shares are sold, and fiduciary duties of directors engaging in the sale of new shares. The purpose of this essay is to consider how different legal systems strike this balance in regulating the issuance of new shares, focusing in particular on preemptive rights. The comparison is not only important for the relevance of the problem, but also because it illuminates some of the fundamental differences in the corporate governance philosophies underlying different legal systems.

[. . .] Focusing on these systems is particularly apt because the two models follow nearly opposite approaches. In the U.S., directors enjoy broad powers in the issuing of new shares, and there is greater freedom of contract in regulating preemptive rights in the corporate charter. Under this system, shareholders are mainly protected through directors' fiduciary duties. In Europe, shareholders are protected through statutory rules that mandate preemptive rights. Shareholders have the power to waive preemptive rights, but only in limited circumstances.

One might argue that European systems still follow the approach adopted in the U.S. until roughly the 1960s, and a possible explanation is that Europe did not experience the same separation between ownership and control that occurred in the U.S. The comparison will allow exploration of a more general difference between shareholder protection in the U.S. and in the civil law systems of continental Europe, namely, the fact that the former jurisdiction relies more on ex-post litigation, and the latter on ex-ante mandatory rules.

[. . .]

Part I: U.S. Law

Competence to Issue New Shares

In the U.S., the power to issue new shares is primarily entrusted to the board of directors. Directors enjoy a great degree of freedom in issuing new shares; however one important limitation is that they can only issue the number of shares authorized by the articles of incorporation. Generally, corporations have outstanding shares, which are shares already sold to shareholders that form the capital of the corporation; but the articles of incorporation provide for additional authorized shares that directors can issue and sell. For example, a corporation can have 100 outstanding shares held by two shareholders, but the articles of incorporation can authorize the issuing of additional 200 shares. If directors want to issue more than the additional 200 shares, they need to obtain shareholders' approval to increase the number of the authorized shares.

This rule gives shareholders some control over the financial structure of the corporation. Sales of shares that might dilute shareholders' ownership of the corporation above the threshold set by the authorized shares must be voted by shareholders as an amendment to the articles of incorporation. The practice, however, is to provide for a number of authorized shares significantly larger than the number of outstanding shares, so that if new financial resources are needed, directors can easily issue new shares. In contrast to European law, issuing new shares in the U.S. is substantially and practically in the hands of directors. In addition, minority shareholders in corporations with a controlling shareholder derive little protection from this rule because majority shareholders can consent to increase the number of authorized shares.

One exception to this allocation of powers is established by M.B.C.A. § 6.21(f), which requires shareholders' approval if (i) the shares are issued for consideration other than cash, and (ii) the voting power of shares that are issued comprises more than 20 percent of the voting power of the outstanding shares. Also in listed corporations, shareholders' approval is necessary when the issuing of new shares might determine a shift in control. Rules enacted by the NYSE, the NASD, and the American Stock Exchange require a vote at the shareholders' meeting when a listed corporation issues an amount of new common shares exceeding 20% of the outstanding ones, if the issuance is not made through a public offer for cash.

Preemptive Rights

Another way to protect shareholders in the event new shares are issued is to grant them a preemptive right to purchase these shares. In this case, shareholders who want to avoid the dilution of their participation can acquire pro-rata the new shares paying the required consideration. Of course, this protection is effective only to the extent that shareholders have the financial means and the willingness to buy the new shares but if they do, no dilution will occur.

The traditional approach in the U.S. was that shareholders enjoyed preemptive rights. . . . More modern corporate statutes [have however abandoned] this approach and generally deny preemptive rights unless the governing documents of the corporation opt for them. The default rule is that shareholders do not have a preemptive right in case of issuance of new shares, unless the articles of incorporation (or sometimes, the bylaws) expressly provide so. In Massachusetts this rule was adopted in 1964, under chapter 156B, section 20 of the general corporation statute. The M.B.C.A. and Delaware law also provide for similar rules.

Notably, there are some differences in how preemptive rights are structured. Some statutes allow shareholders to opt-in to preemptive rights, both in the charter and in the bylaws of the corporation. The effect is obviously different, because if the rule is in the charter, shareholders' approval is necessary to amend it, while if it is in the bylaws, directors could be able to amend it without shareholders' consent. It follows that shareholders' rights are more protected if the preemptive rights are set forth in the articles of incorporation.

Alternatively, a different approach followed by a minority of corporate statutes provides an opt-out mechanism for some corporations. Under this regime, shareholders enjoy preemptive rights as a default rule, but the articles of incorporation can waive them.

[. . .]

Directors' Fiduciary Duties and Other Limitations to the Sale of New Shares

A delicate issue that might arise is whether directors are allowed to freely sell shares only to some shareholders, therefore altering the balance of power within the corporation. In general terms [. . .] when preemptive rights do not apply, directors can sell new shares (or treasury shares) as they see fit. This freedom is, however, not unlimited. Consider, for example, a situation where the charter of the corporation provides for a supermajority of two-thirds of the votes to approve certain extraordinary transactions, such as a merger. One shareholder owns 60% of the outstanding shares, and another one owns 40%. Can the directors sell shares only to the first shareholder, thus bringing his participation above the 66.6% threshold and giving him absolute control over those transactions? In this case, the solution should not be found in preemptive rights, but rather in directors' fiduciary duties and in the principle of equal treatment of shareholders.

Part II: European Law

The European Framework: The Second Company Law Directive

The Second Company Law Directive, enacted in 1977 and amended several times, sets forth a harmonized regulation of the formation of corporations, focusing in particular on legal capital and its maintenance and alteration. Its breadth spans from the minimum amount of capital to eligible contributions and from purchasing of owned shares to distributions to shareholders. For the purposes of this essay the relevant provisions are contained in Articles 25, applicable to publicly held corporations. Two key principles need to be emphasized here. First, Article 25, Paragraph 1, provides that any increase in capital must be decided upon by the general shareholders' meeting. Second, Article 29 establishes that when the capital is increased and the new shares are paid in cash, the shares must be offered on a preemptive basis to shareholders in proportion to the capital represented by their shares.

These two provisions establish a minimum level of harmonization that is very different from, and arguably opposite of, the American regulatory model. The European approach gives more powers to the shareholders' meeting in deciding the issuing of new shares, and mandates preemptive rights as a general rule when shares are issued for a consideration in cash.

To get a clearer sense of how the general provisions of the Second Company Law Directive have been implemented in some Member States, it is helpful to examine some specific European jurisdictions.

Italian Law: Regulation of Issuing of New Shares for a Consideration

The Italian system offers an excellent example of the way in which the regulation of issuing new shares adopted in continental Europe compares with U.S. law. In fact, as we will discuss, the Italian Civil Code (I.C.C.) follows an approach that is considered opposite to the American one, characterized by mandatory regulation that leaves little room for freedom of contract and directors' discretion. Under Italian law, the interests of existing shareholders receive a stronger protection *vis-à-vis* the interest of the corporation to maintain a flexible financial structure so as not to be diluted through a capital increase.

In addition, in light of the partially harmonized regulation at the European level, the Italian system has important similarities with the systems of other major continental European jurisdictions, therefore presenting a good illustration of the European regulatory model.

[. . .]

A first crucial difference between the Italian and American regulation and practice of issuing new shares concerns the competence to decide the increase of capital. Under Italian law, pursuant to the Second Company Law Directive, the power is primarily in the hands of the shareholders. The issuing of new shares for a consideration, in fact, represents an amendment to the corporate charter that can only be approved by the so-called "extraordinary" shareholders' meeting with a supermajority. The matter can be delegated to directors by the shareholders' meeting, pursuant to Article 2443 of the I.C.C. In this case, the situation is similar to the one in which a U.S. corporation has authorized but unissued shares. The delegation to directors, however, can only be given for a maximum period of five years, therefore limiting directors' freedom to issue new shares.

Probably the most crucial difference concerns preemptive rights. In contrast to the U.S.—or, more precisely, in contrast to current U.S. rules, but similar to the traditional U.S. approach—the statutory and mandatory rule generally applicable is that, in any issuing of new shares for a consideration, all shareholders have a preemptive right to purchase the new shares proportionally to their stake in the corporation. Another difference with U.S. law is that, in a closely-held corporation, the shareholders that exercise their preemptive right do not only have the right to buy the new shares pro rata, but they can also exercise an additional preemptive right on the shares that other shareholders have not bought. Hence, if a corporation has two shareholders and only one of them exercises her preemptive right, she has the right to also buy the percentage of shares that the other shareholder refused, increasing her percentage of the corporation's capital. Only if shareholders do not exercise this additional right of preference can directors sell the shares to third parties.

The law is not similarly clear with respect to preemptive rights when it comes to issuing different classes of shares. There is a specific rule for non-voting shares issued by listed corporations: Article 145 of the Consolidated Law on Finance. This rule provides that, in the absence of a different option in the corporate charter, holders of non-voting shares have a preemptive right on shares of the same class. If non-voting shares are not issued, holders of these shares have a preemptive right on the classes of shares that are issued. Most commentators have expressed the view that this rule is the expression of a more general principle, where preemptive rights include the right to subscribe shares of different categories if the capital increase does not respect the proportion between the categories of shares already outstanding.

Statutory Limitations to Preemptive Rights

Preemptive rights can be limited or excluded only in four specific and narrow circumstances, listed in Article 2441 I.C.C. The first circumstance applies when the resolution approving the capital increase provides that the consideration for the new shares must be a contribution in kind. The rationale is the same as that adopted by U.S. courts to limit contractual preemptive rights included in the corporate charter in the absence of a specific provision: the interest of the corporation to receive exactly the property it seeks to acquire trumps the interest of shareholders not to be diluted. The law suggests, however, that, even in this case, it is not sufficient that the resolution indicates a contribution in kind, but also that a specific business purpose for the contribution in kind be shown in order to not elude the right of shareholders to maintain their stake in the corporation.

The second case in which preemptive rights do not apply is, pursuant to Article 2441, Paragraph 5 of the I.C.C., where "the interest of the corporation requires it". The scope of this provision is clearly broader and more blurred, but a few examples can be derived from corporate practice. When a corporation is going public, it needs to have a minimum number of shareholders in order to be admitted to a stock exchange. The initial public offer must, therefore, be made to a broad range of investors, and preemptive rights would be an insurmountable obstacle to the creation of a widespread ownership structure. In this case, the interest of the corporation to be listed arguably requires that preemptive rights be limited. This may occur, for example, when a corporation wants to attract a new shareholder in order to become part of a corporate group, or to exploit the business relationships and expertise of the new shareholder.

[A] third possible exclusion of preemptive rights can be based on an intention to compensate employees with shares of the corporation. Pursuant to Article 2441, Paragraph 8 of the I.C.C., when new shares are offered to employees, a maximum of one-fourth of the new shares can be sold without granting existing shareholders a preemptive right. It should be noted, however, that the limitation on preemptive rights can only affect 25% of the newly issued shares in order to curb the possible dilution of existing shareholders.

The fourth and last situation in which preemptive rights can be limited applies only to listed corporations. This is a relatively recent innovation introduced in 2003 and inspired by German law. Article 2441, Paragraph 4 of the I.C.C. provides that the charter of a listed corporation can opt for the possibility of increasing the amount of outstanding shares up to 10% of their number without granting preemptive rights. The rationale of this rule is to give more flexibility to listed corporations in designing their financial structure by allowing the issuing and selling of new shares without the time-consuming offer to existing shareholders required by preemptive rights. In a listed corporation, when shares are traded on a liquid regulated market, the risk of shareholders' dilution is more limited: existing shareholders that want to maintain their position in the corporation can, in fact, easily buy additional shares on the market.

As mentioned above, these four exceptions to mandatory preemptive rights are the only ones allowed: contribution in kind, interest of the corporation, shares offered to employees, and 10% of the outstanding shares in listed corporations. Only in these cases can the stake of a shareholder in the corporation be diluted if the shareholders' meeting so decides. The law, however, provides for specific rules concerning the issuing price of the new shares in case of limitation or exclusion of preemptive rights, in order to avoid an economic damage to investors. The selling price of the shares cannot, in these cases, be lower than a fair price determined through specific procedures.

More precisely, in the first three cases listed above, the directors must present the shareholders with a proposal indicating the issuing price calculated on the basis of the actual value of the corporation, taking into account, in the case of listed shares, their market price in the last six months.

[. . .]

NOTES AND QUESTIONS

1.   Professor Ventoruzzo's article shows how different systems balance the need to protect existing shareholders against dilutions, and the need to ensure a flexible and efficient management of the financial structure of the corporation. Which system do you think is more efficient? Which one is more protective of shareholders? What do the different approaches tell us about the diverging regulatory techniques, and diverging pressure groups in different jurisdictions?

2.   In systems that mandate pre-emptive rights, when they can be excluded the legislature emphasizes that shares must be issued at a fair price. Sometimes the law also sets a more or less rigid rule for determining the (minimum) issuing price. What is the rationale of this rule? Can it adversely affect the ability of the corporation to quickly raise fresh financial resources?

3.   Imagine that you are advising a client who is acquiring a minority but substantial stake in a corporation in the U.S. and in another one in Italy. What would be your advice to protect him against the risk of dilution in the two different countries?

* * *

As we have seen, in several European countries pre-emptive rights can be excluded only when specific conditions are met, and the issuing price of the new shares must be "fair." These rules raise complex factual issues. Let's move to Germany and take a look at how judges deal with these problems there. Under German law (minority) shareholders are protected in two different ways against an unjustified exclusion of pre-emptive rights. Besides the requirement of a reasonable justification for excluding pre-emptive rights, the new shares also have to be issued at a reasonable or fair price when pre-emptive rights are excluded. If these requirements are violated the shareholders can challenge the shareholders' resolution in court (§ 255 subs. 2 German Stock Corporation Act). The two following cases show the difficulties in the actual application and enforcement of these somehow vague legal requirements.

DEUTSCHE BANK

German Federal Court of Justice, 1994
7 March 1994

Facts

The plaintiffs were shareholders of a large German bank listed on a German stock exchange. At the general meeting in 1991 a resolution was passed to allow the board (*Vorstand*) to increase the capital of the corporation by issuing new shares for an amount of 75,000,000 DM with a complete exclusion of pre-emptive rights of the existing shareholders. At the general meeting the board stated that this increase in capital was necessary in order to increase the number of foreign shareholders abroad especially in the United States to obtain a listing on stock markets in the United States. Moreover the board stated that the issuing price of the new shares would be close to the stock exchange price. The plaintiff claimed that the exclusion of the pre-emptive rights was not justified especially because the exclusion of the pre-emptive rights was not necessary since the listing on a US stock market could also be obtained otherwise. The regional court (Laudgericht) dismissed the case. The appellate court (Oberlaudesgericht) declared the shareholders' resolution void.

Grounds

The court grants the appeal and dismisses the case.

According to decision of the appellate court the pre-emptive rights were excluded by the shareholders' resolution under § 186 German Stock Corporation Law. According to German stock corporation law an exclusion of pre-emptive rights of shareholders is admissible if it is justified taking into account the consequences for the shareholders and the interest of the corporation. This requires a balancing of the interests involved and an application of the principle of proportionality.

[. . .]

It is generally accepted among legal scholars that the listing of a corporation on a foreign stock exchange is in its best interest (*Hüffer*, AktG, 1993, § 186 note 31; *Lutter* in Köler Kommentar zum AktG, 2nd edition, § 186 note 72; *Hefermehl/Bungeroth* in: *Geßiler/Hefermehl/Eckardt/Kropff*, AktG, § 203 note 20; *Heinsius* in: Festschrift Kellermann, 1991, p. 115, 128; *Martens*, liber amicorum Steindorff, 1990, p. 151, 161; *Martens*, ZIP 1992, 1667, 1693 f.; *Liener*, Festschrift Semler, 1993, p. 721, 726 f.; *Kübler*, WuB II A. § 203 AktG 1.93, p. 571 f.; *Kübler/Mendelson/Mundheim*, AG 1990, 461, 463 f.). The advantages of a foreign listing are numerous. The corporation can issue shares in a foreign currency that it might need for international investments. Also it makes it easier for the corporation to obtain loans under more favorable conditions. Moreover an additional foreign listing decreases the volatility of the stock price. Furthermore, an additional listing becomes especially relevant when the domestic capital market of the corporation cannot provide enough capital for the corporation. Also, the corporation becomes more visible in the international context and might strengthen its image. Finally, foreign listings can also attract foreign employees (see also *Liener*, Festschrift Semler, 1993, p. 721, 726 f.).

[. . .]

The defendant, an international bank with several subsidiaries in other countries, would clearly benefit from these advantages. This is the case for the listing in the United States as well as in other countries. The intended listing on foreign capital markets is therefore in the best interest of the corporation.

However the exclusion of the pre-emptive rights of the plaintiff can only be justified when this interest of the corporation respects the principle of proportionality (BGHZ 71, 40, 46). This principle is usually met when the shareholders' meeting believes that the exclusion of the pre-emptive rights is adequate and is the best option to pursue the interest of the corporation (BGHZ 83, 319, 321). [. . .]

The intention of the defendant to enlarge the number of foreign shareholders on foreign stock exchanges requires the issuance of additional shares. It cannot be achieved by granting pre-emptive rights to existing shareholders. Even though some of the shareholders of the defendant are already foreigners, granting pre-emptive rights will not lead to an effective increase of foreign shareholders.

The goal of the defendant to enlarge the number of foreign shareholders on foreign stock exchanges cannot be obtained by listing the existing shares on a foreign stock exchange since this would lead to an imbalance of supply and demand of the stock on the domestic and foreign stock exchanges with the consequence of different prices on the stock exchanges. Moreover the corporation does not own a sufficient amount of stocks for a listing on a foreign stock market and cannot acquire the necessary amount on the stock market due to the limitations set by the system of stated capital [which limits the number of shares that a corporation can purchase].

As a consequence the objective of the defendant to obtain a listing on foreign stock exchanges justifies the exclusion of pre-emptive rights.

[. . .]

* * *

This approach of the Federal Court of Justice was adopted in 1994 by the legislature in the German stock corporation law. § 186 subs. 3 sent. 4 German Stock Corporation Law now states (for listed corporations) that the exclusion of pre-emptive rights is justified when the increase of capital (in cash) is less than 10% of the outstanding shares and the issuing price is not considerably lower than the actual stock exchange price. According to legislative history this requirement should be met when the issuing price is not lower than 3–5% of the stock exchange price.

As mentioned above, in addition to a general justification for the exclusion of shareholders' pre-emptive rights, the exclusion requires the new shares to be issued at a fair price. Also when the shares are listed, and a market price exists, it might be difficult to determine the fair value of the shares, arguing that market prices do not fully reflect the value of the going concern. In addition, even just determining precisely the "stock exchange price" can be problematic: for example, the price on which date? Should an average over a certain period be used? How long should the period be? Should the average price be weighted with volumes traded each day? What if extraordinary events, such as uncontrolled but unfounded rumors affect negatively the market price? To determine the value of non-listed shares, in the absence of an adequate market benchmark, can be even more complex. The following case, decided before the above-mentioned reform of 1994, concerns a contribution in kind of shares in exchange for newly issued shares. It discussed the problems that might arise in evaluating non-listed shares.

KALI UND SALZ
German Federal Court of Justice, 1978
13 March 1978

Facts

The plaintiff is a shareholder of the defendant, a non-listed stock corporation (*Saldetfurth Aktiengesellschaft*). In 1972 the capital of the stock corporation of 125 million DM was increased at a shareholder meeting with a three-quarter majority by 107,112,500 DM and the board was given the authority to increase the capital by another 17,887,500 DM. The pre-emptive rights of the existing shareholder were excluded. Instead two other corporations (*Wintershall AG* and its subsidiary the *Burbach-Kaliwerke AG*) received the new shares for a contribution in kind consisting of shares of the *Kali und Salz AG*. In order to determine the value of the shares of the *Kali und Salz AG* a valuation commission was formed consisting of representatives of the defendant, the *Kali und Salz AG* and certified accountants. In their valuation report the commission determined a certain exchange rate for the new shares and the shares of the *Kali und Salz AG* certifying that these results were rendered according to general business valuation principles. The plaintiff challenged the shareholder resolutions claiming—among other things—that the value of the shares of the *Kali und Salz AG* was actually lower then the value determined by the valutation commission. The Regional Court (Laudgericht) and the Higher Regional Court (Oberlaudesgericht) dismissed the claim.

Grounds

The appeal is denied.

[. . .]

The question whether the consideration for the increase of capital represented by a contribution in kind is reasonable has to be determined not according to stock exchange prices but only based on the real value of the corporation including hidden assets and the inner value (*innerer Geschäftswert*) of the corporation. When newly issued shares are paid with shares of another corporation as a contribution in kind the shareholders can challenge the shareholders' meeting resolution when the shares contributed are overvalued or the newly issued shares of the corporation are undervalued.

[. . .]

In the determination of the value of the newly issued shares and of the shares of *Kali und Salz AG* the valuation committee applied a combination of the following principles. The lower limit of the value was determined by the liquidation value (*Liquidationswert*). If the capitalized earning value (i.e., the net present value of a flow of future estimated earnings, or *Ertragswert*) was higher than the liquidation value (*Liquidationswert*) but below the assets value (*Substanzwert*), the capitalized earnings value (*Ertragswert*) was determining. If the capitalized earning value (*Ertragswert*) was higher than the assets value (*Substanzwert*) the capitalized earning value (*Ertragswert*) was taken into account. [. . .] The Court of Appeals did not hold that the valuation committee applied these standards incorrectly. The court does not object to this holding.

NOTES AND QUESTIONS

1. In the 1994 *Deutsche Bank* case, the German Federal Court of Justice discusses the advantages of cross-listing or dual-listing (*i.e.*, listing on a foreign exchange) for a corporation, in particular considering if the goal of cross-listing can be a legitimate ground to exclude pre-emptive rights. In fact, in order to offer the shares to a sufficient number of investors and reach the number of floating shares necessary for admission to the foreign stock exchange, excluding pre-emptive rights can be necessary. Several European, Asian, and Latin American corporations, especially until 2000, cross-listed in the U.S. What do you think of the pros and cons of listing abroad? Do you think the Court is missing some possible disadvantages, such as the costs of complying with (also) foreign rules? Course participants might be required to conduct a short research of the recent (2014) listing of the Chinese internet giant Alibaba on the NYSE and report in class.

2. In the 1978 *Kali und Salz* decision, the German Federal Court of Justice faced the question of when the value attached to non-listed shares contributed to a corporation in exchange of newly issued shares can be considered fair, and in particular which evaluation techniques are adequate. In a somehow cryptic paragraph, the decision states that there are three basic ways to evaluate a corporation and therefore its shares: (1) the

liquidation value (*Liquidationswert*), which is the value that could be determined winding up the corporation and selling all its assets; (2) the capitalized earnings value (*Ertragswert*), which is determined as the net present value of a flow of earnings (or sometimes cash flows) that the corporation will likely realize in the future; and (3) the assets value (*Substanzwert*), when the value of the corporation is determined based on the actual value of its assets considering the corporation as a going concern (note the difference with the liquidation value: the latter can be lower, for example because a trademark used by the corporation as a going concern, together with its other assets, can have a higher value). The Court says that if the capitalized earnings value (2) is higher than the liquidation value (1) but lower than the assets value (3), it should be determining. On the other hand, if the capitalized earnings value (2) is higher than the assets value (3), it should simply be "taken into account." What does this mean? What is the rationale for such an apparently rigid rule? Does the fact that the capitalized earnings value should be "taken into account" mean that an average between this value and the assets value should be calculated? If so, how should you weight the two elements? Could the rationale of this approach be that the court considers the assets value more reliable and conservative, because it is based on the value of assets owned by the corporation, while the capitalized earning value is less reliable, because it is based on estimates (guesses) on future earnings?

3. More generally, don't you think that the choice of the best evaluation technique should also depend of the type of business and industry? For example, for a real estate corporation, in which the value of the corporation is strictly linked to the value of its real estate, the value should be based on the assets; on the other hand, for an Internet corporation that has very little assets, but huge earnings, the value is more properly determined looking at earnings or cash flows. If the corporation is listed, should the market price, which might be influenced by different elements, including irrational beliefs of investors, also be taken into account? By the way, what is the difference between earnings (or profits) resulting from the financial statement and cash-flows? Why do some consider a net present value of cash flows a more reliable and objective measure of the value of a going concern than the net present value of a stream of earnings?

4. Imagine that a corporation that has issued 1,000 shares is valued $1,000. Would 51% of that corporation be worth $510, or more? Is there a control premium that should be taken into account? And what about a 20% stake, especially if it gives to the shareholders a veto power, for example because major corporate decisions must be taken with a supermajority of 85%? Would this participation be worth $200, or more? Let's imagine that this is a listed corporation, and the market price of one share is $1. A participation of 10% would be worth $100? If you try to sell 10% of the listed shares on the market, don't you think the market price might drop? Should we therefore apply a minority discount in this case? When evaluating shares based on the value of the corporation, or market prices, experts are often

faced with the problem of determining if control or majority premiums or minority premiums or discounts apply.

5.   Although the German Federal Court of Justice held in the *Kali und Salz* decision that the issuing price only meets the requirement of being *fair* when it reflects the *real value* of the corporation determined by the valuation methods mentioned in the decision, it is still unsettled under German stock corporation law whether this also applies in the case of a listed stock corporation. This is particularly important in the case of § 186 subs. 3 sent. 4 German Stock Corporation Law, which allows exclusion of pre-emptive rights for an amount equal to 10% of the outstanding shares but requires the issuing price to be equal to the market price of the shares. Whereas some legal scholars claim that in the case of a listed corporation the actual stock exchange price has always to be considered *fair*, others claim that the stock exchange price is binding only if it is higher than the value determined by the application of the valuation methods mentioned in the *Kali und Salz* decision. This is however also debated, since the issuing of new shares on the stock market requires usually a discount from the actual stock price in order to attract investors (the reason is obvious: why should an investor buy from the corporation newly issued shares that she can buy, at exactly the same price, on the market?).

6.   In 2003, Italy adopted a rule similar to § 186 subs. 3 sent. 4 German Stock Corporation Law: Article 2441, par. 4, of the Italian Civil Code. As discussed in Professor Ventoruzzo's article above, pursuant to this rule the charter of a listed corporation can opt for the possibility of increasing the amount of outstanding shares up to 10% of their number without granting pre-emptive rights. The rationale of this rule is to give more flexibility to listed corporations in designing their financial structure by allowing the issuing and selling of new shares without the time-consuming offer to existing shareholders required by pre-emptive rights. In a listed corporation, when shares are traded on a liquid regulated market, the risk of shareholders' dilution is more limited: existing shareholders that want to maintain their position in the corporation can, in fact, easily buy additional shares on the market. In this case, however, the issuing price must be equal to the market value of the shares, and this should be certified by an independent auditing corporation. Do you think this is an effective way to make sure that the issuing price is fair? Who chooses the auditing corporation and pays it?

* * *

Japanese law in this area, while largely based on U.S. law, contains some rules derived from European systems concerning the issuing price of new shares. Basically, shareholders of public corporations do not have pre-emptive rights, and the board of directors of such a corporation can issue new shares to any third party (Japanese Companies Act Art. 201(1)). When the issuing price is "particularly favorable" to the subscriber of the new shares, however, a special resolution (two-thirds majority) of the shareholders' meeting is necessary (Japanese Companies Act Art. 199(2)(3), Art. 201(1), Art. 309(2)(v)). In addition, when the subscriber, colluding with the directors, subscribed the new shares at an issuing price that was "extremely unfair," the subscriber must pay the difference between the fair price and the actual price paid to the corporation (Japanese Companies Act, Art. 212(1)(i)). This liability of the subscriber can be enforced by shareholders of the corporation with a derivative action (Chapter 7), because directors might be reluctant to sue such subscriber (Japanese Companies Act, Art. 847(1)). Also, shareholders can request an injunction against the issuance of shares when its purpose is to preserve control in the hands of incumbent management (Art. 210(ii)).

The case below deals with a derivative action based on a provision of the former Japanese Commercial Code which corresponds to Japanese Companies Act, Art. 212(1)(i) of the current text. The problem faced by the Court was how to decide when the issuing price can be considered "extremely unfair" in the context of a transaction aimed at turning around a corporation in financial distress.

SONY-AIWA

Tokyo District Court, 1973
27 July 1973, 715 Hanrei Jiho 100

Facts

In 1968, Aiwa, Co., Ltd., an audio-electronics manufacturer, was facing financial difficulties. When Aiwa declared in June 1968 that it was not going to pay dividends for that year, the market price of Aiwa's share on the Tokyo Stock Exchange was 50 JPY per share. Since July of that year, however, there were rumors concerning a possible acquisition or business combination with leading companies such as Sony, and Aiwa's share price increased due to a large volume of speculative buy orders. The share price jumped up in December 1968, and reached 145 JPY at the end of January 9, 1969. In contrast, the share prices of other companies in the same industry registered a downward trend from July through December 1968, although their operating profits were higher than that of Aiwa.

Aiwa's management decided to seek a business combination with a leading company in order to turn around its situation, and had discussions with Sony. On January 10, 1969, the board of directors of Aiwa decided to issue 12 million new shares to Sony Corporation for 70 JPY per share (the number of shares already issued before the issuance to Sony was also 12 million). The share price of Aiwa kept ascending after the announcement of this issuance, reaching 340 JPY on January 6, 1970.

The plaintiff, a shareholder of Aiwa, initiated a "derivative suit" against Sony claiming that the issuing price of 70 JPY per share was "extremely unfair" since the market price on the day before the decision of the board was 145 JPY. The Tokyo District Court dismissed the claim (Tokyo District Court, April 27, 1972, 679 HANREI JIHO 70), and the plaintiff appealed.

The Court's Decision

Appeal dismissed.

[. . .]

When the shares of the issuer corporation are listed the market price usually reflects the value of the assets and the profitability of the corporation, which are at the core of the factors that determine the fair issuing price explained above [. . .]. Therefore, the issuing price of the new shares, determined taking into account other factors beside assets and earnings should generally not be significantly different from the market price (15%). Market prices, however, are also influenced by speculation, and do not always reflect the objective firm value. Therefore, it would be essentially incorrect to always take the market price of shares as the absolute measure when deciding the issuing price of new shares of listed corporations. [. . .]

In this case, the market price of the share of the corporation outside of this suit [Aiwa] at the end of January 9, 1969, which is the day before the day when the issuing price was decided, was 145 JPY per share, this price was influenced mainly by speculation and did not reflect the real value of the firm based on its asset and profitability, as the decision of the lower court had found. Therefore, it is not possible to determine the issuing price based on the market price. In addition, as the decision of the lower court had found, the issuance of new shares in this case was carried out to allow a business combination between the appellee corporations [Sony] and [Aiwa], and the appellee corporation had subscribed all of the 12 million new shares. When considering such facts, it was natural for Sony not to subscribe the new shares at a price that was artificially inflated by speculation.

Considering the points noted above in addition to those raised by the decision of the court below, the issuing price of 70 JPY per share in this case is fair and reasonable.

An "issuing price that is particularly favorable" under Art. 280–2(2) of the Commercial Code is particularly lower than the fair and reasonable price. Since the issuing price of 70 JPY per share in this case is fair and reasonable, as we have already noted, the issuing price above is not "particularly favorable."

NOTES AND QUESTIONS

1.   Basically the Court decides to ignore, or give little consideration, to the market price as an indicator of the fair value of the shares, arguing that speculation can interfere with the formation of market prices. Do you agree with the court's opinion that the Aiwa's share price on January 9, 1969 did not reflect its real value? Didn't it reflect the possibility of Aiwa being rescued by Sony or another corporation? If you believe it did, can you think of any other basis that supports the final decision of the Court?

2.   The standards used in Art. 201 ("particularly favorable") and Art. 212 ("extremely unfair") of the Japanese Companies Act had been considered to be substantially the same by several of the commentators and by the decision cited above. Would you agree with this interpretation, in light of the different wording used by the statute and the different goals of the two provisions? Why yes, or why not?

3.   In the 1960s and 1970s, the rate commonly used as a reasonable discount from the market price was around 10–15%, as mentioned in the decision above. You should understand the rationale for this discount. If you want to sell new shares, and you offer them at the same price available on the market, it would make sense for the buyer to simply buy them on the stock exchange, which is generally easier and quicker. A discount for newly issued shares is therefore often necessary, especially to lure a large investment. Recently, however, the most common discount rate has decreased to 5% or lower. A self-regulatory rule of the Japan Securities Dealers Association regarding private placement of new shares allows a discount of up to 10% of the market price and also the use of the average market price of the previous six months (or shorter) period as the base price. What might be a reason for a lower discount rate? What could be the rationale for using the average market price for a certain period as the base? Do you agree with this approach?

4.   In response to the criticism of foreign and domestic institutional investors with respect to the rules governing the issuance of shares, several reforms have been introduced recently in Japan. First, the time necessary for rights offering (i.e., allotment of transferable share options to all shareholders with effects similar to pre-emptive rights) was shortened. Second, for issuance of shares through which the subscriber becomes a new controlling shareholder by holding more than half of the shares as a result of the issuance, a resolution of the shareholders' meeting is required when shareholders holding more than 10% of the shares object to the issuance. For details and exceptions, *see*, Gen Goto, *The Outline for the Companies Act Reform in Japan and Its Implications*, 35 JOURNAL OF JAPANESE LAW 14, 24–27 (2013).

5.   In contrast to the rules applicable to publicly held corporations, those for closely held corporations (more precisely, corporations that issue only shares with limitations to their transferability) are more "European oriented." In these corporations, a special resolution of the shareholders'

meeting is necessary for any issuance of new shares (Japanese Companies Act, Art. 199(2), Art. 202(3)(iv)), unless it is delegated to the board by a charter provision or by a special resolution of the shareholder's meeting that is effective for only one year. Can you see the rationale of this distinction? Is it similar to the rule adopted in paragraph 4 of Article 2441 of the Italian Civil Code, discussed in Professor Ventoruzzo's article above?

* * *

A very delicate issue combining class voting and pre-emptive right is the following. Consider a legal system in which shareholders do have mandatory pre-emptive rights (or pre-emptive rights are granted by the bylaws). In such a system, if different classes of shares are outstanding, it can happen that a shareholder loses control of the corporation as a consequence of a capital increase. Would the shareholder be entitled to a separate vote on the issuing of new shares? The "Mondadori litigation" in Italy addressed this problem. The case is intriguing also because it involved Mr. Silvio Berlusconi, the well-known Italian media mogul and former Prime Minister. A little bit of additional background is, however, necessary. As we mentioned before, under Italian law (Article 2376 of the Civil Code), when different classes of shares are outstanding, a shareholders' meeting resolution that adversely affects the rights of a class of shareholders must be approved also by a separate vote of only the holders of the shares of the affected class. Now, imagine the following scenario. A corporation XYZ has issued 100 common shares (voting on the election of the board) and 100 limited-voting shares voting only on amendments of the governing documents and the issuance of new shares. All shareholders enjoy mandatory pre-emptive rights, and if only shares of one class are issued, holders of all classes can subscribe them proportionally. Shareholder A owns 60 common shares and controls the corporation because he can appoint the board of directors. Shareholder B, however, owns all the 100 limited-voting shares, and 40 common shares. Consequently, B controls the majority of the votes that can be cast in the general shareholders' meeting of all the shareholders competent to authorize the issuance of new shares (200 shares), since he controls 100 + 40 votes, versus only 60 controlled by A. The general shareholders' meeting, and therefore B, can decide to issue 100 new common shares. If both A and B exercise their pre-emptive rights, A will lose control of the corporation and B will become the new controlling shareholder, owning a majority of the common shares. In fact, A will be entitled to subscribe 60/200 of the 100 new shares (30 shares), while B will be able to subscribe 70 of the new common shares (140/200). As a consequence, after the transaction, A will own 90 common shares (his original 60 plus 30), and B 110 (40 + 70). Under these circumstances, is A entitled to a separate vote only by holders of common shares, to approve the issuance of new shares, arguing the applicability of Article 2376 of the Civil Code?

A CORPORATE LAW SAGA: THE MONDADORI CASE

The "Mondadori case" (from the name of the corporation involved) is extremely long and complex and it is not possible to include a translation of the major judicial decisions here. Instead we will provide an account of the facts and legal issues, and an excerpt of legal opinions written by famous jurists consulting the parties. The litigation originated in 1989 and some parts of it dragged on until 2013 (a fact that also tells you something about the duration of litigation in Italy . . .). The case concerns control over Mondadori, a leading Italian publisher and a listed corporation, and saw a bitter financial and judicial fight between two major Italian entrepreneurs: on the one hand, Silvio Berlusconi and his Fininvest corporation, and on the other hand Carlo De Benedetti and his CIR corporation. They are pictured below.

Silvio Berlusconi

Carlo De Benedetti

The story is known as the "battle of Segrate," from the town near Milan where Mondadori has its headquarters. To make a long story short, in the 1980s Berlusconi and Fininvest acquired a significant stake in Mondadori. At the end of the 1980s, Mondadori had three relevant shareholders: Berlusconi and his group (with roughly 8%), De Benedetti through CIR (roughly 16%), and the Formenton family, relatives of the founder Arnoldo Mondadori and former controlling shareholders, together with Leonardo Mondadori (a little more than 50%). The Formentons executed a contract to transfer their shares to De Benedetti before 1991; pursuant to the agreement De Benedetti would have acquired control of the corporation. In 1989, however, the Formenton family had a change of heart and sold its shares to Berlusconi, who became the new Chairman of Mondadori. De Benedetti challenged the transaction; pursuant to the contract, disputes had to be arbitrated. The arbitration panel, composed of two law professors and a judge of the Italian Supreme Court, found for De Benedetti, holding that the Formentons breached their contract with him. De Benedetti regained control of Mondadori. The arbitration award was however challenged in court, and the Court of Appeal of Rome, in 1991, decided that the agreement between the Formenton family and De Benedetti was at least partially void. The shares returned to Berlusconi. Politicians stepped in: the control of some of the most important Italian newspapers and magazines was at stake. Apparently Giulio Andreotti, then Prime Minister, contributed to broker an agreement according to which some newspapers, such as *La Repubblica*, one of the major Italian newspapers, would be transferred to CIR and the De Benedetti group; while other assets and businesses would go to Berlusconi and Mondadori. Many years later, in 2007, the Italian Supreme Court has concluded that a judge was corrupted in order to obtain an outcome favorable to the Fininvest group in the 1991 decision of the Court of Appeals of Rome, and in 2013 Fininvest was ordered to pay over 540 million euro in damages to CIR.

This is however only the background of our problem. In the years in which the battle of Segrate was going on, between 1989 and 1991, the issuance of new shares that would give control to one party was considered, and this is the question we should focus on.

Mondadori had issued common shares with full voting rights; preferred, limited-voting shares that would only vote in the so-called extraordinary shareholders' meeting also on the issuance of new shares; and some non-voting shares. As in our previous example, and somehow simplifying, at one point of our story Berlusconi and his group had the majority of the common shares, but not of the limited-voting shares; and De Benedetti and his group had the majority of the limited-voting shares. De Benedetti had enough votes to approve the issuance of new common shares with a pre-emptive right for all shareholders, independently of the class of shares they owned; Berlusconi did not own enough common shares to block this resolution. Pursuant to the appellate rules, in fact, in case new shares of only one class were issued, they had to be offered to all shareholders. In the light of the ownership structure, if the capital increase would have been accomplished, De Benedetti, so far holding the majority of the limited-voting shares, would have obtained *also* a majority of the common shares, and acquired control of the corporation and the right to appoint the board of directors. The question was if, in this scenario, holders of common shares had to separately approve the capital increase because it damaged their position (since the controlling shareholder would lose control). If the answer would have been affirmative, Berlusconi could have vetoed the issuance of new shares and kept control.

Pursuant to Article 2376 of the Italian Civil Code, a separate class vote is necessary whenever the general shareholders' meeting approves a resolution that "adversely affects" the "rights" of a class of shareholders. Does the fact that one shareholder loses control due to the issuance of new shares adversely affects the rights of a class of shareholders pursuant to this rule? Due to the conflict among the parties, and the legal uncertainties, the capital increase was not pursued, but several law professors and lawyers issued legal opinions on this matter, and these opinions have been published in law journals.

According to the opinions of some scholars, Article 2376 of the Italian Civil Code does not apply in this scenario:

> "The shareholders' meeting resolution does not envisage the issuance of a new class of shares with preferred rights nor does it determine any change of the current balance between common shares and preferred shares: on the contrary, it increases the number of common shares, which results in a dilution of preferred shares. In this way, it strengthens the position of the common shares with respect both to the voting rights and to the cash-flow rights. Therefore, it cannot be said that the rights attached to the common shares are adversely affected. The opposite is true" (R. COSTI, in *Giur. comm.*, 1990, p. 571).

> "The shareholders' meeting resolution affects only one kind of interest, i.e., the interest attached to the common shares to maintain the same voting power. Such interest shall be protected only by the pre-emption right. Therefore, in this case, Art. 2376 I.C.C. does not apply since there isn't any prejudice to a legal entitlement deemed as 'a right' nor, above all, to 'a right of a class of shares'" (P. FERRO LUZZI—B. LIBONATI, in *Riv. dir. comm.*, 1991, I, p. 708).

Other scholars expressed a different opinion:

"When the capital is raised, the rights of the different classes are not deemed to be affected when the planned issuance and distribution of new shares, together with the exercise of the pre-emptive right, have the effect of maintaining the shareholders in the same position they held before the capital increase (both in terms of voting power and cash-flow rights). When the exercise of the pre-emptive rights would not prevent the alteration of power between classes of shares caused by the distribution of new shares, it would be necessary to call a separate meeting of the holders of the affected stock. In the case discussed hereby, since the exercise of the preemptive right by the holders of common shares is not sufficient in order to maintain the same position as before, a separate meeting of holders of common shares must approve the transaction" (F. D'ALESSANDRO, in *Giur. comm.*, 1990, pp. 587–588).

"In the case described, the extraordinary general meeting's resolution must be approved also by the separate meeting of holders of common shares: in fact, the capital increase determines a shift in the balance of power between different classes of shares and, as a consequence, a change in the voting power of the outstanding common shares" (G.B. PORTALE, in *Riv. dir. comm.*, 1991, I, p. 732).

NOTES AND QUESTIONS

1.   First of all, consider the relevance of opinions by legal scholars and practitioners (so-called *"pro-veritate"* opinions, from Latin *"in the interest of truth"*), especially in some civil law countries. Obviously these opinions have no binding force, but they are often respected by courts and administrative agencies, and can be important also to avoid the risk of liability.

2.   We agree with the first two opinions, Article 2376 of the Italian Civil Code does not apply to this case. As hinted in the excerpts reprinted, the key issue is that the "rights" of a class of shares have not been altered here: this would be the case, for example, if a preference in the payment of dividends would be reduced, or limitations to voting rights would be introduced. In our case, there is only a factual change in the position *not of an entire class*, but *only of one shareholder* who happens to have the majority of the common shares. Obviously this is not desirable for the shareholder losing control, but technically it is not an adverse modification of the rights of one class. A substantive reason also supports this conclusion. Since under Italian (and European) law shareholders have pre-emptive rights, a shareholder having the majority of the common shares and a minority of preferred, limited-voting shares has probably decided or accepted this ownership structure. There must have been a point in time when the shareholder, for

example, decided not to subscribe newly issued limited-voting shares pursuant to his pre-emptive rights, or sold them on the market, or accepted to acquire a majority of the common shares, not caring about limited-voting shares. He should therefore have been aware of, and accepted, the risk that limited-voting shareholders might approve the issuance of new common shares in a way that could affect his control of the corporation. Do you understand this reasoning? Do you agree, or do you find more convincing the different opinions expressed above? Discuss.

3.   According to Article 25, par. 3, of the Second Company Law Directive (Directive 77/91/ECC), applicable at the time of the proposed capital increase: "Where there are several classes of shares, the decision by the general meeting concerning the increase in capital referred to in paragraph 1 or the authorization to increase the capital referred to in paragraph 2, shall be subject to a separate vote at least for each class of shareholder whose rights are affected by the transaction." Compare this wording with that of Art. 2376 of the Italian Civil Code: do you think the Italian rule is consistent with the European one?

4.   How would a similar situation be resolved pursuant to the laws applicable in your jurisdiction?

BONDS AND DEBENTURES

Bonds and debentures are securities representing a fraction of a loan. Generally, in the U.S., the term "bonds" refers to long-term promissory notes, often with duration of 30 years, secured by collateral on the issuer. "Debentures" refers to long-term unsecured promissory notes. Sometimes also the term "notes" is used for shorter-term promissory notes. In the sake of brevity, we can collectively use here the expression "bonds."

There are several reasons why a corporation might prefer to obtain financial resources issuing bonds rather than shares, and similarly several reasons why some investors might prefer to hold bonds. From the perspective of the corporation, in most jurisdictions payments of interests on bonds are tax deductible, while dividends are not. In addition, bonds do not usually carry control rights, and therefore bondholders generally do not interfere with the management of the corporation, even if the issuance of bonds can require certain limitations to the freedom of the corporation (for example, limitations concerning the dividend policy). Of course, however, since generally bondholders are creditors and are entitled to the payment of interests, while shareholders receive a dividend only if the corporation has earnings and directors (or, in some systems, shareholders) decide to pay dividends, the issuance of bonds can be more risky because directors have little discretion on payments of interests on bonds. Recourse to bonds, and in particular bonds paying a fixed interest rate determines a more rigid and unforgiving financial structure. Investors, on the other hand, might prefer bonds because they have a (perceived) lower risk than shares, or for tax reasons.

There is a great deal of flexibility in structuring bondholders' rights: for example, the interest rate can be fixed or floating depending on economic or corporate variables; "zero coupon" bonds that do not pay an interest, but that are remunerated based on the difference between the issuing price and the amount due to the creditor, can also be issued. The repayment of the principal can also be subordinated to the prior payment of other creditors.

When discussing bonds, a first question is if there are rules limiting the maximum amount of bonds that can be issued. Few legal systems provide for a similar rule: Italy is one possible example, but similar limitations also exist under Chinese law. Consider the following provision:

Italian Civil Code Article 2412—Limitations to the Issuing of Bonds

1.   The corporation can issue bonds for an amount not exceeding the double of the capital, of the legal reserve, and of available reserves resulting from the last approved financial statements.

NOTES AND QUESTIONS

1.   Article 161 of the Chinese Company Law similarly provides, among other conditions for the issuance of bonds, that the accumulated value of the bonds issued may not exceed forty percent of the value of the net assets of the company. What do you think is the rationale of this somehow paternalistic rule? Why should the legislature impose a given financial structure? Are these rules aimed at avoiding excessive financial leverage? Is there a rationale to distinguish issuing bonds from other debt, for example to a loan given by a bank or one wealthy individual, and mandate limits for the former, but not the latter?

2.   Do you think this rule can be easily circumvented? Can a corporation subject to such a limitation establish a wholly owned subsidiary in a country where no limitation to the issuance of bonds exists (for example, Luxembourg), and have the subsidiary issue bonds and then transfer the proceeds to the parent corporation (consider the 2003 "Parmalat scandal")? What does this tell us about the limits of municipal law in a globalized economy?

3.   There are exceptions to this rule. For example, a corporation can exceed the limit if the additional bonds are subscribed by a professional investor (for example, a bank), and if the bank transfers the bonds to a non-professional investor, it can be liable in case of insolvency of the issuer. The

limitation also does not apply to bonds listed on a regulated financial market. What do you think is the reason for these two exemptions?

* * *

Different regulatory techniques exist to protect bondholders. In short, in the U.S. the relevant legislation is the Trust Indenture Act of 1939 (TIA), a federal statute enacted as part of the New Deal to protect investors. The TIA only applies to debt issued to the public, not in case of a private placement. It provides the necessary appointment of an independent trustee (generally a bank) that is responsible to act in the interest of the bondholders. For example, the trustee must act if the issuer defaults on the payments, or violates other covenants in the trust indenture. In fact, single bondholders can legally prosecute the issuer only if the trustee, properly notified, does not act. In other systems, for example in civil law jurisdictions, bondholders are protected through a special bondholders' meeting, which must approve any proposed amendment to the indenture.

A typical and simplified trust indenture contains the obligations of the parties, and also a series of additional positive ("thou shalt") and negative ("thou shalt nots") covenants. For example, a common provision is that the corporation is limited in its ability to obtain additional credit that would raise the risk of insolvency, or is limited in dividend payments.

One interesting twist, which is related to our discussion of choice of law in Chapter 2, is that the trust indenture is not necessarily governed by the laws of the state of incorporation of the corporation. Especially in the U.S., for example, it is fairly common that a listed corporation is incorporated in Delaware, and therefore Delaware law governs its internal affairs, but the trust indenture is subject to the laws of New York State, considered by many attorneys more advanced with respect to debt financing. In Europe, Germany has a significant outflow of debt issues, and Luxembourg, the Netherlands, the U.K., and Ireland attract most debt issues either by foreign corporations or by their local subsidiaries. In other legal systems, however, the regulation of bonds is considered at least in part included in the internal affairs of the corporation, and this "decoupling" of legal rules for bonds and other corporate law issues is not possible. An excellent empirical analysis of this phenomenon is offered by Eidenmüller, Engert and Hornuf, *Where Do Firms Issue Debt?* ECGI Finance Working Paper No. 292/2010, available on *www.ssrn.com*. We urge you to read this paper.

One fundamental feature of the regulation of bonds in common law systems stems from the fact that bondholders are creditors, not residual claimants of the corporation. For this reasons, directors do not generally owe fiduciary duties to bondholders (with some possible exceptions when the corporation is nearing insolvency, as we will see in Chapter 6 on Directors' Liability). The protection of bondholders should generally be found in an explicit provision of the trust indenture, even if some courts might infer an implied covenant of good faith in the contract. For this reason, some of the most interesting cases in this area concern the interpretation of the trust indenture, a problem that also allows us to say something about the different possible approaches to contract interpretation in common law and civil law. The following case offers a good discussion on the interpretation of a trust indenture in the U.S.

MORGAN STANLEY & CO., INCORPORATED V. ARCHER DANIELS MIDLAND COMPANY

United States District Court, S.D. New York
570 F.Supp. 1529 (1983)

SAND, DISTRICT JUDGE.

[This suit arose from the redemption by Archer Daniels Midland Company (ADM) of $125 million of debentures bearing an interest rate of 16%. The plaintiff, Morgan Stanley & Company, Inc. (Morgan Stanley), claimed that the redemption violated a contractual prohibition and that it violated certain securities laws, including § 10(b) of the Securities Exchange Act of 1934. The reported decision in this case includes an opinion in support of the court's denial of the plaintiff's request for a preliminary injunction, followed by an opinion on the parties' cross motions for summary judgment. The former opinion, which contains a substantial discussion of the plaintiff's claims under the securities laws, as well as a discussion of its contract-law claims, is omitted.]

[. . .]

Facts

In May, 1981, Archer Daniels issued $125,000,000 of 16% Sinking Fund Debentures due May 15, 2011. The managing underwriters of the Debenture offering were Goldman Sachs & Co., Kidder Peabody & Co., and Merrill Lynch, Pierce, Fenner & Smith, Inc. The Debentures state in relevant part:

> The Debentures are subject to redemption upon not less than 30 nor more than 60 days' notice by mail, at any time, in whole or in part, at the election of the Company. . .

> [P]rior to May 15, 1991, the Company may not redeem any of the Debentures pursuant to such option from the proceeds, or in anticipation, of the issuance of any indebtedness for money borrowed by or for the account of the Company or any Subsidiary (as defined in the Indenture) or from the proceeds, or in anticipation of a sale and leaseback transaction (as defined in

Section 1008 of the Indenture), if, in either case, the interest cost or interest factor applicable thereto (calculated in accordance with generally accepted financial practice) shall be less than 16.08% per annum.

The May 12, 1981 Prospectus and the Indenture pursuant to which the Debentures were issued contain substantially similar language. . . .

In the period since the issuance of the Debentures, ADM also raised money through two common stock offerings. Six million shares of common stock were issued by prospectus dated January 28, 1983, resulting in proceeds of $131,370,000. And by a prospectus supplement dated June 1, 1983, ADM raised an additional $15,450,000 by issuing 600,000 shares of common stock.

Morgan Stanley, the plaintiff in this action, bought $15,518,000 principal amount of the Debentures at $1,252.50 per $1,000 face amount on May 5, 1983, and $500,000 principal amount at $1,200 per $1,000 face amount on May 31, 1983. The next day, June 1, ADM announced that it was calling for the redemption of the 16% Sinking Fund Debentures, effective August 1, 1983. The direct source of funds was . . . the two ADM common stock offerings of January and June, 1983 . . .

[. . .]

Plaintiff [. . .] contends that the proposed redemption is barred by the express terms of the call provisions of the Debenture and the Indenture Agreement, and that consummation of the plan would violate the Trust Indenture Act of 1939 . . . and common law principles of contract law. The plaintiff's claim is founded on the language contained in the Debenture and Trust Indenture that states that the company may not redeem the Debentures "from the proceeds, or in anticipation, of the issuance of any indebtedness . . . if . . . the interest cost or interest factor . . . [is] less than 16.08% per annum." Plaintiff points to the $86,400,000 raised by the Stars transaction within 90 days of the June 1 redemption announcement, and the $50,555,500 raised by the Zeroes transaction in May, 1982—both at interest rates below 16.08%—as proof that the redemption is being funded, at least indirectly, from the proceeds of borrowing in violation of the Debentures and Indenture agreement. The fact that ADM raised sufficient funds to redeem the Debentures entirely through the issuance of common stock is, according to the plaintiffs, an irrelevant "juggling of funds" used to circumvent the protections afforded investors by the redemption provisions of the Debenture. Plaintiff would have the Court interpret the provision as barring redemption during any period when the issuer has borrowing at a rate lower than that prescribed by the Debentures, regardless of whether the direct source of the funds is the issuance of equity, the sale of assets, or merely cash on hand.

The defendant would have the Court construe the language more narrowly as barring redemption only where the direct or indirect source of the funds is a debt instrument issued at a rate lower than that it is paying on the outstanding Debentures. Where, as here, the defendant can point directly to a non-debt source of funds (the issuance of common stock), the defendant is of the view that the general redemption schedule applies.

[. . .]

Contract Claims

The plaintiff's contract claims arise out of alleged violations of state contract law. Section 113 of the Indenture provides that the Indenture and the Debentures shall be governed by New York law. Under New York law, the terms of the Debentures constitute a contract between ADM and the holders of the Debentures, including Morgan Stanley . . .

We note as an initial matter that where, as here, the contract language in dispute is a "boilerplate" provision found in numerous debentures and indenture agreements, the desire to give such language a consistent, uniform interpretation requires that the Court construe the language as a matter of law. *See Sharon Steel Corp. v. Chase Manhattan Bank, N.A.,* 691 F.2d 1039, 1048–49 (2d Cir.1982).

In *Franklin Life Insurance Co. v. Commonwealth Edison Co.,* 451 F.Supp. 602 (S.D.Ill.1978), *aff'd per curiam on the opinion below,* 598 F.2d 1109 (7th Cir.), *rehearing and rehearing en banc denied, id.,* cert. denied, 444 U.S. 900, 100 S.Ct. 210, 62 L.Ed.2d 136 (1979), the district court found, with respect to language nearly identical to that now before us, that an early redemption of preferred stock was lawful where funded directly from the proceeds of a common stock offering.

[. . .]

Morgan Stanley contends [. . .] that *Franklin* was wrongly decided, as a matter of law, and that a fresh examination of the redemption language in light of the applicable New York cases would lead us to reject the "source" rule. In this regard, Morgan Stanley suggests a number of universal axioms of contract construction intended to guide us in construing the redemption language as a matter of first impression. For example, Morgan counsels that we should construe the contract terms in light of their "plain meaning," and should adopt the interpretation that best accords with all the terms of the contract . . . Words are not to be construed as meaningless if they can be made significant by a reasonable construction of the contract . . . Where several constructions are possible, the court may look to the surrounding facts and circumstances to determine the intent of the parties. Finally, Morgan Stanley urges that all ambiguities should be resolved against the party that drafted the agreement. [. . .]

We find these well-accepted and universal principles of contract construction singularly unhelpful in construing the contract language before us. Several factors lead us to this conclusion. First, there is simply no "plain meaning" suggested by the redemption language that would imbue all the contract terms with a significant meaning. Either party's interpretation of the redemption language would dilute the meaning of at least some of the words—either the "indirectly or directly," "in anticipation of" language, were we to adopt defendant's "source" rule, or the "from the proceeds," "as part of a refunding operation" language, were we to adopt the plaintiff's interpretation. Any attempt to divine the "plain meaning" of the redemption language would be disingenuous at best.

Equally fruitless would be an effort to discern the "intent of the parties" under the facts of this case. It may very well be that ADM rejected an absolute no-call provision in its negotiations with the underwriters in favor of language it viewed as providing "greater flexibility." It is also clear, however, that neither the underwriters nor ADM knew whether such "flexibility" encompassed redemption under the facts of this case. The deposition testimony of ADM officials suggesting that they believed at the time they negotiated the Indenture that they could redeem the Debentures at any time except through lower-cost debt merely begs the question. Had ADM management so clearly intended the Indenture to allow refunding under the circumstances of this case, it surely would have considered that option prior to the suggestions of Merrill Lynch, which appears to represent the first time the idea of early redemption funded directly by the proceeds of a stock issue was presented by any of ADM's investment advisors.

Finally, we view this as a most inappropriate case to construe ambiguous contract language against the drafter. The Indenture was negotiated by sophisticated bond counsel on both sides of the bargaining table. There is no suggestion of disparate bargaining power in the drafting of the Indenture, nor could there be. Moreover, even if we were to adopt this rule, it is not at all clear that ADM would be considered the drafter of the Indenture, given the active participation of the managing underwriter. Indeed, it is arguable that the ambiguous language should be construed in favor of ADM. *See Broad v. Rockwell International Corp., supra,* 642 F.2d at 947 n. 20 (purchaser of Debentures may stand in the shoes of the underwriters that originally negotiated and drafted the debentures).

Not only do the rules of contract construction provide little aid on the facts before us, but we find the equities in this action to be more or less in equilibrium. Morgan Stanley now argues, no doubt in good faith, that the redemption is unlawful under the Indenture. Nevertheless, as we noted in our prior opinion, Morgan Stanley employees were fully aware of the uncertain legal status of an early call at the time they purchased the ADM Debentures. To speak of upsetting Morgan's "settled expectations" would thus be rather misleading under the circumstances. By the same token, however, it is also clear that ADM had no expectations with respect to the availability of an early redemption call until the idea was first suggested by Merrill Lynch.

Because we find equitable rules of contract construction so unhelpful on the facts of this case, the decision in *Franklin* takes on added importance. [. . .]

Accordingly, we find that the ADM redemption was lawful under the terms of the Debentures and the Indenture, and that therefore defendant's motion for summary judgment on Counts VI and X through XII is hereby granted.

[. . .]

NOTES AND QUESTIONS

1.   This case revolves around a fairly common covenant in bond indentures. Basically, and somehow simplifying, the covenant states that the corporation can redeem the bonds (anticipate the repayment of the loan), but only if it does not use, for the repayment, funds obtained by borrowing money at an interest rate lower than a set threshold. The goal of this contractual provision is straightforward. If interest rates are lower than a certain threshold in comparison with the interest paid by the bonds, it means that interest rates are going down on the market. This suggests that the bondholders are in a desirable position: they own bonds that pay a high interest rate. If they are repaid in advance, they will unlikely be able to reinvest their funds at the same or better conditions. It is however often difficult to identify the source of the proceeds used to redeem the bonds. In this case, in fact, the corporation (ADM) also issued common stock, and argued that it used the proceeds from this issuance of shares to redeem the bonds. Merrill Lynch, a bondholder, sued. Could you write a hypothetical provision in the trust indenture in a less ambiguous and problematic way?

2.   One of the most interesting parts of the case is the discussion made by the Court of principles of contract interpretation. The Court, based on the complaint, mentions different criteria: plain meaning; not interpreting words as meaningless when reasonable; looking at surrounding facts and circumstances to determine the intent of the parties when different constructions are possible; and, in case of ambiguities, to interpret a rule against the party that drafted the agreement. It is often said that common law courts tend to interpret contracts more "literally," rarely going out of the "four corners" of the contract (and consider, in this respect, the "parol evidence rule"); while for civil law to determine the common intention of the

parties is so important that judges are more willing to use extra-textual evidence. According to some, this is one of the reasons why contracts in the Anglo-Saxon world are generally longer and more detailed. Based on your experience, do you think that this difference really exists? And, if so, could the different approaches, in this case, lead to different outcomes? Even in systems that emphasize a more subjective interpretation approach, corporate charters and bylaws are often interpreted in a more objective, textual and narrow way. Can you tell why?

3.   The Court decided not to follow the rules of contract interpretation proposed by Merrill Lynch, the plaintiff, and rather to follow the precedent of *Franklin*. How did the Court reach this conclusion?

* * *

A fairly common type of bonds are bonds convertible into shares. Holders of these instruments generally have the option, at a certain future date, to convert their bonds into common shares. Basically, they pay the newly issued shares renouncing their credit toward the corporation, and become shareholders. Since they are future shareholders, some legal systems treat them, with respect to some corporate transactions, as shareholders, anticipating the fact that they might or will become shareholders. One interesting problem concerns pre-emptive rights that we discussed in the previous section. Take, for example, the case of Spain, a legal system that, also in accordance with EU law, provides for mandatory pre-emptive rights. Under Spanish law, in case new shares are issued before conversion, convertible bondholders were granted the right to subscribe proportionally the new shares, in order to avoid dilution. But was this provision consistent with EU law mandating pre-emptive rights for shareholders (and, apparently, *only* shareholders)? The next case, a groundbreaking decision of the European Court of Justice handed down in 2008, addresses this issue.

COMMISSION OF THE EUROPEAN COMMUNITIES V. KINGDOM OF SPAIN

European Court of Justice (First Chamber)
Case C–338/06—18 December 2008

[. . .]

By its application, the Commission of the European Communities requests that the Court declare that: . . . by granting the right to pre-emptive subscription rights for bonds convertible into shares not only to shareholders, but also to holders of bonds convertible into shares pertaining to earlier issues, . . . the Kingdom of Spain has failed to fulfil its obligations under Articles 29 and 42 of Second Council Directive 77/91/EEC of 13 December 1976 on coordination of safeguards which, for the protection of the interests of members and others, are required by

Member States of companies within the meaning of the second paragraph of Article [48] of the Treaty, in respect of the formation of public limited liability companies and the maintenance and alteration of their capital, with a view to making such safeguards equivalent (OJ 1977 L 26, p. 1; 'the Second Directive').

Legal context

Community law

The second and fifth recitals in the preamble to the Second Directive, which are legally based on Article 54(3)(g) of the EEC Treaty (subsequently Article 54(3)(g) of the EC Treaty, and now Article 44(2)(g) EC), are worded as follows:

> "Whereas in order to ensure minimum equivalent protection for both shareholders and creditors of [public limited liability companies], the coordination of national provisions relating to their formation and to the maintenance, increase or reduction of their capital is particularly important;
>
> [. . .]
>
> Whereas it is necessary, having regard to the objectives of Article [44(2)(g) EC], that the Member States' laws relating to the increase or reduction of capital ensure that the principles of equal treatment of shareholders in the same position and of protection of creditors whose claims exist prior to the decision on reduction are observed and harmonized."

Article 29 of the Second Directive provides:

> "1. Whenever the capital is increased by consideration in cash, the shares must be offered on a pre-emptive basis to shareholders in proportion to the capital represented by their shares.
>
> [. . .]
>
> 4. The right of pre-emption may not be restricted or withdrawn by the statutes or instrument of incorporation. This may, however, be done by decision of the general meeting. The administrative or management body shall be required to present to such a meeting a written report indicating the reasons for restriction or withdrawal of the right of pre-emption, and justifying the proposed issue price. The general meeting shall act in accordance with the rules for a quorum and a majority laid down in Article 40 . . .
>
> [. . .]
>
> 6. Paragraphs 1 to 5 shall apply to the issue of all securities which are convertible into shares or which carry the right to

subscribe for shares, but not to the conversion of such securities, nor to the exercise of the right to subscribe."

Article 42 of the Second Directive provides:

"For the purposes of the implementation of this Directive, the laws of the Member States shall ensure equal treatment to all shareholders who are in the same position."

National law

Under Article 158(1) of Royal Legislative Decree 1564/1989 of 22 December 1989, which amends the Law on public companies (Real decreto legislativo 1564/1989 por el que se aprueba el texto refundido de la Ley de Sociedades Anónimas) (BOE No 310, of 27 December 1989, p. 679), in the version applicable to the present dispute ('the LSA'):

"Where the capital is increased by means of the issue of new ordinary or preference shares, the shareholders and holders of convertible bonds may . . . exercise their right to subscribe for a number of shares proportionate to the nominal value of the shares which they already hold or, in the case of holders of convertible bonds, which they would hold if, at that time, they exercised their right to conversion."

Article 159 of the LSA provides:

"1. If necessary in the company's interest, the general meeting may, when deciding to increase the capital, resolve to withdraw the right of pre-emptive subscription entirely or partly. For this resolution to be valid, it must conform with the provisions of Article 144 and ensure that:

[. . .]

(b) at the time of convening the meeting, the shareholders shall be provided, in accordance with Article 144(1)(c), with a report drawn up by the directors in which they justify in detail the proposal and the issue price of the shares, giving the names of the persons to whom they are to be allotted, together with a report, for which the directors are liable, prepared by an auditor who is not the company's auditor and is appointed for that purpose by the Commercial Registry, on the fair value of the company's shares, the theoretical value of the rights to pre-emption subscription which it is proposed to withdraw and the accuracy of the information in the directors' report;

(c) the nominal value of the shares to be issued, together with the issue premium, as the case may be, shall correspond to the fair value shown in the auditor's report referred to in (b) above. In the case of a listed company, the fair value shall mean the market value of the company's shares, which shall be presumed to be the stock exchange quotation, unless the contrary is proved.

Nevertheless, in the case of listed companies, the general meeting of shareholders may, as soon as the directors' report and the auditor's report required under (b) above, which must indicate the net asset value of the shares, are available, freely determine the issue price of the new shares, provided that the price is higher than the corresponding net asset value shown in the auditor's report. The general meeting may also confine itself to laying down the procedure for determining the price. [. . .]"

Article 293 of the LSA is worded as follows:

"1.　The shareholders of the company shall have a right of preemption for the convertible bonds.

2.　The holders of convertible bonds issued earlier shall have the same right in the proportion laid down by the rules on the conversion.

3.　The provisions of Article 158 of this law shall apply to the preferential right of subscription for convertible bonds."

[. . .]

The action

[. . .]

Arguments of the parties

By its second and third complaints, which must be examined together, the Commission submits first that Article 158(1) of the LSA gives not only shareholders but also holders of bonds convertible into shares a right of pre-emption for new shares. Secondly, Article 293(2) of that law provides that when there is an issue of bonds convertible into shares, a right of pre-emption for those shares is granted both to shareholders and to holders of earlier issues of convertible bonds.

These provisions of the LSA, it argues, infringe Article 29(1) and (6) of the Second Directive, since the directive requires new shares and convertible bonds to be offered on a pre-emptive basis to shareholders alone.

The Kingdom of Spain and the Republic of Poland dispute the Commission's claim, relying, in particular, on an interpretation of Article 29(1) and (6) on the basis of the directive's purpose and function, which is to protect the holders of convertible bonds as potential shareholders and thus to maintain the value of the shares reserved for them.

Findings of the Court

It is indeed the case, as the Kingdom of Spain submits, that Article 29(1) and (6) of the Second Directive does not provide that both the new shares and the bonds convertible into shares are to be offered exclusively to the shareholders and that they can thus also be offered to holders of earlier issues of convertible bonds.

It must be held, however, that it is apparent from the very wording of that article that the offer must not be made to both of them simultaneously, but 'on a pre-emptive basis' to the shareholders.

Thus, only in so far as the shareholders have not exercised their right of pre-emption can those shares and bonds be offered to other purchasers, including, in particular, the holders of convertible bonds.

Furthermore, if the legislature had wished to extend the right of pre-emption at issue to the latter, it would have done so expressly, in the same way as, in Article 29(6) of the Second Directive, it extended the right of pre-emption to other securities which are convertible into shares or which carry the right to subscribe for shares.

Such an interpretation also accords with the aims of the directive.

As the Advocate General pointed out in point 76 of her Opinion, and as is apparent from point 19 of the judgment in *Siemens*, one of the aims of the Second Directive is to afford shareholders more effective protection, by enabling them—in the event of an increase in capital—to avoid dilution of their stake in the capital represented by their shareholding.

Thus, in order to avoid such a risk, Article 29(1) and (6) of the Second Directive gives precisely to shareholders priority over all other potential purchasers of new shares or of bonds convertible into shares.

It is clear that the achievement of such an objective would be jeopardized if those new securities could also be offered on a pre-emptive basis to a category of purchasers other than that of shareholders, namely the holders of bonds convertible into shares.

It follows that, by granting a pre-emption right in respect of shares in the event of a capital increase by consideration in cash, not only to shareholders, but also to holders of bonds convertible into shares, and a pre-emption right in respect of bonds convertible into shares not only to shareholders, but also to the holders of bonds convertible into shares pertaining to earlier issues, the Kingdom of Spain has failed to fulfill its obligations under Article 29(1) and (6) of the Second Directive.

On those grounds, the Court (First Chamber) hereby:

Declares that the Kingdom of Spain:

– by granting a pre-emption right in respect of shares in the event of a capital increase by consideration in cash, not only to shareholders, but also to holders of bonds convertible into shares;

[. . .]

– has failed to fulfill its obligations under Article 29 of Second Council Directive 77/91/EEC of 13 December 1976 on coordination of safeguards which, for the protection of the interests of members and others, are required by Member States of companies within the meaning of the second paragraph of Article [48] of the Treaty, in respect of the formation of public limited liability companies and the maintenance and alteration of their capital, with a view to making such safeguards equivalent.

NOTES AND QUESTIONS

1.   According to the European Court of Justice, Spain (and other EU Member States) cannot grant pre-emptive rights to convertible bondholders because this would infringe on shareholders' pre-emptive rights. Based on the relevant provisions cited in the decision, do you agree with this outcome?

2.   Would a contractual provision in the bond indenture providing for a different exchange ratio of convertible bonds into shares in case new shares are issued before the conversion be acceptable?

3.   As a research project, you could investigate if currently there are other European countries that provide for pre-emptive rights on newly issued shares for convertible bondholders, notwithstanding this decision. If such countries exist, do they violate European Law in light of the European Court of Justice decision above?

3.   Leaving aside any legal consideration, from an economic standpoint, do you think it makes sense to grant pre-emptive rights to convertible bondholders?

EQUITABLE SUBORDINATION OF SHAREHOLDERS' LOANS

Shareholders are free to provide financial resources to the corporation not only through shares, but also extending loans to the corporation. In other words, they can be both residual claimants (as equity holders) and fixed claimants (as creditors). There could be legitimate reasons to do that, for example tax reasons. The situation in which a shareholder is both a residual claimant and a creditor of the corporation, however, can also lead to abuses, especially when the corporation is approaching insolvency.

Imagine that a corporation is in dire straits, and needs an infusion of cash from its shareholders. If a shareholder buys additional shares, he risks losing his investment if the corporation goes under the water: in case of bankruptcy, creditors will be paid first (and often not entirely), and generally nothing, or very little, will be left for shareholders. The shareholder can therefore decide, together with the directors, that it is preferable to make a loan to the corporation. In this case, at least in theory, his repayment will not be subordinated to the payment of all other external creditors, and he will be paid back pro rata for his loan, together with the other creditors (the Latin expression is "par condicio creditorum"). Especially when the shareholder is exploiting inside information on the financial conditions of the corporation, and maybe is himself a director, this outcome is inequitable and might hinder the confidence of creditors.

Common law courts have thus developed the doctrine of "equitable subordination" of shareholders' loans. Under this theory, when there are indicia of abuse, the claim of a shareholder can be disallowed, or subordinated to other claims. In the U.S., this doctrine is sometimes called the "*Deep Rock*" doctrine, from the 1939 Supreme Court case that first adopted it (*Taylor v. Standard Gas & Electric Co.*). As with all equitable doctrines, its precise contours are not very precisely drawn. Professor Elizabeth Warren referred to it as "murky, rambling doctrine" (The Law of Debtors and Creditors, Aspen, 2009, p. 576).

In a 2001 case decided by the U.S. Court of Appeals for the Sixth Circuit, *In re AutoStyle Plastics, Inc.* (269 F.3d 726), the Court clearly identifies what, in its opinion, should be the elements of equitable subordination:

> "This court has adopted a three-part standard for establishing equitable subordination: (1) the claimant must have engaged in some type of inequitable conduct; (2) the misconduct must have resulted in injury to the creditors of the bankrupt or conferred an unfair advantage on the claimant; and (3) equitable subordination of the claim must not be inconsistent with the provisions of the Bankruptcy Act. [. . .]. Satisfaction of this three-part standard does not mean that a court is *required* to equitably subordinate a claim, but rather that the court is *permitted* to take such action. [. . .]

> When reviewing equitable subordination claims, courts impose a higher standard of conduct upon insiders. Indeed, "[a] claim arising from the dealings between a debtor and an insider is to be rigorously scrutinized by the courts." *In re Fabricators,* 926

F.2d 1458, 1465 (5th Cir.1991); *see also In re Hyperion,* 158 B.R. at 563. Therefore, "if the claimant is an insider, less egregious conduct may support equitable subordination." *In re Herby's Foods, Inc.,* 2 F.3d 128, 131 (5th Cir.1993); *cf. In re Fabricators,* 926 F.2d at 1465 ("If the claimant is not an insider, then evidence of more egregious conduct such as fraud, spoliation or overreaching is necessary."). . . .

While we apply careful scrutiny in our review of an equitable subordination claim involving an insider, we use great caution in applying the remedy: "equitable subordination is an unusual remedy which should be applied in limited circumstances."

The Court also makes a clear distinction between "equitable subordination" and "recharacterization" of a claim:

"The effect of a bankruptcy court's recharacterization of a claim from debt to equity may be similar to the court's subordination of a claim through equitable subordination in that, in both cases, the claim is subordinated below that of other creditors. However, there are important differences between a court's analysis of recharacterization and equitable subordination issues. Not only do recharacterization and equitable subordination serve different *functions,* but the *extent to which a claim is subordinated* under each process may be different. [. . .]. Recharacterization cases "turn on whether a debt actually exists, not on whether the claim should be equitably subordinated." Matthew Nozemack, Note, *Making Sense Out of Bankruptcy Courts' Recharacterization of Claims: Why Not Use § 501(c) Equitable Subordination?,* 56 Wash. & Lee L.Rev. 689, 716 (1999) (criticizing *Pacific Express*). In a recharacterization analysis, if the court determines that the advance of money is equity and not debt, the claim is recharacterized and the *effect* is subordination of the claim "as a proprietary interest because the corporation repays capital contributions only after satisfying all other obligations of the corporation." *Id.* at 719. In an equitable subordination analysis, the court is reviewing whether a legitimate creditor engaged in inequitable conduct, in which case the *remedy* is subordination of the creditor's claim "to that of another creditor *only to the extent necessary* to offset injury or damage suffered by the creditor in whose favor the equitable doctrine may be effective." *In re W.T. Grant Co.,* 4 B.R. 53, 74 (Bankr.S.D.N.Y.1980) (emphasis added). If a claim is recharacterized and, therefore "the advance is not a claim to begin with" and the creditor is not a legitimate one, "then equitable subordination never comes into play."

* * *

Other systems have similar rules. For example, under Italian law, Article 2467 of the Civil Code, applicable to *società a responsabilità limitata* (LLCs), provides that loans made by shareholders to the company are subordinated to creditors' claims, and repayments of shareholders' loans that occur in the year before bankruptcy must be returned to the trustee in bankruptcy. The rule, however, only applies to loans made at a time when "the financial structure of the corporation was not balanced in terms of indebtedness," or when "a capital contribution would have been reasonable": two very ambiguous concepts that require a complex factual analysis and that are clearly difficult to apply. It should also be observed that differently from the American Doctrine of Equitable Subordination, the Italian statutory provision does not seem to require the proof of inequitable conduct. The financial "irrationality" of the loan should be sufficient.

Germany also has both case law and statutory provisions concerning subordination of shareholders' claims. Shareholders' loans are a very controversial issue in Germany. Originally, there were no statutory provisions on this issue. However, in the second half of the twentieth century courts started to apply the provisions on stated capital to shareholder loans, basically holding that a repayment of a shareholder loan constituted a violation of the principles of stated capital if the loan was given by shareholders to a financially distressed corporation (a concept that might be similar to the U.S. idea of "zone of insolvency"). The expression "financial distress" was defined as a situation in which the corporation could not get a loan from third parties at normal market conditions. Shareholders started to circumvent this case law purchasing assets that would be leased to the corporation, and courts started to apply the prohibition also to these leasing agreements. Courts argued that, during a financial crisis, shareholders should finance the corporation with equity, not with additional debt (*Finanzierungsfolgenverantwortung*), and that consequently their loans have to be considered as *de facto equity* (*Eigenkapitalersatz*). This practice might also prolong artificially the life of a corporation with further negative externalities. In this situation, the only legitimate kind of investment of a shareholder would be equity. Therefore, a loan of a shareholder to the corporation during a financial crisis could be (re)qualified as equity.

These developments created legal uncertainty; the German legislature therefore adopted a new approach in 2008 with the Statute to Modernize the Law on Private Limited Companies and Combat Abuses (*Gesetz zur Modernisierung des GmbH-Rechts und zur Bekämpfung von Missbräuchen—MoMiG*). Under these provisions, shareholders are generally not prohibited from extending loans to their corporations. However, in case of bankruptcy, the claims of the shareholder for the restitution of the loans are generally subordinated to the claims of external creditors (§ 39 subs. 1 no. 1 German Insolvency Statute (*Insolvenzordnung*)). Moreover, the bankruptcy trustee can claim a repayment from the shareholders if the loan was repaid to the shareholders in the year preceding the request to open bankruptcy proceedings (§ 135 subs. 1 no. 2 German Insolvency Statute).

Based on this brief discussion of equitable subordination of shareholders loans, try to draft the best possible provision regulating the phenomenon for the fictional country of Lawland, of which you are the benevolent dictator.

CHAPTER 5

CORPORATE GOVERNANCE

■ ■ ■

INTRODUCTION

"Corporate Governance" is an ambiguous term. Narrowly defined, it concerns the powers, rights, and duties of the different corporate bodies (in particular, shareholders' meeting and directors and, when it exists as a separate body, the board of supervisors or auditors), and deals with the internal organizational structure of the corporation and its functioning. In a broader sense, however, it also includes other legal and economic instruments that affect the conduct of directors and shareholders: in this broader sense, for example, the market for corporate control and takeovers regulation is also a governance mechanism, in the sense that the possibility of a takeover can "police" the conduct of directors. More generally one might argue that, directly or indirectly, corporate governance can include all rules that have an effect on the governing bodies of the corporation including, for example, rules concerning the financial structure of the corporation, or shareholders' agreements.

In this chapter, we will focus on corporate governance in a fairly narrow perspective. We will first consider the different corporate governance models that can be found around the world, discuss the composition of the board, and finally focus on one of the fundamental relationships defining the governance of the corporation, the one between the shareholders' meeting and the board of directors. In particular we will discuss the often blurred line that divides the powers and competences of the shareholders from the ones of the directors. Needless to say, as in other parts of this book, it is impossible to cover everything: we selected a few topics to make the discussion more specific, concrete, and relevant.

CORPORATE GOVERNANCE MODELS

If one wants to focus on all the details of existing governance models, it would probably be necessary to conclude that each country has its own system. It is possible, however, to group existing models in three basic families: most legal systems can be considered adopting one variation of these three basic models.

The first one can be defined the "one-tier," "Anglo-Saxon" model, followed in the U.K., the U.S., and most former British colonies, in which the shareholders' meeting appoints a board of directors. Within the board of directors, especially in larger and more complex organizations, several committees are usually established, either because the law mandates them, or because it is a best practice voluntarily followed by most corporations. A particularly important committee is the audit committee, which has a controlling function on the activity of the board and sometimes on accounting and financial issues. A second model is the "two-tier" or "German model," in which the shareholders' meeting appoints a board of supervisors (in German, *Aufsichtsrat*), and the board of supervisors, in turn, appoints (and might revoke) a managing board (in German, *Vorstand*). The first body, as the name suggests, has primarily controlling functions, and sometimes is responsible for approving strategic plans and the financial statements of the corporation; the managing board has the responsibility to carry on the day-to-day business of the corporation (more precisely: to coordinate with and oversee managers and executives concerning the day-to-day activities). A third model could be defined the "traditional Latin model," and has originally developed in France, Italy, Spain, and countries that trace their legal origins to these systems. Japan, China and Taiwan, usually classified as German-law based countries for corporate law, also adopt this model, confirming the diversity determined by legal transplants today. In this case, the shareholders appoint both a board of directors and a separate body entrusted with controlling functions: the "*commissaires aux comptes*" in France, the "*collegio sindacale*" in Italy, the "*auditores*" in Spain, the "*Kausayaku-Kai*" in Japan and the "*jian-shi-hui*" in China. In Taiwan, the members of this body are called "*jian-cha-ren*," but there is no special name for the body because their office, and the way they act, is individual, not collective, in order to ensure greater independence (this is an interesting concept: can the existence of a body somehow affect independence? What about efficacy?)

The following diagrams illustrate the three models.

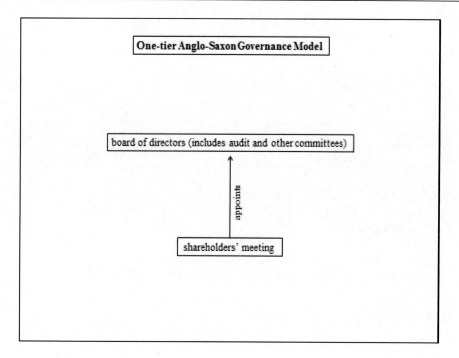

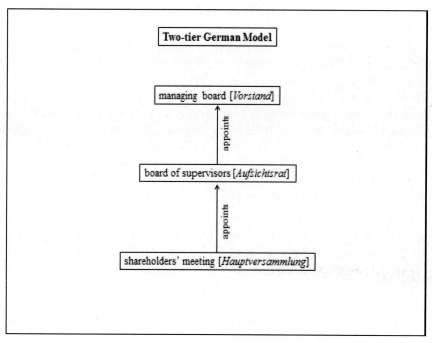

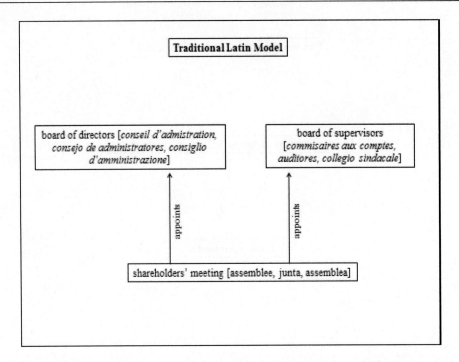

In all three models, there is often also an external and independent auditor, usually mandatory in listed corporations, which audits the financial statements and performs other functions especially concerning evaluations and financial issues (e.g., confirming the fair price of newly issued shares when required). One variation of the Latin model worth mentioning can be found in Brazil, where listed corporations can, as a controlling body, either have a permanent or a temporary "fiscal board" (*conselho fiscal*). For further information on this model, and empirical data on its use, *see* B. S. Black—A. Gledson de Carvalho—É. Gorga, *Corporate Governance in Brazil* (2009), available on *www.ssrn.com*, and also, if you read Portuguese (which you should), É. Gorga, *Direito Societário Atual*, Elsevier, 2013, 263 ff.

In Germany, during the National Socialist dictatorship, a general corporation statute was enacted in 1937 (substituted with a new statute in 1965). In terms of governance, one distinctive feature of the 1937 German Corporation Law was the so-called *Führerprinzip*, or "rule of the leader," according to which—in line with the dominating ideology—the President of the *Vorstand* could adopt decisions also without the consent of the other members of the board and, in addition, the *Vorstand* had to manage the corporation not only in the interest of the shareholders, but also of the people and of the State (§ 70 *AktG* 1937: "*wie der allgemeine Nutzen von Volk und Reich es forden*"). We will come back to this issue later.

One interesting characteristic of the German governance model, partially followed also in other system, is "co-determination" (*"Mitbestimmung"*). The expression refers to the mandatory representation of employees in the board of supervisors of larger corporations. This so-called workers' co-determination as it is structured today was mainly introduced by the Allied Forces after World War II, because the German coal and steel conglomerates had supported the Third Reich and the German military. Arguably, some large mining enterprises, and their controlling shareholders or directors, had facilitated the Nazi rearmament, and one of the ideas underpinning co-determination was that a more "democratic" composition of the board, with workers' representatives, would prevent risky alliances between right-wing dictatorships and industrial potentates to occur again in the future. Consequently, the supervisory boards of several newly formed corporations in the coal and steel industry had to include representatives of the workers. After this restructuring of the coal and steel industry was set into place by the Western allies in the Western sectors of Germany, this structure became legally binding for the entire coal and steel industry in 1951 pursuant to the Mining Co-Determination Act (*Montan-Mitbestimmungsgesetz*), which required all steel and coal companies with more than 1,000 employees to have a supervisory board consisting of eleven members, five of which were appointed by the employees, and five by the shareholders. The eleventh board member had (and has) to be appointed by both groups.

In 1976, workers' co-determination was expanded to all corporations by the Workers Co-Determination Act (*Mitbestimmungsgesetz*). According to this statute, all corporations with more than 2,000 employees must have a supervisory board in which half of the members are appointed by the shareholders and half by the employees. The chairman of the supervisory board, appointed by a two-thirds majority of the members of the board, has a casting vote. If the supervisory board does not reach a two-thirds majority to appoint the chairman, the representatives of the shareholders appoint him or her, and the representatives of the employees appoint the deputy chairman. Moreover, all corporations with more than 500 employees must have a supervisory board in which one-third of board members are appointed by the employees ("One-third Workers Co-Determination Act" or *"Drittelmitbestimmungsgesetz"*). Although generally all German corporations fall under the scope of the workers co-determination, co-determination does not apply to corporations with a political, confessional, charitable, scientific, artistic, or journalistic purpose since this would be considered an unjustified violation of the fundamental rights of the owners of the corporations regarding freedom of speech, religion, press, etc. The German Constitutional Court upheld the Workers Co-Determination Act (*Mitbestimmungsgesetz*) of 1976 by arguing that, for corporations with a different purpose than the ones mentioned above, shareholders' property rights are sufficiently protected by granting a double voting right to the chairman of the supervisory board appointed by the shareholders in the absence of an agreement between shareholders and employees (*see* Constitutional Court as of 1/3/1979—1 BvR 532, 533/77, 419/77, 419/78, 1 BvL 21/78, BVerfGE 50, 290). Although some members of the supervisory board are appointed by shareholders, and some by employees, there is not a distinction concerning the legal duties of board members. Consequently, all members of the supervisory board have to act in the best interest of the corporation and all members of the supervisory board can be held liable for a violation of this duty. Nevertheless one has to consider that German corporate law follows a rather broad definition of the best interest of the corporation taking into account the interest of the workers, the creditors and the shareholders as a whole.

Interestingly enough, several other European legal systems provide for some form of co-determination, of course with notable local variations: Austria, Denmark, Finland, France, Luxembourg, the Netherlands, Poland, and Sweden (in France, for example, the number of representatives of the workers on corporations' boards is lower than in Germany). A proposal for co-determination was even considered in the United Kingdom, just before the "winter of discontent" (the winter of widespread strikes in 1977–1978 that lead to Thatcherism), in the so-called "Bullock Report." The effect of workers' representations in the Anglo-Saxon model would have been even more profound than in Germany because in this latter case the workers only appoint members of the supervisory board, not of the managing board; in the British proposal, on the other hand, the representatives of the workers would have been seated in a board with managing functions. The idea was however abandoned. The European Union also has entertained the idea of harmonized legislation on this issue, but no proposal has ever reached a sufficient level of consensus.

What could be the causes and consequences of co-determination, for example with respect to labor law? The following excerpt offers some interesting insights.

JENS DAMMAN, THE MANDATORY LAW PUZZLE: REDEFINING AMERICAN EXCEPTIONALISM IN CORPORATE LAW
65 HASTINGS L. J. 441 (2014)[1]

[. . .]

One of these reasons relates to the function of codetermination as a disclosure mechanism. As Henry Hansmann has shown in his seminal

---

[1] Footnotes omitted.

work on corporate ownership, a central benefit of codetermination is that it can lower the corporation's contracting costs by reducing informational asymmetries between firms and the labor unions with whom they negotiate. If labor unions lack credible information about their bargaining partners' economic situation, then both sides might resort to costly measures such as strikes or lockouts. Codetermination helps to overcome this problem. Through the employee representatives on corporate boards, the unions have reliable information about the economic situation of firms, greatly reducing the likelihood of strikes and other distributive measures.

The disclosure function of codetermination is now widely recognized. Crucially, it has important implications for explaining transnational differences in codetermination laws. Obviously, the disclosure function can only acquire relevance where firms (or associations of firms) are confronted with labor unions, and where wages are in fact determined by collective bargaining agreements. It is in this context that a further difference between the United States and Europe gains importance. Compared to the United States, European countries rely much more strongly on collective bargaining agreements to set wages.

As of 2011—the most recent year for which data is available—only about 13% of U.S. employees were covered by collective bargaining agreements. This number contrasts rather sharply with the corresponding percentages in European countries: 99% of employees are covered in Austria, 92% in France, 92% in Slovenia, 91% in Sweden, 89.5% in Finland, 62% in Germany, 40% in Slovakia, and 28.9% in Poland.

It follows that one of the central benefits of codetermination—namely its potential to reduce bargaining costs between labor unions and employers—simply has much more relevance in many European countries, such as Germany, France, or Austria, than it does in the United States. This does not per se imply that codetermination is efficient in Europe; even there, its costs might outweigh its benefits. However, the crucial point is that codetermination is likely to be relatively more efficient in Europe than in the United States.

[. . .]

There is also another reason why codetermination might be more efficient in Europe than the United States. In practice, the employee representatives tend to use their role in the supervisory board to voice the concerns of employees and ensure, as they view it, that the latter are treated fairly. The additional protection thus accorded to employees might be the answer to an efficiency problem that arises due to the particular structure of European employment law. In the United States, employees can generally be fired at will. In most European countries, by contrast, the basic rule is that employees cannot be terminated without cause. One can question whether this type of strong employment protection is efficient, but that is beside the point. As a practical matter, for most European countries, far-reaching steps toward the liberalization of employment markets are simply not politically feasible.

One major drawback of the for-cause requirement is that it creates an obvious incentive for harassment and, more generally, bad faith treatment. Seeking to rid themselves of below-average employees, employers have an incentive to make the relevant employees' work environment unpleasant in order to persuade them to quit "voluntarily." This is an issue of great practical importance. Empirical studies in various European countries suggest that workplace bullying is a widespread and serious problem affecting between two and twenty-two percent of employees and that it has significant negative consequences for the health of employees.

Admittedly, one can make a theoretical case that workplace bullying and other bad faith treatment aimed at persuading employees to leave is not necessarily inefficient. After all, if one strongly believes in the efficiency of termination at will, then measures that weaken Europe's for-cause requirements might seem prima facie desirable. However, in light of the significant negative impact that bullying has on the affected employees' health—costs that are not usually reflected in the employer's cost-benefit analysis—such a line of reasoning seems rather implausible.

If, on the other hand, one assumes that bullying aimed at persuading workers to quit is inefficient, then one of codetermination's benefits might be that it provides some protection against such bullying; employee representatives can use their clout in the supervisory board to persuade corporations to respect the rights of the employees. If one further assumes that American employers who can fire their employees at will do not need to rely on bullying to rid themselves of unwanted employees, the relevant protection might be more sorely needed in Europe than in the United States.

In sum, the fact that some European countries protect employees through corporate governance, while the United States does not, can be explained to a certain extent by efficiency considerations. Codetermination might simply be a response to Europe's heavier reliance on collective bargaining agreements and less flexible termination rules.

* * *

It is interesting also to consider the possible effects of co-determination on securities markets. One might argue, for example, that a board that includes representatives of the employees might be particularly adverse to a hostile acquisition or merger, fearing that the transactions will lead (as is often the case) to layoffs. In this respect the

German governance structure, and the use of *Mitbestimmung* in particular, can contribute to explain, according to some commentators, the lower level of takeover activity in Germany as opposed to the U.K. or the U.S.

We have mentioned the three basic governance models, and linked them to their countries of origin. It should be noted, however, that in the last few decades several countries have made available different governance models to their corporations: a corporation can, in its bylaws, opt for one of two or sometimes even three models available in a "menu" offered by the legislatures. Since 1966, for example, in France it is possible to opt between the traditional model discussed above, and a two-tier model with a *conseil de surveillance* and a *directoire* similar to the German system. Some large French corporations have adopted this option. Several other European systems offer two models to choose from, and some even three: this is the case of Italy, after a 2003 reform; and Portugal, after 2006. Also recent reforms in the Czech Republic allow to choose between different models. Japan introduced a second model in 2002, and a third one in 2014. The second one, a variation of the one-tier Anglo-Saxon system, mandates three committees within the Board of Directors (audit, compensation and nomination) with a majority of outside directors. The third model, however, is not based on the German tradition, but is rather a simplified one-tier model with only the audit committee.

The theoretical reasons why a legislature might want to add this level of flexibility are quite obvious—one size doesn't fit all: since all models have pros and cons, and it is probably impossible to define the most desirable model under all circumstances, to let the shareholders or the managers decide, providing adequate protections for minority shareholders and third parties, seems like a good idea. But what could be the practical reasons why a corporation might prefer one particular model? Before continuing reading, pause for a second and try to list possible reasons that you can imagine for adopting one of the three models.

Done? OK, let's see. Of course a first reason might be related to costs. Especially for a small, closely held corporation, some models might require fewer members of the governing bodies and therefore less expenses and a more streamlined organizational structure. The Anglo-Saxon one-tier model seems to fit the bill: it can be structured in a way that minimizes the number of board members.

On the other hand, the two-tier system could ease business combinations, especially in the case of a friendly merger. Anecdotal evidence, for example, shows that it has been adopted by some Italian banks that merged. The reason is simple, and has to do with human ego (something that should not be underestimated when negotiating a business combination): the two-tier system has two boards (even if with different functions), and therefore two "Presidents" or "Chairpersons": one for the board of supervisors, and one for the managing board. This might make it easier to accommodate the desires of the bosses of the merging corporations, granting to each of them a satisfactory position and title. In this perspective it is also possible that the German two-tier system is apt to manage a generational transition at the helm of a family business: the old founders of the corporation can sit on the supervisory board, and retain the power to appoint and remove the managing directors, but not interfere with the day-to-day operations of the business; while the new generation can serve on the managing board.

It might also be desirable for the subsidiary of a foreign parent corporation to adopt a governance structure that mirrors, or is as similar as possible, to the one of the parent. For example, a French subsidiary of a German corporation might adopt the two-tier model: the advantages of a similar governance structure, already familiar to the parent corporation, are self-evident.

Arguably, some governance models might also make hostile takeovers more difficult. For example, with the German two-tier model, if a new shareholder obtains a controlling stake in a corporation, even in the absence of a co-determination mechanism, before being able to control the management of the corporation, the new shareholder must first remove the members of the supervisory board and appoint new ones; second, the new supervisory board must change the composition of the managing board. These steps might take time and resources and contribute to make a hostile acquisition less likely or, at least, more expensive.

Even in light of these possible reasons to adopt a particular model, one should not forget that legal systems have a certain degree of inertia or, as someone prefers to say, path-dependency. Also in countries that have made multiple governance models available, statistically the traditional "local" model tends to be by far the most widely adopted, even years after the introduction of different options (as of 2013, for example, in Italy only six listed corporations—even if fairly large ones—over a total of little less than 300 had adopted the German model). In Japan, as of 2012, only 2.2% of the corporations listed on the Tokyo Stock Exchange adopted the second model introduced in 2002. Can you now understand the reasons for the introduction of the third model in Japan in 2014?

COMPOSITION OF THE BOARD OF DIRECTORS

A central issue in examining governance structures, as indicated by the discussion about co-determination, is the composition of the board of directors. There are different "categories" of directors that perform different roles. The rules concerning the composition of the board can be mandatory and provided by statute or by stock exchange listing rules, adopted voluntarily in the governing documents of the corporation, suggested by a "code of best practices" enacted by different organizations (sometimes pursuant to a "comply or explain" rule, originated in the 1990s in the U.K.), or simply followed as a matter of fact.

It would be impossible to list all the different approaches existing even just in the major jurisdictions, but it is useful to discuss the different "categories" of directors. First of all, we should mention the role of the Chairperson or President of the board. She is generally entrusted with the power and responsibility of running the meetings: calling them (even if in most jurisdictions each member of the board, or at least a qualified minority, can call a meeting), setting the agenda, conducting the discussion and the voting procedures, etc. Sometimes the Chairperson is also the Chief Executive Officer, even if this practice has been criticized by scholars and policy makers because of the concentration of power in the hands of a single individual, especially considering that the Chairperson has also the task of ensuring procedural fairness and circulation of information among board members. Several corporate governance codes require or strongly suggest separating the role of the Chairperson and of the C.E.O. A first important distinction is the one between executive and non-executive (or outside) directors. The first ones, obviously, are also executives of the corporation—which generally means employees with top managerial tasks; while outside directors only sit on the board (and are committee members) but do not have other roles within the organization especially as managers. Non-executive or outside directors are considered more "independent" from the corporation since, as opposed to executive directors, they are not involved in the day-to-day activity of the going concern, and their compensation is generally not or less strongly correlated with the economic performance of the corporation.

At least in some countries and pursuant to some corporate governance codes, however, non-executive directors should be distinguished from "independent" directors. In order to qualify as an independent director, board members must not have (or have had in the recent past) any significant personal, financial, or professional relationship with the corporation in addition, obviously, to their directorship. While generally independent directors must be non-executive directors (and they might lose their status as independent directors if they become executives), not all non-executive directors are also independent: consider, for example, a lawyer of the corporation becoming a non-executive, but also non-independent director.

Independent directors are particularly important, for example, in order to approve (or reject) resolutions in which other board members might have a conflict of interest, or transactions with related parties, as we will discuss more extensively in Chapter 6 on directors' duties.

To make our discussion more concrete, consider the following two provisions from Italy. The Italian statute regulating listed corporations (so-called "Testo Unico della Finanza" or "TUF", which means "Consolidated Law on Finance") requires that if the board of a listed corporation has more than four members—which is virtually always the case—at least one of them must have the independence requirements set forth by Article 148, Par. 3 of the same statute, pursuant to which, in relevant part, independent directors cannot be:

> "b) spouses or relatives up to the fourth degree of kinship of the directors of the company, spouses or relatives up to the fourth degree of kinship of the directors of the companies it controls, the companies it is controlled by and those subject to common control;
>
> c) persons who are linked to the company, the companies it controls, the companies it is controlled by and those subject to common control or to directors of the company or persons referred to in paragraph b) by self-employment or employment relationships or by other relationships of an economic or professional nature that might compromise their independence."

This provision raises interesting questions, demonstrating how difficult it is to write a bright-line rule concerning the concept of independence. For example, in your opinion, based on the above definition, could a non-controlling but important shareholder of a listed corporation, owning 5% of the shares, be considered "independent"?

Interestingly enough, however, one should also consider the Corporate Governance Code sponsored by Borsa Italiana, the Italian Stock Exchange. The Code is not mandatory, in the sense that listed corporations are free to adopt it entirely or in part, but they are required by law to disclose to the market what parts, if any, of the Code they follow (so-called "comply or explain" principle), and might be sanctioned if they misrepresent information in this respect. The Code provides for more rigorous rules concerning independent directors. First of all, it requires that an "adequate" number of directors should be independent; secondly, it contains a definition of independence that is more detailed and possibly more rigorous than the statutory one. The Corporate Governance Code, in other words, indicates best practices that set a higher threshold than the one established by the legislature.

The consequence is that, in light of the very high number of Italian corporations that adopt the Code, independent directors have an important role or, at least, appear frequently on the boards of directors (a different question would be to consider how truly effective they are). For example, in 2013, the average size of the board of directors of an Italian listed corporation was approximately 10 directors (slightly more in financial institutions, 14), and on average the board of directors had 3 executive directors, 3 non-executive directors, and 4 independent (and non-executive) directors (*see* Assonime-Emittenti Titoli. *La corporate governance in Italia: autodisciplina e remunerazioni (Anno 2013)*, available at http://www.assonime.it).

In the last few years, if not decades, the number and relevance of independent (and/or outside) directors have risen in virtually all developed nations. Is this desirable? Does this create the risk of a less cohesive board? Do independent directors without executive roles really have access to all the information, generally guarded by the managers, necessary to oversee the business and ensure the legality of corporate activities? Or should the supervising function of independent directors be welcome? And what are the possible causes of this evolution? In the following excerpt, Professor Gordon offers some possible explanations: even if focusing on the U.S. market, its reasoning is interesting also to consider the phenomenon in other systems.

JEFFREY N. GORDON, THE RISE OF INDEPENDENT DIRECTORS IN THE UNITED STATES, 1950–2005: OF SHAREHOLDER VALUE AND STOCK MARKET PRICES
59 Stan. L. Rev. 1465 (2007)[2]

There is a powerful trend in favor of independent directors for public firms in the United States, yet the empirical evidence adduced thus far gives us no convincing explanation. The Article suggests that this trend reflects two interrelated developments in the U.S. political economy. First is the shift to shareholder value as the primary corporate objective; the second is the greater informativeness of stock market prices. The overriding effect is to commit the firm to a shareholder wealth-maximizing strategy as best measured by stock price performance. Stock prices are taken as the measure of most things. In this environment, independent directors are more valuable than insiders. They are less committed to management and its vision. Instead, they look to outside performance signals and are less captured by the internal perspective, which, as stock prices become more informative, becomes less valuable. They can be more readily mobilized by legal standards to help provide the public goods of more accurate disclosure and better compliance with law. In this way, independent directors are an essential part of a new corporate governance paradigm. In the United States, independent directors have become a complementary institution to an economy of firms directed to maximize shareholder value. Thus, the rise of

---

[2] Footnotes omitted.

independent directors, a very important change in the political economy landscape, should be evaluated in terms of this overall conception of how to maximize social welfare.

Although this new paradigm is bound up with the use of stock market signals in the monitoring of managers, including the evaluation of management's strategic choices, it also opens up space for a distinctive role for the independent board: deciding when prevailing prices misvalue the firm and its strategies. In light of imperfectly efficient capital markets, such a role may be efficiency-based rather than an ineradicable residue of agency costs. For a particular firm, a disfavored strategy may in fact maximize shareholder value over a reasonable time horizon. If the market got it wrong, rejecting its signals may lead to putting the firm's assets to highest and best use. But the most significant efficiency gains (or losses) are systematic: idiosyncratic decisions of an independent board may keep a particular subsector of the economy from converging too rapidly on today's conventional wisdom.

The board's role in this regard is most vividly expressed in the case of an unwanted takeover bid, which, if the board resists, will ultimately be decided through an election contest rather than an immediate market test, under current Delaware law. Presumably the shareholders who would (almost always) accept a premium tender offer would (almost always) vote for directors who would be receptive to the premium offer. The differences between the two mechanisms of acceptance are transaction costs and time. On the imperfectly efficient markets view, this small dose of sand in the gears may give markets the opportunity to test predictions of how to create value before the prescription has been universally applied. Some frictions may be efficient. Note that this element of the new paradigm is not inconsistent with maximizing shareholder value; it merely imagines a somewhat longer horizon for its realization than today's stock price.

NOTES AND QUESTIONS

1. Professor Gordon's explanation is compelling, but when examining this phenomenon in a comparative perspective it might require further consideration. For example, in legal systems characterized by a more concentrated ownership structure, such as in continental Europe, independent directors could be considered important to perform a controlling function on executive directors expressed by the controlling shareholder.

2. Are we sure, however, that independent directors are really more "independent" and have sufficient information, knowledge, and understanding of the business to challenge, if necessary, executive directors? Consider, for a moment, the case of a perfectly independent director, that has no relationships with the corporation at all besides being a member of the board, but imagine that this is her only or primary source of income, and that

she can be removed or not appointed again by the controlling shareholder. Are we sure that she would have the right incentives to oppose a business decision that seems in the best interest of the controlling shareholder, but not of minority shareholders?

3. Japan is an outlier among the developed countries with its low rate of appointment of independent/outside directors. For example, some major Japanese corporations such as Toyota, Canon and Nippon Steel & Sumitomo Metal had appointed no outside (or non-executive) directors until 2013 or 2014. Although the ratio of listed corporations that appoint at least one outside director is increasing and reached 74.2% among those listed in the 1st section of Tokyo Stock Exchange as of June 2014, 39.9% of those corporations appoint only one outside director. When it comes to independent directors, 61.0% appoints at least one, and 21.7% appoints two or more. What would be the reasons of Japanese corporations' reluctance to appoint independent/outside directors? On the other hand, the Japanese government is currently encouraging listed corporations to appoint more of them, through the 2014 reform of the Companies Act and the Corporate Governance Code, which had been discussed under the auspices of the Financial Services Agency and will be adopted by the Tokyo Stock Exchange in 2015. What could be the motives of the government for such a move? See, Japan's Corporate Governance Code [Final Proposal] (March 5, 2015), available at http://www.fsa.go.jp/en/refer/councils/corporategovernance/20150306-1/01. pdf.

* * *

There is, in fact, a fourth category of directors that needs to be considered together with executive, non-executive, and independent directors: directors appointed by minority shareholders. Especially in legal systems in which the ownership structure of listed corporations is more concentrated, in which applying a strict majority rule to appoint the board would give to the controlling group complete control over the composition of the managing body, mandating a system to represent minority shareholders on the board might effectively protect the interests of small and institutional investors. Similarly, in the U.S. and the U.K., vis-à-vis a more widespread ownership structure, there is a risk that directors with strong ties with the managers might be able to self-perpetuate themselves, and minority-appointed directors can mitigate the "incestuous" relationship between managers and board members.

The following article discusses directors' elections in the U.S., explaining why often, at least until recently, shareholders had little control on the nomination of the directors, and advancing a proposal for a system that might ensure the representation of minority shareholders on the board.

MARCO VENTORUZZO, EMPOWERING SHAREHOLDERS IN
DIRECTORS' ELECTIONS: A REVOLUTION IN THE MAKING
7 EUROPEAN COMP. FIN. L. REV. 105 (2010)[3]

A specter is haunting Corporate America—the specter of Directors'
Dictatorship. [. . .] During the *Ancien Régime*, absolute European
monarchs were said to be entitled to the throne solely by the grace of God.
More moderate sovereigns, or sovereigns aspiring (or forced) to appeal to
democratic tendencies, expanded their style to include a reference to their
subjects. Oliver Cromwell, for example, was "Lord Protector" by the Grace
of God, *and the Republic*. The king of Italy, after the reunification of the
country in 1861, was such by the Grace of God, *and the Will of the Nation*.
And today Elizabeth the Second is Queen not only by the Grace of God,
but also "of the United Kingdom of Great Britain and Northern Ireland
and of Her other Realms and Territories." Do American directors reign
over their corporate empires by the will of the shareholders? Can their
tenure really be challenged by disgruntled equity investors? Does their
legitimization come from the shareholders' meeting, or from a quasi-
divine investiture granted by the board itself?

There are several reasons why sitting directors can easily coagulate
enough consensuses to obtain the election of either themselves or their
favourite candidates over candidates advanced by shareholders. In fact,
under the traditional U.S. regulatory framework, the ability of
shareholders to propose nominees to the board is severely constrained.

A first factual explanation might be found in the widespread
ownership structure of listed corporations in the U.S. It is quite difficult
for a multitude of minority shareholders, who are unrelated and hold
relatively small participation, to identify specific candidates and
coordinate to concentrate their votes on those candidates. Collective
action problems, information asymmetries and transactional costs
discourage even institutional investors from following this strategy. In
case of disagreement with the way in which the corporation is managed,
stockholders can more easily sell their shares and thus "vote with their
feet."

In this respect, however, the last decades have seen a peculiar
evolution of the ownership structure of American corporations.
Institutional investors have acquired a more central position and become
some of the most important equity holders. For an institutional investor,
it is not always possible without facing potential significant losses, to
quickly liquidate its investment. A mutual fund holding four percent of a
large listed corporation, for example, can hardly dump its shares without
causing a little earthquake both in the value of its portfolio and in the
market price of the shares. These economic limitations are sometimes

---

[3]   Footnotes omitted.

coupled with even stronger constraints. For example, index funds that replicate a particular market index with a passive investment strategy, holding the shares of the issuers that compose the index, simply cannot alter their portfolio. For these investors in particular, to actively participate in the life of the corporation and have a say in the selection of directors is often the only viable course of action to protect their investment against board's decisions that are perceived as contrary to shareholders' interests. The legal system has not, however, developed as to harmoniously respond to the change in the ownership structure.

Even ignoring the specific needs of large institutional investors, the rules currently applicable to most listed corporations raise serious doubts on directors' accountability to shareholders. Several legal hurdles stand in the way of shareholders seeking to influence the composition of the board.

The first of these hurdles concerns the majority required to appoint a director. Under Delaware law, as well as in most other states, directors are voted one-by-one, and not bundled together. Each individual nominee does not need to receive the positive vote of the majority of the shares represented at the shareholders' meeting to be appointed. Like in political elections, to be elected a plurality of the votes cast is usually sufficient; votes against a specific candidate are not possible and abstentions are not relevant. Simply, the nominees that receive the highest number of positive votes are elected. For example, if 300,000 voting shares are represented at the meeting, nominee John Doe might be elected with as little as 60 votes, if no other individual receives a higher number of positive votes. Under this rule it is easy for sitting directors to obtain the relative highest number of votes for their candidates.

In recent years, largely under the pressure of institutional investors, there has been a shift toward majority voting. In a majority voting system, nominees need to receive the majority of the votes represented at the shareholders' meeting to be elected, and therefore "no" votes or abstentions can affect the outcome of the election. According to a recent study, as of February 2007, roughly 52% of S & P 500 companies had adopted some form of majority voting in their charter or bylaws. The same study, however, demonstrates that the specific provisions implemented in the governing documents of the corporations often water down significantly the intended effects of majority voting in terms of shareholders' empowerment. The reason is that in most cases it is not provided that directors are appointed only if they receive a majority of the votes, but it is simply required that candidates to the board prepare, before their election, a resignation letter renouncing to the position if they are elected but do not obtain the absolute majority of the votes cast. The resignation, however, is subject to approval by the old board. Consequently, the board enjoys a great deal of discretion in overriding the shareholders' meeting outcome by simply rejecting the anticipated resignation.

The traditional regulation of proxy voting provides for another legal basis for the extensive control that current directors hold on the elections of the board. Directors send out proxies using corporate resources and information. Shareholders cannot easily piggy-back on the proxy solicitation conducted by the corporation because, pursuant to Federal law, directors can exclude shareholders' proposals concerning the election of directors from the corporate proxies. Adding nominees to the slot of candidates advanced by the board of directors is considered a matter regarding directors' election, and therefore shareholders can be denied access to corporate proxies in this regard. On the other hand, shareholders could independently solicit their own proxies, but this is unlikely to happen because proxy solicitation can be extremely expensive (also in terms of potential liability for misstatements in the proxy documents). In addition, the corporation is not mandated to reimburse proxy expenses, even in case of complete or partial victory of the dissenting shareholders. On top of that, shareholders might face other procedural obstacles in their proxy fight, such as obtaining an updated lodger of shareholders of record in a timely manner.

[Recent regulatory changes in the area of proxy voting, however, both in Delaware and under Federal law, have now made it easier for shareholders holding a minimum percentage of shares to add their nominees to the corporate proxy statement.]

For these reasons, [until the recent past, in the U.S.] directors' elections [have often been] uncontested, which means that the number of nominees is not greater than the number of available slots on the board, and the only nominees are the ones selected by the existing board. But there is more. Until a recent amendment of NYSE regulation, effective for meetings held on or after January 1, 2010, in uncontested directors elections brokers could vote uninstructed shares. Uncontested elections, more precisely, were considered "routine" matters, and brokers had the discretion to vote the shares in the absence of specific instructions from the beneficial holders of the securities. In these instances, brokers would usually cast their votes according to managers' proposals. [. . .]

As mentioned, however, NYSE Rule 452 has been amended in 2009. According to the new provision, directors' elections will no longer be considered "routine" matters, even when uncontested. Consequently, from January 2010, brokers will no longer be permitted to vote in the absence of specific instructions from the stockholders. The scope of the rule is broad because it applies to all NYSE-registered brokers, independently from the market on which the corporation holding the election is listed.

This innovation will clearly make it somehow more difficult for directors to attract votes under either a plurality or a majority voting system. While institutional investors' campaigns against board nominees are likely to have more chances of success, the concrete effect of new NYSE Rule 452 is not completely clear, especially when plurality vote still applies.

In sum, plurality vote or the "weak" forms of majority vote adopted by some states or companies, limitations to proxy access, the cost of an independent proxy solicitation, and brokers' discretionary vote in uncontested elections have traditionally made it very difficult, for shareholders, to have a strong and independent voice in the appointment of directors. In most situations, with the exclusions of successful hostile takeovers waged either through proxy fights or through the acquisition of a controlling block of shares, directors are *de facto* selected by the existing board and simply "ratified" by a rather passive shareholders' meeting.

A system in which existing directors have a virtually uncontestable power to select their successors on the board and are insulated from shareholders' judgment may deadly wound the fiduciary relationship between shareholders and managers. This peculiar trait of American corporate governance has been denounced by several scholars and interest groups as the cause of lack of directors' accountability to shareholders, and stronger shareholders' democracy has been advocated on both efficiency and political grounds.

[. . .]

[An interesting idea would be to mandate representation of minority shareholders on the board. But] how should a minority representation on the board [. . .] be regulated? In the U.S., the first technical instrument that comes to mind is cumulative voting. Cumulative voting is, historically, the system used to give qualified minority shareholders the possibility to appoint part of the board, and it was, in fact, proposed as a voting mechanism in listed corporations by Jeffrey Gordon in an important article of 1994. In the light of the path dependency of legal systems, cumulative voting has the clear and strong advantage of fitting in the American legal tradition and culture.

[Cumulative voting is, however, very complex and potentially ineffective in listed corporations, where thousands of small shareholders vote. A possible alternative regime, partially inspired by comparative experiences [and in particular by Italian law, is] "list voting".

[. . .]

[W]ith list voting, [. . .] instead of voting on single directors, shareholders would [. . .] vote for alternative lists of directors [submitted by fellow shareholders reaching a minimum percentage of share or by the directors themselves]. A predetermined number of seats on the board (depending on the size of the body) would be reserved for the first candidates of the list that receives the second largest number of votes. For example, if [one] list [receives] 42% of the votes, and [another one,] supported by minority shareholders would rank second receiving 11% of votes, the first nominee(s) from the latter list would also enter the board.

To discuss the technical details of this approach would be beyond the scope of this article. The goal here is to illustrate the overall rationale of the proposed system. It is however necessary to address two important issues. First, a minimum threshold of votes that needs to be reached in order to actually elect the minority director(s) to the board could be imposed either mandatorily by regulation, or on a more flexible basis in the bylaws of the corporation. This would guarantee that minority directors represent a qualified minority. Bylaws or statutory provisions could hypothetically require that the second ranked candidates receive at least one fifth of the votes obtained by the first list, or a fixed threshold, for example 5% of the votes cast.

Second, when it comes to the fine tuning of this proposal, it would need to be ensured that minority directors really represent minority shareholders. There is a risk that a shareholder affiliated with the controlling group might try to "disguise" themselves as an independent investor, with the result that the alleged "minority" director(s) would, in truth, be expressed by the controlling group *"en travesti"*. To avoid this risk is not easy, but a combination of disclosure obligations imposed on the proposing shareholder and her nominees, with a requirement that minority directors are proposed by shareholders independent from the management of the other shareholders that support the managers, could achieve this goal.

NOTES AND QUESTIONS

1. What do you think are the pros and cons of Professor Ventoruzzo's proposal? Do you think it could ever be accepted, also politically, in the United States? Is it really necessary, or at least as useful, in a system with widespread ownership of shares?

2. Is a representation of minority shareholders on the board less "disruptive" than a representation of workers as in the co-determination systems? Is there a risk that a competitor of the corporation would acquire a minority stake just to be able to appoint one director and acquire confidential strategic or marketing information?

3. As indicated in the article, "list voting" is inspired by the Italian experience. In 1998 the Italian legislature introduced this system to appoint the board of auditors, with the idea that the same majority should not entirely determine the composition of both the board of directors and the controlling body. More recently this approach has been extended to the board

of directors. Article 147-*ter* of the TUF, mentioned above, in relevant part provides that: "The Bylaws provide that members of the Board of Directors should be elected on the basis of lists of candidates and defines the minimum participation required for the presentation of a list, not exceeding 2.5% of the capital or the different percentage established by Consob taking into account capitalization, floating shares and ownership structures of listed companies. [. . .] The Bylaws can provide that no director is elected from a list that has not reached a percentage of votes at least equal to half of the participation required for the presentation of the list". Additionally, the same article provides that "at least one member of the Board of Directors must be elected from the minority list that obtained the largest number of votes [after the first one] and that is not linked in any way, even indirectly, with the shareholders who presented or voted the list which resulted first." Do you understand the rationale of these rules? Why do you think it is important to distinguish lists "linked" to the first one, and exclude the nominees included in these lists? Do you think that one director voted by the minority, for example in a board of nine members, is sufficient? One is, in fact, the minimum mandated by law; the bylaws are free to increase the number of minority directors.

4.   What do you think is the difference between an independent director and a minority-appointed director? Is a minority-appointed director necessarily independent pursuant to the legal definitions of independence discussed above?

5.   How do you think the "independent" state of mind of a director can be guaranteed? What arrangements (financial or otherwise) would help achieve this "independence of mind"?

* * *

Talking about the composition of the board, we have discussed the representation of workers and of minority shareholders, different possible "stakeholders" of the corporation. What about the composition of the board in terms of gender or ethnic minorities?

Several countries have adopted a mandatory requirement to ensure representation of both genders on the board, which basically means a mandatory quota for women, a sort of affirmative action in favor of the "last-represented" gender. The following excerpt from an extremely interesting article by Professor Branson discusses the reasons to regulate the presence of women on boards of directors, illustrates the existing regulatory situation in different jurisdictions, and offers some explanations about why mandatory provisions in the U.S. have not been enacted.

DOUGLAS M. BRANSON, INITIATIVES TO PLACE WOMEN ON CORPORATE BOARD OF DIRECTORS—A GLOBAL SNAPSHOT
37 J. Corp. L. 793 (2012)[4]

[. . .]

Arguments abound for an increase of diversity in every profession or calling—law practice, medicine, academe, law enforcement, firefighting, and more. One drumbeat, persistent since the 1990s, has been for an increase in diversity candidates for publicly held corporations' boards of directors—most particularly, women on boards. "[I]f Lehman Brothers were actually Lehman Sisters, the company never would have gone under," is a statement that captures the sentiment. Women are thought to be more sensitive and adverse to the sorts of risk that led to the global financial meltdown of 2008. A greater presence of women on boards of directors may have helped avert many of the debacles which occurred. There are several benefits to corporations from an increase in women directors. First, this increase would provide a positive role model for other women in the middle and lower ranks of corporate organizations. In mid-2011, over 50% of the middle managers in corporate America were women while only 2.6% of CEOs of Fortune 500 companies were female.

Second, boardroom diversity aids in avoidance of "groupthink," the complacency that led to monumental governance failures at Enron and other corporations. The presence of women aids proliferation of the array of perspectives and viewpoints on corporate boards, leading to better assessments of risk and less rubberstamping of CEOs' decisions.

Third, "market reciprocity" means that companies that sell goods and services to the public send positive signals to consumers who might purchase their products. Women account for well over 70% of the purchasing power in our economy. The presence of women in a corporation's senior management would filter out to and sway potential purchasers.

Fourth, corporations will increasingly function in a diverse world. Their governance and the makeup of their boards should reflect this, including more women and persons of color as directors.

Fifth, authoritative international laws and conventions state that "men and women have the same right to employment opportunities," "promotion," and "equal treatment in respect of work for equal value." The latter are sound bites from Article 11 of the United Nations Convention on Elimination of All Forms of Discrimination Against Women (CEDAW). Especially in Europe, fealty to CEDAW and its commands have been influential in consideration of quota laws and other

---

4   Footnotes omitted.

measures to increase the number of women occupying corporate board seats.

Women bring broader perspectives to board service, better use interpersonal skills to promote collaboration among board members and managers, and help expand the context of board discussions. Still other scholars have written extensively about why diversity, including the presence of increased numbers of women directors, is necessary. Only a few view an increased presence in corporate governance through more jaundiced eyes. This Article takes the case for women on boards as a given, turning quickly to a review of the progress and programs contributing to the progress that has occurred around the world.

[. . .]

The statistics indicating the representation of women on corporate boards vary widely throughout the world. Norway, which passed its controversial quota law in 2003, in effect mandated that 40% of a public company's directors be women by 2008—a goal that Norway achieved. In eight years, Norway went from 6.8% to 40.3% female directors on publicly held corporation boards. According to Catalyst, Inc., in the United States, the proportion of women on boards of large publicly held companies stands at 16.1%, but with the proportion stagnant from 2004 onward. Portugal has the fewest females on corporate boards of publicly held corporations, accounting for just 0.6%.

Overall, the 2010 European average was 11.7% but, again, the numbers varied widely. After Norway, the five highest averages were: Sweden (21.9%), Finland (16.8%), Netherlands (7%), Denmark (12.5%), and the United Kingdom (12.2%). Besides Portugal, the laggards included Italy (2.1%) and Germany (7.8%).

The past two years have seen significant change—to between 13% and 14%. France, which adopted a quota law early in 2011, is thought to be responsible for half or more of the EU increase with the percentage of women directors increasing from 12% to 24% in 14 months.

On the Pacific Rim, Australia leads among the countries with available statistics with 13.8%, and New Zealand follows with approximately 10%. Others in the queue include Hong Kong (8.9%) and People's Republic of China (7.2%). The caboose is Japan (0.4%).

[. . .]

Germany reports that approximately 7% of directors are women, but that is the number on supervisory boards. German law requires a two-tiered board structure with a relatively large supervisory board and a relatively small managing board, as corporate laws also provide in several countries with very large populations (e.g., China, Indonesia) and some smaller nations as well (e.g., Slovenia, Netherlands).

Mark Twain wrote that "there are three kinds of lies: lies, damned lies, and statistics." At best, the German statistic is a half-truth. On managing boards (Vorstand), the more exclusive circle in the German system (where "the rubber meets the road") less than 2% of directors are women. Standing alone, without background disclosure, the 7% figure for directors on supervisory boards (Aufsichstrat) seems misleading.

[. . .]

Parliaments in Italy, the Netherlands, and Belgium have enacted gender-based director laws. Norway, the first nation to act, adopted its quota statute in 2003, ordering full compliance by 2008 and setting the level at 40%. Spain, the second to act, ordered achievement of the 40% level by 2016, a significant jump from the 5% level which prevailed in Spain at the time of the adoption of the law. The Spanish statute, though, is largely aspirational, while the Norwegian law has severe penalties. Norwegian companies that do not comply are not only subject to delisting on the stock exchange but to outright dissolution.

France, the third nation to act, adopted a 40% quota law early in 2011. Looking northward to Norway, a deputy of the Assemblée Nationale (Marie-Jo Zimmerman) introduced a 20% quota bill in 2006. Thereafter, the notion of gender parity, at least in French corporate governance, had to negotiate a twisting route.

The Conseil Constitutionnel, a court that renders "advisory" opinions on pending measures, declared the proposed 2006 French legislation unconstitutional. The court found that the 1999 amendments to the French Constitution only permitted enactment of laws aimed at achieving gender parity in elections for political office. The proponents subsequently initiated a movement further to amend the French Constitution, which was achieved in 2008. The amendment provides that French laws shall promote equal access to "positions of professional and social responsibility," as well as to elected offices.

In 2009, adding to the momentum for adoption of a quota statute, the quota measure's supporters found that only 8% of directors in France's largest 100 corporations were women. Further, they bemoaned that in that year, French public companies added only six new women directors to corporate boards.

The recently enacted French quota mandate is staged. Public companies' boards must have 20% women directors within three years of enactment and 40% within six years, by 2017. Thus far, large French corporations are out in front of the 2014 objective, having passed 24% women directors on boards in 2012.

Sweden, Finland, Germany, and the United Kingdom have all come out in opposition to quota laws for various reasons. Sweden (28.2%) and

Finland (26%) already have meaningful representation of women on their boards. On the other hand, Germany and the United Kingdom have middling to poor and mediocre records, respectively, on the issue. Both countries have long traditions of bucking trends and becoming recalcitrant when told what to do.

French reactions to a quota law vary. According to a poll, 71% of citizens favor the quota law. CEO Laurence Parisot favors such a law: "Improvement without a law is so slow that we cannot stay doing nothing." Catherine Chouard, President of the French Equal Opportunities and Anti-Discrimination Commissions, joins in: "It is an excellent way to change mentalities. The law will be first step to a 'new way of life' in companies."

Quota laws also have unintended and adverse consequences. In the rush to name females to directorships, for instance, Norwegian companies named one—no doubt very capable—woman to eleven corporate boards. No one, not even Superwoman, can serve adequately on more than three or perhaps four boards, especially in these post-Sarbanes-Oxley years, versions of which many countries have adopted. Quota laws produce a surfeit of women trophy directors, which may help produce unqualified, figurehead (token) female directors.

Quota laws also may result in a surfeit of celebrity as well as trophy directors, who easily may be regarded as token or figurehead directors. This has allegedly happened in France where board seats have gone to former first lady Bernadette Chirac (from luxury goods retailer LVMH); Nicole Dassault, wife of the controlling shareholder (from Dassault Aviation); Florence Woerth, spouse of the former Minister for Labor (from Hermès); Brigitte Longuet, wife of the former Minister of Defense (broadcaster Canal Plus); and Amélie Oudéa-Castéra, former tennis professional and wife of Société Generale CEO (from the media group Lagardère).

Other consequences thought due to the enactment of a quota law include companies downsizing their boards of directors to reduce the number of women candidates necessary and thus search costs. An extreme consequence is that some companies may go private in order to evade a quota law's requirements altogether.

Opposition to enactment of a quota law is strong in nations such as New Zealand, a country in which women make up 59% of the work force and was recently governed by a female prime minister, yet many corporate executives oppose mandatory or other guidelines. The New Zealand Stock Exchange has publicly stated that it will not even follow its Australian counterpart, the ASX, which has a requirement for companies to set and meet voluntary quotas for increasing the number of women at the top. In the United Kingdom, a recent government report urges a voluntary quota of 25% by 2015, but it pointedly stops short of any recommendation that the United Kingdom adopt a compulsory quota, as France, Spain, Belgium, the Netherlands, Norway, and other states have done.

By contrast, the Malaysian government has imposed a quota that publicly held companies have 30% women directors by 2016. Discussion of proposed or enacted quota laws takes place around the world, is frequent, is at times quite heated, and contains widely divergent, often diametrically opposed, opinions and arguments.

[. . .]

In the United States, as compared to many other developed countries around the world, the ardor for diversity has cooled. Because the fire has not been re-kindled, the fire's embers merely glow. A countertrend to this stall in the United States has been the SEC's new diversity disclosure requirement, which seems to have sprung from the glowing embers. When most U.S. corporations comply with them, the regulations and the disclosures may produce—scofflaws just discussed aside—a significant increase in diversity on corporate boards, re-kindling the fire.

By contrast, a strong countertrend elsewhere—adoption of quota laws imposing quotas for numbers of women on corporate boards—would seem to have little promise for adoption in the United States. Although some Americans are liberal Democrats, and others are conservative Republicans, and still others are in-between those extremes, in my opinion all are libertarians, of sorts, or have a libertarian streak running up their back. My surmise is that most Americans would regard a law dictating how many of each sex must be on a corporation's board of directors as excessively intrusive, far beyond any legitimate role the government could have in regulation of corporations.

* * *

The issue of women on the board has been discussed and debated extensively in the U.K. during the last few years. One notable recent report, namely *Women on Boards: Voluntary Code for Executive Search Firms—Taking the Next Step* (March 2014) highlights recent developments and progress achieved in this area in the U.K. The full report can be found on line.

What follows are excerpts from the Report:

[. . .]

The Voluntary Code of Conduct for Executive Search Firms was launched in July 2011 as a direct result of Lord Davies's review of Women on Boards. The code was created by a number of executive search firms covering relevant search criteria and processes relating to FTSE 350 board level appointments. As at the31st December 2013, 68 executive search firms, covering the whole of the FTSE 350, had become signatories to the code, pledging to adhere to the nine provisions of best practice this sets out.

[. . .]

In January 2014 women accounted for 20.4% of corporate board members of FTSE 100 companies. This continued the positive trend and was up from 19% in 2013, 12.4% in 2010 and 9.4% in 2004. Although the pace of change has increased, and current trends suggest the target of 25% by 2015 set out by Lord Davies in his 2011 report will be achieved we cannot be complacent and assume further progress will be made without further considered focus.

The FTSE 250 has also seen a positive increase in the number of women taking board positions. In January 2014 15.1% of corporate board positions were held by women compared to only 7.8% in 2010.

As at January 2014, 511 further board positions would be required to be taken by women to achieve the target of 25% for FTSE 100 companies, this is assuming that no current female board members step down during that time. For the FTSE 250 to achieve the target, a minimum of 197 board positions would have to be secured by women between now and 2015.

During the 12 months covering January 2013 to January 2014 there were 147 Non-Executive appointments in the FTSE 100, 42 (28.6%) taken by women. Of the FTSE 250, there were 244 Non-Executive appointments of which 74 (30.3%) taken by women. Although these statistics are encouraging, we cannot be complacent about reaching the 25% target.

NOTES AND QUESTIONS

1.   Do you think that diversity on the board of directors, especially gender-wise, is important? Why should the number of female executives matter? If so, do you find it sensible to mandate by statute that a minimum number of directors are women (or, more generally, belong to the less represented gender)?

2.   What about other groups potentially under-represented? Should there be affirmative actions to increase the number of members of ethnic minorities on corporate boards? Religious minorities? People with different sexual orientations (LGBTs)? On the other hand, do you think a private corporation can provide, in its bylaws, for example, that board members must belong to a particular religion? Think, for example, to a corporation doing business primarily or exclusively with the Catholic Church. The answer generally varies in different legal systems, depending on how they strike the balance between the freedom of the corporation to choose its own leadership, and other values such as equality and prohibiting discrimination also by

private parties. In a class with participants from different systems and cultures, this question might lead to an interesting debate.

3. Are you surprised by some of the data presented by Professor Branson concerning different countries? Or not? Do you think that they confirm or contradict stereotypes about different cultures?

4. Do you think diversity of nationalities, experiences, and background is more or less important in this respect? Consider, for example, the following: "According to research by ITAP International, as far as the largest 50 companies in the Fortune 500 are concerned, only around 5% of board members are not American. Moreover, roughly half of US public companies have no non-Americans on their boards at all—despite the fact that fully three-quarters derive some of their revenues from abroad. In contrast, a quarter of board members in Europe's largest company boardrooms, on average, are from cultures other than the company's home country (on an 'average' board of 12 members, two will be European non-nationals and one non-European). This average hides some wide variations, however, with almost three out of ten European boards (28%) having no foreign directors at all, a figure that rises to almost six out of ten in Italy. The most diverse companies are in Switzerland, where half of directors are non-nationals. In the U.K., the figure is 40% whereas in Germany and Spain it is just 10%—the latter perhaps reflecting the fact that language is a major barrier to international diversity in these countries." (Dona Roche-Tarry, *A global board?*, in *Governance* August 2012 Issue 218, p. 8). So is the above an argument for quotas around international diversity? In our globalized world, is having directors from different countries and cultures, with different language skills, an advantage or a disadvantage? Does it matter? Does the U.S. appear chauvinistic in this respect?

5. Speaking about a different type of diversity, concerning educational and professional backgrounds, do you think it is useful, for example, for corporations like Google, Bayer, or Yamaha to have one or more practicing lawyers on the board? Are lawyers on the board a blessing or a curse?

POWERS OF DIRECTORS VS. SHAREHOLDERS

One general question that is often litigated concerns the extension of directors' powers, also *vis-à-vis* shareholders. First of all, it should be considered that the power to manage the corporation is vested in the board of directors, which often delegates it, at least in part, to some executive directors, and to the managers (not board members) of the corporation. The shareholders' meeting has, however, also some competences concerning, broadly speaking, the managing of the corporation, especially when extraordinary transactions (such as a merger or a sale of all the corporation's assets) are concerned. Generally the shareholders have the power to amend the governing documents of the corporation, but here some distinctions are necessary. In the U.S., for example, the approval of the shareholders is necessary to amend the articles of incorporation, but the amendment needs to be proposed ("initiated") by directors. On the other hand, both shareholders and directors have a concurring power to amend the bylaws, even if in some states directors have this power as a default rule (and the governing documents can exclude it), while in other states directors do not have this power as a default rule, unless the governing documents give it to them ("opt-in"). In other jurisdictions, especially in continental Europe and Japan, shareholders have a more extensive and exclusive power on all amendments to the charter and bylaws, both in the sense that they (or at least a qualified minority) can propose an amendment, and that virtually all amendments of the charter and the bylaws require shareholders' approval. This is particularly true in civil law systems with concentrated ownership structures. In these cases, however, the shareholders' meeting can delegate at least some of its powers to the directors (consider, for example, issuing new shares in some systems as discussed in Chapter 4).

It should also be mentioned that in some countries, for example in the U.S., directors have the power to decide the distribution of dividends, while in others, for example in the French civil-law tradition, directors can only make a proposal to the shareholders concerning the destination of earnings, but the shareholders' meeting ultimately decides on the distribution of dividends. Do you see a correlation between ownership structures and the balance of powers between shareholders and managers? For more, *see* the aptly entitled articles by Sofie Cools, *The Real Difference in Corporate Law Between the United States and Continental Europe: Distribution of Powers,* 30 DEL. J. Corp. L. 697 (2005); and Gen Goto, *Legally "Strong" Shareholders of Japan,* 3 MICHIGAN J. PRIVATE EQ. AND VENT. CAP. L. 125 (2014).

Notwithstanding these apparently clear-cut rules, there is a gray area in which it is uncertain if the board of directors or the shareholders' meeting can exercise powers that, at least as a matter of fact, infringe on the competences of each other, as we will see below.

In theory, a general limitation to directors' powers is represented by the corporate purpose as stated in the charter and bylaws. This is, however, often an illusory limitation, for a number of reasons. First of all, in lots of legal systems—typically in common law jurisdictions—the corporate purpose can be defined in extremely broad terms. The corporate purpose is often simply something along the lines of "The Corporation can engage in any legal business" (*see* the example in Chapter 3). In other systems, the corporate purpose must be defined somehow more precisely, for example: "The Corporation is engaged in the business of producing and selling furniture," but the provision also often explicitly encompasses "All other activities directly or indirectly related or necessary to carry on the corporate purpose, including, but not limited to, financial transactions. . ." It is very difficult to decide if a particular act falls outside the purpose: for example, is purchasing an expensive painting by a famous artist included? One might argue that it is necessary to embellish the corporate headquarters, also in order to convey a prestigious and sophisticated image of the corporation to clients, providers, financial partners, etc. In addition, even if the corporate purpose is clearly defined, and the directors exceed it (act *"ultra vires,"* Latin for *"out of powers"*), they might be liable toward the corporation, but specific legal provisions, aimed at ensuring legal certainty, make these contracts binding toward third parties, at least if they did not intentionally take advantage of the ultra vires act being aware of the irregularity.

A more subtle question is what interests the directors need to pursue. More precisely, do they only have to pursue the interests of the shareholders, or can—or must—they take into account also other stakeholders, such as creditors, employees, and the community in general? This question can have important implications: for example, in deciding whether to take into account environmental issues, obviously in the absence of a regulation mandating certain conducts, directors should only aim at maximizing profits, even if this implies a less environmentally friendly business, or can they also consider the impact of corporate activities on the environment? Similarly, in case of a hostile takeover, in deciding whether to accept an offer or to adopt defensive measures, directors should only consider the interests of shareholders, or also, for example, of workers that might lose their jobs if the acquisition is successful?

It's an old question that does not have an easy answer. In some systems and historical periods, emphasizing "shareholders' wealth" as the sole goal of directors has had more traction; in other places and times other stakeholders' interests are also considered relevant. The debate has sometimes been framed in Europe as the juxtaposition of a "contractual" view of the corporation, in which the creation of value for shareholders is the primary obligation of directors, to an "institutional" view, advocating that the interest of the corporation that directors must pursue is not limited only to shareholders' interests. This discussion is famously and nicely captured by an historical anecdote: Walther Rathenau (1867–1922), a German industrialist, politician, and writer, was confronting a group of angry shareholders complaining about low dividends payments by the Norddeutscher Lloyd, a corporation he was involved with. He replied that the purpose of the corporation was not to pay dividends to shareholders, but rather to make boats navigate on the river Rhine. At the extreme opposite of the spectrum, as an example of shareholders' primacy, one might refer to the famous U.S. case Dodge v. Ford Motor, 204 Mich. 459 (1919), in which the court directed Henry Ford to pay dividends rather than retaining the profits. This case, in reality, is quite an outlier and is often misinterpreted: the reality is that also in the U.S. courts are extremely reluctant to interfere with the business decisions of directors concerning dividends.

In any case, the debate goes on. We mentioned before that in Germany, during the Nazi dictatorship, the 1937 Corporate Statute explicitly indicated that the board had to manage the corporation not only in the interest of shareholders, but also of the German people and of the State. References to stakeholders different from shareholders in defining directors' duties are however not the prerogative of totalitarian regimes of the past. An interesting middle course (also known as the 'enlightened shareholder value') can be found in section 172 of the U.K. Companies Act 2006, which provides that:

> 172. *Duty to promote the success of the company.*—(1) A director of a company must act in the way he considers, in good faith, would be most likely to promote the success of the company for the benefit of its members as a whole, and in doing so have regard (amongst other matters) to—
>
> (a) the likely consequences of any decision in the long term,
>
> (b) the interests of the company's employees,
>
> (c) the need to foster the company's business relationships with suppliers, customers, and others,
>
> (d) the impact of the company's operations on the community and the environment,
>
> (e) the desirability of the company maintaining a reputation for high standards of business conduct, and
>
> (f) the need to act fairly as between members of the company.

This discussion is both interesting and relevant, but sometimes it might be quite theoretical, and it does not always have a significant practical impact on the life of the corporation. For example, let's assume that it could be established that the goal of the corporation is to maximize shareholders' wealth. First of all it should be discussed if we mean wealth maximization in the short or in the long term. The difference can obviously be substantial. In any case, it is fairly easy to argue that also a decision that apparently is primarily motivated by the interests of other stakeholders has an effect, at least indirectly, on the economic situation of the corporation. Consider, for example, the decision to make a donation to a charitable or educational institution, or to avoid experiments on animals in the cosmetics industry, and adopt different and more expensive techniques to ensure safety. One might argue that these decisions negatively affect the bottom line of the corporation, at least in the short term, but it is quite easy to respond that they might have a positive impact on public relations, attract more customers, create a better work environment, and ultimately be beneficial *also* in terms of value for the shareholders. Similarly, if one argues that directors can or should take into account different stakeholders, it is not difficult to argue that (legal) profit-maximizing strategies can also benefit constituencies different from shareholders. For example, cutting some jobs today in order to maintain a higher level of profitability can be necessary to save, in the medium term, a larger number of jobs. This is an area in which it is easy to fall into empty rhetoric.

A probably more concrete question concerns the boundary that divides directors' and shareholders' powers. The following two famous U.S. cases illustrate the issue.

BLASIUS INDUSTRIES, INC. V. ATLAS CORP.

Court of Chancery of Delaware
564 A.2d 651 (1988)

Blasius is a new stockholder of Atlas. It began to accumulate Atlas shares for the first time in July, 1987. On October 29, it filed a Schedule 13D with the Securities Exchange Commission disclosing that, with affiliates, it then owed 9.1% of Atlas' common stock.

[. . .]

Immediately after filing its 13D on October 29, Blasius' representatives sought a meeting with the Atlas management. [. . .] At that meeting, [Blasius] suggested that Atlas engage in a leveraged restructuring and distribute cash to shareholders. In such a transaction, which is by this date a commonplace form of transaction, a corporation typically raises cash by sale of assets and significant borrowings and makes a large one-time cash distribution to shareholders. The shareholders are typically left with cash and an equity interest in a smaller, more highly leveraged enterprise. [. . .]

Immediately following the meeting, the Atlas representatives expressed among themselves an initial reaction that the proposal was infeasible. [. . .]

On December 30, 1987, Blasius caused Cede & Co. (the registered owner of its Atlas stock) to deliver to Atlas a signed written consent (1) adopting a precatory resolution recommending that the board develop and implement a restructuring proposal, (2) amending the Atlas bylaws to, among other things, expand the size of the board from seven to fifteen members—the maximum number under Atlas' charter, and (3) electing eight named persons to fill the new directorships. [. . .]

The reaction was immediate. Mr. Weaver [the CEO of Atlas] conferred with Mr. Masinter, the Company's outside counsel and a director, who viewed the consent as an attempt to take control of the Company. They decided to call an emergency meeting of the board, even though a regularly scheduled meeting was to occur only one week hence, on January 6, 1988. The point of the emergency meeting was to act on their conclusion (or to seek to have the board act on their conclusion) "that we should add at least one and probably two directors to the board. . .". A quorum of directors, however, could not be arranged for a telephone meeting that day. A telephone meeting was held the next day. At that meeting, the board voted to amend the bylaws to increase the size of the board from seven to nine and appointed John M. Devaney and Harry J. Winters, Jr. to fill those newly created positions. Atlas' Certificate of Incorporation creates staggered terms for directors; the terms to which Messrs. Devaney and Winters were appointed would expire in 1988 and 1990, respectively.

In increasing the size of Atlas' board by two and filling the newly created positions, the members of the board realized that they were thereby precluding the holders of a majority of the Company's shares from placing a majority of new directors on the board through Blasius' consent solicitation, should they want to do so. Indeed the evidence establishes that that was the principal motivation in so acting. [. . .]

There is testimony in the record to support the proposition that, in acting on December 31, the board was principally motivated simply to implement a plan to expand the Atlas board that preexisted the September, 1987 emergence of Blasius as an active shareholder. I have no doubt that the addition of Mr. Winters, an expert in mining economics, and Mr. Devaney, a financial expert employed by the Company, strengthened the Atlas board and, should anyone ever have reason to review the wisdom of those choices, they would be found to be sensible and prudent. [. . .]

One of the principal thrusts of plaintiffs' argument is that, in acting to appoint two additional persons of their own selection, including an officer of the Company, to the board, defendants were motivated not by any view that Atlas' interest (or those of its shareholders) required that action, but rather they were motivated improperly, by selfish concern to maintain their collective control over the Company. That is, plaintiffs say that the evidence shows there was no policy dispute or issue that really motivated this action, but that asserted policy differences were pretexts for entrenchment for selfish reasons. If this were found to be factually true, one would not need to inquire further. The action taken would constitute a breach of duty. [. . .]

While I am satisfied that the evidence is powerful, indeed compelling, that the board was chiefly motivated on December 31 to forestall or preclude the possibility that a majority of shareholders might place on the Atlas board eight new members sympathetic to the Blasius proposal, it is less clear with respect to the more subtle motivational question: whether the existing members of the board did so because they held a good faith belief that such shareholder action would be self-injurious and shareholders needed to be protected from their own judgment.

On balance, I cannot conclude that the board was acting out of a self-interested motive in any important respect on December 31. I conclude rather that the board saw the "threat" of the Blasius recapitalization proposal as posing vital policy differences between itself and Blasius. It acted, I conclude, in a good faith effort to protect its incumbency, not selfishly, but in order to thwart implementation of the recapitalization that it feared, reasonably, would cause great injury to the Company.

The real question the case presents, to my mind, is whether, in these circumstances, the board, even if it *is* acting with subjective good faith (which will typically, if not always, be a contestable or debatable judicial conclusion), may validly act for the principal purpose of preventing the shareholders from electing a majority of new directors. The question thus posed is not one of intentional wrong (or even negligence), but one of authority *as between the fiduciary and the beneficiary* (not simply legal authority, *i.e.,* as between the fiduciary and the world at large). [. . .]

The shareholder franchise is the ideological underpinning upon which the legitimacy of directorial power rests. Generally, shareholders have only two protections against perceived inadequate business performance. They may sell their stock (which, if done in sufficient numbers, may so affect security prices as to create an incentive for altered managerial performance), or they may vote to replace incumbent board members.

It has, for a long time, been conventional to dismiss the stockholder vote as a vestige or ritual of little practical importance. It may be that we are now witnessing the emergence of new institutional voices and arrangements that will make the stockholder vote a less predictable affair than it has been. Be that as it may, however, whether the vote is seen functionally as an unimportant formalism, or as an important tool of discipline, it is clear that it is critical to the theory that legitimates the exercise of power by some (directors and officers) over vast aggregations of property that they do not own. Thus, when viewed from a broad, institutional perspective, it can be seen that matters involving the integrity of the shareholder voting process involve consideration not present in any other context in which directors exercise delegated power. [. . .]

The board was not faced with a coercive action taken by a powerful shareholder against the interests of a distinct shareholder constituency (such as a public minority). It was presented with a consent solicitation by a 9% shareholder. Moreover, here it had time (and understood that it had time) to inform the shareholders of its views on the merits of the proposal subject to stockholder vote. The only justification that can, in such a situation, be offered for the action taken is that the board knows better than do the shareholders what is in the corporation's best interest. While that premise is no doubt true for any number of matters, it is irrelevant (except insofar as the shareholders wish to be guided by the board's recommendation) when the question is who should comprise the board of directors. The theory of our corporation law confers power upon directors as the agents of the shareholders; it does not create Platonic masters. It may be that the Blasius restructuring proposal was or is unrealistic and would lead to injury to the corporation and its shareholders if pursued. Having heard the evidence, I am inclined to think it was not a sound proposal. The board certainly viewed it that way, and that view, held in good faith, entitled the board to take certain steps to evade the risk it perceived. It could, for example, expend corporate funds to inform shareholders and seek to bring them to a similar point of view. [. . .] But there is a vast difference between expending corporate funds to inform the electorate and exercising power for the primary purpose of foreclosing effective shareholder action. A majority of the shareholders, who were not dominated in any respect, could view the matter differently than did the board. If they do, or did, they are entitled to employ the mechanisms provided by the corporation law and the Atlas certificate of incorporation to advance that view. They are also entitled, in my opinion, to restrain their agents, the board, from acting for the principal purpose of thwarting that action.

I therefore conclude that, even finding the action taken was taken in good faith, it constituted an unintended violation of the duty of loyalty that the board owed to the shareholders. I note parenthetically that the concept of an unintended breach of the duty of loyalty is unusual but not novel.

NOTES AND QUESTIONS

1.   Why would the appointment of two new directors by the board preclude Blasius from obtaining a majority of the board? Could not the total maximum number of directors indicated in the charter (articles of incorporation) be increased?

2.   The Court opines that the directors did not breach any duty, or better that they committed an "unintended breach of the duty of loyalty." This is a somehow strange concept, even if the Court says it is not "novel." In fact, the directors have not breached any specific rule, and have acted, in

principle, within their powers. Their actions are nonetheless considered an unacceptable infringement on the shareholders' franchise. Why? Do you agree with the Court?

3. What alternative course of action would you have suggested to the directors in order to oppose Blasius' proposal?

* * *

INTERNATIONAL BROTHERHOOD OF TEAMSTERS GENERAL FUND V. FLEMING COMPANIES, INC.

Supreme Court of Oklahoma
975 P.2d 907 (1999)

SIMMS, J.

The United States Court of Appeals, Tenth Circuit, John C. Porfilio, Presiding Judge, pursuant to 20 O.S.1991, § 1601, certified to the Oklahoma Supreme Court the following question of law:

Does Oklahoma law [A] restrict the authority to create and implement shareholder rights plans exclusively to the board of directors, or [B] may shareholders propose resolutions requiring that shareholder rights plans be submitted to the shareholders for vote at the succeeding annual meeting?

We answer the first part of the question in the negative and the second part affirmatively. We hold under Oklahoma law there is no exclusive authority granted boards of directors to create and implement shareholder rights plans, where shareholder objection is brought and passed through official channels of corporate governance. We find no Oklahoma law which gives exclusive authority to a corporation's board of directors for the formulation of shareholder rights plans and no authority which precludes shareholders from proposing resolutions or bylaw amendments regarding shareholder rights plans. We hold shareholders may propose bylaws which restrict board implementation of shareholder rights plans, assuming the certificate of incorporation does not provide otherwise.

The International Brotherhood of the Teamsters General Fund [Teamsters] owns sixty-five shares of Fleming Companies, Inc. [Fleming or the company] stock. In 1986, Fleming implemented a shareholder's rights plan with the term of the plan to expire in 1996. The rights plan implemented by Fleming is an anti-takeover mechanism. Such plans give boards of directors authority to adopt and execute discriminatory shareholder rights upon the occurrence of some triggering event, usually when a certain percentage of shares has been amassed by a single shareholder. A board can place "restrictions or conditions on the exercise, transfer or receipt of" shareholder rights which can severely dilute the shareholding power of one seeking control of a company. The defensive plans usually result in entrenching existing management, making a takeover without the approval of incumbent management more difficult. These rights plans can make it far more expensive to effect a takeover. Because the rights plans make the merger of companies more painful for the suitor and assist incumbent management in maintaining control, the plans are often called "poison pill rights plans" or "poison pills."

[Teamsters made a proxy proposal to amend the bylaws eliminating rights plans and providing that the introduction of similar poison pills should be approved by the shareholders, and not left to the board. The directors of Fleming refused to include this proxy proposal, and this lawsuit followed].

This is a case of first impression in Oklahoma and there is little guidance from other states. Oklahoma and Delaware have substantially similar corporation acts, especially with regard to Title 18, §§ 1013 & 1038 which are of primary concern here. [. . .]

In the scheme of corporate governance the role of shareholders has been purposefully indirect. Shareholders' direct authority is limited. [. . .] This is true for obvious reasons. Large corporations with perhaps thousands of stockholders could not function if the daily running of the corporation was subject to the approval of so many relatively attenuated people. However, the authority given a board of directors under the Oklahoma General Corporation Act, 18 O.S.1991 § 1027, is not without shareholder oversight, 18 O.S.1991 § 1013(B).

Fleming's argument relies on this passage, 18 O.S.1991 § 1038 (emphasis added):

> "Subject to any provisions in the certificate of incorporation, *every corporation* may create and issue . . . rights or options entitling the holders thereof to purchase from the corporation any shares of its capital stock of any class or classes, such rights or options to be evidenced by or in such instrument or instruments as shall be approved by the board of directors."

In making its argument, Fleming asserts that the word "corporation" is synonymous with "board of directors" as the term is used in 18 § 1038. Therefore, according to Fleming, "every corporation may create and issue . . . rights and options[.]", can actually be read to say "[every corporation's board of directors] may create and issue . . . rights and options[.]" However, in light of the fact that both terms, "corporation" and "board of directors", are used distinctly throughout the General Corporation Act and within the text of 18 § 1038 itself, this assertion is flawed. Further, the Former Business Corporation Act, 18 § 1.2(1) and (23), defines "corporation" and "director" differently. The statutes indicate our legislature has an understanding of the distinct definitions it assigns to these terms, and we find it unlikely the legislature would interchange them as Fleming contends.

While this Court would agree with Fleming that a corporation may create and issue rights and options within the grant of authority given it in 18 § 1038, it does not automatically translate that the board of directors of that corporation has in itself the same breadth of authority. [. . .]

We find nothing in the Oklahoma General Corporation Act, 18 O.S.1991 § 1001 et seq., or existing case law which indicates the shareholder rights plan is somehow exempt from shareholder adopted bylaws. Fleming argues that only the certificate of incorporation can limit the board's authority to implement such a plan, relying on § 1038. While this Court might agree that a certificate of incorporation, which somehow precludes bylaw amendments directed at shareholder rights plans, could preclude the Teamsters from seeking the bylaw changes which are proposed in this case, neither party has indicated Fleming's certificate speaks in any way to the board's authority or shareholder constraints regarding shareholder rights plans. We find no authority to support the contention that a certificate of incorporation which is silent with regard to shareholder rights plans precludes shareholder enacted bylaws regarding the implementation of rights plans.

A number of states have taken affirmative steps to ensure their domestic corporations, and in many instances the board of directors itself, are able to implement shareholder rights plans to protect the company from takeover. The legislation is typically called a shareholders rights plan endorsement statute. However, the Oklahoma legislature has not passed such legislation. There are at least twenty-four states with these share rights plan endorsement statutes.

[. . .]

This Court understands much of the reasoning behind the enactment of rights plan endorsement statutes and why so many state legislatures are inclined to facilitate this takeover protection for their domestic corporations. In addition, we understand Fleming's desire to have a rights plan available for quick, and more effective, implementation. However, if, as in this case, the certificate of incorporation does not offer directors this broad authority to protect against mergers and takeover, corporations must look to Oklahoma's legislature, not this Court, which is more properly vested with the means to offer boards such authority.

In answering this certified question, we do not suggest all shareholder rights plans are required to submit to shareholder approval, ratification or review; this is not the question presented to us. Instead, we find shareholders may, through the proper channels of corporate governance, restrict the board of directors authority to implement shareholder rights plans.

NOTES AND QUESTIONS

1. What is a "certified question of law"? Where is this case being litigated, and why is it necessary for the Supreme Court of Oklahoma to decide this issue?

2. What is a "Shareholder rights plan"? We will discuss it more extensively in the chapter on takeovers, but basically it is an anti-takeover device that includes three elements: (a) a triggering event generally represented by an unsolicited acquisition of a certain percentage of shares by a third party that is likely aiming at obtaining control of the corporation; (b) a catastrophic consequence that would make the takeover very difficult or financially costly for the acquirer, typically the issuance of shares at a discounted price to existing shareholders; (c) the possibility for the existing board to redeem the plan at a nominal cost. These three features combined create an obstacle for hostile acquisitions, protecting incumbent managers. Shareholders, however, like Teamsters in this case, often do not like these types of poison pills. Can you explain why?

3. In *Blasius v. Atlas*, reprinted before, the Court limited the ability of the directors to interfere with the shareholders' franchise. In *Teamsters v. Fleming* the Court recognizes the power of shareholders to amend the bylaws and restrict the board's discretion with respect to shareholder rights plans. What are the legal grounds to reach this conclusion? Do you think it is always in the best interest of shareholders that directors cannot effectively adopt defensive measures in case of a hostile bid?

4. The Court underlines the reasons why shareholders' direct authority should be limited, but it ultimately decides that in this case shareholders can limit directors' powers. Following the rationale of this decision, do you think it would be admissible, under U.S. law, a bylaws provision requiring the assent of shareholders for every transaction with a value of $50,000 or more?

* * *

Also other countries grapple with the issue of the proper boundary between the powers of the board of directors and of the shareholders' meeting. Germany is an interesting example. Two decisions are particularly crucial: the *Holzmüller* case decided by the Federal Court of Justice in 1982 and, more recently, the *Gelatine* cases of 2004. As a general rule, under German law only the *Vorstand*, the managing board, has the responsibility to run the corporation. The powers of the shareholders to interfere with the management of the corporation are quite limited: they cannot give binding instructions to directors, and the shareholders' meeting can take business decisions only if required by the *Vorstand*. This is also in line with the fact that directors can be liable for damaging decisions (see Chapter 6), while shareholders, at least in practice, rarely are responsible for lack of care. This principle is explained with the adage *"Keine Herrschaft ohne Haftung"* ("No power without responsibility"). In *Holzmüller,* however, a peculiar situation concerning corporations within a group was considered. The *Vorstand* of the corporation decided to spin off the most important assets of the corporation, a harbor-operating business, to an entirely owned subsidiary. The value of the assets transferred was approximately 80% of the total assets of the corporation. The consequence would have been that the directors of the parent corporation would have had extensive control on the assets transferred to the subsidiary, because they exercise the voting rights for the shares of the subsidiary owned by the parent. The Court therefore held that certain key decisions that could be normally taken by the shareholders' meeting of the subsidiary (which, in practice, means by the directors of the parent) require the vote of the shareholders' of the parent, for example in case of issuing of new shares by the subsidiary (which, as we have seen, in civil law systems is generally a competence of the shareholders' meeting—*see* Chapter 4). This is to avoid the result of depriving the shareholders of any control on relevant assets through the use of a corporate group. It's a leading decision because it recognizes, for the first time, non-statutory competences of the shareholders' meeting in a matter traditionally reserved to managing directors. In a way, *Holzmüller* could be considered the German correspondent of *Blasius v. Atlas*: notwithstanding the profound differences of the facts, applicable rules, and holdings, both decisions introduce a limitation to the power of directors to disenfranchise shareholders. This important and somehow revolutionary decision, however, created significant legal uncertainty in terms of its precise meaning and implications, partially addressed in the *Gelatine* case.

In the next few pages, we take a closer look at these decisions.

HOLZMÜLLER

German Federal Court of Justice, 1982
25 February 1982

Facts

The plaintiff was a shareholder holding about 8% of the shares of the defendant which was a corporation in the lumber industry. According to the charter of the defendant corporation, its business purposes were activities in the lumber industry as well as the founding and acquisition of other corporations in this area. Moreover the charter stated that the defendant could allocate parts of its assets to these corporations. In 1972 the board of the defendant founded the *H-KGaA* and transferred all assets of a lumber harbor run by the defendant to this corporation as a contribution in kind in exchange for all the shares of this corporation. The assets of the lumber harbor represented around 80% of all the assets of the defendant. The plaintiff claims that the transfer of all assets of the lumber harbor was void since the general meeting did not approve this transfer and that the transfer constituted a de facto change of the charter. The Regional Court (Laudgericht) and the Court of Appeals (Oberlaudesgericht) dismissed the case.

Grounds

The court grants the appeal but dismisses the case.

[. . .]

The transfer is not void under German corporate law.

[. . .]

The argument of the plaintiff that the transfer of all the assets of the lumber harbor to the *H-KGaA* constituted a de facto change of the charter does not lead to invalidate the transfer. The court of appeals already stated correctly that the transfer of all the assets of the lumber harbor to the *H-KGaA* did not violate any provision of the charter since the charter explicitly allowed the transfer of assets to other corporations. Moreover, the provisions in the charter did not limit these transfers to certain assets or a certain amount of assets. Consequently the provisions of the charter cannot be interpreted as prohibiting the transfer of the major assets of the corporation.

However, this only means that a formal amendment of the charter of the defendant was not necessary. This does not imply that the transfer of all the assets of the lumber harbor to the *H-KGaA* did not require an approval of the shareholders' meeting. If the competences of the shareholders' meeting are governed by mandatory statutory provisions, this only means that the charter cannot attribute this power to the managing board or another corporate body. [. . .] Although it is in the discretion of the managing board whether to obtain an approval of the shareholders' meeting in cases where such an approval is not required by the statute (Sec. 119 subs. 2 German Stock Corporation Law), there are fundamental decisions of the managing board that have a profound impact on the rights of shareholders, and that cannot be adopted without the approval of the shareholders. In these cases the members of the managing board violate their duty of care if they do not refer the decision to the shareholders' meeting.

The transfer of all the assets of the lumber harbor to the *H-KGaA* was such a decision and it required the approval of the shareholders' meeting. This decision had an impact on the core business activity of the defendant, involved the most valuable asset of the defendant and changed its structure completely. Therefore this transfer exceeded the regular scope of business activity of the defendant and had a severe impact on the shareholders of the defendant. Consequently the managing board was not allowed to transfer all the assets of the lumber harbor to the *H-KGaA* without a prior approval of the shareholder meeting of the defendant.

Nevertheless the violation of this duty does not affect the validity of the transfer. According to Sec. 82 German Stock Corporation Law, the power of the managing board to act on behalf of the corporation can only be limited by the bylaws. Although under German law there are two exceptions (abuse of the agent and execution of a contract with a wholly owned subsidiary) of this principle, these exemptions cannot affect the validity of the transfer since the transfer was made as a contribution in kind and therefore does not concern only the internal affairs of the defendant but the affairs of the subsidiary as a separate legal person. In fact a cancellation of the transfer would require a decrease of the legal capital or to dissolve the *H-KGaA*.

[. . .]

The issuance of new shares by a subsidiary corporation paid by transferring the major assets of the parent corporation threatens severely the interest of the shareholder of the parent corporation since it could lead to a decrease of the value of the shares of the parent corporation and to an exclusion of the pre-emptive rights of its shareholders. Consequently, a participation of the shareholders of the parent corporation in future decisions of the subsidiary is essential in order to protect their interest. This also applies in the case that the increase of capital would not be combined with an exclusion of the pre-emptive rights of subscription of the parent corporation (dissenting *Timm*, AG 1980, 183 f.; *Timm*, Die AG als Konzernspitze, p. 174 f.; *Lutter*, in: Festschrift Westermann, p. 365 f.). Even in this case the shareholders of the parent corporation cannot subscribe newly issued shares of the subsidiary directly and make further investments in their business. Every issuance of new shares of the subsidiary increases the probability that it will have new (external) shareholders.

Therefore, the general meeting of the parent corporation must be able to decide if the capital of the *H-KGaA* should be raised and whether the pre-emptive rights should be excluded or be granted to the shareholder of the parent corporation. In this decision, the general meeting of the parent corporation has to vote with the same majority as required at the general meeting of the subsidiary corporation.

* * *

The *Holzmüller* decision caused significant legal uncertainty since the Federal Court of Justice did not clearly define fundamental decisions of the managing board that can have a severe impact on the rights of shareholders, and therefore require specific protections of shareholders. The Court focused on the issuance of new shares by the subsidiary, but what about other transactions that might have similar effects? As a consequence, the precise boundaries of the *Holzmüller* doctrine were debated. Over 20 years after, with *Gelatine*, the German Federal Court of Justice tried to clarify some aspects of the *Holzmüller* principle by generally limiting the *Holzmüller* doctrine to its original version after it had been expanded largely by lower courts.

GELATINE

German Federal Court of Justice, 2004
26 April 2004

Facts

The plaintiffs were four shareholders of the defendant corporation, holding about 29% of the shares of the defendant which was a corporation in the gelatine industry. The defendant held 100% of the shares of a Swedish and a British corporation. While the British corporation had almost no economic impact for the defendant, the Swedish corporation contributed around 30% of the revenues of the defendant. In 1998, the managing board of the defendant transferred all shares of these two corporations to a newly formed corporation in a contribution in kind in exchange for 100% of the shares of this new corporation. At the shareholders' meeting in 2000 the managing board asked the shareholders to approve this transfer and a resolution was passed with a 69% majority. The plaintiffs then challenged the shareholders' meeting resolution claiming that the transfer constituted a violation of the so called *Holzmüller* principles which—according to the plaintiffs—would require an approval of the transfer with a three-fourths majority. The district court (Laudgericht) and the court of appeals (Oberlaudesgericht) dismissed the case.

Grounds

The court rejects the appeal.

[. . .]

The action of the plaintiffs is not well founded. The shareholders' meeting resolution did not require a three-fourths majority. The *Holzmüller* principle does not apply in this case.

In the *Holzmüller* decision (BGHZ 83, 122), this Senat held that a transaction not explicitly listed in the Stock Corporation Law as one that requires the shareholders' vote can also require the approval of the shareholders' meeting. This is the case when the most valuable assets of a corporation are transferred to a subsidiary (BGHZ 83, 122). In this regard this Senat did not refer to the statutory provisions requiring an approval by the shareholders' meeting but only to Sec. 119 subs. 2 of the German

Stock Corporation Law limiting the powers of the managing board (BGHZ 83, 122, 131).

The recognition of such a necessary approval by the shareholders' meeting developed by this Senat was widely accepted by legal scholars (see further references in *Habersack*, in: Emmerich/Habersack, Aktien- und GmbH-Konzernrecht, 3rd edition, vor § 311 note 33 footnote 143). However, the exact scope of this principle remained unclear with respect to its rationale, its legal basis, its precise limits and the required majority of the shareholders' meeting.

[. . .]

It is generally accepted that not every transaction with an effect on shareholders requires the approval of the shareholders' meeting. Therefore it would be consequent—as postulated by some legal scholars— to establish a clearer standard.

However, this Senat refuses to establish such minimum standards. German stock corporation law clearly entrusts the managing board— under the supervision of the supervisory board—with the duty and the right to manage the affairs of the corporation. In contrast, the shareholders' meeting is generally not involved in the management. By considering the experiences until the beginning of the 1930s the legislature explicitly limited the competences of the shareholders' meetings since it was usually not able to fulfil the tasks attributed to it by the former statute. After several years of discussion, legal scholars and practitioners (see further references in Schubert, *Quellen zur Aktienrechtsreform der Weimarer Republik 1926–1931 and Protokolle des Ausschusses für Aktienrecht der Akademie für Deutsches Recht; see also Assmann, in: Großkommentar zum AktG*, 4th edition, Einl. note 133, 156 f., 164) came to the conclusion that the shareholders' meeting cannot be involved in the management of the corporation since its composition was usually not homogenous and random. However, it was also accepted that the shareholders' meeting should be involved in general affairs concerning the fundamental elements of the corporation, such as amendments of the corporate charter, capital increase, the appointment and dismissal of the supervisory board or the discharge of board members (see 1. und 2. Bericht des Vorsitzenden des Ausschusses für Aktienrecht in: Schubert, *Quellen zur Aktienrechtsreform der Weimarer Republik 1926—1931, p. 486, 503 ff.; Amtliche Begründung zum AktG 1937*, Deutscher Reichsanzeiger und Preußischer Staatsanzeiger 1937, Nr. 28 p. 3). These general principles were implemented in the reform of the stock corporation law in 1937 and later also adopted in the reform of 1965— which only extended the competences to business combinations—since they are of such a fundamental importance for the corporation that they cannot be decided by the managing board alone (*Kropff*, Aktiengesetz

1965, vor § 76 p. 95 f.). In a global economy which makes it necessary to take advantage of chances and to react to upcoming risks immediately a too strong engagement of the shareholders' meeting in the corporation would be impractical and only limit the development of the corporation.

Therefore, an involvement of the shareholders' meeting in the management of the corporation can only be justified in very rare circumstances which usually are only met when the foundations of the corporations are affected. This is especially true when the impact of management decisions reaches the level of a change of the corporate charter. This level is argued by some legal scholars as requiring an impact from 10% to 50% on the assets of the corporation (see further references at *Habersack,* in: Emmerich/Habersack, Aktien- und GmbH-Konzernrecht, 3rd edition, vor § 311 note 41; *Kubis,* in: Münchener Kommentar zum AktG, 2nd edition, § 119 note 55; *Krieger,* in: Münchener Handbuch des Gesellschaftsrechts—volume 2, 2nd edition § 69 note 7 f.). In fact it is necessary that these management decisions reach a level similar to the one in the *Holzmüller* decision.

b) If these—exceptional—requirements are met, the managing board must obtain the approval of the shareholders' meeting of its decision with a three-fourths majority although these decisions constitute a management decision and not a change of the corporate charter (see e.g. *Hübner,* Festschrift Stimpel, p. 791, 795 f.; *Priester,* ZHR 163 [1999], 187, 199 f.; *Joost,* ZHR 162 [1999], 164, 172; *Altmeppen,* DB 1998, 49, 51; *Raiser,* Recht der Kapitalgesellschaften, 3rd edition, § 16 note 15; *Habersack,* in: Emmerich/Habersack, Aktien- und GmbH-Konzernrecht, 3rd edition, vor § 311 Rdn. 45 with further references; dissenting *Hüffer,* Festschrift Ulmer, p. 279, 297 ff.; *Semler,* in: Münchener Kommentar zum AktG, 2nd edition, § 34 note 42). The reason is that these management decisions have a severe impact on the position of the shareholders and consequently justify a limitation of the competences of the managing board. This principle is supported by the fact that the stock corporation law also requires an approval of the shareholders' meeting in other cases of management decisions without the change of the corporate charter such as the execution of business combination agreements under the German law of groups of corporations (*Unternehmensverträge*) (see *Kropff,* Aktiengesetz 1965, p. 96), or similar restructurings according to the Law on Mergers. [Therefore, a three-fourth majority is not necessary.]

[. . .]

3. The issue decided by the shareholders' meeting of 2000 in the present dispute does not meet these requirements since it does not have a severe impact on the position of shareholders.

[. . .]

NOTES AND QUESTIONS

1. In *Holzmüller* the court stated that the shareholders of the parent corporation must approve the issuance of new shares by a subsidiary corporation established transferring major assets of the parent corporation to the subsidiary, and also that the shareholders of the parent have to vote on the exclusion of pre-emptive rights when the subsidiary issues new shares. This is quite revolutionary because it grants to the shareholders of a controlling corporation direct powers *vis-à-vis* decisions that, normally, could be taken by the shareholders and directors of the subsidiary (note that here the controlling shareholder is the parent corporation itself, and therefore the directors of the parent, normally, decide how to vote the shares in their subsidiaries). As a rationale the court stated that these rules are necessary in order to protect the interest of the shareholders of the parent corporation. Do you understand why? Do you think that the *Holzmüller* doctrine should be applied only when the subsidiary owns and manages all or substantively all the assets that indirectly belong to the parent, or also in other cases? Can you think of other ways in which the interests of the shareholders of the parent corporation are affected in these situations? What about the possibility to sue directors and managers of the subsidiary?

2. You might have noted (and if you have not, you should read cases more carefully) that in *Holzmüller* the Court observed that by not obtaining the approval of the shareholders, the directors could "violate their duty of care." On the other hand, in *Blasius* (above), the Delaware judges mentioned that by infringing on shareholders' voting rights, directors committed "an unintended violation of the duty of loyalty." We will study in the next chapter the differences between the duty of care and of loyalty. However, in your opinion and based on an intuitive notion of care and loyalty, do you think that infringements on the franchise of the shareholders, as both *Holzmüller* and *Blasius* could be considered, are better described in terms of duty of care or of loyalty?

3. The *Gelatine* decision was largely welcomed by legal scholars as a clarification of the *Holzmüller* doctrine. In contrast, others stated that *Gelatine* actually almost abolished the *Holzmüller* doctrine. Do you think that *Gelatine* really clarified the *Holzmüller* doctrine and established a clear and straightforward rule? Both decisions refer to the rule that allows (not requires) directors to seek the vote of the shareholders on certain decisions (Sec. 119 AKTG). Do you understand why and how?

4. The management of the parent corporation in the *Gelatine* case actually asked the shareholders' meeting to approve the transfer of the Swedish and British corporations to the newly founded corporation, and dissenting shareholders were able to challenge this resolution. How can shareholders actually enforce their right to approve such a transfer, meeting the requirements of the *Holzmüller* doctrine, if the management simply makes this decision without a shareholder approval? What are the possible consequences for the management?

CHAPTER 6

DIRECTORS' LIABILITY AND FIDUCIARY DUTIES

■ ■ ■

INTRODUCTION

Directors are the agents of the corporation and of the shareholders. As such, they owe to their principals fiduciary duties. Although the concept of fiduciary duties is typical of common law systems, directors' duties also in other systems, even if defined differently, substantively are quite similar to common law-style fiduciary duties.

This chapter examines directors' duties and possible consequences of a breach of their duties in terms of liability. Following a traditional and universal distinction, we will focus on the duty of care, *i.e.*, the duty to act diligently in the best interest of the corporation; and the duty of loyalty, which includes different aspects: the duty not to act in conflict of interest, transactions with related parties, and the business opportunity doctrine, holding that a director must offer business opportunities that she became aware of to the corporation before taking advantage of them personally. Some scholars and courts also identify as a separate and specific duty of directors the duty of "good faith," which—somehow simplifying—could be considered a middle ground between the duty of care and of loyalty. Even if, especially more recently, courts in the U.S. have been willing to expand the notion of good faith and use it as a basis to affirm directors' liability, we think that for our purposes it is not necessary to treat this aspect as a separate and independent duty.

Generally speaking, especially in common law systems, directors do not have fiduciary duties toward creditors. Creditors only have contractual rights toward the corporation. This is however not always the case. On the one hand, even in common law systems, when the corporation is nearing insolvency (it is in the so-called "zone of insolvency"), and therefore an almost certain damage to creditors will occur, directors can also have fiduciary duties toward creditors, but the case law is not well settled and varies among different jurisdictions. On the other hand, in several civil law countries specific statutory rules concerning the liability of directors toward creditors exist, sometimes also independently from the insolvency of the corporation (even if they are rarely enforced outside of bankruptcy). We will address this problem in the final part of this chapter. Of course there are also specific remedies in case of bankruptcy, but they are outside the scope of this book.

Specific procedural issues concerning the possibility to sue directors, especially derivatively, will be treated in the following chapter. Here we will consider the substantive definitions of directors' duties and liabilities. One general observation that we can anticipate is that even if in this area comparative differences among the different jurisdictions considered exist and are relevant, some of the basic ideas such as the definition of the duty of care and the business judgment rule, but also the contents of the duty of loyalty, are fairly similar. This is not surprising as the underlying economic issues, and the need to strike a balance between directors' liability and allowing them sufficient latitude to carry on the business and take reasonable risks are similar in all legal systems.

DUTY OF CARE

Basically, as mentioned above, the duty of care is the duty of directors to manage the corporation diligently. In order to understand the content of the duty of care it can be helpful to start from a distinction used in civil law systems, not always familiar to the common law lawyer. In several civil law systems, there is a difference between what might be called, with a somehow loose translation, "obligations of means" and "obligations of result." The former are obligations that are performed simply by being diligent, even if a specific result expected or hoped for by a party is not reached. The latter are, on the other hand, obligations that are performed only if a specific result is achieved: diligence or the absence of negligence do not excuse non-performance and the party is considered to have breached the contract if the promised result is not obtained.

In this perspective, it is essential to understand that directors do not have an obligation of result, but only an obligation of means. They must manage the corporation in compliance with the law and the governing documents of the corporation, and act diligently, but the fact that the corporation does not achieve good economic results, or even that it becomes insolvent or bankrupt, is not automatically a source of liability. The care required by directors, in addition, is primarily a "procedural" care, in the sense that directors that act on an informed basis, devote sufficient time to their decisions, acquire—when necessary—opinions from independent experts on a business decision, and so on, are generally not liable for an honest error of judgment. The emphasis is, in other words, more on the "way" in which a decision has been reached, rather than on the merits of the decision itself. This is so also because, in case of a lawsuit, judges, who are not business experts, are reluctant to substitute their judgment for the one of the directors; in addition, it might be difficult and somehow unfair to second-guess directors' decisions in light of additional elements that might have not been foreseeable when the decision was taken (so-called hindsight bias).

This observation requires, however, a qualification. While it is generally true that the focus is on procedural due care, in egregious circumstances when, based on all the information collected, the actual decision was completely irrational, a breach of the duty of care could be found.

What is the standard of diligence to which directors are held? Based on principles of agency law, it is the vague but universal standard of the "prudent person—better, director—in similar circumstances." Needless to say, this does not require directors to be particularly conservative: managing a corporation requires taking risks; therefore as long as the risks are properly evaluated and balanced by the reasonable expectation of higher returns, directors have significant leeway. Of course this vague standard can only be given a more precise meaning by case law, and the inquiry is always very fact-intensive. Several courts, as we will also see below, limit directors' liability to cases of gross negligence.

A connected and perhaps more complex question is if the diligence standard is objective or subjective; more concretely: if a director has specific knowledge in a certain field, based on her education and past experience, would she be held to a higher standard than the fictional "average director"? For example, let's imagine that the board of a corporation approves both the project to build a bridge, and a complex transaction to finance the project through derivative contracts, and let's imagine that both an engineer and a corporate finance expert sit on the board. If the bridge collapses or the financial transaction turns out to be ruinous, would they be held to different standards based on their professional profiles (so to speak, is the engineer "more liable" for the damages connected to the failure of the bridge, and the financial expert for the loss on derivatives?). In some legal systems, for example under Italian law (Article 2392 of the Italian Civil Code), the corporate statute specifically provides that all directors are held to the standard of diligence of the "average director," but that specific additional competences are taken into account. In other systems this distinction is not so rigid, contrary for example to what happens with the "due diligence" defense in securities cases in the U.S. based on section 11 or 12 of the 1933 Securities Act (*see* Escott v. BarChris Const. Corp., 283 F.Supp. 643 (S.D.N.Y 1968)).

One additional and fundamental concept, especially in common law systems but—as we will see—also in other jurisdictions, is the so-called "business judgment rule." The business judgment rule is basically a presumption that, in carrying out their duties, directors acted in good faith, on an informed basis, and in the best interest of the corporation. In case of dispute, it is up to the plaintiff to overcome this presumption and prove with a preponderance of the evidence that this was not the case. The business judgment rule is a quite powerful protection for directors against liability suits, and from an economic standpoint it is justified, among other reasons, by the need to be able to recruit and retain well-qualified professionals as directors. Can you see why a rigid liability system might cause adverse selection?

There are, however, several circumstances in which the business judgment rule does not apply or, more precisely, can be rebutted. These include situations in which the director breached his duty of loyalty, for example acting in conflict of interest; situations in which the director was completely passive and failed to inform himself on the business of the corporation; or cases of a knowing violation of criminal law. In addition, as mentioned before, the corporations or shareholders suing derivatively can overcome the business judgment rule by demonstrating that a reasonable investigation was missing, or—even if it might be harder—that the decision was (completely) irrational and wasteful.

While most systems recognize that directors are not liable if they exercised good business judgment, and do not hold directors liable for an honest error in judgment, not all systems provide for an explicit presumption that the plaintiff must overcome to prove the lack of care of directors. In many systems this regulatory approach follows from general principles, according to which it is the plaintiff that must prove the basis of her cause of action. Of course, as also the following judicial opinions will illustrate, there is occasionally room for ambiguities. This is the case in China, because the new Company Law of 2005 does not explicitly address the business judgment rule. Commentators have argued that some courts might not apply it, but even some judges seem to embrace the general approach briefly discussed. For example, two Chinese judges have recently written in an article: "The people's courts should not substitute judicial power for the company's ordinary business judgment, but should instead respect the ordinary business judgment" (see Jiang Yu Wang, *Company Law in China: Regulation of Business Organizations in a Socialist Market Economy*, Edward Elgar Publishing, 2014, 214 f.).

Very rarely, in some systems, there is no presumption that directors acted diligently, and if they are sued, they have the burden of proving due care. This seems to be the case in the Czech Republic: see Bohumil Havel, *Czech Corporate Law on its Way*, 12 ECFR 1, 11 (2015).

Needless to say, directors and officers can be liable both for misfeasance, when an improper decision was taken (better: a damaging decision was taken in an improper way), and for nonfeasance, when they failed to supervise or monitor. It is important to point out that most developed legal systems also recognize, as part of the duty of care, a specific duty of directors to put in place adequate internal control systems to prevent or mitigate damages. For example, in the U.S., *see* the famous case *In re Caremark International Inc. Derivative Litigation*, 698 A.2d 959 (Del. Ch. 1996); in Italy *see* Article 2381, Par. 3, Italian Civil Code, stating that directors must evaluate, based on the information received, the adequacy of the organizational, administrative, and accounting systems adopted by the corporation. This duty might be interpreted as including the one of overseeing the internal control system of the corporation, even if oversight liability often requires more serious violations.

With this framework in mind, we can start our comparative analysis. As discussed before, this is an area in which, in our opinion, there are not profound substantive differences among countries. Most jurisdictions limit directors' liability in the sense we have illustrated, and most jurisdictions know, in one form or another, some version of the business judgment rule, putting the burden of proving negligence on the plaintiff. The devil, here more than in other areas, is in the details. There might be differences in the way in which courts interpret and apply the protections for what we have called "honest errors in judgment": some courts might be, as a matter of fact, more or less deferential to directors' business judgment. Let's take a look at three leading cases from the U.S., Germany, and Italy. The first one is the famous 1985 Smith v. Van Gorkom decision of the Supreme Court of Delaware. This is one of the few cases in which a Delaware court found directors liable for a breach of the duty of care, and as we will see in the Notes and Questions following the excerpt of the decision, it triggered a legislative response from the Delaware legislature.

ALDEN SMITH V. JEROME W. VAN GORKOM

Supreme Court of Delaware
488 A.2d 858 (1985)

HORSEY, JUSTICE (for the majority):

This appeal from the Court of Chancery involves a class action brought by shareholders of the defendant Trans Union Corporation ("Trans Union" or "the Company"), originally seeking rescission of a cash-out merger of Trans Union [. . .]

Following trial, the former Chancellor granted judgment for the defendant directors. [. . .] Judgment was based [on a finding] that the Board of Directors had acted in an informed manner so as to be entitled to protection of the business judgment rule in approving the cash-out merger [. . .]

Speaking for the majority of the Court, we conclude that both rulings of the Court of Chancery are clearly erroneous. Therefore, we reverse and direct that judgment be entered in favor of the plaintiffs and against the defendant directors for the fair value of the plaintiffs' stockholdings in Trans Union [. . .]

We hold [. . .] that the Board's decision, reached September 20, 1980, to approve the proposed cash-out merger was not the product of an informed business judgment [. . .]

Beginning in the late 1960's, and continuing through the 1970's, Trans Union pursued a program of acquiring small companies in order to increase available taxable income [against which it could use the investment tax credit (ITC) and depreciation deductions its rail car leasing business generated].

On August 27, 1980, [Chairperson and Chief Executive Officer Jerome] Van Gorkom met with Senior Management of Trans Union. Van Gorkom reported on his lobbying efforts in Washington and his desire to find a solution to the tax credit problem more permanent than a continued program of acquisitions. Various alternatives were suggested and discussed preliminarily, including the sale of Trans Union to a company with a large amount of taxable income.

Donald Romans, Chief Financial Officer of Trans Union, stated that his department had done a "very brief bit of work on the possibility of a leveraged buy-out." This work had been prompted by a media article which Romans had seen regarding a leveraged buy-out by management. The work consisted of a "preliminary study" of the cash which could be generated by the Company if it participated in a leveraged buy-out. As Romans stated, this analysis "was very first and rough cut at seeing whether a cash flow would support what might be considered a high price for this type of transaction."

On September 5, at another Senior Management meeting which Van Gorkom attended, Romans again brought up the idea of a leveraged buy-out as a "possible strategic alternative" to the Company's acquisition program. Romans and Bruce S. Chelberg, President and Chief Operating Officer of Trans Union, had been working on the matter in preparation for the meeting. According to Romans: They did not "come up" with a price for the Company. They merely "ran the numbers" at $50 a share and at $60 a share with the "rough form" of their cash figures at the time. Their "figures indicated that $50 would be very easy to do but $60 would be very difficult to do under those figures." This work did not purport to establish a fair price for either the Company or 100% of the stock. It was intended to determine the cash flow needed to service the debt that would "probably" be incurred in a leveraged buy-out, based on "rough calculations" [. . .]

At this meeting, Van Gorkom stated that he would be willing to take $55 per share for his own 75,000 shares. He vetoed the suggestion of a leveraged buy-out by Management, however, as involving a potential conflict of interest for Management. Van Gorkom, a certified public accountant and lawyer, had been an officer of Trans Union for 24 years, its Chief Executive Officer for more than 17 years, and Chairman of its Board for 2 years. It is noteworthy in this connection that he was then approaching 65 years of age and mandatory retirement.

[. . .]

Van Gorkom decided to meet with Jay A. Pritzker, a well-known corporate takeover specialist and a social acquaintance. However, rather than approaching Pritzker simply to determine his interest in acquiring Trans Union, Van Gorkom assembled a proposed per share price for sale of the Company and a financing structure by which to accomplish the sale. Van Gorkom did so without consulting either his Board or any members of Senior Management except one: Carl Peterson, Trans Union's Controller. Telling Peterson that he wanted no other person on his staff to know what he was doing, but without telling him why, Van Gorkom directed Peterson to calculate the feasibility of a leveraged buy-out at an assumed price per share of $55. Apart from the Company's historic stock market price, and Van Gorkom's long association with Trans Union, the record is devoid of any competent evidence that $55 represented the per share intrinsic value of the Company.

Having thus chosen the $55 figure, based solely on the availability of a leveraged buy-out, Van Gorkom multiplied the price per share by the number of shares outstanding to reach a total value of the Company of $690 million. Van Gorkom told Peterson to use this $690 million figure and to assume a $200 million equity contribution by the buyer. Based on these assumptions, Van Gorkom directed Peterson to determine whether the debt portion of the purchase price could be paid off in five years or less if financed by Trans Union's cash flow as projected in the Five Year Forecast, and by the sale of certain weaker divisions identified in a study done for Trans Union by the Boston Consulting Group ("BCG study"). Peterson reported that, of the purchase price, approximately $50–80 million would remain outstanding after five years. Van Gorkom was disappointed, but decided to meet with Pritzker nevertheless.

Van Gorkom arranged a meeting with Pritzker at the latter's home on Saturday, September 13, 1980. Van Gorkom prefaced his presentation by stating to Pritzker: "Now as far as you are concerned, I can, I think, show how you can pay a substantial premium over the present stock price and pay off most of the loan in the first five years. [. . .] If you could pay $55 for this Company, here is a way in which I think it can be financed."

Van Gorkom then reviewed with Pritzker his calculations based upon his proposed price of $55 per share. Although Pritzker mentioned $50 as a more attractive figure, no other price was mentioned. However, Van

Gorkom stated that to be sure that $55 was the best price obtainable, Trans Union should be free to accept any better offer. Pritzker demurred, stating that his organization would serve as a "stalking horse" for an "auction contest" only if Trans Union would permit Pritzker to buy 1,750,000 shares of Trans Union stock at market price which Pritzker could then sell to any higher bidder. After further discussion on this point, Pritzker told Van Gorkom that he would give him a more definite reaction soon.

On Monday, September 15, Pritzker advised Van Gorkom that he was interested in the $55 cash-out merger proposal and requested more information on Trans Union [. . .]

On Thursday, September 18, Van Gorkom met again with Pritzker. At that time, Van Gorkom knew that Pritzker intended to make a cash-out merger offer at Van Gorkom's proposed $55 per share. Pritzker instructed his attorney, a merger and acquisition specialist, to begin drafting merger documents. There was no further discussion of the $55 price. However, the number of shares of Trans Union's treasury stock to be offered to Pritzker was negotiated down to one million shares; the price was set at $38—75 cents above the per share price at the close of the market on September 19. At this point, Pritzker insisted that the Trans Union Board act on his merger proposal within the next three days.

[. . .]

On Friday, September 19, Van Gorkom called a special meeting of the Trans Union Board for noon the following day. He also called a meeting of the Company's Senior Management to convene at 11:00 a.m., prior to the meeting of the Board. No one, except Chelberg and Peterson, was told the purpose of the meetings. Van Gorkom did not invite Trans Union's investment banker, Salomon Brothers or its Chicago-based partner, to attend.

[A]t the Senior Management meeting on September 20 [. . .] Van Gorkom disclosed the offer and described its terms, but he furnished no copies of the proposed Merger Agreement. Romans announced that his department had done a second study which showed that, for a leveraged buy-out, the price range for Trans Union stock was between $55 and $65 per share. Van Gorkom neither saw the study nor asked Romans to make it available for the Board meeting.

Senior Management's reaction to the Pritzker proposal was completely negative. No member of Management, except Chelberg and Peterson, supported the proposal. Romans objected to the price as being too low; he was critical of the timing and suggested that consideration should be given to the adverse tax consequences of an all-cash deal for low-basis shareholders; and he took the position that the agreement to sell Pritzker one million newly-issued shares at market price would inhibit other offers, as would the prohibitions against soliciting bids and furnishing inside information to other bidders. Romans argued that the Pritzker proposal was a "lock up" [. . .] Nevertheless, Van Gorkom proceeded to the Board meeting as scheduled without further delay.

Ten directors served on the Trans Union Board, five inside (defendants Bonser, O'Boyle, Browder, Chelberg, and Van Gorkom) and five outside (defendants Wallis, Johnson, Lanterman, Morgan and Reneker). All directors were present at the meeting, except O'Boyle who was ill. Of the outside directors, four were corporate chief executive officers and one was the former Dean of the University of Chicago Business School. None was an investment banker or trained financial analyst. All members of the Board were well informed about the Company and its operations as a going concern [. . .]

Van Gorkom began the Special Meeting of the Board with a twenty-minute oral presentation. Copies of the proposed Merger Agreement were delivered too late for study before or during the meeting. He reviewed the Company's ITC and depreciation problems and the efforts theretofore made to solve them. He discussed his initial meeting with Pritzker and his motivation in arranging that meeting. Van Gorkom did not disclose to the Board, however, the methodology by which he alone had arrived at the $55 figure, or the fact that he first proposed the $55 price in his negotiations with Pritzker.

[F]or a period of 90 days, Trans Union could receive, but could not actively solicit, competing offers; the offer had to be acted on by the next evening, Sunday, September 21 [. . .] Trans Union was required to sell to Pritzker one million newly-issued shares of Trans Union at $38 per share.

Van Gorkom took the position that putting Trans Union "up for auction" through a 90-day market test would validate a decision by the Board that $55 was a fair price. He told the Board that the "free market will have an opportunity to judge whether $55 is a fair price." Van Gorkom framed the decision before the Board not as whether $55 per share was the highest price that could be obtained, but as whether the $55 price was a fair price [. . .]

Attorney Brennan advised the members of the Board that they might be sued if they failed to accept the offer and that a fairness opinion was not required as a matter of law.

Romans told the Board that, in his opinion, $55 was "in the range of a fair price," but "at the beginning of the range."

[. . .]

The Board meeting of September 20 lasted about two hours. Based solely upon Van Gorkom's oral presentation [. . .] Romans' oral statement,

Brennan's legal advice, and their knowledge of the market history of the Company's stock, the directors approved the proposed Merger Agreement.

[. . .]

[On] October 9, Trans Union issued a press release announcing: (1) that Pritzker had obtained "the financing commitments necessary to consummate" the merger with Trans Union; (2) that Pritzker had acquired one million shares of Trans Union common stock at $38 per share; (3) that Trans Union was now permitted to actively seek other offers and had retained Salomon Brothers for that purpose; and (4) that if a more favorable offer were not received before February 1, 1981, Trans Union's shareholders would thereafter meet to vote on the Pritzker proposal.

Salomon Brothers' efforts over a three-month period from October 21 to January 21 produced only one serious suitor for Trans Union—General Electric Credit Corporation ("GE Credit"), a subsidiary of the General Electric Company. However, GE Credit was unwilling to make an offer for Trans Union unless Trans Union first rescinded its Merger Agreement with Pritzker. When Pritzker refused, GE Credit terminated further discussions with Trans Union in early January.

In the meantime, in early December, the investment firm of Kohlberg, Kravis, Roberts & Co. ("KKR"), the only other concern to make a firm offer for Trans Union, withdrew its offer under circumstances hereinafter detailed.

On December 19, this litigation was commenced and [. . .] On January 26, Trans Union's Board met and, after a lengthy meeting, voted to proceed with the Pritzker merger. The Board also approved for mailing, "on or about January 27," a Supplement to its Proxy Statement [. . .]

On February 10, the stockholders of Trans Union approved the Pritzker merger proposal. Of the outstanding shares, 69.9% were voted in favor of the merger; 7.25% were voted against the merger; and 22.85% were not voted.

II.

We turn to the issue of the application of the business judgment rule to the September 20 meeting of the Board.

The Court of Chancery concluded from the evidence that the Board of Directors' approval of the Pritzker merger proposal fell within the protection of the business judgment rule. The Court found that the Board had given sufficient time and attention to the transaction, since the directors had considered the Pritzker proposal on three different occasions, on September 20, and on October 8, 1980 and finally on January 26, 1981.

[. . .]

The Court of Chancery made but one finding; i.e., that the Board's conduct over the entire period from September 20 through January 26, 1981 was not reckless or improvident, but informed.

[. . .]

[W]e conclude that the Court's ultimate finding that the Board's conduct was not "reckless or imprudent" is contrary to the record and not the product of a logical and deductive reasoning process.

The plaintiffs contend that the Court of Chancery erred as a matter of law by exonerating the defendant directors under the business judgment rule without first determining whether the rule's threshold condition of "due care and prudence" was satisfied [. . .]

Under Delaware law, the business judgment rule is the offspring of the fundamental principle, codified in 8 *Del.C.* § 141(a), that the business and affairs of a Delaware corporation are managed by or under its board of directors. *Pogostin v. Rice,* Del.Supr., 480 A.2d 619, 624 (1984); *Aronson v. Lewis,* Del.Supr., 473 A.2d 805, 811 (1984) [. . .] In carrying out their managerial roles, directors are charged with an unyielding fiduciary duty to the corporation and its shareholders. *Loft, Inc. v. Guth,* Del.Ch., 2 A.2d 225 (1938), *aff'd,* Del.Supr., 5 A.2d 503 (1939). The business judgment rule exists to protect and promote the full and free exercise of the managerial power granted to Delaware directors. *Zapata Corp. v. Maldonado, supra* at 782. The rule itself "is a presumption that in making a business decision, the directors of a corporation acted on an informed basis, in good faith and in the honest belief that the action taken was in the best interests of the company." *Aronson, supra* at 812. Thus, the party attacking a board decision as uninformed must rebut the presumption that its business judgment was an informed one.

The determination of whether a business judgment is an informed one turns on whether the directors have informed themselves "prior to making a business decision, of all material information reasonably available to them."

Under the business judgment rule there is no protection for directors who have made "an unintelligent or unadvised judgment." *Mitchell v. Highland-Western Glass,* Del.Ch., 167 A. 831, 833 (1933). A director's duty to inform himself in preparation for a decision derives from the fiduciary capacity in which he serves the corporation and its stockholders. *Lutz v. Boas,* Del.Ch., 171 A.2d 381 (1961). *See Weinberger v. UOP, Inc., supra; Guth v. Loft, supra.* Since a director is vested with the responsibility for the management of the affairs of the corporation, he must execute that duty with the recognition that he acts on behalf of others. Such obligation does not tolerate faithlessness or self-dealing. But fulfillment of the fiduciary function requires more than the mere absence of bad faith or fraud. Representation of the financial interests of others imposes on a director an affirmative duty to protect those interests and to proceed with a critical eye in assessing information of the type and under the circumstances present here.

[. . .]

The standard of care applicable to a director's duty of care has also been recently restated by this Court. In *Aronson, supra,* we stated:

> While the Delaware cases use a variety of terms to describe the applicable standard of care, our analysis satisfies us that under the business judgment rule director liability is predicated upon concepts of gross negligence.

We again confirm that view. We think the concept of gross negligence is also the proper standard for determining whether a business judgment reached by a board of directors was an informed one.

In the specific context of a proposed merger of domestic corporations, a director has a duty under 8 *Del.C.* § 251(b), along with his fellow directors, to act in an informed and deliberate manner in determining whether to approve an agreement of merger before submitting the proposal to the stockholders. Certainly in the merger context, a director may not abdicate that duty by leaving to the shareholders alone the decision to approve or disapprove the agreement.

It is against those standards that the conduct of the directors of Trans Union must be tested, as a matter of law and as a matter of fact, regarding their exercise of an informed business judgment in voting to approve the Pritzker merger proposal.

[. . .]

On the record before us, we must conclude that the Board of Directors did not reach an informed business judgment on September 20, 1980 in voting to "sell" the Company for $55 per share pursuant to the Pritzker cash-out merger proposal. Our reasons, in summary, are as follows:

The directors (1) did not adequately inform themselves as to Van Gorkom's role in forcing the "sale" of the Company and in establishing the per share purchase price; (2) were uninformed as to the intrinsic value of the Company; and (3) given these circumstances, at a minimum, were grossly negligent in approving the "sale" of the Company upon two hours' consideration, without prior notice, and without the exigency of a crisis or emergency.

As has been noted, the Board based its September 20 decision to approve the cash-out merger primarily on Van Gorkom's representations.

None of the directors, other than Van Gorkom and Chelberg, had any prior knowledge that the purpose of the meeting was to propose a cash-out merger of Trans Union. No members of Senior Management were present, other than Chelberg, Romans and Peterson; and the latter two had only learned of the proposed sale an hour earlier . . .

Without any documents before them concerning the proposed transaction, the members of the Board were required to rely entirely upon Van Gorkom's 20-minute oral presentation of the proposal. No written summary of the terms of the merger was presented; the directors were given no documentation to support the adequacy of $55 price per share for sale of the Company; and the Board had before it nothing more than Van Gorkom's statement of his understanding of the substance of an agreement which he admittedly had never read, nor which any member of the Board had ever seen.

[. . .]

The defendants rely on the following factors to sustain the Trial Court's finding that the Board's decision was an informed one: (1) the magnitude of the premium or spread between the $55 Pritzker offering price and Trans Union's current market price of $38 per share; (2) the amendment of the Agreement as submitted on September 20 to permit the Board to accept any better offer during the "market test" period. [. . .] We discuss each of these grounds *seriatim:*

[. . .]

A substantial premium may provide one reason to recommend a merger, but in the absence of other sound valuation information, the fact of a premium alone does not provide an adequate basis upon which to assess the fairness of an offering price.

[. . .]

[B]y their own admission they could not rely on the stock price as an accurate measure of value. Yet, also by their own admission, the Board members assumed that Trans Union's market price was adequate to serve as a basis upon which to assess the adequacy of the premium for purposes of the September 20 meeting.

[. . .]

Despite the foregoing facts and circumstances, there was no call by the Board, either on September 20 or thereafter, for any valuation study or documentation of the $55 price per share as a measure of the fair value of the Company in a cash-out context. It is undisputed that the major asset of Trans Union was its cash flow. Yet, at no time did the Board call for a valuation study taking into account that highly significant element of the Company's assets.

We do not imply that an outside valuation study is essential to support an informed business judgment; nor do we state that fairness opinions by independent investment bankers are required as a matter of law. Often insiders familiar with the business of a going concern are in a better position than are outsiders to gather relevant information; and under appropriate circumstances, such directors may be fully protected in relying in good faith upon the valuation reports of their management.

Here, the record establishes that the Board did not request its Chief Financial Officer, Romans, to make any valuation study or review of the proposal to determine the adequacy of $55 per share for sale of the Company. On the record before us: The Board rested on Romans' elicited response that the $55 figure was within a "fair price range" within the context of a leveraged buy-out. No director sought any further information from Romans. No director asked him why he put $55 at the bottom of his range. No director asked Romans for any details as to his study, the reason why it had been undertaken or its depth. No director asked to see the study; and no director asked Romans whether Trans Union's finance department could do a fairness study within the remaining 36-hour period available under the Pritzker offer.

[. . .]

The record also establishes that the Board accepted without scrutiny Van Gorkom's representation as to the fairness of the $55 price per share for sale of the Company—a subject that the Board had never previously considered. The Board thereby failed to discover that Van Gorkom had suggested the $55 price to Pritzker and, most crucially, that Van Gorkom had arrived at the $55 figure based on calculations designed solely to determine the feasibility of a leveraged buy-out [. . .]

We do not say that the Board of Directors was not entitled to give some credence to Van Gorkom's representation that $55 was an adequate or fair price. Under § 141(e), the directors were entitled to rely upon their chairman's opinion of value and adequacy, provided that such opinion was reached on a sound basis. Here, the issue is whether the directors informed themselves as to all information that was reasonably available to them. Had they done so, they would have learned of the source and derivation of the $55 price and could not reasonably have relied thereupon in good faith.

None of the directors, Management or outside, were investment bankers or financial analysts. Yet the Board did not consider recessing the meeting until a later hour that day (or requesting an extension of Pritzker's Sunday evening deadline) to give it time to elicit more information as to the sufficiency of the offer, either from inside Management (in particular Romans) or from Trans Union's own investment banker, Salomon Brothers, whose Chicago specialist in merger and acquisitions was known to the Board and familiar with Trans Union's affairs.

Thus, the record compels the conclusion that on September 20 the Board lacked valuation information adequate to reach an informed business judgment as to the fairness of $55 per share for sale of the Company.

(2)

This brings us to the post-September 20 "market test" upon which the defendants ultimately rely to confirm the reasonableness of their September 20 decision to accept the Pritzker proposal. In this connection, the directors present a two-part argument: (a) that by making a "market test" of Pritzker's $55 per share offer a condition of their September 20 decision to accept his offer, they cannot be found to have acted impulsively or in an uninformed manner on September 20; and (b) that the adequacy of the $17 premium for sale of the Company was conclusively established over the following 90 to 120 days by the most reliable evidence available—the marketplace. Thus, the defendants impliedly contend that the "market test" eliminated the need for the Board to perform any other form of fairness test either on September 20, or thereafter.

[. . .]

The defendants attempt to downplay the significance of the prohibition against Trans Union's actively soliciting competing offers by arguing that the directors "understood that the entire financial community would know that Trans Union was for sale upon the announcement of the Pritzker offer, and anyone desiring to make a better offer was free to do so." Yet, the press release issued on September 22, with the authorization of the Board, stated that Trans Union had entered into "definitive agreements" with the Pritzkers; and the press release did not even disclose Trans Union's limited right to receive and accept higher offers. Accompanying this press release was a further public announcement that Pritzker had been granted an option to purchase at any time one million shares of Trans Union's capital stock at 75 cents above the then-current price per share.

Thus, notwithstanding what several of the outside directors later claimed to have "thought" occurred at the meeting, the record compels the conclusion that Trans Union's Board had no rational basis to conclude on September 20 or in the days immediately following, that the Board's acceptance of Pritzker's offer was conditioned on [. . .] a "market test" of the offer [. . .]

[. . .]

We conclude that Trans Union's Board was grossly negligent in that it failed to act with informed reasonable deliberation in agreeing to the Pritzker merger proposal on September 20; and we further conclude that the Trial Court erred as a matter of law in failing to address that question before determining whether the directors' later conduct was sufficient to cure its initial error.

[. . .]

On remand, the Court of Chancery shall conduct an evidentiary hearing to determine the fair value of the shares represented by the plaintiffs' class, based on the intrinsic value of Trans Union on September 20, 1980 . . . Thereafter, an award of damages may be entered to the extent that the fair value of Trans Union exceeds $55 per share.

REVERSED and REMANDED for proceedings consistent herewith.

NOTES AND QUESTIONS

1.   What is a leveraged buy-out and why can it be considered a risky technique to acquire a corporation?

2.   *Smith v. Van Gorkom* offers almost a laundry list of what a board should *not* do in approving an important corporate transaction. It should be noted that the scrutiny of the court might have been particularly rigorous also because the proposed merger could have been the "last chance" for Trans Union shareholders to cash-in the value of their shares. The board spent too little time on the decision, relied almost exclusively on a brief oral presentation, and did not acquire an independent appraisal of the value of the corporation. The fact that a premium over the market price was paid was not considered sufficient to conclude that the price was fair. In addition, the so-called "market test," the possibility of other offers to be entertained, was not considered sufficient in light of the additional agreements concerning the solicitation of offers (no-shop provision) and the options given to Pritzker, which in the opinion of the court limited the likelihood of more competitive offers. But there is more. On the one hand, even if the court does not discuss this issue explicitly or at length, it is not irrelevant that Van Gorkom desired to sell his shares. One aspect that you should notice is that Van Gorkom and the board seem more focused on identifying a price that would make a leveraged buy-out possible and convenient, rather than on obtaining the best possible price for the shareholders. In this perspective, do you think it is relevant that the merger might be the "last chance" of existing shareholders to obtain the fair value of their investment?

3.   You should note that the price included a premium over market prices, but the court considered this not sufficient to conclude that the price was fair. Why? Does this mean that the court does not believe that market prices are efficient, i.e. correctly assess the value of listed corporations and reflect relevant information available in market prices?

4.   Do you think that the court is more critical of the procedure through which the decision has been taken, or of its substantive outcome?

5.   This decision sent a shiver through U.S. corporate circles. A Delaware court had shown no deference to the business judgment of directors, and in fact some corporations considered reincorporating away from Delaware. In many ways, the decision was somehow unusual and unexpected. The Delaware legislature, shortly after the decision, stepped in. This is an interesting example of the dynamics that can occur between judges and legislatures. To avoid a loss in Delaware's competitive advantage, the legislature adopted section 102(b)(7) of the Delaware General Corporation Law. This provision states, in the relevant part, that the articles of incorporation of a corporation can include

> "[a] provision eliminating or limiting the personal liability of a director to the corporation or its stockholders for monetary damages for breach of fiduciary duty as a director, provided that such provision shall not eliminate or limit the liability of a director (i) for any breach of the director's duty of loyalty to the corporation or its stockholders, (ii) for acts or omissions not in good faith or which involve intentional misconduct or a knowing violation of law, (iii) under section 174 of this Title, or (iv) for any transaction from which the director derived an improper personal benefit. No such provision shall eliminate or limit the liability of a director for any act or omission occurring prior to the date when such provision becomes effective."

A few notes on this rule. First, as you have read, the provision does not cover all violations, in particular when there is a breach of the duty of loyalty or an act in bad faith. Second, the limitation of liability does not apply to executives. Third, it only concerns monetary damages; it is still possible to obtain injunctive relief or other remedies such as rescission. Fourth, it only applies to liability toward the corporation and shareholders, not third parties. Finally, the burden of demonstrating that a director is entitled to this protection is on the defendant. Can you articulate and discuss the rationale for these limitations? Why do you think that the provision should be included in the articles of incorporation, and not in the bylaws?

6.   Consider a legal system in which there is no provision similar to section 102(b)(7) previously discussed. Do you think that a clause limiting or excluding directors' liability toward the corporation in the charter or bylaws might be valid and enforceable? Some arguments to consider in addressing this question: who are the subjects protected (directly or indirectly) by the possibility of the corporation or of the shareholders to sue negligent directors? Are creditors and other third parties included? In case of litigation, can the corporation or the shareholders settle or waive their claims? If so, how? And if the answer is yes, how does this affect the possibility of renouncing suing directors *ex ante* and generally, with a provision in the governing documents?

7.   In addition to Section 102(b)(7) DGCL, directors can also be protected with indemnification agreements, under which the corporation pays, under certain conditions, for litigation expenses that directors might incur as a consequence of their job, and through directors' and officers' insurance. Insurance, however, generally does not cover intentional violations, but only negligence. How do you think this might affect litigation?

* * *

As mentioned above, in most systems courts tend to be reluctant to second-guess the merits of a business decision taken by directors and managers, especially when it is an honest error in judgment. With the exclusion of blatantly irrational decisions, courts tend to focus more on the way in which a decision has been taken (procedural due care, including information and time dedicated to the decision, absence of conflicts of interests, etc.). The degree of deference to the business judgment of the directors varies however in different systems. The following leading German case offers the occasion to discuss the "German version" of the U.S. business judgment rule.

ARAG-GARMENBECK

German Federal Court of Justice, 1997
21 April 1997

Facts

The plaintiffs were members of the supervisory board of the defendant, a stock corporation in the legal protection insurance business. Between 1984 and 1989 the defendant and several subsidiary corporations were engaged in some dubious business relations with a foreign corporation headed by a previously convicted person who was actually running some kind of Ponzi scheme by borrowing money promising very high returns and granting loans with very low interest rates. In the beginning of 1990 this Ponzi scheme collapsed causing a loss for the defendant of more than 80 Million DM since the defendant also granted some loans to this foreign corporation but mainly guaranteed the repayment of loans of this foreign corporation to other lenders. The plaintiffs claimed that the head of the management board of the defendant violated his duty of care and should be held liable. At the meeting of the supervisory board in June 1992 it was decided, without the votes of the plaintiffs, not to pursue any claims for damages against the head of the management board of the defendant. The plaintiffs claimed that this resolution was unlawful and asked the court to declare it void. The Regional Court (Laudgericht) granted the claim. The Court of Appeals (Oberlaudesgericht) dismissed the case.

Grounds

[. . .]

The court grants the appeal. The Court of Appeals unlawfully dismissed the case.

[. . .]

The Court of Appeals stated correctly that the supervisory board has the duty to examine whether the corporation can actually claim damages from the members of the management board for a violation of their duties. This duty can be derived from the general duty of the supervisory board to monitor the activities of the management board (Sec. 111 subs. 1 Stock Corporation Code)—which also includes the review of already completed transactions (BGHZ 114, 127, 129)—and the general authority of the supervisory board to represent the corporation against the members of the management board (Sec. 112 Stock Corporation Code).

[. . .]

The decision of the supervisory board to enforce a claim against a member of the management board requires first of all a determination of a violation of a duty of the members of the management board and an evaluation whether the claim can successfully be litigated. In this evaluation the supervisory board has to take into account that the management board has a wide discretion in the management of the corporation which is essential in order to run the corporation. This includes also the engagement in business transactions with the danger of a misjudgment which is a risk for every manager no matter how carefully he might act. If the supervisory board comes to the conclusion that the corporation is not successfully run by the management board it has to replace the members of the management board. However, the mere fact that the corporation is run unsuccessfully by the management board is not sufficient to establish a claim for damages. This can only be the case when the management board engages in business transactions in an irresponsible way creating a serious risk for the corporation and when these decisions are not based on sufficient information.

The Court of Appeals erred in holding that the discretion of the supervisory board is not subject to judicial review in this case. In determining whether a claim of the corporation can be enforced the supervisory board is in the same position as anybody evaluating the prospects of pursuing litigation. The correctness of this evaluation is subject to a complete judicial review [. . .].

If the supervisory board comes to the conclusion that the corporation is entitled to damages against the members of the management board, the question is whether the supervisory board can refrain from enforcing these claims.

In contrast to the Court of Appeals, this Court does not grant the supervisory board discretion without judicial review in this decision. The freedom to make business decisions is an essential part of the responsibility of the management board to run the corporation. In this regard the supervisory board is limited to certain specific aspects as the appointment or dismissal of the members of the management board or the approval of certain business decisions as stated in the corporate charter (Sec. 111 subs. 4 sent. 2 Stock Corporation Law). However, the decision to sue the managing directors is part of its duty to monitor the management board. In this regard, the supervisory board has to take into account the general discretion of the management board in running the corporation. However, for its own decision to sue the members of the management board the supervisory board has no discretion. Since the enforcement of such claims is usually in the best interest of the corporation because it compensates the damages caused by the members of the management board to the corporation, the supervisory board can only refrain from doing so if there are substantial and compelling reasons indicating that the corporation is better off not enforcing these claims. Therefore, the supervisory board must balance the interest of the corporation to be compensated and these reasons such as a negative impact of the lawsuit on the reputation of the corporation and a non-acceptable interference with the actual activities of the management board. In contrast, aspects like the protection of a long-time board member or social consequences for the families of the board members, are generally not acceptable as a ground for not suing. [. . .]

By considering these principles the enforcement of claims for damages against members of the management board has generally to be the rule and not the exception. Therefore, it requires substantial and compelling arguments to justify the non-enforcement of these claims if the litigation is likely to succeed (*Jaeger*, WiB 1997, 10; *Raiser*, NJW 1996, 552, 545). A general discretion of the supervisory board has only to be taken into account if such substantial and compelling aspect actually exists.

[. . .]

NOTES AND QUESTIONS

1.   The *ARAG* decision is quite unique, and interesting, at a number of levels. First, it offers an occasion to discuss the two-tier governance model explained above, because basically it concerns the relationships between the supervisory board and the managing board. The question is, in fact, if the supervisory board should approve the decision to sue the members of the managing board based on alleged breach of their duty of care. The first thing to notice is that the court seems to limit the discretion of the supervisory board in this decision, arguing that the controlling functions of the members of the supervisory board should "force" them to approve litigation if there is a likelihood of recovery, unless compelling reasons indicated that the litigation

is not in the best interest of the corporation. This approach might appear excessively rigid. The decision to sue should be considered, in a way, a business decision, and it seems reasonable that the pros and cons of this decision should be weighted as in other business decisions. The court, however, seems to mitigate this position by acknowledging that the members of the supervisory board can also take into account other elements, including the effect of a lawsuit on the reputation of the corporation, and goes even further by mentioning a possible comparative evaluation of the damages to the corporation with the effects of a lawsuit on the defendants. Do you find this standard clear? Do you think that there should be a general "duty" to sue a director when there is a likelihood to prevail in court? Isn't this approach somehow dangerous in fostering excessive litigation, or at least very complex to apply in the light of the difficulty of predicting the outcome of litigation? Is it very different from the U.S. standard?

2.   A second reason of interest of this decision, more related to the issues we are discussing here, is that it clearly mentions that the members of the managing board enjoy discretion, and are not necessarily liable in case of damages. The Court, for example, states that "the mere fact that the corporation is run unsuccessfully by the management board cannot establish a claim for damages. This can only be the case when the management board engages in business transactions in an irresponsible way creating a serious risk for the corporation and when these decisions are not being based on a sufficient level of information." While the perspective is not radically different from the U.S. approach, it seems that German courts are less deferential to business decisions of the directors than Delaware courts, and in particular there is no mention of the presumption that directors acted in good faith, on an informed basis, and in the best interest of the corporation (the U.S.-style business judgment rule). Do you see a difference here between German and U.S. law? Which approach do you think makes more sense, in terms of economic efficiency and fairness? Is there a risk of adverse selection of directors, if liability can be imposed too easily?

3.   *ARAG* prompted a discussion in German (and not only) corporate law circles on whether this doctrine should also be adopted by the legislature. After a long discussion, the German legislature finally introduced a sort of business judgment rule in 2004 by enacting Sec. 93 subs. 1 sent. 2 Stock Corporation Law that states: "*They* [the members of the management board] *shall not be deemed to have violated the aforementioned duty* [duty of care of a diligent and conscientious manager] *if, at the time of taking the entrepreneurial decision, they had good reason to assume that they were acting on the basis of adequate information for the benefit of the company.*" Who has the burden of proving that this standard was met?

4.   Italian courts are also reluctant to second-guess the merits of a business decision taken in good faith by informed directors, or at least to hold directors liable for an honest error in judgment. Consider, for example, the holding of this recent decision of the Italian Supreme Court:

"With respect to directors' liability, it is necessary to distinguish between directors' duties that have a specific content determined by statutory law or by the charter of the corporation—for example the procedural rules concerning the way in which corporate decisions must be approved—and duties defined with general provisions, such as the duty to manage the corporation diligently and without conflicts of interest. With respect to the second group of duties, directors' liability requires a violation of the general duty of care, therefore the exercise of due care is sufficient to exclude any breach, independently from the effects of directors' decisions. With respect to specific duties, on the other hand, their violation leads to liability unless the directors can demonstrate that the violation could not have been avoided exercising due care." (*Trustee in Bankruptcy of Giza Corporation v. Campari*, Corte di Cassazione, Section I, March 23, 2004, n. 5718).

In your opinion, is the distinction between duties with a "specific content" "determined by statutory law or by the charter," and duties "defined with general provisions" sufficiently clear and practical? Using a different terminology, it evokes the distinction between "rules" and "standards": for example, not exceeding the 50 mph is a "rule," not driving recklessly is a "standard." What are the effects of these different regulatory strategies in terms of enforcement?

DUTY OF LOYALTY

A director breaches his or her duty of loyalty when he or she acts in conflict of interest with the corporation. The classical notion of conflict of interest concerns situations in which there is a "zero-sum game" between the director and the corporation, *i.e.,* when a gain of the director implies a loss or a lower gain for the corporation. An easy example is a contract for the sale of real estate between the corporation (buyer) and the director (seller). A more subtle situation occurs when the interest of the directors is not in overt conflict with the one of the corporation, but it might still taint his or her ability to exercise independent judgment in the best interest of the corporation. Consider the following simple example: a corporation involved in the business of building and operating golf courses is considering different lots on which to build a new facility; one of the lots is close to the house of the director, the other one is far away. If the corporation builds the golf course near the house of the director, the value of real estate in the proximity of the course will go up. The director might have a bias toward this first option, even if strictly speaking both he and the corporation might gain from the decision (it is not a zero-sum game). The more modern approach is to also take into account these situations. Often, but not always, also indirect interests might be relevant, for example when the conflict is with a close family member of the director or with a corporation owned or managed by the director.

There are basically three regulatory strategies, in theory, to address conflicts of interest of directors. First, all conflicted transactions might simply be prohibited. A similar approach might however deprive the corporation of good business opportunities. It is easy to imagine situations in which the director, for a number of reasons, is willing to pay the fair price for corporate assets, also because she has more information than a third party on the value of the asset. The negotiation and transaction costs might be lower. On the other hand, conflicted transactions might not be regulated at all: there is no need to spend time to explain why no developed economy takes this approach. The usual regulatory strategy is a middle ground: to require that the decision is taken with some procedural protections, such as to delegate the decision to independent and non-conflicted directors fully informed on the situation, or require that the transaction is entirely fair to the corporation.

In this respect, Section 144 of the Delaware General Corporation Law provides as follows:

§ 144   DGCL—Interested directors; quorum.

"(a) No contract or transaction between a corporation and 1 or more of its directors or officers, or between a corporation and any other corporation, partnership, association, or other organization in which 1 or more of its directors or officers, are directors or officers, or have a financial interest, shall be void or voidable solely for this reason, or solely because the director or officer is present at or participates in the meeting of the board or committee which authorizes the contract or transaction, or solely because any such director's or officer's votes are counted for such purpose, if:

(1) The material facts as to the director's or officer's relationship or interest and as to the contract or transaction are disclosed or are known to the board of directors or the committee, and the board or committee in good faith authorizes the contract or transaction by the affirmative votes of a majority of the disinterested directors, even though the disinterested directors be less than a quorum; or

(2) The material facts as to the director's or officer's relationship or interest and as to the contract or transaction are disclosed or are known to the stockholders entitled to vote thereon, and the contract or transaction is specifically approved in good faith by vote of the stockholders; or

(3) The contract or transaction is fair as to the corporation as of the time it is authorized, approved or ratified, by the board of directors, a committee or the stockholders.

(b) Common or interested directors may be counted in determining the presence of a quorum at a meeting of the board of directors or of a committee which authorizes the contract or transaction."

As you can see, the law requires procedural protections in case a director has a conflict of interest: the transaction is "cured" if the decision has been taken by fully informed uninterested directors or shareholders. In case these procedural protections have not been followed, the transaction is still safe if it is "fair" to the corporation when taken. The concept of fairness is not easy to define in the abstract, but clearly it might include an element of fair dealing and fair price. One aspect to keep in mind is that the mere fact that the corporation paid a fair price might not be sufficient to cure the transaction: for example, purchasing goods at a totally fair market price, when the corporation has, however, no need for those goods, it is not fair for the purposes of Section 144. This is an obvious but sometimes overlooked element.

It should be observed that a violation of the above-mentioned rules can also be the basis for a liability suit against a director who breached her duty of loyalty, if the corporation suffered damages.

It is interesting to compare and contrast the Delaware rule with corresponding rules in other systems. Most systems provide for procedural protections, such as the approval of a transaction by independent and informed directors, as a way to insulate a conflict of interest. If those procedural protections are followed, the transaction usually cannot be challenged and no liability can result. In most systems, at the same time, even if procedural protections are not followed, there should be no liability if the transaction was fair to the corporation, also because this generally means that there were no damages for the corporation (but, in these situations, disgorgement of directors' gains can sometimes be obtained). It is less clear if the transaction can be challenged and declared void or voidable, also because the interest of a third party, which might be in good faith, should be considered. The relevance of the fairness of the transaction as an element to "save" a conflicted transaction is, for example, debated under Chinese law. *See*, on this issue, Jiang Yu Wang, *Company Law in China: Regulation of Business Organizations in a Socialist Market Economy*, Edward Elgar Publishing, 2014, 207 f., pointing out that a court could invalidate a transaction in conflict of interest not approved by informed independent directors or shareholders, even if it is fair to the corporation; but also suggesting that courts might adopt a more flexible approach to this issue, and accept "entire fairness" as a possible defense against a claim based on a breach of the duty of loyalty.

Let's take a quick look, in this respect, to Article 2391 of the Italian Civil Code below:

Article 2391 of the Italian Civil Code—Interests of Directors

"1.   Any director must notify the other directors and the board of supervisors of any interest, on his behalf or on behalf of others, which he has in a corporate transaction, indicating the nature, the terms, the origin and the relevance of the interest; directors with delegated powers to act on behalf of the corporation must refrain from entering into the transaction, and invest the board of the decision, in case of a single director he must notify shareholders at the first shareholders' meeting.

2.   In the situations described in Paragraph 1 the resolution of the board must adequately motivate the reasons and the advantages that the corporation derives from the transaction.

3.   If Paragraphs 1 or 2 are not complied with, or in case of a resolution approved with the outcome-determinative vote of an interested director, if the resolution can damage the corporation it can be challenged and voided by the directors and the board of supervisors within 90 days from the resolution; fully informed directors that approved the transaction have no standing to challenge it. In any case the rights acquired by third parties in good faith based on the resolution are not affected by the decision.

4.   Directors are liable for the damages caused to the corporation by their action or omission."

It should be added that also shareholders can challenge the decision of the board, if it affects their rights. As you can see the approach is not radically different from the one adopted in Delaware, even if there are some distinctions. First, under Italian law the director has an affirmative duty to disclose any interest, and the entire board must take the decision, even if nothing prevents the possibility to delegate it to some (non-conflicted) directors. In addition, there is not a general duty of abstention of the interested director. The resolution can only be challenged if: (a.1) the director did not disclose the interest or the board did not motivate; or (a.2) the majority has been reached with the vote of the interested director(s); in addition, in both cases, it is necessary that (b) the resolution can damage the corporation. If you compare it with Delaware law, this is a slightly different way to say that if the transaction has been approved by uninterested fully informed directors, or is entirely fair to the corporation, it shall not be void or voidable; similarly directors are not liable if there is no damage (= the transaction is fair).

It might, however, be argued that the Delaware provision is less broad not including explicitly interests on behalf of third parties and only limiting its scope to contracts between the corporation and the directors or an affiliated party; although a similar result can probably be reached applying the provision. Do you think that, according to a narrow textual interpretation, the above-mentioned hypothetical concerning the golf course, might escape § 144 DGCL, but not Article 2391 of the Italian Civil Code?

The following case offers a classical illustration of a breach of the duty of loyalty, focusing in particular on the issue of the burden of proving entire fairness.

LEWIS V. S.L. & E.

United States Court of Appeals, Second Circuit
629 F.2d 764 (1980)

KEARSE, CIRCUIT JUDGE:

This case arises out of an intra-family dispute over the management of two closely-held affiliated corporations. Plaintiff Donald E. Lewis ("Donald"), a shareholder of S.L. & E., Inc. ("SLE"), appeals from judgments entered against him in the United States District Court for the Western District of New York, Harold P. Burke, Judge, after a bench trial of his derivative claim against directors of SLE, and of a claim asserted against him by the other corporation, Lewis General Tires, Inc. ("LGT"), which intervened in the suit. The defendants Alan E. Lewis ("Alan"), Leon E. Lewis, Jr. ("Leon, Jr."), and Richard E. Lewis ("Richard"), are the brothers of Donald; they were, at pertinent times herein, directors of SLE and officers, directors and shareholders of LGT. Donald charged that his brothers had wasted the assets of SLE by causing SLE to lease business premises to LGT from 1966 to 1972 at an unreasonably low rental. LGT was permitted to intervene in the action, and filed a complaint seeking specific performance of an agreement by Donald to sell his SLE stock to LGT in 1972. The district court held that Donald had failed to prove waste by the defendant directors, and entered judgment in their favor. The court also awarded attorneys' fees to the defendant directors and to SLE, and granted LGT specific performance of Donald's agreement to sell his SLE stock.

On appeal, Donald argues that the district court improperly allocated to him the burden of proving his claims of waste, and that since defendants failed to prove that the transactions in question were fair and reasonable, he was entitled to judgment. Donald also argues that the awards of attorneys' fees were improper. We agree with each of these contentions, and therefore reverse and remand.

I

For many years Leon Lewis, Sr., the father of Donald and the defendant directors, was the principal shareholder of SLE and LGT. LGT, formed in 1933, operated a tire dealership in Rochester, New York. SLE, formed in 1943, owned the land and complex of buildings at 260 East Avenue in Rochester. This property was SLE's only significant asset. Prior to 1956 LGT occupied SLE's premises without benefit of a lease; the rent paid was initially $200 per month, and had increased over the years to $800 per month by 1956, when additional parcels were added. On February 28, 1956, SLE granted LGT a 10-year lease on the newly expanded property ("the Property"), for a rent of $1200 per month, or $14,400 per year. Under the terms of the lease, SLE was responsible for payment of real estate taxes on the Property, while all other current expenses were to be borne by the tenant, LGT.

In 1962, Leon Lewis, Sr., transferred his SLE stock, 90 shares in all, to his six children (defendants Richard, Alan and Leon, Jr., plaintiff Donald, and two daughters, Margaret and Carol), giving 15 shares to each. At that time Richard, Alan and Leon, Jr., were already shareholders, officers and directors of LGT. Contemporaneously with their receipt of SLE stock, all six of the children entered into a "shareholders' agreement" with LGT, under which each child who was not a shareholder of LGT on June 1, 1972 would be required to sell his or her SLE shares to LGT, within 30 days of that date, at a price equal to the book value of the SLE stock as of June 1, 1972.

LGT's lease on the SLE property expired on February 28, 1966. At that time the directors of SLE were Richard, Alan, Leon, Jr., Leon, Sr., and Henry Etsberger; these five were also the directors of LGT. In 1966 Alan owned 44% of LGT, Richard owned 30%, Leon, Jr., owned 19%, and Leon, Sr., owned 7%. From 1967 to 1972 Richard owned 61% of LGT and Leon, Jr., owned the remaining 39%. When the lease expired in 1966, no new lease was entered into. LGT nonetheless continued to occupy the property and to pay SLE at the old rate, $14,400 per year. According to the defendants' testimony at trial, there was never any thought or discussion among the SLE directors of entering into a new lease or of increasing the rent. Richard testified: "We never gave consideration to a new lease." From all that appears, the defendant directors viewed SLE as existing purely for the benefit of LGT. Richard testified, for example, that although real estate taxes rose sharply during the period 1966–1971, from approximately $7,800 to more than $11,000, to be paid by SLE out of its constant $14,400 rental income, raising the rent was never mentioned. He testified that SLE was "only a shell to protect the operating company (LGT)." When this suit was commenced there had not been a formal meeting of either the shareholders or the directors of SLE since 1962. Richard, Alan and Leon, Jr., had largely ignored SLE's separate corporate existence and disregarded the fact that SLE had shareholders who were not shareholders of LGT and who therefore could not profit from actions that used SLE solely for the benefit of LGT.

Neither Donald nor his sisters ever owned LGT stock. As the June 1972 date approached for the required sale of their SLE stock to LGT, Donald apparently came to believe that SLE's book value was lower than it should have been. He sought SLE financial information from Richard, who had been president of SLE since 1967. Richard refused to provide information. Donald therefore refused to sell his SLE shares in 1972, and commenced this shareholders' derivative action in the district court in August 1973, basing jurisdiction on diversity of citizenship. The sole claim raised in the complaint was that the defendant directors had wasted the assets of SLE by "grossly undercharging" LGT for the latter's occupancy and use of the Property. Although the complaint charged such mismanagement for the period 1962 to 1973, plaintiff subsequently limited this claim to the period between February 28, 1966, the date on which the lease expired, and June 1, 1972, the date contractually set for valuation of the SLE shares which plaintiff had agreed to sell to LGT. LGT intervened and demanded specific performance of Donald's agreement to sell his SLE stock. Donald did not contest his ultimate obligation to sell, but took the position that since the book value of the shares would be increased if he prevailed on his derivative claim, specific performance should be granted only after adjudication of that claim.

There ensued an eight-day bench trial, at which plaintiff sought to prove, by the testimony of several expert witnesses, that the fair rental value of the Property was greater than the $14,400 per year that SLE had been paid by LGT. Defendants sought to show that the rental paid was reasonable, by offering evidence concerning the financial straits of LGT, the cost to LGT of operating the Property, the general economic decline of the East Avenue neighborhood, and rentals paid on two other properties in that neighborhood. LGT presented expert testimony that the value of plaintiff's stock as of June 1972, assuming a successful defense of the derivative claims, was $15,650.

The district court subsequently filed lengthy and detailed findings of fact and conclusions of law. Many of the court's findings went to the validity and probative value of the testimony given by plaintiff's expert witnesses, and the court ultimately declined to credit that testimony. On this basis, the court held that Donald had failed to establish the rental value of the Property during the period at issue, and that defendants were therefore entitled to judgment on the derivative claims. Implicit in the district court's ruling, granting judgment for defendants upon plaintiff's failure to prove waste, was a determination that plaintiff bore the burden of proof on that issue. The court also ruled that LGT was entitled to specific performance of Donald's agreement to sell his SLE stock, and that Donald was not entitled to recover attorneys' fees from SLE, but that SLE and the individual defendants were entitled to attorneys' fees from Donald. This appeal followed.

II

Turning first to the question of burden of proof, we conclude that the district court erred in placing upon plaintiff the burden of proving waste. Because the directors of SLE were also officers, directors and/or shareholders of LGT, the burden was on the defendant directors to demonstrate that the transactions between SLE and LGT were fair and reasonable. New York Business Corporation Law ("BCL") s 713(b) (McKinney Supp.1979) (eff. September 1, 1971); BCL s 713(a)(3) (McKinney 1963) (repealed as of September 1, 1971); see Cohen v. Ayers, 596 F.2d 733, 739–40 (7th Cir. 1979) (construing current BCL s 713); Remillard Brick Co. v. Remillard-Dandini Co., 109 Cal.App.2d 405, 241 P.2d 66, 75 (1952) (construing California Corporations Code s 820, upon which the prior BCL s 713 was patterned).

Under normal circumstances the directors of a corporation may determine, in the exercise of their business judgment, what contracts the corporation will enter into and what consideration is adequate, without review of the merits of their decisions by the courts. The business judgment rule places a heavy burden on shareholders who would attack corporate transactions. Galef v. Alexander, 615 F.2d 51, 57–58 (2d Cir. 1980); Auerbach v. Bennett, 47 N.Y.2d 619, 629, 419 N.Y.S.2d 920, 926, 393 N.E.2d 994, 1000 (1979); 3A Fletcher, Cyclopedia of the Law of Private Corporations s 1039 (perm. ed. 1975). But the business judgment rule presupposes that the directors have no conflict of interest. When a shareholder attacks a transaction in which the directors have an interest other than as directors of the corporation, the directors may not escape review of the merits of the transaction. At common law such a transaction was voidable unless shown by its proponent to be fair, and reasonable to the corporation. BCL s 713, in both its current and its prior versions, carries forward this common law principle, and provides special rules for scrutiny of a transaction between the corporation and an entity in which its directors are directors or officers or have a substantial financial interest.

The current version of s 713, which became effective on September 1, 1971, and governs at least so much of the dealing between SLE and LGT as occurred after that date, expressly provides that a contract between a corporation and an entity in which its directors are interested may be set aside unless the proponent of the contract "shall establish affirmatively that the contract or transaction was fair and reasonable as to the corporation at the time it was approved by the board. . . ." s 713(b). Thus when the transaction is challenged in a derivative action against the interested directors, they have the burden of proving that the transaction was fair and reasonable to the corporation. Cohen v. Ayers, supra.

The same was true under the predecessor to s 713(b), former s 713(a)(3), which was in effect prior to September 1, 1971. Section 713(a)(3) was not explicit as to the burden of proof, but simply stated that a transaction with interested directors would not be voidable "If the contract or transaction is fair and reasonable as to the corporation at the time it is approved by the board.... "The consensus among the commentators was that s 713(a)(3) carried forward the common law rule, which placed the burden of proof as to fairness on the interested directors. [. . .]

During the entire period 1966–1972, Richard, Alan and Leon, Jr., were directors of both SLE and LGT; there were no SLE directors who were not also directors of LGT. Richard, Alan and Leon, Jr., were all shareholders of LGT in 1966, and from 1967 to 1972 Richard and Leon, Jr., were the sole shareholders of LGT. Under BCL s 713, therefore, Richard, Alan and Leon, Jr., had the burden of proving that $14,400 was a fair and reasonable annual rent for the SLE property for the period February 28, 1966 through June 1, 1972.

Our review of the record convinces us that defendants failed to carry their burden. At trial, there was no direct testimony as to what would have been a fair rental during the relevant period, i. e., 1966 to 1972, and the evidence that was introduced fell far short of establishing that $14,400 was a fair annual rental value for those years.

Quite clearly Richard, Alan and Leon, Jr., had made no effort to determine contemporaneously what rental would be fair during the years 1966–1972. Their view was that the rent should simply cover expenses and that SLE existed for the benefit of LGT. During this period no appraisals were made; no attempts were made to sell or rent the Property; no thought whatever was given to whether $14,400 was a fair and reasonable rent even when real estate taxes had risen to consume nearly all of that amount.

[The Court discusses at length the evidence concerning the fairness of the rental price.]

We conclude, therefore, that defendants failed to prove that the rental paid by LGT to SLE for the years 1966–1972 was fair and reasonable. Thus, Donald is not required to sell his SLE shares to LGT without such upward adjustment in the June 1, 1972, book value of SLE as may be necessary to reflect the amount by which the fair rental value of the Property exceeded $14,400 in any of the years 1966–1972.

NOTES AND QUESTIONS

1.   Procedurally, the case was brought in a federal court. What are the legal grounds for federal jurisdiction, and what might have been the reasons to opt for a federal court (of course the second part of the question requires you to exercise some imagination)?

2.   This is a fairly easy and straightforward case, but it raises some important points. The first is, obviously, the burden of proving fairness, which the court places on the defendants in light of their conflict of interest. Do you think it is an easy burden for the defendants? To make a connection with the duty of care, do you think that for a plaintiff it is easier to overcome the business judgment rule, or demonstrate the lack of fairness?

3.   The directors of SLE are considered conflicted because they are also directors, officers, and/or shareholders of LGT. Would the result be different if LGT was a wholly owned subsidiary of SLE? And if SLE and LGT had had exactly the same ownership structure? Same shareholders and same percentages?

4.   What other relationships do you think might be relevant? For example, if a corporation enters into a contract with the wife of a director, would the director have a conflict of interest? What about former directors? For example, consider a situation in which A is on the board of X Inc., and X enters into a contract with Y Inc., an unrelated corporation, very advantageous for Y, and shortly after A resigns from the board of X and becomes the CEO of Y. Would there be an issue of duty of loyalty?

* * *

Directors have a duty of loyalty both toward the corporation and the shareholders. One interesting question is if they might be liable also toward shareholders when their action did not cause damage to the corporation, for example if they sold shares of the corporation on behalf of a shareholder to a third party. The case is particularly delicate if directors have some kind of interest in the transaction, also indirectly, and when they do not disclose relevant information. The following (short) excerpt from a French case, one of the first and more important modern ones to deal with the duty of loyalty of directors, offers an occasion to discuss this issue from a particular perspective.

VILGRAIN

French Cass. Com., 1996
12 February 1996, n° 94–11.241

The Court:—According to the decision of the Court of appeals of Paris of January 18, 1994, here challenged by Mr. Bernard Vilgrain, in 1989, Mrs. Alary asked Mr. Bernard Vilgrain, president of the Sté Cie française commerciale et financière (hereinafter, Sté CFCF), to find a purchaser for her shares of Sté CFTC. Mr. Bernard Vilgrain had the shares sold to Francis Vilgrain, Pierre Vilgrain and Guy Vieillevigne (hereafter "the Vilgrain family members"), at the following conditions: 3,321 shares for the price of 3,000 French francs [*around 450 euros*] per share, providing in the contract that if the Vilgrain family members would sell their participation in Sté CFCF before December 31, 1991, 50% of the per share price of 3,500 French francs [*around 530 euros*] would be paid to him. A few days after the sale the Vilgrain family members sold their participation in the Sté CFCF to Bouygues for a price of 8,000 French francs [*around 1,120 euros*] per share. Arguing that her consent had been vitiated, Mrs. Alary filed a suit for damages;

On the first request based on five arguments:—

Mr. Bernard Vilgrain complains that the Court of appeals ordered him to pay damages, on the basis of fraudulent concealment of information [*réticence dolosive* or *dolus malus*], and to pay to Mrs. Alary a sum of 10,461,151 French francs [*around 1,600,000 euros*], with legal interests being computed from 1st October 1989. His complaint raises the following arguments.

On the one hand, the duty to inform which applies to the purchaser, and which is implied in case of fraudulent concealment of information, concerns the elements which can have an influence on the value of the shares, regardless of whether these elements relate to the shares themselves or the assets and liabilities of the company. This duty cannot relate to the activities undertaken by the purchaser in order to sell the shares he has acquired to a third party. In particular this duty does not include offering to the seller the possibility to join the purchaser in parallel negotiation for the sale of his shares to a third party. The purchaser is free to offer or not to offer to the seller to join the negotiation which he has started for the sale to a third party of his participation in the company [. . .]

The decision of the Court of appeals notes, however, that during the meetings that Mrs. Alary had with Mr. Bernard Vilgrain, the latter did not disclose that on September 19th 1989 he entrusted the [*investment bank*] Lazard with the mission to assist the members of his family in looking for a potential buyer for their shares, and did not inform her of an agreement for a sale, at a minimum price of 7,000 French francs per share that he had reached for some minority shareholders. It follows that in intervening in the sale of Mrs. Alary's shares of Sté CFCF at the price of 5,650 French francs, established after a revision, and by purchasing the shares at this price, while at the same time failing to disclose to her the negotiations that he had started for the sale of these same shares at a minimum price of 7,000 French francs, Mr. Bernard Vilgrain violated the duty of loyalty which applies to any senior officer of a company toward any shareholder, especially when he is acting as an intermediary for the sale of his own participation. For these reasons [. . .] the court of appeals could hold that there was a fraudulent concealment of information by Mr. Bernard Vilgrain.

NOTES AND QUESTIONS

1.   This relatively recent French case is reminiscent of a leading but old U.S. case, *Meinhard v. Salmon* (164 N.E. 545), decided in 1928. In that situation, Salmon was managing a hotel based on a joint-venture with Meinhard, who had contributed capital but was not actively involved in the day-to-day business. The lease for the hotel was about to expire, and Salmon did not disclose to Meinhard the possibility of obtaining a new lease; in fact he entered into the contract with the owners of the real estate alone, without his former partner. Judge Cardozo, concluding that Salmon had breached his duty of loyalty by not disclosing the new opportunity, famously remarked that co-adventurers in a business owe to each other the "punctillo of an honor the most sensitive". This case is often mentioned as an early application of the duty of loyalty among fiduciaries. Even if based on a different reasoning, the French Supreme Court, the Cour de cassation, in this 1996 decision, comes to a similar conclusion holding Mr. Vilgrain, the president of a corporation, liable to its shareholders for not having disclosed information concerning the sale of the shares that might have led to a better price. Even worse, in Mr. Vilgrain's case, he improperly favored his own relatives to the detriment of the plaintiff, Mrs. Alary.

2.   It should also be noted that, in this case, the director did not breach his fiduciary duties toward the corporation, but rather toward the shareholders. Based on the same facts, how do you think a court in your jurisdiction (if you are not French) would have resolved the *Vilgrain* case?

3.   Case law developed by the French Supreme Court is very important in the area of duties and liability of directors, since provisions in the French Commercial code on liability are rather general. Therefore, courts have a significant discretion in determining what could be expected of a director or a senior officer in different circumstances. The existence of a duty of loyalty is implicitly recognized by the Commercial code, when it deals with related parties' transactions (Art. L. 225–38 et *seq.*). In addition to this implicit duty of loyalty, an explicit duty of loyalty of the director towards a shareholder has been recognized by the *Vilgrain* case reported above. Do you think that, in the area of fiduciary duties, this is a common feature in different legal systems? In other words, do you agree that in this area often the legislature can only set a somehow general standard, and that it is up to the courts to apply it to specific situations and define more precisely the content of directors' duties? Or are there systems, to your knowledge, in which the statutory provisions are more precise and detailed? Independently from your knowledge of specific systems, if you were the legislature, would you be able

to write a more precise and detailed rule on this issue, or are general standards inevitable?

4.   The duty of loyalty under French law is, according to some scholars, somehow inspired by the American and British duty of loyalty (*see* H. Fleischer, *Legal Transplants in European Company Law—The Case of Fiduciary Duties*, ECFR 2005, 378–397). This is not surprising also considering that the 1867 French Companies Act was influenced by the 1846 British Companies Act. However, it is rare that the French judiciary looks or cites foreign law or decisions (and *see*, on this issue, our discussion in Chapter 1 about citations to foreign cases in courts' decisions). In addition, it is very rare, in the area of corporate law, that courts create new duties without a clear statutory basis. In the *Vilgrain* case, in addition, the duty to disclose inside information, even if applied to a non-listed corporation, has a connection with the prohibition of insider trading which applies in France since 1970.

5.   Since 1996, the existence and scope of the duty of loyalty has been regularly confirmed by case law in France. For instance, it was held by the French Supreme Court in a judgment delivered on May 6, 2008, that a director breached his duty of loyalty by causing a corporation incorporated by him and his spouse to purchase shares of the corporation that he managed without disclosing to the sellers that, based on the actual profits of the corporation, the selling price could have been higher.

6.   However, statutory law, and its use by courts, has evolved. In 1996, the French Supreme Court based the decision reprinted above mainly on general provisions of the Civil Code relating to willful misconduct (*dol*). Then, it turned to article 1382 of the Civil Code on torts. Currently, the Court refers to the specific provisions in the Commercial code relating to the liability of directors, such as article L. 225–251 of the Commercial code.

7.   The duty of loyalty has also been extended to competition and corporate opportunities, and therefore it has been used to protect the corporation itself. The French Commercial Code is silent on competition by directors against the company. However, the French Supreme Court extended the duty of loyalty to a former manager of a private limited company who had left the company and hired former employees (Com. 12 févr. 2002, n° 00–11.602, Bull. civ. IV, n° 32, Revue des sociétés 2002, obs. L. Godon, p. 702). It is not clear how strict this duty is for former managers who have left the company. The decision used for the first time the term "duty of fidelity" which sounds excessive and whose scope was not precisely defined. There is no doubt however that the prohibition also applies to the CEO (*directeur général*) of public limited companies. The duty also applies to directors, but the intensity of their duty is not clear and might be less than for the CEO. All things considered, French case and statutory law, in this area, does not seem as detailed and developed as U.S. law, and still appears to be based more on general and sometimes ambiguous principles. Do you agree?

* * *

A problem closely related to conflicts of interests concerns business opportunities. The situation occurs when a director (or an officer) becomes aware of a business opportunity that could benefit the corporation, but rather than offering it to the corporation, takes advantage of it. The scenario is different from a conflict of interest because in this case we do not have a formal decision influenced and tainted by an interest, but rather a loss of opportunity and gains for the corporation; however, directors clearly have not acted in a loyal fashion toward the corporation and the shareholders, and this breach does not fall squarely within the statutory rules we have just examined concerning conflicted transactions.

In common law systems, the "business opportunity doctrine" was developed to address this problem. If applied too broadly, the business opportunity doctrine could block virtually any activity of a director. As a paradox, consider the situation in which a director is informed of a good deal on a luxury car that could be easily purchased and resold for a profit. Should she disclose this opportunity to the corporation? In theory, the organization could take advantage of this possibility. A rule of reason should apply here: minor transactions not included in the core business of the corporation should not be relevant. To be more precise, however, two basic problems come up in business opportunity cases, and they have been addressed by judges balancing the need to ensure loyalty and the need to leave some latitude to directors. The first is if any information acquired by a director, also when she is not acting in her capacity as director, should be relevant. For example, what if the director learns about an opportunity at a social gathering completely unrelated to her job? Different systems and different courts might take more or less rigorous approaches, but we think that distinguishing between activities carried out "as director" and "personal" ones is very difficult and uncertain. It seems preferable to conclude that when someone is serving as director of a corporation, she must offer all relevant business opportunities that she encounters to the corporation, and take them only if the corporation (*i.e.*, the board) declines them, without distinctions based on how the director learned about the opportunity.

The second, and probably more delicate issue, is what constitutes a business opportunity. Courts have elaborated the so-called "line-of-business-test," which requires that to be subject to the rule, the business opportunity should fall within the activities in which the corporation is actually involved and/or is potentially interested in. Of course this is a highly factual analysis, and to simply rely on the purpose of the corporation as stated in the charter (even when it is defined somehow precisely, which is rare) might not be sufficient. Narrower tests have also been used, such as for example the *Lagarde* test.

A related factor that courts have sometimes considered is the financial ability of the corporation to take the opportunity. For example, if a corporation is in distress, and it is clear that it would not be financially capable of taking advantage of the deal, the director should be free to step in. This is, however, a slippery slope, for the following reason: at least in theory, from a financial point of view, if a project has a sufficient positive net present value, it could be financed borrowing funds or issuing shares. The argument could therefore be made that even a corporation in financial distress might be able to take advantage of the transaction. Of course this is also a complex question of fact that can hardly be resolved in general terms.

Another problem worth mentioning is what should a director who serves on the boards of different corporations, all potentially interested in a business opportunity, do when he becomes aware of it? The best answer is probably that he should disclose the opportunity simultaneously or as soon as possible to all corporations he is involved with. In the decisions on whether to take the opportunity he should be considered having a conflict of interest on behalf of the other entities he is affiliated with.

Empirical analysis suggests that business opportunity disputes generally involve primarily closely held corporations, and that the business opportunity is often in direct competition with the activity of the corporation (*see* Pat K. Chew, *Competing Interests in the Corporate Opportunity Doctrine*, 67 N. C. L. REV. 436 (1989)).

The business opportunity doctrine, developed through case law in common law systems, has also been adopted, sometimes with specific statutory provisions, in other legal systems (*see*, e.g., the last paragraph of Article 2391 of the Italian Civil Code). Let's consider some specific problem with a leading case from the United Kingdom, *Bhullar v. Bhullar*. The case is long and complex, but it is worth examining because it offers a detailed discussion of directors' duties in this area.

BHULLAR V. BHULLAR
[2003] EWCA Civ 424

LORD JUSTICE JONATHAN PARKER:

[. . .]

This is an appeal by the second and third respondents in the proceedings, Inderjit Singh Bhullar ("Inderjit") and Jatinderjit Singh Bhullar ("Jatinderjit") (together "the appellants"), against an order dated 8 May 2002 and made by His Honour Judge Behrens, sitting as a judge of the High Court in the Chancery Division, Leeds District Registry. Permission to appeal was granted by Arden LJ on 26 September 2002, following an oral hearing.

In the proceedings, the appellants' uncle Mohan Singh Bhullar ("Mohan"), his two sons Steven Singh Bhullar and Kalvinder Singh Bhullar (known as Tim) ("Steven" and "Tim" respectively) and his wife Charan Kaur Bhullar petition under section 459 of the Companies Act 1985 ("the 1985 Act") for relief in respect of a family company, Bhullar Bros Ltd ("the Company"). The petitioners (whom I shall call collectively "Mohan's family") together hold 50 per cent of the issued ordinary shares in the Company. The remaining 50 per cent is held by the appellants, their father Sohan Singh Bhullar ("Sohan") and their mother Rajinder Kaur Bhullar (I shall call them collectively "Sohan's family"). The directors of the Company are and have at all material times been Sohan, Mohan, the appellants and Tim. Hence Sohan's family have at all material times had a majority of 3:2 on the board of the Company. The respondents to the petition are Sohan's family and the Company. The Company has not played any independent role in the proceedings.

By the petition, Mohan's family allege that the affairs of the Company have been conducted in a manner which is unfairly prejudicial to their interests, and they seek by way of primary relief an order for the sale to them, or to the Company, of the shares held by Sohan's family at a price to be determined by the court; alternatively, an order giving relief in respect of the various matters of which complaint is made, including an order for the reconstruction or reorganisation of the Company's business. The petition also seeks authority for Mohan's family to bring proceedings in the name of the Company against the appellants for breach of fiduciary duty.

In the result, following a lengthy hearing, the judge declined to grant the primary relief sought by Mohan's family. He did, however, find that the appellants had breached their fiduciary duty to the Company in acquiring for their personal benefit a property known as White Hall Mill ("the Property"), which they had purchased in the name of Silvercrest Trading (GB) Ltd ("Silvercrest"), a company which they own and control. By his order the judge declared that Silvercrest holds the Property on trust for the Company and he ordered that the appellants at their own cost procure that Silvercrest transfer the Property to the Company at the price which was paid for it. He also directed an account of profits. In order to avoid the need for Silvercrest to be joined as a respondent to the petition, counsel for the appellants (Mr Neil Berragan, who also appears for the appellants on this appeal) was also instructed to represent Silvercrest.

The appeal relates only to the relief granted in respect of the purchase of the Property.

[. . .]

THE FACTUAL BACKGROUND

[. . .]

From about the 1950s, Mohan and Sohan ran a grocery shop at 44 Springwood Street, Huddersfield, as equal partners. On 22 October 1964 the Company was incorporated to take over the partnership business. The authorised share capital was £2,000 divided into 2,000 £1 ordinary shares. 1,000 shares were issued to Mohan and 1,000 to Sohan, and they became the first directors of the Company.

After some early loss-making years the Company began to prosper. In addition to its premises at 44 Springwood Street, it acquired a number of other properties in the locality from which it carried on its grocery business. It also acquired an investment property known as Springbank Works, Leeds Road, Huddersfield, which has at all material times been let to UK Superbowl Ltd for the purposes of a bowling operation. It is common ground that the objects of the Company as set out in its Memorandum of Association include the acquisition of property for investment.

On 1 February 1995 Tim and the appellants were appointed directors of the Company, joining Mohan and Sohan on the board.

By about May 1998 relations between Mohan's family and Sohan's family had broken down, and a state of considerable acrimony prevailed (the reasons for this are not material for present purposes). Mohan and Tim decided that the time had come for the two families to go their separate ways. They informed Sohan and the appellants of their decision at a board meeting held in about May 1998, saying that they did not wish any further properties to be acquired by the Company. Sohan's family accepted this decision in principle, and thereafter negotiations took place between the two families with a view to dividing the Company's assets and business between them. Unfortunately, for reasons which I need not go into, the negotiations came to nothing, and in 2001 the petition was issued.

In the meantime, in about June 1999 the appellants discovered by chance that the Property was on the market. The Property is adjacent to Springbank Works, and at that time UK Superbowl Ltd was using part of the Property as a car park. In paragraphs 71 and 72 of his witness statement Inderjit described what happened, as follows:

". . . . During a visit by my uncle from the USA [a Mr Dhesi] and whilst going bowling at UK Bowling on Leeds Road, I noticed a 'Sold' sign on Whitehall Mill. On calling the agents. . . . I was informed that the building was under offer and no further offers would be considered. I insisted on being given a chance to look at the building and my offer being forwarded to the owners. I called

Matthew Scoley of Eddisons Commercial to view the building the following day.

My and [Jatinderjit]'s first offer was rejected but my second, increased offer, was accepted. Both offers were through Eddisons Commercial and from the [outset] I informed them that this was my brother's and my private acquisition. In the meantime I informed Mr Reddington of Barclays Bank plc of our private venture and he gave us his backing. The intention was to place this building in a self-administered pension fund but we were advised there was insufficient time to carry out the necessary paperwork for a pension fund to acquire the property (the seller insisted on a quick sale) and we had no alternative but to place it in the name of [Silvercrest]."

Later in his witness statement, Inderjit states that prior to the acquisition of the Property he sought advice from the Company's solicitor, Mr John Norcliffe, as to whether there was any reason why he and Jatinderjit could not acquire the Property for their personal benefit. Mr Norcliffe's advice was to the effect that there was no difficulty about this.

Contracts were exchanged on 15 July 1999, and the purchase was completed shortly thereafter in the name of Silvercrest.

The appellants did not at that stage disclose the purchase to their co-directors.

[. . .]

THE JUDGE'S JUDGMENT IN RELATION TO THE PURCHASE OF THE PROPERTY

Having set out the relevant facts in paragraphs 161 to 166 of his judgment, the judge addressed the allegation of breach of fiduciary duty in paragraphs 264 to 273 of his judgment, as follows:

"6.7 Diversion of business opportunity

264. Mr Berragan submits that Inderjit and Jatinderjit were not in breach of fiduciary duty in acquiring Whitehall Mill for their pension. He has referred me [to] part of the speech of Lord Macmillan in *Regal Hastings v Gulliver* [1967] 2 AC 134n, 153 where he said directors are liable to account if:

"(i) what the directors did was so related to the affairs of the company that it can properly be said to have been done in the course of their management and in utilisation of their opportunities and special knowledge as directors and (ii) what they did resulted in profit for themselves."

265. He referred me to the decision of Hutchison J in *Island Export v Umunna* [1986] BCLC 460. That was a case where a

claim for exploitation of a business opportunity failed. The learned judge cited extensively from a Canadian case (*Canadian Aero Services v. O'Malley* (1973) 40 DLR (3d) 371 (Can SC), 382—

"Descending from the generality, the fiduciary relationship goes at least this far: a director or a senior officer like [the defendants] is precluded from obtaining for himself, either secretly or without the approval of the company (which would have to be properly manifested on full disclosure of the facts), any property or business advantage either belonging to the company or for which it has been negotiating; and especially is this so when the director or officer is a participant in the negotiations on behalf of the company."

Pausing there, this formulation of the fiduciary duty of a director would appear to be absolutely in accord with the line of authority exemplified by *Regal (Hastings) Ltd v Gulliver*. Laskin J then continues as follows (at 382):

"An examination of the case law in this Court and in the Courts of other like jurisdictions on the fiduciary duties of directors and senior officers shows the pervasiveness of a strict ethic in this area of the law. In my opinion, this ethic disqualifies a director or senior officer from usurping for himself or diverting to another person or company with whom or with which he is associated a maturing business opportunity which his company is actively pursuing; he is also precluded from so acting even after his resignation where the resignation may fairly be said to have been prompted or influenced by a wish to acquire for himself the opportunity sought by the company, or where it was his position with the company rather than a fresh initiative that led him to the opportunity which he later acquired."

[. . .]

THE ISSUES ON THE APPEAL

The appellants challenge the judge's decision that in purchasing the Property through Silvercrest they breached their fiduciary duty to the Company on the ground that he wrongly applied the applicable principles, as laid down by the House of Lords in *Phipps v. Boardman*.

By their respondent's notice, Mohan's family seek to uphold the judge's decision on the following different or additional grounds:

"(1) a director may not, without the consent of the company, during the currency of his directorship exploit for himself a commercial opportunity which is within the company's line of business;

(2) in acquiring [the Property] for themselves (via Silvercrest), [the appellants] placed themselves in a position where their self interest conflicted (or where there was a real, sensible possibility that their self interest did or would conflict) with the duties owed by them to the company as fiduciaries;

(3) the acquisition of [the Property] was an opportunity so closely associated with the existing activities of the company that [the appellants] as directors:

> were under a duty to make the opportunity available to the company, and/or

> in acquiring it without first making it available to the company were under a duty to acquire it only for or on behalf of the company; and/or

> in acquiring it are to be taken to have acquired it as fiduciaries for the company and to hold it on trust on its behalf."

THE ARGUMENTS ON THE APPEAL

Mr Berragan, in his attractively presented submissions, submits that a director of a company is under no duty to offer to the company business opportunities which come to him privately, notwithstanding that the company may be in a position to exploit such opportunities. He submits that the judge was in error in holding that because the Company might possibly have been interested in acquiring the Property, *ergo* the appellants were in breach of their fiduciary duty in acquiring it for themselves. He submits that, applying the principles laid down in *Phipps v Boardman*, the first step is to identify the nature and scope of the appellants' pre-existing duty as fiduciaries in relation to the purchase of the Property. Until the nature and scope of that pre-existing duty has been identified, he submits, one cannot determine whether in purchasing the Property the appellants breached that duty.

He submits, relying on Millett LJ's analysis of constructive trusteeship in *Paragon Finance plc v. Thackerar* [1999] 1 All ER 400 at 408, that it is necessary to distinguish between constructive trusteeship which is said to arise from a wrongful act where there is no pre-existing fiduciary relationship, and a case such as the instant case where the fiduciary relationship predates the allegedly wrongful act. In the latter case, he submits, constructive trusteeship can only arise by reason of some improper dealing by the fiduciary with property belonging to his cestui que trust. Turning to the facts of the instant case, he submits that the opportunity to purchase the Property cannot be regarded as in any sense belonging to the Company, and that the mere fact that the

Company might have been interested in purchasing the Property was not in itself enough to make it so.

In any event, he submits, on the uncontested evidence any interest on the part of the Company in acquiring the Property can only have been an extremely limited one. In support of this submission, he points to the evidence that the Company's main business consisted of operating supermarkets; that it owned only one commercial investment property (albeit adjacent to the Property); and that when the Property was acquired the Company had been trying unsuccessfully to sell one of its supermarkets for some two years. He also points out that there is no evidence that the Company had registered an interest in acquiring commercial investment property with any estate agent, or that Silvercrest acquired the Property on especially advantageous terms.

Mr Berragan submits that the judge's finding (in paragraph 271 of his judgment) that the opportunity to acquire the Property was not a "maturing business opportunity" is sufficient in itself to dispose of the claim based on breach of fiduciary duty; and that no question arises as to a possible conflict of interest. He relies on *Regal Hastings v. Gulliver* [1967] 2 AC 134n for the proposition that directors are only liable for breach of fiduciary duty where they are acting in the course of managing the company's affairs and "in utilisation of their opportunities and special knowledge as directors" (see *ibid.* at 153 per Lord Macmillan). He submits that on the facts as found the appellant's actions in purchasing the Property through Silvercrest were not related to the Company's affairs, nor can they be said to have been done in the course of managing the Company's affairs or to have involved the utilisation of opportunities or special knowledge acquired as directors.

In her written skeleton argument, Miss Rosalind Nicholson (for the Mohan family), relying in particular on the speech of Lord Upjohn in *Phipps v. Boardman*, submits that the equitable rule as to the accountability of directors is not limited to cases in which there is a "maturing business opportunity" but extends to cases in which the director either has or can have (to use the words of Lord Cranworth LC in *Aberdeen Railway Co v. Blaikie* (1854) 1 Macq. 461, 471) "a personal interest conflicting, or which possibly may conflict, with the interests of whose whom he is bound to protect": in other words, as Lord Upjohn explained in *Phipps v. Boardman* (at p.124), where there is "a real sensible possibility of conflict". She submits that on the facts the instant case is such a case. In the instant case, the opportunity to acquire the Property was plainly in the Company's line of business. Relying on the decision of the Privy Council in *New Zealand Netherlands Society "Oranje" Inc v. Laurentius Cornelis Kuys* [1973] 1 WLR 1126, she submits that that is enough to give rise to a real sensible possibility of conflict of interest. She submits that the circumstances in which the opportunity presented itself to the director are immaterial, since accountability does not depend on whether the director happens to be acting as such at the time.

Nor, Miss Nicholson submits, is it necessary that the director should have profited by taking the opportunity which presented itself. In support of this submission she relies on *Parker v. McKenna* (1874) LR 10 Ch 124. Citing *Movitex Ltd v. Bulfield* [1988] BCLC 104 at 117 per Vinelott J, she reminds us that a director faced with such an opportunity may always free himself from the obligation to account by obtaining the company's full and informed consent.

She further submits, relying on *Industrial Development Consultants Ltd v. Cooley* [1972] 1 WLR 443 at 451F per Roskill J, that a director may come under a positive duty to make a business opportunity available to his company if it is in the company's line of business or if the director has been given responsibility to seek out particular opportunities for the company and the opportunity concerned is of such a nature as to fall within the scope of that remit.

CONCLUSIONS

I agree with Mr Berragan that the concept of a conflict between fiduciary duty and personal interest presupposes an existing fiduciary duty. But it does not follow that it is a prerequisite of the accountability of a fiduciary that there should have been some improper dealing with property 'belonging' to the party to whom the fiduciary duty is owed, that is to say with trust property. The relevant rule, which Lord Cranworth LC in *Aberdeen Railway Co v. Blaikie* described as being "of universal application", and which Lord Herschell in *Bray v. Ford* [1896] AC 44 at 51, described as "inflexible", is that (to use Lord Cranworth's formulation) no fiduciary "shall be allowed to enter into engagements in which he has, or can have, a personal interest conflicting, or which may possibly conflict, with the interests of those whom he is bound to protect".

In a case such as the present, where a fiduciary has exploited a commercial opportunity for his own benefit, the relevant question, in my judgment, is not whether the party to whom the duty is owed (the Company, in the instant case) had some kind of beneficial interest in the opportunity: in my judgment that would be too formalistic and restrictive an approach. Rather, the question is simply whether the fiduciary's exploitation of the opportunity is such as to attract the application of the rule. As Lord Upjohn made clear in *Phipps v. Boardman*, flexibility of application is of the essence of the rule. Thus, at *ibid.* p.123 he said:

> "Rules of equity have to be applied to such a great diversity of circumstances that they can be stated only in the most general terms and applied with particular attention to the exact circumstances of each case."

Later in his speech (at p.125) Lord Upjohn gave this warning against attempting to reformulate the rule by reference to the facts of particular cases:

"The whole of the law is laid down in the fundamental principle exemplified in Lord Cranworth's statement [in *Aberdeen Railway Co v. Blaikie*]. But it is applicable, like so many equitable principles which may affect a conscience, however innocent, to such a diversity of different cases that the observations of judges and even in your Lordships' House in cases where this great principle is being applied must be regarded as applicable only to the particular facts of the particular case in question and not regarded as a new and slightly different formulation of the legal principle so well settled."

To my mind that warning is particularly apt in the instant case, given that the joint bundle of authorities which has been placed before us contains no less than 23 authorities, including Australian and American authorities.

As it seems to me, the rule is essentially a simple one, albeit that it may in some cases be difficult to apply. The only qualification which is required to Lord Cranworth's formulation of it is that which was supplied by Lord Upjohn in *Phipps v. Boardman*, where he said this (at p.124):

"The phrase 'possibly may conflict' requires consideration. In my view it means that the reasonable man looking at the relevant facts and circumstances of the particular case would think that there was a real sensible possibility of conflict; not that you could imagine some situation arising which might, in some conceivable possibility in events not contemplated as real sensible possibilities by any reasonable person, result in conflict."

The strictness of the rule, and the flexibility of its application, was stressed by Lord Wilberforce in the Privy Council decision in *New Zealand Netherlands Society etc. v. Kuys*, where he said (at p.1129):

"The obligation not to profit from a position of trust, or, as it sometimes relevant to put it, not to allow a conflict to arise between interest and duty, is one of strictness. The strength, and indeed the severity, of the rule has recently been emphasised by the House of Lords in *Phipps v. Boardman*. . . . It retains its vigour in all jurisdictions where the principles of equity are applied. Naturally it has different applications in different contexts. It applies, in principle, whether the case is one of a trust, express or implied, of partnership, of directorship of a limited company, of principal and agent, or master and servant, but the precise scope of it must be moulded according to the nature of the relationship."

In support of his submission that the rule will only apply where there has been some improper dealing with trust property, Mr Berragan relies on Viscount Dilhorne's reference in *Phipps v. Boardman* (at p.84) to a purchase of trust property by a trustee as an example of impropriety on the part of the trustee in respect of which equity will require him to account. But I cannot read that observation by Viscount Dilhorne as imposing any kind of restriction on the rule as stated by Lord Cranworth.

Mr Berragan also relies on Viscount Dilhorne's references to *Regal (Hastings) v. Gulliver* when concluding (dissenting, with Lord Upjohn, from the majority of their Lordships) that, on the facts of *Phipps v. Boardman*, the appellants were not accountable for the profits they had made. Thus, referring to the *Regal* case, Viscount Dilhorne said this (at p.88):

> "Lord Russell of Killowen in the *Regal* case held that the directors had acquired the shares 'by reason, and only by reason of the fact that they were directors of Regal, and in the course of their execution of that office'. Lord Macmillan said that the directors were accountable for any profit which they made if it was by reason and in virtue of their office. Lord Wright said that an agent must account for profits secretly acquired 'in the course of his agency', and Lord Porter said that 'one occupying a position of trust must not make a profit which he can acquire only by use of his fiduciary position, or, if he does, he must account for the profit so made'.
>
> If the profits made by the appellants [in *Phipps v. Boardman*] had been made as a result of the acquisition of the shares by them in 1957, it could not, in my view, be said that the shares were acquired "only by use of' their 'fiduciary position', or 'in the course of' their "agency" or by reason and only by reason of the fact that they were agents of the trust for certain limited purposes."

Later in his speech Viscount Dilhorne said (at p.94):

> "In this case, as Lord Macmillan said in the *Regal* case, the result depends on issues of fact. Liability to account must depend on their being some breach of duty, some impropriety of conduct on the part of those in a fiduciary position. On the facts of this case I do not consider that there was any breach of duty or impropriety of conduct on the part of the appellants."

As to the *Regal* case, Lord Upjohn said (at p.125) that in his view their Lordships in that case were not attempting to lay down any new view on the applicable law, and (he continued):

".... indeed could not do so for the law was already so well settled."

For the same reason, I cannot regard Viscount Dilhorne (or for that matter any others of their Lordships in *Phipps v. Boardman*) as laying down any new formulation of the rule. The observations on which Mr Berragan relies were made by Viscount Dilhorne in course of applying the rule to the particular facts of *Phipps v. Boardman*.

In so far as reference to authority is of assistance in applying the rule to the facts of any particular case, the authority which (of those cited to us) is nearest on its facts to those of the instant case is the decision of Roskill J in *Industrial Development Consultants Ltd v. Cooley*. In that case, a commercial opportunity was offered to the defendant, who was at the time the managing director of the plaintiff company, in his private capacity. The defendant subsequently obtained his release by the company in order to exploit that opportunity for his own benefit. Had the company known that he had been offered that opportunity, it would not have agreed to release him. He was held accountable for the benefits he had received by exploiting the opportunity. The opportunity was not one which the company could itself have exploited.

Roskill J, after quoting extensively from Lord Upjohn's speech in *Phipps v. Boardman*, observed (plainly correctly, if I may respectfully say so) that although Lord Upjohn dissented (with Viscount Dilhorne) in the result, there was no difference between any of their Lordships as to the applicable principles, but only as to the application of those principles to the facts of the case. Turning to the facts, Roskill J said this (at p.451):

"The first matter that has to be considered is whether or not the defendant was in a fiduciary relationship with his principals, the plaintiffs. [Counsel for the defendant] argued that he was not because he received this information which was communicated to him privately. With respect, I think that argument is wrong. The defendant had one capacity and one capacity only in which he was carrying on business at that time. That capacity was as managing director of the plaintiffs. Information which came to him while he was managing director and which was of concern to the plaintiffs and was relevant for the plaintiffs to know, was information which it was his duty to pass on to the plaintiffs because between himself and the plaintiffs a fiduciary relationship existed. . . ."

Roskill J went on to hold that the defendant had:

".... embarked upon a deliberate policy and course of conduct which put his personal interest . . . in direct conflict with his pre-existing and continuing duty as managing director of [the company]."

He continued, referring to *Keech v. Sandford* (1726) Sel. Cas, t. King 61:

"That is something which for over 200 years the courts have forbidden."

He went on to stress the rigidity with which the rule had since been applied. As confirmation of this, he cited the following well-known passage from the judgment of James LJ in *Parker v. McKenna*:

"I do not think it is necessary, but it appears to me very important, that we should concur in laying down again and again the general principle that in this court no agent in the course of his agency, in the matter of his agency, can be allowed to make any profit without the knowledge and consent of his principal; that that rule is an inflexible rule, and must be applied inexorably by this court, which is not entitled, in my judgment, to receive evidence, or suggestion, or argument as to whether the principal did or did not suffer any injury in fact by reason of the dealing of the agent; for the safety of mankind requires that no agent shall be able to put his principal in the danger of such an inquiry as that."

I turn, then, to the facts of the instant case.

Like the defendant in *Industrial Development Consultants Ltd v. Cooley*, the appellants in the instant case had, at the material time, one capacity and one capacity only in which they were carrying on business, namely as directors of the Company. In that capacity, they were in a fiduciary relationship with the Company. At the material time, the Company was still trading, albeit that negotiations (ultimately unsuccessful) for a division of its assets and business were on foot. As Inderjit accepted in cross-examination, it would have been "worthwhile" for the company to have acquired the Property. Although the reasons why it would have been "worthwhile" were not explored in evidence, it seems obvious that the opportunity to acquire the Property would have been commercially attractive to the Company, given its proximity to Springbank Works. Whether the Company could or would have taken that opportunity, had it been made aware of it, is not to the point: the existence of the opportunity was information which it was relevant for the Company to know, and it follows that the appellants were under a duty to communicate it to the Company. The anxiety which the appellants plainly felt as to the propriety of purchasing the Property through Silvercrest without first disclosing their intentions to their co-directors—anxiety which led Inderjit to seek legal advice from the Company's solicitor—is, in my view, eloquent of the existence of a possible conflict of duty and interest.

I therefore agree with the judge when he said (in paragraph 272 of his judgment) that "reasonable men looking at the facts would think there was a real sensible possibility of conflict".

RESULT

I would dismiss this appeal.

NOTES AND QUESTIONS

1.   Wow. That was a long case. The Court of Appeal suggests that the rule that a fiduciary was not allowed entering into engagements in which he had, or could have, a personal interest conflicting, or which might possibly conflict with the interests he is bound to protect, is both universal and inflexible. In other words, this case illustrates just how wide and strict the no conflict duty is.

2.   The practical difficulty in applying this rule is for directors to identify that a conflict of interest exists, and then avoid it. This might not always be easy. Not to appear too much pro-directors, but there might be situations in which a director, especially someone who is affiliated with several different large corporations and serves on the boards of different business organizations, is not fully aware of all possible conflicts or business opportunities that, in hindsight, would be easy to spot. An answer could be that there should be limits to the number of board positions one single person accepts (something desirable also to ensure that sufficient time and energies are dedicated to each job). In fact, several legal systems provide for limits to the number of positions a director can have, at least in listed corporations. Do you think such limitations are desirable, or might be too rigid?

3.   The question, according to the court, is not whether the party to whom the duty was owed (i.e., the company) had some kind of beneficial interest in the opportunity, but rather whether the fiduciary's exploitation of the opportunity was such as to attract the application of the rule. It did not matter at all that the opportunity in this case was not in the company's line of business. Do you see any danger in such a rigorous approach?

4.   It seems that this case takes a very wide view of what constitutes 'corporate opportunity' and as such represents a very high standard of loyalty to the company. Following this case, do you think a director must pursue *every* opportunity he comes across solely for the company's benefit and not for personal gain? As a legislature or a judge, how would you narrow the range of opportunities prohibited by this rule?

5.   One note concerning judicial style that we already asked for other decisions (we never get tired of this): how do you find the language and organization of this British decision in comparison to other cases we have

discussed? What is distinctive, if anything, in the way the opinion is written and in the way the Court reasons?

* * *

Some countries have adopted, especially for listed corporations, a specific regulation applicable to transactions with related parties. These rules deal with situations in which there are not necessarily one or more directors with a conflict of interest, but there are transactions among affiliated entities, especially within a group, in which a corporation could be unfairly advantaged to the detriment of another one and its shareholders. Even if not strictly related to interested directors, rules concerning transactions with related parties raise issues of fiduciary duties because the board of a corporation might favor another one with which there is a relationship.

One interesting example of regulation of transactions with related parties can be found in Italy. Based on a provision of the Italian Civil Code (Article 2391-*bis*), the Italian SEC (Consob) has enacted, in 2010, a regulation dealing with this problem. The regulation is very long and complex, but in short it basically identifies related parties, and mandates specific disclosure and procedural and substantive rules to mitigate the possible detrimental effects of these transactions. More specifically, a subject is related to another one if it controls it, is controlled by it, or is controlled by the same entity; other relationships are also considered—so, for example, executives are considered related to the corporation they work for, and family members of the above-mentioned subjects are also related parties. The regulation then identifies, in particular, transactions of "major relevance" based on a formula, meaning transactions of particular economic importance, for example transactions whose value exceeds 5% of the equity or the assets of the corporation. In order to approve these transactions, specific procedural and substantive protections must be adopted.

In particular, to simplify, these transactions must be approved by the board of directors (cannot be delegated to one director). A committee of independent directors not related to the corporation must be involved in the negotiation of the transaction, obtain adequate information on it, and is allowed to require further information and give advice. In addition, the board can approve the transaction only after having obtained an opinion by the committee on the interest of the corporation to enter into the transaction, and on its fairness. Alternative procedures can be adopted as long as the majority of the independent and not related directors have a decisive role in approving the transaction. Finally, the board can decide to carry on the transaction also against the advice of the committee, but only obtaining a positive vote of the shareholders (for a more detailed discussion of these rules, including an empirical analysis of the application, *see* M. Bianchi and others, *Regulation and Self-Regulation of*

Related Parties Transactions in Italy, Quaderni di Finanza Consob, 2014, available at www.consob.it).

This regulation is partially inspired by the U.S. approach, in the sense that in the presence of a potential conflict it requires the adoption of procedural safeguards to ensure the fairness of the transaction. One problem worth discussing, however, is whether the regulatory approach, or at least the way in which it is enforced, mixes up procedural and substantive protections. As we have discussed, under U.S. law, if a director has a conflict of interest but the transaction is approved by fully informed independent directors or shareholders, the transaction cannot be challenged. When the procedural protections are not followed, the transaction can be saved only if the defendants prove entire fairness. In other words, the substance of the deal (its fairness) is only examined if there was a procedural failure. In the Italian regulation on related parties' transactions, on the other hand, the committee of independent directors does not simply approve the transaction, but must issue an opinion on its fairness. Is this opinion protected by the business judgment rule? Or can courts and enforcement agencies second-guess the merits of the determination of the independent committee? To what extent can independent directors face liability or sanctions if their decision was not fully informed? This is a very delicate problem that is not clearly resolved by the applicable rules. In our opinion, both the decision of the committee and of the board should be protected by the business judgment rule if effective procedural safeguards have been strictly followed.

* * *

Comparing breaches of the duty of care and of the duty of loyalty, it is interesting to briefly discuss remedies. An insightful observation is offered by Professors Eisenberg and Cox in their casebook on corporations (*Corporations and Other Business Organizations*, Foundation Press, 2011, 726 ff.). They point out how the traditional remedies for violations of the duty of loyalty are restitutionary: rescission of the unfair contract, accounting, or constructive trust in the corporation's favor in case of violation of the business opportunity doctrine. On the other hand, remedies for a breach of the duty of care are generally monetary damages. They observe that as a consequence a director who violated his duty of loyalty might end up not worse off than before the violation, while a director who violated the duty of care could. This might create an incentive to breach the duty of loyalty, if the possibility of not being caught is taken into account. It should be considered, however, that if restitutionary remedies cannot be obtained, the unfaithful director might have to pay damages. In addition he could be terminated for cause, with the obvious reputational consequences. Moreover, occasionally courts have included other remedies, for example mandating the director to repay salary earned and disgorgement of ill-gotten gains; and in some cases punitive damages have been awarded.

Is this a potential problem also in other jurisdictions, especially when courts have more limited flexibility in shaping the proper remedy, as is often the case in civil law countries, where for example punitive damages are generally not admissible? In this analysis it should also be taken into account, however, that often intentional violations especially of the duty of loyalty can also be subject to criminal sanctions.

DIRECTORS' FIDUCIARY DUTIES TOWARD CREDITORS

Generally speaking, in common law systems, directors do not own fiduciary duties to creditors. Creditors can only rely on contractual rights, or on specific anti-fraud provisions (for example, fraudulent conveyances). The situation might change, however, when the corporation approaches insolvency, when it is in the so-called "zone of insolvency." In this situation, which is difficult and fuzzy to define precisely, in several (not all) jurisdictions directors are deemed to have a duty of care and of loyalty also toward creditors. Do you understand the reasons of this shift from a regulatory point of view?

There are however systems in which directors can be liable toward creditors also on other grounds, especially if they damage the financial solidity of the corporation. The following excerpt offers a comparative overview.

JOHN ARMOUR ET AL., TRANSACTIONS WITH CREDITORS, THE ANATOMY OF CORPORATE LAW, 2ND ED.
Oxford, 2009[1]

[. . .]

In each of our jurisdictions, directors, including *de facto* or shadow directors, may be held personally liable for net increases of losses to creditors resulting from the board's negligence or fraud to creditors when the company is, or is nearly, insolvent. Such duties can be framed and enforced with differing levels of intensity, affecting the extent to which they affect directors' incentives. First, as regards the substantive content of the duty, a less onerous standard is triggered by fraud or knowledge of likely harm to creditors, imposing liability only for actions so harmful to creditors as to call into question directors' subjective good faith. A more intensive standard imposes liability for negligently worsening the financial position of the insolvent company. Second, the intensity can be

---

[1] Footnotes omitted.

varied through the trigger for the duty's imposition: the greater the degree of financial distress in which the company must be before the duty kicks in, the more remote will be its effect on incentives. A third dimension over which intensity varies is enforcement. Enforcement is likely to be facilitated if the duties are owed directly to individual creditors, and reduced for duties owned only to the company, which will be unlikely to be enforced unless the company enters bankruptcy proceedings.

The appropriate intensity of such director liability depends on the nature of the debtor firm. Shareholder-creditor agency problems are likely to be most pronounced in firms where managers' and shareholders' interests are closely aligned. For larger firms with dispersed shareholders, managers have fewer incentives to pursue measures that benefit shareholders at creditors' expense; under such circumstances directorial liability based on creditors' interests may over-deter directors, resulting in less risk-taking than is optimal. Directorial liability may therefore be expected to be most useful where shareholders' and managers' interests are aligned. To this there is one important exception. In smaller firms that face financial distress, the owner-managers often have few personal assets beyond their stake in the firm; consequently the threat of liability may not act as a meaningful deterrent. Thus the key factor determining the use of the standards strategy against directors may be expected to be the ownership structure of large firms.

Consistently with these observations, the standard employed for directorial liability to creditors in the U.S. has the lowest intensity among our jurisdictions. Most U.S. states employ the technique of a shift in the content of directors' duty of loyalty in relation to insolvent firms and the duty is owed to the corporation, rather than individual creditors. There has been flirtation in some states with a direct tortuous claim against directors for "deepening insolvency", but this has been explicitly ruled out in Delaware.

In the UK, like in the U.S., there is a shift in the content of the duty of loyalty for directors of insolvent firms, this duty being owned only to the company. In addition, however, the U.K. also imposes negligence-based liability on directors for "wrongful trading" if they fail to take reasonable care in protecting creditors' interests once insolvency proceedings have become inevitable. This duty is, however, only enforceable by a liquidator, and the point at which it is triggered is typically very late—insolvency is usually not "inevitable" unless the firm is cash-flow, as opposed to balance-sheet, insolvent.

Continental European jurisdictions deploy more intensive standards against directors, consistent with the generally more concentrated ownership structure of their large firms. In these countries, directors of financially distressed firms face negligence-based liability, generally based on duties mandated through the company. Moreover, we noted above that French, German, and Italian directors can be held liable simply for failing to take action following serious loss of capital. The draconian nature of this provision is diluted to some degree by the fact that directors often have substantial discretion over whether a going-concern or liquidation valuation is used in compiling the firm's balance sheet, which can enable them to delay the triggering of the obligation. However, we should not make too much of this, for a court is likely to take a dim view *ex post* of any hint of abuse of this discretion.

In Japan, duties to creditors are triggered even earlier, as creditors have standing to sue directors even if the company is solvent. Although directors of a large Japanese company have rarely been held liable under this provision, it is frequently litigated in the case of closely held companies. In addition, the Supreme Court has developed a "director's duty to monitor" doctrine, under which non-executive directors are held liable to creditors when they grossly fail to monitor misbehaving managers. Finally, while increased shareholder litigation during the 1990s prompted statutory change to limit director liability, creditor rights have been left unaffected.

[Article 2394 of the Italian Civil Code also provides for directors' liability to creditors, but only for their failure to comply with obligations related to the maintenance of the value of the assets of the corporation, a somehow ambiguous notion. In addition, creditors can sue only if the assets of the corporation are insufficient to repay the creditors, also a test not always easy to apply, which seems to suggest that the capital is lost. Not surprisingly, this provision is virtually never used outside of a bankruptcy procedure. It would be difficult for a creditor to hold directors liable before insolvency is formally declared.]

NOTES AND QUESTIONS

1.   The authors argue that in corporations with a more concentrated ownership structure it is more important to provide creditors with protections that can be activated before insolvency procedures against misbehaving directors. Do you understand why?

2.   Anticipating the triggering event that allows creditors to sue directors, in terms of the level of financial distress of the firm, can result in a disincentive for directors to take risks. Discuss why this result can be undesirable.

3.   Do you think that creditors could provide, in their contracts with the corporation, additional personal guarantees from directors? Would this be feasible and useful? Would this introduce a sort of fiduciary duty toward (some) creditors? Does this raise a problem in terms of protection of weaker

or involuntary creditors? And what about a hypothetical provision in the bylaws of the corporation that establishes fiduciary duties of directors toward creditors? Obviously, this is largely theoretical: virtually no corporation is interested in doing something like this. But from a purely theoretical perspective, would such a provision be valid and enforceable? You can answer referring to the legal systems you are more familiar with: some of the underlying economic arguments could apply to lots of systems.

* * *

In the United States, an important 1991 Delaware decision (*Credit Lyonnais Bank Nederland, N.V. v. Pathe Communications Corp*) clarified that in a solvent corporation near insolvency directors' duties must take into account creditors' interests (this was also to protect directors from pressures by a controlling shareholder). The decision raises complicated issues, among which in particular the precise boundaries of the "zone of insolvency." The question whether creditors have a direct claim against directors breaching their fiduciary duties, can only sue derivatively on behalf of the corporation (*see* next chapter for a discussion of derivative suits), or have no claim at all, is however far from settled.

Several decisions have held that creditors have a direct claim against directors in the zone of insolvency, for example under Colorado, Illinois, or Louisiana law (*see* respectively *Jetpay Merch. Servs., LLC v. Miller*, 2007 WL 2701636; *Technic Eng'g, Ltd. v. Basic Envirotech, Inc.*, 53 F. Supp. 2d 1007 (1999); and *Lopez v. TDI Servs., Inc.*, 631 So. 2d 679 (1994)). Recent Delaware decisions have however excluded a direct claim of creditors against directors, sometimes recognizing only the possibility to sue derivatively. The following case offers an example of this position.

NORTH AMERICAN CATHOLIC EDUCATIONAL PROGRAMMING FOUNDATION, INC. V. GHEEWALLA AND OTHERS

Supreme Court of Delaware
930 A.2d 92 (2007)

HOLLAND, JUSTICE:

This is the appeal of the plaintiff-appellant, North American Catholic Educational Programming Foundation, Inc. ("NACEPF") from a final judgment of the Court of Chancery that dismissed NACEPF's Complaint for failure to state a claim. NACEPF holds certain radio wave spectrum licenses regulated by the Federal Communications Commission ("FCC"). In March 2001, NACEPF, together with other similar spectrum license-holders, entered into the Master Use and Royalty Agreement (the "Master Agreement") with Clearwire Holdings, Inc. ("Clearwire"), a Delaware corporation. Under the Master Agreement, Clearwire could obtain rights to those licenses as then-existing leases expired and the then-current lessees failed to exercise rights of first refusal.

The defendant-appellees are Rob Gheewalla, Gerry Cardinale, and Jack Daly (collectively, the "Defendants"), who served as directors of Clearwire at the behest of Goldman Sachs & Co. ("Goldman Sachs"). NACEPF's Complaint alleges that the Defendants, even though they comprised less than a majority of the board, were able to control Clearwire because its only source of funding was Goldman Sachs. According to NACEPF, they used that power to favor Goldman Sachs' agenda in derogation of their fiduciary duties as directors of Clearwire. In addition to bringing fiduciary duty claims, NACEPF's Complaint also asserts that the Defendants fraudulently induced it to enter into the Master Agreement with Clearwire and that the Defendants tortiously interfered with NACEPF's business opportunities.

NACEPF is not a shareholder of Clearwire. Instead, NACEPF filed its Complaint in the Court of Chancery as a putative *creditor* of Clearwire. The Complaint alleges *direct,* not derivative, fiduciary duty claims against the Defendants, who served as directors of Clearwire while it was either insolvent or in the "zone of insolvency."

[. . .]

For the reasons set forth in its Opinion, the Court of Chancery concluded: (1) that creditors of a Delaware corporation in the "zone of insolvency" may not assert direct claims for breach of fiduciary duty against the corporation's directors; (2) that the Complaint failed to state a claim for the narrow, if extant, cause of action for direct claims involving breach of fiduciary duty brought by creditors against directors of insolvent Delaware corporations; and (3) that, with dismissal of its fiduciary duty claims, NACEPF had not provided any basis for exercising personal jurisdiction over the Defendants with respect to NACEPF's other claims. Therefore, the Defendants' Motion to Dismiss the Complaint was granted.

In this opinion, we hold that the creditors of a Delaware corporation that is either insolvent or in the zone of insolvency have no right, as a matter of law, to assert direct claims for breach of fiduciary duty against the corporation's directors. Accordingly, we have concluded that the judgments of the Court of Chancery must be affirmed.

[. . .]

NACEPF is an independent lay organization incorporated under the laws of Rhode Island. In 2000, NACEPF joined with Hispanic Information and Telecommunications Network, Inc. ("HITN"), Instructional Telecommunications Foundation, Inc. ("ITF"), and various affiliates of ITF to form the ITFS Spectrum Development Alliance, Inc. (the

"Alliance"). Collectively, the Alliance owned a significant percentage of FCC-approved licenses for microwave signal transmissions ("spectrum") used for educational programs that were known as "Instruction Television Fixed Service" spectrum ("ITFS") licenses.

The Defendants were directors of Clearwire. The Defendants were also all employed by Goldman Sachs and served on the Clearwire Board of Directors at the behest of Goldman Sachs. NACEPF alleges that the Defendants effectively controlled Clearwire through the financial and other influence that Goldman Sachs had over Clearwire.

According to the Complaint, the Defendants represented to NACEPF and the other Alliance members that Clearwire's stated business purpose was to create a national system of wireless connections to the internet. Between 2000 and March 2001, Clearwire negotiated a Master Agreement with the Alliance, which Clearwire and the Alliance members entered into in March 2001. NACEPF asserts that it negotiated the terms of the Master Agreement with several individuals, including the Defendants. NACEPF submits that all of the Defendants purported to be acting on the behalf of Goldman Sachs and the entity that became Clearwire.

Under the terms of the Master Agreement, Clearwire was to acquire the Alliance members' ITFS spectrum licenses when those licenses became available. To do so, Clearwire was obligated to pay NACEPF and other Alliance members more than $24.3 million. The Complaint alleges that the Defendants knew but did not tell NACEPF that Goldman Sachs did not intend to carry out the business plan that was the stated rationale for asking NACEPF to enter into the Master Agreement, i.e., by funding Clearwire.

In June 2002, the market for wireless spectrum collapsed when WorldCom announced its accounting problems. It appeared that there was or soon would be a surplus of spectrum available from WorldCom. Thereafter, Clearwire began negotiations with the members of the Alliance to end Clearwire's obligations to the members. Eventually, Clearwire paid over $2 million to HITN and ITF to settle their claims and; according to NACEPF, was only able to limit its payments to that amount by otherwise threatening to file for bankruptcy protection. These settlements left the NACEPF as the sole remaining member of the Alliance. The Complaint alleges that, by October 2003, Clearwire "had been unable to obtain any further financing and effectively went out of business."

[. . .]

In its Complaint, NACEPF asserts three claims against the Defendants. In Count I of the Complaint, NACEPF alleges that the Defendants fraudulently induced it to enter into the Master Agreement and, thereafter, to continue with the Master Agreement to "preserv[e] its spectrum licenses for acquisition by Clearwire." In Count II, NACEPF alleges that because, at all relevant times, Clearwire was either insolvent or in the "zone of insolvency," the Defendants owed fiduciary duties to NACEPF "as a substantial creditor of Clearwire," and that the Defendants breached those duties by: (1) not preserving the assets of Clearwire for its benefit and that of its creditors when it became apparent that Clearwire would not be able to continue as a going concern and would need to be liquidated and (2) holding on to NACEPF's ITFS license rights when Clearwire would not use them, solely to keep Goldman Sachs's investment "in play."

[. . .]

In order to withstand the Defendant's Rule 12(b)(6) motion to dismiss, the Plaintiff was required to demonstrate that the breach of fiduciary duty claims set forth in Count II are cognizable under Delaware law. This procedural requirement requires us to address a substantive question of first impression that is raised by the present appeal: as a matter of Delaware law, can the *creditor* of a corporation that is operating within the *zone of insolvency* bring a *direct action* against its directors for an alleged *breach of fiduciary* duty?

It is well established that the directors owe their fiduciary obligations to the corporation and its shareholders. While shareholders rely on directors acting as fiduciaries to protect their interests, creditors are afforded protection through contractual agreements, fraud and fraudulent conveyance law, implied covenants of good faith and fair dealing, bankruptcy law, general commercial law and other sources of creditor rights. Delaware courts have traditionally been reluctant to expand existing fiduciary duties. Accordingly, "the general rule is that directors do not owe creditors duties beyond the relevant contractual terms."

In this case, NACEPF argues that when a corporation is in the zone of insolvency, this Court should recognize a new direct right for creditors to challenge directors' exercise of business judgments as breaches of the fiduciary duties owed to them. This Court has never directly addressed the zone of insolvency issue involving directors' purported fiduciary duties to creditors that is presented by NACEPF in this appeal. That subject has been discussed, however, in several judicial opinions and many scholarly articles.

[. . .]

In *Production Resources,* the Court of Chancery remarked that recognition of fiduciary duties to creditors in the "zone of insolvency" context may involve:

"using the law of fiduciary duty to fill gaps that do not exist. Creditors are often protected by strong covenants, liens on assets, and other negotiated contractual protections. The implied covenant of good faith and fair dealing also protects creditors. So does the law of fraudulent conveyance. With these protections, when creditors are unable to prove that a corporation or its directors breached any of the specific legal duties owed to them, one would think that the conceptual room for concluding that the creditors were somehow, nevertheless, injured by inequitable conduct would be extremely small, *if extant*. Having complied with all legal obligations owed to the firm's creditors, the board would, in that scenario, ordinarily be free to take economic risk for the benefit of the firm's equity owners, so long as the directors comply with their fiduciary duties to the firm by selecting and pursuing with fidelity and prudence a plausible strategy to maximize the firm's value."

In this case, the Court of Chancery noted that creditors' existing protections-among which are the protections afforded by their negotiated agreements, their security instruments, the implied covenant of good faith and fair dealing, fraudulent conveyance law, and bankruptcy law-render the imposition of an additional, unique layer of protection through direct claims for breach of fiduciary duty unnecessary. It also noted that "any benefit to be derived by the recognition of such additional direct claims appears minimal, at best, and significantly outweighed by the costs to economic efficiency." The Court of Chancery reasoned that "an otherwise solvent corporation operating in the zone of insolvency is one in most need of effective and proactive leadership-as well as the ability to negotiate in good faith with its creditors-goals which would likely be significantly undermined by the prospect of individual liability arising from the pursuit of direct claims by creditors." We agree.

[. . .]

Delaware corporate law provides for a separation of control and ownership. The directors of Delaware corporations have "the legal responsibility to manage the business of a corporation for the benefit of its shareholders owners."

In this case, the need for providing directors with definitive guidance compels us to hold that no direct claim for breach of fiduciary duties may be asserted by the creditors of a solvent corporation that is operating in the zone of insolvency. When a solvent corporation is navigating in the zone of insolvency, the focus for Delaware directors does not change: directors must continue to discharge their fiduciary duties to the corporation and its shareholders by exercising their business judgment in the best interests of the corporation for the benefit of its shareholder owners. Therefore, we hold the Court of Chancery properly concluded that Count II of the NACEPF Complaint fails to state a claim, as a matter of Delaware law, to the extent that it attempts to assert a direct claim for breach of fiduciary duty to a creditor while Clearwire was operating in the zone of insolvency.

[. . .]

It is well settled that directors owe fiduciary duties to the corporation. When a corporation is *solvent,* those duties may be enforced by its shareholders, who have standing to bring *derivative* actions on behalf of the corporation because they are the ultimate beneficiaries of the corporation's growth and increased value. When a corporation is *insolvent,* however, its creditors take the place of the shareholders as the residual beneficiaries of any increase in value.

[. . .]

Consequently, the creditors of an *insolvent* corporation have standing to maintain derivative claims against directors on behalf of the corporation for breaches of fiduciary duties. The corporation's insolvency "makes the creditors the principal constituency injured by any fiduciary breaches that diminish the firm's value." Therefore, equitable considerations give creditors standing to pursue derivative claims against the directors of an insolvent corporation. Individual creditors of an insolvent corporation have the same incentive to pursue valid derivative claims on its behalf that shareholders have when the corporation is solvent.

NOTES AND QUESTIONS

1.   As we will see in the next chapter, a derivative action is an action brought by an interested subject, especially a shareholder, on behalf of the corporation against directors for a breach of a duty that caused damage to the corporation. In case of victory, the damages awarded go to the corporation. Why does the court deny a direct claim to creditors, but allow a derivative action? What would be the incentives of creditors to bring such an action?

2.   Based on this decision, would creditors have standing to maintain a derivative claim against directors of a corporation that is not insolvent (yet), but is in the "zone of insolvency," meaning that it is approaching insolvency? Why?

3.   Does the rationale of this decision also apply to involuntary creditors, for example victims of a tort? What might be the different considerations, if any, that might support a direct claim of involuntary creditors as opposed to contractual creditors?

4.   Should the conclusion be different in the case of a closely held corporation in which all the shareholders are also directors? If you are not

from the U.S. (or also if you are but you are familiar also with other corporate law systems, or with other U.S. States different from Delaware), do you think the case above could have been decided differently in other jurisdictions?

* * *

As mentioned earlier in the excerpt from "The Anatomy of Corporate Law," a provision of the Japanese Companies Act, Article 429, paragraph 1, prescribes the liability of directors against third parties (i.e., anyone other than the corporation and shareholders), including creditors. According to the Supreme Court of Japan, a director is liable toward a third party for the damage caused by violations of the director's duties to the corporation, when a director violated his duties knowingly or with gross negligence (Supreme Court of Japan, Nov. 26, 1969, 23 SAIKO SAIBANSHO MINJI HANREISHU 2150[2]). In other words, a creditor can sue a director of the corporation directly, not derivatively, although the standard of liability is linked to the violation of the director's duties to the corporation.

Let's take a look at a case decided by a lower court, which judged in favor of a creditor of a bankrupt corporation who sued its president for mismanagement leading to bankruptcy.

TOKYO HIGH COURT, 29 MARCH 1983
29 March 1983, 1079 Hanrei Jiho 92

Facts

By 1969, the corporation outside of the suit, a recycled-tire manufacturer with a stated capital of 32 million JPY, started to experience difficulties due to severe competition in the domestic market. The defendant (the appellant), who was the director with the power to represent the corporation, manipulated the accounting of the corporation to have a temporal relief, and planned to turn around the situation by increasing the production and exporting recycled tires to the Philippines and South Korea. The corporation invested about 150 million JPY in a new factory, mainly financed borrowing funds from a bank, and started operating the new factory and exporting its goods in 1971.

The huge amount of borrowing for the construction of the factory impacted the cash flows of the corporation outside of the suit, and the corporation turned to borrowing at a high-interest rate. After the construction of the factory was completed, the currency exchange system was changed from a fixed rate system to a flexible rate system, and JPY got stronger compared to USD. This change disrupted the initial plan of the corporation to make profits by exporting, and banks refused to extend

---

[2]   This decision regards Article 266–3 of the former Japanese Commercial Code (Sho-ho), before the revision in 2005, which is the predecessor of Article 429 of the current Companies Act.

new loans to the corporation. Thus, the corporation became more dependent on high-interest borrowing.

Although the defendant had been taking care of the cash management of the corporation outside of the suit without consulting other directors, on April 1972, the other directors warned the defendant to correct his behavior, as it would be irrational to continue borrowing at a high-interest rate in order to pay the interest of existing loans, when the corporation showed losses since 1969. The defendant, however, did not listen.

As a result, the financial situation of the corporation outside of the suit deteriorated rapidly. The defendant repaid part of the corporate loans with his personal assets, but was unable to improve the situation. In November 1973, the corporation outside of the suit stopped paying its debts, and was declared bankrupt. The appellant was not able to avoid this result.

The plaintiff (the appellee) is a corporation dealing in rubber and light metals, and is one of the suppliers of the corporation outside of the suit. The plaintiff sued the defendant for the amount of unpaid account receivables to the corporation outside of the suit. The Yokohama District Court judged in favor of the plaintiff. The defendant appealed.

The Court's Decision

Appeal dismissed.

Stock corporations play an important role in the economy and their activity largely depends on the managing of the business by directors, directors owe a duty to promptly and accurately evaluate the situation of their corporation, and to carry on the business properly. According to the facts found above, since 1969, the appellant covered up the deficit of the corporation outside of this suit by manipulating its accounts, depended on high-interest-rate borrowing since 1970 as the corporation faced cash constraints, and did not change this way of management even after the turn-around plan based on a new factory and exporting goods had failed; on the contrary, he caused the corporation to become even more dependent on high-interest-rate loans. Eventually, the appellant forced the corporation outside of this suit to use about one-fourth of the revenues from its sales to pay interests. As a result, the corporation went bankrupt, as the value of its assets decreased while its debt increased rapidly. This made it impossible for the appellee to collect its account receivables from the corporation. Such acts of the appellant clearly violate the duty above. In addition, the appellant did not change his style of management, although he must have recognized that, if he continued such management, sooner or later the assets of the corporation outside of this suit would deteriorate and the corporation would go bankrupt. Therefore, it is clear that the appellant is liable to compensate for the damage suffered by the appellee.

NOTES AND QUESTIONS

1.   According to the Supreme Court of Japan, Nov. 26, 1969, *supra*, which provides the basis of the Tokyo High Court decision above, a director of a corporation is liable for two types of damages. One is "indirect damage," which is a damage suffered by a third party as a consequence of a prejudice suffered by the corporation. Another is "direct damage," which is a damage suffered solely by a third party. An example of the former is the Tokyo High Court case excerpted above. An example of the latter is offered by the 1969 case just mentioned, in which the managing director of a corporation was held liable toward a supplier of the corporation for purchasing goods from that supplier when the financial situation of the corporation was considerably deteriorated, believing that the corporation will be able to pay even though it was easy to predict that the corporation could not do so. Another director, a local politician who had been appointed as the president to add credibility to the corporation but did not participate in the management, was also held liable for overlooking such a transaction. Do you see differences and similarities between the two situations?

2.   Article 429 of the Japanese Companies Act had been used mainly in cases regarding small and medium corporations. Recently, however, some courts imposed liability on directors of large corporations on a theory that the failure of their directors to create an effective internal control system contributed to the wrongdoing of the corporations. These cases imply a "direct damage" to third parties. e.g., Tokyo District Court, Feb. 4, 2009, 2033 HANREI JIHO 3 (liability of directors of a large publisher for defamation in weekly journal); Osaka High Court, May 25, 2013, 1033 RODO HANREI 24 (liability of directors of a listed corporation for death of its employee due to overworking). Why do you think third parties might want to sue the directors in these cases, when the corporation is not insolvent? More generally, does it make sense to distinguish "small" from "large" corporations on these issues? "Closely-held" from "publicly-held"?

3.   A dissenting opinion of the Supreme Court judgment above asserted that the liability of directors toward third parties should be limited to "direct damages." What kind of problem would arise when creditors are allowed to sue directors directly for an "indirect damage" (consider, in particular, the position of shareholders)?

4.   Do you agree with the judgment of the Tokyo High Court above? What about the business judgment rule? Was it possible for the plaintiff-creditor, in this case, to better protect its interests?

5.   Some scholars in Japan tried to provide a more coherent framework for the application of Article 429 by looking to the *Credit Lyonnais* case decided in Delaware and mentioned above, especially with respect to the part of the decision that emphasizes the incentive of shareholders to take

excessive risk when the corporation is close to insolvency. It is important to note, however, that *Credit Lyonnais* was not a case that imposed liability on directors who did not consider the interests of creditors, but rather a case that protected directors who resisted pressure of a large shareholder. Also, as we have seen earlier, the Supreme Court of Delaware denied creditors' direct suits against directors. Therefore, Delaware law would not be a perfect guidance for the interpretation of Article 429. This anecdote shows the usefulness of comparative corporate law as a source of ideas as well as the importance of applying it with proper understandings of the contexts of each jurisdiction.

6.   Overall, what do you think of imposing a duty on directors to consider the interests of creditors when the corporation is near insolvency or is insolvent? Discuss its pros and cons. (For further reference, you can *see* Henry T. C. Hu & Jay Lawrence Westbrook, *Abolition of the Corporate Duty to Creditors*, 107 COLUM. L. REV. 1321 (2007).)

CHAPTER 7

SHAREHOLDERS' LITIGATION

■ ■ ■

INTRODUCTION

As we have seen in the previous chapter, directors can be liable toward the corporation itself, toward single shareholders or third parties, and toward corporate creditors. Whenever directors, breaching their fiduciary duties, damage the corporation, they indirectly damage also shareholders. Clearly enough, if the assets of the corporation are less valuable or the business is less profitable as a consequence of directors' negligence or abuse, also the value of the shares owned by the shareholders is, generally, negatively affected; or at least the return and risk of the investment deteriorate.

When the damage caused affects both the corporation and its shareholders, one problem is who is entitled to sue. The corporation is a separate legal entity from the shareholders, and it has the right to sue and be sued. Generally, if the corporation has a cause of action against someone, it can sue. The decision to sue, if and how to continue litigation, and the management of the dispute, is normally a business decision reserved to directors (sometimes delegated, at least in part, to high-ranking corporate employees). When, however, the potential defendant is one or more current directors, it is unlikely that the top management acting on behalf of the corporation, drags to court one of their own.

Of course there could be situations in which the corporation (i.e., the board of directors) will decide to sue a member of the board, for example in case of an egregious violation of a single director alienating fellow directors, or—more often—when new directors are appointed, possibly after an acquisition, and they realize that the previous board has harmed the corporation. Even this scenario, however, is not very common: there can be a certain degree of reciprocal back-scratching among directors that makes these lawsuits fairly rare.

Shareholders, however, need to be protected. For this reason most modern legal systems have introduced "derivative actions." Even if, as we will see, the role of these procedural devices and the rules governing them differ in different jurisdictions, they share some common features. In a derivative action, shareholders are allowed—meeting certain requirements—to sue corporate directors on behalf of the corporation.

They can, in other words, step in the shoes of the corporation and assert a claim that belongs to the legal entity, in order to overcome the reluctance, when not the conflict of interest, which prevents directors from suing. In case of victory, monetary damages would be awarded to the corporation (with very few exceptions, as we will see), not to the shareholders suing derivatively; and only under certain conditions winning shareholders might be entitled to recover their legal expenses from the corporation.

Based on these elements you might wonder why shareholders bring derivative lawsuits at all. What incentives do they have? On the one hand, even if compensation goes to the corporation, shareholders might indirectly benefit from it: if the assets of the corporation are restored to their original value, this increased value should be reflected in the value and the market price of the shares. Secondly, shareholders might sue also to stop an ongoing abuse (obtaining an injunction), or as part of a strategy aimed at ousting incompetent or unfaithful directors. Finally, derivative litigation can be attorney-driven, especially if lawyers can take the case on a contingency fee basis.

It is important to understand that shareholders can sue derivatively only when the corporation is damaged. There might be situations, however, in which directors, breaching their duties, cause a damage *directly* to the shareholders, a damage that is *not* the consequence of a damage suffered by the corporation. Consider the following example: directors intentionally publish false financial statements or a false prospectus that fools existing shareholders into believing that the economic situation of the corporation is much better than it actually is. Relying on this information, existing shareholders subscribe newly issued shares at a price significantly superior to the fair value of the securities. When the truth is discovered, the price of the shares drops, causing a significant loss to the shareholders. In this situation, you might argue that the breach of the directors has damaged directly (only) the shareholders, not the corporation. You might even go as far as arguing that the corporation not only has suffered no damage, but it has had an advantage because it was able to receive more financial resources for its shares. In this case shareholders have a *direct* cause of action against directors (and a class action or other form of collective redress might be available), but there is no *derivative* lawsuit, since the corporation has not been hurt. As we will see, to distinguish between direct and derivative claims is not always as easy as it might seem.

Keep in mind that, in several jurisdictions, at least in theory, shareholders can sue derivatively on behalf of the corporation also a third party who is not a director and damaged the corporation. This type of suits is however rare, and in any case in this book we only consider derivative actions against directors.

This chapter discusses shareholders' derivative actions, starting with common law systems and in particular U.S. law, and then considering their regulation in other systems. We will investigate how to identify a derivative claim, and the procedural loopholes that shareholders suing derivatively have to jump through to successfully sue the directors of their corporation. On the other hand we will consider how a corporation (and its directors) can effectively avoid or resist derivative lawsuits. We will focus, in particular, on some basic distinctions between common law and civil law systems, and the different role of the shareholders' meeting in these legal families also vis-à-vis directors' liabilities toward the corporation, a difference that might partially be explained in light of the prevailing ownership structures (*see* Chapter 1).

We have mentioned the fact that direct claims of shareholders or investors can sometimes be brought as a class action. A few final pages of this chapter will be devoted to a very brief discussion of class actions in a comparative perspective. Even if class actions are generally more common in the context of violations of the securities laws, they are obviously very important also for corporate law students, scholars, and practitioners. We will therefore dedicate some reflections to this issue.

DERIVATIVE SUITS IN COMMON LAW SYSTEMS: THE U.S. AND THE U.K.

One of the first issues that should be addressed is if the claim of the shareholders is direct (in which case a derivative action is not possible), or if it is derivative, allowing the shareholders to sue the directors on behalf of the corporation. The following leading case examines this question in the U.S.

PATRICK TOOLEY AND KEVIN LEWIS V. DONALDSON, LUFKIN, & JENRETTE, INC., AND OTHERS

Supreme Court of Delaware
845 A.2d 1031 (2004)

[. . .]

VEASEY, CHIEF JUSTICE:

[. . .]

Facts

Patrick Tooley and Kevin Lewis are former minority stockholders of Donaldson, Lufkin & Jenrette, Inc. (DLJ), a Delaware corporation engaged in investment banking. DLJ was acquired by Credit Suisse Group (Credit Suisse) in the Fall of 2000. Before that acquisition, AXA Financial, Inc.(AXA), which owned 71% of DLJ stock, controlled DLJ. Pursuant to a stockholder agreement between AXA and Credit Suisse,

AXA agreed to exchange with Credit Suisse its DLJ stockholdings for a mix of stock and cash. The consideration received by AXA consisted primarily of stock. Cash made up one-third of the purchase price. Credit Suisse intended to acquire the remaining minority interests of publicly-held DLJ stock through a cash tender offer, followed by a merger of DLJ into a Credit Suisse subsidiary.

The tender offer price was set at $90 per share in cash. The tender offer was to expire 20 days after its commencement. The merger agreement, however, authorized two types of extensions. First, Credit Suisse could unilaterally extend the tender offer if certain conditions were not met, such as SEC regulatory approvals or certain payment obligations. Alternatively, DLJ and Credit Suisse could agree to postpone acceptance by Credit Suisse of DLJ stock tendered by the minority stockholders.

Credit Suisse availed itself of both types of extensions to postpone the closing of the tender offer. The tender offer was initially set to expire on October 5, 2000, but Credit Suisse invoked the five-day unilateral extension provided in the agreement. Later, by agreement between DLJ and Credit Suisse, it postponed the merger a second time so that it was then set to close on November 2, 2000.

Plaintiffs challenge the second extension that resulted in a 22-day delay. They contend that this delay was not properly authorized and harmed minority stockholders while improperly benefitting AXA. They claim damages representing the time-value of money lost through the delay.

The Decision of the Court of Chancery

The order of the Court of Chancery dismissing the complaint, and the Memorandum Opinion upon which it is based, state that the dismissal is based on the plaintiffs' lack of standing to bring the claims asserted therein. Thus, when plaintiffs tendered their shares, they lost standing under Court of Chancery Rule 23.1, the contemporaneous holding rule. The ruling before us on appeal is that the plaintiffs' claim is derivative, purportedly brought on behalf of DLJ. The Court of Chancery, relying upon our confusing jurisprudence on the direct/derivative dichotomy, based its dismissal on the following ground: "Because this delay affected all DLJ shareholders equally, plaintiffs' injury was not a special injury, and this action is, thus, a derivative action, at most."

Plaintiffs argue that they have suffered a "special injury" because they had an alleged contractual right to receive the merger consideration of $90 per share without suffering the 22-day delay arising out of the extensions under the merger agreement. But the trial court's opinion convincingly demonstrates that plaintiffs had no such contractual right that had ripened at the time the extensions were entered into:

Here, it is clear that plaintiffs have no separate contractual right to bring a direct claim, and they do not assert contractual rights under the merger agreement. First, the merger agreement specifically disclaims any persons as being third party beneficiaries to the contract. Second, any contractual shareholder right to payment of the merger consideration did not ripen until the conditions of the agreement were met. The agreement stated that Credit Suisse Group was not required to accept any shares for tender, or could extend the offer, under certain conditions-one condition of which included an extension or termination by agreement between Credit Suisse Group and DLJ. *Because Credit Suisse Group and DLJ did in fact agree to extend the tender offer period, any right to payment plaintiffs could have did not ripen until this newly negotiated period was over.* The merger agreement only became binding and mutually enforceable at the time the tendered shares ultimately were accepted for payment by Credit Suisse Group. It is at that moment in time, November 3, 2000, that the company became bound to purchase the tendered shares, making the contract mutually enforceable. *DLJ stockholders had no individual contractual right to payment until November 3, 2000, when their tendered shares were accepted for payment.* Thus, they have no contractual basis to challenge a delay in the closing of the tender offer up until November 3. *Because this is the date the tendered shares were accepted for payment, the contract was not breached and plaintiffs do not have a contractual basis to bring a direct suit.*

Moreover, no other individual right of these stockholder-plaintiffs was alleged to have been violated by the extensions.

That conclusion could have ended the case because it portended a definitive ruling that plaintiffs have no claim whatsoever on the facts alleged. But the defendants chose to argue, and the trial court chose to decide, the standing issue, which is predicated on an assertion that this claim is a derivative one asserted on behalf of the corporation, DLJ.

The Court of Chancery correctly noted that "[t]he Court will independently examine the nature of the wrong alleged and any potential relief to make its own determination of the suit's classification.... Plaintiffs' classification of the suit is not binding." The trial court's analysis was hindered, however, because it focused on the confusing concept of "special injury" as the test for determining whether a claim is derivative or direct. The trial court's premise was as follows:

In order to bring a *direct* claim, a plaintiff must have experienced some "special injury." [citing *Lipton v. News Int'l,*

514 A.2d 1075, 1079 (Del.1986)]. A special injury is a wrong that "is separate and distinct from that suffered by other shareholders, ... or a wrong involving a contractual right of a shareholder, such as the right to vote, or to assert majority control, which exists independently of any right of the corporation." [citing *Moran v. Household Int'l Inc.,* 490 A.2d 1059, 1070 (Del.Ch.1985), *aff'd* 500 A.2d 1346 (Del.1986 [1985])].

In our view, the concept of "special injury" that appears in some Supreme Court and Court of Chancery cases is not helpful to a proper analytical distinction between direct and derivative actions. We now disapprove the use of the concept of "special injury" as a tool in that analysis.

The Proper Analysis to Distinguish Between Direct and Derivative Actions

The analysis must be based solely on the following questions: Who suffered the alleged harm-the corporation or the suing stockholder individually-and who would receive the benefit of the recovery or other remedy? This simple analysis is well imbedded in our jurisprudence, but some cases have complicated it by injection of the amorphous and confusing concept of "special injury."

The Chancellor, in the very recent *Agostino* case, correctly points this out and strongly suggests that we should disavow the concept of "special injury." In a scholarly analysis of this area of the law, he also suggests that the inquiry should be whether the stockholder has demonstrated that he or she has suffered an injury that is not dependent on an injury to the corporation. In the context of a claim for breach of fiduciary duty, the Chancellor articulated the inquiry as follows: "Looking at the body of the complaint and considering the nature of the wrong alleged and the relief requested, has the plaintiff demonstrated that he or she can prevail without showing an injury to the corporation?" We believe that this approach is helpful in analyzing the first prong of the analysis: what person or entity has suffered the alleged harm? The second prong of the analysis should logically follow.

A Brief History of Our Jurisprudence

The derivative suit has been generally described as "one of the most interesting and ingenious of accountability mechanisms for large formal organizations." It enables a stockholder to bring suit on behalf of the corporation for harm done to the corporation. Because a derivative suit is being brought on behalf of the corporation, the recovery, if any, must go to the corporation. A stockholder who is directly injured, however, does retain the right to bring an individual action for injuries affecting his or her legal rights as a stockholder. Such a claim is distinct from an injury caused to the corporation alone. In such individual suits, the recovery or other relief flows directly to the stockholders, not to the corporation.

Determining whether an action is derivative or direct is sometimes difficult and has many legal consequences, some of which may have an expensive impact on the parties to the action. For example, if an action is derivative, the plaintiffs are then required to comply with the requirements of Court of Chancery Rule 23.1, that the stockholder: (a) retain ownership of the shares throughout the litigation; (b) make presuit demand on the board; and (c) obtain court approval of any settlement. Further, the recovery, if any, flows only to the corporation. The decision whether a suit is direct or derivative may be outcome-determinative. Therefore, it is necessary that a standard to distinguish such actions be clear, simple and consistently articulated and applied by our courts.

In *Elster v. American Airlines, Inc.*, the stockholder sought to enjoin the grant and exercise of stock options because they would result in a dilution of her stock personally. In *Elster,* the alleged injury was found to be derivative, not direct, because it was essentially a claim of mismanagement of corporate assets. Then came the complication in the analysis: The Court held that where the alleged injury is to both the corporation *and* to the stockholder, the stockholder must allege a "special injury" to maintain a direct action. The Court did not define "special injury," however. By implication, decisions in later cases have interpreted *Elster* to mean that a "special injury" is alleged where the wrong is inflicted upon the stockholder alone or where the stockholder complains of a wrong affecting a particular right. Examples would be a preemptive right as a stockholder, rights involving control of the corporation or a wrong affecting the stockholder, qua individual holder, and not the corporation.

In *Bokat v. Getty Oil Co.,* a stockholder of a subsidiary brought suit against the director of the parent corporation for causing the subsidiary to invest its resources wastefully, resulting in a loss to the subsidiary. The claim in *Bokat* was essentially for mismanagement of corporate assets. Therefore, the Court held that any recovery must be sought on behalf of the corporation, and the claim was, thus, found to be derivative.

In describing how a court may distinguish direct and derivative actions, the *Bokat* Court stated that a suit must be maintained derivatively if the injury falls equally upon all stockholders. Experience has shown this concept to be confusing and inaccurate. It is confusing because it appears to have been intended to address the fact that an injury to the corporation tends to diminish each share of stock equally because corporate assets or their value are diminished. In that sense, the *indirect* injury to the stockholders arising out of the harm to the corporation comes about solely by virtue of their stockholdings. It does not arise out of any independent or direct harm to the stockholders, individually. That concept is also inaccurate because a direct, individual claim of stockholders that does not depend on harm to the corporation can also fall on all stockholders equally, without the claim thereby becoming a derivative claim.

In *Lipton v. News International, Plc.,* this Court applied the "special injury" test. There, a stockholder began acquiring shares in the defendant corporation presumably to gain control of the corporation. In response, the defendant corporation agreed to an exchange of its shares with a friendly buyer. Due to the exchange and a supermajority voting requirement on certain stockholder actions, the management of the defendant corporation acquired a veto power over any change in management.

The *Lipton* Court concluded that the critical analytical issue in distinguishing direct and derivative actions is whether a "special injury" has been alleged. There, the Court found a "special injury" because the board's manipulation worked an injury upon the plaintiff-stockholder unlike the injury suffered by other stockholders. That was because the plaintiff-stockholder was actively seeking to gain control of the defendant corporation. Therefore, the Court found that the claim was direct. Ironically, the Court could have reached the same correct result by simply concluding that the manipulation directly and individually harmed the stockholders, without injuring the corporation.

In *Kramer v. Western Pacific Industries, Inc.,* this Court found to be derivative a stockholder's challenge to corporate transactions that occurred six months immediately preceding a buy-out merger. The stockholders challenged the decision by the board of directors to grant stock options and golden parachutes to management. The stockholders argued that the claim was direct because their share of the proceeds from the buy-out sale was reduced by the resources used to pay for the options and golden parachutes. Once again, our analysis was that to bring a direct action, the stockholder must allege something other than an injury resulting from a wrong to the corporation. We interpreted *Elster* to require the court to determine the nature of the action based on the "nature of the wrong alleged" and the relief that could result. That was, and is, the correct test. The claim in *Kramer* was essentially for mismanagement of corporate assets. Therefore, we found the claims to be derivative. That was the correct outcome.

In *Grimes v. Donald,* we sought to distinguish between direct and derivative actions in the context of employment agreements granted to certain officers that allegedly caused the board to abdicate its authority. Relying on the *Elster* and *Kramer* precedents that the court must look to the nature of the wrong and to whom the relief will go, we concluded that the plaintiff was not seeking to recover any damages for injury to the corporation. Rather, the plaintiff was seeking a declaration of the invalidity of the agreements on the ground that the board had abdicated its responsibility to the stockholders. Thus, based on the relief requested, we affirmed the judgment of the Court of Chancery that the plaintiff was entitled to pursue a direct action.

Grimes was followed by *Parnes v. Bally Entertainment Corp.*, which held, among other things, that the injury to the stockholders must be "independent of any injury to the corporation." As the Chancellor correctly noted in *Agostino,* neither *Grimes* nor *Parnes* applies the purported "special injury" test.

Thus, two confusing propositions have encumbered our caselaw governing the direct/derivative distinction. The "special injury" concept, applied in cases such as *Lipton,* can be confusing in identifying the nature of the action. The same is true of the proposition that stems from *Bokat*-that an action cannot be direct if all stockholders are equally affected or unless the stockholder's injury is separate and distinct from that suffered by other stockholders. The proper analysis has been and should remain that stated in *Grimes*; *Kramer* and *Parnes*. That is, a court should look to the nature of the wrong and to whom the relief should go. The stockholder's claimed direct injury must be independent of any alleged injury to the corporation. The stockholder must demonstrate that the duty breached was owed to the stockholder and that he or she can prevail without showing an injury to the corporation.

Standard to Be Applied in This Case

In this case it cannot be concluded that the complaint alleges a derivative claim. There is no derivative claim asserting injury to the corporate entity. There is no relief that would go the corporation. Accordingly, there is no basis to hold that the complaint states a derivative claim.

But, it does not necessarily follow that the complaint states a direct, individual claim. While the complaint purports to set forth a direct claim, in reality, it states no claim at all. The trial court analyzed the complaint and correctly concluded that it does not claim that the plaintiffs have any rights that have been injured. Their rights have not yet ripened. The contractual claim is nonexistent until it is ripe, and that claim will not be ripe until the terms of the merger are fulfilled, including the extensions of the closing at issue here. Therefore, there is no direct claim stated in the complaint before us.

Accordingly, the complaint was properly dismissed. But, due to the reliance on the concept of "special injury" by the Court of Chancery, the ground set forth for the dismissal is erroneous, there being no derivative claim. That error is harmless, however, because, in our view, there is no direct claim either.

Conclusion

For purposes of distinguishing between derivative and direct claims, we expressly disapprove both the concept of "special injury" and the concept that a claim is necessarily derivative if it affects all stockholders equally. In our view, the tests going forward should rest on those set forth in this opinion.

We affirm the judgment of the Court of Chancery dismissing the complaint, although on a different ground from that decided by the Court of Chancery. We reverse the dismissal with prejudice and remand this matter to the Court of Chancery to amend the order of dismissal: (a) to state that the complaint is dismissed on the ground that it does not state a claim upon which relief can be granted; and (b) that the dismissal is without prejudice.

NOTES AND QUESTIONS

1.   With this 2004 decision, the Delaware Supreme Court abandoned the concept of "special injury," which had been traditionally used to distinguish derivative suits from direct suits. Under that approach, to bring a direct suit a shareholder had to demonstrate that the alleged breach caused a special damage to his position, different from the one caused to other shareholders. The rationale was that if all shareholders have suffered the same (kind of) damage (proportionally), the damage was done to the corporation, and therefore the action should have been *derivative*, of course if all the other substantive and procedural requirements of a derivative were met. Can you see why the Court rejected this approach? Try to answer before reading the following paragraph.

2.   The answer is that there could be a damage that affects all shareholders equally, but that is not the consequence of a damage suffered by the corporation. Consider a closely held corporation with three shareholders, each of them owning one-third of the outstanding shares. Imagine that the directors, breaching their fiduciary duties, disclose falsely optimistic information that convince the shareholders to subscribe new shares at an overinflated price. You might argue that all the shareholders have suffered the same damage, but clearly this damage is not the reflection of a damage caused to the corporation. Another example could be a situation in which directors, disregarding a mandatory pre-emptive right in favor of existing shareholders, issue and sell shares to a third party: again, the corporation might have suffered no damage (in fact it is even possible that the shares were placed at a better price), but the old shareholders have been diluted. In both cases, the action could only be direct, not derivative, but the "special injury" test would indicate a derivative action because *all* shareholders have been affected, a clearly erroneous result.

3.   The Supreme Court adopts a different test, apparently simpler and almost tautological. You must consider who suffered the alleged harm: if the

corporation, a derivative action is possible; if the shareholders individually (without damage to the corporation), then only a direct action is possible. In other words, the new test shifts the focus of attention from a comparison between the positions of single shareholders (as the "special injury" test used to do), to a comparison between the corporation and the individual shareholders. Can you list pros and cons of this approach versus the previous one?

4.   The second part of the test envisioned by the Supreme Court is, in our opinion, more problematic. The justices indicate that to distinguish between direct and derivative suits you should ask, "Who would receive the benefit of the recovery?" Taken verbatim, this sentence is not very clear. The recovery should go either to the corporation or the individual shareholder depending on whether we have a derivative or direct suit. In other words, who receives the recovery is a consequence of the derivative or direct nature of the claim, it should follow the proper qualification, not be the test used to determine if an action is derivative or direct. Probably the opinion should be interpreted in the sense that if the recovery *should* be paid to the corporation to make it whole, then the action is derivative. In this respect, *see* also below, point 10.

5.   Consider, in the case, the brief but complete overview of the previous jurisprudence on this issue. Do you think that the Supreme Court distinguished the precedents, or simply overruled them based on a different interpretation of the law? If so, how would you reconcile the relative easiness with which the Supreme Court has declined to follow the precedents with the principle that, in a common law system, precedents should be binding?

6.   In this case, after having concluded that there is no derivative claim, the Court also states that there is no direct claim: the fact that the payment of the shares was delayed according to the merger agreement is perfectly lawful, and the shareholders are not entitled to any remedy for the alleged damage due to the financial value of time. Do you agree with this conclusion?

7.   Have you noticed that the corporation (Donaldson) is named as a defendant, together with the directors? The shareholders-plaintiffs, in a derivative action, sue on behalf of the corporation, they act as the "champions" of the corporation, and any benefit deriving from the litigation goes to the corporation. The corporation, however, must generally be a party in the litigation, and it is often indicated as a nominal defendant.

8.   The case briefly refers to the procedural requirements of a derivative action, among which is the "continuous ownership requirement." Although some variations across states are possible, generally this means that a shareholder, in order to bring a derivative action, must have been a beneficial owner of the shares at the time of the alleged breach and damage, and must own the shares throughout the life of the lawsuit. The rationale of this rule has probably something to do with the desire to avoid the possibility that some professional plaintiff buys shares after an alleged breach only to

bring a strike lawsuit; in order to avoid excessive, frivolous, if not blackmail litigation. Also shareholders that receive their shares by operation of law, for example in exchange for the shares of a merged corporation, satisfy the continuous ownership requirement.

9. Keep in mind that shareholders are entitled to bring derivative actions, but directors and creditors are generally not. Courts are divided with respect to convertible bondholders: holders of bonds convertible into shares, before the conversion, are in fact creditors; however they are peculiar creditors because they might become shareholders. If you were a judge or a legislature, would you allow convertible bondholders to file a derivative suit against the directors?

10. We mentioned that a distinctive feature of derivative lawsuits is that any recovery goes to the corporation, not to the shareholders acting on its behalf. There is an important possible exception to this principle, a situation in which shareholders suing derivatively can obtain the damages awarded directly. Can you imagine when this occurs? It is not easy to identify if you are not familiar with the issue, but once it is mentioned it is very obvious. The situation is when some other shareholders, possibly controlling the corporation, are also wrongdoers together with the directors. Consider, for example, a situation in which the controlling shareholder (holding 55% of the voting shares) has pushed the directors to breach their duty of loyalty toward the corporation and all shareholders, participating in the breach, in order to obtain a personal benefit to the detriment of the corporation and other minority shareholders. Now imagine that minority shareholders have successfully managed to bring a derivative suit. If the damages awarded, e.g., $200,000, would be paid by the director to the corporation, the controlling shareholder who participated in the wrongdoing would indirectly benefit proportionally from the increase in the value of the corporation's assets, clearly an illogical and unfair result. In this scenario, therefore, courts can order the damages to be paid directly to minority shareholders.

11. Derivative actions are equitable in nature; the question has been discussed, therefore, if there is a right to a jury trial in derivative actions (since in equity there is no jury). The distinction and the question are not so relevant in Delaware where the Court of Chancery—as the name suggests—is a court of equity and no jury is present. Also the distinction between remedies at law (monetary damages) and in equity (injunctions, specific performance, modification of contract. . .) is today not so relevant, as courts of general jurisdiction can grant both remedies. The question has, however, been addressed in an interesting 1970 Supreme Court case, *Ross v. Bernhard* (396 U.S. 351), which based on the Seventh Amendment of the U.S. Constitution (right to jury trial) has concluded that, at least in federal courts, if the underlying issue could be brought as an action at law by the corporation, the shareholders suing derivatively have a right to a jury trial. We have not included this case, which deals primarily with a procedural law question, but if you are curious to know more check it out!

* * *

Shareholders suing derivatively act on behalf of the corporation. The claim, in truth, belongs to the corporation. To allow shareholders to sue derivatively without giving to the corporation—and therefore to its directors—any chance to control the litigation would seem too extreme. At the same time, it might prompt excessive and futile litigation. The procedural tool used to balance the possibility of shareholders to sue derivatively and corporate control over litigation is the "demand on the board."

The rule requires that shareholders, before bringing a derivative action, must make a proper demand on the board of directors. Basically shareholders must give to directors the opportunity to decide if they want to sue or not. On the one hand, directors might be in the best position to properly evaluate the pros and cons of the litigation in the interest of the corporation, including for example the reputational consequences of a lawsuit against existing or former directors. Needless to say, often directors prefer not to bring a lawsuit against fellow directors, and even more so if the very directors that must decide whether to sue might be implicated in the litigation. Directors, in other words, can have a conflict of interest in deciding whether to sue as required by the shareholders.

Shareholders can challenge the decision of the board, following demand, not to litigate, but the board decision can be protected by the business judgment rule (*see* Chapter 6). To set aside the decision, shareholders would have to overcome the presumption that the decision has been taken in good faith, on an informed basis, and in the best interest of the corporation, for example demonstrating a breach of the duty of loyalty. As we know, it might be difficult to prevail.

On the other hand, there are some situations when the demand requirement, i.e., the rule requiring shareholders to make a demand on the board before bringing a derivative lawsuit, can be excused: shareholders can go directly to court with their derivative claim. This is the case when shareholders can prove—and they have the burden of proving it—that the demand would be futile, because it is almost certain that the board would decide not to litigate, for example in the light of a conflict of interest.

To decide when demand should be excused is not easy, as the following case illustrates. Also for this reason some jurisdictions have preferred to adopt a so-called universal demand rule: demand is never excused. In Delaware, however, demand can be excused, and shareholders often try to have the demand requirement bypassed and go directly to court (on the other hand, the directors would file a motion to dismiss based on failure to make a demand). It is quite important, therefore, to understand when courts would excuse demand. A 1984 Delaware

Supreme Court case, *Aronson v. Lewis*, has established a broadly used but not crystal-clear standard, holding among other things that the mere fact that the directors are named as possible defendants is not sufficient to consider them in conflict of interest and therefore to excuse the demand. If that was the case, it would be too easy for the shareholders-plaintiffs to always avoid demand, simply by naming the existing directors as possible defendants. The court said that in order to consider the demand futile, something more is necessary. More precisely, the court in *Aronson* determined that demand can be excused if shareholders plead particularized facts raising a reasonable doubt that a majority of directors are interested and/or not independent; or that the challenged transaction was not the product of a valid exercise of the board's business judgment. A more recent case decided in 2000 by the Delaware Supreme Court, *Brehm v. Eisner*, illustrates the standard adopted to decide if demand can be excused. The case concerns the epic litigation over the compensation and termination payout of Michael S. Ovitz as President of the Walt Disney Corporation. In short, Ovitz was hired in 1995, but was terminated without fault just over 14 months after, receiving a severance package worth approximately 140 million dollars. Shareholders were not happy, and some of them tried to sue derivatively the directors arguing that demand should be excused. (On the recent corporate story of Disney, we recommend a page-turner: "Disney War" by Pulitzer Prize winner James B. Stewart)

Before reading the case, however, it is important to understand and keep in mind one issue of litigation strategy: from the perspective of shareholders, to make a demand on the board is risky, because the board can refuse to sue, and this decision would be difficult to challenge. On the other hand, if shareholders go straight to court and argue that demand would be futile, they also are in a difficult position: they must satisfy the somehow exacting standard of *Aronson* without having, generally, access to full discovery. In a way, shareholders are caught between the rock of "demand on the board" and the hard place of demonstrating the "futility" of the demand with limited evidence. Notwithstanding this, most plaintiffs prefer to try to argue that demand should be excused. This can cause excessive litigation (and keep in mind, in this respect, that derivative suits are often attorney-driven). For this reason, the American Law Institute before, and the Model Business Corporation Act after (and several states following the MBCA), have suggested or opted for a "universal demand" requirement, mandating that shareholders, in any case, must make a demand on the board.

And, with this, let's take a look at *Brehm v. Eisner*.

BREHM V. EISNER, OVITZ, AND OTHERS

Supreme Court of Delaware
746 A.2d 244 (2000)

[. . .]

VEASEY, CHIEF JUSTICE:

In this appeal from the Court of Chancery, we agree with the holding of the Court of Chancery that the stockholder derivative Complaint was subject to dismissal for failure to set forth particularized facts creating a reasonable doubt that the director defendants were disinterested and independent or that their conduct was protected by the business judgment rule. Our affirmance, however, is in part based on a somewhat different analysis than that of the Court below or the parties. Accordingly, in the interests of justice, we reverse only to the extent of providing that one aspect of the dismissal shall be without prejudice, and we remand to the Court of Chancery to provide plaintiffs a reasonable opportunity to file a further amended complaint consistent with this opinion.

The claims before us are that: (a) the board of directors of The Walt Disney Company ("Disney") as it was constituted in 1995 (the "Old Board") breached its fiduciary duty in approving an extravagant and wasteful Employment Agreement of Michael S. Ovitz as president of Disney; (b) the Disney board of directors as it was constituted in 1996 (the "New Board") breached its fiduciary duty in agreeing to a "non-fault" termination of the Ovitz Employment Agreement, a decision that was extravagant and wasteful; and (c) the directors were not disinterested and independent.

The Complaint, consisting of 88 pages and 285 paragraphs, is a pastiche of prolix invective. It is permeated with conclusory allegations of the pleader and quotations from the media, mostly of an editorial nature (even including a cartoon). A pleader may rely on factual statements in the media as some of the "tools at hand" from which the pleader intends to derive the particularized facts necessary to comply with Chancery Rule 11(b)(3) and Chancery Rule 23.1. But many of the quotations from the media in the Complaint simply echo plaintiffs' conclusory allegations. Accordingly, they serve no purpose other than to complicate the work of reviewing courts.

This is potentially a very troubling case on the merits. On the one hand, it appears from the Complaint that: (a) the compensation and termination payout for Ovitz were exceedingly lucrative, if not luxurious, compared to Ovitz' value to the Company; and (b) the processes of the boards of directors in dealing with the approval and termination of the Ovitz Employment Agreement were casual, if not sloppy and perfunctory. On the other hand, the Complaint is so unartfully drafted that it was properly dismissed under our pleading standards for derivative suits. From what we can ferret out of this deficient pleading, the processes of the Old Board and the New Board were hardly paradigms of good corporate governance practices. Moreover, the sheer size of the payout to Ovitz, as alleged, pushes the envelope of judicial respect for the business judgment of directors in making compensation decisions. Therefore, both as to the processes of the two Boards and the waste test, this is a close case.

But our concerns about lavish executive compensation and our institutional aspirations that boards of directors of Delaware corporations live up to the highest standards of good corporate practices do not translate into a holding that these plaintiffs have set forth particularized facts excusing a pre-suit demand under our law and our pleading requirements.

This appeal presents several important issues, including: (1) the scope of review that this Court applies to an appeal from the dismissal of a derivative suit; (2) the extent to which the pleading standards required by Chancery Rule 23.1 exceed those required by Rule 8 of that Court; and (3) the scope of the business judgment rule as it interacts with the relevant pleading requirements. To some extent, the principles enunciated in this opinion restate and clarify our prior jurisprudence.

Facts

This statement of facts is taken from the Complaint. We have attempted to summarize here the essence of Plaintiffs' factual allegations on the key issues before us, disregarding the many conclusions that are not supported by factual allegations.

A.   The 1995 Ovitz Employment Agreement

By an agreement dated October 1, 1995, Disney hired Ovitz as its president. He was a long-time friend of Disney Chairman and CEO Michael Eisner. At the time, Ovitz was an important talent broker in Hollywood. Although he lacked experience managing a diversified public company, other companies with entertainment operations had been interested in hiring him for high-level executive positions. The Employment Agreement was unilaterally negotiated by Eisner and approved by the Old Board. Their judgment was that Ovitz was a valuable person to hire as president of Disney, and they agreed ultimately with Eisner's recommendation in awarding him an extraordinarily lucrative contract.

Ovitz' Employment Agreement had an initial term of five years and required that Ovitz "devote his full time and best efforts exclusively to the Company," with exceptions for volunteer work, service on the board of another company, and managing his passive investments. In return,

Disney agreed to give Ovitz a base salary of $1 million per year, a discretionary bonus, and two sets of stock options (the "A" options and the "B" options) that collectively would enable Ovitz to purchase 5 million shares of Disney common stock.

The "A" options were scheduled to vest in three annual increments of 1 million shares each, beginning on September 30, 1998 (*i.e.*, at the end of the third full year of employment) and continuing for the following two years (through September 2000). The agreement specifically provided that the "A" options would vest immediately if Disney granted Ovitz a non-fault termination of the Employment Agreement. The "B" options, consisting of 2 million shares, differed in two important respects. Although scheduled to vest annually starting in September 2001 (*i.e.*, the year *after* the last "A" option would vest), the "B" options were conditioned on Ovitz and Disney first having agreed to extend his employment beyond the five-year term of the Employment Agreement. Furthermore, Ovitz would forfeit the right to qualify for the "B" options if his initial employment term of five years ended prematurely for any reason, even if from a non-fault termination.

The Employment Agreement provided for three ways by which Ovitz' employment might end. He might serve his five years and Disney might decide against offering him a new contract. If so, Disney would owe Ovitz a $10 million termination payment. Before the end of the initial term, Disney could terminate Ovitz for "good cause" only if Ovitz committed gross negligence or malfeasance, or if Ovitz resigned voluntarily. Disney would owe Ovitz no additional compensation if it terminated him for "good cause." Termination without cause (non-fault termination) would entitle Ovitz to the present value of his remaining salary payments through September 30, 2000, a $10 million severance payment, an additional $7.5 million for each fiscal year remaining under the agreement, and the immediate vesting of the first 3 million stock options (the "A" Options).

Plaintiffs allege that the Old Board knew that Disney needed a strong second-in-command. Disney had recently made several acquisitions, and questions lingered about Eisner's health due to major heart surgery. The Complaint further alleges that "Eisner had demonstrated little or no capacity to work with important or well-known subordinate executives who wanted to position themselves to succeed him," citing the departures of Disney executives Jeffrey Katzenberg, Richard Frank, and Stephen Bollenbach as examples. Thus, the Board knew that, to increase the chance for long-term success, it had to take extra care in reviewing a decision to hire Disney's new president.

But Eisner's decision that Disney should hire Ovitz as its president was not entirely well-received. When Eisner told three members of the

Old Board in mid-August 1995 that he had decided to hire Ovitz, all three "denounced the decision." Although not entirely clear from the Complaint, the vote of the Old Board approving the Ovitz Employment Agreement two months later appears to have been unanimous. Aside from a conclusory attack that the Old Board followed Eisner's bidding, the Complaint fails to allege any particularized facts that the three directors changed their initial reactions through anything other than the typical process of further discussion and individual contemplation.

The Complaint then alleges that the Old Board failed properly to inform itself about the total costs and incentives of the Ovitz Employment Agreement, especially the severance package. This is the key allegation related to this issue on appeal. Specifically, plaintiffs allege that the Board failed to realize that the contract gave Ovitz an incentive to find a way to exit the Company via a non-fault termination as soon as possible because doing so would permit him to earn more than he could by fulfilling his contract. The Complaint alleges, however, that the Old Board had been advised by a corporate compensation expert, Graef Crystal, in connection with its decision to approve the Ovitz Employment Agreement. Two public statements by Crystal form the basis of the allegation that the Old Board failed to consider the incentives and the total cost of the severance provisions, but these statements by Crystal were not made until after Ovitz left Disney in December 1996, approximately 14 ½ months after being hired.

The first statement, published in a December 23, 1996 article in the web-based magazine *Slate,* quoted Crystal as saying, in part, "Of course, the overall costs of the package would go up sharply in the event of Ovitz's termination (*and I wish now that I'd made a spreadsheet showing just what the deal would total if Ovitz had been fired at any time*)." The second published statement appeared in an article about three weeks later in the January 13, 1997 edition of *California Law Business.* The article appears first to paraphrase Crystal: "With no one expecting failure, the sleeper clauses in Ovitz's contract seemed innocuous, Crystal says, explaining that no one added up the total cost of the severance package." The article then quotes Crystal as saying that the amount of Ovitz' severance was "shocking" and that "*[n]obody quantified this and I wish we had.*" One of the charging paragraphs of the Complaint concludes:

57. As has been conceded by Graef Crystal, the executive compensation consultant who advised the Old Board with respect to the Ovitz Employment Agreement, the Old Board *never* considered the costs that would be incurred by Disney in the event Ovitz was terminated from the Company for a reason other than cause prior to the natural expiration of the Ovtiz Employment Agreement.

Although repeated in various forms in the Complaint, these quoted admissions by Crystal constitute the extent of the factual support for the allegation that the Old Board failed properly to consider the severance elements of the agreement. This Court, however, must juxtapose these allegations with the legal presumption that the Old Board's conduct was a proper exercise of business judgment. That presumption includes the statutory protection for a board that relies in good faith on an expert advising the Board. We must decide whether plaintiffs' factual allegations, if proven, would rebut that presumption.

B. The New Board's Actions in Approving the Non-Fault Termination

Soon after Ovitz began work, problems surfaced and the situation continued to deteriorate during the first year of his employment. To support this allegation, the plaintiffs cite various media reports detailing internal complaints and providing external examples of alleged business mistakes. The Complaint uses these reports to suggest that the New Board had reason to believe that Ovitz' performance and lack of commitment met the gross negligence or malfeasance standards of the termination-for-cause provisions of the contract.

The deteriorating situation, according to the Complaint, led Ovitz to begin seeking alternative employment and to send Eisner a letter in September 1996 that the Complaint paraphrases as stating his dissatisfaction with his role and expressing his desire to leave the Company. The Complaint also admits that Ovitz would not actually resign before negotiating a non-fault severance agreement because he did not want to jeopardize his rights to a lucrative severance in the form of a "non-fault termination" under the terms of the 1995 Employment Agreement.

On December 11, 1996, Eisner and Ovitz agreed to arrange for Ovitz to leave Disney on the non-fault basis provided for in the 1995 Employment Agreement. Eisner then "caused" the New Board "to rubber-stamp his decision (by 'mutual consent')." This decision was implemented by a December 27, 1996 letter to Ovitz from defendant Sanford M. Litvack, an officer and director of Disney. That letter stated:

This will confirm the terms of your agreement with the Company as follows:

1. The Term of your employment under your existing Employment Agreement with The Walt Disney Company will end at the close of business today. Consequently, your signature confirms the end of your service as an officer, and your resignation as a director, of the Company and its affiliates.

2.   This letter will for all purposes of the Employment Agreement be treated as a "Non-Fault Termination." By our mutual agreement, the total amount payable to you under your Employment Agreement, including the amount payable under Section 11(c) in the event of a "Non-Fault Termination," is $38,888,230.77, net of withholding required by law or authorized by you. By your signature on this letter, you acknowledge receipt of all but $1,000,000 of such amount. Pursuant to our mutual agreement, this will confirm that payment of the $1,000,000 balance has been deferred until February 5, 1997, pending final settlement of accounts.

3.   This letter will further confirm that the option to purchase 3,000,000 shares of the Company's Common Stock granted to you pursuant to Option A described in your Employment Agreement will vest as of today and will expire in accordance with its terms on September 30, 2002.

Although the non-fault termination left Ovitz with what essentially was a very lucrative severance agreement, it is important to note that Ovitz and Disney had negotiated for that severance payment at the time they initially contracted in 1995, and in the end the payout to Ovitz did not exceed the 1995 contractual benefits. Consequently, Ovitz received the $10 million termination payment, $7.5 million for part of the fiscal year remaining under the agreement and the immediate vesting of the 3 million stock options (the "A" options). As a result of his termination Ovitz would not receive the 2 million "B" options that he would have been entitled to if he had completed the full term of the Employment Agreement and if his contract were renewed.

The Complaint charges the New Board with waste, computing the value of the severance package agreed to by the Board at over $140 million, consisting of cash payments of about $39 million and the value of the immediately vesting "A" options of over $101 million. The Complaint quotes Crystal, the Old Board's expert, as saying in January 1997 that Ovitz' severance package was a "shocking amount of severance."

The allegation of waste is based on the inference most favorable to plaintiffs that Disney owed Ovitz nothing, either because he had resigned (*de facto*) or because he was unarguably subject to firing for cause. These allegations must be juxtaposed with the presumption that the New Board exercised its business judgment in deciding how to resolve the potentially litigable issues of whether Ovitz had actually resigned or had definitely breached his contract. We must decide whether plaintiffs' factual allegations, if proven, would rebut that presumption.

Scope of Review

Certain dicta in our jurisprudence suggest that this Court will review under a deferential abuse of discretion standard a decision of the Court of

Chancery on a Rule 23.1 motion to dismiss a derivative suit. These statements, apparently beginning in 1984 in *Aronson v. Lewis,* state that the Court of Chancery's decision is discretionary in determining whether the allegations of the complaint support the contention that pre-suit demand is excused.

Our view is that in determining demand futility the Court of Chancery *in the proper exercise of its discretion* must decide whether, under the particularized facts alleged, a reasonable doubt is created that: (1) the directors are disinterested and independent [or] (2) the challenged transaction was otherwise the product of a valid exercise of business judgment.

By implication, therefore, these dicta would suggest that our review is deferential, limited to a determination of whether the Court of Chancery abused its discretion. Indeed, all parties to this appeal agree that our review is for abuse of discretion.

The view we express today, however, is designed to make clear that our review of decisions of the Court of Chancery applying Rule 23.1 is *de novo* and plenary. [. . .]

Therefore, our scope of review must be *de novo.* To the extent *Aronson* and its progeny contain dicta expressing or suggesting an abuse of discretion scope of review, that language is overruled.[. . .]

Pleading Requirements in Derivative Suits

Pleadings in derivative suits are governed by Chancery Rule 23.1, just as pleadings alleging fraud are governed by Chancery Rule 9(b). Those pleadings must comply with stringent requirements of factual particularity that differ substantially from the permissive notice pleadings governed solely by Chancery Rule 8(a). Rule 23.1 is not satisfied by conclusory statements or mere notice pleading. On the other hand, the pleader is not required to plead evidence. What the pleader must set forth are particularized factual statements that are essential to the claim. Such facts are sometimes referred to as "ultimate facts," "principal facts" or "elemental facts." Nevertheless, the particularized factual statements that are required to comply with the Rule 23.1 pleading rules must also comply with the mandate of Chancery Rule 8(e) that they be "simple, concise and direct." A prolix complaint larded with conclusory language, like the Complaint here, does not comply with these fundamental pleading mandates.

Chancery Rule 23.1 requires, in part, that the plaintiff must allege with particularity facts raising a reasonable doubt that the corporate action being questioned was properly the product of business judgment. The rationale of Rule 23.1 is two-fold. On the one hand, it would allow a plaintiff to proceed with discovery and trial if the plaintiff complies with this rule and can articulate a reasonable basis to be entrusted with a claim that belongs to the corporation. On the other hand, the rule does not permit a stockholder to cause the corporation to expend money and resources in discovery and trial in the stockholder's quixotic pursuit of a purported corporate claim based solely on conclusions, opinions or speculation. As we stated in *Grimes v. Donald:*

The demand requirement serves a salutary purpose. First, by requiring exhaustion of intra-corporate remedies, the demand requirement invokes a species of alternative dispute resolution procedure which might avoid litigation altogether. Second, if litigation is beneficial, the corporation can control the proceedings. Third, if demand is excused or wrongfully refused, the stockholder will normally control the proceedings.

The jurisprudence of *Aronson* and its progeny is designed to create a balanced environment which will: (1) on the one hand, deter costly, baseless suits by creating a screening mechanism to eliminate claims where there is only a suspicion expressed solely in conclusory terms; and (2) on the other hand, permit suit by a stockholder who is able to articulate particularized facts showing that there is a reasonable doubt either that (a) a majority of the board is independent for purposes of responding to the demand, or (b) the underlying transaction is protected by the business judgment rule.

[. . .]

Independence of the Disney Board

The test of demand futility is a two-fold test under *Aronson* and its progeny. The first prong of the futility rubric is "whether, under the particularized facts alleged, a reasonable doubt is created that . . . the directors are disinterested and independent." The second prong is whether the pleading creates a reasonable doubt that "the challenged transaction was otherwise the product of a valid exercise of business judgment." These prongs are in the disjunctive. Therefore, if either prong is satisfied, demand is excused.

In this case, the issues of disinterestedness and independence involved in the first prong of *Aronson* are whether a majority of the New Board, which presumably was in office when plaintiffs filed this action, was disinterested and independent. That is, were they incapable, due to personal interest or domination and control, of objectively evaluating a demand, if made, that the Board assert the corporation's claims that are raised by plaintiffs or otherwise remedy the alleged injury? This rule is premised on the principle that a claim of the corporation should be evaluated by the board of directors to determine if pursuit of the claim is in the corporation's best interests. That is the analysis the Court of

Chancery brought to bear on the matter, and it is that analysis we now examine to the extent necessary for appropriate appellate review.

The facts supporting plaintiffs' claim that the New Board was not disinterested or independent turn on plaintiffs' central allegation that a majority of the Board was beholden to Eisner. It is not alleged that they were beholden to Ovitz. Plaintiffs' theory is that Eisner was advancing Ovitz' interests primarily because a lavish contract for Ovtiz would redound to Eisner's benefit since Eisner would thereby gain in his quest to have his own compensation increased lavishly. This theory appears to be in the nature of the old maxim that a "high tide floats all boats." But, in the end, this theory is not supported by well-pleaded facts, only conclusory allegations. Moreover, the Court of Chancery found that these allegations were illogical and counterintuitive:

> Plaintiffs' allegation that Eisner was interested in maximizing his compensation at the expense of Disney and its shareholders cannot reasonably be inferred from the facts alleged in Plaintiffs' amended complaint. At all times material to this litigation, Eisner owned several million options to purchase Disney stock. Therefore, it would not be in Eisner's economic interest to cause the Company to issue millions of additional options unnecessarily and at considerable cost. Such a gesture would not, as Plaintiffs suggest, "maximize" Eisner's own compensation package. Rather, it would dilute the value of Eisner's own very substantial holdings. Even if the impact on Eisner's option value were relatively small, such a large compensation package would, and did, draw largely negative attention to Eisner's own performance and compensation. Accordingly, no reasonable doubt can exist as to Eisner's disinterest in the approval of the Employment Agreement, as a matter of law. Similarly, the Plaintiffs have not demonstrated a reasonable doubt that Eisner was disinterested in granting Ovitz a Non-Fault Termination, thus allowing Ovitz to receive substantial severance benefits under the terms of the Employment Agreement. Nothing alleged by Plaintiffs generates a reasonable inference that Eisner would benefit personally from allowing Ovitz to leave Disney without good cause.

The Court of Chancery held that "no reasonable doubt can exist as to Eisner's disinterest in the approval of the Employment Agreement, as a matter of law," and similarly that plaintiffs "have not demonstrated a reasonable doubt that Eisner was disinterested in granting Ovitz a Non-Fault Termination." Plaintiffs challenge this conclusion, but we agree with the Court of Chancery and we affirm that holding.

The Complaint then proceeds to detail the various associations that each member of the New Board had with Eisner. In an alternative holding, the Court of Chancery proceeded meticulously to analyze each director's ties to Eisner to see if they could have exercised business judgment independent of Eisner. Because we hold that the Complaint fails to create a reasonable doubt that Eisner was disinterested in the Ovitz Employment Agreement, we need not reach or comment on the analysis of the Court of Chancery on the independence of the other directors for this purpose.

In this case, therefore, that part of plaintiffs' Complaint raising the first prong of *Aronson,* even though not pressed by plaintiffs in this Court, has been dismissed with prejudice. Our affirmance of that dismissal is final and dispositive of the first prong of *Aronson.* We now turn to the primary issues in this case that implicate the second prong of *Aronson:* whether the Complaint sets forth particularized facts creating a reasonable doubt that the decisions of the Old Board and the New Board were protected by the business judgment rule.

Analytical Framework for the Informational Component of Directorial Decision-making

Plaintiffs claim that the Court of Chancery erred when it concluded that a board of directors is "not required to be informed of every fact, but rather is required to be reasonably informed." Applying that conclusion, the Court of Chancery held that the Complaint did not create a reasonable doubt that the Old Board had satisfied the requisite informational component when it approved the Ovitz contract in 1995. In effect, Plaintiffs argue that being "reasonably informed" is too lax a standard to satisfy Delaware's legal test for the informational component of board decisions. They contend that the Disney directors on the Old Board did not avail themselves of all material information reasonably available in approving Ovitz' 1995 contract, and thereby violated their fiduciary duty of care.

The "reasonably informed" language used by the Court of Chancery here may have been a short-hand attempt to paraphrase the Delaware jurisprudence that, in making business decisions, directors must consider all material information reasonably available, and that the directors' process is actionable only if grossly negligent. The question is whether the trial court's formulation is consistent with our objective test of reasonableness, the test of materiality and concepts of gross negligence. We agree with the Court of Chancery that the standard for judging the informational component of the directors' decision-making does not mean that the Board must be informed of *every* fact. The Board is responsible for considering only *material* facts that are *reasonably available,* not those that are immaterial or out of the Board's reasonable reach.

We conclude that the formulation of the due care test by the Court of Chancery in this case, while not necessarily inconsistent with our traditional formulation, was too cryptically stated to be a helpful precedent for future cases. Pre-suit demand will be excused in a derivative suit only if the Court of Chancery in the first instance, and this Court in its *de novo* review, conclude that the particularized facts in the complaint create a reasonable doubt that the informational component of the directors' decision-making process, *measured by concepts of gross negligence,* included consideration of all material information reasonably available. Thus, we now apply this analytical framework to the particularized facts pleaded, juxtaposed with the presumption of regularity of the Board's process.

[On these bases, the court examines the conduct of the directors in approving the compensation package and dealing with the termination of Ovitz, and finds that there is no reasonable ground to believe that the board violated procedural or substantive due care, or committed waste].

Conclusion

One can understand why Disney stockholders would be upset with such an extraordinarily lucrative compensation agreement and termination payout awarded a company president who served for only a little over a year and who underperformed to the extent alleged. That said, there is a very large—though not insurmountable—burden on stockholders who believe they should pursue the remedy of a derivative suit instead of selling their stock or seeking to reform or oust these directors from office.

Delaware has pleading rules and an extensive judicial gloss on those rules that must be met in order for a stockholder to pursue the derivative remedy. Sound policy supports these rules, as we have noted. This Complaint, which is a blunderbuss of a mostly conclusory pleading, does not meet that burden, and it was properly dismissed.

[. . .]

NOTES AND QUESTIONS

1. Before considering the specific issues concerning the demand requirement, it should be noted that this case offers an interesting discussion of the possible structure of a compensation agreement, in particular in case of termination, probably a structure that it would not be particularly advisable to adopt after this litigation. We focus here on the procedural aspects of derivative litigation, it is interesting however also to briefly consider the substance of the above decision, which is very telling about fiduciary duties and the reluctance of Delaware courts to hold directors liable. In an interesting recent article, Professor Gevurtz has compared the Disney litigation above with an important German decision in the so-called Mannesmann case. We report parts of his insightful analysis:

"Delaware courts exonerated directors of The Walt Disney Company from liability for damages—despite the directors having paid Michael Ovitz around $130 million in exchange for a year accomplishing little as the number two executive at Disney. At about the same time, the German Federal Supreme Court held that directors of the German company, Mannesmann AG, breached their duty to the company when they awarded a bonus of approximately $17 million to the outgoing CEO—whose actions apparently played an important role in gaining over $50 billion for the Mannesmann shareholders. As a result, the Mannesmann directors ended up paying a multi-million euros settlement for having rewarded success, while their counterparts at Disney avoided liability for paying eight times as much to reward failure. [. . .]. An evident divergence between Delaware law, as illustrated by Disney, and German law, as illustrated by Mannesmann, lies in the degree of deference that the Delaware and the German courts give to directors under the business judgment rule. The factual situations in the two cases are, of course, distinguishable. Nevertheless, the skepticism with which the German court in Mannesmann dissects the question of whether paying the challenged bonus could produce any offsetting advantage for the company seems at odds with the deferential way in which the Delaware courts accept the board's actions in Disney. Both Disney and Mannesmann pay homage to the so-called business judgment rule—the idea that courts should be reticent to second guess the business decisions of disinterested directors. [. . .] Despite its recognition of the business judgment rule, however, the court in Mannesmann held that the directors breached their duty to the corporation in approving the bonus. The court based this holding on the assertion that the bonus could yield no advantage for the company. Essentially, this is the same as a waste claim in the United States." (Franklin A. Gevurtz, *Disney in a Comparative Light*, 55 AM. J. COMP. L. 453 (2007))

This case is a perfect illustration of what we explained in Chapter 6 concerning the substantive scope of fiduciary duty and the business judgment rule in different countries: the idea is there and it is fairly similar in the abstract; the way in which courts interpret the degree of deference due to directors' decisions varies.

2.   The Delaware Supreme Court has quite clearly identified the standard that courts need to apply to decide demand futility: a court must "decide whether, under the particularized facts alleged, a reasonable doubt is created that: (1) the directors are disinterested and independent [or] (2) the challenged transaction was otherwise the product of a valid exercise of business judgment." First of all, notice that the complaint needs to allege "particularized facts": this is also a somehow flexible standard, but it means that the allegations must be sufficiently precise, detailed, and specific. In this case, the court was quite unhappy with the complaint, considering it prolix and vague: the decision contains a quite strong "scolding" of the lawyers.

3.   The first prong of the test concerns the fact that demand can be excused if directors are not disinterested. We suggest considering two aspects

of this element: on the one hand, directors should have been disinterested from the alleged breach of fiduciary duties. The core of the argument of the plaintiff in our case is that the CEO (Eisner) had an interest in an outrageously high compensation for the President (Ovitz), because he thought that this would help also him to obtain a higher compensation; and that the other directors were beholden to the CEO. This argument is considered too weak, speculative, and in any case not sustained by well-pleaded facts. On the other hand, directors can also be non-independent because they would likely be defendants in the lawsuit and possibly liable. In this respect, as we briefly mentioned above, courts tend to exclude that merely naming the existing directors as possible defendants in the lawsuit is sufficient to make them non-independent and excuse demand (otherwise it would be too easy for a plaintiff to avoid demand). There might be situations, however, in which the likelihood of liability is so significant, and alleged with particularized facts, that it is clear that directors cannot serenely decide on the lawsuit. Observe how in this perspective there is a connection between the substantive decision or conduct challenged, and the ability of the directors to independently decide whether to sue.

4.   The second prong of the test tells us that demand can be excused if there is a doubt that the challenged transaction was the product of business judgment. Shareholders wishing to sue derivatively and to have demand excused, in other words, must somehow anticipate the merits of their complaint to convince the court that there is a reasonable possibility that they will prevail. The concept, not profoundly different from the one used to obtain temporary injunctions, was rendered by the Romans with a cool Latin expression: "*fumus boni iuris*," or "smoke of good law", meaning the likelihood of a grouded claim. In the case above, as we have seen, Delaware's judges show the usual (and desirable) deference to business decisions, concluding that the compensation package granted to Ovitz, while very high and probably not advisable, did not amount to a violation of directors' fiduciary duties. We have already mentioned, and we want to stress, that in case shareholders make a demand on the board, and the board decides not to sue, this decision itself can be challenged in court, but it is protected by the business judgment rule. This means, in our opinion, that in this situation directors can prevail (and see their decision not to litigate upheld in court) not only when the challenged transaction appears a valid exercise of business judgment, but also when, for other possible reasons, they reasonably decide not to sue. One example might be helpful: imagine a situation in which shareholders challenge a transaction that appears a breach of the duty of care, and there is a 70% chance (estimated by expert litigators) to prevail and obtain an award of damages for $200,000; a 30% change to lose and have to pay $60,000, and in any case the lawsuit would determine additional costs estimated at $100,000 and a negative impact on the corporation in terms of reputation and a possible consequent decline in share prices, that would cost the corporation approximately $70,000. The value of this litigation is, for the corporation, negative: $140,000 − $18,000 − $100,000 − $70,000 = −$48,000.

In this case, notwithstanding the likelihood to prevail, it would make perfect sense for the corporation (i.e., the directors) not to sue.

5.   From a comparative perspective, contrast this case and especially what we explained above in point 4, with the 1997 decision of the German Federal Court of Justice ARAG/Garmenbeck examined in Chapter 6. And keep in mind Professor Gevurtz's observations on the Mannesmann litigation in Germany reported above in Note 1. What are the differences, if any, between German and American Law with respect to directors' discretion in deciding to sue directors and executives?

* * *

Let's imagine that the shareholders manage to initiate the derivative suit, for example arguing successfully that demand would have been futile. Is there something, at this point, that directors can do if they come to the conclusion that the litigation is potentially very disruptive and damaging for the corporation, and its costs exceed the possible benefits?

One legal device envisioned by corporate law attorneys is the so-called "special litigation committee" (or "SLC"). Directors can appoint a special committee, composed of individuals completely independent from the litigation (sometimes elected to the board after the litigation has commenced specifically for the purpose of serving on the litigation committee) to decide on the opportunity to file a motion to dismiss or otherwise settle the litigation. The decision to voluntarily dismiss or settle a derivative action, under both Federal Rules of Civil Procedure and Delaware Chancery Rules, must be approved by the court. If the committee is truly independent and in good faith and its conclusions are well supported, the court should exercise its own independent business judgment in determining whether the motion should be granted. More precisely, the decision to dismiss or settle of the SLC is upheld by the courts if two conditions are met: (1) the corporation proves that the members of the SLC were independent, in good faith, and conducted a reasonable investigation; and (2) the court determines, exercising its own independent judgment, that the motion to discontinue the litigation should be granted in the light of the best interest of the corporation. In many ways, this is a kind of "watered down" version of the business judgment rule, one in which it is the corporation that has the burden of proving the independence and care of the SLC, and still the court can second-guess the merits of the decision. In this respect it can be argued that the court is allowed more latitude in reviewing the decision of the directors (to dismiss the action) than generally with respect to other business decisions, presumably for two reasons: the delicacy of the matter and the specter of a conflict of interest of directors, or at least of some reciprocal back-scratching with the fellow directors sued; and the fact that judges are likely to be more well-equipped to evaluate a decision to dismiss a lawsuit, rather than other business decisions. Two interesting cases discussing the special litigation committee, which can be suggested as optional readings, are *Zapata v. Maldonado*, 430 A.2d 779 (1981), and *Thompson v. Scientific Atlanta*, 275 Ga.App. 680 (2005). They offer an example of how the special litigation committee should work.

To sum up what we have discussed, here's a diagram that represents the different alternatives that might occur in a derivative action:

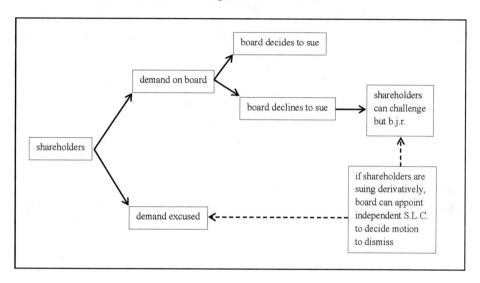

* * *

When we shift our focus on derivative actions in the U.K., the picture emerging is very different than the one in the U.S. Although these actions were recognized as early as the nineteenth century at common law, they were hardly ever used, and even when they were brought, rarely supported by the court. The following extract discusses the current U.K. rules (which since October 2007 are governed by statute), and the reasons why these actions are so rare. But before that we should keep in mind a couple of fundamental differences between the U.S. and U.K., which have a bearing on derivative actions. These relate to attorney's fees and the U.K. loser pays principle (discussed in more detail below), which means that a shareholder in the U.K. who decides to bring a derivative claim must not only fund the action (unless third party funding can be obtained or the court orders the company to indemnify the shareholder against liability for those costs), but also bears the risk of being ordered to pay the defendant directors' costs (subject to the possibility of obtaining an indemnity from the company). This is dissimilar to the position in the U.S., where parties usually bear their own costs. With respect to attorney's fees, whereas these are specifically provided for in the Federal Rules of Civil Procedure and state laws for bringing and continuing an action, in the U.K. the Companies Act 2006 is silent on these as are the

U.K.'s civil procedure rules dealing with group litigation order (a procedure that allows for consolidation of claims and which contains a specific rule for derivative claims). In addition to the above disincentives for a shareholder contemplating a derivative claim in the U.K., under the Companies Act 2006, the shareholder in a derivative claim does not seek relief from directors of the company for itself directly, rather on behalf of the company (very much like in the U.S.), but the English courts, when considering whether to continue the claim, must take into account the possibility 'that the member could pursue [the claim] in his own right rather than on behalf of the company' (see below).

ARAD REISBERG, SHADOWS OF THE PAST AND BACK TO THE FUTURE: PART 11 OF THE UK COMPANIES ACT 2006 (IN) ACTION[1]

2/3 European Company and Financial Law Review 219 (2009)

I.   Introduction

On 1 October 2007 Part 11 (sections 260–269) of the UK Companies Act 2006 ("the Act") came into force. The genesis of the current law in this area can be traced back to the period between 1995 and 1997 when the English Law Commission conducted an extensive inquiry into shareholder remedies. This inquiry led to proposed reforms, which have been further appraised and amplified through the deliberations of the Company Law Review Steering Group between 1998 and 2001. It was then endorsed by the Government and finally implemented by the Companies Act 2006, Part 11, not before being modified at almost each stage of its passage. Following developments in numerous jurisdictions, these provisions provide a statutory basis for the first time for the former common law derivative action with some important changes. The Act provides shareholders with a right to bring a derivative claim against directors on behalf of a company in relation to certain acts or omissions by directors. Any shareholders may bring such a claim provided the court gives it permission. Shareholders may even bring a claim in respect of conduct that occurred before they became a shareholder.

[. . .]

II.   Outline of the new regime

Section 260(1) of the Act defines a derivative claim as proceedings brought by a member of a company and seeking relief on behalf of that company in respect of a cause of action vested in it. Section 260(3) provides that a shareholder may only bring a derivative claim in respect of a cause of action arising from an actual or proposed act or omission involving: negligence; default; breach of trust; or breach of duty, by a

---

[1]   Footnotes and paragraphs numbers omitted.

director of the company. Section 260(3) provides, however, that the cause of action can be against the director or another person (third party) or both. Thus a derivative claim may now be brought, by way of example, against a third party who dishonestly assists a director's breach of fiduciary duty or one who knowingly receives property in breach of a fiduciary duty.

The starting point for considering the statutory derivative claims is through the interaction with the new sections on directors' duties in Part 10 of the Act. Section 170, provides that directors' general duties are owed to the company rather than to individual members. It follows that only the company can enforce them. In line with this, the sections in Part 11 do not formulate a substantive rule to replace the rule in *Foss*, but rather a new procedure for bringing actions based on the existing rules. In other words, the sections *do not* seek to overturn these well-established principles. Instead, they implement the recommendation of the Law Commission that there should be a 'new derivative procedure with more modern, flexible, and accessible criteria for determining whether a shareholder can pursue an action'. In addition to the provisions of Pt 11, Ch.1 of the Act, the Civil Procedure Rules (CPR) have been amended to supplement the Act. CPR, rr.19.9, 19.9A–19.9F deal with derivative claims and a new Practice Direction has been introduced. Once proceedings have been issued the applicant shareholder must apply to the court for permission to continue the claim. The shareholder must notify the company of the proceedings and the application. Notification to the company at this stage is not service and the company is not a party to the permission application. It must, however, be a named defendant in the proceedings in order formally to be a party to the action and be bound by any judgment.

The permission application is a two-stage procedure

Stage one: A prima facie case

Initially a paper hearing will take place where the court will be required to consider the shareholder's evidence. The onus is on the shareholder to demonstrate to the court that it has a prima facie case for permission to continue a derivative claim. If it does not establish a prima facie case then the court will dismiss the application. If the application is dismissed at this stage, the applicant may request the court to reconsider its decision at an oral hearing, although no new evidence will be allowed at this hearing (from the shareholder or the company). The Practice Direction 19C Derivative Claims provides that this stage of the application (whether a paper hearing or a paper and then an oral hearing) will normally be decided <u>without</u> submissions from the company.

Stage two: The permission hearing

If the court does not dismiss the application at stage one, the application will then proceed to a full permission hearing and the court may order the company to provide evidence at this stage. In practice, it is unlikely that the company would not participate at this stage since it will be evidence from the company that is likely to determine whether the derivative claim should proceed. S. 263(2) sets out the factors that the court will consider before deciding whether to grant permission to continue the claim. The court must dismiss the permission application if:

- a person acting in accordance with s.172 (duty to promote the success of the company) would not seek to continue the claim;

- the complaint arises from an act or omission yet to occur, that has been authorised by the company; or where the complaint arises from an act or omission that has occurred, but was authorised before it occurred, or has been ratified since it occurred.

Under s. 263(3) the court must also take into account the following:

- whether the member is acting in good faith;

- the importance a director is likely to attach to pursuing the action;

- whether authorisation or ratification would be likely to occur;

- whether the company has decided not to pursue the claim; and

- whether the shareholder could pursue the action in his own right.

S.263(4) provides further that the court shall have particular regard (but note: not 'must') to the view of members who have no personal interest in the derivative claim.

The full hearing at Stage two is likely to be where many derivative claims fail. The court has considerable discretion, as can be seen from the factors listed above. Where the court dismisses the permission application it may order the shareholder to pay the costs the company has incurred in relation to the hearing. However, this is by no means certain and, in any event, the company's costs in investigating the underlying claim are unlikely to be recoverable from the shareholder. CPR, r.19.9E makes clear that the court may order the company to indemnify the claimant against liability for costs incurred in the permission application or in the derivative claim or both. Therefore, it is possible that the company will be ordered to pay the shareholder's costs in making the application for permission, although this is unlikely where the application has failed.

If the court grants permission to continue a derivative claim, this permission may be conditional on terms including that a claim will not be settled, discontinued or compromised without the court's consent. On the basis that it is the company that ought to benefit from the derivative claim, as noted above, CPR, r.19.9E provides that the court may also order the company to indemnify the shareholder against its liability for costs incurred in the underlying proceedings. Under the former regime the court exercised such power sparingly, requiring the shareholder to prove that such an indemnity was necessary.

III. The new derivative claim procedure
(in)action: shadows from the past?

As I have explained elsewhere recently, it is seriously open to question whether the preference in Part 11 of the Companies Act 2006 for detailed and largely inaccessible criteria supported by wide discretion provided to the judiciary strikes the right balance between managerial freedom and investor protection. This writer believes that the Government favoured the balance being in favour of management, since its clear policy is that derivative claims should be 'exceptional', and is subject to 'tight judicial control at all stages', however permissive the language of the procedure might appear to some commentators. There is no denying that the new statutory restatement of the derivative claim broadens the circumstances in which, at least in theory, it may be brought. In practice, however, it may be doubted whether this will result in any significant extension of the circumstances in which such claims may be expected. Concerns that this will fuel the development of US-style litigation are probably quite far off the mark. A number of reasons combined to ensure that this may not prove to be the case. Courts will continue to retain a wide discretion over whether a derivative claim may proceed. Litigants must therefore still face up to the traditional suspicion of the English courts towards such claims, albeit this time courts are 'armed' with a very restrictive legislation to 'justify' their attitudes. The early case law on the new procedure considered below indeed suggests this is already happening. Secondly, permission to continue a derivative claim will in any event be refused in respect of a claim against a director based upon an act or omission that could be authorised or ratified by the company. In practice, this is likely to exclude the possibility of such claims in respect of ordinary negligence by directors. Finally, and most importantly, the practicalities of financing shareholder litigation will remain a major obstacle. There is nothing in the new procedure that will convince a rational shareholder he should be better off litigating the case on behalf of the company rather than selling his shares. Regrettably, the common law position on costs of derivative claims has not changed. Costs and fees rules need to be re-evaluated if any real change is to occur.

[. . .]

NOTES AND QUESTIONS

1.   The above extensive criteria under the two-stage permission application to continue a derivative claim illustrate well how procedurally and substantively English law has developed to provide disincentives to prospective plaintiffs. Imagine a bona fide shareholder who genuinely contemplates taking an action and reads through this (non-exhaustive, it should be stressed) list. It is no surprise, as the U.K. Law Commission itself admits (Consultation Paper, para 16.43), that the "list may appear to be a set of hurdles which applicants have to overcome and which would deter them. It could easily be seen as maintaining a policy of not favoring derivative actions and as a signal of an over-restrictive approach to shareholders which would over-deter them." Faced with these complexities, the average shareholder will often give up in despair already at this early stage.

2.   The exacting criteria listed above may produce, as did the case law on the common law derivative action, over-cautious judicial decisions (the court is reminded that it 'must' dismiss the application no less than five times in sections 261–264). It could be seen as constraining the flexible exercise of discretion which the Law Commission was anxious to encourage, in that the inclusion of these and the omission of other criteria may suggest that these are the only relevant ones or the most important.

3.   Given the above practical difficulties, do you think there is any value in having a statutory derivative claim procedure under English law at all? What would be lost if this procedure was not available to shareholders?

4.   Do you think U.K. judges should follow U.S. judges and be more willing to allow derivative actions and hence intervene in corporate affairs? If so, what do you think would be the price of such an approach?

* * *

DERIVATIVE SUITS IN CIVIL LAW EUROPEAN SYSTEMS

As mentioned in the Introduction, several continental European systems belonging to the civil law tradition have adopted, more or less recently, rules that might be considered the equivalent of the common-law-style derivative suits. Even if with meaningful differences, these rules share with common-law derivative suits the goal of allowing shareholders "to take matters into their own hands," and sue directors on behalf of the corporation.

Italian law offers, in this perspective, an illustrative example. You might remember that in Chapter 5, discussing corporate governance, but also in other parts of this book, we have observed how in civil law countries, where the ownership structure also of listed corporations is more concentrated or at least there are "stronger" owners and "weaker" managers, the shareholders' meeting often has more powers *vis-à-vis* the board of directors when compared to common law systems. This basic difference can also be seen in the area of directors' liability, specifically considering Italian law as a representative example of these jurisdictions. As a general rule, under Italian law, the decision to sue directors is entrusted to the shareholders' meeting, not to the directors (as any other lawsuit would be). This approach makes a lot of sense, because it should resolve the conflict of interest that directors can have if they have to sue themselves or their fellow directors. But, there is a but . . . In a system with large shareholders often holding a controlling stake in the corporation, the real conflict of interest is between controlling and minority shareholders. Controlling shareholders are often directors themselves, or in any case directors have a strong allegiance to them: block holders appoint and remove directors, determine their compensation, and often give more or less strict directions. In practice, this means that the controlling shareholders who have appointed the directors will rarely sue them, especially if the alleged directors' breach was damaging for minority shareholders but not for controlling shareholders.

To balance this possible agency problem, the Italian Civil Code allows also a qualified minority to sue derivatively. Consider the following Article 2393-*bis*:

"1. Shareholders representing at least one-fifth of the outstanding shares or the different percentage established in the bylaws, not to exceed one-third, can sue the directors for damages caused to the corporation.

2. In publicly held corporations, shareholders representing at least 2.5% of the outstanding shares, or the lower threshold established in the bylaws, can exercise the action regulated by the previous paragraph.

3. The corporation must be served of process and can be a party in the lawsuit. The complaint must be notified also to the president of the supervisory board.

4. The shareholders intending to sue must appoint, through a majority vote, one or more lead plaintiffs.

5. In case of victory of the shareholders, the corporation reimburses the plaintiffs for the expenses of the litigation that the judge has not ordered the losing defendants to pay or that is not possible to recuperate from them.

6. The shareholders that have promoted the litigation can dismiss or settle the dispute; any compensation for the dismissal or settling of the dispute should be paid to the corporation."

It should be noted that the corporation can dismiss or settle the litigation; however, the decision must be taken by the shareholders' meeting. Needless to say, if the controlling shareholder, holding the majority of the votes, would be able to dismiss or settle the dispute notwithstanding the opposition of the minority that brought the derivative suit, the entire provision allowing the minority to bring a derivative suit would be nugatory. Article 2393 of the Italian Civil Code therefore provides that the shareholders' meeting resolution approving the dismissal or settlement of the lawsuit is only valid if the proposal does not receive a percentage of "no" votes equal to the percentage required to bring the derivative lawsuit (20% of the capital in closely held corporations and 2.5% in listed ones, unless the bylaws provide for a different threshold within the limits set by the statute). This means that if the minority shareholder(s) who brought the lawsuit, for example holding 6% in a listed corporation, oppose dismissal or settlement, the controlling shareholder (or the directors) will not be able to overrule them and block the litigation.

NOTES AND QUESTIONS

1. Based on this brief information about the Italian system, compare it to the American one considered above. Which system do you find more effective? Which system do you think achieves the best balance between the need to protect minority shareholders against negligent or unfaithful directors and avoiding excessive and frivolous litigation? Or would you rather say that each system is better suited to the business scenario of the different countries, especially with respect to different ownership structures?

2. As we mentioned, there is no demand requirement in the Italian system and, for that matter, generally in civil law systems. The power to bring a derivative lawsuit is given to qualified minorities. What do you think are the advantages and disadvantages of this approach? Is it preferable to allow only qualified minorities to bring a derivative lawsuit, as in the Italian system, or is it preferable to allow each shareholder, independently from the percentage of shares owned, to sue?

3. The absence of a formal demand requirement, however, does not prevent shareholders from informally "suggesting" the lawsuit to directors. This suggestion can be particularly persuasive if made by institutional investors or other qualified minorities holding enough shares to sue derivatively. Do you think that directors should take this possibility into account when deciding whether to sue or not?

4. Comparing the US and the Italian approach (but, as we will see, other jurisdictions follow the Italian system), two models for derivative litigation emerge: in the first one, normally directors have the power to decide to sue directors, but shareholders can sue derivatively subject to demand on the board or if demand can be excused because it would be futile.

In the second model, the shareholders' meeting normally has the power to decide to sue directors, but a qualified minority of shareholders can exercise the action on behalf of the corporation. To the extent that these two models represent the two extremes of a spectrum, where does your system fall?

* * *

Also Spanish law allows a qualified minority to promote a lawsuit against directors, and sue them derivatively, when the shareholders' meeting does not act. Pursuant to Article 239 of the Spanish Real Decreto 1/2010, shareholders representing 5% of the capital can call a shareholders' meeting to decide whether to sue the directors, and they can sue the directors if they do not call a shareholders' meeting notwithstanding the request of the qualified minority, or when the lawsuit is not brought notwithstanding the resolution of the shareholders' meeting.

One very interesting European system, in this respect, is the French one. In France, a single shareholder, independently from the number of shares she owns, can bring an "*action sociale* ut singuli," a claim against directors on behalf of the corporation (Articles L. 225–252 of the French Commercial Code). This possibility has been recognized under French law since the nineteenth century. The 1867 Companies Act mentioned that the "*action sociale* ut singuli" could be brought by a minority representing 5% of the shareholders, which was already rather low (Articles 17 and 39). However, as soon as 1872 case law admitted that this action could also be brought on an individual basis (Cass., 7 May 1872, Dal. 72, I, 273). The reasoning of the French Supreme Court was that the 5% threshold was simply designed to create an incentive for shareholders to group together to appoint one of them to file a derivative action. It was a cost-sharing provision. In addition, the fact that the corporation is a separate legal person from the shareholders should not be invoked to the detriment of shareholders, since the principle was established for their benefit. Therefore, shareholders should be entitled to sue on behalf of the corporation. From a systematic point of view, moreover, Article 17 of the 1867 Act mentioned explicitly the right of any shareholder to act in his personal interest. This somehow ambiguous language would have been unnecessary if it covered only individual damages, since the right of a single shareholder to sue to recover direct damages is already recognized by general tort law provisions in the French Civil Code. This interpretation was formally embraced by the 1966 Commercial Companies Act and is now included in the Commercial Code. The "*action sociale* ut singuli" remains a derivative action, meaning for example that a shareholder cannot act when the company has already filed a suit. However, differently from U.S. law, there is no demand requirement under French law. The shareholder must only notify the directors of the company.

Because the costs of suing the directors can be significant, it is possible for a group of shareholders to join together. The Commercial Code currently allows shareholders representing a certain amount of the capital to act together and, in listed companies, for an association of shareholders to act, but these provisions are seldom used.

One rule that hinders the use of derivative suits under French law, however, is that, differently from other systems, in case of victory the costs of the litigation remain with the shareholder, whereas the benefit goes to the corporation. Some scholars have, in this respect, argued to adopt the Italian or other similar approaches. Unsurprisingly, listed companies strenuously oppose such a development. Therefore, derivative actions continue to be quite rare.

One interesting question under French law is the coordination between a lawsuit brought against directors by the corporation, following a shareholders' meeting resolution, and one brought by a single shareholder on behalf of the corporation. This issue was considered in the following case.

TESTUT

French Cass. Crim., 2000
12 December 2000, n° 97–83470

Considering articles L. 225–252 of the Commercial Code (*article 245 of the 24 July 1966 Act at the time the decision was rendered*) and 509 of the Code of criminal procedure;

Whereas a shareholder is entitled to sue on behalf of the corporation pursuant to Article L. 225–252 of the Commercial Code;

Whereas it results from the first degree judgment and the decision of the court of appeals that following the filing of a criminal suit by Alain X, shareholder of the Testut company, both in his own name and on behalf of the corporation, in application of Article L. 225–252 of the Commercial Code, the prosecutor decided to start criminal proceedings against the following persons: Elie Y, Bruno Z and Bernard A, former directors, the first for abuse of corporate assets, forgery and use of forged documents, the second for being an accomplice to abuse of corporate assets, the third for abuse of corporate assets and concealment; Bernard B, a lawyer, for being an accomplice to abuse of corporate assets and use of forged documents; Michel C, former CEO of the *Société de Banque Occidentale* (SDBO), for being an accomplice to abuse of corporate assets;

Whereas [. . .] the Testut company requested the sentencing of the defendants and of SDBO, civilly liable for the act of its CEO Michel C;

Whereas the first degree commercial court [. . .] rejected the claims of the Testut company and the ones of Alain X on behalf of the corporation, and decided on the claims concerning the direct damages he suffered;

Whereas the court has held that Alain X, the only appellant, cannot act on behalf of the corporation because the Testut company has, on the same grounds, brought an action for directors' liability and not appealed the first degree decision;

The action of the corporation cannot deprive the single shareholder of his right to sue the directors on behalf of the corporation, therefore the court of appeals misinterpreted the meaning and scope of the above-mentioned provisions;

For this reason, this Court voids and nullifies the decision of the court of appeal

[. . .]

NOTES AND QUESTIONS

1.   This case, even if brought in criminal court and dealing (also) with criminal liability, addresses civil liabilities of directors for criminal violations and derivative suits. In France, as in many other systems where criminal and civil courts are separated, criminal courts within a proceeding for alleged criminal violations can in fact also decide on damages since a criminal violation is generally also a source of civil liability. To somehow clarify the partially cryptic style of French Supreme Court decisions, it is necessary to point out that the Testut company had sued some of its former directors for damages connected with embezzlement. An aggrieved shareholder, Alain X, also sued derivatively. The Court holds that the shareholder was entitled to file an appeal even if the corporation itself was also a party to the litigation and decided not to appeal the lower court's decision. The French Supreme Court's interpretation is very protective of shareholders. It essentially holds that a company can sue both through its legal representative and through any shareholder, and that the complaint of the shareholder is not subordinated to the complaint of the company. Each shareholder has a concurrent right with the corporation to sue the directors for the benefit of the company. The rationale of this approach is to avoid the risk that the corporation might litigate the issue to prevent the shareholders from suing derivatively, only to accept a sweetheart settlement with the directors. It is, however, very different from the rules we have considered, for example, in the U.S. or Italy, and might lead to multiple and contradictory results.

2.   Do you think that the broad possibility attributed to single shareholders to bring a derivative suit under French law is an effective tool to curb directors' abuses? What could be the drawbacks of this approach?

3.   A 1989 Brazilian statute authorizes prosecutors, sometimes with the assistance of the *Comissão de Valores Mobiliários*, the Brazilian

Securities and Exchange Commission, to bring a lawsuit aimed at avoiding or recovering damages for investors in securities (a so-called *Ação Civil Pública*). The damages awarded, in this case, are supposed to be distributed among investors upon proof that they were in the "class" protected. The action has both the goal of compensating injured investors and indirectly protect the market also because of its deterrence. In this perspective, it might evoke the American concept of attorney general, but this action also shows a similarity with a derivative action, in the sense that the prosecutor is litigating on behalf of the investors, who will receive the benefits of the litigation, if any. Based on these few elements, can you try to guess if the *Ação Civil Pública* has been often used in Brazil, and has been an effective instrument for investors' protection? Why? (For further information *see* Viviane Muller Prado, *The protection of minority investor and compensation for their losses in Brazilian capital markets* (2015) unpublished paper sent by the author to M. Ventoruzzo, on file with the authors.)

4.   Considering the Brazilian institute mentioned above, it is worth mentioning that also other systems attribute specific powers to prosecutors, in addition to criminal enforcement, allowing them to intervene to protect minority shareholders and investors. Can you make an example concerning a system you are familiar with?

* * *

While legal instruments that can be compared with the U.S.-style derivative suit now exist in most European systems, empirical evidence suggests that derivative suits in Europe are much less common than in the U.S. What are the reasons for this divergence? We have already mentioned some possible explanations under French Law, but take, as another example, German law. In Germany derivative suits have very limited relevance. Although case law developed derivative suits for almost all other business organizations, until recently no case law existed establishing the right of shareholders of a stock corporations to sue derivatively. Only in 2005 the German legislature introduced derivative suits in the German stock corporation law in Sec. 148 which is loosely based on the American model, even if additional loopholes and obstacles exist for shareholders. The German legislature did not want to encourage attorney-driven litigation, and there are almost no cases applying Sec. 148 of the German stock corporation law. In addition, the German stock corporation law, as well as other statutes in Europe, provides another possibility for shareholders to pursue claims of the corporation against the directors. According to Sec. 147 of the German stock corporation law the shareholders' meeting can appoint a so-called special representative (*besonderer Vertreter*) who has the task only to assert claims against the members of the managing and supervisory boards and (in certain occasions) against other shareholders. Although this appointment of the special representative requires a shareholder resolution with a (simple) majority, which can be difficult to reach for minority shareholders, this rule was used quite often in the last few years when shareholders want to appoint a special representative not only to assert claims against the directors, but also against the majority shareholder. In this case, the latter cannot vote. In addition, also pursuant to Section 147 of the Aktiengesetz, 10% shareholders can obtain with the approval of the court, the appointment of special representatives. Besides this recent development the enforcement of liability claims of the corporation against directors is traditionally not the domain of shareholders.

This, however, does not mean that shareholders' litigation is not used as a governance tool in Germany. Typically, shareholders react to perceived abuses by challenging the shareholders' meeting resolutions, as the following excerpt illustrates. Sometimes shareholders use these claims, more or less legitimately, to pressure the corporation and/or the managers to settle the claim.

More generally, considering the European situation, in the following article, Professor Gelter identifies some interesting and compelling explanations why derivative suits are not very often used in Europe, and in doing so he also challenges some commonly held beliefs. The article offers a good overview of different European-style derivative suits regimes.

MARTIN GELTER, WHY DO SHAREHOLDER DERIVATIVE SUITS REMAIN RARE IN CONTINENTAL EUROPE?[2]
37 Brook. J. Int'l L. 843 (2012)

[. . .]

INTRODUCTION

The objective of this symposium piece is to explore why shareholder derivative suits are rare in Continental Europe. I mainly focus on Germany, France, and Italy, and further provide less extensive references regarding derivative suits in Austria, Belgium, the Netherlands, Spain, and Switzerland. In doing so, I compare the Continental European situation with the one in the United States and Japan, where derivative suits are important mechanisms of corporate governance enforcement. It is sometimes thought that shareholder litigation and litigiousness in general are cultural features of U.S. society. In Japan—where shareholder derivative suits have also become common since the early 1990s—cultural theories gave way to theories emphasizing economic incentives that were more strongly supported by the evidence, as no discernible cultural shift occurred when suits became widespread. I also emphasize economic incentives set by the legal framework to explain the scarcity of derivative suits in Continental Europe. This explanation, similar to the explanation provided for Japan, is also only cultural as far as legal and structural constraints setting these incentives are part of the respective culture. [. . .]

---

[2]　Footnotes and paragraphs numbers omitted.

In his Pulitzer Prize-winning book *Guns, Germs and Steel*, geographer and biologist Jared Diamond popularized the "Anna Karenina Principle" based on the first line of Leo Tolstoy's classic novel. Tolstoy suggested that happy families share a number of core characteristics that must all be present to ensure happy family life. Diamond varies the idea to explain that an animal species needs to meet a list of criteria, including diet, social behavior, and breeding habits, to be susceptible to domestication by humans. The relatively small number of domesticable species can thus be explained by the observation that if even one criterion on the list is not met, the species would be too onerous to employ for human purposes. Likewise, only the United States and Japan seem to "get it right" with respect to all necessary criteria to make derivative litigation a successful model for shareholders. By contrast, no single factor suffices to account for the scarcity of derivative litigation in Continental Europe—or even a single country. I survey the available and some additional explanations, and suggest that several criteria have to be met to make derivative suits attractive.

[. . .]

The European evidence is fragmentary, but commentators that discuss individual countries uniformly confirm that the number of suits is very low. In the United Kingdom, an investigation by Armour et al., spanning 2004 through 2006, brought to light only twenty-six suits in which directors were named as the defendants. I am not aware of any systematic evidence for Continental Europe. Cheffins and Black report only two suits against German supervisory board members before 1997 in which damages were awarded at trial. Ulmer reports only two published German cases awarding damages on the basis of a submission by shareholders between 1965 and 1999. Pierre-Henri Conac, Luca Enriques, and I began to compile a database of published French, German, and Italian cases decided between 2000 and 2007 where self-dealing by controlling shareholders is alleged. While this can provide us only with a limited (and maybe not even the main) subset of derivative suits, it is still interesting to note that we have so far found only two such suits in Germany (one of which related to a GmbH, roughly the equivalent of an LLC), two in Italy, and one in France. [. . .]

[. . .]

THE ANNA KARENINA PRINCIPLE: EXPLANATIONS FOR THE ABSENCE OF SUITS

I focus on four issues to explain the scarcity of derivative litigation in spite of its availability in principle. In analogy to the Anna Karenina principle, countries need to "get it right" in at least four dimensions to allow shareholder suits to proliferate. The four dimensions are as follows: there must be favorable standing requirements that do not include a minimum ownership threshold (Section 2.1); the litigation risk must be allocated favorably to overcome minority shareholders' rational apathy (Section 2.2); potential plaintiffs must have sufficient access to information to litigate (Section 2.3); and the enforcement model must make it possible for shareholders to derivatively sue potential wrongdoers, which not only includes directors, but also controlling shareholders (Section 2.4).

Minimum Share Ownership Requirements

A number of Continental European jurisdictions require that shareholders (or groups of shareholders) hold a qualified percentage of the company's shares or a specified amount of capital to bring a derivative suit. Percentage limits can be rationalized as a screening mechanism against abusive lawsuits on the grounds that the incentive for a shareholder with a small amount of shares to bring a legitimate suit is very likely small. Given that any shareholder's benefits from the results of a successful suit consist only of a proportionate share in the rise of the value of the corporation, it seems hard to imagine why a shareholder with only a few shares would sue for a legitimate reason. For a small investor, a suit would seem to be rational only when the investor can somehow coerce management into an abusive settlement that constitutes an effective bribe to make the investor go away, i.e., the litigation equivalent of greenmail. Theory cannot explain what particular percentage should provide the cutoff, which could be set at 1%, 5%, 10%, or any other number with almost equal justification. A plaintiff's motives are presumably legitimate when the benefits of the lawsuit, multiplied by the probability of its success, exceed the costs of litigation, including nonmonetary cost. Any percentage limit is, to some extent, arbitrary and can preclude some legitimate suits. The requirement to retain a relatively large number of shares while the suit is pending may act as a further deterrent.

Grechenig and Sekyra suggest that percentage limits are to blame for the absence of derivative suits in Continental Europe. Their mathematical model captures a simple intuition: in order to avoid a lawsuit, potential defendant managers only need to deal with those shareholders above the applicable threshold. In order to "bribe" these large shareholders, managers would have to offer these shareholders an advantage that exceeds their losses from managerial wrongdoing. Large shareholders, therefore, do not monitor management, but become accomplices of management in actions exploiting investors whose share is below the threshold.

In recent years, Germany and Italy have reduced minimum ownership thresholds. The traditional German enforcement mechanism required a qualified minority of 10% or DM 2,000,000 until 1998, when it was lowered to 5% or € 500,000 for cases where shareholders could establish facts indicating dishonesty or serious violations of the law or the corporate charter. The derivative suit introduced in 2005 requires only 1% or €100,000. To prevent abusive litigation, the German legislature introduced a special judicial "lawsuit admission procedure," or *Klagezulas-sungsverfahren*, during the course of which plaintiffs must show that they demanded that directors bring the suit. Shareholders have to establish facts indicating dishonesty or serious violations of the law or the corporate charter, and the court must determine whether litigation would be in the interest of the company before allowing it to proceed beyond this stage.

In 1998, when derivative suits were introduced, Italian law started out with a 5% threshold. Since the mechanism was never used, the 2003 reform eliminated the six month ownership requirement and extended it to unlisted stock corporations. In unlisted corporations, the suit is restricted to shareholders owning at least 20%, unless the corporate charter provides an even higher threshold of up to 33.3%. For publicly traded firms, the threshold was reduced from 5% to 2.5% in 2006, again because derivative suits failed to emerge in practice.

Whereas Belgian law also only requires 1% or a nominal capital share of € 1,250,000 for a derivative suit, the thresholds are higher in Spain (5%) and Austria (10%). [. . .]

The percentage limit theory cannot explain the cases of France and Switzerland, where—as in the United States and Japan—individual shareholders can enforce liability claims against directors without holding a minimum stake. These laws also do not have the additional procedural hurdles of German law, such as the demand requirement and admission procedure. The German situation is not well explained by the theory, since there is a special derivative mechanism available to every shareholder in the law of corporate groups, but the mechanism has also failed to produce litigation. [. . .]

Costs and the Allocation of Litigation Risk

Law Firm Driven Litigation in the United States

[. . .]

The high frequency of derivative (and other shareholder) litigation is typically credited to the entrepreneurial and specialized plaintiff bar. This bar actually has quite a strong incentive to bring derivative suits given that contingency fees resulting from an award or settlement could be as high as one third of the amount. Even when the settlement does not contain a monetary award, and only requires changing the firm's corporate governance practices (e.g., more independent directors), the law firm can receive a considerable award under the "substantial benefits" doctrine. Specialized law firms therefore only need to find a suitable plaintiff and sometimes actually hold a stock portfolio to be able to sue once they hear about a possible claim. This situation may result in a "race to the courthouse" between law firms since, traditionally, the first firm to file is assigned the role of lead counsel in the case and thus receives most of the fee. However, since about the year 2000, Delaware courts have begun to rely on a variety of factors to determine lead counsel, including the size of the plaintiff's stake and the quality of the pleadings filed. While this may marginally diminish suits or induce plaintiffs to take cases out of Delaware, this further illustrates that the incentive to sue rests almost entirely with the law firm.

The "Loser Pays" Principle

European countries generally apply what in the United States is often called the "English Rule": the losing party has to reimburse the winning party for litigation costs. Since the outcome of a lawsuit is rarely certain, it is often suggested that the most important factor deterring derivative suits is that shareholders will not be willing to take the risk of having to pay for the defendants fees. The argument appears persuasive at first glance. Fees often depend on the complexity of the case, which is high if it involves intricate business issues. Moreover, to the extent that fees depend on the amount in dispute, court fees will also be very high in a derivative suit given the high value at stake in such suits.

[. . .]

Moreover, European reimbursement systems are often closer to the American Rule in practice than in theory. In several countries, including Germany and Italy, reimbursement is limited to court fees plus expenses for lawyers, according to the official tariff promulgated by the bar association. Reimbursement by the loser is even more limited in France; while court fees are usually reimbursed, lawyers' fees normally are not. These are automatically borne by the losing party only when retention of an attorney is mandatory, which is generally not the case in commercial courts, where corporate cases are litigated. French judges can grant lawyers' fees to the winning party under equitable considerations, but, if fees are granted in practice, the amount tends to be much lower than what lawyers actually charged.

Several jurisdictions have special rules regarding litigation costs for shareholder derivative suits, all of which slightly improve the position of plaintiff shareholders compared to the basic "loser pays" principle.

No Contingency Fees

Besides the "English Rule," the other classic difference that could explain the rarity of derivative suits in Europe is the absence of contingency fees. In contrast to the United States, contingency fees are uncommon and often illegal. Contingency fees have traditionally been rejected because they are thought to distort the incentives of lawyers to represent clients' interests. Although the cultural aversion to a more entrepreneurial view of the legal profession may be receding, this has not yet resulted in the emergence of a plaintiff bar comparable to the American one.

[. . .] By itself, however, the contingency fee prohibition does not seem to explain the absence of derivative litigation either. Hertig and McCahery suggest that contingency fees already are "a common but concealed practice throughout Europe." The new Italian law seems to allow at least conditional fees, and derivative suits still have not emerged as a prominent factor. This is illustrated by the emergence of derivative suits in Japan in the early 1990s. Two-part tariffs consisting of a fixed retainer and a fee conditional on success—either in the form of a judgment or a settlement—were seemingly enough to encourage derivative litigation. For Japanese firms representing shareholders, retainers tend to be low and success fees high.

[. . .]

Access to Information

[. . .] [I]n the United States, plaintiffs with a thin basis of evidence can avail themselves of pretrial discovery, in the course of which the defendant is required to disclose pertinent information to the plaintiff. Once the suit passes the demand requirement on the basis of relatively limited notice pleading, plaintiffs may rely on information gathered in discovery to coerce the defendant to settle or go to trial. In Europe, a party to a civil suit must generally identify specific documents and ask the court to order the other party to produce them; furthermore, it must explain why these documents are necessary and where they are located. The absence of a wide-ranging discovery procedure is often thought to make derivative suits, particularly strike suits, more difficult in Europe. Fishing expeditions are typically not permitted, while "the opponent's obligations to cooperate are usually strict and quite restrictive."

Is there a Continental European functional equivalent that makes up for this "information gap"? While there is no obvious or complete one, a mechanism that is sometimes brought up by Continental European observers is the appointment of a "special auditor" by a court upon application by minority shareholders. The auditor, who will typically be an accounting professional or other certified expert, is tasked with reviewing problematic or suspicious management activities and subsequently submits a report at the shareholder meeting. The information compiled by the auditor can—at least in theory—form the basis for a lawsuit.

[. . .]

As a true functional equivalent to discovery, special audits seem to fail by and large. The instrument is relatively popular in France, partly because the minority right can be exercised by a shareholder association. Furthermore, under the general law of civil procedure, individual shareholders can also ask the court to appoint an expert even before a trial to establish facts. Elsewhere, special auditors are not appointed frequently, although appointments happen occasionally. Both in Germany and Italy, requirements to show "serious" irregularities put a heavy burden of proof on the petitioner, which rules out fishing expeditions. [. . .]

Limitations Regarding Potential Defendants

[. . .]

In all of the countries surveyed here, the legal basis for derivative suits is, in all cases, found in a section of the respective corporate law governing directors' liability. This fact has two important consequences. First, derivative suits are only available for claims to damages. The French courts, for example, found that derivative actions are not available for injunctions. The potential of derivative litigation to prevent harmful corporate behavior ex ante and to put pressure on those actually in control of the corporation is therefore low. [. . .]

Second, possible defendants in Continental European derivative suits are limited to directors (including supervisory board members), and in some cases corporate officers, auditors, or the founders of the corporation. The opportunity to engage with controlling shareholders is therefore limited. True, sometimes controlling shareholders may be sued because they are also directors, and in rare cases a director can be successfully sued for failing to prevent illicit self-dealing by controlling shareholders; the limitation may still, however, prevent litigation that would otherwise be brought.

[. . .]

NOTES AND QUESTIONS

1. Professor Gelter offers several reasons that might explain the more limited use of derivative suits in Europe, when compared to the U.S. What is particularly valuable in this analysis is that he does not rely on general and sometimes vague "cultural" differences, but on specific technical, legal, and economic differences. This is not to say that cultural and social elements are not relevant in explaining comparative differences, but it is very important to identify precise legal rules and institutes that might account for comparative differences. Can you think of any other possible elements that can influence the use of derivative lawsuits? For example, is the fact that corporations rely more or less on equity markets, and therefore on shareholders, to finance

their operation, rather than banks, an element that might affect at least the "settlement value" of a derivative lawsuit?

2.   Note that one of the reasons that might explain a more litigious attitude of U.S. shareholders is the absence of the so-called "loser pays" rule, pursuant to which the losing party bears most of the costs of litigation. This rule, provided for example under English law, clearly discourages in particular plaintiffs without large economic resources, and also lawsuits based on somehow new, innovative, and untested legal theories. Some scholars, in fact, have argued that U.S. case law is more "progressive" than British case law also because of this difference. This article was however published in 2012. An interesting 2013 Delaware decision might change this scenario. In *ATP Tour, Inc. v. Deutscher Tennis Bund* (91 A.3d 554 (Del. 2013)), the court concluded that the bylaws of a Delaware corporation can adopt the English "loser pays" rule, therefore shifting litigation costs to unsuccessful plaintiffs. The plaintiffs' bar immediately lobbied for a statutory provision that would prohibit, or limit, the ability of corporations to take advantage of this provision, but as of 2014 it appears that the corporate lobby successfully blocked the legislative amendment, urging the need to curb "frivolous litigation." What impact do you think this might have? What does it tell us in terms of the effects of regulatory competition, how corporate laws are concocted, and race to the top or bottom? To complicate things, however, consider that the distinction between countries that require the losing party to pay for the expenses of litigation and countries that do not is not always clear: in the former, sometimes expenses can be "compensated;" and in the latter courts can sometimes ask the losing party to pay for the expenses, also a sort of "sanction" for frivolous suits. (For an interesting discussion, *see* Sean J. Griffith, *Correcting Corporate Benefit: How to Fix Shareholder Litigation by Shifting the Doctrine on Fees*, forthcoming *Boston College Law Review*, 2015, available on www.ssrn.com.)

3.   Do you think that a limited use of derivative lawsuits causes an inefficient underenforcement of corporate laws? Or, on the other hand, do you fear the costs and possible inequities of excessive litigation, and therefore you think it is desirable to limit derivative suits?

4.   In another part of the article reprinted above, not excerpted here, Martin Gelter points out how in Europe, and continental Europe in particular, shareholders' litigation often concerns actions for the "nullification" of a shareholders' meeting resolution or sometimes—even if probably more rarely—a decision or an action of directors. These kinds of actions, while possible also in the U.S., are quite less common in this system. Based on what you know concerning ownership structures (Chapter 1) and the division of powers between shareholders and directors (Chapter 5), can you elaborate on this idea? What could be possible explanations for this comparative difference? You can also research this issue before class.

* * *

DERIVATIVE SUITS IN ASIA

Now shifting our attention to Asia, and speaking about the possible "cultural" explanations for the more or less widespread use of derivative actions and corporate litigation more generally, the following excerpt from an illuminating article by Professor Dan Puchniak offers a unique perspective on the topic. The article is interesting also because it offers broad and important methodological insights with respect to different attitudes toward comparative (corporate) law.

DAN W. PUCHNIAK, THE DERIVATIVE ACTION IN ASIA: A COMPLEX REALITY[3]
9 Berkeley Bus. L.J. 1 (2012)

The derivative action in Asia presents a tantalizing topic for comparative corporate law scholarship. To start, the derivative action, which has its historic roots in the United States and United Kingdom, has become a ubiquitous feature in the corporate law regimes of Asia's leading economies. Indeed, the derivative action has been implemented and more recently has captured the attention of corporate stakeholders, legislatures, courts, and scholars in Asia's three largest (i.e., China, Japan and India) and four "tiger" (i.e., Korea, Taiwan, Hong Kong and Singapore) economies. These seven jurisdictions account for approximately eighty percent of Asia's economic output, are home to its nine largest stock exchanges and are consistently recognized as the region's most important and/or dynamic economies. As such, an accurate understanding of the derivative action in these seven leading Asian economies provides an important window into how the historically Anglo-American derivative action functions within and impacts upon corporate governance in Asia.

The reality of the derivative action in Asia's leading economies can be summed up in one word: complex. This complex reality debunks the popular notion that shareholder litigation in Asia can be easily or meaningfully understood through the monolithic lens of Asia's ostensibly "non-litigious culture." To the contrary, an accurate understanding of the derivative action in Asia's leading economies turns the theory of Asia's non-litigious culture on its head.

Japan, which is often portrayed as the archetype of Asia's non-litigious culture, has become a world leader in derivative litigation and in doing so makes most Western countries (aside from the United States) appear squeamishly non-litigious. Korea, with an increase in economic

---

[3]   Footnotes omitted.

incentives for derivative litigation and the emergence of a powerful shareholder activist group, has experienced a notable increase in derivative litigation without a noteworthy change in its traditional culture. China, in spite of not formally having a derivative action in its Company Law until 2006, has had a robust level of derivative ligation for over a decade. Yet, derivative litigation in *large public* Chinese companies is virtually nonexistent largely due to the political constraints placed on such actions. India, with almost 30 million cases pending before its courts, makes a mockery of the non-litigious Asian theory. However, for a variety of complex reasons, derivative actions in India remain scarce.

The point is simple. There are a myriad of complex factors which result in varying levels of derivative litigation in Asia's leading economies. Ironically, the one factor that is conspicuously absent as a defining force of derivative litigation in *all* of Asia's leading economies is Asia's ostensibly non-litigious culture. This suggests that the cultural theory of Asian non-litigiousness provides scant explanatory or predictive value for either the evolution or function of the derivative action in Asia's leading economies.

In addition to lacking probative value, the overly simplistic and often tautological nature of the non-litigious Asian culture theory risks providing a seductively convenient, but wholly uninformative, rationale for explaining away behavior of Asian shareholders when it does not conform to "Western" norms. This risk is highlighted by the common trope of citing an Asian country's low level of shareholder litigation as evidence of its non-litigious Asian culture and then claiming that the same country's non-litigious Asian culture explains its low rate of shareholder litigation. As such, from the outset, this Article suggests that for the purpose of understanding the derivative action in Asia's leading economies, the non-litigious Asian culture theory should be relegated to the dustbin of academic history.

Without the black box of Asian culture to erroneously explain away potential differences between "Asian" and "Western" derivative actions, the reality of the derivative action in Asia's leading economies becomes markedly more important. Indeed, if one views evidence from these seven leading Asian jurisdictions as evidence of how the derivative action functions in seven *leading global* economies (rather than seven *idiosyncratically Asian* ones) such evidence becomes a valuable litmus test for a number of comparative corporate law's most influential theories. As will be explained in detail below, such a litmus test is woefully lacking in the current literature.

[. . .]

Turning the legal origins theory on its head

In terms of understanding the derivative action in Asia's leading economies, whether a jurisdiction has a common law or civil law legal origin appears to matter little and risks confusing a lot. The grand universal theory that the common law provides better protection for shareholders than the civil law (i.e., the common law superiority theory) is built on the more general assumption that there are predictable differences between how corporate law functions in common law and civil law jurisdictions. Evidence from the derivative action in Asia's leading economies undermines the general assumption that there are predictable differences between how corporate law functions in common law and civil law jurisdictions and illustrates how the more specific claim of common law superiority terribly misleads.

One of the most basic theoretical divides between civil law and common law systems is the prominence of codified law in the former and case law in the latter. This clear theoretical divide does not exist in the derivative actions of Asia's three leading common law (i.e., India, Hong Kong and Singapore) and four leading civil law (i.e., China, Japan, Korea and Taiwan) jurisdictions. To the contrary, in all of Asia's leading economies, except for India, the fundamental legal rules governing the derivative action are contained in statutory law—not case law. In this sense, one of the most basic points of demarcation between how the corporate law "predictably" differs in common law and civil law jurisdictions is blurred.

Even more surprisingly, it appears that many of the most important recent changes in the derivative actions regimes of Asia's leading common law and civil law jurisdictions have occurred as a result of statutory amendments in the former and judicial decisions in the latter. Without dispute, over the last two decades, the most important changes in the derivative actions regimes of Hong Kong and Singapore—two of Asia's leading common law jurisdictions—have been the implementation of the statutory derivative action through amendments to their respective Companies Acts. In stark contrast, in China, Korea and, more recently, Japan—three of Asia's leading civil law jurisdictions—court decisions, which have often been made by activist judges, have been critically important in the evolution of their respective derivative actions regimes. The critical importance of statutory amendments in Asia's leading common law jurisdictions and judicial decisions in their civil law counterparts further confounds the idea that there are predictable differences between how corporate law functions in common law and civil law jurisdictions. In fact, it arguably turns what one would predict on its head.

The more specific common law superiority theory is similarly confounded by the reality of the derivative action in Asia's leading economies. On balance, evidence from Asia's leading economies suggests that shareholders in civil law jurisdictions have been better protected by the derivative action than their common law counterparts. Indeed, minority shareholders in Japan, a civil law jurisdiction, have utilized the derivative action far more than their counterparts in any of Asia's common law jurisdictions (or, for that matter, any jurisdiction in the world aside from the United States). Similarly, Korea, another civil law jurisdiction, is the only Asian leading economy, aside from Japan, to have a significant number of derivative actions involving large listed companies—making the derivative action in its Asian common law counterparts appear somewhat inept.

In light of the common law superiority theory it is ironic that the most likely culprit for the moribund nature of the derivative action in Asia's leading common law countries has, in fact, been their common law origin. The English common law Rule in *Foss*, which was directly transplanted into all of Asia's leading common law jurisdictions, is perhaps the most formidable restriction on derivative litigation in Asia's leading economies. Indeed, both Singapore and, more recently, Hong Kong have implemented statutory derivative actions specifically aimed at providing minority shareholders with a way around the Rule in *Foss*. These statutory amendments have resulted in the derivative action being a considerably more powerful tool for minority shareholder protection. In a similar vein, India, which is the only leading Asian jurisdiction without a codified derivative action, has almost no derivative litigation and the English Rule in *Foss* seems to be significantly to blame. In short, rather than providing better minority shareholder protection, which is what the common law superiority theory predicts, it appears that in terms of the derivative action the common law in Asia's leading economies has served to thwart minority shareholder protection.

As such, it is clear that the legal origins theory fails to make sense out of the derivative action in Asia's leading economies. Indeed, in many respects, evidence from the derivative action in Asia's leading economies turns the legal origins theory on its head. This demonstrates that the blunt civil/common law divide appears to be of little value in explaining or predicting how the derivative action functions in Asia. It also illustrates how the complexity of the derivative action in Asia's leading economies befuddles the academy's unyielding lust for grand universal theories.

[. . .]

In sum, this Article illustrates that there are no grand universal theories that can accurately explain or predict how the derivative action functions in Asia. The assumption that the rate of derivative litigation will necessarily be modest merely because a jurisdiction has an "Asian culture" is absurd. The fact that a jurisdiction follows either the civil law or common law tradition does not necessarily allow us to predict whether judicial decisions or statutory provisions will be more influential, or whether the derivative action will provide strong protection for minority shareholders. [. . .] Moreover, the fact that Asia's leading jurisdictions seem to have adopted some general shareholder-friendly measures in their derivative actions regimes does not necessarily suggest convergence, as all of the jurisdictions remain functionally diverse, do not appear to evolve in a unidirectional fashion, and a static American endpoint model does not even appear to exist.

In this sense, the truth revealed in this Article is an "inconvenient one." The fact is that the forces that drive derivative actions in Asia's leading economies (and, most likely, everywhere else) are far too complex and varied to conform to any one grand universal theory. This means that to accurately understand how the derivative action functions in Asia's leading economies it is necessary to consider a myriad of local factors including the specific regulatory framework, case law, economic forces, corporate governance institutions, and sociopolitical environment that affect derivative actions in each individual jurisdiction.

Such an approach may seem like common sense—because it is. However, unfortunately, the field of comparative corporate law has increasingly moved away from such research towards using leximetrics in large multijurisdictional studies or broad taxonomies of abstract corporate law principles which are normally only based on a cursory analysis of how specific aspects of the corporate law function in practice.

NOTES AND QUESTIONS

1.   This article contains an interesting critique of what we have called the "law & finance" approach epitomized by the work of "LLSV" discussed in Chapter 1. Also in the light of Professor Puchniak's insights, what do you think about it?

2.   The other interesting lesson of this excerpt is, obviously, to be wary of stereotypes, especially of cultural stereotypes such as the alleged non-litigious nature of Asian cultures. International lawyers, businesspeople and comparativists should be particularly careful to avoid the illusory short-cuts often offered by generalizations, even if sometimes they capture at least some part of the truth. Also based on the last two articles, what do you think are the most important factors that can incentivize derivative lawsuits against directors?

3.   Puchniak explains that in common law Asian systems, such as Hong Kong and Singapore, derivative actions were introduced and developed primarily through statutory reform; while in civil law Asian jurisdictions

(China, Korea, and Japan), case law activist judges have had a major role. Do you find this surprising or counter-intuitive? Comment.

* * *

As mentioned by Professor Puchniak, Japan has probably used shareholders' derivative suits as a governance and enforcement tool more than any other country in the world except the U.S. Several characteristics of Japanese law account for this phenomenon. First, there is no minimum share ownership requirement to bring a derivative lawsuit (Art. 847(1), Companies Act). Holding just one share is sufficient. Second, although a plaintiff must have held her share(s) consecutively for six months before bringing a derivative suit (Art. 847(1)), she does not need to be a shareholder at the time of alleged wrongdoing by a director. Thus, one can purchase a share after noticing a wrongdoing, wait six months and then sue. Third, although a shareholder must demand that the corporation sue the director in the first place, the shareholder can bring a derivative suit if the corporation does not sue the director within 60 days of that demand (Art. 847(3)). There is no need to establish that there was a wrongful refusal or that making the demand was futile. Fourth, the plaintiff/shareholder does not have to pay the lawyers' fees of defendants if she loses, and she can get a reasonable amount of reimbursement of her lawyer's fee from the corporation when she wins (Art. 852). As a whole, it is very easy for shareholders of a Japanese corporation to bring a derivative suit!

This easiness might give rise to strike suits (by the way, what constitutes a "strike suit" that should be deterred is a debatable problem). What can Japanese courts do to limit them? First, and quite obviously, the court will dismiss a derivative suit when the purpose of the plaintiff/shareholder is to seek unlawful gains or inflict damage on the corporation (Art. 847(1) proviso). For example (and not surprisingly), a derivative suit against directors of a bank by a corporate racketeer who had been trying to blackmail the bank was dismissed as it was used as a measure to extract personal gains unrelated to the plaintiff's status as a shareholder (Nagasaki District Court, February 19, 1991, 1393 Hanrei Jiho 138). Dismissal based on the decision of special litigation committee, like in the U.S., however, is not permitted. Second, courts can order the plaintiff to deposit a security if the defendant presented a prima facie case that the derivative suit has been filed "in bad faith" (Art. 847–4, (2)(3)). The sum deposited can be used to compensate the defendants if the derivative suit is deemed a tortious action, and is often set at 3–10 million JPY (approximately 30–100 thousand USD) per defendant, which is not a trifle amount. The suit will be dismissed when the plaintiff cannot place the required deposit (Art. 78 and 81, Code of Civil Procedure). The usefulness of this measure hinges upon the interpretation of "in bad faith," which was discussed by the Osaka High Court in the case below.

IN RE DAIWA BANK SHAREHOLDERS LITIGATION, PETITION FOR ORDER ON PLACEMENT OF DEPOSIT

Osaka Hight Court
November 18, 1997, 1628 HANREI JIHO 133

Facts

In September 1995, Daiwa Bank, Ltd. was criminally prosecuted in the U.S. for deliberately not reporting to the competent authorities its loss of approximately 1.1 billion USD from unauthorized off-balance dealing for 11 years by an employee in its New York office. After admitting some of the charges, in February 1996, Daiwa Bank was fined 340 million USD for the violation of US federal banking regulations. On March 1996, two individual shareholders of Daiwa Bank requested it to sue its current and former directors and statutory auditors for damages of 350 million USD (fine plus legal fees) caused by their breach of duties. As Daiwa Bank did not do so within 6 months, these shareholders brought the derivative suit against 48 defendants asking them to pay 350 million USD to Daiwa Bank. Defendants petitioned to order placement of deposit asserting that the suit was filed in bad faith.

The court below ordered the plaintiffs to deposit 20 million JPY (approximately 200 thousand USD) per defendant, holding that, the plaintiffs brought the lawsuit relying solely on news in the media, without gathering additional evidence, and had not sufficiently pleaded the breaches of each one of the defendants. For these reasons, the court concluded that it was reasonable to assume that the plaintiffs brought the suit knowing that there was no chance to prevail without a substantial modification of the claims (Osaka District Court, April 18, 1997, 1604 Hanrei Jiho 146). The plaintiffs appealed.

Court's Decision

Decision of the court below vacated, petition for order on placement of deposit denied.

II.   The meaning of "bad faith"

According to our interpretation of "bad faith" under Article 106, paragraph 2 of the Commercial Code, which is applied correspondingly to Article 267, paragraph 6 of the same code that prescribes the conditions for order on placement of deposit regarding shareholders' derivative suits [currently, Art. 847–4(2) of the Companies Act], plaintiff should be found to have filed a shareholder's derivative suit "in bad faith" when she brought the suit knowing that there was no factual or legal ground to support the liability of the defendant, or when she brought the suit with a wrongful purpose knowing that the suit would damage the defendant.

[. . .]

A prima facie case of lack of factual or legal grounds to support the liability of the defendant is established, for example, when the argument of the plaintiff does not make sense as a matter of law, when there is a remarkable reason to expect that it is extremely unlikely for the plaintiff to succeed in establishing facts supporting the claim, or when the defenses of the defendant are likely to succeed. When there is a prima facie case that the plaintiff raised the suit knowing the situation above, it can be assumed that the plaintiff knew that there were no factual or legal grounds to support the liability of the defendant. The court, however, must be cautious, as these matters might pre-empt deliberations to be made in trial on merits, as shareholders' right must not be unduly limited by ordering placement of deposit, and as petitions on placement of deposit are decided upon prima facie evidence.

III. On these bases, we will consider the present case.

[. . .]

As the court below points out, the arguments of the plaintiffs are indeed very unsatisfactory, because they do not specify the essence of the breach of duties of each defendant in terms of mismanagement or inadequate control. These arguments, however, do claim liability for mismanagement or inadequate monitoring. Based on the records, Daiwa Bank was prosecuted on September 26, 1995 for 24 charges in relation to the accident in this case [the loss of approximately 1.1 billion USD from unauthorized off-balance dealing by an employee]; it entered into a plea bargain agreement paying a fine of 340 million USD and admitted responsibility for 16 charges. It is likely that some of the defendants are liable for the loss. Thus, whether or not the defendants are liable is a question that should be carefully decided in a trial on the merits. At this moment, considering the difficulty shareholders face in gathering information and evidence, we do not think that the arguments of the plaintiff, even if somehow general, do not make sense as a matter of law.

[. . .]

[W]e do not think that the plaintiffs have raised this suit knowing that there is no factual or legal ground for the liability of the defendant against the corporation.

[. . .]

NOTES AND QUESTIONS

1. To request the plaintiff to deposit a sum of money in case of loss is a fairly common technique used to curb frivolous or abusive litigation. In the decision above, you can see an application of this technique. Do you think that the discretion given to the court is too broad, or is it adequate? Is there a risk to anticipate, at a pre-trial phase, a discussion of the merits of the lawsuit without giving to the parties the opportunity to present evidence? Is discovery (or the lack thereof) relevant in this case?

2. How different is the role of Japanese courts from that of Delaware courts in screening derivative suits? Compare the factors being considered in the case cited above with those in *Eisner v. Brehm, supra.*

3. In Japan, claims enforceable by derivative suit are limited to those against incorporators, directors, statutory auditors, executive officers, outside auditors, and liquidators of the corporation and several special statutory claims (Art. 847(1), Companies Act). Claims of the corporation against its controlling shareholders are not included. What is the rationale of these rules?

4. Does the plaintiff have a duty to gather sufficient evidence before trial? How is discovery relevant in this perspective?

5. A significant percentage of derivative suits in Japan are brought by shareholders and attorneys to achieve social or political goals, such as protection of the environment or promoting compliance with laws and regulations. See Dan W. Puchniak & Masafumi Nakahigashi, *Japan's Love for Derivative Actions: Irrational Behavior and Non-Economic Motives as Rational Explanations for Shareholder Litigation*, 45 VAND. J. TRANSNATIONAL L. 1, 53–58 (2012). For example, in Nagoya High Court, November 15, 1995, 892 Hanrei Taimuzu 121, a group of anti-nuclear-power-plant activists holding shares of an electric power company, derivatively sued its directors for expenditures regarding a project for a nuclear power plant against which they were protesting. The court ordered placement of 10 million JPY as deposit for each one of the seven defendants, holding that a deposit is necessary when the plaintiff-shareholder brings a derivative suit solely or primarily for the purpose of achieving its personal political or social goals, even if there is a prima facie case that the plaintiff's argument itself does not lack factual or legal grounds and thus is not wrongful. What do you think of this ruling? And of Japanese law on derivative suits generally?

* * *

BRIEF OBSERVATIONS ON CLASS ACTIONS FROM A COMPARATIVE PERSPECTIVE

This chapter focuses on derivative litigation, but as we mentioned when shareholders suffer a damage directly, *i.e.,* not the consequence of a damage suffered by the corporation, they of course have a direct claim against the directors, or sometimes even the corporation and other persons. This is often the case in the area of securities regulation, an area very close to corporate law, which however is largely beyond the scope of this casebook. In particular, direct claims often arise when the directors or other managers disclose false, incomplete, or misleading information concerning a corporation and/or the securities it has issued, and investors purchase those securities at an inflated price, only to lose money once the truth is discovered. In these situations another important procedural tool that investors can use is the class action. The class action allows several plaintiffs to proceed as a class against a defendant who, allegedly, injured them all. The class action is a very powerful tool because it allows grouping together many plaintiffs whose individual claims might be too small to be economically litigated separately. For example, if 3,000 small shareholders all have a direct claim against the directors of a corporation worth approximately $12,000, it might be impossible, or too risky and expensive for one of them to sue individually: only the lawyer is likely to cost much more than the possible award, and no good lawyer is probably interested in taking such a small case on a contingency fee basis. If, however, the shareholders can join their forces in a collective action, all of a sudden the claim is worth 36 million dollars and it can be extremely attractive for a plaintiff's lawyer (a contingency fee paying her 30% in case of victory would translate into a fee of over 10 million dollars, not too bad).

Class actions developed in the common law world, and if on the one hand in many cases they allow plaintiffs that would be otherwise unprotected to access justice, they also raise many problems in terms of excessive litigation, attorney-driven litigation, and so on. Relevant and delicate issues that play a role in the balance between the interests of justice and frivolous suits concern, for example, the selection of the leading plaintiff, the requirements to certify a class, the pleading standards, the structure of the compensation of the lawyers, and so on. In the United States, for example, legislation in the 1990s has been enacted to curb excessive litigation in the area of securities regulation.

In the last few years, collective redress systems that might apparently resemble U.S.-style class actions have been adopted in several European countries notwithstanding their traditional hostility toward this device (among others: Denmark, the U.K., France, Germany, Italy, the Netherlands, Poland, Portugal, and Spain; in addition, the European Union has enacted a non-binding recommendation on collective redress systems in 2014). Of course there are several and profound differences between the collective redress rules enacted in these jurisdictions and U.S.-style class actions; even in a European common law country such as the U.K., U.S.-style class actions are unknown and considered with skepticism. One of the most typical and important comparative differences is the "opt-out" vs. "opt-in" approach. In the U.S., plaintiffs (and/or their lawyers) that are trying to bring a class action can rely on an opt-out system: simplifying, they can advertise the existence of the class action and invite all potential plaintiffs that fit in the class (e.g., investors who have purchased bonds issued by corporation X between December 1, 2010, and March 31, 2011) to contact them and join the class. If potential class members do not opt out of the class, however, they are bound by the decision of the court and cannot bring additional claims based on the same facts. In other words, if they want to differentiate their position from that of the members of the class, they have to actively "opt out" of the class. This is very important to facilitate class actions, both because it makes it easier to form the class, and because it allows the potential defendants to negotiate a settlement with the representatives of the class without fearing other possible lawsuits (therefore increasing the settlement value of the class action).

In most European systems that have adopted some form of collective redress, on the other hand, general principles—according to some, in certain systems, constitutional principles—do not allow the "opt-out" approach because the individual decision of each person to sue must be explicitly expressed. On the contrary, they adopt an "opt-in" rule, according to which potential members of the class that want to join the collective litigation must actively do so, and generally the judgment does not bind the potential plaintiffs that, remaining passive, did not join the collective litigation. It should be fairly clear why this difference might significantly affect the possibility of creating large classes of plaintiffs.

Japan introduced its collective redress procedure for damages suffered by consumers in 2013 (Act on Special Provisions Regarding Civil Procedure for Collective Redress of Property Damages to Consumers, Law No.96 of 2013). This procedure is a two-step opt-in system, in which class members opt in to the suit in the second step after the liability of the defendant is confirmed based on common issues in the first step. This new procedure, however, is limited to claims for compensation of damages suffered by consumers and related to consumer contracts. Thus, it is generally unavailable for investors in the secondary market or shareholders in a merger context. In these situations, some law firms try to bring together a large group of plaintiffs by setting up websites to invite "victims" to join the suit. Although this unofficial opt-in style suit is growing in Japan, it has very little in common with U.S.-style class actions.

Of course it cannot be argued that class actions are always desirable and that substantive and procedural rules facilitating them should be encouraged in every system. Excessive litigation in the U.S. has probably led to undesirable and sometimes also unfair results. In addition, other legal systems rely less on private enforcement, and more on other legal techniques to ensure compliance with the applicable laws, such as *ex ante* administrative controls. It is, however, important to point out these differences concerning class actions.

This chapter does not really have the ambition to discuss class actions in any detail. As we mentioned, class actions are probably more relevant in other areas such as securities regulation, torts, etc., than in corporate law; in addition even class actions in securities regulation, one of the areas closer to corporate law, are not necessarily "shareholders' litigation," since the plaintiffs can also be investors in securities other than shares. We thought, however, that it would be interesting to briefly mention class actions, also to distinguish them from derivative lawsuits. The following excerpt offers a concise discussion of some comparative differences concerning collective litigation in the U.S. and in the E.U., and points at some possible reasons for the limited development of class actions in Europe.

MANNING GILBERT WARREN, III, THE PROSPECTS FOR CONVERGENCE OF COLLECTIVE REDRESS REMEDIES IN THE EUROPEAN UNION[4]

47 Int'l Law. 325 (2013)

Among EU Member States, there has been no fundamental shift from public enforcement to private enforcement of laws protecting various classes of consumers. According to a recent EU report, sixteen Member States have enacted collective redress schemes. These schemes provide "a complex legal patchwork of solutions" but, according to the report, these schemes are "not effective due to disparities and low participation rates." As defined in the report, the term "collective redress" encompasses "any mechanism that may accomplish the cessation or prevention of unlawful business practices which affect a multitude of claimants or the compensation for the harm caused by such practices" and that provides either for injunctive or compensatory relief. The report concludes that these collective redress schemes all "stop markedly short of full-fledged embrace of U.S.-style class actions."

The collective redress schemes adopted thus far by EU Member States barely resemble each other and are remotely different from the U.S.-style class action procedure. Unlike the U.S. class action, most of the Member State schemes are subject to opt-in requirements, thus denying defendant wrongdoers the preclusive effect against potential plaintiffs who do not formally consent to inclusion in a given class. Many of these schemes are not horizontally applicable to remedies in all areas of law, as in the United States, but are sectoral and thus limited by sectoral scope to consumer protection, product liability, or antitrust violations. These

---

[4]   Footnotes and paragraphs numbers omitted.

Member State schemes also have widely disparate standing requirements. Some only vest government authorities with the power to institute collective proceedings while others grant standing only to non-profit foundations and consumer organizations. Moreover, these collective redress schemes have been enacted in a legal context rich in oppositional legal traditions. The impediments that are inherent in these traditions are the single most important barrier to convergence. At the risk of oversimplification, I will highlight the most significant obstacles to convergence, including, first, those that arise from those legal traditions and, second, those that are integral to the extant collective redress schemes in the Member States. The following summary of characteristics of the Member States' legal systems clearly demonstrates why the U.S.-style class action is unlikely to serve as a model to be replicated either on a national or pan-European level in the EU.

Cultural Aversion to Private Litigation

The EU's Member States have legal cultures that are largely abhorrent to the adversarial legal system and litigious culture of the United States. They generally share a cultural aversion to litigation and have traditionally favored regulation and public enforcement over private litigation. Europe has a "historical preference for a regulatory rather than a citizen driven litigious response to widespread wrongdoing," and this preference "remains strong despite recent developments in collective redress litigation." The first reaction by a European grievously harmed is not, "I'll sic my lawyer on you" but, rather, "I'll denounce you to the police." This cultural aversion to private litigation operates largely independent of the costs attendant to retaining lawyers to pursue private or collective claims. Those costs only compound the cultural aversion.

The Absence of Contingency Fees

Contingency legal fees, the engine of the class action remedy in the United States, have been largely rejected by the EU's Member States. Fees based on a proportion of the sum recovered, pactum de quota litis, are prohibited in Germany, France, the Netherlands, Portugal, Austria, Belgium, Cypress, Malta, the Czech Republic, Denmark, Luxembourg, Greece, Ireland, Poland, Romania, and the United Kingdom. Some Member States do provide for conditional or success fees, payable only upon the successful conclusion of the litigation. In addition, such fees may include an uplift over normal rates but cannot include a proportion of the recovered damages. The prohibition of contingency fees not only serves to restrain aggrieved consumers financially unable to pursue expensive litigation, but also works as a fundamental restraint on the entrepreneurial zeal of their counsel.

The Loser Pays

The "English rule," commonly referenced to as the "loser pays," imposes on the losing party in litigation the obligation to pay the winning party's costs. This rule has been adopted by every EU Member State except Luxembourg. It is based on a culturally consistent policy of imposing financial risks on potential plaintiffs in order to discourage unnecessary litigation and of promoting out-of-court settlements. Consequently, European lawyers are prompted by the rule to analyze diligently the reasonable prospects for a successful outcome and the reasonable measure of damages to be sought through a lawsuit. By imposing the burden of both sides' costs on the party bringing the litigation, only claims that are clearly meritorious are likely to be filed by plaintiffs' counsel. Obviously, the loser pays rule seriously discourages access to justice. On the other hand, from the European perspective, it avoids the costliness and coercive settlements of weak claims endemic in the U.S. system. The loser pays rule will continue to be a substantial deterrent to consumer claims, whether brought individually or collectively.

Limitations on Discovery

In stark contrast to the liberal discovery procedures for document production and deposition testimony provided by U.S. courts, discovery is largely unavailable to the parties in litigation brought in the EU Member States. Instead, the Member States largely subscribe to the civil law tradition that the gathering of evidence is strictly a judicial function. Consequently, there is virtually no documentary or deposition discovery in the vast majority of EU Member States and only limited document discovery in the United Kingdom and Ireland. Discovery in the United Kingdom has been described as a "push" rather than a "pull" system, requiring attorneys, as officers of the court, to provide to the adverse party all documents that support either party's position in the litigation. Accordingly, the discovery process is not dependent on the parties' requests for production and responses to those requests. In the continental Member States, litigation is administered by the presiding judge, and, thus, the parties' counsels have no authority to manage the discovery process. The liberal discovery procedures in the United States are, in sum, quite alien to European litigation.

The Absence of Jury Trials

No Member State in continental Europe provides the right to a jury trial in civil litigation. It is rarely used in Scotland and is available in England only for very limited categories of civil litigation. As Lord Denning noted in Ward v. James, jury trials in even personal injury cases are unsuitable because juries generally do not have the necessary expertise and experience to assess damages. Consequently, the success or failure of plaintiffs' claims must be determined by non-elected jurists who generally have the expertise and experience to determine both the facts and the law in civil litigation. The absence of fact finding by jurors, with limited understanding of legal and factual issues and with possible biases favoring loss-suffering consumers, precludes plaintiffs' counsel's appeals to jury sympathies and otherwise indeterminate outcomes. In other words, plaintiffs' counsels, aware that all civil cases are bench trials, are much less willing to roll the dice and file marginal claims.

The Absence of Punitive Damages

In the EU Member States, punitive damages generally are unavailable to wronged litigants, no matter how wanton the conduct of defendants. Accordingly, it is largely impossible for plaintiffs to secure punitive damage awards against defendants in the EU Member States. This prohibition of punitive damages is based primarily on the public policy that civil lawsuits should only permit compensatory damages. Punishment of wrongdoers is solely the promise of the criminal justice system. Again, in stark contrast to the U.S. civil justice system, punitive damage awards are universally disfavored in the EU and most jurisdictions worldwide.

The foregoing characteristics of the civil law legal systems in the EU Member States are, of course, sufficient in themselves to discourage, if not foreclose, even the least risk-averse plaintiffs' lawyers from pursuing civil claims on behalf of aggrieved consumers in the EU. The barriers these legal traditions pose are further heightened for those lawyers considering the filing of claims through a collective class action mechanism, even where one has been adopted by a particular Member State. The following completes my summary of the legal obstacles to the EU's replication of the U.S. class action model.

Sectoral Application

Most of the collective redress schemes adopted by the EU's Member States are limited in applicability to certain sectors of the law. Consequently, the Member States' class action devices are largely unavailable to plaintiffs who would assert claims under statutes or regulations not specifically addressed by a particular collective redress scheme. Although some of the adopted collective redress schemes are horizontal and thus have broad scopes of application, most are limited sectorally to consumer protection claims, product liability claims, antitrust (competition) claims, or some combination of these limited areas of application. As a result, claims made on behalf of a specified group of claimants for violation of statutes or regulations not within the scope of a given collective redress scheme—e.g., securities law violations—may not be asserted through collective redress. In such cases, those claims can only be pursued as individual cases under a given Member State's applicable law.

Restrictive Standing Requirements

The collective redress schemes enacted by various EU Member States generally provide standing to bring collective actions only to governmental authorities, consumer associations, and other specified organizations. In other words, most of the adopted collective redress schemes do not permit, as in the United States, any aggrieved plaintiff to act as a class representative, assuming his adequacy to protect the interests of the aggrieved class, to file a collective action against the wrongdoer. Accordingly, individuals without specifically authorized standing are unable to pursue claims on behalf of the subject class. Instead, they are relegated to individual actions, where the amount at stake may be insufficient to justify the time and expense of litigation, not to mention the other barriers discussed above.

Opt-in Requirements

The majority of collective redress schemes adopted thus far by the EU Member States require that all claimants in a given class on whose behalf a collective action has been filed actually opt-in to the represented class. All claimants must be individually identified, either at the time the collective action is filed or at some later stage of the proceedings. Any settlement agreement reached or judgment rendered will only bind those claimants who have expressly consented to the proceedings. The defendants remain subject to all claims that may be brought by injured consumers who have not opted-in to the litigation. Consequently, defendants are denied their highly coveted finality and thus cannot achieve any national or global peace through settlement with the representative of the particular class. These commonly applicable opt-in requirements generally foreclose the preclusive effect that incentivizes settlements by defendants in U.S. class actions. Indeed, the opt-out system that facilitates the U.S. class action procedure has been essentially a procedural gift to corporate defendants. Regardless of the underlying merits of a given class action, defendants are positioned to sidestep litigation risks by agreeing to insurance-funded settlements with plaintiffs' counsel, including generous concessions on attorney fees, and achieve finality even where a majority or more class members fail to file proofs of claim with settlement claims administrators. The filing of claims by small stakeholders has long been categorized as an onerous process, in which, dependent on the length of the litigation, claims documentation may be impossible as a practical matter. The U.S. class action system is, in reality, an opt-in system in the sense that unless a class member opts-in, at least at the post-settlement stage, that class member will receive no distribution whatsoever and, compounding the tragedy, will be precluded forever from filing claims against the defendants. The U.S. opt-out system perversely encourages class action lawsuits, providing finality for defendants and denying access to justice for a significant percentage, if not a majority, of aggrieved class members.

The foregoing summary, both of traditional, long-established civil litigation principles in Europe and the restrictive provisions of the collective redress schemes thus far adopted by the EU's Member States, should illustrate just how far apart the Member States of the EU are from the U.S. class action model. Both the European Commission and the European Parliament have rejected the U.S. model out of hand [. . .].

NOTES AND QUESTIONS

1.   Several of the procedural rules listed in the excerpt above allegedly limiting the development of collective redress mechanisms in the European Union are similar to the ones considered affecting the recourse to derivative lawsuits. Can you, however, identify some possible different reasons for the more limited use of collective redress systems and derivative lawsuits in Europe as opposed to the U.S.?

2.   What do you think are the crucial elements fostering collective redress systems?

3.   Do you think that U.S.-style class actions are an efficient tool to police directors and managers? Or do the costs of litigation exceed the benefits? Discuss.

4.   The case of class actions and collective redress systems in Europe is a good example of the problems of "legal transplants," situations in which an institute developed in one legal system and culture is "exported" to another one. Can you name one example of a legal transplant in which a new rule or institute has been introduced in your jurisdiction from abroad, or has been adopted abroad from your jurisdiction, which has not worked? And can you mention one example that has worked? For an interesting discussion of legal transplants more generally, *see* Michele Graziadei *Comparative Law as the Study of Transplants and Receptions*, in *The Oxford Handbook of Comparative Law* (Reimann and Zimmermann editors), 2006, Oxford University Press. The contribution can be purchased and downloaded on-line at www.oxfordhandbooks.com.

5.   We mentioned that class actions are not very often used to vindicate a corporate law claim. Can you, however, identify a typical corporate law claim, based for example on the breach of a fiduciary duty of a director, which might lead to a class action?

CHAPTER 8

SHAREHOLDERS' AGREEMENTS

■ ■ ■

INTRODUCTION

Shareholders' agreements are contracts among some (or sometimes all) shareholders regulating their relationships or the exercise of their rights; in some cases the corporation itself is also a party to the agreement. The best way to illustrate a shareholders' agreement is to consider two of the most common types of pacts that we will discuss more extensively below: limitations to the free transferability of the shares; and voting agreements, which govern the way in which the shareholders exercise their voting rights.

It is important to underline that shareholders' agreements constitute a separate contract, distinct from the corporate contract embodied in the articles of incorporation and the bylaws, and a contract that generally only binds the specific shareholders that have executed it (while the articles and bylaws generally bind all shareholders). The substantive provisions of a shareholders' agreement can often also be included in the articles or bylaws, representing in this case a clause of the governing documents. This option might have some advantages: for instance, in France, in a simplified public limited liability company (*société par actions simplifiée*) transferring the shares in violation of a charter provision would be invalid (Article L. 227–15 of the French commercial code); on the contrary a breach of a separate shareholders' agreement would only lead to the payment of damages (the transfer would be valid). Italian law is similar in this respect. There are, however, very good reasons why shareholders might prefer, when they have an option, to enter into a separate contract. For example, shareholders might want to be bound only with *some* other shareholders, not with *all*, and/or they might want to keep the agreement confidential: in some systems shareholders' agreements, especially in a listed corporation, must be disclosed, but often they can be kept confidential and unknown to other shareholders, especially in a closely held corporation. As we will see, there might also be other and more technical reasons why shareholders prefer to include, for example, a pre-emptive right in case of a sale of shares in a separate contract, rather than in the bylaws; reasons concerning how the agreement can be modified, or the available remedies in case of breach. In addition, the law might prohibit including certain provisions in the charter or bylaws: in this case a separate agreement is the only option. Finally, in some systems, there might be tax reasons to execute a shareholders' agreement, because transferring the shares among members of the agreement might reduce or exclude donation or inheritance taxes, something that might be important especially in a family-owned business.

In this chapter we will examine restrictive stock transfer agreements first, and voting agreements (and more generally agreements affecting the governance of the corporation) next, comparing and contrasting rules and practices existing in different jurisdictions. We will also discuss the legal effects of shareholders' agreements, focusing in particular on the consequences in case of breach, distinguishing the different effects of a clause included in a separate shareholders' agreement, or in the bylaws. As we will see, in the U.S. and U.K., shareholders' agreements are generally discussed almost exclusively in the context of closely held corporations, and are not particularly common in publicly held corporations. If you look at a U.S. corporate law casebook or manual, the chapter on shareholders' agreement will often be in the part discussing closely held corporations. In other systems, however—in particular in continental European systems, but not only—shareholders' agreements are broadly used also in publicly held and listed corporations. We will explore possible reasons for this difference.

One final point is that shareholders' agreements are extremely common in corporate practice, and are often used in international transactions, for example when establishing a joint venture in a foreign country. The ability to negotiate, understand, and litigate a shareholders' agreement is an important tool for any lawyer practicing nationally or internationally.

LIMITATIONS ON THE FREE TRANSFERABILITY OF THE SHARES

To become a voting member of a partnership, as a default rule, it is generally necessary to have the consent of the other partners. This is only natural, because partners normally have joint and several liability for the obligation of the partnership (with some exceptions), and because the governing rules envision an active involvement of partners in the management of the business enterprise. The Latin expression sometimes used to express the fact that the individual characteristics of the contracting parties are essential in partnerships is *"intuitu personae"* (literally, "because of the person"). On the other hand, free transferability of the shares is the general rule in corporations; indeed, as we noted in Chapter 3, free transferability of the shares is one of the defining features of corporations. Limited liability and the governance structure of the corporation make less relevant for fellow shareholders, creditors and other stakeholders who the shareholders are. This, at least, is how the theory goes.

In practice, however, things are quite different. Notwithstanding limited liability, especially in a closely held corporation, it is obviously very important for shareholders to know and trust their fellow shareholders. Just imagine a situation in which a corporation, in order to avoid insolvency, needs fresh financial resources in terms of equity: to be sure that your fellow shareholders are capable and willing to provide new funds can be essential. Similarly, there might be several reasons why you are willing to be in business with one person, from mutual trust to her skills and experience, but not with others.

Restrictive stock transfer agreements represent one way to eliminate or reduce the risk that fellow shareholders will transfer their participation to unwelcomed new investors. But they can be used also to achieve other connected goals, such as maintaining the existing "balance of power" among shareholders, protect minority shareholders against changes in the economic situation of the corporation, and so on.

The advantages of limitations to the free transferability of the shares are quite obvious. Their risks should also be clear: first of all, they might make some shareholders, as the French put it, *"prisonniers de la société"* ("prisoners of the corporation"), by creating insurmountable obstacles to the alienation of the shares, something that can be unfair and inefficient. On the other hand, especially when (as we will see in the next paragraph) combined with a voting agreement, these pacts can entrench some shareholders in a position of strength, allowing them to control the corporation even with a limited investment. They can contribute, in other words, to separate ownership and control in a way that causes agency costs and facilitate the extraction of private benefits from the corporation. Statutes and courts must therefore find the right balance between freedom of contract and the need to avoid undesirable results, especially in order to protect small investors.

There are different types of shareholders' agreements limiting the free transferability of the shares. The following "families" capture some of the most common ones that you might encounter; of course keep in mind that the following list is not carved in stone: the labels we use are just conventions, and sometimes different names might be used. As always, to understand the substance of the provisions is more important than to commit their names to heart.

Right of first offer provisions: these clauses provide that a shareholder, before executing a transfer of shares to a third party, must offer the shares to fellow members of the shareholders' agreement. Under a right of first offer provision, basically, shareholders who are parties to the agreement have a call option (right to buy) on the shares that another shareholder intends to sell. Right of first offer provisions can be generally divided into *right of first option*, pursuant to which the shares might be acquired by the offeree-shareholder paying a consideration calculated on the basis of a formula, or under the same conditions that the third party is willing to pay; and *right of first refusal*, pursuant to which the price at which the option can be exercised is fixed in the contract. Keep in mind, however, that different sources might use this terminology in a different way: for example, some people define a right of first offer as simply an obligation to negotiate with one party before others, and a right of first refusal as a call option under specified conditions. Again, do not sweat these semantic distinctions.

"Russian roulette" provisions: this colorful name refers to agreements providing that if shareholder X finds a potential buyer willing to buy the shares, upon request of other shareholders she must purchase their shares under the same conditions that the buyer is willing to pay her. The idea is that if fellow shareholders are dissatisfied with the possible new shareholders, they can exit the corporation alienating the shares at the same (and possibly fair) price offered by a third party.

Consent restraint provisions: these clauses provide that, before transferring shares to a third party, the alienating shareholder must secure the consent or approval of other shareholders or corporate bodies, typically the board of directors. The contract can be more or less narrow in terms of possible reasons to withhold consent, and the decision can be entirely discretionary and not subject to any duty to justify the denial of the consent. Needless to say, a broad provision might cause a shareholder to become a prisoner of the corporation, for example if the board of directors systematically and for no good reasons denies its permission to sell the shares. For this reason, in several systems completely discretionary restraint provisions are disliked by courts, or specific statutory protections are mandated (e.g., appraisal rights in case of prohibition to sell).

Limitations to certain possible buyers: in this case a provision might limit the freedom of existing shareholders to transfer the shares only to individuals that meet certain requirements in terms of education and experience, for example only to investors holding a college degree in chemistry for a closely held corporation managing a lab. The existence of the desired requirement might have to be evaluated by a body of the corporation, for example the board of directors, and in this case the provision is similar to a consent restraint in which the consent is dependent on certain more or less objective requirements. One interesting question, in this respect, is whether limitations to certain categories of people are lawful and enforceable. For example, what about a provision allowing the transfer of shares only to "Caucasian males younger than 45 years old," or to "Chinese citizens and people of Chinese descent" or to members of the "African Methodist Episcopal Church"? We are not going to answer this question, but you can discuss it in class. Hints for the discussion: Are discriminating clauses, in a private agreement, void per se? To the extent that the government could not discriminate, would prohibitions of discriminations also apply to private organizations, such as corporations? Would a court in your country enforce similar provisions?

Absolute prohibitions to transfer the shares: as the name suggests, in this case the clause would simply prohibit any alienation of the shares, at least for a certain period (these are also called "lock-up provisions," and sometimes are used when a corporation goes public, to ensure that controlling shareholders remain committed to the investment for a period of time). Courts and corporate law systems have little tolerance, however, for unreasonable restraints to the possibility to sell the shares.

Drag-along and tag-along provisions: a tag-along right assures that if a party (generally the majority shareholder) sells his shares, minority shareholders have the right to join the sale and sell their stake to the third party under the same conditions. More precisely, since the third-party buyer is generally not bound by the agreement, the majority seller has the duty to assure that the buyer will also purchase the shares of the minority. A drag-along is the opposite: it is the obligation of a party (generally the minority shareholder) to sell her shares together with the seller (generally the majority shareholder) to a buyer under the same conditions. The two provisions serve different purposes: a tag-along right protects non-selling shareholders from the risk of becoming fellow shareholders of someone they do not like, offering them a presumably fair way out. It is somehow similar to what we have called a "Russian roulette" provision, the difference being that in the case of the Russian roulette clause the seller of the shares to a third party must buy the shares of the other members of the agreement; in the case of a tag-along, the selling member of the agreement must convince the third-party buyer to purchase, in addition to his shares, also the ones of the other members of the agreement. A drag-along provision, on the other hand, can facilitate the sale of the shares (of the controlling shareholder), in case a buyer is only interested in acquiring a large stake in the corporation that includes the shares of all the parties of the agreement. Keep in mind, in this perspective, that the purchaser of a controlling stake in a corporation often wants to be able to buy out the minorities in order to avoid having to deal with them.

Of course all the above-mentioned provisions can be combined in different ways; therefore it is far from uncommon to have a shareholders' agreement that includes both a right of first refusal, and a tag-along: the parties have the right to either buy the shares that someone else is considering selling, or have their shares bought from the third party (from a financial point of view, it is like a collar, or call-put option triggered by the intention to sell the shares).

The bottom line here is that contractual freedom, in this area, is quite broad; and the fantasy of the parties can envision all sorts of different rules applicable in case of a transfer of shares. As mentioned before, a critical limitation to contractual freedom, often expressed in mandatory statutory provisions or judicial precedents, derives from the need to avoid freezing the market for the shares and reducing shareholders to prisoners of the corporation. The magic expression here is "unreasonable restraint to the free transferability of the shares." In most legal systems, therefore, absolute restrictions or restrictions that make it almost impossible to disinvest from the corporation are unlawful or at least unenforceable. For example, either based on general principles or on specific statutory provisions, most courts would not uphold absolute prohibitions to alienate the shares that are not limited to a reasonable period (e.g., three years). As we will see, some statutes prescribe the maximum duration of shareholders' agreements limiting the free transferability of the shares (and also other shareholders' agreements), or provide that they are not binding when certain events occur, for example when a tender offer is launched.

One question that sometimes people unfamiliar with these provisions ask is why a shareholder would accept these limitations to her freedom. Of course when the provision is enforced, there might always be a shareholder who would prefer not to encounter any limitation. The reason, obviously, is that *ex ante* the agreement might have been desirable or, at least, necessary to secure an investment. For example, imagine that shareholder A is interested in investing in XYZ Inc. with B, a controlling shareholder, but is afraid that in the future B might decide to sell the shares to someone else. It might make sense for A to accept to invest only if she and B enter into a tag-along provision, so that she is sure that if B sells to a third party, A can also sell the shares at the same conditions. At the same time, if for B it is important to have A as a shareholder (he might need the funds that A is able to provide), B might accept to sign the agreement. It can happen, however, that after a couple of years A decides to sell the shares, and the tag-along provision would apply to her sale too. She might not be happy about that, but still to execute the agreement might have been the best option *ex ante*.

THE JIMINY CORPORATION HYPOTHETICAL

Rather than a more extensive general and abstract discussion on restrictive stock transfer agreements, and before considering some cases, we propose a brief hypothetical, which we believe might help you to become more familiar with these agreements. Imagine the following scenario. You are a lawyer sitting in your office and, one fine day, a new client walks in seeking your advice. We will call him Mr. Pinocchio. Mr. Pinocchio tells you that he has been contacted by Mr. Cat and Ms. Fox, who have made him an interesting business proposition. He would become a minority shareholder holding 20% of the common shares of Jiminy Corporation; Mr. Cat and Ms. Fox will hold, respectively, 55% and 25%. Mr. Pinocchio is interested in this opportunity, envisioning the new enterprise as a profitable one. He also tells you that he is fine being a minority investor, and that the ownership structure is not negotiable. He trusts Mr. Cat and Ms. Fox, considering them honest and capable partners, but his real concern is that after a while one or both of them might sell the shares to a third party that he does not trust, in particular he is afraid that either Mr. Stromboli or Mr. Lampwick might acquire the shares: in Pinocchio's own words, two "goons" he does not respect. Pinocchio tells you that Cat and Fox have accepted to sign a right of first refusal agreement, and that they have prepared a draft. Your task as Pinocchio's lawyer is to read the proposed draft and point out all possible problems and pitfalls, suggesting—if necessary—how to rewrite the agreement in order to improve it. In doing so, keep in mind that the goal of your client is to avoid the possibility that the ownership structure of the corporation might change in a way he does not like, without having the opportunity to purchase the shares before other possible investors. Your task, therefore, is to make the agreement as strong as possible, and avoid any possible circumvention. Pinocchio also tells you that in this negotiation phase Cat and Fox are very likely to accept most proposed changes, as long as they are reasonable and fair, because they desperately need his five gold pieces to start the business.

The following is the draft agreement that Pinocchio shows you. Read it carefully, and try to identify its shortcomings, suggesting how to change it. ATTENTION, the answer is below, in the "Notes and Questions" section: if you want the exercise to be meaningful, make sure not to look at it before reasoning on this provision and/or discussing it in class.

"No stockholder shall sell to third parties his stock or any portion thereof without first having given written notice of such intention to this Corporation and to each other stockholder.

During the fifteen days succeeding the announcement each other stockholder shall have the right to purchase such stock, proportionally to his stake in the capital, at the same conditions offered by third parties."

NOTES AND QUESTIONS

1.   Needless to say, the draft provision above is oversimplified and there might be several valid improvements that you could suggest. We want to focus, however, on three potential problems. The first one is that the provision refers only to "sales" of shares and appears to be triggered only when a shareholder "sells" his shares. There are however many different ways to transfer ownership in the shares, and a sale is only one of them. The shares can be exchanged (bartered), contributed to another corporation, gifted, inherited, and so on. In this respect, therefore, if Pinocchio wants to enjoy a pre-emptive right anytime fellow shareholders intend to transfer the shares, the provision should be broader. Of course the problem is how to apply a call option when the consideration that the seller might obtain from a third party is not fungible cash, but a specific asset; or there is no consideration at all. If, for example, Cat wants to exchange his shares with an apartment owned by Stromboli, Pinocchio cannot—obviously—offer the same apartment. The shareholders' agreement must, therefore, provide for a mechanism to allow Pinocchio to exercise his option with a payment in cash: for example, in this situation, an independent expert must be appointed in order to determine the market value of the apartment, and Pinocchio will be allowed to purchase the shares paying a price equal to that value. The question might be even more difficult when the shares are donated or inherited. In some legal systems it might be questionable to allow Pinocchio to prevail and obtain the shares, paying a sum of money, because this might be considered an unacceptable limitation to the freedom to gift specific property to specific people or to dispose of personal property after death.

2.   A second problem is that the proposed text provides that the right of first refusal only applies when the shares are sold to "third parties." The reference to "third parties" is ambiguous: on the one hand, it might be interpreted as limited to transfers to buyers that are not shareholders and/or not members of the shareholders' agreement; on the other hand, it could be interpreted in a broader sense, as referring to any transfer to a buyer different from the seller. If the first—and quite likely—interpretation is followed, however, there is something that needs to be clarified with Pinocchio: if he wants the option to also apply if a fellow shareholder sells to another fellow shareholder, for example if Cat sells to Fox. The question is very important because it might be different, for Pinocchio (and any minority shareholder) to participate in a corporation with two other shareholders holding, respectively, 55% and 25% of the shares, or only with another controlling shareholder holding 80% of the shares. A minority shareholder might want to avoid a situation in which one single large shareholder owns almost all the shares and is able to take unilateral decisions without substantively being challenged by the minority. If this is the case, you might want to suggest to Pinocchio to clarify in the agreement that the option right is triggered in any case of transfer of the shares, both to shareholders and to third parties (non-shareholders).

3.   Finally, there is a problem with the fact that the option right can be exercised under the "same conditions" offered by a third party. Imagine that, give or take, considering the relevant elements, the fair value of the 25% participation of Fox is $100,000. What if Cat finds a completely naïve investor willing to pay an exorbitant price, for example $200,000? Pinocchio would be between a rock and a hard place: he either accepts to pay an excessive price to prevent the sale, or renounces exercising the option but accepts a new and possibly undesirable (if nothing else, because he has demonstrated not to be business-savvy) new shareholder. The solution to this problem is to provide that, in case of disagreement on the fairness of the price, the parties can initiate an evaluation procedure pursuant to which an independent expert will determine the fair price of the shares, and the parties will be allowed to exercise the option under the conditions determined by the expert. A few suggestions on how to write a similar provision: first, avoid identifying the expert *ex ante* in the contract. The reason should be obvious: imagine you indicate as an expert a famous professor of finance from the best business school in your country, which appears to be independent. At the time of the appraisal, the expert might be dead, might have married the selling shareholder thus losing her independence due to a clear conflict of interest, might have become incapacitated. . . . You should instead provide for a neutral appointment mechanism writing, for example, that the expert will be selected by the president of the court sitting where the corporation has its seat, or by dean of a renowned business school, among experts presenting certain requirements in terms of independence and competences. No system is perfect, and also in this case there is the possibility that the appointing person might lack independence, but in this way you should be able to avoid major problems.

4.   Based on these three suggestions, here's an improved version of the agreement:

> "No stockholder shall sell or otherwise transfer his stock or any portion thereof without first having given written notice of such intention and of the conditions of the transfer to this Corporation and to each other stockholder.
>
> During the fifteen days succeeding such notice each stockholder might require the Corporation to notify the Dean of XYZ Business School, who will appoint an independent appraiser among tenured professors of corporate finance in order to determine the fair value of the shares . . .
>
> Within ten days after the appraiser has indicated the fair value of the shares, each other stockholder shall have the right to purchase such stock, proportionally to his stake in the capital, at the price set forth by the appraiser . . ."

5.   An additional issue that you might want to discuss with your client is how shares would be divided in case more than one person exercise the option. In the previous example, if a shareholder owning 10 shares intends to

sell, and two shareholders each owning 15% decide to buy, each of them will be entitled to receive 5 shares. If only one of them exercises the option, he will be allowed (but also will have) to buy all the 10 shares. This seems fair because it might be difficult, for the seller, to find another buyer interested in only 5 shares. The structure of the provision in this respect is, however, negotiable also subject to the bargaining power of the parties. It is possible to give more or less flexibility to the shareholders intending to exercise the option with respect to the percentage of shares that they can/must buy. Try to imagine situations in which deviations from this approach might be desirable for one party, and explain them.

* * *

Hopefully the previous exercise contributed to make you understand more clearly the possible content of a right of first refusal and other similar limitations to the free transferability of the shares, including strategic considerations about how to negotiate and draft them. The exercise does not however entail, in itself, comparative considerations. We dare to say, in fact, that in terms of drafting limitations to the free transferability of the shares, there are comparative differences, but they are not particularly profound. Or, more precisely, we think that what you have discussed and learned in the Jiminy Corporation Hypothetical could be useful in different jurisdictions. From a comparative perspective, you will probably find more differences, in this area, concerning contract interpretation techniques, specific rules governing the disclosure and duration of this type of agreements, available remedies in case of breach, and whether they bear against third parties.

In this perspective, let's start with one case combining the problem of unreasonable restraints to the transfer of shares and contract interpretation. It is a famous U.S. case, which offers the occasion to compare U.S. law with other systems.

IN RE ESTATE OF GILBERT MATHER

Supreme Court of Pennsylvania
410 Pa. 361 (1963)

BELL, CHIEF JUSTICE.

The Executors of the Estate of Gilbert Mather took this appeal from a decree which entered judgment on the pleadings and ordered specific performance of a written stock option agreement. The Executors claim the agreement was invalid as *an unreasonable restraint on alienation*, because the optional purchase price was fixed at $1.00 per share, which was only a small fraction of the stock's actual value.

In order to decide this question a review of the relevant facts is necessary.

Prior to 1926 Mather & Co. was a partnership consisting of Charles E. Mather, his two sons Victor C. Mather and Gilbert Mather, and his daughter Josephine C. Mather. In December, 1926, the partners incorporated their insurance business under the name of 'Mather & Co.'

Of the 1,000 authorized shares of common stock, 800 were issued as follows:

Charles E. Mather: 250 shares

Victor C. Mather: 250 shares

Gilbert Mather: 250 shares

Josephine C. Mather 50 shares

On December 22, 1926, the four stockholders entered into a written agreement which provided, inter alia, that if any one of the four die or desire to sell his (or her) participation, would first have to offer it to the others at $50 per share.

Charles E. Mather died October 31, 1928. Victor and Gilbert exercised their respective options and bought the stock which was owned by (the executors of) Charles E. Mather for $50 per share. As a result of these purchases

Victor C. Mather: 375 shares

Gilbert Mather: 375 shares

Josephine C. Mather 50 shares

On or about January 9, 1933, 50 shares of stock held in the treasury but previously unissued, were issued to Charles E. Mather II, the son of Victor C. Mather.

On November 6, 1939, Victor C. Mather, Gilbert Mather and Josephine C. Mather entered into a written agreement which provided' [. . .] the said contract of December 22, 1926 is hereby canceled and terminated by the unanimous consent of Victor C. Mather, Gilbert Mather and Josephine C. Mather insofar as the Fifty Shares of Common Stock of the said Mather & Co., held by the said Josephine C. Mather, is concerned, to the end that the said Josephine C. Mather may enter into an Agreement with Mather & Co. relative to and touching upon said Fifty Shares of Common Stock held by her.'

On the same day, viz., November 6, 1939, Josephine C. Mather and Mather & Co. entered into a written agreement which pertinently provided: 'That the said Josephine C. Mather agrees to sell and the said Mather & Co. agrees to buy said Fifty shares of Common Stock of Mather & Co., a Pennsylvania Corporation, from the personal representatives of the said Josephine C. Mather at her death at the rate of Fifty Dollars ($50.00) per share, the payment for same and the transfer of same to be consummated within thirty days of the death of Josephine C. Mather. And the said Josephine C. Mather on her part agrees not to sell said Fifty Shares of Common Stock of Mather & Co. during her lifetime to any person or corporation other than the said Mather & Co. without first obtaining from the said Mather & Co. its consent in writing to such sale and transfer.'

On the same day, viz., November 6, 1939, Victor, Charles II and Gilbert entered into a written agreement which pertinently provided:

'2.   That in the event of the death of Gilbert Mather, or in the event of his offering his stock for sale during his life, he, for himself, his heirs, executors and administrators, agrees to sell, and Victor C. Mather and Charles E. Mather, 2nd agree to buy, in equal proportions, at One Dollar ($1.00) per share, any or all of the Common Stock holdings of the said Gilbert Mather.

'4.   That as to any or all of the above three provisions, the survivors or survivor among the class of purchasers in each case shall be entitled to the entire rights given the purchasers in each case.

'5.   That in the event that any of the aforesaid stock, when for sale by the stockholder, or his estate, is not purchased by those entitled to purchase, as aforesaid, then the holder of said stock, or his personal representatives shall have the right to sell same upon the open market without restrictions.

'9.   That the parties hereto further agree that the provisions of the aforesaid agreement and the rights to purchase thereunder shall accrue in each case not only as to the original holdings of each of the signatories hereto, but also to any and all additional holdings of common stock as may come into the ownership of any of the signatories hereto by operation of this agreement, or otherwise.

'10. That the parties hereto further agree not to at any time sign or hypothecate or make any effort to transfer shares of Common Stock of Mather & Co. contrary to the terms of this agreement.

'11. That the parties further agree that this agreement shall be binding upon the heirs, executors and administrators of the parties hereto * * *.'

Following the death of Victor C. Mather, his executors sold and Gilbert and Charles II, purchased on July 16, 1943, in equal proportions at $1.00 per share, all of the common stock of Victor, in accordance with the aforementioned agreement of November 6, 1939. After this purchase, the stock was held as follows:

Gilbert Mather: 562½ shares

Charles E. Mather, II: 273½ shares

Josephine C. Mather: 50 shares

On June 5, 1950, *Gilbert* sold 61 1/2 shares to Charles II at $1.00 per share, making the holdings:

Charles E. Mather, II: 299 shares

Gilbert Mather: 501 shares

Josephine C. Mather: 50 shares

Josephine C. Mather died August 12, 1953, and her 50 shares were sold to Mather & Co. at $50 per share, as per the above mentioned agreement between her and Mather & Co. dated November 6, 1939.

Following the death of Gilbert on October 23, 1959, Charles II tendered $501 to the Executors of the Estate of Gilbert Mather for the purchase of Gilbert's stock. At the time of the tender, the stock of Mather & Co. was carried on the books at $444.92, and its actual value was not less than $1,060 per share. After the tender had been refused Charles E. Mather II filed a petition in the Orphans' Court asking for specific performance of the aforesaid agreement of November 6, 1939.

[. . .] In order to determine the meaning of the agreement, we must examine the entire contract since it is well settled that in construing a contract the intention of the parties governs and that intention must be ascertained from the entire instrument taking into consideration the surrounding circumstances, the situation of the parties when the contract was made and the objects they apparently had in view and the nature of the subject matter. [. . .]

In addition to the hereinabove recited provisions, this agreement provided:

'WHEREAS: The parties, *for their mutual benefit*, desire to perpetuate the business of Mather & Co., and the ownership of the Common Stock thereof in the *Mather family*.'

When the family changed the form of the family business from a partnership to a corporation their language and intent was crystal clear— they wanted and intended to keep the stock of Mather & Co. in the Mather family if any Mather wanted it; and to carry out this intent they gave the options, rights and obligations so clearly and specifically set forth in the aforesaid agreements.

[. . .]

The aforesaid written agreements, including the one in suit, were made between mature members of a close family and it is conceded that there was no overreaching or fraud or deceit. The facts and the lawfulness of the purpose were admitted by appellants. However, appellants argue that the agreement was *an invalid restraint on alienation* because the price was clearly very *unfair* and *unchangeable*. The contention that a stock option or purchase price must be flexible is unrealistic and utterly devoid of merit, even if we overlook the fact that the price was not unchangeable since in 1939 the parties entered into the present written agreement changing the price on options, purchases and sales from $50 to $1.00. Moreover, we repeat, the agreement clearly and expressly set forth the *intention* of all the parties—they wanted to keep the family business in the Mather family and to give each other and their personal representatives the options, rights and obligations hereinabove recited. There was a limited but not an absolute restriction on sale, since if the option was not exercised by a living signatory to the family agreement 'the holder of said stock or his personal representatives shall have the right to sell same upon the open market without restrictions.' In this free land of ours where even a State can not impair the obligations of a contract, we cannot understand how it can be seriously contended that this written family agreement—and family agreements are always favored in the law—when made by adult business men without any overreaching or fraud, is 'a scrap of paper.'

Not only was there no overreaching or fraud but *Gilbert Mather himself* in 1950 bought from Victor Mather's executors 187 1/2 shares at $1.00 per share and in 1950 sold 61 1/2 shares of Mather & Co. stock at a price of one dollar a share to Charles E. Mather, II. In the light of this, it seems anomalous that Gilbert's executors contend that the agreement was valid for Gilbert, but invalid for Charles.

Appellants contend, we repeat, that this agreement is an unreasonable restraint on alienation.

[. . .]

A similar question was raised in Allen et al., Executors v. Biltmore Tissue Corporation (Court of Appeals of New York, April 4, 1957), 2 N.Y.2d 534, 161 N.Y.S.2d 418, 141 N.E.2d 812, 61 A.L.R.2d 1309, where the Court said:

'The question posed, therefore, is whether the provision, according the corporation a right or first option to purchase the stock at the price which it originally received for it, amounts to an unreasonable restraint. In our judgment, it does not.

'The courts have almost uniformly held valid and enforceable the first option provision, in charter or by-law, whereby a shareholder desirous of selling his stock is required to afford the corporation, his fellow stockholders or both an opportunity to buy it before he is free to offer it to outsiders. [. . .] In Doss v. Yingling, supra, 95 Ind.App. 494, 172 N.E. 801 a leading case on the subject and one frequently cited throughout the country, a by-law provision against transfer by any stockholder—there were three—of any shares until they had first been offered for sale to other stockholders at *book value*, was sustained as reasonable and valid, 95 Ind.App. at page 500, 172 N.E. at page 803: 'The weight of authority is to the effect that a corporate by-law which requires the owner of the stock to give the other stockholders of the corporation * * * *an option to purchase the same at an agreed price or the then-existing book value before offering the stock for sale to an outsider, is a valid and reasonable restriction and binding upon the stockholders.*"

[. . .] To summarize: We find no merit in appellants' contention that where there is no overreaching or fraud, the great difference between the sale price and the actual value of the stock is sufficient, alone or with the aforesaid additional facts, to invalidate the agreement or defeat specific performance.

Decree affirmed, costs to be paid by appellants.

COHEN, JUSTICE (dissenting).

The majority here fails to recognize, and hence does not discuss, the manner in which this agreement differs from the usual first option agreement. Here, the agreement creates an absolute restraint against transfers and provides for a first refusal price which is unconscionably nominal in relation to the value of the shares *at the time the arrangement was made*. I would hold where an agreement entered into at a time when the actual value of the stock is $50 or more a share, which agreement prohibits the sale of shares by any party during his life-time without first offering the same to the other shareholders at a price of $1.00 per share, that the imposition of this nominal and unvariable pre-emption price creates an unreasonable restraint upon the alienability of the shares and imposes an invalid restriction on their transfer. See Sparks, 'Future Interests' 32 N.Y.U.Law Rev. 1434 (1957); Baker and Cary, Cases and Materials on Corporations, 322–26 (3rd ed. 1958).

The fact that the parties have entered into the agreement of their own free will cannot validate provisions which are void as against public policy; nor does the fact that there was no overreaching or that Gilbert Mather himself bought shares at $1.00 per share from Victor Mather's executors legalize an unreasonable restraint on alienation.

I dissent.

NOTES AND QUESTIONS

1.   In this case the Court decided that a right of first refusal that gives to shareholders the option to purchase shares at a nominal price, significantly below their fair value, was not an unreasonable restraint on the transferability of the shares. In reaching this conclusion, the Court relied on principles of contract interpretation: it pointed out the need to investigate the intention of the parties. The majority observed that: "in construing a contract the intention of the parties governs and that intention must be ascertained from the entire instrument taking into consideration the surrounding circumstances, the situation of the parties when the contract was made and the objects they apparently had in view and the nature of the subject matter." A first question for you is if this attitude is consistent with the one of the court in *Morgan Stanley v. ADM*, discussed in Chapter 4 and concerning the interpretation of a trust indenture.

2.   Since no fraud was found in this case, an agreement among consenting adults pursuing the goal of keeping the ownership of the corporation within the family was upheld, and contractual freedom trumpeted the fact that the exercise of the option was very advantageous for the buyers. The short dissenting opinion, however, is also quite powerful, arguing that public policy arguments should prevail over contractual freedom. Do you side with the majority or with the dissenting judge? Could you explain why? Do you think it would be easier or more difficult to argue the invalidity or unenforceability of the agreement in the hypothetical case that, when it was executed, the fair value of the shares was, in fact, $1.00 (the strike price of the option)?

3.   It is sometimes observed that common law judges and jurists tend to adopt a more objective approach in interpreting contracts, in the sense that—simplifying—there is a more strict adherence to the written text of the agreement (and consider the "four corners" approach and the "parol-evidence rule"). On the other hand, in civil law systems, figuring out the common intention of the parties using also extra-textual elements of interpretation is considered more important, or at least more widely accepted and encouraged (subjective interpretation). According to some observers, this difference is also related to the tendency to have longer, more detailed contracts in common law systems than in civil law systems. To the extent that there is some truth in this assertion, where do you think *In re Estate of Mather* decision falls on the objective-subjective interpretation dichotomy? In this respect, please keep in mind, however, that even in systems that adopt a more subjective interpretation approach, this is generally used for contracts such as shareholders' agreements, but not for so-called "open contracts," such as the articles of incorporation and the bylaws of a corporation. The reason, clearly enough, is that in the case of "open contracts" new parties (*i.e.*, new shareholders) can become members of the organization *after* the governing documents have been executed, and often the parties at a given time are different from the founding shareholders. It would seem illogical and unfair, therefore, to interpret the corporate contract in a way consistent with the

intent of its drafter: objective interpretation seems preferable to subjective interpretation. For a concise but excellent discussion of differences in contract interpretation rules and techniques in civil law and common law systems *see* Catherine Valcke, *Contractual Interpretation at Common Law and Civil Law: An Exercise in Comparative Legal Rhetoric*, in EXPLORING CONTRACT LAW, J. Neyers, ed., Hart Publisher, 2008 (also available on www.ssrn.com).

4. If you are not from the U.S., also based on the above-mentioned distinction between contractual interpretation styles in common law and civil law systems, how do you think the *Mather* case could have been resolved in your system? A partially similar case was decided in Japan. If you are interested, try to find it (this could also be a research project to learn how to find cases; of course if you are familiar with the Japanese systems it would be very easy), and compare it with the *Mather* case: Supreme Court of Japan, February 17, 2009, 2038 Hanrei Jiho 144.

* * *

Let's briefly talk about remedies in case of breach. Shareholders' agreements are contracts among parties, and in case of breach, generally speaking, the typical remedy would be damages. If a share transfer limitation is breached, and the shares sold to a non-member of the agreement, therefore, it is impossible to get back the shares from the buyer, at least in the absence of bad faith. Russia is a good example: Article 32.1 of the Federal Corporate Law provides that "Shareholders' agreements are only binding for the parties. A contract executed by one of the parties in violation of the agreement can be voided by the judge, upon the request of an interested party, only if it is proved that the other party knew or should have known the limitations provided by the agreement."

Going back to our Pinocchio hypothetical, therefore, imagine that Fox breaches the agreement and sells the shares to Lampwick. What can Pinocchio do? Of course he can sue Fox for breach of contract, but one problem is the calculation of damages. What is the damage suffered by Pinocchio because a new shareholder has entered the corporation and/or because he was not allowed to exercise his option? Clearly, it might be very difficult to tell, and this could lead to extensive litigation. One idea to mitigate this problem, and to create a disincentive to a breach, would be to include a liquidated damages clause in the agreement, possibly setting a measure of damages that would discourage the parties from violating the contract. In most jurisdictions, courts enforce liquidated damages and/or penalty provisions if they are not inequitably high. Damages could however be a very dissatisfactory remedy: the real goal of Pinocchio is to keep Lampwick out of the corporation. It might also be important, in this respect, if the parties stipulate in the agreement that a breach would determine an irreparable harm; in several jurisdictions this might help to obtain a restraining order or other injunctive relief against

Fox; but if the shares have *already* been transferred to a third party, it might be very difficult—indeed, often impossible—to claim the right to own the shares. The third-party buyer is not part of the shareholders' agreement, and the agreement is not enforceable against him.

We want to underline one important comparative distinction in this respect. A stock transfer restriction can be included in a separate shareholders' agreement, or can be included in the bylaws of the corporation. In the first case, what we have mentioned above in terms of unenforceability toward third parties is true in most legal systems; but if the provision is included in the governing documents, in some systems (especially in civil law systems, for example in France, Italy, Spain) it also bears against third parties. The rationale is that the bylaws, in these systems, are a public document, and a third party, before buying the shares, can obtain a copy: therefore there is a sort of constructive knowledge of the agreement by the third party. In this case, the third party might be forced to relinquish ownership of the shares and our friend Pinocchio might be able to claim them; alternatively the transfer in violation of the bylaws provision might be considered void. A good example is German law. The German Corporation Law offers two ways to limit the transferability of the shares. First, the charter of the corporation can state that the transfer of the share requires the approval of the corporation (Sec. 68 German Stock Corporation Act). In this case a contract transferring the shares without the approval of the corporation would be void. However, this limitation, called *Vinkulierung* (from Latin *vinculum*, meaning "chain"), can only be used for registered shares (*Namensaktien*). For bearer shares (*Inhaberaktien*) such a limitation can only be established in a shareholder agreement on a contractual basis, and in case of violation only damages would be available. A provision limiting the transferability of bearer shares in the charter would be considered void.

In the U.S., the inclusion of stock transfer limitations in the bylaws does not make them automatically binding on third parties. Limitations to the free transferability of the shares might be binding on third parties if they are noted conspicuously on the share certificates, but inclusion in the bylaws (which are often not a public document) does not suffice, by itself, to bind third parties.

Based on this additional piece of information, let's go back to our hypothetical. Put yourself once again in the shoes of Pinocchio's counselor, and imagine that you are in a civil law system that follows the above-mentioned approach (for example, Italy). Your client tells you: "Hey, Fox and Cat have told me that for them it's the same to include the right of first refusal in a separate shareholders' agreement, or in the bylaws. What do you suggest to do to make the provision as strong and effective as possible?"

Think about it for a moment (hint: consider the percentage of shares held by the three shareholders).

You might be tempted to suggest including the clause in the bylaws. After all, if this makes it binding on third parties, the bylaws option has the advantage that Pinocchio will be able to recover the shares from Lampwick or any undesired new shareholder. There is however a twist that you can think about. Even if you know nothing about the jurisdiction we are considering, there is a question that you should ask yourself.

The question is: what are the rules to amend a separate shareholders' agreement, and to amend the bylaws? A separate contract normally can only be amended with the unanimous agreement of all parties; the default rule to amend the bylaws, on the other hand, is a majority vote. In our case, remember that Pinocchio only has 20% of the shares, while Cat has 55% and Fox 25% It is true that, in a way, a stock transfer restriction in the bylaws is "stronger" for the above-mentioned reasons; however, Pinocchio should be aware that, other things being equal, if the clause is part of the bylaws, Cat and Fox (and possibly even Cat alone) could change the bylaws and eliminate or modify the rule in a way that would allow them to sell the shares. The idea, here, is that to answer this question you must know the rules governing amendments of contracts generally (usually, unanimity), and of that particular contract that is the bylaws of a corporation (usually, majority).

It is however possible to have the best of both worlds. If the other shareholders (or enough shareholders to reach a majority) agree, you can include the restriction in the bylaws, but also provide for a supermajority requirement to eliminate or amend the restriction. For example, in our case, if a supermajority of 85% is necessary to amend the right of first refusal, Pinocchio will have a veto power to prevent any undesired modification. Also, you should make sure that in the jurisdiction you are operating a supermajority requirement like this one is lawful and enforceable (in some systems very high supermajority requirements, or unanimity requirements in corporate bylaws, are not acceptable for fear of a deadlock). But once you have established this, you might help your client. Be also aware that in some countries the corporate statute itself, for some business organizations, might attribute a veto power on amendments of the governing documents to minority shareholders. For example, in a French simplified public limited company (*société par actions simplifiée*), provisions like the one we are discussing can only be introduced in and removed from the governing documents by unanimous vote (Article L. 227–19 of the French commercial code).

A smart lawyer's suggestion, in any case, would be—if possible—to actually have both: a separate shareholders' agreement *and* a provision in the bylaws containing a stock transfer restriction.

One final insight. Also if your only option is a separate contract with other shareholders, and you cannot include the restraint in the bylaws, there might be other techniques to make a breach less likely. We have already mentioned the liquidated damages provision, and that is for sure useful. Something else you might consider is to require the parties to deposit the shares with a trusted independent third party, e.g., an attorney or a bank, who will undertake the obligation not to deliver the shares to a third-party buyer unless it is established that the pre-emptive right has been offered to and refused by other shareholders. In jurisdictions in which it is possible to establish a trust, a trust can also be used to achieve this goal.

* * *

VOTING AGREEMENTS

Voting agreements are another common type of contract among shareholders. Shareholders participating in a voting agreement basically agree to vote at the shareholders' meeting of the corporation in a certain way and following certain rules. In this respect, we can distinguish three basic types of voting agreements. Ranking them from the less intrusive on the shareholders' franchise to the more intrusive, they are: consultation agreements, unanimity agreements, and majority agreements.

Pursuant to the first type, the only obligation that shareholders undertake is to get together and consult among themselves before any occasion in which they have to vote, either at a convened meeting, or by written consent. The purpose of this "weak" type of agreement is simply to facilitate the adoption of a shared voting strategy, but no specific obligation concerning how to vote is envisioned.

In a unanimity agreement, shareholders are bound to vote in the shareholders' meeting according to the outcome of a "pre-vote," but only if they all agreed on how to vote at the upcoming meeting. Consider for example a closely held corporation with five shareholders. Three of them, A, B, and C, holding respectively 30, 20 and 5% of the shares, execute a unanimity voting agreement. Pursuant to the agreement, before the date of a shareholders' meeting called, for example, to approve a merger, the parties will get together or otherwise communicate according to what has been established in the agreement. If the three of them agree that they should vote in favor of the merger, this "pre-meeting" decision becomes binding, and A, B, and C will have to participate either in person or by proxy to the meeting, and vote accordingly (in favor of the merger). If they do not, they have breached the agreement and might be liable for damages. On the other hand, if even just one of them, for example C with only a 5% stake, is contrary to the merger, without unanimity there is no binding decision, and each shareholder is free to vote as he or she sees fit in the following meeting. In other words, each member of the agreement has the right to veto a shared and binding decision. Also in this case the goal is to foster the ability of a group of shareholders to follow a common strategy, and the effects of the agreement are stronger than in the case of a mere consultation agreement; however, there is a binding decision only if all the contracting parties see the issue eye-to-eye.

Finally, in a majority voting pact, the decision of the majority of the members of the agreement becomes binding also on dissenting shareholders: based on the contract, all of the members must align themselves to the will of the majority in voting at the shareholders' meeting. Using again the example of A, B, and C, pursuant to a majority agreement the three of them will have to get together before the shareholders' meeting that must vote on a merger. If A, holding 30% is in favor of the merger, and B and C, jointly owning 25% oppose it, the majority (of the participants in the agreement) supports the merger, and therefore all three shareholders must vote in favor. If they do not, they have breached the agreement.

Needleless to say, majority voting agreements are often the most attractive for the parties, but also the most controversial. They are a typical control enhancing device: in the previous example A, with a participation of only 30% thanks to the agreement controls, in fact, 55% of the votes. A's control is not absolute, in the sense that B or C might decide to breach the agreement, but there might be legal strategies, such as a liquidated damages provision or others that we will consider below, to make breach unlikely, if not impossible. The consequence is a possible alteration of the proportionality between economic interest and voting power. For this reason, some authors have even suggested the unlawfulness of voting agreements, but as interesting as this position might be from a policy perspective, it has rarely gained significant traction in most modern corporate law systems. Two Italian scholars, for example, have in the past considered with skepticism these agreements: Tullio Ascarelli, at least since the 1950s, and more recently Guido Rossi, possibly also in light of the widespread use (and one might say abuse) of this device in their own national system. Statutes have however recently expressly regulated shareholders' agreements, providing for rules concerning their duration and disclosure, as we will see below, with the consequence that today, in most jurisdictions, it is impossibile to argue the unlawfulness of shareholders' agreements *per se*, while criticisms in a reform perspective is naturally still possible.

You might once again wonder why a minority shareholder, for example C in the previous example, would join a majority voting agreement limiting his voting freedom. There might be several reasons: family ties suggesting to some shareholders to establish a formal way to coordinate their voting strategies. Alternatively, C might have been allowed to purchase shares in the corporation only under the condition that he would sign the voting agreement. Again, there might be a mutual benefit because, for example, C is the majority shareholder in another corporation participated by A and B with minority stakes. Entering into shareholders' agreements for both corporations, C makes A's position stronger in the first one, and A makes C's position stronger in the second one.

A couple of additional observations concerning voting agreements are in order. Differently from stock transfer restrictions, which might be included in a separate agreement only among shareholders and in the bylaws of the corporation, voting agreements are rarely included in the bylaws. One of the reasons, at least in some systems, is simply that voting agreements are valid and enforceable as a separate contract, not binding for the corporation, but are not valid and enforceable in the bylaws because they might violate mandatory corporate governance rules. In addition, as you can imagine, while a stock transfer restriction might make sense also without a voting agreement, a voting agreement is hardly effective if it is not accompanied by a limitation to the free transferability of the shares. In fact, if shareholders A and B are bound by a voting agreement, but one of them can sell the shares to a third party that is obviously not bound by the voting agreement, the whole purpose of the voting agreement would be frustrated. It is therefore fairly rare to have a voting agreement not coupled with a limitation to the transferability of the shares. This can however happen in situations in which the shareholders with the right to vote are already clearly identified, and the parties want to bind themselves only for the upcoming shareholders' meeting.

A simple "vote pooling agreement" binds the parties, and the party breaching the agreement might be required to pay damages. As we will consider below, since damages are difficult to determine in these situations, a liquidated damages provision might be very important. Additionally, as we also see below, sometimes courts might order specific performance of the agreement. Damages are however clearly an inadequate remedy: the parties want to ensure that the shares are voted according to the agreement. Some legal techniques to reinforce voting agreements, therefore, include depositing the shares with a trusted third party, granting him an irrevocable proxy (to the extent that this is possible) to vote the shares pursuant to the contract. Alternatively, in systems that recognize the trust, one possibility is to transfer the shares to a trust, and instruct the trustee to vote them according to the agreement. The trust creates a separation between ownership and voting rights because the trustee has exclusive power to vote the shares, and therefore voting trusts are subject to certain limitations. For example, in the U.S., under the Model Business Corporation Act, the voting trust agreement must be formed with certain formalities, delivered to the corporation, and—most importantly—is only valid for ten years unless extended (we will come back to duration of voting agreements below).

A very important and delicate issue concerning voting agreements is if shareholders can bind themselves not only to vote in a certain manner in the shareholders' meeting, but also to vote or act in a certain way as directors. A typical scenario is the following: shareholders A and B not only want to bind themselves to appoint each other as director, but also to vote, as members of the board of directors, to appoint A CEO of the corporation, or to approve a certain compensation package for executives. Can they do that? Would the agreement be valid and enforceable? The first part of the agreement (how to vote *as shareholders*) is generally not a problem, but it is more uncertain if they can also bind themselves *as directors*. As we know from Chapter 6, an argument against this possibility is that directors have the duty to act diligently in the best interest of the corporation and the shareholders, a duty that also implies a risk of liability. In order to carry on their duties, directors should be free to decide the best course of action based on all the existing and variable circumstances, and cannot be bound by an agreement that limits their freedom. Courts appear sometimes to take a less rigid approach, and uphold these agreements, subject to certain conditions. The following two cases, one from the U.S., and one from an Italian arbitration, provide the framework to discuss this issue. You can find the Notes and Questions for both decisions after the second one.

CLARK V. DODGE ET AL.

Court of Appeals of New York
269 N.Y. 410 (1936)

CROUCH, JUDGE.

[The facts], briefly stated, are as follows: The two corporate defendants are New Jersey corporations manufacturing medicinal preparations by secret formulae. The main office, factory, and assets of both corporations are located in the state of New York. In 1921, and at all times since, Clark owned 25 per cent and Dodge 75 per cent of the stock of each corporation. Dodge took no active part in the business, although he was a director, and through ownership of their qualifying shares, controlled the other directors of both corporations. He was the president of Bell & Co., Inc., and nominally general manager of Hollings-Smith Company, Inc. The plaintiff, Clark, was a director and held the offices of treasurer and general manager of Bell & Co., Inc., and also had charge of the major portion of the business of Hollings-Smith Company, Inc. The formulae and methods of manufacture of the medicinal preparations were known to him alone. Under date of February 15, 1921, Dodge and Clark, the sole owners of the stock of both corporations, entered into a written agreement under seal, which after reciting the stock ownership of both parties, the desire of Dodge that Clark should continue in the efficient management and control of the business of Bell & Co., Inc., so long as he should 'remain faithful, efficient and competent to so manage and control the said business'; and his further desire that Clark should not be the sole custodian of a specified formula, but should share his knowledge thereof and of the method of manufacture with a son of Dodge, provided, in substance, as follows: That Dodge during his lifetime and, after his death, a trustee to be appointed by his will, would so vote his stock and so vote as a director that the plaintiff (a) should continue to be a director of Bell & Co., Inc.; and (b) should continue as its general manager so long as he should be 'faithful, efficient and competent'; (c) should during his life receive one-fourth of the net income of the corporations either by way of salary or dividends; and (d) that no unreasonable or incommensurate salaries should be paid to other officers or agents which would so reduce the net income as materially to affect Clark's profits. Clark on his part agreed to disclose the specified formula to the son and to instruct him in the details and methods of manufacture; and, further, at the end of his life to bequeath his stock—if no issue survived him—to the wife and children of Dodge.

It was further provided that the provisions in regard to the division of net profits and the regulation of salaries should also apply to the Hollings-Smith Company.

The complaint alleges due performance of the contract by Clark and breach thereof by Dodge in that he has failed to use his stock control to continue Clark as a director and as general manager, and has prevented Clark from receiving his proportion of the income, while taking his own, by causing the employment of incompetent persons at excessive salaries, and otherwise.

The relief sought is reinstatement as director and general manager and an accounting by Dodge and by the corporations for waste and for the proportion of net income due plaintiff, with an injunction against further violations.

The only question which need be discussed is whether the contract is illegal as against public policy within the decision in McQuade v. Stoneham, 263 N.Y. 323, 189 N.E. 234, upon the authority of which the complaint was dismissed by the Appellate Division.

'The business of a corporation shall be managed by its board of directors.' General Corporation Law (Consol.Laws, c. 23) § 27. That is the statutory norm. Are we committed by the McQuade Case to the doctrine that there may be no variation, however slight or innocuous, from that norm, where salaries or policies or the retention of individuals in office are concerned? There is ample authority supporting that doctrine. E. g.,

West v. Camden, 135 U.S. 507, 10 S.Ct. 838, 34 L.Ed. 254; Jackson v. Hooper, 76 N.J.Eq. 592, 75 A. 568, 27 L.R.A. (N.S.) 658. But cf. Salomon v. Salomon & Co., [1897] A.C. 22, 44, and something may be said for it, since it furnishes a simple, if arbitrary, test. Apart from its practical administrative convenience, the reasons upon which it is said to rest are more or less nebulous. Public policy, the intention of the Legislature, detriment to the corporation, are phrases which in this connection mean little. Possible harm to bona fide purchasers of stock or to creditors or to stockholding minorities have more substance; but such harms are absent in many instances. If the enforcement of a particular contract damages nobody—not even, in any perceptible degree, the public—one sees no reason for holding it illegal, even though it impinges slightly upon the broad provision of section 27. [. . .] Where the directors are the sole stockholders, there seems to be no objection to enforcing an agreement among them to vote for certain people as officers. [. . .]

Except for the broad dicta in the McQuade opinion, we think there can be no doubt that the agreement here in question was legal and that the complaint states a cause of action. There was no attempt to sterilize the board of directors, as in the Manson and McQuade Cases. The only restrictions on Dodge were (a) that as a stockholder he should vote for Clark as a director—a perfectly legal contract; (b) that as director he should continue Clark as general manager, so long as he proved faithful, efficient, and competent—an agreement which could harm nobody; (c) that Clark should always receive as salary or dividends one-fourth of the 'net income.' For the purposes of this motion, it is only just to construe that phrase as meaning whatever was left for distribution after the directors had in good faith set aside whatever they deemed wise; (d) that no salaries to other officers should be paid, unreasonable in amount or incommensurate with services rendered—a beneficial and not a harmful agreement.

If there was any invasion of the powers of the directorate under that agreement, it is so slight as to be negligible; and certainly there is no damage suffered by or threatened to anybody. [. . .]

MR. A v. XYZ

Arbitral Tribunal, 2011
November 2011

Arbitrators: B. Cavallone (President), G. Rossi, G. De Nova

[. . .]

Facts

XYZ is a corporation listed on the stock exchange managed by Borsa Italian s.p.a. since March 2007.

The shareholders' meeting of the corporation, on December 19, 2006, adopted the so-called "two-tier governance system," appointed the first members of the Board of Supervisors, and Mrs. A, B, and C as members of the Managing Board (hereinafter also called, collectively, "Managing Partners"). A, B, and C can be considered the founding shareholders of XYZ.

[. . .]

A few days after the above-mentioned resolution, and precisely on December 22, 2006, Mrs. A, B, and C, together with other shareholders of XYZ, executed a shareholders' agreement pursuant to which, in addition to other provisions aimed at coordinating the appointment of the members of the Board of Supervisors, the parties agreed to "employ their best efforts in order to cause the Board of Supervisors of XYZ to appoint Mrs. A, B, and C as the only members of the Managing Board."

[One additional agreement (the "Collaboration Agreement") signed by the President of the Board of Supervisors on behalf of XYZ and by Mr. A provided that XYZ would use its best efforts to cause Mr. A to be appointed managing director of XYZ from 2007 through 2012, with a set compensation, and an additional provision establishing that in case of revocation or termination of Mr. A without cause before December 31, 2012, he would have been entitled to liquidated damages equal to five times his annual compensation.]

[. . .]

After the first term of three years of tenure of the governing bodies of the corporation, the newly appointed Board of Supervisors, with its resolution of March 12, 2010, raised the number of the members of the Managing Board to five, confirming Mrs. A, B, and C and appointing Mrs. L and M as independent directors. [. . .]

On March 22, 2010, the new Managing Board appointed as managing directors only Mrs. B and C, not Mr. A, and instructed Mr. B to prepare a document for the Board of Supervisors concerning the compensation of the directors.

In its meeting on May 25, 2010, the Board of Supervisors approved, for the year 2010, a compensation of euro 250,000 for each of the two managing directors (Mrs. B and C), and of euro 35,000 for each of the non-executive members of the Managing Board (Mrs. A, L, and M).

[. . .]

Mr. A initiated this arbitration procedure against XYZ on June 16, 2010 [claiming that XYZ breached the Collaboration Agreement.] On November 10, 2010 the Board of Supervisors of XYZ revoked Mr. A from his position as member of the Managing Board for cause, based on an opinion by law professor Mr. Bonelli.

[. . .]

Analysis

[. . .]

On the unlawfulness of the Collaboration Agreement as Against Public Policy

Article 2409-novies of the Italian Civil Code (hereinafter, "ICC"), with a provision identical to the one set forth by Article 2383 ICC for the board of directors of corporations adopting the traditional governance model, provides that "the members of the managing board [. . .] are appointed for a period not exceeding three years," and can be "reappointed." Similarly, the bylaws of XYZ provides that "the members of the managing board are appointed for a term [. . .] not exceeding three years" (Article 21.5) and that they can be "reappointed" (Article 21.6).

According to the defendant corporation, these rules establishing the maximum duration of the tenure of directors are mandatory and cannot be contracted around. An agreement resulting in an appointment exceeding the maximum duration (such as the Collaboration Agreement in the present case) would be null and void.

At first sight, the above-mentioned provisions of the Collaboration Agreement might seem contrary to a mandatory provision, and therefore null and void.

A more careful exam of the matter leads, however, to a different conclusion.

First of all, the Collaboration Agreement does not, in itself, imply a violation of the above-mentioned rules. It is simply a bilateral agreement between the corporation and Mr. A, under which the corporation has undertaken the obligation to use its best efforts to cause the competent corporate bodies to appoint again Mr. A as managing director of XYZ for the period 2010–2013. The Board of Supervisors and the other competent corporate bodies would need to appoint Mr. A for another term, and Article 2409-novies of the ICC would not be violated.

[. . .]

We should consider however if the Collaboration Agreement contains, as a matter of fact, an obligation for XYZ and its corporate bodies to appoint Mr. A managing director for six years, and this obligation is not compatible with the freedom of corporate directors, necessary to allow them to take their decisions in the best interest of the corporation, in the light of the liquidated damages provision.

The answer, according to the majority of the arbitral tribunal, must be negative.

In deciding the appointment or revocation of a fellow director, directors might be influenced by the possible adverse economic effects of the liquidated damages provision, but this possibility is somehow inevitable and also regulated by the statute, since Article 2409-novies ICC provides that the members of the managing board can be revoked at any time by the board of supervisors, but they are entitled to damages if the revocation is without cause. There is no doubt that these statutory rules do not determine an obligation not to revoke directors: on the contrary, they allow revocation. Similarly, both case law and scholars have recognized that it is possible to delegate specific powers to the members of the managing board (*see* Tribunal of Milan, decision No. 6137 of May 12 2010 and C. Conforti, Nomina e revoca degli amministratori di società, Milano, 2007, p. 792). A contract providing for a penalty or indemnity in case of revocation of the delegated powers does not, in itself, unreasonably limit the freedom of directors to decide the revocation.

[. . .]

It should be also pointed out that the relevant provisions of the Collaboration Agreement appear in line with a widespread use in the corporate world, in particular within banks and financial intermediaries, aimed at facilitating the hiring and retention of qualified managers by ensuring them that in case of early termination they would be given an adequate compensation.

[The arbitral tribunal discusses several examples of similar provisions in other agreements, and also examines regulatory provisions in the banking industry confirming that it is lawful to provide for a "golden parachute" for directors in case of early termination.]

[. . .]

Arbitrator Professor De Nova dissents from the decision of the majority, for the following reasons. He agrees with the majority that the Collaboration Agreement binds the corporation and Mr. A, and that a mandatory provision protects the freedom of the corporation, at a minimum every three years, to decide whether to confirm Mr. A as managing director. He does not agree, however, with the arguments that lead the majority to conclude for the validity of the agreement.

The Collaboration Agreement cannot be interpreted, as the majority does, in the sense that XYZ Corporation was not bound to appoint Mr. A as managing director also after the first three years, through 2012 [. . .].

For These Reasons

The majority of the arbitration tribunal:

- Recognizes a credit of Mr. A, plaintiff, toward XYZ Corporation, defendant, of euro 2,400,000, plus legal interests from March 22, 2010 through payment;

- Condemns XYZ s.p.a. to pay the amount of euro 2,400,000, plus legal interests from March 22, 2010 through payment to Mr. A.

[. . .]

NOTES AND QUESTIONS

1.   The two cases present several similarities, but also important differences. In *Clark v. Dodge*, shareholders agreed to appoint themselves to the board of directors, and to vote, as directors, to appoint one of them general manager, subject to certain conditions. Also in *Mr. A v. XYZ* (note that since this was an arbitration, confidentiality of the parties had to be protected) shareholders agreed to appoint certain individuals as members of the Supervisory Board, and to use their best efforts in order to cause the Supervisory Board to appoint certain individuals—among whom Mr. A—on the Managing Board (the Italian corporation had adopted the "two-tier," German model, *see* Chapter 5). In addition, in *Mr. A v. XYZ*, the plaintiff and the defendant corporation had also agreed that the corporation would have used its best efforts to have Mr. A appointed as managing director among the members of the Managing Board, to keep him in that position for a certain number of years, and to pay him a predetermined compensation/damages in case of early termination in breach of the agreement. In both cases, therefore, the crucial legal issue is if the agreements, and the possibility to pay damages in case of breach, create an unacceptable limitation to the freedom of corporate directors to decide who to appoint in key managerial roles. Both courts decided that the agreements were valid, but there are subtle and important differences in their reasoning. Can you identify them? One possible answer is below.

2.   First of all, of course, there are some factual distinctions. The American agreement concerns a closely held corporation, and all the shareholders have accepted the agreement. The Italian agreement concerns a listed corporation, and only some shareholders are members of the agreement. The American agreement provided that Clark had to be appointed director, and general manager, as long as he should be "faithful, efficient and competent," and also included some provisions concerning compensation and additional obligations of the parties; the agreement did not, however, have a specified duration. The Italian agreement was also aimed at retaining Mr. A for a minimum period as managing director, but it did not provide a similar condition. It should be remembered, however, that under the Italian agreement the liquidated damages would be paid to Mr. A

only in case of early termination *without cause*, therefore also under the Italian agreement, at least in principle, if he had become "unfaithful, inefficient or incompetent" he could have been terminated. In addition, the obligations under the Italian agreement were limited to a six year period. Another important difference is that the American agreement was among shareholders, and shareholders in their capacity as directors; of the two Italian agreements, on the other hand, one was among shareholders (concerning the appointment of the Board of Supervisors and of the Managing Board), and the other one between the corporation and Mr. A (concerning his appointment as managing director within the Managing Board).

3.   Also in light of these differences, it is interesting to consider the reasoning of the two adjudicating bodies. Both underline the general principle that the board should be allowed to make its decisions in the best interest of the corporation, and both conclude that these agreements do not infringe on this power in a way that could be considered contrary to public policy. Note, however, that the New York Court of Appeals focuses on the fact that the agreement does not "harm anybody." How could such an agreement harm someone? For example, if it would force the appointment of an incompetent director, you might argue that it could harm creditors and other stakeholders. In this perspective it is probably important that the retention of Clark is subject to his being faithful, efficient and competent. The Italian Arbitral Tribunal, on the other hand, seems to focus more on whether the risk of paying a penalty in case of early termination of Mr. A would impair the freedom and ability of the directors to exercise their duties in appointing and/or revoking the executives. The Arbitral Tribunal concludes that it does not; also because under general provisions of Italian law, any time a director is revoked without cause, she should be indemnified. Can you pinpoint other comparative differences between the two decisions? For example, the Italian Arbitral Tribunal seems less concerned about the possibility that the agreement might harm third parties, or is it? Is the fact that the U.S. corporation is closely held, and that all shareholders accepted the agreement, while the Italian corporation is listed and the agreement is only among some shareholders, relevant? Imagine for a moment that the New York court would have been presented with the facts of the Italian case, and vice versa the Italian Arbitration Tribunal with the facts of the U.S. case: applying their rationales, would the outcomes have been different? Hint for the discussion: look up Section 7.32(a)(1) of the Model Business Corporation Act.

4.   Also other courts and other systems have faced a question not too different from the one epitomized by *Clark v. Dodge*. In Germany, for example, one important Supreme Court decision has concluded that shareholders cannot be bound by a voting agreement to appoint certain members of the Supervisory Board, if they reasonably believe that the nominee is incompetent, untrustworthy, or lacks the necessary skills for the job (RGZ 133, 90, 96). In *Clark v. Dodge* the court held the agreement valid, also because it would only operate as long as the nominee would remain "faithful, efficient and competent." Do you see a difference in these positions?

5.   Under French law, the Commercial code does not regulate shareholders' agreements but recognizes implicitly their validity provided that they conform to the "interest of the corporation" (a concept debated by corporate law pundits as, from a practical perspective, vague and not particularly helpful). French courts consider valid and enforceable voting agreements relating to the appointment of directors, provided that their duration is "reasonable." The duration of the agreement in *Clark v. Dodge*, for example, would have likely been considered excessive by a French court: agreements lasting over 10 years are not advised. If you are interested in French case law on these issues, you might read Cass. Com. 19 dec. 1983, *Rev. sociétés* 1985. 105, note D. Schmidt; Com. 2 juill. 1985, Bull. Joly 1986. 374; or Appel Paris, 30 June 1995, JCP E 1996. 795, note J.-J. Daigre.

6.   Note a few things about arbitration in the *Mr. A v. XYZ* decision: (a) the anonymity of the parties: confidentiality is often an important reason to opt for arbitration, also in the corporate context; (b) dissenting opinion: in most civil law countries judges are not allowed to write a dissenting opinion, the court only issues one opinion. In arbitration, on the other hand, also in these systems, dissenting opinions are generally allowed and fairly often used. Consider whether the possibility to write a dissenting opinion facilitates or not reaching a decision. And by the way, do you agree with the majority or the dissenting arbitrator in the case above?; (c) consider also the length of the procedure. In *Mr. A v. XYZ*, the dispute arose in the late spring of 2010, and the decision was handed down in November 2011, a little bit over a year later. Not bad, especially for a system in which civil litigation, on average, often lasts several years. Here's another possible reason to opt for arbitration. These ideas will be briefly examined in our last chapter.

7.   Finally, with respect to the second case, we would like you to consider the relevance of a liquidated damages and penalties clause in most shareholders' agreements. As we mentioned before, it is often difficult to determine damages in case of breach of a voting agreement, or of a stock transfer restriction. Liquidated damages, if not considered excessive and inequitable by the adjudicators, can be a way to address this problem and reinforce the agreement.

8.   The fact that these two decisions are quite liberal with respect to the scope of voting agreements does obviously not mean that all voting agreements are valid and enforceable. Under German law, for example, agreements under which a shareholder has to vote in a certain way in exchange for a monetary payment ("vote buying") are illegal and null and void because they violate Section 134 of the German Civil Code and can be punished with a fine of up to 25.000 €; (Sec. 405 subs. 3 no. 7 Stock Corporation Law); the same is true in France in order to protect shareholders' ability to decide without bias (Article L. 242–9 of the French commercial code). Similarly, pursuant to Section 136, paragraph 2 of the German Stock Corporation Act, a voting agreement obligating a shareholder to vote following the instructions of the directors would be unlawful. The rationale is to avoid an "incestuous" relationship in which the directors control

shareholders' voting without having invested in the corporation themselves. What do you think of these limitations? Is the underlying public policy argument convincing? What about your own system? Is vote buying allowed? Is an agreement pursuant to which shareholders have to vote as instructed by directors valid? Discuss.

9. Interestingly enough, occasionally an otherwise invalid shareholders' agreement might be considered valid as a type of voting agreement. In the U.K, the House of Lords decision in *Russell v Northern Bank Development Corp.*, [1992] 1 WLR 588; [1992] 3 All ER 161, offers an interesting example. The litigation concerned an extensive shareholder agreement, clause 3 of which provided that "no further share capital should be created without the written consent of each of the parties to the agreement." The directors were proposing to issue more shares and the claimant sought an injunction to restrain this. He was not strongly opposed to their proposal, but wanted to test the efficacy of clause 3 because he feared that the directors might on a future occasion try to issue more shares in circumstances which might lead to a reduction of his voting power. The House of Lords held that, in so far as the clause purported to bind the company, it was void as being contrary to statutory provisions (Section 617 of the Companies Act 2006 gives to a company the power to increase its capital). Clause 3 of the shareholder agreement purported to take this power away and accordingly, in so far as it bound the company, which was a party to the shareholder agreement, then it was void. However, the House of Lords upheld the validity of the clause and its enforceability among shareholders on the basis that it could be interpreted as operating as a voting agreement. It being well established in the case law that a voting agreement was valid, this provided a way of upholding the shareholder agreement to a considerable extent. The case is significant because it shows a marked lack of judicial hostility to the concept of a complex shareholder agreement operating as a third governing document of the company (in addition to the articles of incorporation and the bylaws). The part of the agreement in conflict with mandatory company law provisions was considered invalid, but the rigidity of corporate law did not prevent the shareholders' agreement to be considered valid as a sort of voting agreement.

* * *

We have discussed the validity of both stock transfer restrictions and voting agreements, and possible consequences of the violation of a stock transfer restriction. But what remedies are available in case of violation of a voting agreement? As mentioned above, it is clear that in case of breach of any shareholders' agreement, damages are available, and we have also explained why a liquidated damages clause might be particularly important in this context. We have also mentioned that a shareholders' agreement is generally only binding among the parties that executed it, and cannot be enforced against third parties. If, for example, a shareholder sells her shares in breach of a right of first refusal, the other members of the agreement might obtain damages, but generally cannot recover the ownership of the shares from a buyer who is not a party to the agreement unless certain conditions are met. Similarly, if a shareholder votes in violation of a voting agreement, there might be damages, but especially in civil law systems the vote is generally valid and the shareholders' meeting resolution cannot be challenged based on the breach of the agreement (but, alas, there are exceptions). An example of this approach can be found in Russia where, pursuant to Article 32.1 of the Federal Corporation Law, the breach of a voting agreement is explicitly excluded from the list of the grounds for voidability of a shareholders' meeting resolution. We have also mentioned that in some systems, especially in civil law countries, if a stock transfer restriction is included in the bylaws of the corporation, it can be binding on third parties, and the third party who acquired the shares from a shareholder breaching, for example, a right of first offer, might be prevented from exercising her rights as shareholder. In the U.S., on the other hand, inserting the provision in the bylaws might not be sufficient to enforce it against third parties; it is generally necessary to note the limitation conspicuously on the share certificate.

One question that deserves further consideration with respect to a voting agreement is if a party may obtain specific performance, *i.e.,* if a court can order to vote in accordance with the agreement. Some U.S. courts have ruled that specific performance is possible: one interesting decision in this respect is *Ringling v. Ringling Bros.* (29 Del.Ch. 318 (1946)), a fascinating case involving the famous circus (you can read the story of this litigation and of the circus in J. Mark Ramseyer, *The Story of Ringling Bros. v. Ringling: Nepotism and Cycling at the Circus*, in J. Mark Ramseyer (editor), CORPORATE LAW STORIES (2009), 135). According to the court, a "shareholders' pooling agreement":

> "does not preclude the granting of specific performance, e. g., see Clark v. Dodge, 269 N.Y. 410, 199 N.E. 641. Indeed, the granting of such relief here is well within the spirit of certain principles laid down by our courts in cases granting specific performance of contracts to sell stock which would give the vendee voting control. See G. W. Baker Mach. Co. v. United States Fire Apparatus Co., 11 Del.Ch. 386, 97 A. 613; Francis et al. v. Medill, 16 Del.Ch. 129, 141 A. 697. Obviously, to deny specific performance here would be tantamount to declaring the Agreement invalid. Since petitioner's rights in this respect were properly preserved at the stockholders' meeting, the meeting was a nullity to the extent that it failed to give effect to the provisions of the Agreement here involved. However, I believe it preferable to hold a new election rather than attempt to

reconstruct the contested meeting. In this way the parties will be acting with explicit knowledge of their rights."

It should be added that section 7.31 of the Model Business Corporation Act explicitly provides that voting agreements are specifically enforceable.

In France, some lower courts have ordered specific performance of a shareholders' agreement, but the French Supreme Court is reluctant to accept this as a general principle. Practically speaking, the violation of shareholders' agreement is sanctioned through damages.

Another interesting example is Brazil. In this system, "If a shareholder agreement is filed with the company and made public, votes at a shareholder meeting by control group members, which violate the agreement, will not be counted." (Bernard S. Black, Antonio Gledson de Carvalho, Érica Gorga, *Corporate Governance in Brazil* (2009), available on *www.ssrn.com*). In this country, in other words, shareholders' agreements become binding for the corporation and specific performance is possible when they are properly filed with the corporation and therefore disclosed. Do you understand the possible rationale of such a rule?

In other systems, however, the validity of a vote in violation of a shareholders' agreement *vis-à-vis* the corporation is an established principle, because shareholders' agreements are only governed by the law of contracts and only have effects among the parties of the agreement (the issue might be more tricky if the corporation is also a party to the agreement). This is, for example, the case in Spain, France, and Italy.

Generally, also under German law shareholders' agreements are only binding for the participating shareholders. In case of breach, damages are available; however, in at least one case a kind of specific performance has been ordered. The German Federal Court of Justice, in the following decision, allowed shareholders to challenge a shareholders' meeting resolution on the grounds that it was approved in violation of a shareholders' agreement.

GERMAN FEDERAL COURT OF JUSTICE, 20 JANUARY 1983
20 January 1983—II ZR 243/81, NJW 1983, 1910

Facts

The plaintiff was a shareholder of the defendant, a corporation (A) with the business purpose of producing machinery equipment. In addition to the plaintiff the defendant corporation had three other shareholders. These shareholders and the plaintiff were also shareholders of another corporation (B) which was also producing machinery equipment. The plaintiff and the other shareholders had a contractual agreement pursuant to which the defendant corporation could invest in other businesses as long as these businesses did not interfere with the business purpose of B. At the shareholders' meeting of the defendant in 1979 a resolution was passed with the votes of the other shareholders but with the opposition of the plaintiff to acquire 50% of the shares of a company producing the same goods as B. The plaintiff claims that this shareholders' resolution is void since it constitutes a violation of the contractual agreement among the shareholders.

[. . .]

Grounds

The court grants the claim and declares the shareholder resolution void.

[. . .]

Sec. 243 German Stock Corporation Law states that a shareholders' resolution is void when it violates a provision of the charter of the corporation or of the Stock Corporation Law. Although the shareholders' resolution of the 1979 general meeting does not meet these requirements, it nevertheless has to be declared void. Generally shareholders of a corporation have the contractual freedom to bind each other to vote at the shareholder meeting in a certain way. Therefore the contractual agreement between the plaintiff and the other shareholders according to which the defendant can invest in other businesses as long as they do not interfere with the business purpose of B is valid and binding. The violation of such a contractual agreement of the shareholders generally does not entitle the other shareholders to challenge the shareholders' meeting resolution passed in violation of such an agreement, since the violation affects only the contractual relation among the shareholders and does not concern the corporation. However, the right of a shareholder to challenge a shareholders' meeting resolution passed in violation of a shareholders' agreement has to be recognized when all shareholders are parties to the shareholders' agreement. In this case the agreement must be considered binding for the corporation although the corporation is not a party of the agreement and the shareholders' agreement is not part to the corporate charter. It would constitute an unnecessary formality to force the shareholders to sue the shareholder violating the shareholders' agreement in order to enforce the shareholders' agreement and to pass another shareholders' resolution in which the shareholders originally violating the agreement vote in accordance with it. Instead the other shareholders can challenge the shareholders' meeting resolution directly.

NOTES AND QUESTIONS

1.   The decision of the German Federal Court of Justice dealt with a LLC (more precisely, a GmbH). However, it is generally accepted by legal

scholars in Germany that these principles can also apply to stock corporations. Could you think of any reasons why the application of the principles in the decision should be limited to LLC or closely held corporations?

2.   Why does the Court opt for a special treatment of a shareholders' agreement when all shareholders are a party to the agreement? Does this requirement make sense, or do you think that also the violation of a shareholders' agreement among only some of the shareholders should allow the performing members of the agreement to challenge the resolution of the shareholders' meeting adopted with votes expressed in violation of the agreement?

3.   In this case the shareholder of the corporation limited the business purpose of the corporation with a contractual agreement, although they could have limited it also with a charter provision. What are the advantages and disadvantages of regulating this issue in the corporate charter and in a shareholders' agreement?

* * *

In contrast, it is unclear whether specific performance of voting agreement is available in Japan, because of the scarcity of case law on the matter. (This does not imply the scarcity of shareholders' agreements, which are widely used in family-owned corporations and joint ventures.) The following controversial case is the only published decision referring to this subject to date. In an *obiter dictum*, it restricted the availability of an injunction against the exercise of voting rights in violation of shareholders' agreement.

SUZUKEN CORP. V. KOBAYASHI PHARMACEUTICAL CORP.

Nagoya District Court, 2007
12 November 2007, 1319 Kinyu Shoji Hanrei 50

Facts

Suzuken Corporation, the petitioner, became a 20% shareholder of Kobasho Corporation, a subsidiary of Kobayashi Pharmaceutical Corporation, the petitionee, as Suzuken sold its subsidiary to Kobasho by a share-exchange procedure (a statutory procedure similar to a merger, in which a corporation acquires all shares of another corporation and makes the latter its 100% subsidiary, and the shareholders of the latter corporation receive consideration, often in form of the shares of the former corporation). Kobayashi owns 80% of Kobasho's shares. At the same time, Suzuken and Kobayashi entered into shareholders' agreement (hereinafter "the Agreement"). Art. 17(1) of the Agreement stated that "Unless otherwise provided in (2), the parties shall not transfer all or a part of their respective shares of Kobasho to others," and Art.17(2) provided a right of first offer in case one of the parties intended to transfer its shares after five years have passed.

Three years later, Kobayashi decided to make Kobasho a 100% subsidiary of Mediceo Paltac Holdings by using share-exchange procedure.

Suzuken sought for injunctive relief to prohibit Kobayashi from voting in favor of this share-exchange at the Kobasho's special shareholders' meeting, asserting that a statutory share-exchange violates Art. 17(1) of the Agreement because Kobayashi will be transferring its shares of Kobasho for consideration in this procedure.

Court's Decision

Under general usage of the Japanese language, it is not impossible to interpret "transfer of shares" under Art.17 of the Agreement to include all kinds of transfer of shares including those by share-exchange procedure. On the other hand, at the time of the Agreement, share-exchange, which is a procedure under corporate law, was generally regarded to be different from transfer of shares by contract.

Thus, there are two possible ways of textual interpretations of "transfer of shares" under Art. 17 of the Agreement. To interpret a contractual provision, a reasonable reading that takes into account factors such as the nature of the parties and the content of the contract should be adopted.

Both parties are large listed corporations at the 1st Section of Tokyo Stock Exchange and have experience of M & As. [. . .] It is unthinkable that such parties have drafted the Agreement not using the expression "transfer of shares" in its technical legal sense, but just in its general meaning in Japanese. [. . .]

Thus, the petitioner failed to provide prima facie evidence that "transfer of shares" under Art. 17 of the Agreement has the meaning that the petitioner asserts.

Even if the defendant owes a duty not to exercise its voting rights under Article 17 of the Agreement in this case, a different question is whether the petitioner can ask for injunctive relief.

When a party owes such a duty, there is no reason to deny its effect between the parties of the Agreement (i.e., the liability for damage resulting from violation of this duty). An injunction for the exercise of the voting rights, however, will affect not only the plaintiff and the defendant, who are the parties of the Agreement, but also other shareholders of Kobasho. Injunctive relief might also disturb legal certainty because there was no case law on the availability of such relief at the time of the Agreement [. . .]

It follows that an injunction of the exercise of voting rights shall not be ordered as a rule, even if the petitionee owes a duty not to exercise its voting rights under Article 17 of the Agreement in this case. Injunctive relief may be granted as an exception only when (i) all shareholders are parties to the voting agreement, and, (ii) the Agreement clearly requires shareholders not to exercise their voting rights in a certain manner.

NOTES AND QUESTIONS

1.   As mentioned above, the restrictions of the availability of injunctive relief are *obiter dictum*, as the court denied that Art. 17(1) of the contract executed by the shareholders covered the transaction in question. Compare the approach to contractual interpretation of the Nagoya District Court to the one followed in *In re Estate of Mather*: what do you think are the most remarkable differences, if any?

2.   Do the restrictions on availability of injunctive relief imposed by the Nagoya District Court make sense? Why yes, or why not? Note that Japan, as a civil law jurisdiction, permits specific performance in principle as a matter of general contract law (Art. 414, Japanese Civil Code).

3.   Even if specific performance of voting agreement in form of injunction to vote in violation of the agreement is available, the validity (or invalidity) of a vote in violation of shareholders' agreement vis-à-vis the corporation is a different problem. This is because shareholders' agreements are only governed by the law of contracts and only have effects among the parties of the agreement (the issue might be more complex if the corporation is also a party to the agreement). As mentioned, this is generally, and somehow simplifying, also the case in countries such as France, Spain, and Italy.

4.   Does the position of the Nagoya District Court offer any argument with respect to the question of the validity of a vote in violation of shareholders' agreement vis-à-vis the corporation?

DISCLOSURE AND DURATION OF SHAREHOLDERS' AGREEMENTS. INTERNATIONAL LAW ASPECTS

Shareholders' agreements, especially stock transfer restrictions and voting agreements, have an impact on the ownership structure of the corporation. As we have discussed, a shareholder can use these legal devices to control a number of votes significantly higher than the ones he would be entitled to on the basis of the shares he owns. Voting agreements, in other words, can separate ownership and control. Stock transfer restrictions, on the other hand, can freeze the ownership structure of the corporation, and impede or make difficult third-party acquisitions of control. Especially in listed corporations, this can be a problem.

Most legislatures, however, rather than prohibiting or narrowly limiting shareholders' agreements (a rigid solution that might be difficult to enforce and contrast with contractual freedom), have opted for allowing these contracts, but regulating them mandating disclosure of shareholders' agreements and limiting their maximum duration. Disclosure and duration provisions are considered to achieve a desirable compromise between contractual freedom and the need to protect shareholders and third parties.

Disclosure obligations are generally provided for listed or publicly held corporations, not for closely held ones, for the obvious reason that transparency of the ownership structure and of the distribution of power is particularly important when the shares are traded on the market and investors can acquire them. At a minimum, disclosure requirements are much stricter for listed than for closely-held corporations. For example, under Italian law, most stock transfer limitations and voting agreements in listed corporations are null and void if they are not disclosed to the Italian Securities and Exchange Commission (Consob) within five days after execution, published in a national newspaper within ten days after execution, and filed with a public register within fifteen days from execution. If these disclosure obligations are not complied with, voting rights cannot be exercised, and if they are the resolution of the shareholders' meeting can be challenged also by Consob (Article 122 of the Italian Consolidated Law on Financial Markets). In addition, in publicly held corporations shareholders' agreements must also be deposited with the corporation, and the existence of shareholders' agreements must be disclosed at the beginning of any shareholders' meeting (Article 2341-ter of the Italian Civil Code). In France, any clause in a shareholders' agreement allowing preferential terms and conditions to be applied to the sale and purchase of shares which are admitted to trading on a regulated market and that amount to at least 0.5% of the capital or voting rights must be submitted to the Financial Markets Authority (*Autorité des marchés financiers*, or AMF). Failing such submission, the effects of that clause are suspended, and the parties are released from their undertakings while any public offer of sale is in progress. These provisions are made public by the AMF. Note that only the relevant provisions have to be communicated to the AMF and the public, not the entire shareholders' agreement.

Again under Italian law, the duration of shareholders' agreements cannot exceed three years in listed corporations, and five years in closely held ones (Articles 123 of the Italian Consolidated Law on Financial Markets and 2341-bis of the Italian Civil Code). Agreements can be renewed after they have expired for an additional three or five years, but shareholders have an opportunity to decide if they want to continue to be bound, thus avoiding the risk of becoming prisoners of the corporation. In France there is not such a short limit to the duration of shareholders' agreements in listed corporations but, as mentioned before, case law indicates that agreements with excessive duration are not upheld, typically over ten years.

As previously stated, also in the United States there are statutory limitations to the duration of some shareholders' agreements, in particular for those agreements that take the form of a voting trust. Pursuant to Section 7.30 of the Model Business Corporation Act, for example, a voting trust "is valid for not more than 10 years after its effective date unless extended" with the written consent of the parties. Occasionally courts have concluded that a pooling agreement combined with the deposit of the shares and an irrevocable proxy should be treated as a voting trust with respect to maximum duration (*see Abercrombie v. Davies*, 130 A.2d 338 (Del. 1957)).

It is probably clear that the rationale underlying the maximum duration provisions relates also to the desire to foster a market for corporate control, since it prevents entrenchment of some shareholders. One interesting rule at the European level, in this respect, is the breakthrough provision set forth by Article 11 of Directive 2004/25 on takeovers. We will discuss takeovers and tender offers in Chapter 10, but it might be interesting to anticipate something about this rule. Clearly enough, shareholders' agreements can hinder the possible success of a tender offer. To the extent that an efficient market for corporate control is desirable, therefore, the European regulation of tender offers limits the effects of stock transfer restrictions (both in the bylaws and in a separate agreement) and of voting agreements when a public offer is launched. Consider this rule:

Article 11, Paragraphs 2 and 3, Directive 2004/25/CE

"2. Any restrictions on the transfer of securities provided for in the articles of association of the offeree company shall not apply vis-à-vis the offeror during the time allowed for acceptance of the bid laid down in Article 7(1).

Any restrictions on the transfer of securities provided for in contractual agreements between the offeree company and holders of its securities, or in contractual agreements between holders of the offeree company's securities entered into after the adoption of this Directive, shall not apply vis-à-vis the offeror during the time allowed for acceptance of the bid laid down in Article 7(1).

3. Restrictions on voting rights provided for in the articles of association of the offeree company shall not have effect at the

general meeting of shareholders which decides on any defensive measures in accordance with Article 9.

Restrictions on voting rights provided for in contractual agreements between the offeree company and holders of its securities, or in contractual agreements between holders of the offeree company's securities entered into after the adoption of this Directive, shall not have effect at the general meeting of shareholders which decides on any defensive measures in accordance with Article 9."

NOTES AND QUESTIONS

1. How different are the rules regarding extending the duration of shareholders' agreements under Italian law and under the MBCA? Also, limitations of duration of shareholders' agreements could be provided not by statutes but by case law. For example, one Japanese lower court held that shareholders should not be bound by a voting agreement after "a period of considerable length" has passed (10 years in the case), also considering the intent of the parties. (Tokyo High Court, May 30, 2000, 1750 Hanrei Jiho169). It is preferable to adopt a rigid statutory rule, or a more flexible standard that courts can apply in this area?

2. Comment on the breakthrough provision above with respect to "restrictions to the transfer of securities." What does it mean, and how broad is the provision? For example, a covenant that would require one shareholder to pay 5% of the selling price of her shares to other shareholders if she decides to sell them, is a "restriction" pursuant to Article 11 above? What is the rationale of the rule?

3. What about voting agreements? As we will see in Chapter 10, under European law defensive measures in case of a tender offer, defined as any measure that might frustrate the success of the bid (e.g., purchasing own shares, issuing new shares, selling assets, etc.), must be approved by the shareholders' meeting. This is to allow shareholders to decide if they want to tender their shares or, if the offer is not value-maximizing, if they prefer to resist it. In this scenario, the Directive provides that voting agreements are not binding with respect to the shareholders' meeting called to vote on defensive measures. Can you explain why the European legislature has adopted this rule?

4. Pursuant to Article 12 of Directive 2004/25, the rules reprinted above are not mandatory but optional. In implementing the Directive, Member States, as we will discuss more extensively in Chapter 10, had the option to adopt the breakthrough provision or to opt out of it (and in this case single corporations could decide to introduce it in their bylaws). The vast majority of European countries has *not* mandated the breakthrough rule. Only three States have mandated the breakthrough rule: Estonia, Latvia, and Lithuania—not the most important financial markets of the Union. The

consequence is that most shareholders' agreements would remain binding also in the case of a tender offer. Can you think of possible reasons why Member States have decided to avoid the breakthrough rule?

* * *

A shareholders' agreement is, as we now know very well, a separate contract, distinct from the charter and bylaws of the corporation. In principle it can include a choice of law provision pursuant to which parties can subject the agreement to the laws of a system different from the one that governs the internal affairs of the corporation (at least if the provision does not indirectly affect the structure of the corporation). Similarly, the parties can give jurisdiction over disputes arising out of the shareholders' agreement to courts of a different country or to an arbitration panel.

As for choice of law, in the absence of an explicit provision most courts would apply the laws that govern the corporation. As you will remember from Chapter 2, this means the laws of the state of incorporation but, in some systems, it might mean the laws of the country where the corporation has its "real seat." In the U.S., when a choice of law clause has not been included, sometimes parties have tried to argue that the shareholders' agreement was subject to the laws of the state where the agreement was executed, or where it had to be performed, if different from the state where the corporation was incorporated. Courts have however generally declined to follow this approach, and applied the laws applicable to the internal affairs of the corporation (for a brief discussion of this principle, *see* again *Ringling v. Ringling Bros.* (29 Del.Ch. 318 (1946)).

Choice of forum or arbitration clauses are generally admissible, if they do not undermine the public policies of the country in which the decision will have to be enforced. The previous *Mr. A v. XYZ* arbitration is a fitting example. We will discuss more broadly jurisdictional issues and alternative dispute resolution mechanisms with respect to the internal affairs of the corporation in Chapter 12.

FOCUS ON SHAREHOLDERS' AGREEMENTS IN LISTED CORPORATIONS

In Chapter 4, discussing multiple voting shares, we cited a study on the Proportionality Principle in the European Union, commissioned by the European Commission to Sherman & Sterling, ISS, and ECGI published in 2007.[1] The same study presents interesting data on the use of shareholders' agreements in listed European corporations. The data, in

---

[1]   Available at http://ec.europa.eu/internal_market/company/docs/shareholders/study/final_report_en.pdf.

fact, take only into account the largest listed corporations, therefore they do not tell the whole story, but are still significant:

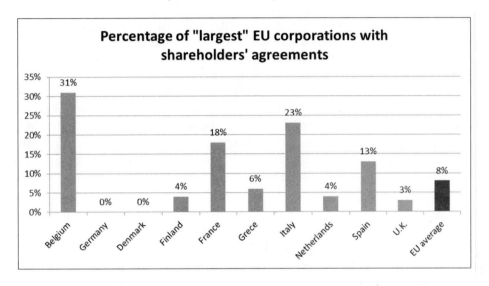

As mentioned, the data offer an interesting, but partial picture. For example no shareholders' agreements are listed for Germany, a country in which they are used also in listed corporation, because the research only considered the largest 20-DAX corporations, excluding corporations such as Henkel, Metro, and Porsche, which have shareholders' agreements. In any case, the data reported clearly indicate that shareholders' agreements in European listed corporations are quite widespread, especially in civil law countries with a more concentrated ownership structure (Belgium, France, Italy, Spain), and less in the U.K., a common law system with a more widespread ownership structure. In the U.S., as mentioned before, most manuals, casebooks, and treatises only discuss shareholders' agreements in the context of closely held corporations, or at least consider them a typical feature of this type of organizations. Japan might again lie in the middle. In this country, discussions regarding shareholders' agreements center on closely held corporations, as in the U.S.; but voting agreements in public corporations have been reported. In addition, as noted in Chapter 1, cross-shareholdings are fairly common in Japan; for example, a public corporation often has many shareholders, each holding less than 5% of shares, who have business relationships with the corporation. The corporation, in return, also holds the shares of these shareholders. Although there is no formal shareholders' agreement among these shareholders, it could be argued that they act under an implicit understanding to support the incumbent management if a hostile shareholder appears.

The limited diffusion of shareholders' agreements as a control enhancing device in the U.K. and in the U.S., as well as in other common law systems, is confirmed also by recent empirical analysis. H. Masullo, *Shareholder Agreement in Publicly Traded Companies: A Comparison Between the U.S. and Brazil* (2015), available on *www.ssrn.com*, notes that in the period between 2010 and 2012, 54 Brazilian publicly-traded corporations had signed 64 shareholders agreements, and 65 U.S. ones signed 69 ones. Considering that as of 2012 there were approximately 353 listed corporations in Brazil and 4,102 in the U.S., it is clear how relatively uncommon these agreements are in the U.S. in comparison to other (civil law) systems. This poses an interesting conundrum. Shareholders agreements might be very desirable for some shareholders, to limit the risk of hostile takeovers, reinforce control, or also simply coordinate with fellow shareholders. Why are they therefore not used (or not so commonly used) in the U.S.?

One explanation is for sure based on ownership structures. Shareholders agreements tend to be less common where ownership structures are more widespread, if nothing else because it is less important—and more difficult—to gather a minimum number of shareholders with enough shares to render the execution of a shareholders' agreement an effective control enhancing device. In addition, shareholders' agreements tend to be more used in systems in which a relative small number of shareholders own significant cross-holdings in different corporations. For obvious reasons it is easier, in these systems, that two or more parties enjoy a reciprocal advantage by entering into several shareholders' agreements, and it is easier to coordinate a small group of influential shareholders.

In addition, at least in the U.S., some state statutes prohibit certain types of voting agreements in public companies. Section 7.32 of the Model Business Corporation Act lists several voting agreements that "cease to be effective when the corporation becomes a public corporation": for example, agreements restricting the discretion or powers of the board of directors (like the one in *Clark v. Dodge*), allowing distributions to shareholders not proportional to the shares owned, requiring dissolution of the corporation at the request of one or more shareholders or upon the occurrence of a specified contingency, and so on. Also the Florida Business Corporation Act, just to give another example, provides that some shareholders agreements cease to be binding if the corporation is listed.

Widespread ownership structure and rules akin to 7.32 of the MBCA do not, however, seem completely satisfying explanations for the limited use of shareholders' agreements in the U.S. In the following excerpt from an essay, Professor Ventoruzzo offers some possible specific *legal* reasons why shareholders' agreements are not widespread among listed corporations in the U.S.

MARCO VENTORUZZO, WHY SHAREHOLDERS' AGREEMENTS
ARE NOT USED IN U.S. LISTED CORPORATIONS: A
CONUNDRUM IN SEARCH OF AN EXPLANATION

Penn State Law Research Paper No. 42–2013 (available on www.ssrn.com)

It is [interesting] to explore other, specific rules that might create a disincentive to the diffusion of shareholders' agreements [in the United States]. This exercise, to my knowledge, has not been attempted before, so I will try to offer some food for thoughts.

First of all, entering into a shareholder agreement can trigger a poison pill. A poison pill can take different forms, but generally and in its more common shape it provides a catastrophic event triggered by the acquisition, without board's approval, of a set threshold of shares. For example, in a typical pill, acquisition of a 15% stake in the corporation would allow all shareholders, with the exception of the ones triggering the pill, to exercise options rights on common stock at a price below the market price. Poison pills are often triggered by the acquisition of the set threshold by one single investor, but can also be triggered by a "group" of investors acting in concert. Since the parties of a shareholders' agreements can be considered members of a group, the stipulation of a shareholders' agreement can trigger a poison pill and have very negative consequences on the corporation and on the members of the agreement. The relationship between shareholders' agreements and poison pills has not been studied very much, but I posit that the fear of triggering a pill might be a powerful disincentive to the stipulation of shareholders' agreements.

Secondly, pursuant to the Williams Act, beneficial owners of 5% or more of common stock must disclose their participations, indicating also the purpose of their acquisition, and disclosing any 1% or more increase or decrease of their participation. The members of a shareholders' agreement will generally be considered a "group" for disclosure purposes, and therefore be required to comply with the disclosure provisions if collectively they cross the 5% threshold. This can also create a disincentive to enter into a shareholders' agreement, especially because U.S. law requires disclosure of the purposes of the beneficial owner. Both institutional investors and entrepreneurs might be very reluctant to disclose their strategies in this context. Hence another possible disincentive to shareholders' agreements.

One additional and overlooked explanation for the limited use of shareholders' agreements as control-enhancing devices could be found in section 16(b) of the Exchange Act, the original insider trading provision that regulates what are called "short-swing profits." In a nutshell, section 16(b) provides that if "insiders" realize a profit on a purchase and sale, or a sale and purchase, of beneficially owned stock of the company within any six-month period, the profit is recoverable by the company. For example, if the CEO of a corporation buys one share at $5 and sells it three months later at $7, she will have to disgorge any profit ($2) back to the corporation. Basically, there is a presumption that the profit was obtained using inside information. For the purposes of this rule, "insiders" include directors, officers, and beneficial owners of more than 10% of the common stock. One crucial question is if members of a shareholders' agreement could be considered as a single beneficial owner of shares for the application of this rule. If the answer is affirmative, any shareholder owning less than 10% will be reluctant to enter into a shareholders' agreement that aggregates more than 10% of the shares, because her ability to profit from trading on the shares would be significantly limited.

Also corporate law statutes, at the state level, can deter the stipulation of shareholders' agreements. In this case, obviously, Delaware law is particularly relevant. Space constraints force me to oversimplify the issue, but to give an example section 203 of the DGCL provides, in relevant part, that stockholders who acquire beneficial ownership of more than 15% of the stock of the corporation without prior board approval become "interested stockholders." Such interested stockholders cannot enter into business combinations such as mergers, consolidations, but also other transactions with the corporation for a period of 3 years without supermajority approvals. The act of entering into an agreement, arrangement or understanding with other stockholders could cause the stockholders to be attributed ownership of the other shares subject to the agreement, which would limit the possibility to do business with the corporation.

NOTES AND QUESTIONS

1.   What do you think of these possible explanations for the limited role of shareholders' agreements in U.S. financial markets?

2.   Based on our discussion, do you think that shareholders' agreements should be prohibited in listed corporations? What are the pros and cons of shareholders' agreements, also considering the broader interest to have well-functioning financial markets? A suggested exercise is the following: imagine the class is the parliament of a country of your choice, and divide the students into two groups. One group has to support a bill prohibiting shareholders' agreements in listed corporations, the other one should oppose the bill, and suggest instead that shareholders' agreements should be allowed but, possibly, regulated with respect to duration and disclosure. What would be the most compelling arguments? Is it relevant if the bill is discussed in a country with concentrated or widespread ownership structures?

CHAPTER 9

MERGERS AND ACQUISITIONS

■ ■ ■

INTRODUCTION

This chapter addresses extraordinary financial transactions, in particular mergers and acquisitions (M&As). Acquisitions of a controlling stake in a listed corporation through a public offer and other takeover issues will be discussed in the next chapter.

The regulation of M&As in the jurisdictions we will be considering presents profound comparative differences, but also important similarities. In Europe, for example, several aspects of the rules concerning mergers (and spin-offs) have been harmonized with Directive 78/855 (and Directive 82/891). The topic we are tackling here is extremely broad, and it is not possible to treat it in a comprehensive way in the space we have. As in other chapters, therefore, we have selected some specific issues that we consider particularly interesting or relevant for this course, both practically and theoretically. The chapter is organized as follows. First, by way of general introduction, we will take a look at mergers and acquisitions from an economic perspective. This introductory part will not discuss specific comparative differences, but rather concentrate on three issues: what distinguishes different acquisition techniques (sale of shares, sale of assets, contributions in kind, mergers, and spin-offs), but also what they have in common; the basic economic structure of a merger and the meaning and calculation of the exchange ratio; and some empirical evidence concerning M&As. Second, we will discuss sales of all or substantively all the assets, focusing in particular on the so-called de facto merger doctrine. Third, we will talk about leveraged buyouts, a particular type of acquisition technique involving debt and mergers. Finally, we will concentrate on cash-out mergers and freeze-out transactions, illustrating some interesting differences between U.S., European and Japanese law.

AN OVERVIEW OF MERGERS AND ACQUISITIONS

A merger is a transaction in which the assets and liabilities of a corporation (A) are transferred to another one (B). A is extinguished as a consequence of the merger, and B issues new shares to the former shareholders of A. A variation is a consolidation, in which the assets and liabilities of two corporations (for example, A and B) are transferred to a third newly incorporated entity (C), A and B are extinguished by operation of law, and C issues new shares for the former shareholders of A and B. Consolidations are much rarer than mergers, essentially for tax and practical reasons (in most systems, consolidations are less advantageous than mergers) and for practical reasons. We will therefore focus on mergers.

In a merger, B, the surviving corporation, acquires A, the corporation merged with and into B; or, more precisely, acquires its assets and liabilities. The consideration paid to the shareholders of the acquired corporation is generally newly issued shares of B, with the consequence that the ownership structure of B after the merger will change, and its shareholders will include both the old shareholders of B, and the new ones who owned shares of A. As we will see, however, at least in some systems, the shareholders of the corporation extinguished as a consequence of the merger might also be liquidated in cash (cash-out merger). In addition, sometimes a wholly owned subsidiary of a corporation is merged with and into the parent. In this case, no new shares are issued and the transaction is generally simplified.

A first basic concept that should be understood is that a merger is one way to acquire the business of another corporation, and in this perspective it can be compared and contrasted with other similar transactions. Consider the following example. Corporation A has two shareholders, X and Y, and corporation B has only one shareholder, Z. Now imagine that B and its shareholder Z want to acquire the business of A, meaning its assets and liabilities.

One possibility, obviously, is for Z to acquire the shares of A from X and Y. In this case the transaction will result in Z being the sole shareholder of the two corporations. Alternatively, the shares of A could be purchased by B, with the consequence of creating a group of corporations in which Z controls B, and B controls A. Another option would be for A to transfer its assets and liabilities to B. The assets and liabilities can be sold to B for cash, with the consequence that A will only own cash and B the business that used to be managed through A (at which point A might invest the proceeds of the sale in a new business, or dissolve and distribute the sums received to X and Y). A could, however, also transfer its assets and liabilities to B with a spin-off and a contribution in kind to B (*see* Chapter 3): in this case, B will issue new shares to A. Note the similarities and differences with other scenarios: here, once again, B will own the business of A, but A (and indirectly its owners X and Y), becomes a new shareholder of B, together with Z. Finally, in a merger, the assets and liabilities of A are transferred to B, A is extinguished, and B issues shares directly to the former shareholders of

A, X, and Y. In this case, the ownership structure of B after the merger will include X, Y, and Z.

Needless to say, these different transactions have profoundly different legal, tax, financial, economic, and organizational consequences. Other important consequences might be determined by antitrust issues (antitrust is often relevant in large acquisitions), or labor and industrial relationships. One particular road might be preferable for a broad range of reasons. In a way, however, they also all have something in common: they allow the combination of the businesses of A and B, and often (not always) imply the acquisition or the control of the business of A by the group controlled by Z that includes B. As a lawyer, your obligation is frequently to identify creatively the way to acquire a business that better serves the interests of your client, also keeping in mind the interests of the other parties and stakeholders. Just consider, for example, the possible different consequences in terms of liability toward corporate creditors of the different alternative transactions briefly described above. The complexity of the variables that you must consider is magnified when the acquisition has an international dimension, typically because the corporations involved are located in different jurisdictions and are subject to different corporate laws. Like in a game of three-dimensional chess, you need to be able to figure out the best strategy based on the different moving pieces, and carry it on effectively.

Zeroing in on mergers, we need to underline that a merger is a process, a procedure, and that to successfully complete a merger several steps are necessary, and also—as a general rule—the approval of different corporate bodies of the corporations involved (boards of directors and shareholders' meetings) must be obtained. Roughly speaking, in most jurisdictions the merger procedure requires three steps. First, the boards of directors of both corporations must approve the merger according to a document sometimes referred to as the merger project or plan. The plan endorsed by the boards must then be approved by the shareholders' meetings of the two corporations, sometimes with supermajority requirements. Finally a formal deed of merger must be prepared and filed with the secretary of state or similar public register, in order for the legal effects of the merger to occur.

There are two important observations on this procedure. First, this is the default rule. A "simplified" procedure (sometimes also called "short-form merger") might be available, for example when the surviving corporation owns a significant stake of the merged one (often 90% or more), in which case the approval of the shareholders is not always necessary, as we will discuss more analytically below. Second, in the real world the negotiations preceding the formal approval of the merger by the boards, often conducted by the CEOs and other top executives, are extremely important. In this phase of the process some crucial and delicate agreements are often reached among the directors and officers of the corporations. For example, confidentiality agreements are signed to ensure that business secrets and other important information that need to be exchanged during a negotiation will not be disclosed to third parties or used to the detriment of the party making the disclosures. Often the parties will also execute no-shop provisions, aimed at limiting the ability of one party to seek or receive other offers from possible buyers or sellers: the rationale here is to prevent a party from being used as a stalking horse (do you remember that in *Smith v. Van Gorkom* in Chapter 6, there was a no-shop provision?). Sometimes "material adverse change" agreements are entered into, to protect in particular the buyer from possible unpleasant surprises down the road concerning the conditions and value of the target. Finally, the parties might provide for penalties in case the deal is not consummated or for other interruptions of negotiations. These provisions are delicate because, as you can imagine, they somehow limit the freedom of the board of directors or of the shareholders to reject a proposed transaction, and therefore might be considered an infringement on the franchise of these bodies (*see* Chapter 5).

In order to understand the nuts and bolts of a merger, and its economic and legal consequences, one crucial issue is to understand what the exchange ratio is and how it is determined. As we mentioned, with the exclusion of cash-out mergers, the consideration paid to shareholders of a corporation merged with and into another one, and therefore extinguished, are shares of the surviving corporation. The exchange ratio indicates how many shares of the surviving corporation the shareholders of the merged corporation should obtain, for each share of the merged corporation that they owned. If A is merged into B, and the exchange ratio is 2, for example, for each share of A its shareholders will obtain two shares of B. If it is ½, they will obtain one share of B for every two shares of A. The exchange ratio can be considered the "price" of the merger, and determines the relative economic and administrative powers that the shareholders of the merged corporation will have in the new venture. Obviously, it must be calculated based on the relative values of the two corporations. It is extremely important to clearly understand how the exchange ratio is determined. We know that (most) law students freak out when they see some numbers, but we still want to offer you a numeric example to explain this concept. We promise that if you understand the following example, understanding merger negotiations and litigation will be enormously easier. If you went through fifth grade, you know enough math to follow us.

Consider two corporations, X and Y, with the following simplified balance sheets and ownership structures:

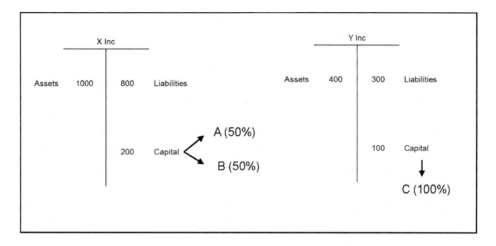

The shareholders of X are A and B, holding 50% of the outstanding shares each, while all the shares of Y are owned by C. Imagine that the directors and the shareholders of X and Y agree to merge Y with and into X: the assets and liabilities of Y will be transferred to X by operation of law, Y will be extinguished, and C will receive newly issued shares of X. How many shares of X should C receive for each share that he owns in Y? In other words, what is the exchange ratio?

To answer this question, we need some additional information. First, we need to know the number of outstanding shares of both corporations. Let's assume that X has 200 shares outstanding with a par value or accounting value of $1 each, and that Y has 100 shares outstanding, also with a par or accounting value of $1. (We have not discussed the concept of par or accounting value, which is not particularly important for our purposes and that would require a long explanation. Just consider this as a conventional value attributed to each share, which is however different from, and generally lower of, the price or actual value of the shares.)

The other important information that we need to have is the "fair value" of X and Y. From an accounting perspective, the values of the two corporations, simply determined by subtracting the accounting value of the liabilities from the accounting value of the assets, are respectively 200 for X and 100 for Y. The accounting values, however, do not represent the "fair" values of these businesses. Accounting principles, in fact, often underestimate the real value of a corporation, because accounting rules are conservative. For example, several assets might be registered in the financial statements at their historical cost, i.e., the price that the corporation paid to acquire them, reduced with depreciation. Their actual value, however, might be significantly higher. Consider, for example, a patent: its historical cost might include only the expenditures in research and development occurred by a business to secure the patent, plus some additional legal and administrative fees necessary to register it. A few years after the patent has been registered, however, its commercial value might increase dramatically due to a new technological development that makes the patent extremely precious. Its actual value, at this point, might be ten times its historical costs, but the financial statements will still indicate the historical cost. In addition, the balance sheet generally does not take into account the "goodwill" or the "badwill" of a business, i.e., that part of its value derived from its ability to generate a flow of earnings or a cash flow, or a loss, in the future. If you take into account these phenomena, it should be clear that the actual value of a business might be significantly higher—or, more rarely, lower—than its accounting value.

How can you therefore determine the "fair value" of X and Y? There are several criteria that can be adopted, depending also on the industry and type of business, to determine the value of a business. Some criteria are simply based on the evaluation of the single assets and liabilities, independently from their accounting value. Other criteria take into account the goodwill (or badwill) by calculating the value of the firm as the value of any investment, by determining the net present value of the flow of future earnings or future cash flows that the business is expected to generate. If the corporation is listed and there is an active market for the shares, market prices can (and should) also be considered. In most cases financial experts must be hired to find the appropriate formula and determine the fair value, often a very complex calculation that inevitably depends on several assumptions on which reasonable minds can disagree. It is therefore accurate to say that there is not such a thing as a single and precise "fair" value, but rather a range of values that could be considered acceptable. In addition, also keep in mind that even if based on the opinions of the experts, the parties will negotiate. In our example, C will try to convince X and its shareholders that the value of his corporation, Y, is as high as possible; and vice versa A and B will argue that the value of X is as high as possible.

In any case, for our purposes, we can take the fair values of X and Y as given. Let's imagine, therefore, that after obtaining opinions from qualified and independent experts, and negotiating the transaction, all the parties involved agree that the fair value of X is $300 ($100 more than its accounting value), and that the fair value of Y is also $300 ($200 more than its accounting value).

Now we are ready to calculate the exchange ratio. The formula that should be used is the following:

$$exchange\ ratio = \frac{\dfrac{fair\ value\ of\ merged\ corporation\ (Y)}{number\ of\ outstanding\ shares\ of\ merged\ corporation\ (Y)}}{\dfrac{fair\ value\ of\ surviving\ corporation\ (X)}{number\ of\ outstanding\ shares\ of\ surviving\ corporation\ (X)}}$$

Substituting the numbers, we have:

$$exchange\ ratio = \frac{\dfrac{300}{100}}{\dfrac{300}{200}} = 3 \times \frac{2}{3} = 2$$

The exchange ratio is 2, meaning that C will obtain 2 shares of X for each share of Y. Does it make sense? It's not rocket science. Consider the formula above: it basically compares the fair value of one share of Y with the fair value of one share of X. If one share of X is worth half of the value of one share of Y, it follows that, for each share of Y, the former shareholders of Y must receive two shares of X.

Is this enough to determine what X, the acquiring corporation, will look like after the merger? No, we also need to determine the capital increase that X must realize to complete the merger. Basically this requires determining the number of new shares that must be issued and factor in their dollar value. The following formula can be used:

capital increase for merger
        = exchange ratio × number of shares of merged corporation (y)
        × accounting or par value of one share of surviving corporation (x)

Based on our numbers we have:

$$capital\ increase\ for\ merger = 2 \times 100 \times \$1 = \$200$$

Once again, the idea is very simple: 100 shares of Y will be cancelled as a consequence of the merger (Y will disappear), for each one of those shares the (former) shareholders of Y must receive 2 shares of X, and the accounting or par value of one share of X (attention, *not* its fair value) is $1. Consequently, X must issue 200 shares with an accounting or par value equal to $200. After the merger, this is what X will look like:

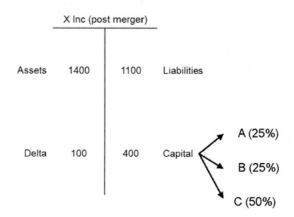

As you can see, the assets and liabilities of Y have been transferred to X and, in X's balance sheet, the value of the assets and liabilities is the sum of the value of the assets and liabilities of the two merged corporations: assets = 1000 (assets of X) + 400 (assets of Y) = 1400; liabilities = 800 (liabilities of X) + 300 (liabilities of Y) = 1100. The new capital is $400, determined as the old capital of X ($200), plus the $200 that we have just determined as capital increase based on the exchange ratio. The 200 newly issued shares have been given to C, the former shareholder of Y, who now owns half of the outstanding shares of X.

Pause here for a second to consider this: does it make sense from a substantive economic standpoint? Of course yes: if you look at the new joint venture, you can argue that C "brought" with him "something" (the business of Y) that was worth $300. Also what A and B brought together to the common enterprise, corporation Y, was worth $300. It is therefore correct and fair that the former shareholder of Y will control half of the new business of X, and that the other half is divided among the old shareholders of X.

But wait a minute. What is that "Delta" of $100 indicated in the balance sheet of X after the merger, above? Simplifying complex accounting rules, that number can be considered an expression of the difference between the fair values of the two corporations and their accounting values, a sort of goodwill that the merger allows and requires to recognize and indicate in the financial statements.

This simplified explanation has hopefully made you more aware of what a merger is and how it works. As simple as this is, if you keep in mind these basic concepts it will be much easier to understand any merger transaction that you will encounter (as an exercise, try to calculate the exchange ratio and the capital increase of a merger of Y with and into X in the previous example, assuming however that X has issued 50 shares with an accounting value of $4 each, Y has issued 200 shares with an accounting value of $0.5 each, that the fair value of X is $600 and that the fair value of Y is $150). The answers, which you should look at only after having tried to determine the values yourself, are in the footnote.[1]

A merger is often a receipt for litigation. Shareholders might complain that the exchange ratio or the cash consideration received is not fair, that the transaction was tainted by conflict of interest, and so forth. What are major remedies that can be invoked by shareholders in case of an allegedly unfair merger or, more generally, frequently litigated issues in the merger context?

---

[1] $exchange\ ratio = \dfrac{1}{16}; capital\ increase = \$50$

First of all, dissenting shareholders can challenge the transaction alleging a breach of the fiduciary duties of the directors, or—to the extent that it might be relevant—of other shareholders, or other substantive or procedural violations. Based on these allegations, shareholders can seek monetary damages, to set aside the merger (but in most jurisdictions, to protect third parties and legal certainty, this is not possible after the merger deed), or an injunction to prevent the completion of the merger. In civil law countries, as we discussed previously, shareholders challenge the validity of the shareholders' meeting resolution approving the merger, a remedy not so often invoked in common law systems. Especially when the corporations involved are listed, shareholders can also sue for violations of the securities laws, for example omissions or misstatements in the proxy solicited for approving the merger. One of the more distinctive remedies is, however, the appraisal right, which in different forms exists in most jurisdictions. To understand this remedy, we need to take a step back in history.

Until the end of the XIX century or the beginning of the XX century, in several legal systems, fundamental transactions such as mergers, which have a profound and lasting impact on the structure of the corporations involved, traditionally required unanimity of the shareholders. Unanimity is, however, a problem: even a single small shareholder can veto an efficient and otherwise desirable transaction. Most legislatures therefore, in the last century, abandoned unanimity requirements and provided that most fundamental transactions, including mergers, could be approved with the majority of the votes (sometimes a supermajority). In order to compensate minority dissenting shareholders, the appraisal right was created. Dissenting shareholders can ask the court to "appraise" their shares, to determine their fair value, and the corporation (or sometimes other shareholders) will have to purchase the shares of the dissenting minority at the price determined by the court or by an expert appointed in other ways.

As pointed out by Professor Thompson in an interesting article (Robert B. Thompson, *Exit, Liquidity, and Majority Rule: Appraisal's Role in Corporate Law*, 84 GEO. L.J. 1 (1995)), however, the appraisal remedy, especially in the U.S., is not particularly effective, for several reasons. For example, in some jurisdictions the appraisal remedy is not available in listed corporations (the idea being that shareholders can easily sell the shares on the market), in addition shareholders must jump through several procedural loopholes to exercise the right (for example, notify the corporation of their intention to dissent before the shareholders' meeting called to approve the merger, and actually dissent or abstain at the meeting). Valuation criteria used by experts might not maximize the value of the shares, and the appraisal procedure is often long and expensive, and its costs often fall on dissenting shareholders.

In terms of remedies, one interesting comparative distinction concerns the role of shareholders' actions challenging the validity of the shareholders' meeting resolution approving a merger. As we briefly mentioned in Chapter 7 discussing shareholders' litigation (*see* the "Notes and Questions" section after the excerpt of Professor Gelter's article in that chapter), in civil law systems often shareholders bring an action for the nullification of the shareholders' resolution approving the merger, arguing for example that procedural rules have been breached, that the resolution passed thanks to the votes of a conflicted shareholder, or that the exchange ratio was unfair. In this perspective, it is particularly important to underline that under the harmonized European rules set forth by Directive 78/855 an external independent expert has to examine the merger project drafted by the directors and take a position on the fairness of the exchange ratio. The report of the expert must be deposited with the corporation before the shareholders' vote on the merger, to allow shareholders to consider it. Article 10 of the Directive provides, in fact, that:

> "1.   One or more experts, acting on behalf of each of the merging companies but independent of them, appointed or approved by a judicial or administrative authority, shall examine the draft terms of merger and draw up a written report to the shareholders. However, the laws of a Member State may provide for the appointment of one or more independent experts for all the merging companies, if such appointment is made by a judicial or administrative authority at the joint request of those companies. Such experts may, depending on the laws of each Member State, be natural or legal persons or companies or firms.
>
> 2.   In the report mentioned in paragraph 1 the experts must in any case state whether in their opinion the share exchange ratio is fair and reasonable. Their statement must at least:
>
> (a) indicate the method or methods used to arrive at the share exchange ratio proposed;
>
> (b) state whether such method or methods are adequate in the case in question, indicate the values arrived at using each such method and give an opinion on the relative importance attributed to such methods in arriving at the value decided on.
>
> The report shall also describe any special valuation difficulties which have arisen.
>
> 3.   Each expert shall be entitled to obtain from the merging companies all relevant information and documents and to carry out all necessary investigations."

It is interesting to point out that even in systems in which it is not mandated by the legislature (such as in several common law systems), the opinion of a qualified and independent expert on the fairness of a major corporate transaction is often obtained. The reason has to do with directors' and managers' possible liabilities: an independent opinion is often an indispensable tool to reduce the risk of being accused of a breach of the duty of care or of loyalty (once again, do you remember *Smith v. Van Gorkom* on this specific issue?).

Challenging the shareholders' meeting resolution is possible but not very frequent in common laws systems, where the most utilized remedies are monetary damages or appraisal rights. You should be aware, however, of the fact that even in systems in which challenging the validity of the shareholders' meeting is more common, such as in continental Europe, the legislature generally only allows this before the merger deed is filed with the public register or the secretary of state (this generally means only within a few weeks after the shareholders' vote). After that moment, only monetary damages are available. The rationale is legal certainty and protection of third parties that might rely on the validity of the merger, and also the high costs—and sometimes impossibility—of untangling a business combination. In these systems, also the creditors of the corporation involved in the merger can enjoin the transaction in the period preceding the publication of the merger deed, if they can demonstrate that they will suffer a prejudice as a consequence of the merger, but after that moment they are only entitled to damages.

Mergers and acquisitions tend to come in waves. This is partially natural, as changing economic and legal conditions influence the convenience of business combinations. For example, in a period of low interest rates, in which obtaining fresh financial resources to acquire other corporations might be easier, M&As can peak; similarly if market price are down, and corporations are (perceived to be) undervalued, acquisitions might become more common. Also legal developments might hinder or foster mergers, for example more liberal rules on defensive measures or more rigorous enforcing of the antitrust laws might reduce the number of acquisitions, not to mention tax considerations. The following graph, even if only referring to mergers involving U.K. corporations, confirms the existence of "merger waves" (source: U.K. Office for National Statistics, 2014).

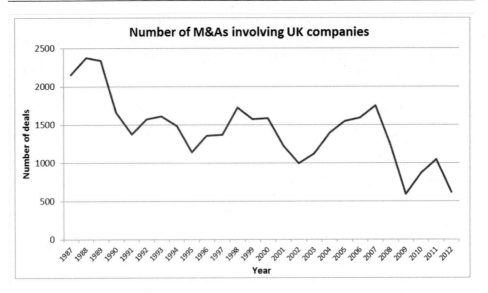

In this section we have considered mergers as one particular type of business combination, and compared them with other alternative transactions. We have then explained a typical merger procedure, focusing in particular on the different steps necessary to complete the transactions. Next we wanted to clarify the economics of a merger, and in particular the determination of the exchange ratio, something that we have done with some basic accounting and numbers, hopefully without traumatizing the readers. We have finally mentioned possible remedies in case of an alleged unfair merger, and made a reference to "merger waves." The framework that we laid down in this chapter is, more or less, valid for most modern jurisdictions, even if of course there are important differences. We believe, however, that this common background will be helpful—in fact, essential—for the following comparative analysis.

SALES OF ALL OR SUBSTANTIVELY ALL THE ASSETS

As we have mentioned, in the United States as well as in many other jurisdictions, several "extraordinary financial transactions," including mergers, generally require the approval of both the directors and the shareholders of the corporations involved. The idea is that these transactions are fundamental amendments to the articles of incorporation and/or have effects similar to the winding up of a corporation, and therefore cannot be approved without the consent of the shareholders. A merger might significantly alter the risk/return of the investment of shareholders, and they must have a voice in these decisions. Selling some of the assets of a corporation, on the other hand, is generally considered a business decision that falls within the competences of the board of directors. In the absence of a different provision in the charter or bylaws, directors are generally free to sell specific assets, and of course potentially liable for their decision.

This general rule, however, has exceptions or, more precisely, raises a particular problem. What if directors sell all or substantively all the assets of a corporation, therefore materially modifying the purpose of the corporation and its economic perspectives? Is a shareholders' vote necessary? Are the protections existing for minority shareholders in case of merger also available in this case?

We touched on a related problem in Chapter 5, discussing corporate governance and in particular the relative powers of directors and shareholders. You might remember (or go back and review) the German case *Holzmüller* we discussed there. The question raised by that case was whether directors, spinning off assets to a different controlled corporation, infringed the shareholders' franchise because, after the spin-off, directors would be able to manage the assets that had been transferred without shareholders' supervision. We now examine a partially similar issue with respect to sales of assets and mergers.

The problem is particularly evident when the sale of assets has economic effects very similar to a merger. Consider the following example: the directors of corporation X sell all the assets of X to Y, an independent corporation, for cash. With the proceeds of the sale, X buys shares of Y from one of its shareholders. At this point, X is dissolved, creditors are paid, and the shares of Y owned by X are distributed among X's shareholders. As you can see, the practical consequences are almost identical to the ones of a merger of X with and into Y: X will disappear, its assets will be transferred to Y, and the former shareholders of X will become shareholders of Y. Formally, however, the transaction is not a merger. Should it be treated as a *de facto* merger for some purposes? For example, should dissenting shareholders of X be entitled to exercise their appraisal rights, if appraisal rights are not explicitly provided by the applicable statute in case of sale of assets? From a broader perspective, this is a typical problem that lawyers and judges encounter all the time: should the substance of the transaction (the fact that the economic effects are similar to a merger) prevail over its form (the transaction is technically not a merger), and shareholders be treated and protected as in case of merger?

The following case illustrates the Delaware approach to this problem.

MARTIN HARITON V. ARCO ELECTRONICS, INC.

Court of Chancery of Delaware
40 Del. Ch. 326 (1962)

SHORT, VICE CHANCELLOR.

Plaintiff is a stockholder of defendant Arco Electronics, Inc., a Delaware corporation. The complaint challenges the validity of the purchase by Loral Electronics Corporation, a New York corporation, of all the assets of Arco. Two causes of action are asserted, namely (1) that the transaction is unfair to Arco stockholders, and (2) that the transaction constituted a de facto merger and is unlawful since the merger provisions of the Delaware law were not complied with.

Defendant has moved to dismiss the complaint and for summary judgment on the ground that the transaction was fair to Arco stockholders and was, in fact, one of purchase and sale and not a merger.

Plaintiff now concedes that he is unable to sustain the charge of unfairness. The only issue before the court, therefore, is whether the transaction was by its nature a de facto merger with a consequent right of appraisal in plaintiff.

Prior to the transaction of which plaintiff complains Arco was principally engaged in the business of the wholesale distribution of components or parts for electronics and electrical equipment. It had outstanding 486,500 shares of Class A common stock and 362,500 shares of Class B common stock. The rights of the holders of the Class A and Class B common stock differed only as to preferences in dividends. Arco's balance sheet as of September 30, 1961 shows total assets of $3,013,642. Its net income for the preceding year was $273,466.

Loral was engaged, primarily, in the research, development and production of electronic equipment. Its balance sheet shows total assets of $16,453,479. Its net income for the year ending March 31, 1961 was $1,301,618.

In the summer of 1961 Arco commenced negotiations with Loral with a view to the purchase by Loral of all of the assets of Arco in exchange for shares of Loral common stock. I think it fair to say that the record establishes that the negotiations which ultimately led to the transaction involved were conducted by the representatives of the two corporations at arm's length. There is no suggestion that any representative of Arco had any interest whatever in Loral, or vice versa. In any event, Arco rejected two offers made by Loral of a purchase price based upon certain ratios of Loral shares for Arco shares. Finally, on October 11, 1961, Loral offered a purchase price based on the ratio of one share of Loral common stock for three shares of Arco common stock. This offer was accepted by the representatives of Arco on October 24, 1961 and an agreement for the purchase was entered into between Loral and Arco on October 27, 1961. This agreement provides, among other things, as follows:

1.　Arco will convey and transfer to Loral all of its assets and property of every kind, tangible and intangible; and will grant to Loral the use of its name and slogans.

2.　Loral will assume and pay all of Arco's debts and liabilities.

3.　Loral will issue to Arco 283,000 shares of its common stock.

4.　Upon the closing of the transaction Arco will dissolve and distribute to its shareholders, pro rata, the shares of the common stock of Loral.

5.　Arco will call a meeting of its stockholders to be held December 21, 1961 to authorize and approve the conveyance and delivery of all the assets of Arco to Loral.

6.　After the closing date Arco will not engage in any business or activity except as may be required to complete the liquidation and dissolution of Arco.

Pursuant to its undertaking in the agreement for purchase and sale Arco caused a special meeting of its stockholders to be called for December 27, 1961. The notice of such meeting set forth three specific purposes therefor: (1) to vote upon a proposal to ratify the agreement of purchase and sale, a copy of which was attached to the notice; (2) to vote upon a proposal to change the name of the corporation; and (3) if Proposals (1) and (2) should be adopted, to vote upon a proposal to liquidate and dissolve the corporation and to distribute the Loral shares to Arco shareholders. Proxies for this special meeting were not solicited. At the meeting 652,050 shares were voted in favor of the sale and none against. The proposals to change the name of the corporation and to dissolve it and distribute the Loral stock were also approved. The transaction was thereafter consummated.

Plaintiff contends that the transaction, though in form a sale of assets of Arco, is in substance and effect a merger, and that it is unlawful because the merger statute has not been complied with, thereby depriving plaintiff of his right of appraisal.

Defendant contends that since all the formalities of a sale of assets pursuant to 8 Del.C. § 271 have been complied with the transaction is in fact a sale of assets and not a merger. In this connection it is to be noted that plaintiff nowhere allege or claim that defendant has not complied to the letter with the provisions of said section.

The question here presented is one which has not been heretofore passed upon by any court in this state. [. . .]

The doctrine of de facto merger in comparable circumstances has been recognized and applied by the Pennsylvania courts, both state and federal. Lauman v. Lebanon Valley Railroad Co., 30 Pa. 42; Marks v. Autocar Co., D.C., 153 F.Supp. 768; Farris v. Glen Alden Corporation, 393 Pa. 427, 143 A.2d 25. The two cases last cited are founded upon the holding in the case first cited which was decided on common law principles. [. . .]

The right of appraisal accorded to a dissenting stockholder by the merger statutes is in compensation for the right which he had at common law to prevent a merger. [. . .] At common law a single dissenting stockholder could also prevent a sale of all of the assets of a corporation. 18 C.J.S. Corporations § 515, p. 1194. The Legislatures of many states have seen fit to grant the appraisal right to a dissenting stockholder not only under the merger statutes but as well under the sale of assets statutes. Our Legislature has seen fit to expressly grant the appraisal right only under the merger statutes. This difference in treatment of the rights of dissenting stockholders may well have been deliberate, in order 'to allow even greater freedom of action to corporate majorities in arranging combinations than is possible under the merger statutes.' 72 Harv.L.Rev. 1132, 'The Right of Shareholders Dissenting From Corporate Combinations To Demand Cash Payment For Their Shares.'

While plaintiff's contention that the doctrine of de facto merger should be applied in the present circumstances is not without appeal, the subject is one which, in my opinion, is within the legislative domain. Moreover it is difficult to differentiate between a case such as the present and one where the reorganization plan contemplates the ultimate dissolution of the selling corporation but does not formally require such procedure in express terms. [. . .]

There is authority in decisions of courts of this state for the proposition that the various sections of the Delaware Corporation Law conferring authority for corporate action are independent of each other and that a given result may be accomplished by proceeding under one section which is not possible, or is even forbidden under another. For example, dividends which have accrued to preferred stockholders may not be eliminated by an amendment to the corporate charter under § 242, Title 8. Keller v. Wilson & Co., 21 Del.Ch. 391, 190 A. 115. On the other hand, such accrued dividends may be eliminated by a merger between the corporation and a wholly owned subsidiary. Federal United Corporation v. Havender, 24 Del.Ch. 318, 11 A.2d 331; Hottenstein v. York Ice Machinery Corp., D.C.Del., 45 F.Supp. 436, Id., 3 Cir., 136 F.2d 944. In Langfelder v. Universal Laboratories, D.C., 68 F.Supp. 209, Judge Leahy commented upon these holdings as follows:

' * * * Havender v. Federal United Corporation, Del.Sup., 11 A.2d 331 and Hottenstein v. York Ice Machinery Corp., D.C.Del., 45 F.Supp. 436; Id., 3 Cir., 136 F.2d 944 hold that in Delaware a parent may merge with a wholly owned subsidiary and thereby cancel old preferred stock and the rights of the holders thereof to the unpaid, accumulated dividends, by substituting in lieu thereof stocks of the surviving corporation. Under Delaware law, accrued dividends after the passage of time mature into a debt and can not be eliminated by an amendment to the corporate charter under Sec. 26 of the Delaware Corporation Law, Rev.Code 1935, § 2058. But the right to be paid in full for such dividends, notwithstanding provisions in the charter contract, may be eliminated by means of a merger which meets the standard of fairness. The rationale is that a merger is an act of independent legal significance, and when it meets the requirements of fairness and all other statutory requirements, the merger is valid and not subordinate or dependent upon any other section of the Delaware Corporation Law.'

In a footnote to Judge Leahy's opinion the following comment appears:

'The text is but a particularization of the general theory of the Delaware Corporation Law that action taken pursuant to the authority of the various sections of that law constitute acts of independent legal significance and their validity is not dependent on other sections of the Act. Havender v. Federal United Corporation proves the correctness of this interpretation. Under Keller v. Wilson & Co. accrued dividends are regarded as matured rights and must be paid. But, this does not prevent a merger, good under the provisions of Sec. 59, from having the incidental effect of wiping out such dividend rights, i. e., Sec. 59 is complete in itself and is not dependent upon any other section, absent fraud. The same thing is true with most other sections of the Corporation Law.'

The situation posed by the present case is even stronger than that presented in the Havender and York Ice cases. In those cases the court permitted the circumvention of matured rights by proceeding under the merger statute. Here, the stockholder has no rights unless another and independent statute is invoked to create a right. A holding in the stockholder's favor would be directly contrary to the theory of the cited cases.

I conclude that the transaction complained of was not a de facto merger, either in the sense that there was a failure to comply with one or more of the requirements of § 271 of the Delaware Corporation Law, or that the result accomplished was in effect a merger entitling plaintiff to a right of appraisal.

Defendant's motion for summary judgment is granted.

NOTES AND QUESTIONS

1.   Why is the plaintiff trying to have the transaction treated as a merger?

2.   The Delaware Chancery Court rejects the de facto merger doctrine which, at the time of this decision, was for example followed in Pennsylvania (the legislature later intervened to abolish the doctrine). Do you think that this approach is too formalistic? Or do you find the reasoning of the Court convincing?

3.   What do you think are the crucial and related arguments on which the Court relies? How would you describe the concept of "independent legal significance"? Why is the *Havender* precedent relevant?

4.   What do you think might be the risks of the *de facto* merger theory? What about, for example, legal uncertainty and protection of third parties, such as creditors?

5.   This case is, obviously, about applying to a sale of assets all the rules that should be applicable to a merger to a sale of assets, including in particular appraisal rights. Please keep in mind that, in most U.S. jurisdictions, a sale of all or substantively all the assets generally requires the approval of shareholders. The delicate factual problem here is to define what constitutes a sale of "substantively" all the assets. There is a grey area in which it is not so easy to decide if the type, amount, and value of the assets sold is "substantial" enough to mandate a shareholders' resolution. Different tests have been developed, some based more on a bright-line rule taking into account the value of the assets transferred (80% of the total? 90%?), others using a more qualitative approach, considering for example the strategic relevance of certain assets, and whether transferring them would significantly impact the business of the corporation.

6.   It is interesting to note that the de facto merger doctrine does not exist in the U.K. Instead, one should examine similar doctrines dealing with successor liability. Professors Andreas Cahn and David C. Donald (*Comparative Company Law: Text and Cases on the Laws Governing Corporations* (CUP 2010), pp. 659–660)) explain: "Neither the Companies Act 2006 nor the UK case law directly provides a procedure to approve a sale of all or substantially all of a company's assets. Inclusion of such a provision was specifically recommended by a committee of experts as far back as 1962, but has not been followed. In cases in which such transactions arose, it was common in the past that U.K. companies had from the outset provided that for the sale of the 'whole of the company's undertaking' in the memorandum and make such sale contingent upon a special resolution of shareholders . . . because the 2006 Act no longer requires that registering companies specify a

corporate objective, this possibility of introducing shareholder control will diminish as new companies are formed and old ones are liquidated. . . . FSA [now FCA] listing rules contain highly detailed regulations specifying transactions that require shareholder approval based on the percentage of gross assets, profits, the capital they entail or the consideration paid, and such transactions include major asset sales. . . .".

* * *

In other legal systems, the problem raised by the sale of all assets is approached from different perspectives. One interesting example, which is also connected to another comparative distinction that we have mentioned in Chapter 3, concerns the "purpose" of the corporation. As you will remember, the governing documents of the corporation must indicate the business purpose. This provision can be extremely broad in some jurisdictions, typically in common law systems, where a corporation can be established to "engage in any lawful act and activity." Some countries however require a more precisely defined purpose, for example "the production and sale of medical equipment, and all related activities." Also these provisions tend to be quite broad, especially because they include activities related and instrumental to the core business, such as financial activities. There are therefore few acts that might be deemed outside the business purpose, and in any case directors and top executives are generally considered to have at least apparent authority to act on behalf of the corporation. If, however, directors sell all (or substantively all) the assets without the consent of the shareholders, possibly to use the proceeds for different goals, the transaction might be considered a de facto amendment of the corporate purpose. Since an amendment of the corporate purpose requires shareholders' approval (and often triggers appraisal or withdrawal rights of dissenting shareholders), a de facto amendment decided only by the directors might be unlawful. One application of this general principle is Article 2361 of the Italian Civil Code: this rule provides that even if the bylaws include in the corporate purpose the acquisition of participations in other business organizations, it is forbidden to acquire participations that substantially modify the corporate purpose indicated in the bylaws.

Differently from Italy, French courts do not generally follow the doctrine of de facto amendments of the corporate purpose. For example, in a 1994 case, the board of directors of a close corporation sold real estate owned by the corporation. A minority shareholder sued arguing that the sale made impossible pursuing the corporation's business purpose and could only be approved with a vote of the shareholders' meeting. The French Supreme Court rejected the request holding that the sale of real estate did not represent a modification of the purpose of the corporation (Cour de cassation, February 1er 1994, Francis Carricaburu c/ SCGC, Revue des sociétés 1994 p. 697, note Y. Chaput.). In this decision the

French Supreme Court took a quite formalistic approach, basically ignoring the substantive, actual effects of the sale on the activity carried on by the corporation. In order to better protect investors, one scholar has suggested that, at least for listed corporations, the French legislature should provide that a sale of all or substantively all the assets is equivalent to an amendment of the articles of incorporation and requires a vote of the shareholders. The rule could apply, for example, when over 80% of the assets in terms of book value are sold (*see* Pierre-Henri Conac, *Cession de l'essentiel des actifs d'une société cotée: plaidoyer pour la compétence de l'assemblée générale extraordinaire (AGE)*, REVUE DES SOCIÉTÉS 598 (2014)).

Under German law the sale of all or substantively all the assets requires a shareholder resolution with ¾ majority at the shareholder meeting in order to protect minority shareholders (Sec. 179a German Stock Corporation Law). A contract executed without the approval of the shareholders is void and the corporation can claim back the assets.

Wrapping up, selling all or substantively all the assets (and liabilities) of a corporation is a risky transaction for shareholders, because it allows directors to profoundly alter the investment of the shareholders. Different regulatory techniques or arguments might be used to protect shareholders. One possibility is to say that if the sale has effects similar to a different transaction that offers better protections for shareholders (for example, resembles a merger that requires a vote of the shareholders and in which shareholders could invoke appraisal rights), the same protections existing for the latter should be extended to the sale with a legal analogy. This approach, which is the de facto merger theory, hinders however legal certainty, applying the regime set forth for one type of transaction to other transactions not precisely defined. Courts, at least in Delaware, are reluctant to do that. Another option, followed in Germany, is to specifically attribute the competence to approve a sale of all the assets to the shareholders, either by statute or with a provision in the bylaws, and possibly provide for additional protections, such as appraisal rights for dissenters. When a similar provision does not exist, it might be possible to argue that directors infringed in the shareholders' franchise by altering substantially the purpose of the corporation, something that would normally require a positive vote of the shareholders to modify the charter.

Do you think protections for shareholders are necessary in case of a sale of all the assets? If so, which one of the above mentioned regulatory strategies do you find preferable? Is it necessary to also take into account the need to give directors sufficient flexibility?

LEVERAGED BUYOUTS

Do you remember *Smith v. Van Gorkom*, the case on directors' duty of care that we discussed in Chapter 6? If you do (and if you do not we suggest you review it), you will remember that the underlying facts concerned a leveraged buyout, and in fact one of the criticism of the decision of the directors is that they did not maximize the sale price of the shares, but rather accepted a price that would have made the leveraged buyout possible for the buyer.

It is now time to discuss a little more extensively leveraged buyouts and their regulation. Basically, a leveraged buyout ("LBO") is an acquisition in which the buying corporation obtains a loan or other credit in order to have the financial resources necessary to obtain control of the target. Often the acquiring corporation is an empty shell incorporated specifically for the transaction, and before the acquisition its financial statements will only show the debt as liability and the proceeds obtained from the creditors as assets. Once control of the target is acquired, the target is merged with and into the vehicle that the buyer is using. The result is generally a corporation that looks very similar to the target, but has a much higher leverage (more debt).

Consider the following example. A, a listed corporation, wants to acquire B, another listed corporation. For a number of reasons, A might decide that it needs credit to complete the transaction: for example, A might not have the required financial resources, or a loan might make sense to take advantage of low interest rates. Consequently, A incorporates a new corporation, X, essentially a vehicle used to complete the acquisition. X generally has little capital. At this point A will try to convince a bank or other investors to lend it the money needed to launch a tender offer on B. If the loan is secured, with the proceeds X will launch a tender offer on B. Once control is acquired, B will be merged into X.

The transaction can be illustrated with the following example:

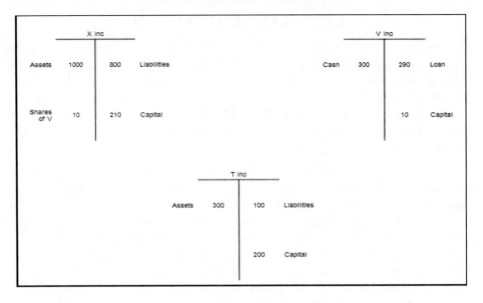

In our example, X incorporates V, the "vehicle" for the LBO, with an initial capital of 10, entirely owned by X. X and V obtain a significant loan that will be used to finance the acquisition of the "target" T, equal to 290. As you can see, V is a highly indebted corporation. At this point the cash of V is used to launch a tender offer on T. Imagine the bid is successful and, for sake of simplicity, imagine that V obtains all the shares of T. At this point T is merged into V. With some simplification, after the merger, which represents the second step of the acquisition, V will have the following financial structure:

	V Inc		
Assets	300	390	Liabilities
Delta	100	10	Capital

The surviving corporation has the assets of the target T, and its liabilities are represented by the old liabilities of T, plus the loan originally granted to V in order to finance the acquisition, which still need to be repaid. After the LBO, the resulting corporation is also a highly leveraged corporation, with a fairly low capital vis-à-vis debt. This is a typical consequence of an LBO and, if you think about it, you might argue that the generic "guarantee" that was offered to the creditors that extended the loan to V was represented by the assets and business of the target, T. In other words, the business proposition that V (and its controlling shareholder X) made to the creditors was: "give me credit that I can use to buy the target; once I will be the new controlling shareholder, I will manage the target so well that I will be able to pay back the debt, and still make a profit."

Clearly enough, the LBO is a highly risky transaction. If the target corporation is not managed effectively, it can easily become insolvent because it is loaded with debt. The situation is even more delicate when the creditors are not represented by sophisticated counterparties such as banks, but rather bondholders. To finance acquisitions in this way, issuing bonds, became fairly common in the 1980s, especially in the United States, during a takeover frenzy. These bonds, even if promised high yields, became known as "junk bonds" due to their highly risky nature (in the 1980s, one of the "kings" of junk bonds was financier Michael Milken, who ended up spending time in prison for insider trading). LBOs are, however, certainly older, as demonstrated by the wonderful, Shakespearian movie "High and Low," a 1963 crime drama by Akira Kurosawa, in which the main character Kingo Gondo is a Japanese manager planning a leveraged buyout.

Some legislatures do not see it as their job to limit or regulate LBOs. They might require full disclosure on the transaction in order to inform investors purchasing junk bonds of the highly speculative nature of the transaction, but these rules are generally confined in the area of securities regulation. Substantive corporate law provisions limiting or regulating the acquisition are not enacted. In other systems, the legislature has introduced specific rules designed to give to shareholders and creditors a deeper understanding of the transaction, and more control on the decision. For example, pursuant to Article 2501-bis of the Italian Civil Code, in case of a merger in which one corporation has obtained credit to acquire control of the merged one (basically, the definition of an LBO), the directors must present to the shareholders (and also make available for creditors) a detailed plan indicating how the debt will be repaid. Not only that, but an external independent expert must prepare an opinion on the reasonableness of the plan proposed by the directors. What do you think of a similar rule? Is it useful or pointless? Is it excessively patronizing? Is it easy to define precisely when it should apply?

FREEZE-OUTS, CASH-OUT MERGERS, AND GOING PRIVATE TRANSACTIONS

The United States and Europe have a radically different approach to the regulation of "cash-out" mergers. This difference is as important as is poorly understood. As the name suggests, a cash-out merger is a merger in which some or all the shareholders receive, instead of shares of the surviving corporation as in a regular merger, cash or other consideration. These transactions are very delicate because shareholders, and minority shareholders in particular, are "expropriated" of their shares, and only receive the value of their investment. The fairness of a cash-out merger is, therefore, extremely important: for many investors, it represents the last chance to receive the value of their investment. Cash-out mergers are so controversial that, as we will see, several jurisdictions prohibit or significantly restrict them, and also where they are allowed, they often cause litigation and are governed by extensive statutory and judge-made rules designed to protect minorities.

The complexity of this area of the law makes it difficult to gain a comprehensive understanding by only considering a few cases. For this reason, we have decided to tackle this issue with a somehow longer excerpt of an article comparing cash-out mergers, and more generally "freeze-out transactions" (transactions in which minority shareholders are bought out) in listed corporations, in the U.S. and in Europe. The excerpt also examines some of the most important decisions in this area.

Marco Ventoruzzo, Freeze-Outs: Transcontinental Analysis and Reform Proposals[2]
50 Va. J. Int'l L. 841

One of the most crucial, but systematically neglected, comparative differences between corporate law systems in Europe and the United States concerns regulation governing freeze-out transactions in listed corporations. [. . .] [F]reeze-outs can be defined as transactions in which the controlling shareholder exercises a legal right to buy out the shares of the minority, consequently delisting the corporation and bringing it private. Beyond this essential definition, the systems diverge profoundly.

Few studies have undertaken to examine the differences between the European and U.S. approaches to minority freeze-outs, despite the fact that they are among the most debated issues in corporate law, the public media, a vast body of scholarly work, and case law in the United States and Europe. In light of the relevance of the subject and the extensive and growing number of transatlantic mergers in which the acquiring corporations and target corporations are subject to different legal

---

[2]   Footnotes omitted.

regimes, the dearth of research focused on comparing the European and American approaches to minority freeze-outs is startling.

[. . .]

There are numerous combinations of transactions that allow controlling shareholders to appropriate the equity interests of minority shareholders. In the United States, the different techniques are distilled into four major categories: asset sales, reverse stock splits, (cash-out) mergers, and tender offers. [. . .] The two more common techniques are mergers and tender offers. More specifically, under Delaware law, two approaches have become increasingly popular: the "long-form merger," (or "one-step freeze-out") and the "tender-offer/short-form merger" (or "two-step freeze-out"). In the long-form merger, controlling shareholders simply approve a merger in which the consideration offered to minority shareholders is cash or other nonequity securities, rather than shares of the surviving entity. The tender offer/short-form merger, a more recent development, consists of two steps: a voluntary tender offer on all the outstanding shares launched by the parent corporation, generally aimed at acquiring at least 90% of the outstanding shares, followed by a short-form, cash-out merger.

[. . .]

[M]inority shareholders often challenge a merger on the basis of some illegality, in particular for breach of directors' fiduciary duties or disclosure violations of federal securities laws. The bulk of cases that shape the law of going-private transactions in the United States deal with these types of allegations.

[. . .]

Delaware courts frequently adjudicate minority shareholders' claims of breach of fiduciary duties, or other illegalities, in connection with cash-out transactions. In deciding these disputes, Delaware courts have attempted to balance the power of the directors and the majority shareholders on one hand with the protection of minority shareholders on the other. Too much of the latter prevents efficient, value-maximizing transactions, whereas too much of the former leads to injustice. Courts are frequently reluctant to grapple with elusive standards of substantive fairness, particularly because the legislature has already attempted to strike the balance through procedural protections. Notwithstanding the complexity of the issue, courts have weighed in, and the resulting legal framework [can be] illustrated through seven leading cases, each of which adds to the mosaic of regulation governing going-private transactions. These cases are: Weinberger v. UOP, Inc., Rosenblatt v. Getty Oil Co., Kahn v. Lynch Communication Systems, Inc., Solomon v. Pathe Communications Corp., In re Siliconix Inc. Shareholders Litigation, Glassman v. Unocal Exploration Corp., and In re Pure Resources, Inc.,

Shareholders Litigation. The first three cases dealt with long-form mergers; the last four addressed short-form mergers.

Delaware Case Law on Challenges to Long-Form Cash-Out Mergers from Weinberger to Getty Oil

In Weinberger, UOP, a subsidiary of Signal Companies (Signal, holding 50.5% of the outstanding voting shares), was merged into the parent corporation through a long-form, cash-out merger. Dissenting minority shareholders refused cash consideration and brought a class action suit against the subsidiary and the parent, directors of the two companies, and the investment bank Lehman Brothers, challenging the fairness of the transaction and seeking injunctive relief or, alternatively, monetary damages.

The key factual issues leading to approval of the merger are worth recounting. In the early 1980s, Signal sought investment opportunities. After considering different alternatives, the company's board of directors concluded that the best option was to acquire the totality of shares of its subsidiary, UOP, through a cash-out merger. Signal's executive committee informed James V. Crawford, UOP's president, CEO, and long-time Signal group executive, of this intention and quoted a price per share between $20 and $21. Evidence at trial showed that, during the discussion, Crawford agreed that the price was fair but concentrated his attention on the consequences of the acquisition for personnel. Following this conversation, Signal's board of directors approved a merger proposal offering $21 per share to minority shareholders, a figure significantly above market price, which fluctuated around $15. The proposal provided that the merger would be completed only if it satisfied a double condition: the totality of the votes cast in favor of the merger would be greater than or equal to two-thirds of the entire voting capital, and a majority of the minority shareholders (constituting 49.5% of all shares) would vote in favor.

The UOP board approved these terms and recommended the merger. In making its decision, the board relied upon, among other things, a fairness opinion issued by Lehman Brothers, which, at trial, the court determined to have been hastily prepared. The trial also revealed that two UOP directors (who were also employees of the acquiring corporation Signal), had prepared a report quoting a price of up to $24 as a "good investment" for Signal. This higher price would have had minor consequences on the financial structure of the deal for Signal, but would have created substantial additional benefit for UOP's shareholders. The report was never disclosed to UOP's outside directors and was only shared with Signal's board.

Notwithstanding the revelation of the $24 per share recommendation, the Chancery Court considered the merger fair and found for the defendants. On appeal, however, the Supreme Court of Delaware reversed the lower court's ruling and took the occasion to discuss, and partially resolve, several different issues, including share evaluation techniques.

Weinberger held that under Delaware law, as in other U.S. jurisdictions, freeze-out transactions conducted by controlling shareholders amount to self-dealing. Thus, freeze-out transactions are subject to "entire fairness" review. The decision explored the concept of entire fairness in the merger context, arguing that it encompasses both "fair dealing" and "fair price." The former is a procedural element, concerned with the way in which the acquisition is negotiated; the latter is a substantive element, taking into account the economic rationale behind the deal.

The most relevant part of the decision for the current analysis, however, is dicta buried in a footnote, where the Supreme Court of Delaware proscribed the means by which the entire fairness requirement would be met: the corporation considering a cash-out merger should appoint a special committee of independent directors, entrusted with the task of negotiating the merger at arm's length.

The court's laconic observation stirred a theoretical debate. Supporters of outside directors' ability to ensure truly independent decisions in the best interest of all shareholders clashed with critics that doubted the efficacy of a special committee with veto powers. At a more practical level, however, many corporations soon followed the path pointed out by Weinberger, and litigation erupted on the precise consequences of the committee's approval.

Two answers were possible, and the judges of the Delaware Chancery Court split. By one approach, the committee's decision would be measured by the "business judgment rule." In other words, the resolution of the independent directors would be presumed to have been made on an informed basis, in good faith, and in the honest belief that the action was in the best interest of the corporation. Alternatively, the special committee's decision would simply shift the burden to the plaintiff to prove the absence of entire fairness. This school of thought was more favourable to plaintiffs because to prove that a transaction is not entirely fair, either for lack of fair dealing or fair price, is less cumbersome than overcoming the highly deferential business judgment rule.

The Delaware Supreme Court addressed the issue left open in Weinberger in two pivotal cases: Rosenblatt v. Getty Oil and Kahn v. Lynch. In both decisions, and under different circumstances, the court embraced the view that if merging companies complied with specific procedural safeguards intended to protect minority shareholders, review would be limited to the entire fairness test, with the burden of proof transferred from the defendant to the plaintiff.

Getty Oil settled the question concerning the effect of a majority of the minority shareholders' approval of a merger. In the 1960s, Getty Oil, an oil behemoth created by Jean Paul Getty, became a majority stockholder of Skelly, another big player in the industry, owning directly 7.42% of the outstanding voting shares, and indirectly, through its controlled subsidiary Mission, an additional 72.6%. Jean Paul Getty opposed any further integration between the two companies, believing that a certain degree of competition between them was beneficial to their own strength and profitable for the shareholders. Soon after his death, however, Getty Oil's executive vice-president, Harold E. Berg, contacted Skelly President James H. Hara to discuss combining Getty Oil, Skelly, and Mission.

The directors of Skelly and Getty Oil engaged in an extensive hard-bargaining process to determine the proper exchange ratio for outstanding stock. Skelly's representatives were very determined to obtain the best possible conditions for their shareholders, focusing extensively on the application of the Delaware Block Method. Eventually, the boards agreed on an exchange ratio of 0.5875 Getty Oil shares for every Skelly share. With the boards' unanimous approval, the deal was submitted to the shareholders of the corporations involved and conditioned on the approval of the majority of the minority stockholders. Almost 90% of the minority shares present at the meeting, representing 58% of all the outstanding minority shares, voted in favour of integration, which was subsequently completed. The merger was, however, challenged by disgruntled Skelly shareholders, who brought a class action suit claiming the exchange ratio was unfair. After a lengthy and complicated trial, the Chancery Court found the deal entirely fair and entered judgment for the defendants. On appeal, the Delaware Supreme Court affirmed.

Applying Weinberger, the Delaware Supreme Court evaluated issues of both fair dealing and fair price. Its decision offers an insightful discussion of the Delaware Block Method and proper disclosure of all material facts in a proxy statement. For current purposes, however, it resolved what significance should be attributed to the minority shareholders' vote:

Clearly, Getty, as majority shareholder of Skelly, stood on both sides of this transaction and bore the initial burden of establishing its entire fairness. However, approval of a merger, as here, by an informed vote of a majority of the minority shareholders, while not a legal prerequisite, shifts the burden of proving the unfairness of the merger entirely to the plaintiffs.

Utilizing this procedural protection simply shifted the burden of proving the fairness of the transaction. It did not alter the standard of review to the business judgment rule, with its more deferential treatment of managers and its less favourable disposition towards minority shareholders.

In Kahn v. Lynch, decided nine years after Getty Oil, the Delaware Supreme Court reached a consistent conclusion where the procedural protection afforded minority shareholders was approval of the merger by a committee of independent directors.

In Kahn, Alcatel, holding almost 44% of Lynch, pursued a freeze-out merger with Lynch, whose board of directors instituted a special committee to negotiate the terms of the acquisition. Alcatel proposed a cash price for minorities of $14 per share; Lynch representatives countered at $17. Finally, the board endorsed a price of $15.50 per share, but only after Alcatel executives informed the committee that they were considering a hostile tender offer directly to minority shareholders at a lower price.

The Chancery Court ruled that the negotiation between the acquiring corporation and the special committee was, in fact, conducted at arm's length, and that the burden of proving unfairness of the $15.50 price therefore shifted to the plaintiffs. Moreover, the court concluded that the plaintiffs had not satisfied their burden. On appeal, the Delaware Supreme Court reversed but, in doing so, endorsed the general rule that approval by an independent committee shifted the onus of proving unfairness to the plaintiff. Having subscribed to this view, the court nonetheless considered what effect the threat of a hostile tender offer had on the directors' ability to negotiate independently and determined that the plaintiffs had made a prima facie showing of unfairness. Simply put, the directors' capitulation in the face of a possible hostile tender offer belied their ability to operate independently and to adequately protect the interests of minority shareholders. The case was therefore remanded to the lower court, with the burden of proving entire fairness shifted back to the defendant.

Thus, by the mid-nineties, Delaware case law on long-form, freeze-out mergers was well settled. As in any arm's-length transaction, courts would review a merger conducted by controlling shareholders against the two-pronged entire fairness test (Weinberger). Under normal entire fairness review, the defendants shoulder the burden of proving fairness. However, in the context of a freeze-out where certain procedural protections are afforded to minority shareholders—for example, when there is approval by a truly independent special committee (Lynch), or approval by the majority of the minority stockholders (Getty)—the burden of proving unfairness shifts to the plaintiff.

This doctrinal framework has been applied extensively and consistently, even if more recent decisions have added further specifications and, in some cases, suggested possible reforms.

Tender Offers Followed by Short-Form Mergers from Pathe to Pure

The second technique used to achieve a freeze-out of minority shareholders, the tender-offer followed by a short-form merger, was anticipated by Alcatel's alleged threat in Kahn v. Lynch to launch a tender offer directly to the shareholders, bypassing the board of directors. The essential question for a court to consider in such a situation is straightforward: When a majority shareholder launches a public bid to purchase the outstanding minority shares of a controlled corporation, is the offer subject to the entire fairness standard?

In 1996, the Delaware Supreme Court answered in the negative. Solomon v. Pathe Communications Corp. involved a complex financial transaction with global ramifications. Pathe financed its acquisition of the movie company MGM/UA with loans from the Dutch bank Credit Lyonnaise Banque Nederland N.V. (CLBN). The loans were guaranteed by security interests in 89% of Pathe's shares and 98% of MGM/UA shares. CLBN also obtained control over 89.5% of Pathe's shares through voting trusts. Not long after the acquisition, CLBN voted to remove four Pathe directors, among them CEO Giancarlo Parretti. An Italian court found Parretti's removal improper, and while the legal grounds and possible consequences of the ruling in the United States were unclear, CLBT nonetheless decided to foreclose its security. Pathe and CLBN reached an agreement pursuant to which the former would not delay the foreclosure, and the latter would extend an offer to buy the publicly held shares of Pathe for $1.50 per share. A committee of independent directors approved the merger, supported by financial and legal advisors.

The likely motivation for Pathe's directors to launch a tender offer on all the shares was to reduce potential liabilities toward shareholders. Nonetheless, Solomon, representing the class of Pathe's shareholders that tendered the shares, brought suit alleging that the directors breached their duty of care in failing to resist the foreclosure and not negotiating effectively the price of the tender offer. This second failure, according to the plaintiff, also represented a breach of the directors' duty of fair dealing.

The Delaware Supreme Court confirmed the Chancery Court's decision, rejecting the plaintiff's theory: In the case of totally voluntary tender offers, as here, courts do not impose any right of the shareholders to receive a particular price. Delaware law recognizes that, as to allegedly voluntary tender offers (in contrast to cash-out mergers), the determinative factor as to voluntariness is whether coercion is present, or whether there is [sic] "materially false or misleading disclosures made to shareholders in connection with the offer."

The decision came as a surprise to the legal community. Prior to Solomon, the common understanding was that a tender offer launched by a controlling shareholder presented a conflict of interest and was, therefore, subject to the entire fairness requirement. This point of view emphasized the role of the board of directors of the subsidiary in negotiating the terms of the bid with the parent corporation. The court reasoned, however, that the two parties of the deal are the bidder on the one hand, and the minority shareholders on the other. They are unrelated parties and, in the absence of coercion and disclosure violations, single investors are free to accept or refuse the proposed price.

Notwithstanding the very specific facts of Solomon, transactional lawyers and their clients started to consider tender offers a less treacherous pathway for the elimination of minorities than the traditional long-form cash-out merger. Any remaining doubts were eliminated by the Delaware Supreme Court's holdings in In re Siliconix Inc. Shareholders Litigation and Glassman v. Unocal Exploration Corp., both decided in 2001.

In Siliconix, the vice-chancellor determined that a bidder voluntarily launching a tender offer followed by a short-form merger is not obliged to offer a fair price. Siliconix Inc. was active in the semiconductors industry and listed on the NASDAQ. Vishay, listed on the New York Stock Exchange, was its controlling shareholder, with an 80.4% equity interest. In 2000, the market price of Siliconix's shares was subject to significant volatility, hitting a low in December. The company's fundamentals were also looking grim: sales and profits were decreasing at an alarming rate.

In February 2001, Vishay proposed a cash tender offer on Siliconix for $28.82 per share. The quoted price included a 10% premium over the market price. Vishay also announced that if it reached a 90% controlling stake, it would proceed to merge Siliconix into one of its subsidiaries through a short-form, cash-out merger at the same $28.82 price. Siliconix's board appointed a two-member special committee to evaluate the offer. Although questions were raised on the actual independence of the committee's members because of their relationships with the controlling stockholder, the committee found that the price offered was inadequate. By then, Siliconix's shares had risen above $28.82.

When the committee rejected the initial offer, Vishay started considering a less financially burdensome stock-for-stock offer which was announced in May 2001, with no opportunity provided for the special committee to evaluate the fairness of the transaction. The exchange ratio was calculated simply by dividing the price of Siliconix and Vishay shares on February 22, 2001, and was fixed at 1.5 Vishay shares for each Siliconix share. No premium above the market price was considered.

In the public disclosure documents concerning the acquisition, Vishay included a majority of the minority nonwaivable condition, stating that the offer would be finalized only if a majority of the nonaffiliated investors tendered their securities. In addition, Vishay informed the public that, following the offer, it might proceed to a cash-out short-form merger for the same consideration offered in the bid, but specified that it would follow through only if certain conditions were met. Siliconix, on the other hand, stated in its Schedule 14D–9 form that the special committee was neutral with respect to the offer, not having issued a recommendation. It also declared that no fairness opinion had been provided by an outside financial advisor.

Raymond L. Fitzgerald, a qualified minority shareholder holding 6% of Siliconix's outstanding shares, sued asserting individual claims both on his own behalf and on behalf of a class of Siliconix's minority shareholders. He also filed a derivative action on behalf of the corporation seeking, in particular, to enjoin the transaction.

Relying on Solomon, the court denied Fitzgerald's petitions. For [our purposes] it is sufficient to note that the court distinguished mergers (where corporate boards are the primary negotiators, with extensive power to structure and bring forward the deal) from tender offers (where the counterpart to the bidder consists of minority shareholders with power to decline the proposal if inadequate). In other words, the tender offer does not entail the conflicts of interest that arise when directors and officers elected by the controlling acquiring corporation promulgate a merger. On this basis, the court determined that a tender offer is not subject to entire fairness review.

Siliconix focused on the front-end of the new freeze-out technique, the tender offer. In contrast, Glassman v. Unocal Exploration Corp. addressed the back-end, the subsequent short-form, cash-out merger. In fact, no tender offer ever took place in Glassman. When Unocal initiated the short-form merger of its subsidiary UXC, it already owned 96% of UXC's outstanding shares and proceeded directly to the short-form merger pursuant to Section 253 of the Delaware General Corporation Law (DGCL). Dissenting minority shareholders brought a class action suit alleging an unfair exchange ratio.

Crucially, the court considered the statutory procedure for a short-form merger set forth by Section 253 inherently incompatible with equitable relief based on entire fairness review. In a short-form merger, the board of directors and the shareholders of the merged subsidiary have no voice, are not involved in the decision, and do not even receive advance notice of the transaction. This exceptionally truncated process, which allows the parent company's board of directors to unilaterally determine the transaction, is based on a clear policy rationale: the relatively small dimension of minority interests fails to justify a lengthy and more costly procedure, such as that required in a long-form merger. In the court's own words: "The equitable claim plainly conflicts with the statute. If a corporate fiduciary follows the truncated process authorized by § 253, it will not be able to establish the fair dealing prong of entire fairness. If, instead, the corporate fiduciary sets up negotiating committees, hires independent financial and legal experts, etc., then it will have lost the very benefit provided by the statute—a simple, fast and inexpensive process for accomplishing a merger. We resolve this conflict by giving effect the intent of the General Assembly. In order to serve its purpose, § 253 must be construed to obviate the requirement to establish entire fairness."

Applying its own precedents, the court reasoned that, in the specific context of a short-form merger, minorities are sufficiently protected by the appraisal remedy available to "dissenting" shareholders even if technically they do not vote and, therefore, cannot "dissent" in the general sense. Equitable relief through an entire fairness claim is therefore not available in the context of short-form mergers.

Siliconix and Glassman combined to clear the way for going-private transactions through a tender offer followed by a short-form merger: neither of the two components of the transaction would be subject to the demanding standard of entire fairness.

The resulting doctrinal picture was subject to criticism, particularly by academics. Two types of transactions aimed at the same substantive result of eliminating minority shareholders—the long-form merger and the tender-offer followed by a short-form merger—were held to radically different standards of review. One-step mergers (i.e., long-form mergers) were subject to the entire fairness standard, more protective of minority investors. Two-step mergers (i.e., tender offers/short-form mergers), however, were subject to the pro-manager business judgment rule absent proof of coercion and disclosure violations.

In 2002, with In re Pure Resources, the Chancery Court attempted to reconcile these differences by establishing further protections for minority shareholders in two-step mergers. In Pure, Unocal, the controlling shareholder of the corporation that gives its name to the case, launched a stock-for-stock tender offer on the common stock of its subsidiary. The exchange offer, as in Siliconix, was conditioned on the majority of the minority nonaffiliated shareholders tendering their shares and was also subject to the waivable condition that Unocal secure at least 90% of all Pure shares before it initiated a short-form merger pursuant to DGCL Section 253. Unocal also stated that it would proceed with the merger as soon as possible after completion of the tender offer, at the same exchange ratio as the front-end offer.

The special committee instituted by Pure to evaluate the transaction prepared a 14D–9 communication recommending that minority shareholders not tender their shares. A class action followed, with dissenting minority shareholders seeking to enjoin the transaction. The plaintiffs proffered the usual argument: The offer did not meet the entire fairness standard because it was coercive and material information was not properly disclosed.

The court ruled in favor of the plaintiffs, enjoining the offer. [. . .] [T]he court, for the first time, distinguished clearly between the one-step merger (subject to the entire fairness standard) and the two-step merger (subject to the business judgment rule in light of the greater freedom of minority shareholders to accept the front-end offer). The court was not, however, oblivious to the risk that a two-step merger might sometimes confront minority investors with a prisoner's dilemma, forcing them to accept less-than-optimal consideration for their shares. Coercion of the minority would be more subtle in a two-step merger than in a one-step merger, but still present. Therefore, to level the playing field, Pure established three conditions that must be met in order to exclude the transaction from entire fairness review: (1) the offer must be subject to a nonwaivable condition of approval (expressed through tendering) by the majority of the minority; (2) the bidder must guarantee to promptly consummate a short-form merger at the same conditions of the tender offer in terms of price and/or exchange ratio; and (3) the bidder can make no retributive threats in dealing with the target's directors.

[. . .]

To sum up the discussion thus far, Delaware law provides two primary modes by which controlling shareholders can freeze-out minorities. The first is the one-step, long-term, cash-out merger, subject to the entire fairness standard of review. Absent certain procedures to protect minority shareholders, the burden to prove fairness is on the defendants. The burden is shifted to the plaintiffs, however, if a truly independent special committee of the controlled corporation is instituted to negotiate the deal, or if a majority of the minority unaffiliated shareholders of the acquired corporation approve the merger. Alternatively, controlling shareholders can employ a two-step tender offer followed by a short-form merger, where entire fairness review applies only if the three Pure conditions are not satisfied.

[. . .]

Unavailability of Cash-Out Mergers in Europe

Cash-out mergers are generally not permitted in Europe.109 Articles 3 and 4 of the Third Council Directive Concerning Mergers of Public Limited Liability Companies (Third Directive) provide that in a "merger by acquisition" and in a "merger by the formation of a new company," shareholders of the constituent corporations must receive shares of the surviving corporation according to an exchange ratio agreed upon by the boards of directors and approved by the shareholders. They can also receive a cash payment, but "not exceeding 10% of the nominal value of the shares . . . issued or, where they have no nominal value, of their accounting par value."

Thus, shareholders of the corporation extinguished by the merger are entitled to receive at least some shares of the surviving company and cannot simply be cashed out. In other words, under European law, a merger with an entirely cash consideration for some shareholders is unacceptable. This rule is the expression of a more general principle, still reflected in the national laws of most Member States, that a shareholder's participation right cannot be taken away without her consent.

To be sure, the exchange ratio could theoretically be set so high that minority shareholders of the acquired corporation will not, as a matter of fact, obtain shares of the acquiring corporation, similar to what can happen in a reverse stock split, or share consolidation. Consider, for instance, a situation where the controlling shareholder owns 51,000 shares, and no other shareholder matches this equity interest. If the exchange ratio is set at one share of the surviving corporation for every 51,000 shares of the merged corporation, only the majority shareholder is able to obtain equity of the surviving entity.

The exchange ratio cannot be set arbitrarily but must express a fair relationship between the value of the two constituent corporations and their shares. According to the Third Directive, in all Member States, before the draft terms of a merger are presented to the shareholders, a judicially-appointed independent expert must examine the exchange ratio and issue an opinion on its intrinsic fairness. This provision embodies in many respects one of the fundamental differences between European, and in particular civil law based systems, and U.S. law. The former rely more on ex ante procedural protections regulated by the legislature; the latter is a litigation-based system where directors enjoy greater freedom in structuring the deal but are subject to potentially extensive review through ex post lawsuits. Interestingly, in the United States, the outcome of litigation often backfires on the process, suggesting procedural protections for minorities that can avoid or reduce the risk of a class action.

According to European rules, a listed corporation will virtually never be allowed to pursue a merger with an exchange ratio so high as to freeze out minority shareholders. It is possible that some small investors may have insufficient shares to obtain even a single share of the resulting corporation, and in this case, the constituent corporations offer to buy the shares. The vast majority of minority shareholders, however, are entitled to maintain their status in the new corporation. The limitation on cash consideration ensures this result.

Consider, for example a merger in which the par value of the shares of both corporations is €1, the real value for one share of P (the parent/acquiring corporation) is €2, and the real value of one share of S (the subsidiary/target) is €1.10. The exchange ratio would be 0.55 (1.10/2), meaning that for each share of S, an investor is entitled to 0.55 shares of P. This will result in many shareholders of S being entitled only to a fraction of P's shares, with obvious complications for the merger process. European law allows reducing the exchange ratio by offering consideration partially in cash. The cash consideration cannot, however, exceed 10% of the par value of P's shares. In this example, it would be possible to provide that for each S share, an investor is entitled to €0.10 cash (10% of the €1 par value) on top of the exchange ratio, consequently setting the exchange ratio at 0.5 (2/1), a more manageable figure.

These adjustments, however, are very limited and, as a practical matter, are simply used to round up the exchange ratio, not to cash out minorities. In this respect, the European approach resembles the one prevalent in the United States before the mid-1930s, when corporate statutes were just beginning to allow cash-out mergers.

Statutory Freeze-Out in Europe: Takeover Directive, Article 15

The fact that cash-out mergers are not the principal method by which to conduct going-private transactions in Europe does not mean that freeze-outs are impossible. A freeze-out can, in fact, be accomplished through a different legal technique, explicitly regulated by Article 15 of the Thirteenth Directive on Takeovers (Takeover Directive).

In short, Article 15, under certain conditions, grants any shareholder acquiring at least 90% of the voting shares of a listed corporation through a tender offer the right to cash out minorities at a fair price. In these general terms, the overall structure of the provision recalls a U.S.-style short-form merger. Upon closer analysis, however, important and profound differences emerge. First, pursuant to Article 15, minorities are cashed out without merging the target into the parent corporation. After the majority shareholder exercises the freeze-out right, the delisted target can either maintain its corporate identity as a wholly-owned subsidiary or can be completely merged into the parent.

[. . .]

Alternative Ways to Freeze Out Minority Shareholders in Some European Jurisdictions

Before providing a critical comparison of the different systems, a few more words are necessary on freeze-outs in European countries. In some jurisdictions, freeze-out rights based on Takeover Directive Article 15 are not the exclusive means by which controlling shareholders can unilaterally cash out minorities. Two examples of additional procedures are the United Kingdom's "scheme of arrangement," and Germany's Aktiengesetz (AktG) Articles 327a ff. Each is briefly considered.

Pursuant to British law: "A "scheme of arrangement" or a "reconstruction" under [Companies Act] 2006, Part 26 and Part 27 (additional requirements for public companies) enables a company to effect mergers and amalgamations, and also to alter the rights of its members or its creditors, with the sanction of the court. The provisions are sufficiently wide to accommodate schemes having a considerable diversity of objectives and range of complexity, which may involve more than one company. . . . Unless the court orders otherwise, the members or creditors who dissent are nevertheless bound to accept the terms of the scheme."

Thus, a "scheme of arrangement" is a flexible procedure used to reach a broad variety of outcomes with the approval of a court. Theoretically, this technique can be employed to cash out minorities. Existing case law is limited on the subject, however, and doubts remain as to whether the procedure is as streamlined as a short-form merger in the United States. An example of a case where the scheme of arrangement was employed is In re Hellenic & General Trust Ltd., where Hambros intended to buy all of the outstanding shares of Hellenic. The transaction was approved at the general shareholders' meeting by a large majority of the votes. It was opposed, however, by minority shareholders, in particular, the National Greek Bank, which held 14% of the shares. The court did not sanction this scheme. Rather, it required a positive vote of the majority of the (nonaffiliated) minority as a "different class." The case is illustrative of a certain reluctance to allow a scheme of arrangement for freeze-out purposes when shareholders could otherwise be cashed out pursuant to Article 974ff of the Companies Act of 2006, implemented pursuant to Takeover Directive Article 15. The British scheme of arrangement therefore does not appear equivalent to the U.S. cash-out merger and can be considered a much more uncertain, lengthy, and potentially expensive cash-out technique, if it is one at all.

Sections 327a through 327f of the German AktG also provide a means by which to freeze out minorities outside the scope of Takeover Directive Article 15, while at the same time granting meaningful protections for minority shareholders. This procedure is available when a shareholder holds 95% of the shares. In short, the controlling shareholder convenes a meeting of all shareholders to approve the cash-out procedure. Because the squeeze-out is not preceded by any tender offer, the fairness of the cash-out price cannot be determined based on presumptions regarding the price of the triggering offer. Rather, a court-appointed expert evaluates the fairness of the proposed price. The expert's positive opinion limits the possibility of challenging the transaction in court.

While this particular procedure clearly broadens the possibility to squeeze out minorities and is quite flexible, it is still significantly stricter than the American short-form merger. The controlling shareholder, in fact, must own a very high percentage of shares, close to 100%, in order to exercise her freeze-out right.

In conclusion, Article 15 of the Takeover Directive is not the exclusive freeze-out provision in all European jurisdictions. But, to the extent that other rules exist in Member States, they are significantly less liberal than in the United States. This follows naturally from the bedrock European principle that minority shareholders enjoy a quasi-absolute right to remain members of the corporation in which they have invested. Because these additional freeze-out provisions are generally ineffectual, exist in only a handful of Member States, and lack harmonization, they do not undermine the reform proposals advanced in the final Part of this Article.

[. . .]

Causes and Consequences of the Diverging Approaches

Different overlapping elements explain the origins of different approaches to freeze-outs in the United States and in Europe. [. . .] Four explanations for the comparative differences can be identified: (1) the federal structure of the American corporate law system and the related chartering competition among states, (2) the risks and costs of litigation associated with the status of listed corporations, (3) the potential role of freeze-out rules or the absence thereof as a springboard for hostile corporate acquisitions or a protection for entrenched shareholders, and (4) a path-dependency phenomenon linked to how the legal system and local culture have traditionally envisioned the property rights of shareholders.

The first reason that explains the existence of a more flexible freeze-out regime in the United States can be found in regulatory competition among states and the existence of a market for corporate charters. The scholarly debate has largely explained the different dynamics of regulatory competition in the United States and Europe, to the extent that corporate mobility exists in Europe. There is little doubt that a regime that facilitates going private can be appealing for decision-makers when selecting the jurisdiction of incorporation. This conclusion holds both because freeze-out rules can be an important driver for regulatory competition and because corporate jurisdictions generally characterized by a more permissive approach are likely to offer more flexible rules concerning freeze-outs. The limited role of the market for corporate charters in Europe, especially with respect to public corporations or corporations considering going public, which could potentially be more interested in going private in the future, supports the conclusion that legislatures and policy makers have few incentives to facilitate these types of transactions.

The second, and related, explanation concerns the risk of litigation. To the extent that a system relies on litigation to enforce shareholder rights, going private will be an attractive option to controlling shareholders. In the United States more than in Europe, buying out minority shareholders eliminates the risk of future derivative suits and class actions, and its value is directly correlated with the potential costs associated with these events for the corporation, its controlling shareholders, directors, and managers. It is true that going private itself is often a catalyst for litigation. Nonetheless, corporate insiders might prefer to face a "controlled" risk of litigation for one specific transaction, minimizing the risk by complying with the now well-established Delaware case law, rather than remaining exposed to potential lawsuits as a listed corporation.

Vis-à-vis the higher potential relevance of litigation associated with publicly-held status, it is therefore not surprising that freeze-out rules emerged as a pivotal issue in the United States earlier and more forcefully than in Europe. For American legislatures and judges it became crucial, especially in light of regulatory competition among states, to facilitate going-private transactions while protecting the value of the investment of minority shareholders.

This last motivation for the different development of freeze-out rules opens the door to a more general, and probably more cynical, remark from a public choice perspective. The idea that in most civil law systems private benefits of control are higher than in the United States is coherent with the observation that legislatures face less pressure from controlling shareholders, managers, and their lobbies to facilitate going-private transactions. A lower level of minority protection reduces the risks and costs associated with the status of a publicly held corporation. In other words, and more bluntly: In Europe, controlling shareholders and directors might be less eager to buy out minority shareholders because the likelihood of litigation (and losing this litigation) is low while the possibility of exploiting the private benefits of control are more significant than in the United States.

But there is even more. Barriers to going-private transactions might have a protective effect for incumbent controlling shareholders against hostile acquisitions. It can be a sort of implied antitakeover measure, which has not really been examined by scholars and policy makers. It is intuitive that many hostile acquisitions in the form of leveraged buyouts and management buyouts can be sustained financially only by bringing the corporation private and cashing out minorities. This might be the case for different reasons, perhaps because of the tax benefits of substituting equity with debt, or because the debt incurred to take over the corporation can be serviced only by cutting compliance expenses, or because the corporation needs an organizational turnaround that cannot be effectively and efficiently accomplished in the presence of minority shareholders.

When potential buyers know that achieving a position in which they can unilaterally cash out minorities is difficult, especially with the opposition of the existing controlling shareholder, the risk of not being able to obtain 100% of the outstanding shares might discourage hostile acquisitions. It can therefore be argued that, in states with concentrated ownership structures that do not favor the proliferation of hostile acquisitions, stricter rules concerning freeze-outs might also serve as an indirect, but relatively effective, deterrent to some takeovers, to the advantage of existing controlling shareholders.

A fourth and final explanation for the different approaches to freeze-outs in the United States and Europe can be found in a cultural relic concerning the legal qualification of the interests of minority shareholders in the corporation. Most continental European systems emphasize the property rights of the single shareholder over the shares she owns and consider most forced acquisitions an infringement of the right to own property. In some Member States, freeze-out statutory rights have even raised constitutional law challenges on the grounds that they might be considered unconstitutional takings based on private, rather than public, interests.

Allowing controlling shareholders to unilaterally buy out minorities is at odds with this view. In Europe, it is still the dominant view that cashing-out minorities should be possible only in extreme circumstances. This approach assumes that the best protection of minority shareholders consists in allowing them to hold on to their shares.

In the United States, on the other hand, the prevailing perspective is that minority shareholders are primarily investors with a financial interest in the corporation. Accordingly, the appropriate form of protection for minority shareholders is to guarantee a fair value on their investment. Additional flexibility for controlling shareholders and managers in designing the financial structure of the corporation, including the option to exit the equity market, is compatible with the interests of the minority, so long as minority interests are liquidated at fair value in a coercion-free environment. This view assumes that with the consideration received, minority shareholders can find alternative investments in a robust, efficient market.

NOTES AND QUESTIONS

1.　Do you find the American jurisprudence on cash-out mergers and freeze-out discussed in the first part of Professor Ventoruzzo's work reasonable and coherent? Can you identify possible criticisms? For example, why the tender offer followed by the short-form merger does not require entire fairness review only if the three conditions established in *In re Pure*?

2.　In your opinion, is the U.S. or the European approach to cash-out mergers and freeze-outs preferable? Why? Is there a reason to facilitate the acquisition of all shares by the controlling shareholder, also against the will of the minority shareholders?

3.　Professor Ventoruzzo offers some possible explanations for the different approaches followed on the two sides of the Atlantic. Do you find these explanations compelling? Are there other possible reasons for this divergence that you could suggest? Are any of the explanations offered particularly weak, or particularly strong?

4.　The article above discusses the general framework of cash-out mergers and freeze-out transactions. While it delves into some technicalities, of course there are other details that could be examined. If you are from one of the jurisdictions considered, is there any additional issue that you would suggest to consider? And if you are from a different jurisdiction, how are cash-out mergers and freeze-out transactions regulated in your system if they are regulated at all? Are they allowed? Where the line between managerial flexibility and protection of minority shareholders should be drawn?

* * *

Japanese law on freeze-out transactions is an interesting addition to our discussion. The Japanese approach in this area presents elements of both the European approach and the U.S. approach, but has also its own specific features. Before 2005, in fact, freeze-out transactions were generally unavailable. The Companies Act of 2005 opened the door to these transactions, first by allowing cash-out mergers (Art. 749(1)(iii) Companies Act), both as long-form mergers in which a supermajority vote of the shareholders is required (Art. 783(1) and Art. 309(2)(xii) Companies Act), and as short-form mergers in which the surviving corporation holds 90% or more of the target corporation and no vote of the shareholders of the target is necessary (Art. 784(1) Companies Act). Due to an unfavorable tax treatment, however, cash-out mergers are rarely used.

To achieve similar goals, practitioners have developed a complex procedure, using a special class of shares called "class-shares subject to wholly-call" (Art. 108(1)(vii) Companies Act). This strangely-named class of shares, originally envisioned to facilitate out-of-court reorganizations of distressed corporations, is a kind of redeemable shares, but differs from usual redeemable shares in that the corporation must redeem all of the shares in that class at the same time by a two-thirds majority vote of the shareholders' meeting (Art. 171 and Art. 309(2)(iii) Companies Act). Simplifying, the procedure is initiated with a tender offer in which the offeror aims to obtain a large percentage of the shares, typically over 90%. After the tender offer, the corporation convenes a shareholders' meeting, in order to amend its charter to authorize the corporation to issue class-shares subject to wholly-call, to convert the ordinary shares into the newly-authorized shares subject to wholly-call, and to redeem all of these shares, offering, as consideration, ordinary shares in exchange. The exchange ratio, however, is calculated in such a way that only the controlling shareholder receives one or more ordinary shares, while minority shareholders who would receive less than one share are compensated in cash (Art. 234 Companies Act). As you can see, this elaborate procedure results, in fact, in a freeze-out.

The problem of this complex, and arguably somehow baroque procedure is that even when the controlling shareholder holds 90% or more of the shares, a special resolution of the shareholders' meeting is required. Under Japanese law, procedurally, this takes nearly a month and in this period minority shareholders who did not tender their shares in the front-end offer are in a delicate position, and undue pressure to tender in the front-end offer is possible.

In response to this problem, the Companies Act Reform of 2014 introduced a special procedure for freeze-outs that does not require a shareholders' meeting resolution. Pursuant to this new procedure, called "request for sale of shares," a controlling shareholder holding 90% or more of a corporation can, with the approval of the directors, force minority shareholders to sell their shares of the corporation (Art. 179(1) and 179-3 Companies Act). This approach resembles the European squeeze-out right discussed above. In order to approve the request of the controlling shareholder, the board of directors must consider the fairness of the conditions offered and the interests of minority shareholders, even though the board is controlled by the majority shareholder.

The major protection for minority shareholders in these situations is represented by appraisal rights (Art. 785 of the Companies Act in case of merger; Art. 172 when the issuance of class-shares subject to wholly-call is involved; Art. 179–8 in case of a "request for sale of shares"). Differently from U.S. law discussed earlier in this chapter, this remedy is available also for shareholders of listed corporations in Japan. Indeed, appraisal remedy has been used quite extensively since 2005.

The main issue in appraisal proceedings is, not surprisingly, the determination of the "fair price." As we mentioned before, in a typical freeze-out transaction, the one who seeks to buy out all the shares of a corporation launches a tender offer at a price higher than the market price. After that the bidder follows one of the procedures described above to freeze-out the remaining minority shareholders. Under which circumstances can the price of the front-end tender offer be considered a "fair price" also for appraisal purposes? If you have read the previous excerpt by Professor Ventoruzzo, you will recognize that this problem is quite similar to the one addressed in the *In re Pure* case in Delaware, and more generally concerns the question of how protecting the minority in case of a tender offer followed by a cash-out, short-form merger.

The following Japanese case deals with this problem in the context of a management buyout (MBO). The decision of the Supreme Court itself was very short, but one of the judges wrote an interesting supplementary opinion.

IN RE REX HOLDINGS CO., INC.

Supreme Court of Japan, 2009
29 May 2009, 1326 Kinyu Shoji Hanrei 35

Facts

Rex Holdings Co., Inc. was a holding company of a group that included businesses such as restaurants, convenience stores, and supermarkets, and its shares were listed on the JASDAQ Stock Exchange. The plaintiffs were shareholders of Rex Holdings Co., Inc.

On August 21, 2006, Rex Holdings announced an extraordinary loss and restated its projections for 2006. The market price of the shares of Rex Holdings, which was 304,000 JPY per share at the end of August 21, 2006, dropped to 144,000 JPY on September 26, 2006, and then rebounded to 219,000 JPY on November 10, 2006.

On this day, AP8, Inc., the defendant, which is a special purpose vehicle established and completely owned by an investment fund, announced a tender offer on all shares of Rex Holdings for 230,000 JPY per share. This price was calculated by adding a premium of 13.9% to 202,000 JPY, the average market price in the one-month period from October 10, 2006 to November 9, 2006. At the same time, the board of Rex Holdings announced its support of the offer by AP8, that the offer was part of an MBO, and that its CEO planned to hold 33.4% of the shares of AP8 and to continue to manage Rex Holdings for at least five years, and that it planned to freeze-out shareholders who did not tender their shares through the issuance of class-shares subject to wholly-call [the second type of transaction discussed above] at a price based on the price of the tender offer. As a result of the tender offer, AP8 obtained 91.51% of the existing shares of Rex Holdings.

At the annual shareholders' meeting of Rex Holdings held on March 28, 2007, the board of directors of Rex Holdings proposed 1) to amend its charter to enable Rex Holdings to issue both ordinary shares and a new redeemable class of shares (subject to wholly-call); 2) to convert all existing ordinary shares into the new class of shares subject to wholly-call, which could be redeemed by Rex Holdings with a consideration of 0.00004547 ordinary shares per one class-share subject to wholly-call; and 3) to redeem all the class-share subject to wholly-call on May 9, 2007. All proposals were approved by the shareholders' meeting. According to this resolution, Rex Holdings acquired the shares of the remaining shareholders on May 9, 2007.

Meanwhile, the plaintiffs, who had objected to the proposals above at the annual shareholders' meeting and had notified their intention to exercise appraisal rights to Rex Holdings before the meeting, filed petitions for appraisal in the Tokyo District Court on April 4 and April 12, 2007. On September 1, 2007, Rex Holdings was merged into AP8, and AP8 changed its name to "Rex Holdings Co., Inc."

The Tokyo District Court (December 19, 2007, 2001 Hanrei Jiho109) held that the fair appraisal value was 230,000 JPY per share, the same amount as the tender offer price. The plaintiffs appealed. The Tokyo High Court (September 12, 2008, 1301 Kinyu Shoji Hanrei 28) rejected the tender offer price as inadequate and held that the appraisal value was 336,996 JPY per share. The defendant appealed.

Court's decision

Considering the facts of the present case, the decision of the court below can be confirmed as it is within its discretion. The decision of the court below does not contradict the current case law as the appellant [Rex Holdings] asserts. Assertions of the appellant cannot be adopted. Appeal dismissed.

Supplementary opinion by Judge Mutsuo Tahara

Appraisal of the acquisition price. When a shareholder listed under Article 172(1) of the Companies Act petitions for appraisal of the acquisition price of shares, the court must determine the fair price of those shares by exercising its reasonable discretion considering the purpose of the appraisal remedy. Since the appraisal remedy intends to compensate dissenting shareholders whose shares are expropriated by a management buyout (MBO), the appraisal price should be calculated by adding (1) the value of the shares in the absence of the MBO and (2) the part of the value of the shares increased by the MBO that should be enjoyed by the shareholders.

[. . .]

The party carrying out an MBO is required to secure transparency of the process for all shareholders, including dissenting shareholders, since the structure of an MBO, which is the purchase of shares of a corporation by its management, implies a risk of a conflict of interest between shareholders and the management, and the MBO procedure could have coercive effects on shareholders (see Corporate Value Study Group, "Report Regarding Management Buyouts (MBO) for the Purposes of Enhancement of Corporate Value and Ensuring Fair Procedure" (August 2, 2007, hereinafter "MBO Report"), which was commissioned by the Ministry of Economy, Trade and Industry). Therefore, when appraising the acquisition price, the court considers the transparency of the MBO procedure.

The decision of the court below and judicial discretion in this area

[. . .]

In the MBO in the present case, third party's evaluations or opinions, used by the bidder in determining the price of the front-end tender offer, were not disclosed. To be sure, the bidder was not obliged as a matter of law to make such disclosure [because the reform of the Financial Instruments and Exchange Act that requires such disclosure was not applicable in the present case]. The MBO Report, however, notes that it is desirable to provide shareholders with the opportunity to consider the fairness of the price of the tender offer by disclosing business plans and evaluations of the value of the shares used by the bidder.

In an MBO procedure it is also important to allow shareholders to make an informed decision and avoid any coercion. In this respect, the bidder and the target both informed the public that shareholders not tendering their shares in the front end would only receive a fraction of one ordinary share in the back end, and that it was uncertain that dissenting shareholders could have exercised appraisal rights [. . .]. These statements could have a "coercive effect," which should be avoided according to the MBO Report. The court below, taking into account the details of the MBO, determined the value of the shares on the day of the acquisition as the average of the market price at the end of the day of the six-months period from May 10, 2006 to November 9, 2006, which is the day before the announcement of the tender offer in the present case. [. . .]

Then, considering that the appellant had not disclosed its business plan after the MBO and its evaluation of the share price based on the due diligence made by the bidder on the former Rex Holdings, despite repeated requests by the appellee, and referring to other cases of MBO in the same period, the court below decided that, in order to calculate the fair appraisal value, 20% should be added to the average market price calculated as mentioned above.

Such decision by the court below, based on the details of the MBO in the present case, can be approved in light of the available evidence, and the measure used for appraisal was within the range of the court's discretion.

NOTES AND QUESTIONS

1.   According to the second prong of Judge Tahara's dichotomy, dissenting shareholders exercising their appraisal rights cannot obtain the entire value created through the MBO, but just a part of it. What would be the reason for this restriction? Think how freezing-out minority shareholders with an MBO can increase the value of corporation. With the answer to this question in mind, can you criticize the decision of the Tokyo High Court in *Rex Holdings*?

2.   Judge Tahara emphasizes the importance of transparent and non-coercive procedures for MBOs. In particular, he criticizes threatening statements made in relation to the tender offer as they might have a coercive effect on shareholders. It has been reported that such statements have largely disappeared in current practice after the Supreme Court decision. In other words, Judge Tahara's opinion functioned as guidance to better practice. Can you see the similarities and differences with the *In re Pure* Delaware decision discussed above, in Professor Ventoruzzo's article?

3.   In a similar vein, the MBO Report of the METI's Corporate Value Study Group, cited in Judge Tahara's opinion, suggested several measures to address conflicts of interests between shareholders and managers in MBO transactions. One popular measure in current practice is to establish a special committee consisting of outside directors and/or other independent persons and to consult the committee about the fairness of the price offered by the bidder. In a case regarding the MBO of CYBIRD Holdings Co., Inc., the Tokyo District Court approved the creation of such a committee (September 18, 2009, 1329 Kinyu Shoji Hanrei 45). This decision, however, was reversed by the Tokyo High Court, which slightly raised the price determined by the committee increasing the premium over market prices (Judge Tahara's second prong) from 17.34% to 20%. (October 27, 2010, 322 Shiryoban Shoji Homu 174). This decision has been criticized for adopting the "20% premium" used in the *Rex Holdings* case passively. Of course, the use of a special committee of independent directors is not enough to solve all conflicts of interests. Based on our previous analysis, discuss the pros and cons of the use of a special committee in cash-out mergers in the United States. For further discussion of Japanese law on this issue, *see* Wataru Tanaka, *Going Private and the Role of Courts: A Comparison of Delaware and Japan*, 3 UT SOFT LAW REVIEW 12 (2011).

4.   Recently, other remedies designed to protect minorities developed in Japan, sometimes inspired by the U.S. experience. First, the 2014 reform introduced the possibility to obtain an injunction against a freeze-out transaction, which will be granted to shareholders when their interest is

likely to be harmed by a "violation of law or charter provision" (Art. 171–3, 179–7, and 784–2 Companies Act). This standard, however, does not include violation of directors' fiduciary duties or mere unfairness of the consideration offered to shareholders. How this new remedy will be used in practice remains to be seen. Second, disgruntled shareholders can sue directors under Article 429 of Companies Act (*see* Chapters 6 and 7) or under general tort law. Interestingly enough, in a suit filed by the shareholders of Rex Holdings, the Tokyo High Court denied liability of directors of Rex Holdings, even if it generally acknowledged that approving a MBO at a low price that does not adequately reflect the value of the corporation constitutes a violation of directors' duty of care (Tokyo High Court, April 17, 2013, 2190 Hanrei Jiho 96). The plaintiffs in this case also argued that directors had the duty to maximize the sale price of the corporation in case of a MBO, referring to *Revlon, Inc. v. MacAndrews & Forbes Holdings, Inc.*, 506 A.2d 173 (Del. 1986), a famous American case that we will discuss in our next chapter.

5.   Now that we have guided you through cash-out transactions in the U.S., Europe and Japan, it is your turn to be a comparativist. Explain to your classmates the underlying problem, the different regulatory techniques, and their pros and cons.

CHAPTER 10

TAKEOVERS AND TENDER OFFERS, HOSTILE ACQUISITIONS, AND DEFENSIVE MEASURES

■ ■ ■

TAKEOVERS: THE ECONOMIC AND LEGAL BASIC IDEAS

Takeovers, and the dramatic battles for corporate control that they entail, are one of the few corporate law topics entertaining enough to make it into movies. Hollywood blockbusters depicting takeovers include *Wall Street* (1987), *Other People's Money* (1990), and *Pretty Woman* (1990), portraying more-or-less unforgettable corporate raiders such as Gordon Gekko (Michael Douglas), Larry The Liquidator (Danny DeVito), and Edward Lewis (Richard Gere). OK, maybe they are not all considered masterpieces by movie buffs, but if you haven't yet, we suggest you watch them as part of your cultural background on takeovers.

When a corporation is listed (and in this chapter we only focus on listed corporations), someone interested in obtaining control must, first of all, decide if a friendly acquisition is possible, or if it is possible—and necessary—a hostile acquisition. By "friendly" acquisition we refer to a transaction in which control is transferred with the consent of the existing controlling shareholder and/or management of the target corporation; by contrast, and obviously enough, a "hostile" acquisition occurs when the existing controlling shareholder and/or management of the corporation opposes the takeover: in this situation the incumbents and the buyer engage in a legal and financial duel. This distinction is not always as clear-cut as it might appear. For example, a "friendly" acquisition might be conducted under the more-or-less overt threat that a hostile one could be successfully launched. In addition, in a "friendly" acquisition other stakeholders, different from major shareholders and top management, might oppose the plans of the acquirer: employees and unions, creditors, sometimes even the government. Generally, however, we distinguish between hostile and friendly acquisitions based on whether the incumbent is willing to transfer control or not.

If a controlling shareholder owning an absolute majority of the shares exist, it is generally very difficult to obtain control without her consent. A 60% shareholder, for example, can prevent a takeover simply by not selling her shares. In reality, to obtain control in this situation might be very difficult, but not entirely impossible. Think, for example, to the battle for controlling Mondadori, which we discussed in Chapter 4, talking about different classes of shares (do you remember? It was the case involving former Italian Prime Minister Berlusconi). In that case shareholders holding limited voting shares could possibly obtain control notwithstanding the opposition of the then controlling shareholder. But those are fairly unique situations, and if someone owns the majority of the outstanding shares the only way to obtain control is, generally, to convince her to sell you some or all her shares.

There might, however, be a shareholder able to control the corporation without holding an absolute majority of the shares. For example, imagine a situation in which the largest shareholder owns 33% of the common stock, the next largest shareholder after him is an institutional investor with 5%, then three other smaller shareholders with 2% each, and then the rest of the shares are widespread among investors holding tiny participations (not more than 0.3% each). In this case, because of the "rational apathy" of minority shareholders, who generally do not actively participate in the governance of the corporation due to information asymmetries, transaction costs, and so on (*see* Chapter 5), our 33% shareholder is likely able to appoint the majority of the directors, influence the management of the corporation, and unilaterally adopt most shareholders' meeting resolutions.

The position of the controlling shareholder, in this situation, is however vulnerable. A third party might try to acquire control with his consent, persuading him to sell his shares, but could also try a hostile acquisition. In fact, if a third party manages, for example, to buy 45% of the voting shares from the minority shareholders, the third party might become the new controlling shareholder. Of course the same is true in a corporation with a very widespread ownership structure with no strong controlling shareholder, a real "public corporation" controlled, as a matter of fact, by its managers and directors.

Now, what are the possible techniques to acquire control? First, the acquirer can buy in private transactions, not on the stock exchange, large participations from the existing controlling shareholder or from qualified minorities. This technique obviously requires the existence and willingness to sell of relatively large shareholders. Second, the acquirer might simply start purchasing shares on the market, trying to obtain the desired threshold, for example 51% of the voting shares (with or without the consent of the incumbents). Open market purchases, however, can be problematic for the acquirer.

To understand why, we need to take a step back and briefly illustrate the rationale of the acquisition. Imagine a corporation whose shares, in the last two months, have had a relatively stable market price of approximately $3. The buyer is generally motivated to obtain control because, basically, he thinks that the corporation is undervalued, or more generally that he can make a profit. For example, he might think that if he obtains control, by managing the corporation more effectively and efficiently, the value of the corporation will increase and the market price will reflect that, for example reaching the $7 level. At that point, he could sell the shares and reap a large gain. Alternatively, the buyer might think that by merging the target with other business activities he is involved with and exploiting economies of scale, or by breaking up the target and selling the different parts, he can make a profit. The bottom line, however, is that as in any business transaction there is a "reservation price," a price above which for the buyer, based on his plans and projections, the deal is no longer profitable. In our previous example, if the acquirer hopes to be able to push the prices to $7, he might still be willing to buy shares for $6.5, even if at this point his marginal profit will be lower, but not for $7.5.

With this in mind, let's go back to the idea of obtaining control through open market purchases. Acquisitions of control by buying shares on the market, without making a public offer, are sometimes also called "creeping acquisitions." Especially if the buyer needs to acquire a large number of shares, his activity will put a significant pressure on market prices: the demand for the shares might be very relevant. In addition, as we will see, most legal systems impose specific disclosure requirements on whoever acquires certain thresholds of listed corporations, in order to ensure that investors are informed on the ownership structure. Under these conditions, the market price might skyrocket, also irrationally: other investors, realizing that someone is trying to obtain control, might also start buying shares, and since they do not know the reservation price of the buyer, the price could easily exceed the $7 limit in our previous example. For this reason, acquiring control through open market purchases might be difficult, expensive, lengthy, and in short not feasible.

Another option available for the acquirer, therefore, is to launch a public tender offer. With a tender offer the buyer invites all existing shareholders to tender their shares, offering the same conditions to everyone. Of course, to be successful, he must offer a price above the market price, but the advantage is that he can "cap" the price and plan accordingly. Going back once again to the numbers of the previous example, our acquirer might launch a tender offer paying $4.5 per share, a quite significant premium over current market prices of $3, but still significantly lower than the $7 value that he attaches to the shares. The terms of the tender offer might vary, for example it might be an offer for all the outstanding shares, or just limited to a certain percentage of shares; it might be conditioned to reaching a set threshold (typically, a controlling participation), or not; it might be open for a longer or shorter period, and so on. As we will see, most legislatures regulate quite precisely these aspects, especially to ensure that sufficient information is disclosed to investors by the offeror, and to limit coercive offers (for example, offers only opened for a very short period, designed at putting undue pressure to tender on the offerees, or partial offers on a first-come, first-served basis).

You can find here one of the most important and striking comparative differences with respect to the regulation of control acquisitions. In some countries, under certain conditions, it is mandatory to launch a tender offer on all (or part of) the outstanding shares, at a set minimum price, in order to obtain control, or after having acquired control. This is the case in the European Union, pursuant to the Thirteenth Directive modelled after the U.K. approach, but also—of course with significant variations—in countries as diverse as Japan, China, and Brazil. Other systems, and specifically the United States, at least at the federal level, do not provide any such mandatory bid rule, and allow much more freedom on how to conduct an acquisition. What is the rationale of the mandatory tender offer? How is it regulated? What are its effects, also based on the prevailing ownership structures? These are some of the questions that this chapter will address.

In addition to negotiated, over-the-counter purchases from large shareholders, market transactions, and tender offers, there are also other possible ways to acquire control or, more precisely, to substitute the members of the board. One example is proxy fights, in systems that allow them. With a proxy fight, someone simply tries to convince—with a solicitation of proxies—a majority of the voting shareholders to vote for certain candidates to the board and oust the existing board, or to vote on certain corporate transactions in a way different from what is suggested by the existing incumbents. Even if proxy fights might be a way to oppose controlling shareholders or managers, they do not involve the acquisition of shares (actually, they can be a preliminary step to a future acquisition of shares), and therefore we will not consider them here, even if you should keep them in mind as a possible alternative to other takeover techniques.

We have so far considered the "weapons" that can be used by someone aiming at obtaining control. Let's now consider the perspective of the target corporation in case of a threatened or launched hostile acquisition. An existing controlling shareholder, or the directors and managers of a target corporation, might vehemently oppose a non-negotiated acquisition. Generally the new controlling shareholder will remove the existing directors and substitute them with directors she trusts, and the new board will probably replace the top executives. The former controlling shareholder might be put in a corner, and lose his privileged position. After all, very often the primary motivation for a takeover is to change the way in which the corporation is run and turn it around.

What are the legal tools that the incumbent can use to resist an unsolicited, and unwelcome, acquisition? What are, in other words, the possible "weapons" of this battle? Before reading further, try to come up with a list of possible corporate actions that can frustrate the goals of a corporate raider.

The list is long, but even limiting ourselves to the most common ones we should mention the following. Having the corporation purchase own shares could be a way to put serious obstacles in the path of a hostile bidder. On the one hand, this strategy pushes market prices up; on the other hand, there would be fewer shares outstanding, and therefore it might be harder to acquire a majority stake. A somehow opposite, but potentially effective alternative is for the corporation to issue new shares to existing shareholders, at a carefully determined price. Also this transaction can make it harder for the bidder to acquire control, for example because in order to reach the necessary threshold he might need to acquire a higher number of shares. Merging a subsidiary with and into the target-parent corporation might have similar consequences, since—as we have seen in Chapter 9—a merger requires the issuance of new shares according to the exchange ratio.

The target can also be rescued by a "white knight," a friendly corporation that might launch a competing tender offer at more attractive conditions, with the understanding that in case of success it will not substitute the management, or otherwise displace whoever controls the corporation. The original hostile bidder must either match the second offer, or retreat. Another defensive measure with a colorful name is called "selling the jewels of the crown": the idea here is that directors might sell some crucial assets, considered very important by the hostile bidder, for example a trademark or a portfolio of patents, therefore making the target corporation much less attractive and valuable. Of course in this case the risk is to damage the target corporation by giving away its most precious assets, and generally the technique requires selling the assets to a friendly third party that will sell them back when—hopefully, for the target—the danger is gone.

A particular variation of this technique might involve the so-called Dutch "*stichting*", a sort of foundation or trust in which some assets or shares can be placed. In practice, when threatened with a takeover, a corporation can create a *stichting* and transfer to it its more valuable assets, e.g. a business unit. The *stichting* is an independent entity whose directors are appointed by the target for a fixed term and cannot be removed or changed. The directors have specific instructions concerning the assets, such as for example not selling them to anyone and only transfer them back to the target if and when the risk of hostile acquisition is over. The instrument can however also be used in other ways, for example granting it an option to purchase shares of the target, engineered in a way that would make the acquisition too expensive or impossible for the bidder (with effects somehow similar to a poison pill, *see* below). As "trustees", the directors of the *stichting* must comply with the instructions given by the target and the purpose written in its governing document, and the *stichting* cannot be "undone", even if the bidder obtains control of the target, at least for a period of time. The legal status of the *stichting* is still debated, but it has been used as a defense in some notorious battles for control, e.g. the (eventually successful) acquisition of steel giant Arcelor by the Indian Mittal group, or more recently in the Teva-Mylan deal.

Again, a corporation might adopt the so-called "Pac-Man" defense, from the name of the famous arcade game of the 1980s. Like the character of the game, Pac-Man could turn around and eat the enemies that were chasing him after touching a power-pellet, this defense consists of a counter tender offer or purchase of shares of the hostile bidder by the target: the prey turns around and attacks the predator. This defense, however, only works if the bidder or its controlling corporation are listed and vulnerable to hostile acquisitions; in addition lots of legal systems put limitations on cross-holdings of shares: since the bidder often already has a participation in the target before launching a tender offer, in some jurisdictions the law limits the ability of the target to acquire voting shares of the bidder.

Another type of defense is represented by the introduction of very large compensations for directors and managers in case of a non-negotiated change of control, so called "golden parachutes." The inhibiting effect of golden parachutes is due to the potentially huge payments to former executives. In addition, even if generally the bidder wants to change *part* of the management, he often does not want to find replacements for *all* the managers, something that might be difficult to do in a short period of time. Other "shark repellents" (the expression clearly betrays a negative view of hostile acquisitions, which is not necessarily justified) include staggered boards provisions, under which a new controlling shareholder might need more time to obtain a majority of the directors, and supermajority requirements that might make the approval of mergers or other extraordinary transactions difficult.

One last defense that we should mentioned, particularly common in the U.S., is the aptly named "poison pill," aka "shareholders' rights plan." We encountered it in Chapter 5. The poison pill, in fact, is a family of defenses that share certain features but also present some distinctions. In essence, the "pill" is a set of rules generally included in the governing documents of the corporation and adopted by the board of directors, characterized by three elements: (a) a triggering event; (b) a catastrophic (from the point of view of the hostile bidder) consequence; and (c) the possibility to be redeemed at nominal costs by the directors. The triggering event is often represented by the acquisition of a certain threshold of shares by a shareholder, for example 20%, signaling a likely intention to acquire control (disclosure is mandated by the securities laws). Once the triggering event occurs, shareholders can exercise some kind of right that makes the acquisition much more difficult for the bidder. For example, in a "flip-in" pill shareholders of the target can acquire additional shares from the corporation at discounted price; while in a "flip-over" pill shareholders of the target can have the right to obtain shares of the bidder if, after the acquisition, it wants to merge with the target. The bottom line is that the pill is calibrated to grant to existing shareholders advantages that frustrates the goals of the bidder.

The pill—which, as we have seen, is basically a right granted to shareholders—can however be redeemed by the directors at a very low price, for example they can "cancel" the rights for one cent per share. If you consider the effects of these three elements, the result is that an acquirer can only hope to obtain control with the agreement of the existing board, which must redeem the pill (interestingly enough, bylaws provisions only allow continuing directors to redeem the pill, in order to avoid that new directors appointed through a proxy fight could get rid of this defense, even if the permissibility of these "dead-hand" pills is excluded in several jurisdictions, including Delaware).

As you can clearly see, defensive measures comprise a gamut of different and heterogeneous techniques, ranging from purchase of own shares to seeking a white knight. Some of them can be adopted after a hostile takeover has been launched; others work better if introduced before any declaration of war. From a legal point of view, in different legal systems, these measures might be within the competence of the shareholders' meeting or of the directors, and they basically have only one thing in common: they are designed to frustrate a hostile offer.

The key issue is that the adoption of defensive measures, in particular by directors, presents an inherent conflict of interest. Directors might be adopting a defense not because it is in the best interest of the corporation or the shareholders, but simply to save their own . . . seat. Fearing that a new controlling shareholder might fire them, directors could frustrate an offer that would actually be fair and desirable for the shareholders, and economically efficient, simply to entrench themselves. What is even more delicate is that, in deploying their defenses, directors use—and might destroy—corporate resources. Let's go back to the example of the tender offer for $4.5 on the shares of a corporation that floats at around $3. The offer might be value-maximizing for shareholders, who might be happy to accept it; the bidder might in fact have a chance to manage the corporation more effectively, and see the market price go up to $7, but only after having removed the incompetent existing directors. Everyone would be happier with the offer (Pareto-efficiency), but the directors. They have the power to block the offer, for example selling the jewels of the crown. By doing so they might succeed in discouraging the bidder, and keep their job for a few more years, but they would also have impoverished the corporation. It would be as if the defenders of a citadel under siege, in order to repel the barbarians at the gates, would set fire to the riches of their community.

If this is the case, why don't corporate law systems simply prohibit directors from adopting defensive measures? The answer is that there are, in fact, situations in which defensive measures are desirable from the point of view of shareholders and other stakeholders, and the proposed tender offer is not value maximizing. Consider again our previous example. You might imagine a situation in which the market price of the shares is unreasonably low, for example it is depressed in a period of extraordinary high interest rates that cause lots of investors to sell equity and buy bonds. Under these circumstances, the directors of the target might genuinely and correctly believe that the actual value of the shares is at least $6, not $3 (the current market price), but not even $4.5 (the price offered by the bidder). They might believe that if the shareholders hold on to their shares, wait a few months and let them carry on their strategy, the market will adjust and prices will go up. Shareholders, obviously, would not be better off tendering the shares now for $4.5; if the offer is successful they might not have the opportunity to enjoy the full possible capital gain. In addition, the bidder might be using techniques designed to create a pressure to tender, to the extent that the legal system allows them, such as giving a very short timeframe to accept the offer. In this scenario, you might argue that it is not only legitimate and in the best interest of shareholders that existing directors adopt defensive measures, but that directors have a duty to protect the corporate bastion. Using again a military metaphor, when the attackers threaten to sack the city, the captain of the guards must throw some arrows and boiling oil at them. If nothing else, a defensive measure might force the bidder to improve the terms of the offer.

As you can see, the regulation of defensive measures must strike a complex balance between two opposing goals: preventing the incumbents from adopting frustrating measures not in the best interest of the corporation and the shareholders, but at the same time do not tie their hands so tightly that they cannot adopt defenses necessary to react to inadequate, damaging and coercive offers.

Legal systems around the world struggle to find the optimal equilibrium, but once again here we find an interesting comparative divide. Some countries (including all the E.U. Member States) follow the U.K. approach, adopting some kind of "passivity" or "no-frustration" rule. The idea, here, is that to address the conflict of interest of directors in case of hostile takeover the best option is to take any decision concerning defenses away from them, and let shareholders decide, since they are the ones that can be primarily benefitted or harmed by the offer. The passivity rule, therefore, simply says that when an offer is pending the shareholders' meeting, and not the directors, must approve any action that might frustrate the goals of the bidder. We will discuss how and under which conditions this simple and ingenious solution can work well, and when it can be ineffective, or even counterproductive. On the other end of the spectrum, in the U.S., the way in which this problem is addressed is primarily through directors' fiduciary duties. In the takeover context, in other words, a modified duty of care and duty of loyalty dictate what directors can and cannot do in terms of defensive measures. This difference is interesting because it shows, once again, a defining feature of American corporate law, its reliance on litigation and ex post measures to regulate corporate governance.

To sum up this unusually long but necessary introduction, looking at different strategies to regulate takeovers you can come up with a matrix in which you can have fun trying to fit different systems:

		board neutrality rule	
		yes	no
mandatory bid	no		United States
	yes	European Union (but often board neutrality is optional)	Japan

Needless to say, this matrix oversimplifies the reality. As we will partially see later, for example, the passivity rule has been adopted in different ways, more or less rigorously, in different European countries, and also in the United States there might be some rules at the state level, or in the governing documents of the corporation, which have effects not dissimilar from the ones of a mandatory tender offer (so-called "cash-out statutes"). As with all simplified models, however, it captures nicely some basic alternative regulatory approaches.

To explore further the regulation of takeovers, the chapter proceeds as follows. First, we will take a closer look at the regulation of tender offers, and particularly mandatory tender offers, and defensive measures, in different countries. In this perspective, we will consider the effects of the adoption of the U.K. approach, based on mandatory tender offer and passivity rule, in systems with a very different ownership structure, such as Italy or France: It is an interesting example of legal transplant and possible unintended consequences. Second, we will focus on the European situation, to consider if the Thirteenth Directive on Tender Offers has really harmonized takeover rules, or if the differences among European States are still profound. Third, we will move back to the U.S., to briefly discuss another interesting effect of regulatory competition among states (remember Chapter 2?): anti-takeover statutes. Finally, we will consider the Japanese experience, particularly interesting because Japan followed a sort of hybrid approach between the European and American ones.

TENDER OFFERS AND DEFENSIVE MEASURES: UNINTENDED CONSEQUENCES?

Tender offers, both voluntary and mandatory, are subject to rules designed to protect investors. These rules focus on disclosure, mandating that whoever intends to launch a tender offer must provide certain key information to the market and the offerees (and sometimes other stakeholders, e.g., workers), concerning the conditions of the offer and his plans for the corporation, in an offering document generally filed with the competent financial markets authority. Additional rules govern certain substantive aspects of the offer, for example its timing (the offer must be open for more than a certain minimum number of days and less than a certain maximum), and equal treatment of offerees ("pro-rata," "all-holders" and "best-price" rules), and so on. The goal of these provisions is, in many ways, connected to and instrumental in disclosure, and is to avoid excessive pressure to tender on the offerees, in order to allow them to objectively evaluate the offer and take a rational and unbiased decision.

In the United States, most of these rules are included in the Securities and Exchange Act, and more precisely in the part introduced in 1968 with the so-called Williams Act (section 14). In Europe they are regulated in the Thirteenth Directive, and further specified in national statutes and regulations enacted by the Member States. In Japan, relevant legislation are Articles 27–2 to 27–22–4 of the Financial Instruments and Exchange Act and related secondary rules.

One important provision to understand the mechanics of takeovers is the requirement that whoever acquires a qualified participation in a listed corporation must disclose her acquisition. For example, in the U.S., under section 13(d) of the Williams Act, anyone who becomes the beneficial owner of 5% of any class of equity securities must file with the SEC a Form 13D within 10 days of the acquisition, indicating in particular the source of the funds used for the purchase, and her intentions with respect to the corporation, and specifically, if she aims at obtaining control. Similar provisions exist in most developed financial markets, even if the triggering threshold might vary (for example, in some European countries it is 2% and the scope of disclosure is not identical).

This provision is very interesting because it demonstrates quite well the double-edged nature of most takeover rules: on the one hand, they can protect minority shareholders and investors, but on the other hand they can protect the incumbent managers or controlling shareholder. Mandating to disclose the acquisition of a participation allows, obviously, the market and therefore investors to have a more complete picture of the ownership structure of the corporation, and informs them on possible impending takeovers that might drive the market price of the shares up. The disclosure, however, also represents a wake-up call for managers and large shareholders on the possibility of a hostile attempt to acquire the corporation, giving them the time to react and implement defensive measures. In this perspective, for example, the 10-day window that section 13(d) of the Williams Act allows between the acquisition and the filing of Form 13D can be precious for the buyer to accumulate shares in excess of 5% unbeknownst to the incumbents.

In any case, in the United States, with the exception of some possible anti-takeover provisions at the state or corporate level, no mandatory bid is required. Let's consider, however, the opposite approach, and read the provision of the Thirteenth Directive (2004/25/EC) mandating a tender offer:

Article 5—*Protection of minority shareholders, the mandatory bid and the equitable price*

1. Where a natural or legal person, as a result of his/her own acquisition or the acquisition by persons acting in concert with him/her, holds securities of a company [regulated by the laws of a Member State and whose securities are listed in a Member State] which, added to any existing holdings of those securities of his/hers and the holdings of those securities of persons acting in concert with him/her, directly or indirectly give him/her a specified percentage of voting rights in that company, giving him/her control of that company, Member States shall ensure

that such a person is required to make a bid as a means of protecting the minority shareholders of that company. Such a bid shall be addressed at the earliest opportunity to all the holders of those securities for all their holdings at the equitable price as defined in paragraph 4.

[. . .]

3.   The percentage of voting rights which confers control for the purposes of paragraph 1 and the method of its calculation shall be determined by the rules of the Member State in which the company has its registered office.

4.   The highest price paid for the same securities by the offeror, or by persons acting in concert with him/her, over a period, to be determined by Member States, of not less than six months and not more than 12 before the bid referred to in paragraph 1 shall be regarded as the equitable price. If, after the bid has been made public and before the offer closes for acceptance, the offeror or any person acting in concert with him/her purchases securities at a price higher than the offer price, the offeror shall increase his/her offer so that it is not less than the highest price paid for the securities so acquired.

NOTES AND QUESTIONS

1.   The rationale of the mandatory tender offer is twofold: to spread, at least partially, the "control premium" among all shareholders, and to grant to minority shareholders a possible fair exit in case of change of control. First of all, what is the "control premium" and why should it be shared by all shareholders? Consider a situation in which the existing controlling shareholder owns 33% of the common stock. Imagine, for sake of simplicity, that the corporation has 100 outstanding common shares, and that the market price of one share is $3. The 33% control participation is likely to have a value and a price higher than $99 ($3 x 33 shares), for example $132, equal to $4 per share. The reason has to do with the fact that having control of a listed corporation has certain obvious perks, for example power, prestige, and—in a darker perspective—the possibility to extract "private benefits" from the corporation. Now imagine a friendly acquisition: if the buyer would simply be allowed to negotiate with the existing controlling shareholder the acquisition of her 33%, he would pay her $132, but all minority shareholders would be left out in the cold and could not capitalize on the transaction. Similarly, in case of a hostile tender offer, without the mandatory bid mechanism the bidder might launch an offer only for 40% of the shares at $4, purchasing pro-rata the securities tendered. Also in this case some shareholders would not be able to sell all their shares at the highest price. The mandatory bid forces the buyer to pay at least part of the control premium to all shareholders (note that, due to the minimum price of the

mandatory bid, not necessarily the entire premium is offered). On the other hand, without the mandatory bid, some shareholders might be "stuck" in a corporation that, because of the new controlling shareholder, has a lower value. Imagine that the buyer obtains control in a private transaction with the previous controlling shareholder, paying her $4 per share. Immediately after that, the market might decide that the new controlling shareholder will destroy value (for example, she is notoriously incompetent or corrupt), and the market price might drop from $3 to $1. In this perspective, the mandatory bid offers a reasonable way out to investors. Of course, the idea that the control premium should be distributed to all shareholders and that they must have a fair way out is both buttressed by some economic reasons in terms of efficiency, but it is also a political decision based on fairness arguments. Can you articulate these possible arguments in favor of a mandatory bid regime (efficiency and fairness)? Is there a risk that investors might abandon the market if a mandatory bid does not ensure benefits in case of a change of control? Or does, in your opinion, the premium for control only belong to the controlling shareholder, and the law should not be concerned about spreading it among investors? Anticipating something that we will discuss below, do you think that the mandatory tender offer might raise the costs of hostile acquisitions and be a protection for the incumbents?

2.   Article 5 of Directive 2004/25 is inspired, as we will study more extensively below, by the U.K. regulatory approach. You might have noticed that the controlling threshold that triggers the mandatory offer shall be determined by Member States. Most Member States, again following the British experience, have opted for a "fixed" threshold, generally between 30 and 33% of the voting shares. Anyone acquiring more than the threshold must launch a tender offer. Why 30–33%? The idea is that this percentage often indicates a controlling participation; it is a sort of "presumption" of control. This approach might however appear very rigid: after all it is not difficult to imagine situations in which, notwithstanding the acquisition of the relevant participation, there are compelling reasons not to mandate a tender offer, and situations in which the rationale underlying the mandatory offer suggests mandating one even if the threshold has not been passed. For this reason, Member States have enacted what we might call "exemptions from" and "extensions of" the mandatory tender offer. Italian law (the so-called *Testo Unico della Finanza*" or "Consolidated Law on Financial Markets") offers a good illustration of these rules, but similar provisions exist in most European systems. Two examples of "exemptions" are the following. Consider a listed corporation in which the controlling shareholder, X, owns 55% of the voting shares, and another investor, Y, owns 29% Under Italian law, the threshold triggering the mandatory offer is 30% (with some exceptions that we will mention soon). Imagine that Y buys another 5%, to strengthen his position. In a situation in which X does not intend to give up his absolute control, forcing Y to launch a tender offer would add insult to injury: Y would have no chance to gain control (because X keeps his 55%), but would have to incur the costs of a tender offer. For this reason, when another shareholder already has absolute control, there is no obligation to launch a

tender offer even if the "magic" threshold is passed. Another example is a merger. Imagine that X owns 25% of a listed corporation, K; and that an unrelated corporation, Z, owns 10% of K. If Z is merged into X, its assets are obviously transferred to the surviving company X (*see* Chapter 9), including its 10% of K, with the consequence that X ends up holding 35% of K. This might trigger a mandatory tender offer on K's shares, but the costs of the offer could be so substantial as to prevent the merger between X and Z. Since mergers often are desirable because they lead to economies of scale and more efficient management, to mandate the tender offer would frustrate efficient transactions. For this reason another exemption can apply, at least when the merger has a valid business purpose and is not only an elusive device to circumvent the mandatory tender offer.

3.   On the other hand, also "extensions" of the mandatory tender offer are necessary. Consider, for example, a situation in which two formally separate subjects acting in a coordinated way (in concert) acquire more than 30% but none of them individually passes the threshold. For example, corporation A buys 25% of listed corporation C, and A's wholly owned subsidiary B acquires an additional 10% Even if formally none has more than 30%, it is clear that the group lead by A substantively controls more than 30% Therefore, under the so-called "action in concert" rule, when different persons linked by specific relationships (parent-subsidiary, members of a shareholders' agreement, etc.) acquire participations, they are treated, for the purposes of the mandatory bid, as one single entity. It is, once again, a question of substance over form.

4.   As we have seen, exemptions and extensions help curb the rigidity and possibly irrational consequences of the compulsory bid mechanism based on the acquisition of a fixed threshold. Based on the brief examples provided above, put yourself in the shoes of the legislature. Can you imagine other situations in which an exemption or an extension would be required either because of the inherent rationale of the mandatory bid, or because of other, conflicting public policy goals? (Hints: turn-around of distressed corporations and acquisitions of non-listed entities owing shares of a listed corporation.)

5.   Read Article 5 Paragraph 4 of the directive above, which deals with the minimum price requirement. Does the minimum price fully reflect the control premium? Why do you think the European legislature has used this formula? Any suggestion on a better one?

6.   What happens if someone who, in theory, would be required to launch a mandatory tender offer does not? Consider the following scenario: A and B have a secret shareholders' agreement (in violation of applicable rules, they have not disclosed it to the market) to vote their shares in C as A indicates. A buys 25% of C, and B buys 10%. They should launch a tender offer under the "action in concert" rule mentioned above, but since none knows about their agreement, it looks like two independent persons have acquired participations that, individually considered, do not trigger any obligation. If the agreement is later discovered, of course there might be

administrative, and in some cases also criminal sanctions, but do shareholders have a private cause of action to recover the alleged damages (in terms of lost profits) caused by the violation of the mandatory bid rule? The Italian Supreme Court, in 2012, has concluded that they do (Corte di Cassazione, No. 14392, 14399 e 14400 of August 10, 2012).

7.   Under Brazilian law, a tender offer on all voting shares is mandatory when someone aquires "control" of a listed corporation. There is no fixed triggering threshold, but the existence of an obligation to launch a public bid depends on the fact that the amount of shares purchased constitutes control of the target corporation. Naturally, the controlling threshold varies for each corporation, depending on the overall ownership structure and other relevant circumstances (for example, A might control corporation X with 30% of the voting shares if the next largest shareholder holds 5% and minority shareholders are dispersed, while the same participation might not represent control if there are two shareholders holding 16% each and bound by a voting agreement). In order to understand if a mandatory offer is necessary, it is preliminarily necessary to investigate the situation of each single corporation. The approach is in many ways rationale: only when someone acquires control there is a need to protect minority shareholders. This rule, however, is very difficult to apply. Can you explain why? Interestingly enough this approach was followed in several European countries before the implementation of the Thirteenth Directive, but it has been largely abandoned. The mandatory tender offer that, under Brazilian law, must be launched on all remaining voting shares after having acquired control, must be launched at a price not lower than 80% of the price paid for obtaining control. Why 80% and not 100%? For more information on Brazilian takeover law a good source (in Portuguese) is N. Eizirik at al., *Mercado de Capitais. Regime Jurídico*, 3rd ed., Renovar, 2011, 604 ff.

* * *

In systems that provide a statutory mandatory tender offer in case of acquisition of control (such as in the European Union), what are the consequences if a shareholder obtains the triggering threshold but does not launch a tender offer? In principle, damages should be available for minority shareholders, at least if they can demonstrate that they would have tendered the shares in case of a mandatory bid and, based on the minimum price of the offer, they would have made a profit (some cases in Italy, for example, have addressed this issue). This is in fact the rule in several systems. German case law, however, opted for a different answer. The following German case, criticized by several scholars, examines this question.

BKN

German Federal Court of Justice, 2013
11 June 2013

Facts

The plaintiff and the defendant were both shareholders of a corporation listed on a German stock exchange. In 2009 the corporation went bankrupt. The plaintiff asserts that from 2003 to 2005 the defendant acquired directly and indirectly more than 50% of the shares of the corporation without complying with Sec. 35 of the German Securities Acquisition and Takeover Act, (Wertpapiererwerbs – und Übernahmegesetz) a provision stating that any person who gains control of a target company directly or indirectly must, without undue delay and within seven calendar days at the latest, disclose this circumstance, file an offering document with the Supervisory Authority and launch a mandatory offer. The plaintiff sued the defendant for damages in the amount of 980,000 € in exchange for her shares of the corporation, claiming that the violation of Sec. 35 of the German Securities Acquisition and Takeover Act entitles the non-controlling shareholders to damages since they would have accepted the mandatory offer and would not have been affected by the insolvency of the corporation. The Regional Court (Laudgericht) dismissed the case. The Higher Regional Court (Oberlaudesgericht) denied the appeal.

Grounds

[. . .]

The court dismisses the case.

[. . .]

The court of appeals did not have to decide whether the defendant was a controlling shareholder because German law does not provide a cause of action for damages in the case of a violation of Sec. 35 of the German Securities Acquisition and Takeover Act.

However, some legal scholars hold the view that such a cause of action actually exists based on Sec. 35 of the German Securities Acquisition and Takeover Act (*Seibt*, ZIP 2003, 1865, 1876; *Ekkenga/Hofschroer*, DStR 2002, 768, 777; *Wagner*, NZG 2003, 718, 719) or based on an obligation of the controlling shareholder (*Mülbert/U. H. Schneider*, WM 2003, 2301, 2308). Nevertheless the majority of legal scholars denies such a claim (*Habersack*, ZHR 166 [2002], 619, 621 f.; *Habersack*, in: Emmerich/Habersack, Aktien- und GmbH-Konzernrecht, 6th edition, vor § 311 note 24; [. . .].

b) The court agrees with the latter opinion.

[. . .]

Such a claim cannot be based on the wording of Sec. 35 of the German Securities Acquisition and Takeover Act. Sec. 35 subs. 1 of the German Securities Acquisition and Takeover Act imposes only the duty to publish the fact that a shareholder actually became a controlling shareholder. According to Sec. 35 subs. 2 of the German Securities Acquisition and Takeover Act the controlling shareholder also has the duty to submit an offer document to the Supervisory Authority. Sec. 35 of the German Securities Acquisition and Takeover Act does not mention a specific claim of the non-controlling shareholders for the case of a violation of these duties. The official comment to Sec. 35 of the German Securities Acquisition and Takeover Act prepared by the legislature does not include any reference to actions for damages of the non-controlling shareholders in case of violation of these duties. In fact, the legislative history only refers to the sanctions explicitly stated in the German Securities Acquisition and Takeover Act, such as the possibility of the Supervisory Authority to fine the controlling shareholder, or a possible claim of interested shareholders in case of a delay in the publication of the mandatory offer. An action for damages of minority shareholders in the case of non-compliance with the duties of Sec. 35 of the German Securities Acquisition and Takeover Act is not mentioned.

[. . .] This interpretation is also in accordance with the regulatory purpose of Sec. 35 of the German Securities Acquisition and Takeover Act. The purpose of this Act is to create a general framework for takeovers and other public offers for the acquisition of shares on German stock markets in order to meet the requirements of globalization and international financial markets and to improve the position of the German capital market in the international competition of capital markets. As a consequence the German Securities Acquisition and Takeover Act has to be considered only as a capital market regulation (*Kleindiek*, ZGR 2002, 546, 558 ff.; *Habersack,* in: Emmerich/Habersack, Aktien- und GmbH-Konzernrecht, 6th edition, vor § 311 note 10, 25; dissenting *Altmeppen*, ZIP 2001, 1073, 1082; compromising *Hopt*, ZHR 166 [2002], 383, 38). Therefore, it [. . .] cannot determine the liability of the controlling shareholder.

The fact that Sec. 35 of the German Securities Acquisition and Takeover Act does not provide a claim for minority shareholders is also coherent with the fact that the German Supervisory Authority acts only in the general public interest (Sec. 4 subs. 2 German Securities Acquisition and Takeover Act). This illustrates that the German Securities Acquisition and Takeover Act mainly focuses on the protection of the capital market as an institution and not on the protection of single shareholders.

Moreover, this interpretation is also supported by systematic arguments.

The German Securities Acquisition and Takeover Act provides sufficient instruments in order to force a controlling shareholder to comply with the duties of its Sec. 35. If the controlling shareholder does not comply, according to Sec. 59 of the same Act she cannot vote her shares. Consequently all shareholder resolutions approved with the vote of the controlling shareholder can be challenged by other shareholders. [. . .] Moreover the controlling shareholder in violation of the duties of Sec. 60 of the German Securities Acquisition and Takeover Act can be sanctioned by the Supervisory authority with a fine up to one million Euro. Although the Supervisory Authority acts only in the public interest the shareholders can ask the Regulator to intervene.

[. . .] Finally, the Takeover Directive does not allow a different interpretation. According to Art. 3 subs. 1a of the Takeover Directive, shareholders must be protected in case of change of control. This protection does not, however, necessarily require a private cause of action for damages for non-controlling shareholders when a mandatory bid has not been launched (Art. 4 subs. 6 Takeover Directive). Moreover, Art. 17 of the Directive states that the sanctions provided by national legislatures shall be effective, proportionate, and dissuasive. These requirements are already met without granting a cause of action for damages to non-controlling shareholders (*Habersack*, ZHR 166 [2002], 619, 622).

NOTES AND QUESTIONS

1.   In this decision the court states that the German Securities Acquisition and Takeover Act constitutes only a capital market law, and not a corporate group or general corporate law. This distinction, used to exclude a private cause of action, might seem, especially to readers not familiar with German law, quite formalistic. Could you think of any general legal principles of corporate law providing the basis for a claim for the plaintiff in this case? Do you think that the argument of the court is convincing and that this distinction between "capital market rules" and "corporate law rules" is possible?

2.   The Court states that there are several other sanctions under German law applicable to the controlling shareholder violating the duty to make a mandatory bid. Do you think that these sanctions are efficient and adequate? Consider also that the Takeover Directive states that the sanctions provided for shall be effective, proportionate, and dissuasive.

3.   Take a closer look at the argument used by the Court with respect to public interest. Do you find it convincing? One the one hand, the Court raises a quite formalistic point observing that the rules at hand are designed to regulate financial markets, and only corporate law rules can impose liability on the controlling shareholder. This argument, which is based on general German law principles concerning different sources of the law and the distinction between "securities regulation" and "corporate law," might be

hard to understand for an outsider. The second but connected argument, however, is in some ways more clear, and also—in our opinion—very problematic. The Court says that single shareholders do not have a cause of action because the relevant rules are designed to protect capital markets as institutions, not single shareholders. But isn't protecting single shareholders, who are investors, a way to protect the integrity of capital markets? The fact that capital markets can be protected independently from the protection granted, also through private causes of actions, to single shareholders, seems to us very abstract. Aren't shareholders-investors exactly the class that the legislature needs to protect in order to foster financial markets?

4.   One reason justifying the reluctance of the German judges in establishing a private cause of action available to minority shareholders damaged by the violation of the duty to launch a tender offer might be found in the fact that German law, differently from Italian and French law, and somehow more similarly to the original Roman law approach and also to the common law system of "writs," has opted for a narrower approach to tort (*unerlaubte Handlung*) liability, avoiding a general and broad private cause of action for any damage caused. Intentionally or negligently, by a wrongful act (a notion that can include violations of a statute). The only exception of this principle concerns certain violations of criminal law. In this perspective, the discussion is not dissimilar, for example, from the question, under U.S. law, if investors have a private cause of action for damages due to misstatements and omissions under section 10b of the Securities and Exchange Act (you can research this on the Internet and compare). For sure, not granting minority shareholders a direct remedy for damages seems quite harsh. Do you think it affects the relevance of the mandatory tender offer requirement?

5.   In the last part of the excerpt above, the German Federal Court of Justice considers the compatibility of their interpretation (no private cause of action for failure to launch a mandatory offer) with European law. Why do they do this? Do you find the conclusion, in this respect, convincing?

* * *

In the regulation of tender offers Japan has taken a sort of mixed approach combining aspects of the U.S. and the European Union regulations. The rules enacted in 1971 were clearly inspired by the U.S. experience and by the Williams Act in particular, but later reforms in 1990 and 2006 brought the Japanese approach closer to the British and European ones. In fact, also under Japanese law a mandatory tender offer is required to acquire control, with the basic threshold being one-third of the shares. There are, however, also significant and profound differences with the "European-style" mandatory tender offer. Professor Fujita, in an interesting article, points out some of these differences (Tomotaka Fujita, *The Takeover Regulation in Japan: Peculiar Developments in the Mandatory Offer Rule*, 3 UT SOFT LAW REVIEW 24 (2011)): (a) under Japanese law, the mandatory tender offer does not follow the acquisition of control, but control should be acquired through a tender offer; (b) while European law provides for a minimum price at which the mandatory offer must be launched, determined by taking into account the price paid by the offeror for previous purchases and market prices, Japanese law does not require a minimum price: if the price is too low, the offer will not succeed and the offeror will not acquire control; (c) under Japanese law, no offer is mandated if control is acquired purchasing shares on the market, only privately negotiated acquisitions of shares trigger the mandatory tender offer. European rules, on the other hand, impose a tender offer also when control is obtained on the market; (d) the Thirteenth Directive, in Europe, provides that—with few and limited exceptions—the mandatory tender offer must include all outstanding shares, in order to grant all shareholders the opportunity to sell their shares. In Japan, before 2006, the mandatory offer could be partial and not extended to all shares (shares will be purchased on a pro-rata basis). With the 2006 reform, a mandatory bid on all the outstanding shares has been introduced, but it is only triggered by the acquisition of two-thirds of all the voting shares. Based on these differences, we can observe that Japanese law, similarly to European law and differently from U.S. law, provides for an exit right designed to protect minority shareholders in case of change of control. Differently from Europe, however, the mandatory tender offer is not necessarily extended to all the outstanding shares, and there is no required minimum price. Do you think this approach, compared to the European and U.S. ones, is more or less protective of investors? Does it facilitate an active market for control? Comparing the Japanese and the European rules listed above, what do you think their rationales are?

* * *

Shifting now our attention to defensive measures in case of hostile takeovers, we have already mentioned in the first section of this chapter the basic conflict of interest that their adoption determines for directors. The U.K., since the 1960s, adopted the so-called "passivity" or "no-frustration" rule, pursuant to which directors cannot adopt defensive measures if not specifically authorized by the shareholders' meeting. They must, in other words, stay on the side-lines and toss the ball to the shareholders, directly interested in the tender offer. This approach has been (partially) embraced by the European Takeover Directive, whose Article 9 provides that:

Article 9—*Obligations of the board of the offeree company*

[. . .]

2.   During the period referred to in the second subparagraph, the board of the offeree company shall obtain the prior authorisation of the general meeting of shareholders given for

this purpose before taking any action, other than seeking alternative bids, which may result in the frustration of the bid and in particular before issuing any shares which may result in a lasting impediment to the offeror's acquiring control of the offeree company.

Such authorization shall be mandatory at least from the time the board of the offeree company receives the information [. . .] concerning the bid and until the result of the bid is made public or the bid lapses. Member States may require that such authorisation be obtained at an earlier stage, for example as soon as the board of the offeree company becomes aware that the bid is imminent.

3. As regards decisions taken before the beginning of the period referred to in the second subparagraph of paragraph 2 and not yet partly or fully implemented, the general meeting of shareholders shall approve or confirm any decision which does not form part of the normal course of the company's business and the implementation of which may result in the frustration of the bid.

[. . .]

This provision is not mandatory: Member States, pursuant to Article 12 of the Directive, can in fact opt out of it and leave corporations free to adopt board neutrality or not in their bylaws. This optional regime was necessary as a compromise to approve the Directive (it's the so-called "Portuguese compromise"), since some Member States strenuously opposed the passivity rule, being concerned that it could make national corporations vulnerable to attacks from foreign raiders not subject to the same restrictions. We will consider later the effects of this rule and of its optional nature. For now, can you pinpoint the rationale of Paragraph 3 of Article 9 above?

As we mentioned, in the U.S. the issue of directors adopting defensive measures vis-à-vis a hostile takeover is not addressed shifting decision-making authority to shareholders, but through that malleable and powerful, but sometimes confusing, legal tool represented by fiduciary duties. Recognizing the peculiarity of the takeover context, courts—and in particular Delaware courts—have developed specific fiduciary duties of directors. This difference is also interesting, from a comparative perspective, because it says a lot about the preference, in the U.S., to regulate through ex post case law, rather than through ex ante regulatory provisions ("we will cross that bridge when we come to it").

The following two cases, *Unocal v. Mesa* and *Revlon v. MacAndrews & Forbes*, are two of the leading decisions that define what directors can and cannot do to defend the corporate citadel under Delaware law. To be sure, as we will briefly illustrate, these cases only show one side of the issue, and some of their conclusion have been refined or even modified with successive decisions or statutory and regulatory provisions. They still offer, however, a general sense of the U.S. approach to defensive measures. The cases are so famous that you might already be familiar with them, but a quick review cannot hurt.

UNOCAL CORP. V. MESA PETROLEUM CO.

Supreme Court of Delaware
493 A.2d 946

MOORE, JUSTICE.

We confront an issue of first impression in Delaware—the validity of a corporation's self-tender for its own shares which excludes from participation a stockholder making a hostile tender offer for the company's stock.

The Court of Chancery granted a preliminary injunction to the plaintiffs, Mesa Petroleum Co., Mesa Asset Co., Mesa Partners II, and Mesa Eastern, Inc. (collectively "Mesa"), enjoining an exchange offer of the defendant, Unocal Corporation (Unocal) for its own stock. The trial court concluded that a selective exchange offer, excluding Mesa, was legally impermissible. We cannot agree with such a blanket rule. The factual findings of the Vice Chancellor, fully supported by the record, establish that Unocal's board, consisting of a majority of independent directors, acted in good faith, and after reasonable investigation found that Mesa's tender offer was both inadequate and coercive. Under the circumstances the board had both the power and duty to oppose a bid it perceived to be harmful to the corporate enterprise. On this record we are satisfied that the device Unocal adopted is reasonable in relation to the threat posed, and that the board acted in the proper exercise of sound business judgment. We will not substitute our views for those of the board if the latter's decision can be "attributed to any rational business purpose." *Sinclair Oil Corp. v. Levien,* Del.Supr., 280 A.2d 717, 720 (1971). Accordingly, we reverse the decision of the Court of Chancery and order the preliminary injunction vacated.

I.

The factual background of this matter bears a significant relationship to its ultimate outcome.

On April 8, 1985, Mesa, the owner of approximately 13% of Unocal's stock, commenced a two-tier "front loaded" cash tender offer for 64 million shares, or approximately 37%, of Unocal's outstanding stock at a price of $54 per share. The "back-end" was designed to eliminate the remaining publicly held shares by an exchange of securities purportedly worth $54 per share. However, pursuant to an order entered by the United States District Court for the Central District of California on April 26, 1985, Mesa issued a supplemental proxy statement to Unocal's stockholders disclosing that the securities offered in the second-step merger would be highly subordinated, and that Unocal's capitalization would differ significantly from its present structure. Unocal has rather aptly termed such securities "junk bonds".

Unocal's board consists of eight independent outside directors and six insiders. It met on April 13, 1985, to consider the Mesa tender offer. Thirteen directors were present, and the meeting lasted nine and one-half hours. The directors were given no agenda or written materials prior to the session. However, detailed presentations were made by legal counsel regarding the board's obligations under both Delaware corporate law and the federal securities laws. The board then received a presentation from Peter Sachs on behalf of Goldman Sachs & Co. (Goldman Sachs) and Dillon, Read & Co. (Dillon Read) discussing the bases for their opinions that the Mesa proposal was wholly inadequate. Mr. Sachs opined that the minimum cash value that could be expected from a sale or orderly liquidation for 100% of Unocal's stock was in excess of $60 per share. In making his presentation, Mr. Sachs showed slides outlining the valuation techniques used by the financial advisors, and others, depicting recent business combinations in the oil and gas industry. The Court of Chancery found that the Sachs presentation was designed to apprise the directors of the scope of the analyses performed rather than the facts and numbers used in reaching the conclusion that Mesa's tender offer price was inadequate.

Mr. Sachs also presented various defensive strategies available to the board if it concluded that Mesa's two-step tender offer was inadequate and should be opposed. One of the devices outlined was a self-tender by Unocal for its own stock with a reasonable price range of $70 to $75 per share. The cost of such a proposal would cause the company to incur $6.1—6.5 billion of additional debt, and a presentation was made informing the board of Unocal's ability to handle it. The directors were told that the primary effect of this obligation would be to reduce exploratory drilling, but that the company would nonetheless remain a viable entity.

The eight outside directors, comprising a clear majority of the thirteen members present, then met separately with Unocal's financial advisors and attorneys. Thereafter, they unanimously agreed to advise the board that it should reject Mesa's tender offer as inadequate, and that Unocal should pursue a self-tender to provide the stockholders with a fairly priced alternative to the Mesa proposal. The board then reconvened and unanimously adopted a resolution rejecting as grossly inadequate Mesa's tender offer. Despite the nine and one-half hour length of the meeting, no formal decision was made on the proposed defensive self-tender.

On April 15, the board met again with four of the directors present by telephone and one member still absent. This session lasted two hours. Unocal's Vice President of Finance and its Assistant General Counsel made a detailed presentation of the proposed terms of the exchange offer. A price range between $70 and $80 per share was considered, and ultimately the directors agreed upon $72. The board was also advised about the debt securities that would be issued, and the necessity of placing restrictive covenants upon certain corporate activities until the obligations were paid. The board's decisions were made in reliance on the advice of its investment bankers, including the terms and conditions upon which the securities were to be issued. Based upon this advice, and the board's own deliberations, the directors unanimously approved the exchange offer. Their resolution provided that if Mesa acquired 64 million shares of Unocal stock through its own offer (the Mesa Purchase Condition), Unocal would buy the remaining 49% outstanding for an exchange of debt securities having an aggregate par value of $72 per share. The board resolution also stated that the offer would be subject to other conditions that had been described to the board at the meeting, or which were deemed necessary by Unocal's officers, including the exclusion of Mesa from the proposal (the Mesa exclusion). Any such conditions were required to be in accordance with the "purport and intent" of the offer.

Unocal's exchange offer was commenced on April 17, 1985, and Mesa promptly challenged it by filing this suit in the Court of Chancery. [. . .]

II.

The issues we address involve these fundamental questions: Did the Unocal board have the power and duty to oppose a takeover threat it reasonably perceived to be harmful to the corporate enterprise, and if so, is its action here entitled to the protection of the business judgment rule?

Mesa contends that the discriminatory exchange offer violates the fiduciary duties Unocal owes it. Mesa argues that because of the Mesa exclusion the business judgment rule is inapplicable, because the directors by tendering their own shares will derive a financial benefit that is not available to *all* Unocal stockholders. Thus, it is Mesa's ultimate contention that Unocal cannot establish that the exchange offer is fair to *all* shareholders, and argues that the Court of Chancery was correct in concluding that Unocal was unable to meet this burden.

Unocal answers that it does not owe a duty of "fairness" to Mesa, given the facts here. Specifically, Unocal contends that its board of directors reasonably and in good faith concluded that Mesa's $54 two-tier tender offer was coercive and inadequate, and that Mesa sought selective treatment for itself. Furthermore, Unocal argues that the board's approval of the exchange offer was made in good faith, on an informed basis, and in the exercise of due care. Under these circumstances, Unocal contends that its directors properly employed this device to protect the company and its stockholders from Mesa's harmful tactics.

III.

We begin with the basic issue of the power of a board of directors of a Delaware corporation to adopt a defensive measure of this type. Absent such authority, all other questions are moot. Neither issues of fairness nor business judgment are pertinent without the basic underpinning of a board's legal power to act.

The board has a large reservoir of authority upon which to draw. Its duties and responsibilities proceed from the inherent powers conferred by 8 *Del.C.* § 141(a), respecting management of the corporation's "business and affairs". [. . .]

Finally, the board's power to act derives from its fundamental duty and obligation to protect the corporate enterprise, which includes stockholders, from harm reasonably perceived, irrespective of its source. [. . .]

Given the foregoing principles, we turn to the standards by which director action is to be measured. [. . .] The business judgment rule is a "presumption that in making a business decision the directors of a corporation acted on an informed basis, in good faith and in the honest belief that the action taken was in the best interests of the company." *Aronson v. Lewis,* Del.Supr., 473 A.2d 805, 812 (1984) (citations omitted). A hallmark of the business judgment rule is that a court will not substitute its judgment for that of the board if the latter's decision can be "attributed to any rational business purpose." *Sinclair Oil Corp. v. Levien,* Del.Supr., 280 A.2d 717, 720 (1971).

When a board addresses a pending takeover bid it has an obligation to determine whether the offer is in the best interests of the corporation and its shareholders. In that respect a board's duty is no different from any other responsibility it shoulders, and its decisions should be no less entitled to the respect they otherwise would be accorded in the realm of business judgment. *See also Johnson v. Trueblood,* 629 F.2d 287, 292–293 (3d Cir.1980). There are, however, certain caveats to a proper exercise of this function. Because of the omnipresent specter that a board may be acting primarily in its own interests, rather than those of the corporation and its shareholders, there is an enhanced duty which calls for judicial examination at the threshold before the protections of the business judgment rule may be conferred.

IV.

In the board's exercise of corporate power to forestall a takeover bid our analysis begins with the basic principle that corporate directors have a fiduciary duty to act in the best interests of the corporation's stockholders. *Guth v. Loft, Inc.,* Del.Supr., 5 A.2d 503, 510 (1939). As we have noted, their duty of care extends to protecting the corporation and its owners from perceived harm whether a threat originates from third parties or other shareholders. But such powers are not absolute. A corporation does not have unbridled discretion to defeat any perceived threat by any Draconian means available.

The restriction placed upon a selective stock repurchase is that the directors may not have acted solely or primarily out of a desire to perpetuate themselves in office.

A further aspect is the element of balance. If a defensive measure is to come within the ambit of the business judgment rule, it must be reasonable in relation to the threat posed. This entails an analysis by the directors of the nature of the takeover bid and its effect on the corporate enterprise. Examples of such concerns may include: inadequacy of the price offered, nature and timing of the offer, questions of illegality, the impact on "constituencies" other than shareholders (i.e., creditors, customers, employees, and perhaps even the community generally), the risk of nonconsummation, and the quality of securities being offered in the exchange.

Specifically, the Unocal directors had concluded that the value of Unocal was substantially above the $54 per share offered in cash at the front end. Furthermore, they determined that the subordinated securities to be exchanged in Mesa's announced squeeze out of the remaining shareholders in the "back-end" merger were "junk bonds" worth far less than $54. It is now well recognized that such offers are a classic coercive measure designed to stampede shareholders into tendering at the first tier, even if the price is inadequate, out of fear of what they will receive at the back end of the transaction. Wholly beyond the coercive aspect of an inadequate two-tier tender offer, the threat was posed by a corporate raider with a national reputation as a "greenmailer".

In adopting the selective exchange offer, the board stated that its objective was either to defeat the inadequate Mesa offer or, should the offer still succeed, provide the 49% of its stockholders, who would otherwise be forced to accept "junk bonds", with $72 worth of senior debt. We find that both purposes are valid.

However, such efforts would have been thwarted by Mesa's participation in the exchange offer. First, if Mesa could tender its shares, Unocal would effectively be subsidizing the former's continuing effort to buy Unocal stock at $54 per share. Second, Mesa could not, by definition, fit within the class of shareholders being protected from its own coercive and inadequate tender offer.

Thus, we are satisfied that the selective exchange offer is reasonably related to the threats posed. [. . .]

V.

Mesa contends that it is unlawful, and the trial court agreed, for a corporation to discriminate in this fashion against one shareholder. It argues correctly that no case has ever sanctioned a device that precludes a raider from sharing in a benefit available to all other stockholders. However, as we have noted earlier, the principle of selective stock repurchases by a Delaware corporation is neither unknown nor unauthorized. [. . .]

[W]hile the exchange offer is a form of selective treatment, given the nature of the threat posed here the response is neither unlawful nor unreasonable. If the board of directors is disinterested, has acted in good faith and with due care, its decision in the absence of an abuse of discretion will be upheld as a proper exercise of business judgment.

To this Mesa responds that the board is not disinterested, because the directors are receiving a benefit from the tender of their own shares, which because of the Mesa exclusion, does not devolve upon *all* stockholders equally. [. . .] The answer of course is that the exclusion is valid, and the directors' participation in the exchange offer does not rise to the level of a disqualifying interest. [. . .]

Nor does this become an "interested" director transaction merely because certain board members are large stockholders. As this Court has previously noted, that fact alone does not create a disqualifying "personal pecuniary interest" to defeat the operation of the business judgment rule. [. . .]

Mesa also argues that the exclusion permits the directors to abdicate the fiduciary duties they owe it. However, that is not so. The board continues to owe Mesa the duties of due care and loyalty. But in the face of the destructive threat Mesa's tender offer was perceived to pose, the board had a supervening duty to protect the corporate enterprise, which includes the other shareholders, from threatened harm.

[. . .]

VI.

In conclusion, there was directorial power to oppose the Mesa tender offer, and to undertake a selective stock exchange made in good faith and upon a reasonable investigation pursuant to a clear duty to protect the corporate enterprise. Further, the selective stock repurchase plan chosen by Unocal is reasonable in relation to the threat that the board rationally and reasonably believed was posed by Mesa's inadequate and coercive two-tier tender offer. Under those circumstances the board's action is entitled to be measured by the standards of the business judgment rule.

[. . .]

The decision of the Court of Chancery is therefore REVERSED, and the preliminary injunction is VACATED.

NOTES AND QUESTIONS

1. This decision set forth one important principle. Somehow simplifying, the actions of the board of directors in a hostile takeover scenario are protected by the business judgment rule (therefore, as you will remember from Chapter 6, they can hardly be attacked) if two conditions are met: (1) directors had a reasonable ground to believe that the takeover would not be in the best interest of the corporation and its shareholders; and (2) the defensive measure is reasonable in relation to the threat posed, in other words it does not unnecessarily waste corporate resources. The court applies a sort of modified business judgment rule, if you will. Why a modified business judgment rule is necessary? Of course this principle is fairly easy to state, but can be difficult to apply. It sets a somehow vague standard that requires a very factually intense, case-by-case analysis. What is interesting to observe, from a comparative perspective, is both the broad freedom granted to directors under Delaware law, and the regulatory technique used, i.e., fiduciary duties.

2. In *Unocal v. Mesa*, the court upholds a selective stock repurchase plan excluding the hostile bidder. This raises a question in terms of equal treatment of shareholders, but the court considers that Mesa was "responsible" for having launched a coercive offer, and therefore is not entitled to equal treatment in this perspective. A different solution, argued the court, would basically have resulted in Unocal financing the very unfair offer that it was trying to defeat. Shortly after the decision, the SEC introduced, however, the so-called "all-holders" rule, pursuant to which public offers cannot discriminate against a shareholder. It is an interesting example of federal intervention to correct state law and, even if today this rule limits the ability of a target corporation to use a selective offer as a defense, the core holding of the decision, based on the nature of the threat and the proportionality of the response above mentioned, is still valid.

3. In the U.S., the adoption of unreasonable or disproportionate defensive measures can lead to directors' liability. Let's go back for a moment to the board neutrality rule embodied in Article 9 of the European Thirteenth Directive, reprinted above. If a defensive measure is approved by fully informed shareholders, and directors implement the defensive transactions that received the green light, but it turns out to cause damage to the corporation, could directors still be liable? Do you think that the shareholders' meeting's resolution exculpates them? Under Italian law,

apparently, directors can be liable also if they implement a shareholders-approved defense if it is clearly damaging. Article 104 of the Italian Consolidated Law on Financial Markets, in fact, provides that notwithstanding a shareholders' resolution authorizing a defensive measure, "Directors are responsible for their acts and transactions." The idea is that directors must, in a sense, "oversee" shareholders' decisions, and refrain from carrying them out if they are detrimental to the corporation. What do you think of this provision and its effects? As a side note, however, it should be observed that notwithstanding this provision, from a practical perspective, most judges will not consider totally irrelevant, in evaluating possible directors' breaches, that they acted on the basis of a shareholders' meeting resolution, especially if the shareholders' decision was fully informed. Can you argue, based on this last observation, that also in systems that provide for board neutrality, directors' duties and potential liability are still important to regulate takeovers?

* * *

REVLON, INC. v. MacANDREWS & FORBES HOLDINGS, INC.

Supreme Court of Delaware
506 A.2d 173

MOORE, JUSTICE:

In this battle for corporate control of Revlon, Inc. (Revlon), the Court of Chancery enjoined certain transactions designed to thwart the efforts of Pantry Pride, Inc. (Pantry Pride) to acquire Revlon. The defendants are Revlon, its board of directors, and Forstmann Little & Co. and the latter's affiliated limited partnership (collectively, Forstmann). The injunction barred consummation of an option granted Forstmann to purchase certain Revlon assets (the lock-up option), a promise by Revlon to deal exclusively with Forstmann in the face of a takeover (the no-shop provision), and the payment of a $25 million cancellation fee to Forstmann if the transaction was aborted. The Court of Chancery found that the Revlon directors had breached their duty of care by entering into the foregoing transactions and effectively ending an active auction for the company. The trial court ruled that such arrangements are not illegal *per se* under Delaware law, but that their use under the circumstances here was impermissible. We agree. *See MacAndrews & Forbes Holdings, Inc. v. Revlon, Inc.,* Del.Ch., 501 A.2d 1239 (1985). Thus, we granted this expedited interlocutory appeal to consider for the first time the validity of such defensive measures in the face of an active bidding contest for corporate control. Additionally, we address for the first time the extent to which a corporation may consider the impact of a takeover threat on constituencies other than shareholders. *See Unocal Corp. v. Mesa Petroleum Co.,* Del.Supr., 493 A.2d 946, 955 (1985).

In our view, lock-ups and related agreements are permitted under Delaware law where their adoption is untainted by director interest or other breaches of fiduciary duty. The actions taken by the Revlon directors, however, did not meet this standard. Moreover, while concern for various corporate constituencies is proper when addressing a takeover threat, that principle is limited by the requirement that there be some rationally related benefit accruing to the stockholders. We find no such benefit here.

Thus, under all the circumstances we must agree with the Court of Chancery that the enjoined Revlon defensive measures were inconsistent with the directors' duties to the stockholders. Accordingly, we affirm.

I.

The somewhat complex manoeuvres of the parties necessitate a rather detailed examination of the facts. The prelude to this controversy began in June 1985, when Ronald O. Perelman, chairman of the board and chief executive officer of Pantry Pride, met with his counterpart at Revlon, Michel C. Bergerac, to discuss a friendly acquisition of Revlon by Pantry Pride. Perelman suggested a price in the range of $40–50 per share, but the meeting ended with Bergerac dismissing those figures as considerably below Revlon's intrinsic value. All subsequent Pantry Pride overtures were rebuffed, perhaps in part based on Mr. Bergerac's strong personal antipathy to Mr. Perelman.

Thus, on August 14, Pantry Pride's board authorized Perelman to acquire Revlon, either through negotiation in the $42–$43 per share range, or by making a hostile tender offer at $45. Perelman then met with Bergerac and outlined Pantry Pride's alternate approaches. Bergerac remained adamantly opposed to such schemes and conditioned any further discussions of the matter on Pantry Pride executing a standstill agreement prohibiting it from acquiring Revlon without the latter's prior approval.

On August 19, the Revlon board met specially to consider the impending threat of a hostile bid by Pantry Pride. At the meeting, Lazard Freres, Revlon's investment banker, advised the directors that $45 per share was a grossly inadequate price for the company. Felix Rohatyn and William Loomis of Lazard Freres explained to the board that Pantry Pride's financial strategy for acquiring Revlon would be through "junk bond" financing followed by a break-up of Revlon and the disposition of its assets. With proper timing, according to the experts, such transactions could produce a return to Pantry Pride of $60 to $70 per share, while a sale of the company as a whole would be in the "mid 50" dollar range. Martin Lipton, special counsel for Revlon, recommended two defensive measures: first, that the company repurchase up to 5 million of its nearly 30 million outstanding shares; and second, that it adopt a Note Purchase

Rights Plan. Under this plan, each Revlon shareholder would receive as a dividend one Note Purchase Right (the Rights) for each share of common stock, with the Rights entitling the holder to exchange one common share for a $65 principal Revlon note at 12% interest with a one-year maturity. The Rights would become effective whenever anyone acquired beneficial ownership of 20% or more of Revlon's shares, unless the purchaser acquired all the company's stock for cash at $65 or more per share. In addition, the Rights would not be available to the acquirer, and prior to the 20% triggering event the Revlon board could redeem the rights for 10 cents each. Both proposals were unanimously adopted.

Pantry Pride made its first hostile move on August 23 with a cash tender offer for any and all shares of Revlon at $47.50 per common share and $26.67 per preferred share, subject to (1) Pantry Pride's obtaining financing for the purchase, and (2) the Rights being redeemed, rescinded or voided.

The Revlon board met again on August 26. The directors advised the stockholders to reject the offer. Further defensive measures also were planned.

[At this point, Pantry Pride and Revlon engage in a battle in which Pantry Pride responds to different defensive measures adopted by Revlon substantially improving the conditions of the offer in order to make it more attractive for Revlon's shareholders. Eventually, Pantry Pride finds an alternative offeror that the directors prefer, Forstmann, and Revlon's directors approve certain conditions of a proposed offer by Forstmann.]

[. . .] On October 12, Forstmann made a new $57.25 per share offer, based on several conditions. The principal demand was a lock-up option to purchase Revlon's Vision Care and National Health Laboratories divisions for $525 million, some $100–$175 million below the value ascribed to them by Lazard Freres, if another acquiror got 40% of Revlon's shares. Revlon also was required to accept a no-shop provision. The Rights and Notes covenants had to be removed as in the October 3 agreement. There would be a $25 million cancellation fee to be placed in escrow, and released to Forstmann if the new agreement terminated or if another acquiror got more than 19.9% of Revlon's stock. Finally, there would be no participation by Revlon management in the merger. In return, Forstmann agreed to support the par value of the Notes, which had faltered in the market, by an exchange of new notes. Forstmann also demanded immediate acceptance of its offer, or it would be withdrawn. The board unanimously approved Forstmann's proposal because: (1) it was for a higher price than the Pantry Pride bid, (2) it protected the noteholders, and (3) Forstmann's financing was firmly in place. The board further agreed to redeem the rights and waive the covenants on the preferred stock in response to any offer above $57 cash per share. The covenants were waived, contingent upon receipt of an investment banking opinion that the Notes would trade near par value once the offer was consummated.

Pantry Pride, which had initially sought injunctive relief from the Rights plan on August 22, filed an amended complaint on October 14 challenging the lock-up, the cancellation fee, and the exercise of the Rights and the Notes covenants. Pantry Pride also sought a temporary restraining order to prevent Revlon from placing any assets in escrow or transferring them to Forstmann. Moreover, on October 22, Pantry Pride again raised its bid, with a cash offer of $58 per share conditioned upon nullification of the Rights, waiver of the covenants, and an injunction of the Forstmann lock-up.

On October 15, the Court of Chancery prohibited the further transfer of assets, and eight days later enjoined the lock-up, no-shop, and cancellation fee provisions of the agreement. The trial court concluded that the Revlon directors had breached their duty of loyalty by making concessions to Forstmann, out of concern for their liability to the noteholders, rather than maximizing the sale price of the company for the stockholders' benefit. *MacAndrews & Forbes Holdings, Inc. v. Revlon, Inc.*, 501 A.2d at 1249–50.

II.

To obtain a preliminary injunction, a plaintiff must demonstrate both a reasonable probability of success on the merits and some irreparable harm which will occur absent the injunction. [. . .]

We turn first to Pantry Pride's probability of success on the merits. [. . .]

[W]hen Pantry Pride increased its offer to $50 per share, and then to $53, it became apparent to all that the break-up of the company was inevitable. The Revlon board's authorization permitting management to negotiate a merger or buyout with a third party was a recognition that the company was for sale. The duty of the board had thus changed from the preservation of Revlon as a corporate entity to the maximization of the company's value at a sale for the stockholders' benefit. This significantly altered the board's responsibilities under the *Unocal* standards. It no longer faced threats to corporate policy and effectiveness, or to the stockholders' interests, from a grossly inadequate bid. The whole question of defensive measures became moot. The directors' role changed from defenders of the corporate bastion to auctioneers charged with getting the best price for the stockholders at a sale of the company.

III.

This brings us to the lock-up with Forstmann [. . .]

A lock-up is not *per se* illegal under Delaware law [. . .]. Such options can entice other bidders to enter a contest for control of the corporation, creating an auction for the company and maximizing shareholder profit. Current economic conditions in the takeover market are such that a "white knight" like Forstmann might only enter the bidding for the target company if it receives some form of compensation to cover the risks and costs involved. [. . .]

Forstmann had already been drawn into the contest on a preferred basis, so the result of the lock-up was not to foster bidding, but to destroy it. The board's stated reasons for approving the transactions were: (1) better financing, (2) noteholder protection, and (3) higher price. As the Court of Chancery found, and we agree, any distinctions between the rival bidders' methods of financing the proposal were nominal at best, and such a consideration has little or no significance in a cash offer for any and all shares. The principal object, contrary to the board's duty of care, appears to have been protection of the noteholders over the shareholders' interests.

While Forstmann's $57.25 offer was objectively higher than Pantry Pride's $56.25 bid, the margin of superiority is less when the Forstmann price is adjusted for the time value of money. In reality, the Revlon board ended the auction in return for very little actual improvement in the final bid. The principal benefit went to the directors, who avoided personal liability to a class of creditors to whom the board owed no further duty under the circumstances. Thus, when a board ends an intense bidding contest on an insubstantial basis, and where a significant by-product of that action is to protect the directors against a perceived threat of personal liability for consequences stemming from the adoption of previous defensive measures, the action cannot withstand the enhanced scrutiny which *Unocal* requires of director conduct. [. . .]

In addition to the lock-up option, the Court of Chancery enjoined the no-shop provision as part of the attempt to foreclose further bidding by Pantry Pride. [. . .] The no-shop provision, like the lock-up option, while not *per se* illegal, is impermissible under the *Unocal* standards when a board's primary duty becomes that of an auctioneer responsible for selling the company to the highest bidder. The agreement to negotiate only with Forstmann ended rather than intensified the board's involvement in the bidding contest.

[. . .]

The court below similarly enjoined the payment of the cancellation fee, pending a resolution of the merits, because the fee was part of the overall plan to thwart Pantry Pride's efforts. We find no abuse of discretion in that ruling.

IV.

Having concluded that Pantry Pride has shown a reasonable probability of success on the merits, we address the issue of irreparable harm. The Court of Chancery ruled that unless the lock-up and other aspects of the agreement were enjoined, Pantry Pride's opportunity to bid for Revlon was lost. The court also held that the need for both bidders to compete in the marketplace outweighed any injury to Forstmann. Given the complexity of the proposed transaction between Revlon and Forstmann, the obstacles to Pantry Pride obtaining a meaningful legal remedy are immense. We are satisfied that the plaintiff has shown the need for an injunction to protect it from irreparable harm, which need outweighs any harm to the defendants.

V.

In conclusion, the Revlon board was confronted with a situation not uncommon in the current wave of corporate takeovers. A hostile and determined bidder sought the company at a price the board was convinced was inadequate. [. . .] However, in granting an asset option lock-up to Forstmann, we must conclude that under all the circumstances the directors allowed considerations other than the maximization of shareholder profit to affect their judgment, and followed a course that ended the auction for Revlon, absent court intervention, to the ultimate detriment of its shareholders. No such defensive measure can be sustained when it represents a breach of the directors' fundamental duty of care. *See Smith v. Van Gorkom,* Del.Supr., 488 A.2d 858, 874 (1985). In that context the board's action is not entitled to the deference accorded it by the business judgment rule. The measures were properly enjoined. The decision of the Court of Chancery, therefore, is AFFIRMED.

NOTES AND QUESTIONS

1. According to the court, lock-up option, no-shop provision, and cancellation fee in favor of Forstmann stopped an auction that could have further benefitted Revlon's shareholders, cutting out Pantry Pride. The defensive measure is, therefore, considered illegitimate. It is essential, however, that the decision had been taken at a time when the corporation was "for sale" and it had become clear that a new controlling shareholder would have acquired control. This is the famous "*Revlon* moment," in which directors become auctioneers. How do you think the *Revlon* moment can be precisely identified? Is this yet another theoretically clear standard that however, when applied to actual facts, becomes blurry and determines uncertainties?

2. Another important principle stated by the court is that directors are not allowed to take into account the interests of other stakeholders besides shareholders (in this case, noteholders) when deciding defensive measures. In other words, even if you could demonstrate that a successful takeover would

cause damages to the employees greater than the benefits to shareholders, directors cannot oppose the takeover simply on this basis. This evokes a broader issue concerning corporate social responsibility: to what extent can—or must—directors and managers also consider the position of stakeholders different from shareholders? To what extent is profit and value maximization ("shareholders' primacy") the only legitimate purpose of corporate directors? This discussion is often slippery, also because a skilled lawyer, in this respect, can fairly easily, at least in most situations, argue everything and its opposite. For example, even assuming that directors must only maximize shareholders' value, it does not follow automatically that the decision to be environmentally responsible, also if not mandated by law, and to take into account the interest of other stakeholders, contradicts value maximization. You could for example argue that respect for the environment produces good will with customers and the community, avoids risks of liability should the applicable rules change, and so on, therefore ultimately being coherent with shareholders' wealth maximization in the medium term, even if it is costly in the short term. Going back to takeovers, in any case, it is interesting to point out that several U.S. States (approximately 30) have enacted so-called "other constituencies' statutes" that explicitly allow directors to take into account the interests of different stakeholders besides shareholders in taking certain decisions. As we have seen, this approach has been adopted also in the U.K. with the 2006 Companies Act (in section 172 of the Act), but in this country it is less relevant in the takeover context since, as we mentioned, the board neutrality rule applies. "Other constituencies' statutes" appear, in this respect, to reject *Revlon*. What do you think: can, or must, directors consider the impact of an acquisition on workers, customers, creditors, and on the community generally? What about other legal systems you are familiar with?

3.   To decide which one is the better offer among several offers might not be always easy. As the court says in *Revlon*, price is not the only element. One important variable could be the type of consideration offered. Do you think that a cash offer is always superior to an exchange offer in which other securities are used as a consideration for the shares of the target? Imagine, in other words, two bids, one offering $3 per share, the other offering for each share a fixed interest rate bond traded on a regulated market and whose price, in the last two weeks, has been $4, with very minor variations. Which offer is superior? Does it depend? If so, on which variables does it depend? Can the answer be different for different offerees? In such a situation, how can directors make sure that they are not facilitating an inadequate offer, or preventing a value-maximizing one?

* * *

Japan started regulating defensive measures quite late. In 2004, some takeover battles attracted the attention of regulators, and in 2005 the Ministry of Economy, Trade and Industry and the Ministry of Justice jointly issued the "Guidelines Regarding Takeover Defense for the Purposes of Protection and Enhancement of Corporate Value and

Shareholders' Common Interests (May 27, 2005)", also called "METI-MOJ Guidelines." The Guidelines, which do not have any formal binging force, are based on the following principles. First, the adoption, implementation, and termination of defensive measures must have the goal of maximizing the value of the corporation and therefore shareholders' wealth. Second, when takeover defense measures are adopted, their purpose and terms should be specifically disclosed and such measures should reflect the reasonable will of the shareholders. Third, defenses adopted in response to a takeover threat must be necessary and reasonable in relation to the threat posed.

Based on these Guidelines, a large number of listed corporations have adopted so-called "advance-warning rights plan," or "Japanese poison pill," through a shareholders' meeting resolution and in the absence of a concrete hostile acquisition attempt. This measure allows the board of directors of a corporation to allot all shareholders options to purchase shares. The options cannot be exercised by shareholders holding 20% or more of the shares of the issuer, and are triggered by the acquisition of 20% of the shares by a shareholder without the consent of the board. Corporations are required to disclose the details of defensive measures in annual reports (Art.118 (iii), Ministerial Order for Implementation of the Companies Act).

The validity of these "poison pills" is, however, still uncertain, both because courts are not bound by the above-mentioned Guidelines, and because there is so far no specific precedent. With respect to defensive measure more generally, some lower courts have denied the validity of defensive measures adopted by the sole decision of the board of directors, while acknowledging the power of the board to adopt defensive measures to protect and enhance the value of the corporation and shareholders' interests (*see*, Tokyo High Court, March 23, 2005, 1899 HANREI JIHO 56 (Livedoor v. Nippon Broadcasting), and Tokyo High Court, May 12, 2008, 1282 HANREI TAIMUZU 273). This is an interesting approach which indicates that Japan does not follow the board neutrality rule adopted in the U.K., pursuant to which all defenses that might frustrate a tender offer must be approved by the shareholders, but allows defenses approved by directors alone, without a vote of the shareholders, only when they are value-maximizing. Needless to say, the standard embraced is slippery and difficult to define in the abstract and apply consistently to specific cases. In a way, it might evoke the intermediate standard used in the U.S., but it is of course an original criteria to balance shareholders' interests and directors' duties.

One decision of the Supreme Court, excerpted below, upheld the validity of a defensive measure similar to the advance-warning rights plan described above, but the defense was approved by the shareholders after a hostile bidder had appeared.

STEEL PARTNERS JAPAN STRATEGIC FUND (OFFSHORE), L.P. v. BULL-DOG SAUCE CO., INC.

Supreme Court of Japan, 2007
7 August 2007, Saiko Saibansho Minji Hanreishu, 2215

Facts

Bull-dog Sauce Co., Inc., the defendant, is a manufacturer of sauces and other condiments, listed in the Second Section of the Tokyo Stock Exchange. Steel Partners Japan Strategic Fund L.P. (SPJ), the plaintiff, is an investment fund that holds approximately 10.25% of the existing shares of the defendant, as of May 18, 2007, together with its related entities.

On May 18, 2007, a special purpose vehicle established and completely owned by the SPJ launched a tender offer with the intent of acquiring all the outstanding shares of Bull-dog Sauce. The original price of the offer, 1,584 JPY per share, was calculated by adding a premium to the average price of the shares in a period preceding the offer. The premium ranged from approximately 12.82% to 18.56% depending on the period considered. The price was eventually raised to 1,700 JPY per share.

On June 7, the board of directors of Bull-dog Sauce decided to resist the tender offer because, in its opinion, it would harm the value of the corporation and the common interest of its shareholders, and to propose a defensive measure using allotment of share options to the annual shareholders' meeting on June 24. The content of this defensive measure was as follows. The defendant, Bull-dog Sauce, allots three options per share to all shareholders as of July 10. Shareholders can exercise these options at a price of 1 JPY each, and obtain one new share for each option. The plaintiff SPJ and its affiliates, including the special purpose vehicle, however, are not permitted to exercise their options. At the same time, the defendant had the option to acquire the share options from all shareholders paying 396 JPY per option, which is one-fourth of the original price of the tender offer, to SPJ and its related party, and issuing one share per option to the other shareholders. At the annual shareholders' meeting, the proposal regarding the above defensive measure was approved with approximately 88.7% of the votes of the shareholders present at the meeting representing 83.4% of the capital.

On June 13, before the annual shareholders' meeting, the plaintiff petitioned for preliminary injunction the Tokyo District Court, asserting that Article 247 of the Companies Act, which regulates the issuance of share options, is also applicable to the allotment of share options at hand and that the proposed defense violated the law and the principle of equal treatment of shareholders.

Both the Tokyo District Court and the Tokyo High Court rejected this petition. The SPJ appealed.

Court's decision

Appeal dismissed.

[. . .]

Equal treatment of shareholders is a principle that obliges a corporation to treat all its shareholders equally based on the rights and amount of shares they hold in order to protect the interest of individual shareholders. As the interest of individual shareholders depends on the well-being and the growth of the corporation in general, however, it is not against such principle to treat a particular shareholder in a different manner, when there is a risk that the value of the corporation and the common interest of the shareholders will be prejudiced if that shareholder obtains control of the corporation, and such treatment is necessary to avoid such risk, as long as such treatment is neither inequitable nor unreasonable. Whether the value of the corporation and the common interest of the shareholders will be destroyed if a particular shareholder obtains control of the corporation should be determined by the shareholders themselves. A decision by the shareholders' meeting in this regard should be respected as long as there is no significant element indicating the unfairness of the decision, such as that it was based on a false premise.

[The defensive measure in the present case] was adopted by a 83.4% majority, which means that almost all shareholders of the defendant, with the exception of the plaintiff and its affiliates, believed that the value of the corporation and the common interest of its shareholders would have been harmed if the plaintiff had obtained control of the defendant. [. . .] There is no significant element denying the fairness of that decision.

Thus, this court will examine whether the allotment of share options in the present case is inequitable or unreasonable.

[. . .]

The participation of the affiliates of the plaintiff will decline significantly due to the defensive measure discussed here, because they can neither exercise the options, nor receive shares in exchange of their options. The allotment of share options in the present case, however, was approved by almost all shareholders of the defendant except the related party of the plaintiff as a necessary measure to prevent the negative effects on the value of the target corporation that its shareholders believed would have been caused by the acquisition of control by the plaintiff. This decision was taken at a shareholders' meeting in which the group of the plaintiff had the opportunity to express its opinion. Also, the affiliates of the plaintiff can receive cash when the defendant acquires share options. [. . .] The amount of this consideration is determined based on the price of the tender offer, and is proportionate to the value of the share options. From these facts, the allotment of share options in the present case is not inequitable or unreasonable, even when considering the effect on the group of the plaintiff. [. . .]

NOTES AND QUESTIONS

1.   What was the function of the defensive measure used in the *Bull-dog Sauce* case? Was it used by the management of the target corporation to obtain a higher price from the bidder?

2.   One feature of the defensive measure in the Bull-dog Sauce case was a payment of cash by Bull-dog Sauce to SPJ to compensate for the dilution of its participation. Why do you think this payment was provided? Why did almost all shareholders of Bull-dog Sauce approve such payment, even though it could have a negative effect on the value of Bull-dog Sauce, as the Supreme Court points out? From the viewpoint of SPJ, was the hostile bid against Bull-dog Sauce a success or a failure? Such payment was heavily criticized in Japan (can you tell why?) and is not used in the current practice.

3.   This case is somehow similar to *Unocal v. Mesa*, discussed above. Also in *Unocal*, the legitimacy of a selective counteroffer that excluded the hostile bidder was discussed. Compare the two cases. Was the standard adopted by the Japanese court different? If so, how?

4.   In the *Bull-dog Sauce* case the Court seems to think that the approval of a defensive measure by the shareholders is very important. How do you think this perspective can be compared with the European Union board neutrality rule?

5.   The Court indicates deference to defensive measures approved by the shareholders when there are, in its own words, "no significant element indicating the unfairness of the decision," and the defense is neither "inequitable" nor "unreasonable." Are these concepts clear? How would you articulate them? How do they compare to concepts used in *Unocal*? In the first prong of the test ("unfairness"), do you see a connection with rules on the duty of loyalty? Does this decision evoke the European no-frustration rule?

6.   Both the METI-MOJ Guidelines and the *Bull-dog Sauce* decision refer to "negative effects on the value of the corporation and on the common interest of shareholders" as the main standard to define the legitimacy of defensive measures. The Supreme Court in *Bull-dog Sauce* did not need to clarify this standard because it was able to defer to the assessment made by the shareholders themselves after the bid had been launched. But can the board of directors decide unilaterally that an offer is damaging, and therefore adopt a defensive measure? If so, how should the standard be defined? Take this as a research project: find an English translation of the METI-MOJ

Guidelines, look for additional sources, and discuss this question in class or in your study group.

* * *

You hopefully now have a good understanding of the basic differences among alternative approaches to takeovers, and more precisely of the rules governing mandatory tender offers and defensive measures in the U.S., the European Union, and Japan. It's time for two even more fascinating questions. Keeping in mind that what we have called the "European" approach has been largely inspired by U.K. law, a first question is why the U.S. and the U.K., two legal systems that share several features (common law tradition, existence of a fairly large number of listed corporations with a widespread ownership structure, advanced and competitive financial markets) have developed so radically diverse rules? And, secondly, what are the effects of having extended the U.K. approach to continental European systems, with a much more concentrated ownership structure? The first question is tackled in an interesting article by John Armour and David Skeel (*Who Writes the Rules for Hostile Takeovers, and Why?—The Peculiar Divergence of U.S. and U.K. Takeover Regulation*, 95 GEO. L. J. 1727 (2007)), and the second in another article by Marco Ventoruzzo. Since the latter also refers to the former, consider the following excerpt.

MARCO VENTORUZZO, TAKEOVER REGULATION AS A WOLF IN SHEEP'S CLOTHING: TAKING U.K. RULES TO CONTINENTAL EUROPE[1]
11 U. Pa. J. Bus. & Emp. L. 135 (2008)

[. . .]

In [an] insightful work, John Armour and David Skeel address the reasons why takeovers in the U.K. and in the United States of America (U.S.) are regulated so differently. More specifically, their work demonstrates how historical events and the economic, legal, and political climate—particularly the role of lobbying groups—in the U.S. and the U.K. have affected both the content of substantive takeover rules, and the processes through which they are created and enforced.

[I]n the U.K., acquisition of a set threshold of the voting shares (thirty percent) requires the buyer to launch a mandatory tender offer on all the outstanding shares at the highest price paid for those shares. No laws or regulations of this sort are provided under U.S. law at the federal level, even if some states provide for "best-price rules" whose effects are similar to the U.K. mandatory bid rule. Similarly, the British "City Code" imposes a ban on directors' actions that might frustrate a hostile bid

---

[1]   Footnotes omitted.

without shareholder approval, which contrasts starkly with the relative freedom that U.S. directors have to resist a hostile acquisition.

Armour and Skeel explain these differences by pointing to the fact that, notwithstanding the widespread ownership structure that both systems have in common, the role of institutional investors in the U.K. as shareholders and as an organized group influencing the policy makers, is absent in the U.S. Instead, in the U.S., direct investment by small and disorganized shareholders is more common. Armour and Skeel also examine why corporate directors and managers, in the context of American federalism, have a more effective role than their British counterparts in shaping takeover rules.

The most original part of their contribution underlines the importance of the rule-making process in determining the substantive regulatory outcome. In this respect, Armour and Skeel juxtapose British "coerced self-regulation, made under a clear governmental threat of intervention" favored also by the geographical proximity of the major actors in the City, with the U.S. legislative and case-law processes, which are largely derived from litigation and judge-made rules. Combining these and other elements, they conclude that, in the U.K., coordinated and influential institutional investors were able to promote a private takeover regime particularly favorable to minority investors. The pillars of this regime are the mandatory bid and the non-frustration rule. In the U.S., by contrast, incumbent directors and managers were able to obtain more leeway to resist takeovers thanks to a number of factors ranging from U.S. federalism that (borrowing the image used by Armour and Skeel) amplifies the voice of corporate managers to the lesser impact of institutional investors' lobbying efforts on the development of case-law.

The story told by Armour and Skeel is not only well grounded and convincing from an historical perspective, it is also consistent with modern public-choice models that analyze the role of lobbying groups in determining the level of investors' protection in different jurisdictions [. . .].

But, therein lays the rub. If it is true that the U.K. approach to takeovers favors institutional investors in systems with a significant degree of dispersed ownership structure, why would the essential pillars of this approach be spontaneously adopted, well before the Thirteenth Directive, in several continental European countries that have concentrated ownership structures? In these systems, entrenched controlling shareholders and the associations representing their interests are among the most influential pressure groups in the political arena, and institutional investors play a comparatively less relevant role. In this context, Armour and Skeel's analysis leads to additional questions: Who are the lobbying groups that promoted this legislation? Or, is it possible that the legislatures were merely particularly attentive to the need of protection of minority investors? Why were countries such as France and Italy among the first, dating back to the 1990s, to embrace the British regime when they have otherwise been slower in legislative protection of minority investors?

[. . .]

Mandatory bid, the best price rule, board neutrality, and breakthrough provisions, which represent the entire panoply of what is considered to be effective takeover regulation, might have very different effects when applied in systems with concentrated ownership instead of dispersed ownership. This hypothesis has been largely overlooked, especially in the public debate, notwithstanding the fact that it is quite intuitive.

Consider mandatory bids. In very broad terms, this rule provides that when a bidder acquires a set threshold of voting shares of a listed corporation (let's say 30 percent), it must launch an offer on all the outstanding shares at an equitable price. Now imagine how this rule would apply in a system with a very dispersed ownership structure in which, for example, the average participation necessary to have de facto control of a corporation is ten percent. In that context, a raider can easily succeed in a hostile acquisition without triggering the mandatory bid. If the current controlling shareholder holds ten percent of the voting shares, it might be sufficient to acquire, for example, eighteen percent to be in the driver's seat. And this can be done with a partial tender offer, by buying shares on the market, or by negotiating blocks of shares outside the market with qualified minority shareholders. In any case, by not exceeding the thirty percent threshold, no mandatory bid is required on all the shares.

The important implication is that, in a system with widespread ownership, the real goal of the mandatory bid is not so much the one of protecting minority investors from any change in control, but rather from a change in control when the resulting ownership structure of the corporation is characterized by the presence of a large block-holder. The importance of this protection is that a new large block-holder weakens the potential disciplining role of the market. In other words, mandatory bids provide a fair exit to shareholders when a change of control takes place that is not easy to reverse.

Compare the same rule in a system in which the ownership structure is concentrated, and the largest shareholders typically hold a percentage higher than the threshold triggering the mandatory bid. In that context, the practical effect of the rule is that whoever aims at obtaining control must be ready to buy all the outstanding shares. Needless to say, rendering the acquisition more expensive might help the controlling shareholder to fend off an undesired suitor.

In a similar vein, the board neutrality rule can also lead to dramatically different consequences depending on the ownership structure of the corporation. This rule provides that when a tender offer is launched, the directors of the target corporation cannot initiate or continue any action that might frustrate the success of the offer without obtaining the approval of the shareholders' meeting. Once again, when the ownership structure is widespread, and the real agency problem is between directors and managers as against relatively dispersed shareholders, required approval by shareholders' meeting empowers the investors. This is especially true if—as Armour and Skeel show to be the case in the U.K.—organized and competent institutional investors, able to make informed decisions, are present and actively participate in the shareholders' meeting.

Conversely, when the ownership structure is concentrated and there are strong controlling shareholders, the real agency problem is not between directors and managers, on the one hand, and dispersed equity investors, on the other, but rather between majority and minority shareholders. A resolution of the shareholders' meeting in that context does not really address the crucial issue. More simply, when there is a controlling shareholder holding more than forty percent of the voting shares, a defensive measure against a hostile bid voted by the shareholders' meeting is unlikely to resolve the inherent conflict of interest between incumbent, entrenched controllers able to extract private benefits from the corporation and minority investors that might welcome a value-maximizing bid.

[. . .]

[T]he mandatory bid might appear favorable to minority shareholders in the case of a friendly acquisition where the existing controlling shareholder sells its participation, or a significant part thereof, to an acquirer. In such a scenario, the same price per share recognized by the seller must be offered to all of the shareholders. However, the parties will take this element into account in their negotiations, thus raising as a preliminary issue whether the new rule might also deter friendly takeovers.

[. . .]

Together with the mandatory bid mechanism, the non-frustration prohibition—also called "board neutrality" or the "passivity rule"—is the landmark difference between U.S. and U.K. approaches to takeovers. The degree of freedom enjoyed by American directors in structuring and deploying pre- and post-bid defenses, with the only substantive limitation being their fiduciary duties, is unknown in the U.K. and in those

European countries that have adopted the U.K. approach. The non-frustration prohibition of the General Principle 3 of Rule 21 of the U.K. Takeover Code prevents directors from either adopting or setting into motion most post-bid defenses. It also requires an explicit vote by the general shareholders' meeting. Extensive debate exists whether greater leeway in resisting a takeover—as is the case in the U.S.—favors shareholders. However, with a caveat that will be discussed later, it cannot be denied that board neutrality and shareholder choice in the U.K. were perceived and introduced as protections against directors' and managers' conflicts of interest in a takeover contest. This purpose is confirmed in the legislative history of the provision.

A recent and insightful analysis, however, questions whether this rule is truly important or merely illusory. David Kershaw persuasively argues that in the very jurisdiction where the non-frustration rule developed, most takeover defenses would also require shareholder approval in the absence of this rule. General company law principles, he argues, end up requiring the same. More precisely, Kershaw concludes that "in the absence of the non-frustration prohibition not only would post-bid, directors-controlled [takeover defenses] require pre-bid shareholders consent but when made available there is limited scope to use them for entrenchment purposes".

To the extent that this theory is well-grounded in the U.K., even without a detailed analysis of corporate law in civil law systems, it is fair to say that in countries such as Italy, a similar conclusion would be even more justified. In these systems, the extent and relevance of the competences of the shareholders' meeting versus the directors are even broader than in common law systems. [. . .] The issuing of option rights to subscribe or acquire the target's shares at a discount, as well as most business combinations (e.g., mergers, spin-offs, contributions in kind), are used to increase the corporation's capital. These [actions, in most European continental systems] are [generally] subject to shareholders' approval independent of the passivity rule. [. . .]

Independent of the scope of the non-frustration rule, the crucial point is that determining at shareholders' meetings whether defenses in systems where the most important agency problem is between controlling shareholders holding a majority of the shares and minority investors may not be in the best interest of the minority shareholders.

Needless to say, such a rule is better than nothing. The fact that a defense must be approved (or re-approved) by the shareholders' meeting implies several important advantages for minorities. First and foremost, it has the advantage of increasing the transparency of the adoption of a frustrating action. In fact, even if a defense adopted unilaterally by the directors would also be subject to specific disclosure obligations if it involved price-sensitive information, passage through the shareholders' meeting allows organized minorities to discuss the measure and to obtain further information from the directors. In addition, the existence of a shareholders' meeting resolution creates at least the potential for legal action, such as challenging the resolution. It may create the potential for obtaining a preliminary injunction from the court inhibiting the adoption of the defense. The resolution might be challenged, for instance, on the grounds that the majority shareholder has a conflict of interest or that it is exercising its power in an abusive manner. Even if sustaining claims of this type would be very difficult, it is at least less improbable than if the decision were taken only by the directors.

NOTES AND QUESTIONS

1.   Do you find that the explanation offered by Professors Armour and Skeel for the differences between takeover regulation in the U.S. and in the U.K. is convincing? Have you ever thought how geographical proximity or dispersion of legislatures, regulators, judges and lobbies can influence the rule-making process? Discuss.

2.   Professor Ventoruzzo argues, basically, that the mandatory bid can be a defensive tool *en travesti*: when the controlling shareholder owns more than the triggering threshold, the mandatory bid can help entrench the incumbents. Similarly, he argues that in a system with concentrated ownership, letting the shareholders' meeting—which basically means the controlling shareholder—decide on defensive measures might be like asking the fox to guard the henhouse. Do you agree? To be fair, he also indicates some possible positive effects for minority shareholders of the mandatory bid and the board neutrality rule: can you identify them?

3.   The empirical evidence seems to confirm, or at least not to disprove, Professor Ventoruzzo's claims. Consider, for example, the low number of hostile tender offers launched in Italy from the 1990s through today: this data might be interpreted as a sign of the fact that, under the European rules, incumbents can entrench themselves and scare away any hostile bidder.

4.   Based on what you know of the Japanese law on takeovers, do you think that the considerations of Armour, Skeel, and Ventoruzzo might also apply to this system?

5.   To conclude our analysis of defensive measures, before moving to other systems, we want to mention one additional idea worth of consideration. As it should be clear, there are some defenses that a corporation can adopt before going public, such as the poison pill and other measures designed to entrench control (e.g. multiple voting shares). One scholar has considered the adoption of takeover defenses at the IPO stage from a market perspective: Sharon Hannes, *The Market for Takeover Defenses*, 101 NW. U. L. REV. 125 (2007). In this fascinating study, in short, Professor Hannes argues that when a corporation decides to go public with or without defenses ("shielded" or "unshielded"), it does not (or should not) take

this decision in a vacuum, but also in light of the prevailing structure of listed corporations in this respect. If most corporations are shielded, bidders will be willing to pay a higher price and premium for the few unshielded ones, other things being equal. At least in the absence of a controlling shareholder, therefore, when not many unshielded corporations are present, there might be a stronger incentive to go public without—or with weaker—defenses. More specifically, investors purchasing shares in the IPO will be willing to pay a higher price for unshielded (potential) targets. This dynamic might result in oscillations around a market equilibrium in terms of shielded versus unshielded listed corporations. This insightful theoretical intuition seems to be at least partially confirmed by empirical evidence (*see* Kose John & Dalisa Kadyrzhanova, *Does Board Classification Matter for Industry Rivals? Evidence of Spillover Effects in the Market for Corporate Control*, 2009, working paper on file with Authors).

TAKEOVER REGULATION, HARMONIZATION, REGULATORY COMPETITION, AND LEGAL TRANSPLANTS: EUROPE, U.S., CHINA, INDIA, AND BRAZIL

What is the effect of regulatory competition and harmonization efforts on the regulation of takeovers? Let's start with European law. So far we have referred primarily to the 2004 Takeover Directive, which offers a good sense of the European regulatory approach in this area; there are, however, some important caveats we have to make with respect to the way in which the Directive has been implemented in the different Member States. The Directive had been embroiled in political controversy for almost twenty years, especially due to concerns of some governments that the new rules could make national champions vulnerable to takeovers by foreign firms. In fact, approval of the Directive was only possible thanks to compromise, in the form of making the most contentious rules not mandatory, but simply optional. The Directive, in other words, sets forth a common legal framework, but leaves to Member States lots of freedom on if and how to implement the different rules. It provides, in other words, a quite minimal level of harmonization and in fact, according to some, no real harmonization at all; while others even argue that the Article 12 option, creating as it does a two-track regulatory environment for takeovers, has made the Directive pointless. Whatever the case may be, there is flexibility with respect—for example—to the definition of "control" that triggers the mandatory offer on all the outstanding shares, on the calculation of the minimum price of the mandatory offer, on the exemptions and extensions of the obligation to launch an offer, and—particularly important for our purposes—even on the adoption of the board neutrality rule, one of the "pillars" of the U.K.

approach which inspired the Directive. In addition, also another rule designed to facilitate efficient hostile takeovers, the "breakthrough rule" set forth in Article 11 of the Thirteenth Directive, is optional.

We have not previously explained the breakthrough rule, so let's open a parenthesis here and spend a few moments on this rule. The board neutrality rules deals with defenses decided and adopted during a hostile offer; a corporation or its controlling shareholders can however implement many other legal devices before any hostile takeover is attempted, designed to entrench control or at least make a non-negotiated acquisition very difficult. Some of these devices can be effective without any need for specific action when a hostile takeover is launched. We have seen examples of these "control enhancing devices" throughout this book: shareholders' agreements limiting the free transferability of the shares, dual-class share structures with multiple voting shares, supermajority requirements to approve transactions often necessary to complete an acquisition, such as a merger, and so on. The very existence of similar provisions can deter potential suitors.

The breakthrough rule aims at curbing the paralyzing effect of these devices on the market for corporate control, limiting the powers of the incumbents. The rule was also intended to level the playing field across Europe, since the corporate law systems of different countries allow different control enhancing devices. In order to achieve these goals, Article 11 of the Thirteenth Directive provides two things. First, when an offer is made public, restrictions on the transfer of shares and voting agreements, either provided in the bylaws of the target corporation or in shareholders' agreements, are not enforceable until the end of the offer. In other words, for example, a shareholder normally bound by a right of first refusal would be free to tender the shares to the bidder without incurring any negative legal consequence. Second, if the offer has been particularly successful (i.e., more than 75% of the outstanding voting shares have been tendered), most restrictions designed to undermine the position of the successful bidder are suspended: voting caps, multiple voting rights, supermajority requirements, and the like, are neutralized, therefore sterilizing defenses that could hinder the reorganizational goals of the new controlling shareholder.

That's all interesting in theory, however, as you can imagine, also the breakthrough rule (as the board neutrality one) prompted significant opposition from some legislatures. The consequence? In this case as well, the rule has been made optional, and Member States are not required to mandate it (again the "Portuguese compromise").

Therefore, both the board neutrality rules and the breakthrough rule are optional, and Member States can decide not to mandate them: in this case, however, they must allow corporations to adopt these provisions in their bylaws (the idea being that if the market appreciates them, managers and shareholders might be inclined to opt-in those provisions). In addition, if the national legislature mandates either board neutrality or breakthrough rule, it can make them applicable only if reciprocity is respected, meaning only if the bidder is subject to similar restrictions limiting its ability to resist hostile acquisitions (Article 12 of the Directive). The result is that very, very few European companies are subject to the breakthrough rule.

Going back to our panoramic view, the bottom line here is that most provisions of the Directive are, in fact, optional, or at least Member States have significant flexibility in implementing them. Let's take a general look, with the help of the following table, at how some of the major provisions of Directive 2004/25 have been implemented in different Member States (please note that the table requires some inevitable simplification, and some more nuanced details of the different systems are not indicated; the overall picture is, however, accurate).

	France	Germany	Italy	Spain	United Kingdom
event triggering mandatory tender offer	purchase of 30% of voting rights	purchase of 30% of voting rights	purchase of 30% of voting rights or 25% of voting rights on the appointment of or removal of directors small and medium corporations can opt in their bylaws for a different threshold, between 25 and 40%	purchase of 30% of voting rights or appointment of more than half the directors in 24 months	purchase of 30% of voting rights
minimum price	highest price paid by the bidder for the shares in the last 12 months	highest price paid by the bidder for the shares in the last 6 months	highest price paid by the bidder for the shares in the last 12 months	highest price paid by the bidder for the shares in the last 12 months	highest price paid by the bidder for the shares in the last 12 months

board neutrality rule	not mandated by law, issuers can adopt it in the bylaws, and in this case can decide if it is subject to reciprocity or not (before 2014 mandated by law, but subject to reciprocity)	not mandated by law, issuers can adopt it in the bylaws, and in this case it is subject to reciprocity	provided by law as a default rule, and subject to reciprocity, but issuers can opt out in their bylaws	mandated by law, but subject to reciprocity	mandated by law, not subject to reciprocity
breakthrough rule	not mandated by law, issuers can adopt it in the bylaws, and in this case it is subject to reciprocity	not mandated by law, issuers can adopt it in the bylaws, and in this case it is subject to reciprocity	not mandated by law, issuers can adopt it in the bylaws, and in this case it is subject to reciprocity (but in case of tender offer shareholders' agreements are not enforceable)	not mandated by law, issuers can adopt it in the bylaws, and in this case it is subject to reciprocity	not mandated by law

As even this partial sketch makes clear, the degree of harmonization achieved by the directive is limited, and local departures from the default rules of the directive can be interpreted as a form of regulatory competition: Member States have adopted rules that they consider protective of national interests, in particular designed at fencing out a foreign hostile bidder that might take over local corporations and possibly adversely affect employment.

A particularly interesting example of how Member States can use the flexibility embedded in the Directive is the recent (August 2014) Italian reform of the mandatory bid rules. Before these new rules, under Italian law whoever acquired 30% of the voting shares of a listed corporation had to launch a tender offer on all the voting shares. This rule is still applicable, but one additional threshold triggering the bid had been added: 25%, when no other shareholder owns more. More relevant for us here, the new rules allow the bylaws of small and medium listed corporations (defined based on gross sales and market capitalization) to provide for a different threshold triggering the mandatory bid, in between 20 and 40% of the voting shares. By lowering the triggering threshold, mandatory bids are made more likely and hostile acquisitions more expensive. The new provisions can be interpreted as a protection of controlling shareholders against unwelcomed suitors, and allow shareholders to control the corporation with a smaller investment. In fact, as we have discussed above, the mandatory bid can represent a sort of defensive measure, especially when the existing controlling shareholder owns a participation higher than the triggering threshold (not surprisingly, in some U.S. States, provisions that have effects similar to the mandatory tender offer rule are regarded as defensive measures). In this perspective, consider the case of a listed corporation controlled by a shareholder owning 23% of the voting shares. Under the previous regime, which set the triggering threshold at 30%, in theory a hostile acquisition could have been successful without triggering the mandatory tender offer, if the buyer would have obtained, for example, 28% of the voting rights. Under the new approach, on the other hand, the controlling shareholder could set the triggering threshold at 20% and therefore be protected from hostile acquisitions by the mandatory bid mechanism. It will be interesting to test empirically, in the next few years, if Italian small and medium corporations—or, better, their shareholders—will take advantage of this new option.

The recent Italian reform is also interesting because it allows bylaws, and therefore a private contract, to define the triggering threshold of the offer. This raises two questions: one of compatibility with European law, and a more general theoretical question on the role of private ordering in this area. With respect to the former, Article 5 of the Takeover Directive states, "The percentage of voting rights which confers control for the purposes of [mandating the tender offer on all the voting shares] and the method of its calculation shall be determined by the rules of the Member State in which the company has its registered office." Someone has therefore objected that the legislature, and *not* the governing documents of the corporation, should determine the triggering threshold. This interpretation seems, however, too narrow and one might reply that the Directive simply requires the Member State to set the rules to calculate "control": it does not seem to prevent a Member State from doing so by "delegating" the definition of control to corporate bylaws.

The second, more theoretical question, is to what extent it is desirable that the statutory regulation of takeovers does not include mandatory provisions, but only default ones, therefore leaving the matter to contractual freedom. Should the takeover regime be determined at the level of the single corporation? The answer, of course, depends on your faith in the efficiency of the "market for corporate bylaws." It depends, in other words, on whether you think that investors can effectively appreciate takeovers rules articulated in the bylaws of single corporations, effectively "price" them, and therefore effectively cause incumbents to internalize their preferences and opt for Pareto-efficient rules. Some authors believe in this ability of the market, and therefore suggest the adoption of almost entirely optional rules (*see*, for example, L. Enriques, R. J. Gilson, and A. Pacces, *The Case for an Unbiased Takeover Law (With an Application to the European Union)*, 4 HARVARD BUS. L. REV. 85 (2014)). We are more skeptical about the virtues of private ordering in this area, but the issue offers the occasion for an interesting discussion. For example, if takeover rules should be flexible, do you find preferable to have a default rule in favor of incumbents, and corporations can opt-in a rule more protective of investors, or the other way around? If the level of protections against hostile takeovers is set by a resolution of the shareholders' meeting, what is the role of supermajority provisions?

France has also used the flexibility of the Directive to enact rules designed to protect incumbents against takeovers. To begin with, it reduced the threshold for a mandatory bid from 33% to 30% in 2010: as we have seen, a lower triggering participation might mean more expensive hostile takeovers. In 2014, the board neutrality rule was abandoned and the right of information of the employees' council strengthened. Also the fact that "loyalty shares" (discussed in Chapter 4) have become the default rule in 2014 can be considered an anti-takeover device: when the shareholders' meeting votes on a defensive measure, long-term shareholders will have proportionately more influence than more recent ones, including the bidder. The breakthrough rule (Article 11 of the Takeover Directive) could curb the effect of loyalty shares, but as seen in the above table, the rules is not mandatory in France.

As French loyalty shares suggest, the barriers to takeovers do not only depend on takeover rules, but also on other corporate law rules. There are countless examples. Consider, for instance, corporate governance rules that we have studied in Chapter 5. As we mentioned in that part of the book, many commentators have argued that the two-tier German system of governance represents, in itself, a possible protection against takeovers, because a new shareholder, before being able to control the management of the corporation, not only has to change the composition of the supervisory board, but must also wait for the new members of the supervisory board to change the members of the managing board. According to some, this apparently minor glitch could contribute to raising the cost of a takeover. In addition, and probably more substantively, German *Mitbestimmung*, the mandatory representation of employees in the supervisory board, can also make German boards particularly averse to hostile takeovers. Employees' representatives, quite clearly, will not be particularly pleased with acquisition plans aiming at "greater efficiency," if this means layoffs.

We discussed that optional rules and differences in the corporate laws of the Member States have significantly limited the harmonizing effects of the Takeover Directive. Should it, however, be considered a total failure for the purposes of creating a levelled playing field? We believe a similar evaluation would be too harsh. There are other less controversial features of the Directive that have helped or will help to bring about a level playing field for takeovers in Europe. If nothing else, the Directive has contributed to the development, in Europe, of a "common language" on takeover among businesspeople, policy makers, judges, practitioners, and legal and economic scholars. It has contributed to identifying crucial aspects of takeover regulation, and to more easily classifying alternative takeover regimes and rules as more or less in favor of the different stakeholders. That might be considered a not particularly rich consolation prize, but we believe it is not irrelevant.

It should be noted, on the other hand, that also in the U.S. states have competed to attract corporations through the enactment of rules designed to protect incumbents against hostile takeovers. We refer, of course, to so-called "anti-takeover statutes." Some of the earlier versions of these statutes, based on merit review of hostile offers by state bodies, have been held unconstitutional because they were in violation of the commerce clause and pre-empted by the Williams Act (*see* Edgar v. Mite Corp., 457 U.S. 624 (1982)); subsequent generations of anti-takeover statutes, based on corporate governance rules, have however been upheld in court (*see* CTS Corp. v. Dynamics Corp. of Am., 481 U.S. 69, 94 (1987)), and they offer a broad variety of techniques to protect incumbents. We find "control share acquisition" statutes, providing limitations to the voting rights of whoever acquires a certain threshold of shares, unless the other shareholders approve the acquisition; "fair price" statutes, pursuant to which business combinations with relevant shareholders (for example, holding more than 15% of the shares) must be approved by a supermajority vote unless they offer a minimum price to existing shareholders; "cash-out" statutes, according to which if a person obtains control, she must offer to purchase the remaining shares at the highest price paid (as you can see, the economic effects of these provisions are similar to the ones of the mandatory tender offer); and "business combination" statutes, which limit the ability of large shareholders to carry on mergers and other transactions for a few years after the acquisition of the shares unless those transactions are approved with a supermajority vote.

But what about other legal systems, and in particular "BRIC" countries? Have the regulatory approaches adopted in Europe or in the U.S. been successfully exported to those jurisdictions? The following excerpt very effectively, even if briefly, illustrates the situation in China, India, and Brazil.

JOHN ARMOUR, JACK B. JACOBS, CURTIS J. MILHAUPT, THE
EVOLUTION OF HOSTILE TAKEOVER REGIMES IN DEVELOPED
AND EMERGING MARKETS: AN ANALYTICAL FRAMEWORK[1]

52 Harv. Int'l L.J. 219 (2011)

Despite the absence of market activity, the institutional landscape for hostile takeovers in the three emerging markets we examine is far from barren, as we sketch below.

1. China

State ownership of enterprise and regulatory requirements for major investments in Chinese firms creates an environment where there is little immediate prospect of a market for corporate control developing in China. The transformation of state-owned enterprises into publicly traded companies in the process of China's market opening has only been partial—indeed, the term used is corporatization, not privatization. Organs of the central and provincial governments, or related affiliates, still control a majority of the shares of most companies listed on the Shanghai and Shenzhen stock exchanges. Until recently, shares held by the state were not even legally tradable except to other state-affiliated investors. In addition, the approvals of various government agencies, such as the Ministry of Commerce and the China Securities Regulatory Commission ("CSRC"), are required to complete a major investment in a Chinese listed company. Ministry approvals, in turn, are predicated on board and shareholder approval of the transaction. Thus, without the cooperation of the state, an outside investor cannot gain control of a publicly traded Chinese firm.

Nevertheless, China has a highly developed takeover regime, at least as a formal matter. China's approach, like that of Japan, is a blend of the U.K. and Delaware models, refracted through distinctive national institutions. The Securities Law ("China Securities Law") and related rules of the CSRC contain a partial mandatory bid rule triggered by thirty percent share ownership. Under the CSRC's Takeover Rules ("CSRC Rules"), however, the agency can waive the mandatory bid rule for negotiated share acquisitions; it frequently uses this power. This exemption is significant because negotiated share acquisitions are a common means of merging state-owned or state-affiliated enterprises in China, at the instruction of high-level government bodies such as the State Council (China's cabinet) or the State-Owned Assets Supervision and Administration Commission ("SASAC") (the state agency that acts as a holding company and monitor for the largest state-owned enterprises). Moreover, since 2006, a mandatory bid need only be for a minimum of five percent of the outstanding shares, which greatly dilutes its effect. These measures avoid the problem of mandatory bid rules stifling takeovers in

---

[1]   Footnotes omitted.

countries where there are controlling shareholders by requiring control premia to be offered to minority shareholders as well.

Consistent with the U.K. approach, the CSRC Rules permit target company boards to take post-bid defensive measures only if approved by shareholders. At the same time, however, the CSRC Rules also contain Delaware-like fiduciary standards that govern the adoption of defenses. They require target boards of directors to meet their "duties of loyalty and diligence to the company" and "treat all offerors fairly." They further specify that defensive measures "shall be beneficial to the interests of the company and its shareholders," and that "directors shall not abuse their power to create obstacles to takeovers." While at first glance these rules may resemble a potentially unruly mix of the U.K. and Delaware approaches, it should be recalled that although U.K. directors are also subject to fiduciary duties regarding the adoption of takeover defenses, these duties are rarely enforced because compliance with the more exacting board neutrality standard necessarily subsumes compliance with the underlying fiduciary duties. Still, it is noteworthy that Chinese lawmakers have included explicit reference to fiduciary duties in the CSRC Rules.

As in Japan, China's approach to enforcement is mixed. However, instead of a Japanese-style blend of ex ante stock exchange approval and ex post judicial review, China has engrafted a U.K.-style specialized panel model upon more traditional regulatory approaches featuring high levels of state control. In U.K. fashion, a specialized panel handles interpretive issues arising out of takeover transactions and considers revisions to takeover regulations. However, unlike the U.K. Takeover Panel, the Chinese panel is not an independent organ. Rather, it is under the jurisdiction of the CSRC. The panel has only advisory authority, leaving the CSRC as the ultimate enforcement agent. At this stage, it is not clear whether Chinese courts would accept cases involving contests for corporate control.

2.   India

India has to date experienced only a handful of unsolicited takeover attempts, all of which have failed. The primary obstacle to hostile bids in India is the pervasive control of public firms by founding families. Family ownership is buttressed by the attitudes of Indian financial institutions, which have historically been staunch supporters of controlling shareholders, valuing business and personal relations over financial returns based solely on share ownership. These obstacles have been reinforced by a foreign investment regulatory regime that is highly protective of incumbent management.

India's legal regime for hostile takeovers, like that of China, bears a superficial resemblance to the City Code. India's Takeover Code ("India

Takeover Code") was first introduced in 1997. The India Takeover Code contains restrictions on the conduct of target managers once a bid has been launched and an "open offer" (mandatory bid) rule requiring a general offer to be made by persons exceeding a specified control threshold, set since 1998 at fifteen percent, at a price no lower than the best price paid by the acquirer for the target's shares in the previous six months. The Code is also promulgated and enforced by a specialist agency, the Securities Exchange Board of India ("SEBI"). Moreover, SEBI regulations generally prohibit issuance of warrants with an exercise price below a specified minimum linked to the recent trading price of the target company stock, thereby eliminating the possibility of adopting a U.S.-style poison pill at the pre-bid stage.

Despite its ostensible similarity to the U.K. approach, the Indian Takeover Code is highly attuned to Indian shareholding structures, which, as noted, center on controlling shareholders, typically families (known under Indian corporate law as "promoters"). In contrast to the United Kingdom's mandatory bid rule, acquirers that trigger an open offer requirement under the Indian Takeover Code need only offer to acquire an additional twenty percent, as opposed to all, of the remaining shares. A full-blown mandatory bid rule can hinder control transactions where there are blockholders, as it requires bidders to offer the same premium to all minority shareholders as is offered to a blockholder. Thus, like the Chinese rule, the Indian rule is a compromise that requires only a partial sharing of premia with minority shareholders.

At the same time, the Indian Takeover Code contains several channels through which blockholders in public firms may consolidate their holdings and successfully resist foreign takeovers. The principal mechanism for promoter protection is an exemption from the open offer requirement for "creeping acquisitions." Under the Code, a shareholder that owns between fifteen percent and fifty-five percent of a company's shares may continue to acquire up to five percent of the company's stock each year without making an open offer. Other exemptions from the open offer requirement provide similar ways for controlling families to strengthen their positions. One exemption that was removed from the Code in 2002 permitted preferential share allotments to promoters. An exemption still exists for "inter se" transfers of shares among family members or group companies. Observing this pattern, one commentator concluded that the ostensible similarity to the U.K. City Code was highly misleading: "Far from legitimising [sic] the contestability of control, India's takeover regulation has been the single most important enabling factor in the consolidation of promoter stakes against any possible takeover threat."

3.   Brazil

As in India, the chief obstacle to hostile bids in Brazil is the presence
of a controlling shareholder, typically the founding family, in many
Brazilian publicly traded firms. Also, as in India, corporate law is highly
protective of controlling shareholders. Indeed, a major policy goal of
Brazilian corporate law has historically been to foster minority
investment without jeopardizing founder control. The Corporations Law
of 1976 allowed up to two-thirds of a public company's outstanding shares
to be non-voting. A legislative reform in 2001 reduced the allowable
maximum of non-voting stock to fifty percent, but firms that were already
publicly traded as of that date were exempted from the more stringent
regime. A mandatory bid rule was instituted in the 2001 legal reform, but
the rule only applies to voting stock, and the bid price may be as low as
eighty percent of the price paid for the control block. Brazilian corporate
law contains no specific provisions on takeover defenses, but given the
situation just described, there has been no particular need for defensive
measures. Brazil has experienced almost no hostile takeover activity in
its history.

Developments over the past five years, however, have altered this
institutional landscape. A new segment of the São Paulo Stock Exchange
("Novo Mercado," or New Market) was established in December 2000 to
promote the growth of companies not tied to established corporate groups
and to improve the corporate governance of public companies in Brazil.
The Novo Mercado has higher corporate governance standards than the
traditional Exchange, including requirements that all shares be voting
shares and that financial statements comply with either U.S. or
International GAAP. A wave of IPOs on the Novo Mercado in the mid-
2000s created a meaningful number of publicly traded firms with more
dispersed share ownership than the typical Brazilian public corporation,
creating at least the potential for future hostile takeover activity.

Many of the companies that went public on the Novo Mercado, as
well as publicly traded firms on other sections of the Brazilian Stock
Exchange without controlling shareholders, adopted anti-takeover
measures in their by-laws. Known as the "Brazilian poison pill," these
measures require a shareholder who reaches a specified threshold of
share ownership (generally ten to thirty-five percent) to make a
mandatory bid for all remaining shares at a specified price, typically a
substantial premium over the current trading price of the target
company's stock. Shareholders who vote to remove the by-law provision
are also required to make an offer to purchase all outstanding shares. In
response to investor lobbying, the Brazilian securities regulatory
authority Comissão de Valores Mobiliários ("CVM"), issued a policy
statement ("Parecer Normativo" or Normative Rule) in 2009 indicating
that it would not enforce this mandatory bid rule against shareholders

voting to eliminate the by-law provision, on the grounds that the cost of potential entrenchment posed by such provisions would outweigh the benefits. The policy statement is nonbinding, however, and the legal status of such by-law provisions is not entirely clear as of this writing.

NOTES AND QUESTIONS

1.   Based on the above observations, do you think that the U.K./European regulatory approach or the American one has been more successfully transplanted in other systems? Why? Is it easier to "export" to a foreign jurisdiction a few statutory provisions, or doctrines and principles distilled through decades of judicial precedents? Do you think this factor might be relevant in this perspective?

2.   What economic, political, and cultural factors might concur to explain how China, India, and Brazil regulate takeovers, and how takeovers rules are actually enforced? Consider, in particular, the fairly extensive powers of the Chinese regulatory authorities to waive the mandatory bid requirement. What do you think might be reasons for such a provision, and what are its consequences? In India, on the other hand, the mandatory bid is triggered when someone acquires a certain threshold of shares and does not extend to all the outstanding shares, but only to 20% of them (partial offer). What do you think are the possible negative consequences of this provision from the perspective of shareholders, and the possible positive ones to stimulate an active market for control?

3.   What do you think might be the determinants of the failure or success of a legal transplant? And how do you define "failure" and "success" in this area? Corporate law and takeover rules in particular, as seen in this Chapter, have often been transplanted. Why? For further ideas on legal transplants in corporate law, see M. Ventoruzzo, *The Role of Comparative Law in Shaping Corporate Statutory Reforms,* 52 DUQ. L. REV. 151 (2014), also available as a paper on www.ssrn.com.

CHAPTER 11

INSIDER TRADING

■ ■ ■

INTRODUCTION

We started the previous chapter with the observation that takeovers are one of the few corporate law issues that have attracted the attention of moviemakers and moviegoers. Another one is insider trading, sometimes referred to also as "insider dealing." In fact, in Oliver Stone's *Wall Street* (spoiler alert!), the demise of villain-hero Gordon Gekko is due to insider trading charges. Also in the comedy *Trading Places* (1983) the plot involves insider trading and market manipulations on nothing less than frozen orange juice future contracts.

But what is insider trading? To use a very general definition, it is the prohibition to trade in securities while in possession of "inside" information: price sensitive information not publicly available, but rather obtained by reasons of a professional position of trust. The director of a listed corporation, for example, aware that his firm is about to patent a revolutionary (but still secret) procedure to produce steel, cannot purchase shares before the information is disclosed, hoping to obtain large gains when, after the innovation will become public, share prices will jump up. Violations of the prohibition can result in criminal and administrative sanctions, and in civil liability. Most modern legal systems prohibit insider trading, even if, as we will see, the regulatory approaches and specific rules vary significantly. Interestingly enough, in addition, notwithstanding growing enforcement efforts and harsh penalties, insider trading remains one of the most common violations of the securities laws worldwide (for a recent discussion of enforcement of insider trading in the Middle East and North Africa, for example, *see* A. Amico, *Corporate Governance Enforcement in the Middle East and North Africa: Evidence and Priorities*, OECD Corporate Governance Working Papers, No. 15, 2014).

As we discuss the materials in this chapter, please keep in mind—as we will see also below—that in most legal systems insider trading can result in both criminal and administrative sanctions, and can also be enforced by private litigants claiming damages. In fact, the combination or tension between public (both by prosecutors and regulatory agencies) and private enforcement of insider trading rules is itself an interesting comparative issue. Do not be surprised or confused, therefore, if in the following pages you will find both criminal and civil cases.

THE RATIONALES FOR THE INSIDER TRADING PROHIBITION

There are two basic rationales to prohibit insider trading. The first one is ethical. It seems unfair that insiders use privileged information to speculate, reaping large profits while other investors cannot benefit of similar positions. But there is also an explanation based on the efficiency and integrity of the market. Allowing insider trading might undermine investors' trust in the possibility to gain trading in securities, something that could hinder the attractiveness of financial markets and raise the cost of capital.

A way to look at the regulation of insider trading is through the lenses of the economist Eugene Fama, Nobel-prize laureate in 2013. In 1970 he published in the Journal of Finance an article entitled "*Efficient Capital Markets: A Review of Theory and Empirical Work*," based on his Ph.D. dissertation. In this work Fama distinguished three "levels" of information efficiency of a market, depending on the information that market prices incorporate. At the lower end of the spectrum there are markets with weak-form efficiency: in this case, market prices reflect effectively only information on historical prices, which means that it is impossible to earn extra profits simply relying on past price movements or, more precisely, that an analyst cannot predict the future better than other investors simply looking at past prices and, therefore, cannot beat the market in this way. Semi-strong (or semi-weak) efficient markets are markets in which the prices fully reflect all publicly available information, such as for example macroeconomic conditions and financial statements published by issuers. This means that the market is so quick ("efficient") in reacting to public information and adjusting prices that it is not possible to beat the market, or make extra profits, using publicly available information. Finally, a strongly efficient market is so good at processing information that prices reflect also private information, information not publicly available. In such a market, insiders cannot make a profit exploiting their information advantage, because the market is extremely effective in adjusting prices. As soon as an insider, e.g., starts buying, by doing this he is also disclosing his expectations on price movements, and in a strongly-efficient market other traders are so able in picking up this trend that prices immediately jump to the level that reflects the inside information As a side note, we should mention that economists have argued that the distinction between private and public information is more blurred than often imagined, and that most information falls in a continuum between these two extremes (K. R.

French, and R. Roll, *Stock Return Variances: The Arrival of Information and the Reaction of Traders*, 17 J. FIN. ECON. 5 (1986)).

But how good are markets in identifying and correctly pricing information? In other words, are markets efficient? Anecdotal evidence does not allow answering this question, but is very interesting. A tragic but interesting possible example of information efficiency is connected with the explosion of the space shuttle Challenger in 1986. The event was totally unexpected, and experts took several months to determine the causes of the accident (a faulty O-ring in one of the two rocket boosters), and identify the contractor who provided the defective component (Morton Thiokol, a listed corporation). However, on the very day of the accident, shortly after the worldwide televised disaster, the securities of Morton Thiokol were being massively sold. By the end of the trading day, Morton Thiokol daily stock return was almost −12%, a significant loss in comparison with the previous three months. The stock of other NASA contractors involved in the space shuttle project, such as Lockheed and Martin Marietta, also experienced some sales on the day of the accident, but nothing comparable to Morton Thiokol: the market allocated responsibility correctly in a matter of minutes (an interesting article on this case, and its meaning in terms of information efficiency, is M. T. Maloney, J. H. Mulherin, *The complexity of price discovery in an efficient market: the stock market reaction to the Challenger crash*, 9 Journal of Corporate Finance 453 (2003)). Market efficiency, or a case of insider trading?

Counterexamples of cases in which, on the other hand, markets have not been able to detect the truth, and insiders have reaped huge profits, also abound. One of the most enthralling, for its momentous historical relevance, is the story of how Nathan Rothschild, of the notorious banking (and wine, they own Château Lafite) dynasty, profited from Napoleon's defeat at Waterloo in 1815. According to one account, the 38-year-old Nathan, already an established trader and entrepreneur in London, was informed very early of the victory of Wellington by one of his agents on the continent. In the words of Frederic Morton (*The Rothschilds: A Family Portrait*, 1962):

> "A moment later he was on his way to London (beating Wellington's envoy by many hours) to tell the government that Napoleon had been crushed: but his news was not believed, because the government had just heard of the English defeat at Quatre Bras. Then he proceeded to the Stock Exchange.
>
> Another man in his position would have sunk his work into consols [British government bonds], already weak because of Quatre Bras. But this was Nathan Rothschild. He leaned against "his" pillar. He did not invest. He sold. He dumped consols.

Consols dropped still more. "Rothschild knows," the whisper rippled through the 'Change. "Waterloo is lost." Nathan kept on selling, consols plummeted—until, a split second before it was too late, Nathan suddenly bought a giant parcel for a song. Moments afterwards the great news broke, to send consols soaring. We cannot guess the number of hopes and savings wiped out by this engineered panic."

The story sounds too good to be true, and in fact historians consider it apocryphal and based on an anti-Semitic pamphlet of the nineteenth century. But there are plenty of real examples of market failures to process information, beginning with the 2007–2008 Global Financial Crisis.

Leaving aside intriguing anecdotes, and going back to Fama's classification, more systematic empirical studies suggest that most markets have weak-form efficiency, while it is to this day highly debated if developed financial markets are efficient in the semi-strong sense. No market, however, is efficient in the strong sense: insiders trading on the basis of secret information can always obtain extra profits. In a way, the legal prohibition against insider trading is designed to "correct" the lack of strong efficiency in financial markets or, better, to prevent insiders from taking advantage of this feature of the market.

In many countries, however, insider trading was not illegal until fairly recently, and on the contrary it was quite common and largely considered not only socially acceptable, but a necessary form of additional compensation for business executives. Even in the United States, one of the first legal systems to regulate the phenomenon, insider trading was rampant through the 1920s. In that period, for example, Joe Kennedy, the father of future U.S. President JFK and himself the future first chairman of the Securities and Exchange Commission, while a member of the brokerage firm Hayden, Stone & Co., allegedly engaged extensively in practices that by today's standards would be considered illegal insider trading and market manipulation (so much so that apparently, when Franklin D. Roosevelt appointed him to the newly created SEC, somebody asked him why he had picked such a crook. Roosevelt's reply: "Takes one to catch one"). In fact, the idea that information transparency and efficiency were not only unimportant, but potentially damaging for the market, was so engraved in the industry's culture that when the New Deal introduced rules designed to protect investors, including insider trading, several professionals lamented that "grass would grow on Wall Street."

Prominent scholars have clad these sentiments in a scientific vest, and a minority of scholars still advocates that insider trading should not be banned. Among others, and with different arguments, this position has been taken by Henry Manne, Milton Friedman (also a winner of the Nobel prize in Economics), Daniel Fischel, and Frank H. Easterbrook. Take a look at the following 1983 article.

DENNIS W. CARLTONA AND DANIEL R. FISCHEL, THE REGULATION OF INSIDER TRADING[1]

35 Stan. L. Rev. 857 (1983)

[. . .]

Since the firm's shareholders value the ability to control information that flows to the stock market, they may also value insider trading because it gives the firm an additional method of communicating and controlling information. If insiders trade, the share price will move closer to what it would have been had the information been disclosed. How close will depend on the amount of "noise" surrounding the trade. The greater the ability of market participants to identify insider trading, the more information such trading will convey. At the extreme, trading by insiders is as fully revealing as complete disclosure. But since insiders will limit the size of their positions because of risk aversion and will camouflage their trading to some degree, they convey less information by trading than that conveyed by (credible) full disclosure.

Several reasons explain why communicating information through insider trading may be of value to the firm. Through insider trading, a firm can convey information it could not feasibly announce publicly because an announcement would destroy the value of the information, would be too expensive, not believable, or—owing to the uncertainty of the information—would subject the firm to massive damage liability if it turned out ex post to be incorrect. Conversely, firms also could use insider trading to limit the amount of information to be reflected in price. Controlling the number of traders who have access to information may be easier than controlling how much information gets announced over time. In other words, announcement of information need not be continuous, while trading on inside information can be. Thus, insider trading gives firms a tool either to increase or to decrease the amount of information that is contained in share prices.

[. . .]

NOTES AND QUESTIONS

1.   The idea suggested by this excerpt is that trading by insiders is another way to convey information to the market. The very act of purchasing and selling shares "gives away" the expectations of the insiders and therefore, implicitly, their private information. The question, of course, is how quickly

---

[1]   Footnotes omitted.

and efficiently markets react, and how many investors might not be able to profit from the information effect. A possible answer is that if insider trading is prohibited, and in fact no one trades on inside information that is kept confidential, none will benefit from it. This might be true, but again the problem with insider trading is that *some* people gain much more than *others*. The "*others*" are generally not happy. You might argue that the prohibition against insider trading is an equalizer. In addition, supporters of free insider trading opine that even if insiders make a profit, it is generally not large enough to cause investors to flee the market. To this, others retort that if insider trading was allowed, insiders could easily obtain large financial resources from creditors to speculate, and that this behavior would in fact drive disadvantaged investors away from the market (George W. Dent, Jr., *Why Legalized Insider Trading Would Be a Disaster*, 38 DEL. J. CORP. L. 247 (2013)). What do you think?

2.   Can you come up with other possible arguments to legalize insider trading? Try answering this before continuing reading, and discuss this in class. One argument might be that insider trading is a so-called "victimless" crime. No one is really hurt: two consenting parties exchange securities with unequal information, one of them ends up with a larger gain, but this happens all the time for all sorts of possible reasons. Is this a good argument? Another argument to legalize insider trading is that in many markets different from securities ones, it is perfectly legal to strike a deal based on asymmetric information. Think, for example, of real estate: if I know that a little field hides a lucrative oil reservoir, I can purchase it without—at least in many legal systems—disclosing anything to the ignorant seller (unless I owe some kind of specific duty to the seller, for example if I have been hired to determine the value of the land). In fact, also in commodities markets insider trading laws are either absent or weakly enforced. Is this "special treatment" for shares, bonds, and other securities justified? On what basis? Others have even tinkered with free speech arguments: are prohibitions of insider trading (think, in particular, of prohibitions against tipping) a form of censorship? Does this idea fly? Is there a difference with other confidential obligations imposed by contract or statute? Finally, do you think it might make sense to distinguish between information that reflects negatively on market prices, and information that reflects positively, limiting insider trading prohibitions to the latter? (Hint: is negative information about corporation X less likely to be disclosed by corporation X? Additional hint for the discussion: is it always easy to distinguish, ex ante, how information will affect market prices?).

3.   Supporters of legalized insider trading are probably less vociferous than supporters of legalized marijuana, and probably less likely to be successful. As mentioned, most legal systems prohibit insider trading, and a change does not appear possible in the foreseeable future. A somehow related violation is market manipulation, in particular "information" market manipulation, consisting in disclosing false or misleading information in order to profit from the induced effect on market prices (to go back to *Trading*

Places, cited above, Dan Aykroyd and Eddie Murphy dupe the Duke brothers into buying frozen orange juice futures with a forged report on orange crops, a typical example of market manipulation). Under European law, as we will see, insider trading and market manipulation, although clearly different, are regulated in a coherent way under the common label of "market abuses." Well, after our discussion on the rationales for prohibiting insider trading, imagine for a moment that you are the enlightened dictator of a fictitious country and you must choose whether to prohibit market manipulations or insider trading, but you cannot prohibit both. Which one would you prohibit? Which one seems more dangerous and socially reprehensible? The question is not as fantastic as it might sound. You might not (we hope you do not) become the dictator of a fictitious country, but you might be an executive of a regulatory agency or a prosecutor with limited resources, and have a certain discretion in deciding whether to investigate and prosecute insider trading, market manipulations, or other violations.

* * *

A COMPARATIVE PERSPECTIVE ON INSIDER TRADING

In order to compare the U.S. and European Union approaches to insider trading, let's start with an overview of American law in the following article.

MARCO VENTORUZZO, COMPARING INSIDER TRADING IN THE UNITED STATES AND IN THE EUROPEAN UNION: HISTORY AND RECENT DEVELOPMENTS[2]

11 European Company and Financial Law Review 554 (2015)

In the European Union insider trading has been regulated much more recently than in the United States, and it can be argued that, at least traditionally, it has been more aggressively and successfully enforced in the United States than in the European Union. Several different explanations have been offered for this difference in enforcement attitudes, focusing in particular on resources of regulators devoted to contrasting this practice, but also diverging cultural attitudes toward insiders. This situation has evolved, however, and the prohibition of insider trading has gained traction also in Europe. Few studies have however focused on the substantive differences in the regulation of the phenomenon, especially with respect to their underlying tenets. [. . .]

The overly complex structure of the regulation of insider trading in the United States under section 10(b) of the 1934 Exchange Act and Rule 10b–5 is largely the product of case law and administrative regulations enacted by the SEC. Its defining feature is the questionable theory

---

[2]   Footnotes and paragraph numbers omitted.

embraced by the Supreme Court in the seminal U.S. v. Chiarella decision, pursuant to which insider trading requires the violation of a fiduciary duty. This notion has not only enormously complicated this important area of the law, but has also hindered enforcement actions and has led to the enactment of convoluted regulations to cover conducts that clearly conflict with the rationale of prohibiting insider trading. A more simple, elegant, and effective regulation would simply provide that anyone who obtains material non-public information concerning an issuer or a security because of his professional activity, or misappropriates it, should either disclose it (when allowed) or abstain from trading, and that tippees aware of the material and non-public nature of the information received should also disclose it or abstain from trading. This regulatory approach, generally referred to as "parity-of-information" theory, is the foundation of the prohibition against insider trading in the European Union. Interestingly enough, the parity-of-information theory was originally adopted also in the United States in the 1960s, only to be rejected by the Supreme Court in favor of the current fiduciary-duty based approach. [. . .]

It should however also be noted that, notwithstanding the different theoretical underpinnings of insider trading in the U.S. and in Europe, the practical scope of the two systems are largely similar, especially in the most egregious cases, even if important differences still exist. In the U.S., however, this result is reached through a [sometimes mind-boggling] web of case law, legislation and regulation. [. . .]

INSIDER TRADING IN THE U.S.: FROM PARITY OF INFORMATION TO BREACH OF FIDUCIARY DUTIES, TO MISAPPROPRIATION

Rule 10b–5 and Insider Trading: The Rise and Fall of the Equal Access to Information Theory.

The prohibition of insider trading based on Section 10(b) of the Exchange Act and rule 10b–5 thereunder developed through a non-systematic and sometimes contradictory series of cases, legislative acts and S.E.C. regulations. For this reason, the current prohibition can only be properly understood in the light of its historical context. We will therefore adopt an historic perspective to examine the applicable rules.

A first starting point is that when in 1942 the S.E.C. enacted Rule 10b–5 under Exchange Act section 10(b), it did not explicitly address insider trading; the rule, in fact, does not even contain a reference to this type of conduct, but is a broad and general anti-fraud provision. In relevant part, Rule 10b–5 makes it unlawful, for any person in connection with the purchase or sale of a security:

"(a) to employ any device, scheme, or artifice to defraud, (b) to make any untrue statement of a material fact or to omit to state a material fact necessary to make the statements made . . . not misleading, or (c) to engage in any act, practice or course of business which operates or would operate as a fraud or deceit on any person."

The history of how the provision was introduced confirms that when the S.E.C. adopted it, it did not consider its possible application to insider trading. Only in the 1960s the Commission started using rule 10b–5 to prosecute insider trading occurring on impersonal markets in an administrative procedure, *In re Cady, Roberts & Co.*

In this case the director of a registered corporation, J. Cheever Cowdin, was also a partner of Cady, Roberts & Co., a stock brokerage firm. In his capacity as director, Cowdin learned that the corporation was about to reduce its dividend, and shared this information with Robert M. Gintel, another partner of the brokerage firm. Gintel sold his clients' shares of the corporation before the dividend cut was announced, thus avoiding significant losses they might have otherwise suffered. The S.E.C. sanctioned Cady, Roberts & Co., arguing that a violation of Rule 10b–5 had occurred because Gintel traded while in possession of material, non-public information. This was the first instance in which the Commission introduced the concept of "disclose or abstain", and was based on the principle of equal access to information, according to which trading on the basis of material, non-public information was fraudulent under Rule 10b–5.

[. . .]

A couple of years after, in 1963, however, the Second Circuit adopted the principle of equal access to information in *S.E.C. v. Texas Gulf Sulphur*. The facts of this case, as with many other insider trading litigations, evoke the plot of a movie. In short, since 1959, Texas Gulf Sulphur began secretly to investigate the presence of precious minerals in an area in Ontario. Employees of the corporation involved with the surveys were explicitly asked to keep information concerning the possible discovery confidential. The surveys confirmed the presence of a rich ore deposit, and the corporation started acquiring land where the minerals could be mined. In 1963, when the information was still secret, employees of Texas Gulf Sulphur began to buy stock or options on stock of the corporation and tipped outsiders about the possible appreciation of the shares of the corporation. In fact, as news about the discovery began to become public, the price of the shares soared, granting to employees and their tippees a substantial profit. The S.E.C. brought a suit against the insiders alleging a violation of Rule 10b–5.

The Second Circuit [. . .] embraced the position of the S.E.C., holding that an insider in possession of material, non-public information, had to either disclose the information to the public or abstain from trading. The rationale for this decision was, once again, a theory of equality of access to information, according to which insiders could not take advantage of undisclosed information and all investors should be granted a similar set of information when trading.

This expansive notion of insider trading sent a shiver in financial and legal circles. The fear was that such a broad approach would result in unfair results that might hinder the development of active markets. When, seven years later, the Supreme Court considered the issue in the seminal case of *Chiarella v. U.S.*, the justices rejected the equality of access to information approach and curbed its potentially broad reach. In order to do so, the Court refused to accept that simply possessing material, non-public information imposed the duty to disclose or abstain, and required something more in order to find insider trading liability: a breach of a fiduciary duty owed by the insider to the investors with which he traded.

Fiduciary-Duty Based Insider Trading.

Even if well-known, the facts of *Chiarella* deserve a brief description. Pandrick Press, a financial printer that prepared tender offer materials for bidders, used codes to conceal the names of the corporations involved. Notwithstanding this precaution, one of Pandrick's employees, Vincent Chiarella, managed to figure out the name of the target corporation in a tender offer and bought securities in the corporation before the bid was announced. Obviously after the announcement the price of the shares of the target rose, and Chiarella sold them at a significant premium. Chiarella was found guilty of illegal insider trading both by the district court and the court of appeals of the Second Circuit on the basis of the equal access to information theory.

The Supreme Court, however, acquitted Chiarella, clearly stating that it refused to impose a general duty of all investors not to trade based on material, nonpublic information. In order to incur in liability for insider trading, the defendant needed also to have a duty to speak based on a fiduciary relationship with the party on the other side of the transaction. Pursuant to this view, Chiarella had no relationship with the shareholders of the target corporation from whom he bought the shares, and was therefore free to use the information he had. According to this approach, in other words, for insider trading liability two conditions need to be met: (a) trading on the basis of material, nonpublic information; (b) and violating a fiduciary duty to the investors with which the trade occurs. It follows that, for example, directors of an issuer might violate Rule 10b–5 by trading with their shareholders on the basis of inside information, but only because they owe them a fiduciary duty.

With this and following decisions, insider trading in the U.S. became indissolubly intertwined with the elusive concept of fiduciary duties, a circumstance that raised (and in many ways still raises) delicate legal issues, tension with other precedents, and a regulatory chase between the S.E.C. and judicial decisions in order to define the scope of the prohibition.

Probably the best example of this struggle is the adoption by the S.E.C. of rule 14e–3 under section 14(e) of the Williams Act just six months after Chiarella. Under the fiduciary duty theory introduced with Chiarella, supporters of a stricter regulation of insider trading clearly identified a void in the regulation of the phenomenon. To many it seemed unacceptable that Vincent Chiarella would escape liability; more generally, insider trading was basically not applicable in the context of tender offers. Non-insiders of the target who had access to information concerning an imminent tender offer could freely speculate on this information beating the market, because they had no fiduciary duties toward the shareholders of the target. The S.E.C. stepped in with rule 14e–3, which prohibits insiders of the bidder and target to tip confidential information on a tender offer, and any person possessing information on a tender offer from trading in the target's securities if substantial steps towards the commencement of the bid have been made. It is important to point out that rule 14e–3 is applicable independently from any violation of fiduciary duties, in fact it completely ignores the issue of breach of fiduciary duties in order to effectively regulate insider trading in relationship to a tender offer.

Rule 14e–3, however, enacted under the Williams Act, only covers cases in which the acquisition technique is a tender offer. Consider the situation in which the buyer attempts to gain control of a target through acquisitions of shares on the open market, or through a proxy fight. In these instances, investors that are not in a fiduciary relationship with the target's shareholders and whoever becomes aware of the confidential information about the acquisition could be able to speculate without incurring in liability. This result seems inconsistent with rule 14e–3: the different treatment that these cases receive simply because of the different acquisition technique used does not appear fair or rationale. Rule 14e–3, while probably helpful to fill a void left open by Chiarella and the fiduciary-duty standard, is simply a patch of an otherwise incomplete and asystematic approach to insider trading.

In the wake of Chiarella, the Supreme Court decided in 1983 the second seminal case on insider trading, Dirks v. S.E.C., this time dealing with the controversial issue of tippees' liability. Also in this case, the opinion written by Justice Powell remained entrenched on the idea that insider trading requires a violation of fiduciary duties. The decision held that a tippee dealing on the basis of inside information can be liable only if (a) the tipper breached a fiduciary duty by disclosing the information and receiving a personal benefit from tipping, and (b) the tippee knows or has reason to know of the breach of the duty. *Dirks* was coherent with *Chiarella*, but it also contributed to constrain the application of the prohibition against insider trading by requiring, as a pre-condition for the violation, a breach of a fiduciary duty.

Dirks has also somehow clarified the notion of constructive insiders, as opposed to mere tippees. These are subjects external to the issuer, who however become fiduciaries of the issuer (and its shareholders) by reason of their professional relation with the issuer. Among constructive insiders, the Court listed underwriters, accountants, lawyers and consultants working for the corporation.

The Misappropriation Theory of Insider Trading.

Both *Chiarella* and *Dirks* did not, however, resolve a more general issue, only partially addressed by rule 14e–3 with respect to the tender offer setting: what happens to defendants that trade on the basis of inside information not obtained from an issuer or the insider of an issuer, but somehow illegally obtained or used?

The response to this concern is the so-called misappropriation theory advocated by the S.E.C. to regain the ground lost after *Chiarella* and *Dirks*. The theory is simple to state, but raises several interpretative issues. It posits that whenever a fiduciary uses information belonging to his principal for personal gain, without disclosing the use, he commits fraud in connection with the purchase or sale of a security and is liable under Rule 10b–5. The Supreme Court endorsed this theory in *U.S. v. O'Hagan* in 1997. The facts of the case neatly illustrate the point. Grand Metropolitan PLC was contemplating a tender offer on the common stock of Pillsbury Company, and it retained the law firm of Dorsey & Whitney for representation in the planned acquisition. One of the partners of the law firm, O'Hagan, not involved in the representation, came to know of the pending tender offer and, undisclosed to the law firm, purchased shares of the target corporation. When the tender offer was announced, the price of Pillsbury stock rose and O'Hagan pocketed a profit of over four million dollars. The district court sentenced O'Hagan to a prison term for violating Rules 10b–5 and 14e–3. On appeal, the Eight Circuit however reversed the judgment holding that the alleged violation of Rule 10b–5 could not be based on the misappropriation theory, and that Rule 14e–3 was invalid because it did not contain a breach of fiduciary duty requirement.

Justice Ginsburg, writing for the majority of the Court, affirmed two important principles. On the one hand, she affirmed the legitimacy of Rule 14e–3. More relevant to the point at issue here, however, the court also made the misappropriation theory the law of the land. The Court, in fact, held that:

"In this case, the indictment alleged that O'Hagan, in breach of a duty of trust and confidence he owed to his law firm, Dorsey & Whitney, and to its client, Grand Met, traded on the basis of nonpublic information regarding Grand Met's planned tender offer for Pillsbury common stock. [. . .] This conduct, the Government charged, constituted a fraudulent device in connection with the purchase and sale of securities. We agree with the Government that misappropriation, as just defined, satisfies § 10(b)'s requirement that chargeable conduct involve a "deceptive device or contrivance" used "in connection with" the purchase or sale of securities. We observe, first, that misappropriators, as the Government describes them, deal in deception. A fiduciary who "[pretends] loyalty to the principal while secretly converting the principal's information for personal gain," [. . .] "dupes" or defrauds the principal".

One interesting question that *O'Hagan* raised is whether, under the misappropriation theory, *Chiarella* would have been held liable. The answer is probably affirmative, because Chiarella could be considered having a fiduciary relationship with his employer, Pandrick Press. The problem with *O'Hagan* and the misappropriation theory more generally, however, is once again that it ties illegal insider trading with a violation of a fiduciary duty. The existence and scope of fiduciary duties is often a murky subject, and therefore immediately after the *O'Hagan* decision in 1997 it became apparent that further guidance was needed to define relevant relationships that might determine insider trading liability.

Consider, for example, the hypothetical of the C.E.O. of a corporation that discloses to her spouse inside information. If the spouse trades on the basis of this information, is he liable? One possibility might be to argue that, under *Dirks*, he is a tippee, but in this case a violation would occur only if the plaintiff can prove that the tipper breached a fiduciary duty, and that the tippee knew or had reason to know about the violation, which might not be the case. The second option, under the misappropriation theory, would be to hold the husband liable because he misappropriated the information as a fiduciary. The delicate question on the table, however, would be if a family relationship creates a fiduciary duty.

This is exactly the question that the Second Circuit faced in *U.S. v. Chestman*. In this case, the Court held that a fiduciary duty cannot be imposed unilaterally by entrusting a person with confidential information», and—with a certain involuntary irony—that «marriage does not, without more, create a fiduciary relationship». Once again, the choice made by U.S. jurisprudence to base insider trading on the violation of a fiduciary duty poses complex interpretative conundrums and leads to potentially absurd results, because the very notion of fiduciary duties is enveloped in the mists of the common law. We can, for example, surely recognize a fiduciary relationship between «attorney and client, executor and heir, guardian and ward, principal and agent, trustee and trust beneficiary, and senior corporate officer and shareholder», but outside of these typical relationships the question whether the misappropriation theory applies can be a difficult one.

Once again, in the aftermath of *Chestman* the S.E.C. felt the need to intervene through its rule-making power to dissipate part of the mist and reduce uncertainty, and to ensure a sufficiently broad reach of insider trading rules. The Commission, in fact, adopted Rule 10b5–2 in order to clarify which relationships might be considered to determine if the fiduciary misappropriated the information belonging to his source. According to this provision, application of the misappropriation theory is triggered when the recipient of the information trades or tips when: (a) he explicitly agreed to maintain the confidentiality of the information; (b) he had a history, practice or pattern of sharing confidences with the source of the information; (c) he is a spouse, child, parent or sibling of the source of the information (subject to an affirmative defense that there was no reasonable expectation of confidentiality). While this rule seems to shed some light on the scope of application of the misappropriation theory, at the practical level it does not always provide clear guidance. For example, what about confidential information given to a physician, bound to keep confidential health issues, but not necessarily other types of information?

NOTES AND QUESTIONS

1. The "quest" for the perfect regulation of insider trading, in the U.S., has seen these basic steps: parity of information theory, fiduciary-based theory, and misappropriation theory. Can you summarize them based on the discussion above? Which one of these three approaches seems to you more coherent with the goal of limiting the negative consequence of the lack of "strong-efficiency" (as defined by Fama) of the market?

2. Insider trading regulation in the U.S. originates from the fairly short and very broad Rule 10b–5, which is also the basis, among other things, for most lawsuits for civil liability for omissions or misstatements in connection with securities transactions. Justice Rehnquist, the Supreme Court Chief Justice, in a famous 1975 opinion wrote that litigation based on Rule 10b–5 is "a judicial oak which has grown from little more than a legislative acorn." What do you think it means? Why so much litigation—and consequently judicial opinions—on this provision? How many "judicial oaks," in the area of corporate law and securities regulation, are born out of a "legislative acorn"?

3. The evolution described in the excerpt illustrates very well the dynamics of the rule-making process in a "decentralized" system like the U.S.: what do you think about the tension between the SEC and the courts,

and more generally the interplay of legislative provisions, cases, and administrative rules and procedures? Is it healthy or are its costs in terms of uncertainty excessive?

4. Based on what you have learned so far, do you think that the American approach to insider trading could be easily "exported" to other countries? If so, why? If not, why not?

5. You receive a phone call in the middle of the night. It's your friend Tom, a taxi driver, who has been arrested and is calling you from the police station. He seeks your help because he is being accused of insider trading. You run to the station to confer with him, and he tells you that in fact, a couple of months ago, he gave a ride to two top executives he picked up in front of the headquarter of Banana Corporation, the manufacturer of the ubiquitous b-Phone. As Tom was driving them to the airport, he overheard their conversation: they mentioned that unexpectedly all the very serious antitrust charges against Banana had been dropped, which was a huge relief for them since there were rumors that the corporation might have received harsh sanctions and be split in two smaller competitors. They pointed out how this meant significant and unexpected profits, differently from their announcements, for next year, but also remarked that the decision was not final yet and therefore they had to keep it strictly confidential. Tom, who is putting himself through business school and has a fixation for finance, tells you that that very night he traded online and invested all his savings, $35,000, in Banana shares. A couple of days later, the news on the antitrust case became public, Banana shares jumped considerably, and Tom pocketed $20,000 in profits when he sold his shares. For some reason, the prosecutor came to know this and indicted him. Based on what we have discussed on insider trading in the U.S., should Tom be worried? Under which one of the three theories that we have seen above, if any, could he be liable?

6. A couple of additional observations. Insider trading violations also require the inside information to be "material," which means relevant for the reasonable investor in taking an investment decision. This definition, however, is not entirely clear. In addition, insider violations require "scienter," also a concept on which there is some disagreement. And finally, another element of uncertainty is if liability requires the demonstration that the trader *used* the information, i.e., she invested based on it (for example, if she has positive information, she bought shares), or it is sufficient that she traded while in *possession* of the information. More, on some of these issues, will follow.

* * *

What if, in the U.S. system, someone "steals" confidential information, without, however, owing or breaching any fiduciary duty to the (involuntary) source? Would this be considered misappropriation and therefore be relevant for insider trading purposes? In other words, to what extent is a breach of a fiduciary duty always necessary to claim an insider trading violation? A recent and interesting case addressing this issue has been decided by the Second Circuit in *SEC v. Dorozhko*; let's take a look.

S.E.C. v. DOROZHKO

United States Court of Appeals, Second Circuit
574 F.3d 42 (2009)

JOSÉ A. CABRANES, CIRCUIT JUDGE:

We are asked to consider whether, in a civil enforcement lawsuit brought by the United States Securities and Exchange Commission ("SEC") under Section 10(b) of the Securities Exchange Act of 1934 ("Section 10(b)"), computer hacking may be "deceptive" where the hacker did not breach a fiduciary duty in fraudulently obtaining material, nonpublic information used in connection with the purchase or sale of securities. For the reasons stated herein, we answer the question in the affirmative.

BACKGROUND

In early October 2007, defendant Oleksandr Dorozhko, a Ukrainian national and resident, opened an online trading account with Interactive Brokers LLC ("Interactive Brokers") and deposited $42,500 into that account. At about the same time, IMS Health, Inc. ("IMS") announced that it would release its third-quarter earnings during an analyst conference call scheduled for October 17, 2007 at 5 p.m.—that is, after the close of the securities markets in New York City. IMS had hired Thomson Financial, Inc. ("Thomson") to provide investor relations and web-hosting services, which included managing the online release of IMS's earnings reports.

Beginning at 8:06 a.m. on October 17, and continuing several times during the morning and early afternoon, an anonymous computer hacker attempted to gain access to the IMS earnings report by hacking into a secure server at Thomson prior to the report's official release. At 2:15 p.m.—minutes after Thomson actually received the IMS data—that hacker successfully located and downloaded the IMS data from Thomson's secure server.

Beginning at 2:52 p.m., defendant—who had not previously used his Interactive Brokers account to trade—purchased $41,670.90 worth of IMS "put" options that would expire on October 25 and 30, 2007. These purchases represented approximately 90% of all purchases of "put" options for IMS stock for the six weeks prior to October 17. In purchasing these options, which the SEC describes as "extremely risky," defendant was betting that IMS's stock price would decline precipitously (within a two-day expiration period) and significantly (by greater than 20%).

At 4:33 p.m.—slightly ahead of the analyst call—IMS announced that its earnings per share were 28% below "Street" expectations, *i.e.,* the expectations of many Wall Street analysts. When the market opened the next morning, October 18, at 9:30 a.m., IMS's stock price sank approximately 28% almost immediately—from $29.56 to $21.20 per share. Within six minutes of the market opening, defendant had sold all of his IMS options, realizing a net profit of $286,456.59 overnight.

Interactive Brokers noticed the irregular trading activity and referred the matter to the SEC, which now alleges that defendant was the hacker. [. . .]. On October 29, 2007, the SEC sought and received from the United States District Court for the Southern District of New York a temporary restraining order freezing the proceeds of the "put" option transactions in defendant's brokerage account.

[The District Court denied SEC's request holding that computer hacking was no deceptive within the meaning of Section 10(b). This appeal followed].

DISCUSSION

[. . .]

"Section 10(b) prohibits the use or employ, in connection with the purchase or sale of any security . . ., [of] any manipulative or deceptive device or contrivance in contravention of such rules and regulations as the [SEC] may prescribe." 15 U.S.C. § 78j(b). The instant case requires us to decide whether the "device" in this case—computer hacking—could be "deceptive."

In construing the text of any federal statute, we first consider the precedents that bind us as an intermediate appellate court—namely, the holdings of the Supreme Court and those of prior panels of this Court, which provide definitive interpretations of otherwise ambiguous language. Insofar as those precedents fail to resolve an apparent ambiguity, we examine the text of the statute itself, interpreting provisions in light of their ordinary meaning and their contextual setting. [. . .] Where the statutory language remains ambiguous, "we resort to canons of construction and, if the meaning still remains ambiguous, to legislative history." [. . .]

The District Court determined that the Supreme Court has interpreted the "deceptive" element of Section 10(b) to require a breach of a fiduciary duty. [. . .] The District Court reached this conclusion by relying principally on three Supreme Court opinions: *Chiarella v. United States* (1980), *United States v. O'Hagan* (1997), *SEC v. Zandford* (2002). We consider each of these cases in turn.

In *Chiarella,* the defendant was employed by a financial printer and used information passing through his office to trade securities offered by acquiring and target companies. In a criminal prosecution, the government alleged that the defendant committed fraud by not disclosing to the market that he was trading on the basis of material, nonpublic information. The Supreme Court held that defendant's "silence," or nondisclosure, was not fraud because he was under no obligation to disclose his knowledge of inside information. [. . .]

In *O'Hagan,* the defendant was an attorney who traded in securities based on material, nonpublic information regarding his firm's clients. As in *Chiarella,* the government alleged that the defendant had committed fraud through "silence" because the defendant had a duty to disclose to the source of the information (his client) that he would trade on the information. The Supreme Court agreed, noting that "[d]eception through nondisclosure is central to the theory of liability for which the Government seeks recognition." [. . .]

In *Zandford,* the defendant was a securities broker who traded under a client's account and transferred the proceeds to his own account. The Fourth Circuit held that the defendant's fraud was not "in connection with" the purchase or sale of a security because it was mere theft that happened to involve securities, rather than true securities fraud. The Supreme Court reversed in a unanimous opinion, observing that Section 10(b) "should be construed not technically and restrictively, but flexibly to effectuate its remedial purposes." [. . .] In a final footnote, the Court offered the following observation: "[I]f the broker told his client he was stealing the client's assets, that breach of fiduciary duty might be in connection with a sale of securities, but it would not involve a deceptive device or fraud." [. . .] In the instant case, the District Court interpreted the *Zandford* footnote as an "explicit[ ] acknowledg[ment] that Zandford would not be liable under § 10(b) if he *had* disclosed to Wood that he was planning to steal his money."

The District Court concluded that in *Chiarella, O'Hagan*, and *Zandford,* the Supreme Court developed a requirement that any "deceptive device" requires a breach of a fiduciary duty. In applying that interpretation to the instant case, the District Court ruled that "[a]lthough [defendant] may have broken the law, he is not liable in a civil action under § 10(b) because he owed no fiduciary or similar duty either to the source of his information or to those he transacted within the market." [. . .]

In our view, none of the Supreme Court opinions relied upon by the District Court—much less the sum of all three opinions—establishes a fiduciary-duty requirement as an element of every violation of Section 10(b). In *Chiarella, O'Hagan*, and *Zandford,* the theory of fraud was silence or nondisclosure, not an affirmative misrepresentation. The Supreme Court held that remaining silent was actionable only where there was a duty to speak, arising from a fiduciary relationship. In *Chiarella,* the Supreme Court held that there was no deception in an employee's silence because he did not have duty to speak. [. . .] In *O'Hagan,* an attorney who traded on client secrets had a fiduciary duty to inform his firm that he was trading on the basis of the confidential information. [. . .] Even in *Zandford,* which dealt principally with the statutory requirement that a deceptive device be used "in connection with" the purchase or sale of a security, the defendant's fraud consisted of not telling his brokerage client—to whom he owed a fiduciary duty—that he was stealing assets from the account. [. . .]

Chiarella, O'Hagan, and *Zandford* all stand for the proposition that nondisclosure in breach of a fiduciary duty "satisfies § 10(b)'s requirement . . . [of] a 'deceptive device or contrivance,'" [. . .]. However, what is sufficient is not always what is necessary, and none of the Supreme Court opinions considered by the District Court *require* a fiduciary relationship as an element of an actionable securities claim under Section 10(b). [. . .]

In this case, the SEC [. . .] argues that defendant affirmatively misrepresented himself in order to gain access to material, nonpublic information, which he then used to trade. We are aware of no precedent of the Supreme Court or our Court that forecloses or prohibits the SEC's straightforward theory of fraud. [. . .]

Having established that the SEC need not demonstrate a breach of fiduciary duty, we now remand to the District Court to consider, in the first instance, whether the computer hacking in this case involved a fraudulent misrepresentation that was "deceptive" within the ordinary meaning of Section 10(b). The District Court may, in its informed discretion, enter a new order on the basis of the existing record or reopen the preliminary injunction hearing to consider such additional testimony regarding the nature of the hacking in this particular case as it deems appropriate in the circumstances.

NOTES AND QUESTIONS

1. The Second Circuit argues, in this case, that *Chiarella* does not hold that a breach of a fiduciary duty is an essential element of any insider trading violation, but rather that silence constitutes deception only when it breaches a fiduciary duty; in the absence of a fiduciary duty there is no obligation to disclose, and therefore no deception and no insider trading violation. According to the Second Circuit the precedents do not stand for the proposition that a breach of a fiduciary duty is always necessary for any insider trading violation, but simply that a breach of a fiduciary duty can be sufficient for insider trading purposes. This interpretation of the Second Circuit of the jurisprudence of the Supreme Court is very intelligent, but we feel that it is based more on a rhetorical trick than on an accurate reading of the cases. If it was true, as the Second Circuit holds here, that even at the

time of *Chiarella* the Supreme Court thought that a breach of a fiduciary duty is sufficient, but not necessary to commit insider trading, and that other "deceptions" are prohibited, the Court could have easily found a ground to hold Vincent Chiarella liable. It seems hard to maintain that his sneaky techniques to figure out the name of the target corporation, circumventing the precautions taken by his employer, and specifically violating the instructions of the employer (or at least their gist), could not be considered deceptive and a misappropriation of information. Somehow similarly, it is certainly true that O'Hagan was found guilty because he breached a fiduciary duty to the law firm he was a member of, and it can be true that narrowly interpreted, this only means that a fiduciary breach is sufficient for insider trading, but not that it is necessary. However, if the Supreme Court considered *also* other deceptions or fraudulent actions relevant for insider trading purposes, why was it necessary, in *O'Hagan*, to spend so much time and energy to argue for a breach of a fiduciary duty? Couldn't you simply say that grabbing clearly confidential information disclosed in an attorney-client relationship, and not to him but to another partner of the firm, and using it for personal gain against the rules of the law firm and of professional responsibility, was a deception? Again, if *Chiarella* could be read as not limiting insider violations to fiduciary duties violations, why was it necessary for the SEC to introduce specific rules to cover insider trading in connection with tender offers?

2. In any case, what is interesting about *Dorozhko* is that it seems to aim at disentangling insider trading violations from fiduciary duties and broaden the scope of Section 10(b) and Rule 10b–5 thereunder. Note that the court simply says that a fiduciary duty is not necessary for insider trading, but it does not decide if computer hacking is a deception. The issue is left to the District Court on remand. Why? What is your opinion on the deceptive nature of computer hacking? What about breaking and entering a locked building, stealing some paper documents from the drawer of the CEO, and using the information so acquired to trade? Another question: if Mr. Dorozhko would have not traded, but simply tipped the information to an acquaintance, not disclosing that he had obtained them hacking a computer, could the acquaintance trade? Would your answer be different if the acquaintance, in fact, knew about the hacking or even without knowing, would understand the confidential nature of the information? And if Tom simply suggests to his cousin to buy shares of the Banana Corporation, without giving any reason, and the cousin buys because he trusts Tom's acumen? (Try to use the precedents referred to in Professor Ventoruzzo's article above.)

3. Rule 10b–5 is not the only provision dealing with insider trading. Another important rule, quite unique to the U.S. system, is Section 16(b) of the 1934 Securities and Exchange Act, the so-called prohibition against short-swing profits by insiders, which is the original and only provision in the securities laws explicitly addressing insider trading. Differently from Rule 10b–5, Section 16(b) is a prophylactic and crude rule of thumb that targets

specific transactions by only three categories of insiders: directors, officers, and 10% shareholders that purchase and sell, or sell and purchase, equity securities of an issuer within six months. Any profit that these insiders make through these transactions must be disgorged to the issuer. The provision has given rise to numerous and complex interpretative questions that have been the object of extensive scholarly work and great attention by practitioners. The rationale is that these profits are likely based on the use of inside information: it is, as mentioned, a crude absolute presumption that has a prophylactic function. It should be noted that the "profits" that need to be disgorged under this rule are calculated in a peculiar way. Notwithstanding some conflicting precedents, in case of multiple sales, often courts match the lowest purchase price against the highest sale price in the relevant period. The effect is that liability can exceed the actual profits realized, and sometimes "profits" can be deemed to have occurred also if the insider actually lost money. Some commentators have argued that this appears to be a measure of punitive damages, exceeding actual damages in violation of Section 28(a) of the Securities and Exchange Act. Another aspect to mention is interesting in the prospective of private vs. public enforcement. Insider violations under Rule 10b–5 can lead to criminal sanctions, civil fines imposed by the SEC, and civil liability toward investors. For several reasons, including the difficulty of obtaining evidence in insider trading cases without having the investigative powers and resources of the government, private investors rarely bring a civil lawsuit for damages based on insider trading violations based on Rule 10b–5, at least if the SEC or the prosecutor has not already brought an action. The bulk of the enforcement, with respect to Rule 10b–5, is done by the SEC and the DOJ (you might have noticed that all the cases cited in Ventoruzzo's article above and reprinted have the SEC or the U.S. as plaintiff). On the other hand, actions based on Section 16(b) are generally brought by private investors, even if the profits disgorged go the issuer. The reason is twofold: on the one hand, investors want to recover the ill-gotten gains for the corporation, therefore indirectly benefitting from the award; but on the other hand, this is often attorney-driven litigation: the plaintiff bar might have an incentive to bring these actions. Do you think that this particular combination of public and private enforcement is an effective regulatory strategy? Is there a risk of over-enforcement? If you are not from the U.S. (or also if you are from the U.S. but are familiar with other systems), in the legal systems you know better, is there a provision similar to Section 16(b)? Is insider trading—if proscribed—enforced more by governmental agencies and prosecutors, or by private litigants?

* * *

Let's now jump on a plane and head to Europe. How is insider trading regulated there? While there are not insignificant differences among single systems, the European Union has enacted harmonized rules with respect to both insider trading and market manipulation. For our purposes, since we want to outline the major "philosophical" regulatory differences, we can concentrate on E.U. rules. The following excerpt discusses the 2003 Market Abuse Directive. In 2014, the Directive has been updated (with a new Directive and a Regulation) and some important changes have been introduced; however, the general principles discussed below are still valid also under the new regulatory framework.

MARCO VENTORUZZO, COMPARING INSIDER TRADING IN THE UNITED STATES AND IN THE EUROPEAN UNION: HISTORY AND RECENT DEVELOPMENTS[3]

11 European Company and Financial Law Review 554 (2015)

THE EUROPEAN APPROACH TO INSIDER TRADING: PARITY OF INFORMATION.

European Regulation of Insider Trading: The Market Abuse Directive of 2003.

In Europe, a crucial concern behind the regulation of insider trading is market egalitarianism. As [Niamh Moloney has observed], "[i]f investor confidence and the efficient operation of the market are the dominant objectives, the source of the inside information is largely irrelevant, although it is central if the prohibition is based on fiduciary concepts". This statement nicely captures the key difference between regulation of insider trading in the US and in Europe.

The core concept of the Market Abuse Directive of 2003 ("MAD") is the definition of "inside information". This is information of a precise nature that has not been made public relating, directly or indirectly, to one or more issuers or one or more securities. The characterization of inside information as precise is necessary to exclude opinions or rumors from the definition. More specifically, according to the directive, information is precise if it indicates a set of circumstances which exists or may reasonably be expected to come into existence or an event that has occurred or may reasonably be expected to occur and is specific enough to allow a conclusion on the possible effects on the prices of the securities. The information has also to be price sensitive in the sense that, if made public, it would likely have a significant effect on the price of the securities. Similarly to the U.S., information is deemed price-sensitive under Article 1(2) of the directive if a reasonable investor would be likely to use it as a basis for her investment decisions.

The definition of information relevant for insider trading purposes, and also for disclosure obligations (as we will see below, in paragraph 3, under EU law inside information must be disclosed to the market unless there is a valid reason to delay disclosure), has been addressed in several cases decided by the European Court of Justice. One of the most relevant ones is *Geltl v. Daimler AG*, which raised the issue of when information

---

[3]   Footnotes and paragraph numbers omitted.

concerning a possible future event becomes relevant for insider trading and should be disclosed. The case reminds of Basic v. Levinson, the U.S. Supreme Court decision that hold that information concerning possible future events becomes material when, based on a "probability-magnitude" test, it appears to be relevant for investors. The U.S. Supreme Court, in other words, in this respect held that the likelihood of a future event (e.g. a merger, the launch of a tender offer, a court's decision, etc.) should be factored in with its possible effects on market prices to decide if information is material. Under this approach, also a relatively unlikely event, which however could have a profound impact on the market, should be disclosed.

Geltl dealt with the resignation of the CEO of DaimlerChrysler AG, Mr. Schrempp, in 2005. To make a long story short, the decision to resign, and the related resolutions of the corporation, developed over a period of several weeks. The information was however disclosed to the market only when the board of supervisors formally approved the resignation and appointed a new CEO, on July 28, 2005. The price of the shares increased after the announcement, and Mr. Geltl, a shareholder who had sold the shares before it, sued claiming that the information should have been disclosed before the formal decision of the board of supervisors. The *BaFin*, the German regulator, also imposed sanctions. The issue reached the German Federal Supreme Court, the *Bundesgerichtshof*, which raised two certified questions for the European Court of Justice. The first was whether the "intermediate steps" that lead to a future specific event could be considered precise information for the purposes of the MAD directive; the second was whether in considering the relevance of an information, its likelihood could be combined with its potential effect on the market; in other words, if a "probability-magnitude" test could or should be applied. The European Court answered the first question in the affirmative, but rejected the use of a "probability-magnitude" test (contrary to the opinion of the Advocate General), holding that in order to decide if an information concerning a future event must be disclosed it is necessary to consider if there is a realistic prospect that the event will occur. In fact the Court has not clarified the degree of likelihood that is relevant, but the key point here is the rejection of the U.S.-style probability-magnitude test.

[. . .]

We dedicated some space to the notion of inside information under EU law, in the light of its statutory definition and its central role in the application of the relevant rules. For the purposes of our comparison with U.S. law, however, we should now focus on the fact that the Directive contains broad provisions (in Articles 2 and 3) that prohibit persons in possession of inside information from: (a) dealing in the securities to which the information relates using inside information; (b) disclosing inside information to third parties unless the disclosure is made in the normal course of employment, profession or duties; (c) recommending or inducing other persons, on the basis of inside information, to trade.

One important difference with the U.S. approach emerges considering the persons subject to the prohibition. They can be divided in primary and constructive insiders, defined in Article 2 of the Directive, and other persons, defined in Article 4. The formers are persons who possess the information by virtue of (a) their membership in the administrative, management or supervisory bodies of the issuer; (b) their holding in the capital of the issuer; (c) their employment, profession or duties; (d) criminal activities. It is interesting to compare this list with the list of possible insiders under U.S. law. Persons indicated from (a) through (c) would, in all likelihood, be considered primary or constructive insiders also under U.S. law under rule 10b–5. [. . .] It is however questionable if, under U.S. law, persons possessing inside information by virtue of criminal activities would be considered insiders if they did not breach a specific fiduciary duty, even if obviously they might be sanctioned through the application of other rules. The above mentioned *Dorozhko* case suggests that they would be.

The key difference between the two approaches emerges, however, when we consider Article 4 of the MAD. Under this provision, the prohibitions set forth by Articles 2 and 3 also extend to anyone "who possesses inside information while that person knows, or ought to have known, that it is inside information".

This provision clearly demonstrates that the European prohibition of insider trading is based on an equal access to information theory, and not on fiduciary duties. Consider the following example based on the facts of *Texas Gulf Sulphur*. Imagine that an agent of the corporation meets a farmer owning land that the corporation wishes to buy because of the non-public discovery of the ore deposit. If the agent shares the inside information with the farmer, without any specific confidentiality obligation, and the farmer buys the securities at a low price and sells them at a higher one once the information becomes public, he would probably not be guilty of insider trading under U.S. law. More precisely, he could be liable under Dirks but only if it could be proven that the insider breached a fiduciary duty for his personal gain, and that the tippee knew or should have known about the breach. On the contrary, in Europe the farmer would have violated the prohibition against insider trading: the only element that needs to be proved is that he ought to know of the inside nature of the information received by the corporation's agent.

It should be noted that, under European law, the tippee does not need to have received the information from an insider that has breached a fiduciary duty. Even if the inside information is revealed to a third party through a long chain of tippees-tippers, the person trading might be liable as long as she trades on the basis of inside information being aware of the inside nature of the information.

NOTES AND QUESTIONS

1.　Let's go back for a second to the case of Tom, the taxi driver who calls you in the middle of the night in the hypothetical case above after the discussion of the U.S. situation. Based on what you have just read on European law, would Tom be liable? Consider a different situation: after driving a customer to the airport, Tom finds on the back seat, clearly forgotten, a confidential report discussing financial problems of a listed company. Can Tom trade using this information in Europe? And in the U.S.?

2.　Do you find the American or the European approach to insider trading, as discussed above, more effective? Why? Can you see any possible problem in the potentially very broad scope of the European rules?

3.　It is possible to argue that European rules are too broad. The European legislature is, in fact, aware of this problem, and has introduced some exemptions from the prohibition against insider trading. One example concerns takeovers. The bidder, before launching a tender offer, possesses inside information concerning the target, including its very decision to launch the public offer. If you could conclude that, because of that, the bidder cannot trade, insider trading rules would hinder the market for corporate control. The use of inside information in the context of a public offer or of M&As is therefore partially excluded from the prohibition. It is worth mentioning this because it clearly shows a difference between the U.S. and European approaches to insider trading also in terms of regulatory structure. If insider trading is predicated upon the violation of a fiduciary duty, as the U.S. Supreme Court held in *Chiarella*, the bidder or persons knowing about the impending bid would never violate insider trading provisions because they are not fiduciaries of the investors in the target corporation. At a minimum, also based on different theories such as misappropriation, it would be hard to find and demonstrate a violation. This is why the SEC had to introduce a specific prohibition with rule 14e–3 discussed above. In Europe we find an opposite approach: the general prohibition of insider trading, based on parity of information, is very broad and would extend to the tender offer context. It is therefore necessary to explicitly carve out exemptions in order to allow tender offers.

4.　In the previous pages the "probability-magnitude" test has been mentioned. Can you summarize what it is used for and what it provides? Do you see any problem with this test that might explain why the European Court of Justice has not adopted it?

5.　As briefly mentioned, in 2014 the European Union adopted two pieces of legislation that partially reform market abuse rules: a Regulation (directly applicable in Member States) on insider trading and market manipulation, including also disclosure obligations of listed corporations and administrative sanctions, and a Directive dealing with criminal sanctions for the violation of the applicable rules. The new rules include several important innovations, but the overall framework, the underlying "philosophy" of the rules discussed above did not change. It is worth mentioning, however, that the new rules expand the scope of market abuses to include other securities and also securities traded on multilateral trading systems, not on stock exchanges; new additional and harmonized investigative and enforcement powers are also given to regulatory agencies. The new rules also provide for a clearer distinction between information that must be disclosed to the market, and inside, price-sensitive information relevant for insider trading purposes (*see* Note 6 below).

6.   Insider trading prohibits trading while in possession of private, price-sensitive information. The rule, in fact, is sometimes expressed as "disclose or abstain": you can either disclose the information (meaning make it broadly available to the market, for example through a public statement in a press conference), and therefore make it public and no longer "inside," or you must refrain from trading. Of course this does not mean that disclosing confidential information is always permissible; there might be legal grounds why disclosure might violate other rules, for example a contractual confidentiality agreement. The consequence is simply that trading is not possible. A separate question, however, is if there is a general duty to disclose price-sensitive information. While some legal systems provide such a broad provision (with some exceptions, to protect valuable business secrets of the issuer), others prefer to analytically indicate corporate events and transactions that require disclosure (even if the disclosure obligations are generally quite extensive also in these systems). A full discussion of this would take too much space, and it has more to do with securities regulation than with corporate law. However, you can discuss this in class: which one of the two models briefly described do the jurisdictions you are more familiar with follow? Is there a general duty to disclose all price-sensitive information (with exceptions), or are there specific, statutory and regulatory defined obligations to disclose particular events and transactions?

7.   One fascinating question is if "political" information can be inside information. For example, if a congresswoman or a member of parliament learns about the imminent approval of a legislative amendment that would be extremely detrimental to one corporation, and for some reason the information is not public, can she sell the shares of the corporation before the public learns about the new rule, and therefore avoid serious losses? (A somehow similar question can be asked with respect to administrative agencies activity or court decisions.) In some countries, specific legislation has been enacted to address this phenomenon. Applying the general rules that we have considered before, what do you think could be the answer in different systems, assuming that no specific legislation has been enacted in this respect?

8.   Consider financial analysts. An analyst who collects lots of dispersed information, talks with different sources familiar with a

corporation, and, by putting together the different pieces, figures out that a corporation is in trouble, is he subject to the disclosure or abstain rule? In other words, if examining not-private information, through research and analysis, someone understands or predicts how a security might do, is this information inside information? And, to walk a very fine line, what if an analyst obtains from different sources three clearly confidential pieces of information that however—pay close attention—individually considered are not sufficiently precise to allow any inference on market prices. The three separate pieces of information, combined and properly interpreted, allow the analyst to understand that a drop of market prices is to be expected, and he sells. Any violation?

9. And what about journalists? If you are an editor of *The New York Times*, and you are about to publish a piece that will negatively affect the price of the shares of General Motors, can you trade? Is the very information that the article is about to be published inside information? What about fiduciary duties?

10. Pamela is the very successful CEO of a major listed corporation. Her skills, understanding of the industry, vision and charisma are clearly considered by investors and consumers, and with good reasons, the primary factor in the success of the corporation for the last 15 years. Unfortunately Pamela is diagnosed with a terminal illness and given not more than six months. She decides to resign and spend her remaining time with her family in their country house. Before announcing her intention to resign and the reason, however, she sells a significant amount of shares that she owned in the corporation. After the announcement the price of the shares drops. Has Pamela committed insider trading? Would your answer be different if Pamela would announce the resignation, but not disclose her illness and simply mention personal reasons? Is Pamela's illness or impending resignation inside, price-sensitive information?

* * *

A delicate issue in insider trading cases is if it is necessary to prove that the accused has traded *using* inside information, or is it sufficient to demonstrate that she traded while in *possession* of inside information. One example might clarify. Alexis, the CFO of X, a pharmaceutical corporation, is told that X is about to register a patent for a revolutionary and extremely lucrative drug. Before the information is public she purchases shares of X that soar after the announcement. This is clearly a case of insider trading, and it is not difficult to argue that Alexis used the information she obtained. But what if rather than buying shares, Alexis sells some shares she has, possibly because she urgently needs funds to avoid a foreclosure on her house? In this case you might argue that Alexis possessed inside information, but she did not *use* it, she did not take advantage of it; in fact, she sold shares, which is contrary to what an insider exploiting her position would have done. This is, with an example, the *use* vs. *possession* debate.

From a policy perspective, choosing between use and possession of information as an element of insider trading is complicated. To demonstrate *use* can be difficult, therefore *use* can lead to under-enforcement. On the other hand, *possession* can clearly lead to over-enforcement, and it might seem unfair to punish insiders when they do not exploit inside information.

Most legal systems provide for some exemption to avoid the risk of punishment at least in the cases in which it is clear that the insider cannot be blamed (for example, if the insider already had the obligation to trade the securities because he sold a call option well before any inside, price-sensitive information was available). But what about the more general issue of use vs. possession?

In the United States, in the 1990s the Second Circuit adopted the "possession theory," arguing that information does not "lie idle in the human brain" (*United States v. Teicher*, 987 F.2d 112, 120 (2nd Cir. 1993)). The possession theory, however, might be considered incompatible with the scienter requirement of section 10(b). Other circuits have held that a proof of use of inside information is necessary, and the Supreme Court in *Dirks* has indicated that mere possession of confidential inside information is insufficient to impose the disclose or abstain rule. The SEC in 2000 adopted Rule 10b5–1 to address this issue. Basically, the provision states that a person is liable when trading while "aware" of inside information. This is a sort of presumption of use of inside information, even if liability is excluded if the insider purchases or sells on the basis of pre-existing plans, contracts, or instructions, therefore not because of material non-public information.

In Europe, most national legislatures seem to consider necessary the use of inside information. In the U.K., for example, Section 118(2) of the Financial Services and Markets Act 2000 requires insiders to deal "on the basis" of inside information; in Germany § 14(1) of the *Wertpapierhandelsgesetz* provides that insiders must "use" the information; and in Italy, Article 184 of the Italian *Testo Unico della Finanza* prohibits trading using ("utilizzando") inside information.

In the case of *Spector Photo Group NV*, however, the European Court of Justice has taken a broader approach. The decision involved a Belgian corporation that had purchased its own shares in order to carry on an employee stock-option plan, but later announced its financial results and an acquisition plan that affected positively its market prices. One of the questions raised by the Belgian courts was if the Market Abuse Directive (MAD) had to be interpreted as prohibiting trading using, or also only possessing, inside information. The European Court of Justice gave a somehow ambiguous answer, but it seems basically to consider that possession of material inside information implies a presumption of use if the insider deals in securities. The presumption, however, can be rebutted, in particular because the Court held that only use that conflicts with the purpose of granting equal access to information to all investors, one of the goals of the Directive, is prohibited.

SPECTOR PHOTO GROUP NV, CHRIS VAN RAEMDONCK V. COMMISSIE VOOR HET BANK-, FINANCIE-EN ASSURANTIEWEZEN (CBFA)
JUDGMENT OF THE COURT (Third Chamber)
Case C–45/08, 23 December 2009

THE COURT (Third Chamber),

[. . .]

By its second and third questions, which need to be examined together and prior to the others, the referring court requests the Court of Justice to interpret the expression 'use of inside information' in Article 2(1) of Directive 2003/6. That provision provides that the Member States are to prohibit any person referred to in the second subparagraph thereof (a 'primary insider') who 'possesses inside information from using that information by acquiring or disposing of, . . . for his own account or for the account of a third party, either directly or indirectly, the financial instruments to which that information relates' or from trying to enter into such a transaction on the market. More precisely, the referring court seeks to determine whether it is sufficient, for a transaction to be classed as prohibited insider dealing, that a primary insider in possession of inside information trades on the market in financial instruments to which that information relates or whether it is necessary, in addition, to establish that that person has 'used' that information 'with full knowledge'.

Article 2(1) of Directive 2003/6 does not stipulate that prohibited transactions must be carried out 'with full knowledge of the facts' but merely prohibits primary insiders from using inside information when entering into market transactions. That article defines the constituent elements of such prohibited transactions by referring expressly to two such elements, namely, the persons likely to fall within its scope and the material actions which constitute that transaction.

By contrast, that provision does not expressly set out the subjective conditions in relation to the intention behind those material actions. Article 2(1) of Directive 2003/6 does not state whether the primary insider must have been driven by a speculative intention, must have had a fraudulent intention or must have acted either deliberately or negligently. That article does not expressly state whether it is necessary to establish that the inside information was decisive in the decision to enter into the market transaction at issue, or whether the primary insider had to be aware that the information in his possession was inside information.

[...]

The fact that Article 2(1) of Directive 2003/6 does not expressly provide for a mental element can be explained, first, by the specific nature of insider dealing, which enables a presumption of that mental element once the constituent elements referred to in that provision are present. To begin with, the relationship of confidence which links the primary insiders referred to in Article 2(1)(a) to (c) to the issuer of the financial instruments to which the inside information relates implies, on their part, a specific responsibility in that regard. Next, entering into a market transaction is necessarily the result of a series of decisions forming part of a complex context which, in principle, makes it possible to exclude the possibility that the author of that transaction could have acted without being aware of his actions. Finally, where such a market transaction is entered into while the author of that transaction is in possession of inside information, that information must, in principle, be deemed to have played a role in his decision-making.

[...]

Once the constituent elements of insider dealing laid down in Article 2(1) of Directive 2003/6 are satisfied, it is thus possible to assume an intention on the part of the author of that transaction.

Such a presumption does not, however, infringe fundamental rights and, in particular, the principle of the presumption of innocence laid down, inter alia, in Article 6(2) of the European Convention for the Protection of Human Rights and Fundamental Freedoms, signed in Rome on 4 November 1950 ('the ECHR').

It should be noted in that regard that, according to settled case-law, fundamental rights form an integral part of the general principles of law whose observance the Court ensures (Joined Cases C–402/05 P and C–415/05 P Kadi and Al Barakaat International Foundation v Council and Commission [2008] ECR I–6351, paragraph 283).

[...]

The establishment of an effective and uniform system to prevent and sanction insider dealing with the legitimate aim of protecting the integrity of financial markets has thus led the Community legislature to adopt an objective definition of the constituent elements of prohibited insider dealing. The fact that Article 2(1) of Directive 2003/6 does not expressly provide for a mental element does not, however, mean that that provision needs to be interpreted in such a way that any primary insider in possession of inside information who enters into a market transaction, automatically falls within the prohibition on insider dealing.

As pointed out by the Italian and United Kingdom Governments, such an extensive interpretation of Article 2(1) of Directive 2003/6 would entail the risk of extending the scope of that prohibition beyond what is appropriate and necessary to attain the goals pursued by that directive. Such an interpretation could, in practice, lead to the prohibition of certain market transactions which do not necessarily infringe the interests protected by that directive. It is therefore necessary to distinguish 'uses of inside information' which are capable of infringing those interests from those which are not.

[. . .] [P]rohibition on insider dealing applies where a primary insider who is in possession of inside information takes unfair advantage of the benefit gained from that information by entering into a market transaction in accordance with that information.

It follows that the fact that a primary insider who holds inside information trades on the market in financial instruments to which that information relates implies that that person 'used that information' within the meaning of Article 2(1) of Directive 2003/6, but without prejudice to the rights of the defence and, in particular, the right to be able to rebut that presumption.

However, in order not to extend the scope of the prohibition laid down in Article 2(1) of Directive 2003/6 beyond what is appropriate and necessary to attain the goals pursued by that directive, certain situations may require a thorough examination of the factual circumstances enabling it to be ensured that the use of the inside information is actually unfair so as to be prohibited by the directive in the name of the integrity of financial markets and investor confidence.

In should be noted, in that regard, that the preamble to Directive 2003/6 provides several examples of situations in which the fact that a primary insider in possession of inside information enters into a transaction on the market should not in itself constitute 'use of inside information' for the purposes of Article 2(1) of that directive.

Thus, the 18th recital in the preamble to Directive 2003/6 states that use of inside information 'can consist in the acquisition or disposal of financial instruments by a person who knows, or ought to have known, that the information possessed is inside information'. That hypothesis is expressly provided for in Article 4 of that directive, which extends the prohibition on insider dealing to persons who know, or ought to have known, that the information in their possession is inside information. None the less, the automatic application of those criteria to certain professionals in the financial markets, who are required to hold inside information relating to transactions carried out on the market by third parties, risks leading to a situation in which such persons are prohibited from carrying out their activity, an activity which is both legitimate and useful for the efficient functioning of the financial markets. The 18th recital in the preamble to that directive states, in that regard, that the assessment of what a reasonable person knows or should have known 'in the circumstances' is to be carried out by the competent authorities.

[. . .]

It follows from the above that the question whether a primary insider in possession of inside information 'uses that information' within the meaning of Article 2(1) of Directive 2003/6 must be determined in the light of the purpose of that directive, which is to protect the integrity of the financial markets and to enhance investor confidence. That confidence is based, in particular, on the assurance that they will be placed on an equal footing and protected from the misuse of inside information. Only usage which goes against that purpose constitutes prohibited insider dealing.

Therefore, the answer to the second and third questions must be that, on a proper interpretation of Article 2(1) of Directive 2003/6, the fact that a person as referred to in the second subparagraph of that provision, in possession of inside information, acquires or disposes of, or tries to acquire or dispose of, for his own account or for the account of a third party, either directly or indirectly, the financial instruments to which that information relates implies that that person has 'used that information' within the meaning of that provision, but without prejudice to the rights of the defence and, in particular, to the right to be able to rebut that presumption. The question whether that person has infringed the prohibition on insider dealing must be analysed in the light of the purpose of that directive, which is to protect the integrity of the financial markets and to enhance investor confidence, which is based, in particular, on the assurance that investors will be placed on an equal footing and protected from the misuse of inside information.

NOTES AND QUESTIONS

1.   In this case, the European Court of Justice adopts a sort of presumption of use of inside information that the accused can rebut. Do you find this approach sensible? Is it similar or different from the approach adopted in the U.S. by the SEC in 2000 and mentioned above?

2.   What do you think might be the practical problems (if any) of the *Spector* decision?

3.   If an insider sells shares when all the inside information that she possesses indicates an imminent jump up in the prices of the shares, is she using the information?

4.   In your opinion, would there be any reason to treat primary insiders and tippees differently with respect to the possession vs. use question?

5. Another interesting issue is if relevant inside information must be "precise" enough so that a specific inference on how market prices will be affected is necessary, or not. If, for example, the information is that the corporation will be involved in a massive lawsuit because it intends to sue another business for breach of contract, but the outcome of the litigation is uncertain, it might be argued that it is unclear if market prices will react positively or negatively. Doe trading on the basis of this information lead to liability? In the *Lafonta* case, the European Court of Justice, answering a certified preliminary question raised by the French Supreme Court on the basis of the European MAD, has very recently concluded that information can be "precise" also if it is not unequivocal the direction in which market prices will move after the information is disclosed (Case C-628/13) decided March 11, 2015). This very broad reading of the provisions further extends the reach of European insider trading prohibitions, and is somehow questionable. For example, don't you think that if no inference is possible on market prices, it is impossible to "use" an information that is not precise? In any case, the decision can help you address the question we proposed in Note 8 above, after Professor Ventoruzzo's article discussing insider trading in the E.U.

* * *

Japanese law on insider trading, which was introduced by a reform of the Securities and Exchange Act (now called Financial Instruments and Exchange Act, hereinafter also "FIEA") in 1988, follows an approach more similar to the European one than that of the U.S. This similarity is apparent, first of all, in the fact that the regulation is primarily based on statutory provisions and not on gradual development of case law. Needless to say, as we have mentioned since the beginning in Chapter 1, the role of courts in interpreting the statutes is also extremely important in Japan, but their role is not as broad and creative, at least in this area, as in the U.S. One difference from the E.U. approach is that the relevant provisions of the Financial Instruments and Exchange Act are more detailed and specific than those in the Market Abuse Directive, even if we should not forget that, in Europe, directives are implemented at the Member State level, and national legislatures and regulatory agencies have added further details to the European regulatory framework.

Persons who are subject to insider trading regulation are explicitly listed, and can be classified into three categories. The first category includes corporate insiders, who are prohibited to trade on insider information regarding the issuer. They are: (a) directors, statutory auditors, executive officers, representatives, and employees of the issuer (Art. 166(1)(i) FIEA); (b) shareholders holding the right to inspect corporate records, in principle holding 3% or more of the voting rights of the issuer (Art. 166(1)(ii) FIEA); (c) civil servants with powers over the issuer, such as for example government officials exercising control over the issuer (Art. 166(1)(iii) FIEA); (d) whoever has concluded, or is negotiating a contract with the issuer (Art. 166(1)(iv) FIEA) (exceptions for non-material contracts and information are provided); and (e) directors, statutory auditors, executive officers, representatives, and employees of organizations falling in the above-mentioned (b) or (d) categories (Art. 166(1)(v) FIEA). The second category consists of persons having a relationship with an offeror, who cannot trade on information regarding a tender offer. The third category is tippees. Differently from the E.U., however, this category is limited to direct tippees receiving a tip from persons in the first two categories; when the direct tippee belongs to an organization, the prohibition also extends to the directors, statutory auditors, executive officers, representatives, and employees of the organization (Art. 166(3) and Art. 167(3) FIEA). This shows that Japanese law does not completely adopt the "parity-of-information" approach. At the same time, however, Japan does not follow the complex fiduciary-duties or misappropriation theories followed in the U.S.

Inside information relevant for insider trading purposes is, in essence, information regarding the issuer or its subsidiaries that may have a significant influence on investors' investment decisions (Art. 166(2)(iv)(viii) FIEA). The FIEA enumerates in detail different types of information that fall into this broad category, but also provides for several safe harbors. These categories can be listed as follows: (a) information on important decisions made by the issuer or its subsidiaries, such as issuance of shares, decrease of legal capital, distributions to shareholders, mergers and acquisitions, dissolution, launch of a new product or business, etc.; (b) other financially relevant events such as damages due to catastrophic events, change of major shareholders, lawsuits and litigations, etc.; and (c) certain forward-looking forecasts (Art. 166(2)(i)(ii)(iii)(v)(vi)(vii) FIEA, Art. 28–Art. 29–2 Cabinet Order for Implementation of Financial Instruments and Exchange Act).

Corporate insiders, persons related to the tender offeror and their tippees cannot trade in the securities if the inside information is not disclosed to the public (Art. 166(1) and Art. 167(1) FIEA). This is a typical "disclose or abstain" rule, and of course the persons mentioned do not have a duty to disclose the information (and, in fact, might be prohibited from disclosing it, for example due to confidentiality obligations, in which case they will not be able to trade).

In addition to the prohibition of insider trading, FIEA also requires directors, statutory auditors, executive officers, representatives, and employees of the issuer and shareholders of the issuer holding 10% or more of voting rights to report their trading activity on the securities of the issuer (Art. 163 FIEA), and allows the issuer to obtain the disgorgement of profits from some types of short-swing trades (Art. 164 FIEA).

In terms of sanctions against violations of insider trading rules, Japan used to rely only on criminal measures (currently a prison term of up to 5 years and/or fines of up to 5 million JPY, and a fine of up to 500 million JPY for legal persons). Criminal sanctions, for a number of self-evident reasons, are not always the best option, if nothing else because of the complexity of a criminal trial. For this reason, the possibility to impose administrative fines was introduced in 2004 (Art. 175 FIEA). Since then, the Japanese Securities and Exchange Surveillance Commission (SESC) and Financial Services Agency (FSA) have been enforcing insider trading quite vigorously. For example, in 2013, the SESC recommended that FSA imposes administrative fines in 32 cases. Criminal sanctions are however imposed in more egregious cases. The presence of both administrative and criminal sanctions will be discussed further, below, considering the European and American situation. On the other hand, private enforcement by investors is very rare in Japan, primarily because of the difficulty of proving that the plaintiffs were the counterparties of the insiders.

Let's go back to the discussion on style of insider trading regulation. The Japanese rules were adopted because it was thought necessary to provide clear guidance, as violations of insider trading regulation could lead to criminal sanctions and, when criminal sanctions are involved, statutory provisions must be clear and detailed. Although this approach eliminates some of the uncertainties that we have discussed with respect to the U.S., there are also shortcomings. One problem, which is described in the following excerpt from *The Economist*, is that the regulation can be under-inclusive.

MUDDY WATERS—THE DEEP ROOTS OF INSIDER TRADING
Economist, June 16, 2012
http://www.economist.com/node/21556947

THE cult of the insider in Japan is rooted in its paddy fields, some scholars argue. To cultivate wet rice, villagers need to work together, sharing land, labour, water and gossip. Anyone not in the group is out of the loop. There is something of the rice paddy about Japan's capital markets, too.

A string of insider-trading scandals in recent weeks suggests that restricted information has been flowing between underwriters and hedge funds as freely as water down a sluiceway. And the puny punishments imposed may be as likely to encourage law-breaking as to deter it.

On June 8th Japan's Securities and Exchange Surveillance Commission (SESC) proposed its first fine for insider-trading against a foreign firm, First New York Securities. The penalty of $185,000 is harsh by Japanese standards, but negligible by others (Raj Rajaratnam, a hedge fund boss convicted of insider dealing in America, was sentenced to 11 years in prison last year).

On the same day Nomura, Japan's biggest investment bank, admitted that its employees had leaked non-public information in three cases, including the First New York Securities one. Though Nomura said it was still under scrutiny by the SESC, it has not been penalised—and may never be. Under Japanese law, insider-trading rules only apply to those who receive the tip, not to the tipster.

Fines are tiddly because they are based on the commission earned by those trading on the news, not the profits they generate. So the proposed penalties in three other insider-trading cases levied against Japanese firms this year were as low as 50,000 yen ($630)—"a candlelit dinner for two" as Nicholas Smith of CLSA, a brokerage, puts it.

Mr Smith, who has written extensively on insider trading in Japan, says the problem is rampant. According to his estimates, in Japan share prices in 2011 typically fell for two weeks before a public issue, sharply lagging the rest of the stockmarket—suggesting information leaks. By comparison, in America shares outperformed (see chart). He says there has been a similar pattern in Japan since 2008.

The power of information

Share-price performance during capital raisings

2011 average, day of announcement=100

Days since announcement

Source: CLSA

The problem occurs when underwriters are marketing company shares to potential investors. In a letter last year to the Financial Services Agency, Japan's main stockmarket regulator, the Hong Kong-based Asian Corporate Governance Association, which represents institutional shareholders, said that some brokers were enabling a few favoured hedge funds to profit from insider trading.

On June 14th the ruling Democratic Party said it wanted to tighten up the rules. But there are other ways the government could signal its displeasure—for instance by excluding chastened brokers like Nomura from the forthcoming sale of the government's stake in Japan Tobacco. It is an important time for Japan's capital markets: next year, the government hopes to merge the Tokyo and Osaka stock exchanges to create a huge pool of capital for Asia. Just as in the paddy fields, a hint of ostracism could be a powerful corrective tool.

NOTES AND QUESTIONS

1.   One week after the publication of this article, the Japanese government excluded Nomura from the sale of the government's stake in Japan Tobacco, although a government official suggested that the problem described in the article above was not the decisive factor.[4]

2.   Do you agree with the article's proposal to exclude Nomura from the sale of government's stake in Japan Tobacco as a sanction against Nomura's inappropriate but not illegal behavior? Any counter-arguments?

3.   As a response to the problem described in the article above, the Financial Instruments and Exchange Act was reformed in 2013 to prohibit corporate insiders and persons related to a tender offeror from sharing inside information or advice based on inside information with third parties. If tippees trade, tippers can be subject to criminal sanctions (Art. 197–2(xiv)(xv) FIEA) and administrative fines (Art. 175–2 FIEA). Even when tippees do not act, tipping itself constitutes a violation of the FIEA and tippers can also be sanctioned, especially if they are registered securities brokers. The 2013 reform also introduced a new measure of enforcement: public disclosure of the name of individual who violated FIEA (Art. 192–2 FIEA). What is your take on these measures? In particular, what do you think of disclosure of the name of a violator as a sanction? Is the possible social blame a sufficient sanction, in your opinion, in all systems and cultures?

4.   Considering the article above, does it make sense, in your opinion, to calculate fines based on trading commissions, rather than on profits? Discuss.

---

[4]   See, Hiroyuki Kachi and Kana Inagaki, Nomura Left Out of Japan Tobacco Share Sale, Wall Street Journal, June 18, 2012 12:31 p.m. ET, available at http://www.wsj.com/articles/SB10001424052702303379204577474103669207334.

5.   The article of *The Economists* refers to cultural elements influencing attitudes toward insider trading (rice paddy). Do you think cultural elements and personal relationships are particularly important in this area? Why?

6.   One scholar has argued that notwithstanding the differences in insider trading prohibitions around the world, they have been introduced outside the United States largely as a consequence of political pressure from the U.S., where the prohibition is also based, as we have seen, on cultural notions of egalitarianism and fair play (Amir N. Licht, *Games Commissions Play: 2x2 Games of International Securities Regulation*, 24 YALE J. INT'L L. 61 (1999)). Professor Licht calls this a case of "Ideological Hegemony." It is difficult to conclude with certainty that the widespread adoption of insider trading rules has been determined by U.S. political pressure, and influenced by American legal and economic culture (and what are precisely the boundaries of this, e.g. requests of American institutional investors). Assuming, however, that U.S. political pressure contributed to the adoption of the prohibition and criminal sanctions in other systems, we can ask: If insider trading is in fact beneficial for the markets, enhances efficiency and reinforces investors' confidence, why was it necessary for the U.S. to push other legislatures to regulate it? Can you come with an explanation based on pressure groups influence?

* * *

INSIDER TRADING, DOUBLE JEOPARDY, AND HUMAN RIGHTS

In this section we tackle one issue that has been addressed in a recent and important decision of the European Court of Human Rights in the context of enforcement of market abuse rules, but that has a broader relevance. The issue is the following: as briefly mentioned above, insider trading and market manipulation (as well as many other violations) can be sanctioned both with criminal and civil (or administrative) penalties. Does the possibility of receiving both administrative sanctions from the market regulator, and criminal sanctions, violate the prohibition of double jeopardy, or *ne bis in idem*? Double jeopardy, or *ne bis in idem*, states that none should be subject to prosecution, tried or punished *criminally* twice for the same conducts, and is a well-established principle at common law; it is enshrined in the American Constitution (in the Fifth Amendment), and is set forth in the European Convention on Human Rights, among others. Most modern constitutions, or at least criminal statutes, embrace this principle. The problem, in our case, is whether the sanctions formally defined by the legislatures as "administrative" should, in fact, substantively be considered "criminal," in light of their severity, their punitive goals, and other elements. If the answer is affirmative, then the full protection of the double jeopardy prohibition should apply.

Needless to say this question can be extremely relevant any time different sanctions for the same conduct can be cumulated.

The European Court of Human Rights (ECHR)—actually confirming its precedents, but applying them in a new area—has recently concluded that, in this respect, market abuse rules violate the *ne bis in idem* requirement in *Grande Stevens and Others v. Italy*. A very similar question was decided by the U.S. Supreme Court in two important decisions of the 1980s and 1990s, the latter (*Hudson v. U.S.*) overruling the former (*U.S. v. Halper*) and adopting a somehow more narrow and formalistic approach than the one followed by the ECHR. Below we reprint two excerpts from *Grande Stevens* and *Hudson*, and offer some comments in the "Notes and Questions" session. The cases are very interesting, bringing together the apparently distant fields of market abuse and protection of human rights.

The *Grande Stevens* decision is very long and complex; therefore before reading the judgment of the ECHR a brief overview of the facts and the procedural history can be useful. In short, in 2002 the Italian listed corporation Fiat (way before the merger that created Chrysler-Fiat) negotiated a loan with a pool of banks that would have expired in 2005. At the expiration date, in case Fiat could have not repaid the capital, the banks would have obtained Fiat's shares and offered them to existing shareholders. Due to technicalities that it is not worth examining here, in the spring of 2005 it became clear that Fiat could not repay the loan, and the consequence would have been a dilution of the controlling shareholder. To avoid this outcome, several executives and consultants of the Fiat group negotiated an equity swap with physical settlement with Merrill Lynch: pursuant to the agreement Merrill Lynch would have delivered a certain amount of Fiat shares to the controlling shareholders, thus avoiding the dilution. The Italian financial markets regulator, Consob, initiated a sanctioning procedure against Fiat's executives and consultants, among whom was Mr. Grande Stevens, arguing that the equity swap agreement had not been properly and timely disclosed to the market, and that the group issued misleading communications to the market representing an unlawful manipulation. Several individuals received very heavy administrative sanctions, up to 3 million euro, and temporary professional debarments.

Market abuse and insider trading violations, under Italian law at the time (but still now as this books goes to print), could be sanctioned both with an administrative penalty and a criminal penalty. The same is true in most European countries, in the U.S., and in other systems, for example Brazil. In fact, this possibility was not explicitly authorized by the applicable European directive, but did not seem to be explicitly prohibited either. The Italian legislature therefore, as well as other European and non-European legislatures, had provided both civil and criminal penalties. In our case, in 2008, as the administrative procedure and trials were still going on, the prosecutors charged Mr. Grande Stevens and others with criminal violations of market abuse rules. Eventually the Italian Supreme Court, in 2013, acquitted them based on the expiration of the statute of limitation, but in the meantime the accused sued the Italian government in the ECHR in Strasbourg arguing a violation of due process requirements established by the European Convention of Human Rights (one aspect that we do not focus on here), and of the *ne bis in idem* principle. The ECHR has jurisdiction over alleged violations of the European Convention on Human Rights by governments that have ratified the Convention. The Court's reasoning is premised on the idea that the "administrative" sanctions should, in fact, be considered criminal notwithstanding the "label" assigned to them by the legislature, in the light of their severity and their retributive and deterrence functions. Consequently, the Italian government had violated both the due process provision (Article 6) and the double jeopardy provision (Article 4, Protocol No.7) of the European Convention on Human Rights.

Keep in mind that the decision is relevant also for non E.U. countries. In fact, signatories of the European Convention on Human Rights also include countries that are not part of the European Union, for example Turkey. But the case is also an excellent opportunity to discuss a broader issue. And after Grande Stevens we publish an excerpt of *Hudson v. U.S.* decided by the U.S. Supreme Court in the 1990s.

GRANDE STEVENS AND OTHERS V. ITALY

European Court of Human Rights
Second Section
(Cases No. 18640/10, 18647/10, 18663/10, 18668/10 e 18698/10)
Strasbourg, March 4, 2014

[. . .]

According to established precedents of the Court, in order to establish the existence of a "criminal accusation" three criteria must be considered: the qualification of the penalty under national law, the nature and the severity of the "sanction" (Engel and Others v. Netherland, June 8, 1976). [. . .]

[As for the qualification of the penalty under Italian law, the Court acknowledges that it is classified as an administrative sanction, but points out how this is not decisive since the label given to a penalty by the national legislature cannot correspond to the substance of the penalty under the Convention.]

As for the nature of the violations, the aim of the provisions considered is to ensure the integrity of financial markets and public trust in financial transactions. Consob, the independent regulatory agency, has among its institutional goals investors' protection and the good functioning, transparency, and development of stock exchanges. These are general interests of the society normally protected with criminal sanctions [. . .]. In addition, in the opinion of the Court the monetary penalties inflicted had primarily punitive and deterrence goals. [. . .] Contrary to what the Italian Government has argued, the goals of the sanctions were not uniquely to restore a financial damage. It is noteworthy that the penalties are inflicted by the Consob proportionally to the seriousness of the conduct, not to the damage caused to investors.

As for the severity of the sanction that can be inflicted, the Court agrees with the Government that the monetary fines could not be substituted with a prison term. However, the Consob could inflict a monetary sanction up to 5,000,000 euro, and this amount could, under certain circumstances, be trebled or raised up to ten times the ill-gotten gains. The infliction of the mentioned monetary sanctions determines, for the representatives of the corporations involved, the temporary loss of their honor and, if the corporations are listed, a temporary inability to serve as executives or directors of listed corporations from two months to three years. Consob can also prohibit listed corporations from availing themselves of the professional services of the violator up to three years, and can require professional organizations to suspend the violator. Finally, the infliction of monetary sanctions implies the confiscation of the profit of the violation and of the instrumentalities used to commit the violation.

It is true that in this case the maximum sanctions have not been inflicted [. . .]. However, the criminal nature of a proceeding depends on the possible sanction, not on the sanction actually inflicted. In addition, in this case the petitioners have been sanctioned with fines between 500,000 and 3,000,000 euro, and Gabetti, Grande Stevens, and Marrone have been suspended from the ability to serve as directors and executives of listed corporations for a period between two and four months. This sanction affected the professional standing of the accused, and the fines, considering their amount, were undeniably severe and had important economic consequences.

In the light of the above and of the amount of the sanctions the Court concludes that these sanctions are criminal.

[. . .]

[This Court has already established that] Article 4 of Protocol No. 7 [of the Convention] must be interpreted in the sense that it prohibits trying or judging a person for a second "violation" if it is predicated on the same facts of the ones of a previous prosecution.

The protection of Article 4 of Protocol No. 7 applies when a verdict has been rendered. [. . .]

The decision on the new accusations is irrelevant because Article 4 of Protocol No. 7 protects against new prosecutions or the risk of new prosecutions, and does not only prohibit a second guilty verdict.

[Notwithstanding the infliction of sanctions by the Consob, later partially confirmed in court, the district attorney initiated and continued the criminal prosecution even if the petitioners had to be considered already criminally sanctioned].

We just need to decide if the prosecution by the district attorney was based on the same facts on which the previous sanctions had been inflicted. Contrary to what the Government seems to opine, it is irrelevant that some of the elements of the statutory definitions for the infliction of the "administrative" [however also considered "criminal" by this Court] and of the "criminal" sanctions are different [because, for example, the "criminal" violation, differently from the "administrative" one, requires intent], since the conduct is the same.

Consob prosecuted the petitioners, substantially, for not having properly disclosed the renegotiation of the equity swap agreement with Merrill Lynch in the press releases of August 24, 2005. The accusations of the prosecutor are based on the same facts.

According to the Court this is clearly the same conduct of the same people on the same date, as confirmed also by the Turin Court of Appeals. It follows that the second prosecution concerned a "violation" based on the same conducts that led to the infliction of the first sanctions.

This is sufficient to conclude that Article 4 of Protocol No. 7 was violated.

JOHN HUDSON V. UNITED STATES

Supreme Court of the United States
118 S.Ct. 488 (1997)

CHIEF JUSTICE REHNQUIST delivered the opinion of the Court.

The Government administratively imposed monetary penalties and occupational debarment on petitioners for violation of federal banking statutes, and later criminally indicted them for essentially the same conduct. We hold that the Double Jeopardy Clause of the Fifth Amendment is not a bar to the later criminal prosecution because the administrative proceedings were civil, not criminal. Our reasons for so holding in large part disavow the method of analysis used in *United States v. Halper,* 490 U.S. 435 (1989), and reaffirm the previously established rule exemplified in *United States v. Ward,* 448 U.S. 242 (1980).

During the early and mid-1980's, petitioner John Hudson was the chairman and controlling shareholder of the First National Bank of Tipton (Tipton) and the First National Bank of Hammon (Hammon). During the same period, petitioner Jack Rackley was president of Tipton and a member of the board of directors of Hammon, and petitioner Larry Baresel was a member of the board of directors of both Tipton and Hammon.

An examination of Tipton and Hammon led the Office of the Comptroller of the Currency (OCC) to conclude that petitioners had used their bank positions to arrange a series of loans to third parties in violation of various federal banking statutes and regulations. According to the OCC, those loans, while nominally made to third parties, were in reality made to Hudson in order to enable him to redeem bank stock that he had pledged as collateral on defaulted loans.

On February 13, 1989, OCC issued a "Notice of Assessment of Civil Money Penalty." The notice alleged that petitioners had violated 12 U.S.C. §§ 84(a)(1) and 375b (1982 ed.) and 12 CFR §§ 31.2(b) and 215.4(b) (1986) by causing the banks with which they were associated to make loans to nominee borrowers in a manner that unlawfully allowed Hudson to receive the benefit of the loans. [. . .] The notice also alleged that the illegal loans resulted in losses to Tipton and Hammon of almost $900,000 and contributed to the failure of those banks. [. . .] However, the notice contained no allegation of any harm to the Government as a result of petitioners' conduct. "After taking into account the size of the financial resources and the good faith of [petitioners], the gravity of the violations, the history of previous violations and other matters as justice may require, as required by 12 U.S.C. §§ 93(b)(2) and 504(b)," OCC assessed penalties of $100,000 against Hudson and $50,000 each against Rackley and Baresel. [. . .] On August 31, 1989, OCC also issued a "Notice of Intention to Prohibit Further Participation" against each petitioner. [. . .] These notices, which were premised on the identical allegations that formed the basis for the previous notices, informed petitioners that OCC intended to bar them from further participation in the conduct of "any insured depository institution." [. . .]

In October 1989, petitioners resolved the OCC proceedings against them by each entering into a "Stipulation and Consent Order." These consent orders provided that Hudson, Baresel, and Rackley would pay assessments of $16,500, $15,000, and $12,500 respectively. [. . .] In addition, each petitioner agreed not to "participate in any manner" in the affairs of any banking institution without the written authorization of the OCC and all other relevant regulatory agencies. [. . .]

In August 1992, petitioners were indicted in the Western District of Oklahoma in a 22-count indictment on charges of conspiracy, 18 U.S.C.

§ 371, misapplication of bank funds, §§ 656 and 2, and making false bank entries, § 1005. The violations charged in the indictment rested on the same lending transactions that formed the basis for the prior administrative actions brought by OCC. Petitioners moved to dismiss the indictment on double jeopardy grounds, but the District Court denied the motions. The Court of Appeals affirmed the District Court's holding on the nonparticipation sanction issue, but vacated and remanded to the District Court on the money sanction issue. [. . .] The District Court on remand granted petitioners' motion to dismiss the indictments. This time the Government appealed, and the Court of Appeals reversed. [. . .] That court held, following *Halper,* that the actual fines imposed by the Government were not so grossly disproportional to the proved damages to the Government as to render the sanctions "punishment" for double jeopardy purposes. We granted certiorari [. . .], because of concerns about the wide variety of novel double jeopardy claims spawned in the wake of *Halper.* We now affirm, but for different reasons.

The Double Jeopardy Clause provides that no "person [shall] be subject for the same offence to be twice put in jeopardy of life or limb." We have long recognized that the Double Jeopardy Clause does not prohibit the imposition of all additional sanctions that could, " 'in common parlance,' " be described as punishment. [. . .]

Whether a particular punishment is criminal or civil is, at least initially, a matter of statutory construction. [. . .] A court must first ask whether the legislature, "in establishing the penalizing mechanism, indicated either expressly or impliedly a preference for one label or the other." *Ward,* 448 U.S., at 248. Even in those cases where the legislature "has indicated an intention to establish a civil penalty, we have inquired further whether the statutory scheme was so punitive either in purpose or effect," [. . .] as to "transfor[m] what was clearly intended as a civil remedy into a criminal penalty" (1956).

In making this latter determination, the factors listed in *Kennedy v. Mendoza-Martinez,* 372 U.S. 144 (1963), provide useful guideposts, including: (1) "[w]hether the sanction involves an affirmative disability or restraint"; (2) "whether it has historically been regarded as a punishment"; (3) "whether it comes into play only on a finding of *scienter*"; (4) "whether its operation will promote the traditional aims of punishment-retribution and deterrence"; (5) "whether the behavior to which it applies is already a crime"; (6) "whether an alternative purpose to which it may rationally be connected is assignable for it"; and (7) "whether it appears excessive in relation to the alternative purpose assigned." It is important to note, however, that "these factors must be considered in relation to the statute on its face," [. . .], and "only the clearest proof" will suffice to override legislative intent and transform what has been denominated a civil remedy into a criminal penalty.

Our opinion in *United States v. Halper* marked the first time we applied the Double Jeopardy Clause to a sanction without first determining that it was criminal in nature. [. . .]

The analysis applied by the *Halper* Court deviated from our traditional double jeopardy doctrine in two key respects. First, the *Halper* Court bypassed the threshold question: whether the successive punishment at issue is a "criminal" punishment. Instead, it focused on whether the sanction, regardless of whether it was civil or criminal, was so grossly disproportionate to the harm caused as to constitute "punishment." In so doing, the Court elevated a single *Kennedy* factor—whether the sanction appeared excessive in relation to its nonpunitive purposes—to dispositive status. But as we emphasized in *Kennedy* itself, no one factor should be considered controlling [. . .] The second significant departure in *Halper* was the Court's decision to "asses[s] the character of the actual sanctions imposed," 490 U.S., at 447, rather than, as *Kennedy* demanded, evaluating the "statute on its face" to determine whether it provided for what amounted to a criminal sanction [. . .].

We believe that *Halper*'s deviation from longstanding double jeopardy principles was ill considered. As subsequent cases have demonstrated, *Halper*'s test for determining whether a particular sanction is "punitive," and thus subject to the strictures of the Double Jeopardy Clause, has proved unworkable. We have since recognized that all civil penalties have some deterrent effect. [. . .] If a sanction must be "solely" remedial (*i.e.,* entirely nondeterrent) to avoid implicating the Double Jeopardy Clause, then no civil penalties are beyond the scope of the Clause. [. . .]

Finally, it should be noted that some of the ills at which *Halper* was directed are addressed by other constitutional provisions. The Due Process and Equal Protection Clauses already protect individuals from sanctions which are downright irrational. [. . .] The Eighth Amendment protects against excessive civil fines, including forfeitures. [. . .] The additional protection afforded by extending double jeopardy protections to proceedings heretofore thought to be civil is more than offset by the confusion created by attempting to distinguish between "punitive" and "nonpunitive" penalties.

Applying traditional double jeopardy principles to the facts of this case, it is clear that the criminal prosecution of these petitioners would not violate the Double Jeopardy Clause. It is evident that Congress intended the OCC money penalties and debarment sanctions imposed for violations of 12 U.S.C. §§ 84 and 375b to be civil in nature. As for the money penalties, both §§ 93(b)(1) and 504(a), which authorize the imposition of monetary penalties for violations of §§ 84 and 375b respectively, expressly provide that such penalties are "civil." [. . .]

Turning to the second stage of the *Ward* test, we find that there is little evidence, much less the clearest proof that we require, suggesting that either OCC money penalties or debarment sanctions are "so punitive in form and effect as to render them criminal despite Congress' intent to the contrary." [. . .] We have long recognized that "revocation of a privilege voluntarily granted," such as a debarment, "is characteristically free of the punitive criminal element." *Helvering,* 303 U.S., at 399. Similarly, "the payment of fixed or variable sums of money [is a] sanction which ha[s] been recognized as enforceable by civil proceedings since the original revenue law of 1789." *Id.,* at 400, 58 S.Ct., at 633.

Second, the sanctions imposed do not involve an "affirmative disability or restraint," as that term is normally understood. While petitioners have been prohibited from further participating in the banking industry, this is "certainly nothing approaching the 'infamous punishment' of imprisonment." *Flemming v. Nestor,* 363 U.S. 603, 617 (1960). [. . .]

Finally, we recognize that the imposition of both money penalties and debarment sanctions will deter others from emulating petitioners' conduct, a traditional goal of criminal punishment. But the mere presence of this purpose is insufficient to render a sanction criminal, as deterrence "may serve civil as well as criminal goals." [. . .]

In sum, there simply is very little showing, to say nothing of the "clearest proof" required by *Ward,* that OCC money penalties and debarment sanctions are criminal. The Double Jeopardy Clause is therefore no obstacle to their trial on the pending indictments, and it may proceed.

The judgment of the Court of Appeals for the Tenth Circuit is accordingly affirmed.

NOTES AND QUESTIONS

1. Compare and contrast the decisions of the ECHR and the U.S. Supreme Court: which Court, in your opinion, has a more "formalistic" approach in identifying "criminal" sanctions that trigger the double jeopardy protection? Which approach do you find more convincing? Does the U.S. Supreme Court leave the door ajar allowing to conclude for the criminal nature of a penalty, notwithstanding the legislative "label" attached to it? Can you explain the difference between the *Halper* and *Hudson* decisions of the U.S. Supreme Court? Don't you think that double jeopardy protections, in the United States and in other systems, might also limit or prohibit the awarding of punitive damages in civil lawsuits? After all, the function of punitive damages is exactly and by definition to punish; they are unrelated to the actual damages suffered and to any compensatory consideration. Do you think that punitive damages in civil matters might run afoul of double jeopardy protections? Research and comment.

2.   The composition of the U.S. Supreme Court, when it decided *Hudson*, was more conservative (more justices appointed by Republican presidents and/or with a conservative background and track-record); when it decided *Halper* was more liberal. Do you think this "ideology" element might have played a role?

3.   Needless to say, the possibility to cumulate administrative sanctions and criminal sanctions, particularly in the area of insider trading, could be important to achieve deterrence, especially because the former are inflicted by an administrative agency (even if the administrative agency's determination can be challenged in court), and the latter by a court in an adversarial procedure. Following the ECHR's decision, however, how would you distinguish violations that can only lead to administrative sanctions from violations that might lead to a criminal sanction? One idea could be to provide that intentional violations only determine criminal liability and negligent violation only administrative liability, but this distinction would be very problematic, because obviously "negligent" insider trading seems an oxymoron. Another option could be to provide criminal liability depending on the damage caused in insider trading cases, and on the effect on market prices in market manipulation cases. But this option would also be very problematic: can you tell why? (Hint: think about how damages and effect on prices could be determined).

4.   In addition, even if the relevant elements of the crime and of the administrative violation could be clearly and precisely distinguished, avoiding possible overlapping, this would not entirely resolve the problem. A "race" to the courthouse between the regulatory agency and the prosecutor might still develop, for example with the former arguing that a violation is negligent, and the second that it is intentional, because as we have seen double prosecution—not only double punishment—is also prohibited by the *ne bis in idem* principle.

5.   The opinion of the ECHR also held that the administrative procedure followed by Consob violated the due process clause of the European Convention on Human Rights. This was due, first of all, to the fact that the accusation is made by one office of the Consob, but the final decision is taken by the Commission itself, the apex of the Consob, but still the same agency. Consequently, for the Court, there was no sufficient separation between the accusing and the adjudicating bodies. In addition the accused had limited access to the accusing documents, and limited rights to be heard and present evidence to the adjudicating Commission. In this perspective, therefore, the Strasbourg Court concluded that there was not sufficient separation between accuser and judge. In other cases, the Court also concluded that this deficiency of the administrative procedure (common with many administrative sanctions) could be cured if the sanctions could be challenged in court, and a full and fair trial would follow. The ECHR, however, concluded that in this case there was not a fair trial, essentially because the following trial did not involve any public hearing (in a concurring opinion, however, two ECHR judges observed that the problem was not simply the

lack of a public hearing, but more generally that the following court proceeding did not allow the defendants to fully debate the facts of the case). We did not focus on the due process claim, but what do you think about this issue? Is it common, in "administrative" sanctioning procedures, that judge and accuser are part of the same regulatory agency? Is it common that the rights of the accused are less extensive than in court for criminal violations? Just to complete: as this book is about to be finalized, Consob is amending its sanctioning procedure.

6. The *Spector* decision of the European Court of Justice in Luxembourg excerpted above had, in many ways, anticipated the conclusions of the ECHR in the *Grande Stevens* case. It should be noted, in addition, that also Italian law prohibits double jeopardy; the problem, however, is that the "administrative" sanctions were not considered "criminal," and double jeopardy only applies to criminal sanctions.

7. The reform of the Market Abuse Directive in 2014 seems to suggest that Member States cannot cumulate criminal and administrative sanctions for insider trading and market manipulations, but frankly it is not perfectly clear on this issue. This principle will become even stronger if the European Union will access the European Convention on Human Rights. So far, in fact, only single States have ratified the Convention, but not the European Union.

8. An interesting recent Spanish decision, evoking the problems of the intertwine between criminal and administrative procedures in this area, has held that the *ne bis in idem* prohibition does not exclude the possibility that the facts of a corporate transaction could be interpreted differently in a criminal trial and in a subsequent administrative procedure (Audience National, April 15, 2014, Case No. 398/2009). The general relevance of the decision is, however, dubious because the criminal and administrative procedures concerned different defendants: individuals in the first case, and the corporation they were working for in the second case. The question raised is, however, interesting: do you think that double jeopardy provisions should affect the ability of two distinct adjudicators to differently interpret the same facts? Is there an issue of "res judicata?"

9. Based on what you have read, if you are from a system different from Italy or the United States, do you think that a problem concerning double jeopardy similar to the one decided in *Grande Stevens* and in *Hudson* would be relevant in your country? Comment.

CHAPTER 12

INTERNATIONAL CORPORATE LITIGATION AND ARBITRATION

■ ■ ■

INTRODUCTION

We have almost reached the end, and we all deserve a break. This final chapter will be, in fact, fairly short. Throughout the book we have focused on substantive rules governing corporations in different jurisdictions; our goal here is simply to offer some ideas concerning issues of international litigation that might come up in your law practice. As you surely know, the three "pillars" of international private law are choice of law (determining the applicable substantive rules), jurisdiction (determining the adjudicator with the power to resolve a dispute), and enforcement of foreign judgments or arbitral awards.

We have already, in fact, discussed choice of law in Chapter 2, in which we have addressed the incorporation and real seat approaches to the regulation of the internal affairs of a corporation, their exceptions and historical evolution, and the dynamics that they might determine in terms of regulatory competition. Also in that chapter, from a jurisdictional perspective, we have briefly referred to choice of forum provisions in the governing documents of a corporation. In the following pages we just want to add something from a comparative perspective on jurisdiction, arbitration, and enforcement of judgments.

This is where international law meets comparative law, and the resulting whirlpool can be quite confusing. As promised, however, we will keep it short and simple. In exchange we only request your awareness that the aspiration of these last pages is simply to provide some general ideas and food for thought on this complex area of the law, and surely not cover in any systematic way the many technical details that could be relevant.

JURISDICTION AND ARBITRATION

Needless to say, jurisdiction is different from applicable laws (and, also needless to say, here we use the term "jurisdiction" in the sense of "power to adjudicate," not to refer to a state or government, or the extent of legislative or regulatory powers, as we have done in other parts of the book). The criteria to identify the applicable law do not coincide with the ones used to determine which court has jurisdiction. It can happen that the courts of state X have to decide a corporate dispute applying the laws of state Y.

In the United States, this happens fairly frequently. Choice of law rules generally point at one specific system (as we know, the state of incorporation, e.g., Delaware), but jurisdiction can be established in different ways (there is generally jurisdiction in the state of incorporation, but also in the state where the corporation does business, etc.). Often more than one state court can have the power to adjudicate a dispute, which might cause a "race to the courthouse" between plaintiffs and defendants, especially when the different courts have—or are perceived to have—different attitudes or procedural rules. This might result in parallel proceedings based on identical or similar facts, a circumstance under which a court might "stay" its proceedings and wait for the decision of a sister court. Attempting to litigate in different courts can also be a way, for the plaintiff, to raise the settlement value of the suit.

Jurisdiction in the U.S., also due to its federal structure, is an extremely complicated issue. Several classes of a first-year civil procedure course are dedicated only to jurisdiction. For our purposes, it is sufficient to know that a basic distinction is between subject matter jurisdiction, and personal jurisdiction. Subject matter jurisdiction concerns the power to adjudicate certain types of disputes. In terms of subject matter, State courts have general jurisdiction, meaning that they can hear any controversy except the ones explicitly excluded and attributed to the jurisdiction of other courts. This means that State courts generally can hear almost all disputes concerning the internal affairs of a corporation. On the other hand, courts of exclusive jurisdiction can only decide the types of disputes attributed to them by the legislature: federal courts are one example, since they can only decide controversies in which a federal question is raised (a violation of the U.S. Constitution, of federal law, or of a treaty), or in diversity cases (when the parties are citizens of different U.S. States or foreign citizens, and the claim exceeds $75,000). Another example of courts of exclusive jurisdiction are bankruptcy courts or were the Courts of Customs and Patent Appeals until 1982.

If subject matter jurisdiction concerns the power to decide on certain facts applying certain laws, personal jurisdiction, on the other hand, determines the power of a court to exercise jurisdiction over the parties of a lawsuit. There are different possible ways to establish personal jurisdiction: for example, if the parties have consented through a forum selection agreement, or if the person has sufficient contacts with the jurisdiction. To exercise jurisdiction, also proper notice must be given, which basically means service of process. In addition, personal jurisdiction can be *in personam* (on a person or legal entity), and *in rem* (on a thing, such as over real estate).

Another distinction is between original and appellate jurisdiction, depending on whether the court has the authority to hear the case in first instance, or only to review the judgment of a lower court. It should be noted, however, that sometimes the same court can have both original and appellate jurisdiction depending on the issue: the U.S. Supreme Court, for example, has appellate jurisdiction over judgments of the federal courts of appeals and of the state supreme courts, but original (and exclusive) jurisdiction over controversies among states, and original (but non-exclusive) jurisdiction over controversies between the federal government and the states or the states and foreign citizens or countries. Finally, sometimes jurisdiction can be discretionary, in the sense that the court has a more or less broad discretion to hear a case over which it has jurisdiction, generally through a writ of certiorari: this is famously the case, once again, for the U.S. Supreme Court; but lower courts generally *must* adjudicate controversies over which they have jurisdiction.

Jurisdiction concerns the authority to adjudicate, and is predicated on constitutional law principles; venue, on the other hand, deals with the proper geographical location of the competent court; the analysis to determine venue is usually conducted in parallel with the one concerning personal jurisdiction, since the two concepts are related. For example, once, based on subject matter jurisdiction and personal jurisdiction, you determine that a federal or state court can adjudicate one particular dispute, you need to find in which district (for federal courts) or in which county (in state courts, with the exception of Louisiana, where there are no "counties" but "parishes") there is venue.

In the international context, other important concepts are comity and forum non conveniens. These expressions refer to situations in which a court has jurisdiction, but declines to entertain the litigation deferring to a foreign court in which also jurisdiction can be established, either for reasons of comity ("reciprocity"), or because the costs and impracticalities of litigating in one country would greatly outweigh the benefits: this is the case, for example, if all the evidence, including the witnesses, is located abroad and difficult to obtain for a court in another country, it is difficult to enforce the judgment, and so on.

With this background in mind, a first problem to consider is if a forum selection clause in the governing documents of the corporation can effectively force plaintiffs to sue in the selected courts. As we have seen in Chapter 2, this is becoming more and more frequent in the U.S., and it is generally done to select Delaware courts (to apply Delaware law), avoiding multiple lawsuits. Some courts are willing to enforce this kind of provision, also when adopted by the board of directors. Consider the following case.

NORTH V. MCNAMARA

United States District Court, S.D. Ohio
2014 WL 4684377 (2014)

MICHAEL R. BARRETT, DISTRICT JUDGE.

This is a shareholder derivative action brought by Plaintiff Mildred North, an Illinois resident, against nominal Defendant Chemed Corporation and Individual Defendants Kevin McNamara, David Williams, Timothy O'Toole, Joel Gemunder, Patrick Grace, Walter Krebs, Andrea Lindell, Thomas Rice, Donald Saunders, George Walsh III, Frank Wood, and Thomas Hutton. Plaintiff, derivatively on behalf of Chemed, asserts claims for breach of fiduciary duty, abuse of control, gross mismanagement, unjust enrichment, and insider trading arising between February 2010 and the present in relation to the VITAS Innovative Hospice Care ("VITAS") segment of Chemed's business. Plaintiff contends that Individual Defendants caused VITAS to submit improper claims to Medicare and Medicaid. Plaintiff further contends that Individual Defendants caused Chemed to make false and misleading statements to the investing public, and that Chemed was damaged when its stock plummeted and it was subjected to numerous lawsuits, including a lawsuit by the United States. Department of Justice and a securities-fraud class action in this Court.

Chemed is a corporation that is incorporated under the laws of Delaware with its principal place of business in Cincinnati, Ohio. It is a publicly-traded company. VITAS is a subsidiary of Chemed that is the largest provider of hospice services in the United States. VITAS's principal place of business is Miami, Florida, but it operates in sixteen states, including Ohio and Delaware. VITAS's largest markets are Florida and California. Individual Defendants McNamara, Williams, Saunders, and Wood are residents of Ohio, Individual Defendants Grace and Walsh are residents of New York, Individual Defendant Rice is a resident of Maryland, Individual Defendants O'Toole and Gemunder are residents of Florida, Individual Defendant Lindell is a resident of North Carolina, and Individual Defendant Krebs is a resident of Kentucky.

Chemed's Certificate of Incorporation is dated March 26, 1970. It was filed on November 26, 1991 along with Form S–3. The Certificate of Incorporation provides, in pertinent part:

In furtherance and not in limitation of the powers conferred upon the board of directors by statute, the board of directors is expressly authorized, without any vote or other action by stockholders other than such as at the time shall be expressly required by statute or by the provisions hereof or the by-laws, to exercise all of the powers, rights and privileges of the corporation (whether expressed or implied herein or conferred by statute) and do all acts and things which may be done by the corporation, including but not limited to, the authority to make, adopt, alter, amend and repeal from time to time by-laws of the corporation, subject to the right of stockholders entitled to vote with respect thereto to alter and repeal by-laws made by the board of directors.

In 2010, Plaintiff purchased stocks in Chemed and has continuously been a shareholder since that time. On August 2, 2013, Chemed amended its Bylaws to include Bylaw 8.07. Bylaw 8.07 states:

Unless the corporation consents in writing to the selection of an alternative forum, a state or federal court located within the State of Delaware shall be the sole and exclusive forum for (i) any derivative action or proceeding brought on behalf of the corporation, (ii) any action asserting a claim for breach of a fiduciary duty owed by any director, officer or other employee of the corporation to the corporation or the corporation's stockholders, (iii) any actions asserting a claim arising pursuant to any provision of the Delaware General Corporation Law, the certificate of incorporation or the by-laws of the corporation or (iv) any action asserting a claim governed by the internal affairs doctrine, in each such case subject to such court having personal jurisdiction over the indispensable parties named as defendants therein.

On November 6, 2013, Plaintiff KBC Asset Management NV filed a shareholder derivative suit against certain Chemed officers and directors in the United States District Court for the District of Delaware. On November 14, 2013, Plaintiff filed this shareholder derivative suit against nominal Defendant Chemed and twelve Individual Defendants, all of whom were named as defendants in the Delaware action.

The parties [dispute] the enforceability of Bylaw 8.07 [. . .].

The determination as to the enforceability of the forum-selection clause is governed by federal law. *Wong v. PartyGaming, Ltd.,* 589 F.3d 821, 828 (6th Cir.2009). Generally, a "forum selection clause should be upheld absent a strong showing that it should be set aside." *Id.* In the Sixth Circuit, three considerations govern the enforceability determination: "1) whether the clause was obtained by fraud, duress, or other unconscionable means; 2) whether the designated forum would ineffectively or unfairly handle the suit; and 3) whether the designated forum would be so seriously inconvenient such that requiring the plaintiff to bring suit there would be unjust." *Id.* (citing *Sec. Watch, Inc. v. Sentinel*

Sys., Inc., 176 F.3d 369, 375 (6th Cir.1999)). "The party opposing the forum selection clause bears the burden of showing that the clause should not be enforced." *Wong,* 589 F.3d at 828 (citing *Shell v. R.W. Sturge, Ltd.,* 55 F.3d 1227, 1229 (6th Cir.1995)).

Plaintiff makes three primary arguments as to why Bylaw 8.07 should not be enforced. First, she argues that she did not knowingly and willing consent to the bylaw. Second, she argues that the bylaw was adopted for an improper purpose. Third, she argues that forcing her to litigate in the United States District Court for the District of Delaware would be "seriously inconvenient." Each of those arguments is addressed below.

1. Consent

Plaintiff argues that Bylaw 8.07 should not be enforced because the shareholders did not knowingly and willingly consent to it. Plaintiff points to the statement of the Sixth Circuit in *Wong* suggesting that a forum-selection clause will not be enforced if the agreement to that clause was obtained unknowingly or unwillingly. *Wong,* 589 F.3d at 828. Plaintiff indicates that a forum-selection clause cannot be obtained with the knowing and willing consent of shareholders when it is adopted unilaterally by the board of directors after the shareholders purchased their shares, after the claims arose, and without notice. [. . .]

While Defendants do not dispute that Bylaw 8.07 was adopted by the board without the shareholders' contemporaneous consent, Defendants contend that the board received the necessary consent at the time Plaintiff purchased her shares because Plaintiff agreed to be bound by the Certificate of Incorporation that permitted the board to unilaterally adopt bylaws. [. . .]

[T]he shareholders of Chemed consented to the Delaware corporate framework by buying shares in a Delaware corporation and agreeing to the certificate of incorporation that allowed the board to unilaterally adopt bylaws. The board acted in accordance with the contractual framework and the certificate of incorporation when it amended the bylaws to include the forum-selection clause. While the shareholders did not provide contemporaneous consent to the amendment, they previously chose to be bound by those bylaws adopted unilaterally by the board. [. . .]

Lastly, Plaintiff appears to rely on *Galaviz* and *In re Facebook* to support an argument that Bylaw 8.07 cannot bind her because it attempts to regulate claims that arose before its adoption and before any consent had been provided. Beyond citing to those cases, however, she does not elaborate on why the adoption of a bylaw after the purported wrongdoing should render it unenforceable.

Courts are divided on how to handle the adoption of a forum-selection bylaw after the purported wrongdoing. [. . .]

Upon considering the issue, the Court concludes that the forum-selection bylaw does not become unenforceable simply because it was adopted after the purported wrongdoing. The Court [A] corporation may enact a forum-selection bylaw that is reasonable and fair, even in circumstances such as those presented here, for the purpose of consolidating litigation—particularly litigation brought on behalf of the corporation—into a single forum to reduce costs and prevent duplication. Not only would such consolidation be in the interests of the corporation, it also would be in the interests of shareholders to have the issues resolved efficiently and consistently. Moreover, as discussed above, binding a shareholder to such a bylaw is not unreasonable or unjust given that the shareholders were on notice at the time they purchased their shares in the Delaware corporation of the broad powers conferred upon the board to make, adopt, alter, amend, or repeal the bylaws from time to time. As such, the Court does not find the fact that the claims arose primarily before the adoption of the bylaw to render that bylaw unenforceable.

2. *Improper Purpose*

Plaintiff appears to make several arguments that suggest Bylaw 8.07 should not be enforced because it was adopted for an improper purpose. The Court is not persuaded by those arguments.

[. . .] Plaintiff argues that Bylaw 8.07 "discourages the pursuit of derivative claims by increasing the difficulty and costs of such litigation." That argument is conclusory, however, and is insufficient to demonstrate an improper purpose. The argument also focuses on the difficulty and costs of the litigation for an individual plaintiff proceeding on behalf of the corporation, fails to recognize that a shareholder derivative lawsuit already was filed in Delaware, and fails to recognize the cost and efficiency benefits that inure to the corporation and its shareholders by streamlining litigation into a single forum, even if it means having to incur some costs for discovery in Ohio or from Ohio-based witnesses.

Likewise, Plaintiff's argument that the adoption of Bylaw 8.07 was a defensive maneuver aimed at protecting the Individual Defendants by "limiting the shareholders' ability to bring derivative actions" does not persuade the Court to set aside the forum-selection clause. Bylaw 8.07 does not insulate the Individual Defendants from suit; rather, it limits the forum in which shareholders may bring such an action. Plaintiff has not shown that shareholders would be precluded from bringing a shareholder derivative action in Delaware, and as mentioned previously, such an action currently is pending there. Nor has Plaintiff provided any other information or explanation that would demonstrate how proceeding in Delaware courts would be unfairly advantageous to the interests of the

Individual Defendants. Without more, the Court cannot conclude that Plaintiff met her burden of showing that the adoption of Bylaw 8.07 rose to the level of unfairness that makes it necessary to set the bylaw aside.

3. Seriously Inconvenient

Plaintiff argues that forcing her to bring suit in Delaware is "seriously inconvenient." Plaintiff cites to the fact that she is an Illinois resident, she will be forced "to retain Delaware counsel," Chemed is headquartered in Ohio with several VITAS facilities in Ohio, and she will have to incur increased difficulty and costs. A finding of serious inconvenience, however, must be based on more than the mere inconvenience of the party seek to avoid the clause. [. . .] Instead, it must appear that the enforcement of the clause would effectively deprive the plaintiffs of "a meaningful day in court." [. . .] The Sixth Circuit has previously held that a party does not satisfy this standard even where the clause was not negotiated, the plaintiffs were not sophisticated business entities, or the selected forum was in a foreign country where the possibility of a jury trial and a class-action suit was foreclosed. *Wong,* 589 F.3d at 829.

Here, the Court finds that Plaintiff has not met her "heavy burden" of showing that enforcing the forum-selection clause would be seriously inconvenient. She chose to purchase shares in the Delaware corporation, she provided the necessary consent and agreement to bind her to Bylaw 8.07, and she has not shown fraud, improper purpose, or other serious inequities as to proceeding in the District of Delaware that would weigh against enforcement of the bylaw. [. . .] As such, the Court finds the circumstances do not warrant setting aside Bylaw 8.07.

[. . .]

Consistent with the foregoing analysis, the Court hereby GRANTS Defendants' Motion to Transfer Venue Pursuant to 28 U.S.C. § 1404(a) (Doc. 13). This case shall hereby be TRANSFERRED to the United States District Court for the District of Delaware.

NOTES AND QUESTIONS

1.   Do you agree with the decision, or do you think that forum selection clauses (FSCs) adopted by directors can jeopardize investors' protection?

2.   Do you think it is relevant, for this opinion, the fact that the plaintiffs are suing derivatively? And that the corporation is listed? Could or should the conclusion be different in case, for example, of an individual shareholder suing another shareholder in a closely held corporation for an alleged breach of a fiduciary duty?

3.   How do you reconcile this case with what we have discussed in Chapter 5 with respect to the "separation of powers" of directors and

shareholders, and the issue of directors' infringing on the franchise of the shareholders?

4.   Based on the rationale of this decision, do you think that a FSC opting for a foreign court, e.g., the Commercial Division of the Supreme Court of the Commonwealth of the Bahamas, should be valid and enforceable? And what about a FSC opting for the Judicatoria of Cahul in the Republic of Moldova? (Suggestion for the Instructor: you might actually assign this question as a short take-home research).

* * *

What about jurisdiction over corporate disputes and choice of forum provisions in other systems? The European Brussels I Regulation, for example, contains the rules that European Union Member States must follow to establish jurisdiction. Let's consider how these rules would apply to corporations.

To begin with, in disputes concerning the validity of the constitution, the nullity or the dissolution of a corporation with its seat in a Member State, or the validity of the decisions of its bodies, exclusive jurisdiction is given to the courts of the state in which the corporation has its seat as determined by the rules of private international law. Needless to say, countries that are not bound by the Brussels I Regulation do not need to respect its exclusive forum requirements. For other controversies, for example claims concerning the liability of directors or shareholders, the general principle is that the courts of the state where the defendant has its domicile have jurisdiction. This general rule obviously reflects the brocard *actor sequitur forum rei*, Latin for "the plaintiff follows the forum of the defendant." But is it admissible, and to what extent, under European law, to have a forum selection clause in the bylaws? How would *North v. McNamara* be decided in Europe? The following decision of the European Court of Justice offers some ideas.

POWELL DUFFRYN PLC v. WOLFGANG PETEREIT

European Court of Justice
Case C–214/89, 10 March 1992

By order of 1 June 1989, which was received at the Court on 10 July 1989, the *Oberlandesgericht* (Higher Regional Court) Koblenz referred to the Court for a preliminary ruling pursuant to the Protocol of 3 June 1971 on the interpretation by the Court of Justice of the Convention of 27 September 1968 on Jurisdiction and the Enforcement of Judgments in Civil and Commercial Matters a number of questions on the interpretation of Article 17 of that convention, as amended by the 1978 Accession Convention (Official Journal 1978 L 304, p. 1, hereinafter referred to as the "Brussels Convention").

The questions arose in proceedings between W. Petereit, acting as liquidator of the company IBH-Holding AG, in liquidation, and Powell Duffryn plc (hereinafter referred to as "Powell Duffryn"). It appears from the papers in the case that Powell Duffryn, a company under English law, had subscribed for registered shares in IBH-Holding AG (hereinafter referred to as "IBH-Holding"), a company limited by shares under German law, when the latter's capital was increased in September 1979. On 28 July 1980 Powell Duffryn participated in the proceedings of a general meeting of IBH-Holding during which, by a show of hands, the shareholders adopted resolutions amending the statutes of IBH, in particular by inserting into them the following clause:

> "By subscribing for or acquiring shares or interim certificates the shareholder submits, with regard to all disputes between himself and the company or its organs, to the jurisdiction of the courts ordinarily competent to entertain suits concerning the company."

In 1981 and 1982 Powell Duffryn subscribed for further shares on successive increases in the capital of IBH-Holding and also received dividends. In 1983 IBH-Holding was put into liquidation and Mr Petereit, acting as liquidator, brought an action before the *Landgericht* Mainz claiming that Powell Duffryn had not fulfilled its obligations to IBH-Holding to make the cash payments due in respect of the increases in capital. He also sought to recover dividends which he maintained had been wrongly paid to Powell Duffryn.

The *Landgericht* dismissed the plea of lack of jurisdiction raised by Powell Duffryn whereupon the latter appealed to the *Oberlandesgericht* Koblenz. That court considered that the dispute raised a question of interpretation of Article 17 of the Brussels Convention, stayed the proceedings and referred the following questions to the Court of Justice for a preliminary ruling:

> "Does the rule contained in the statutes of a company limited by shares on the basis of which the shareholder by subscribing for or acquiring shares submits, with regard to all disputes with the company or its organs, to the jurisdiction of the courts ordinarily competent to entertain suits concerning the company constitute an agreement conferring jurisdiction within the meaning of Article 17 of the Brussels Convention which is concluded between the shareholder and the company?"

[. . .]

Article 17 of the Brussels Convention provides that if the parties, one or more of whom is domiciled in a Contracting State, have agreed that a court of a Contracting State is to have jurisdiction to settle any disputes which have arisen or which may arise in connection with a particular legal relationship, that court is to have exclusive jurisdiction.

It is necessary to examine whether a clause conferring jurisdiction inserted in the statutes of a company limited by shares constitutes an agreement within the meaning of Article 17 between the company and its shareholders.

Powell Duffryn maintains that a clause conferring jurisdiction contained in the statutes of a company limited by shares cannot constitute an agreement because the statutes are normative by nature and thus the contents are not open to discussion by shareholders; shareholders even face the risk of clauses being introduced against their express wishes if such a possibility is provided for in the statutes or the applicable national law.

In contrast, Mr Petereit and the Commission argue, on the basis of German law and in particular the provisions of the German *Aktiengesetz* (Law on stock corporations), that the statutes are contractual by nature and therefore a clause conferring jurisdiction contained therein constitutes an agreement within the meaning of Article 17 of the Brussels Convention.

In that regard, it appears from a comparative examination of the different legal systems of the Contracting States that the characterization of the nature of the relationship between a company limited by shares and its shareholders is not always the same. In some legal systems the relationship is characterized as contractual and in others it is regarded as institutional, normative or *sui generis*.

[W]hen it was requested to interpret the concept of "matters relating to a contract", referred to in Article 5 of the Convention, the Court held that the obligations imposed on a person in his capacity as member of an association were to be considered to be contractual obligations, on the ground that membership of an association created between the members close links of the same kind as those which are created between the parties to a contract (*see* the judgment in Case 34/82 *Peters v ZNAV*, referred to above, paragraph 13).

Similarly, the links between the shareholders of a company are comparable to those between the parties to a contract. The setting up of a company is the expression of the existence of a community of interests between the shareholders in the pursuit of a common objective. In order to achieve that objective each shareholder is assigned, as regards other shareholders and the organs of the company, rights and obligations set out in the company's statutes. It follows that, for the purposes of the application of the Brussels Convention, the company's statutes must be regarded as a contract covering both the relations between the shareholders and also the relations between them and the company they set up.

It follows that a clause conferring jurisdiction in the statutes of a company limited by shares is an agreement, within the meaning of Article 17 of the Brussels Convention, which is binding on all the shareholders.

It is immaterial that the shareholder against whom the clause conferring jurisdiction is invoked opposed the adoption of the clause or that he became a shareholder after the clause was adopted.

By becoming and by remaining a shareholder in a company, the shareholder agrees to be subject to all the provisions appearing in the statutes of the company and to the decisions adopted by the organs of the company, in accordance with the provisions of the applicable national law and the statutes, even if he does not agree with some of those provisions or decisions.

Any other interpretation of Article 17 of the Brussels Convention would lead to a multiplication of the heads of jurisdiction for disputes arising from the same legal and factual relationship between the company and its shareholders and would run counter to the principle of legal certainty.

Consequently, the reply to the national court's [. . .] question must be that a clause contained in the statutes of a company limited by shares and adopted in accordance with the provisions of the applicable national law and those statutes themselves conferring jurisdiction on a court of a Contracting State to settle disputes between that company and its shareholders constitutes an agreement conferring jurisdiction within the meaning of Article 17 of the Brussels Convention.

NOTES AND QUESTIONS

1.   The European Court of Justice spends quite some time in arguing that the bylaws of a corporation (here called "statutes") are a contract, and that the relationships among shareholders and between shareholders and the corporation are contractual in nature. Do you think this discussion is necessary? Is it really questionable whether a corporation is (also) a contract? In answering this question, keep in mind that the controversy was decided in 1992. In any case, why is it so important, to answer the certified question received from the *Oberlandesgericht* of Koblenz, to decide if bylaws can be considered a contract?

2.   In this case the dispute arose from the subscription of newly issued shares of IBH by Powell Duffryn. Do you think the solution would or should have been different if Powell Duffryn would have bought shares already outstanding from another shareholder? Should the Court take into account whether the FSC was introduced before or after the alleged wrongdoing? Would the FSC apply to a dispute between two shareholders? In case you answered negatively, would a FSC explicitly covering disputes among shareholders included in the bylaws be valid and enforceable?

3. Comparing *North v. McNamara* and *Powell Duffryn v. Wolfgang Petereit,* what are the similarities and differences between the U.S. and European approaches to jurisdiction in our area?

* * *

We have considered above the admissibility and enforceability of forum selection clauses in the governing documents of a corporation. But what about arbitration clauses? Are controversies concerning the internal affairs of a corporation arbitrable? What policy considerations does this question entail? The advantages of arbitration vis-à-vis judicial litigation are well-known: greater speed, lower costs, confidentiality, and more expertise of the adjudicators in some areas (of course not everybody agrees on these advantages, and they do not always exist). In the international context, in addition, arbitration can appear as more neutral than a national court to parties from different countries.

G. RICHARD SHELL, ARBITRATION AND CORPORATE GOVERNANCE[1]
67 N.C. L. Rev. 517 (1989)

Although arbitration of shareholder claims is a novelty for the public corporation, this dispute resolution system is well established in the context of another class of corporate entities, that of the privately held or 'close' corporation. The close corporation is the predominant form of corporate enterprise in the United States. Only about 4,000 corporations have securities listed on a national securities exchange. Another 4,000 corporations are unlisted but report regularly to the SEC. That leaves an estimated 2,500,000 corporations that do not fit into either of these regimes. Close corporations differ in four principal ways from their public counterparts. First, close corporations tend to be small businesses with few assets, whereas public corporations tend to be very large multifaceted enterprises. Second, ownership and control of the close corporation are often integrated. The stock of close corporations tends to be held by a few individuals, most of whom are actively involved in the management of the business. By contrast, public shareholders typically play no role in the management of the corporation. Third, because the stockholders are the managers, the stock of close corporations is usually 'restricted,' that is, stockholders may not sell it without first offering the stock for sale to the remaining stockholders. It follows that, in contrast to the highly liquid nature of the public shareholder's investment, there is no readily available market for close corporation shares. The absence of such a market makes valuation of shares difficult for both insiders and would-be purchasers, leads to conflicts over dividend and distribution policies, and eliminates the discipline of an active market for corporate

---

[1] Footnotes and paragraph numbers and titles omitted.

control of the close corporation. Finally, the owners of close corporations, while legally entitled to the benefit of limited liability, in practice must frequently waive this protection to gain access to credit markets. Thus, shareholders of a close corporation, unlike public shareholders, risk losing considerably more than their investment should the enterprise fail.

[. . .]

Surprisingly, in light of the facts that close and public corporations are entirely distinct forms of business enterprise and close corporations greatly outnumber public corporations, states have until recently chosen to regulate all corporations with a single set of rules drafted 'almost exclusively' with large, public corporations in mind. Thus, close corporations have been subject to the same corporate laws as public corporations for the greater part of the last 100 years and have had to cope, as best they could, with statutory norms that have sometimes proven to be ill-suited to their economic needs. In recent years many states have moved to provide close corporations with specially tailored statutory rules. Legislatures have added flexibility to general corporation statutes, legal experts have drafted entire model codes dedicated solely to close corporations, and courts have developed corporate common-law rules applicable only to close corporations. The story of how arbitration has come to be an acceptable remedy for close corporations exemplifies this legal evolution.

[. . .]

Although commentators have questioned the utility of arbitration in the close corporation setting, investors in close corporations have included arbitration clauses in negotiated shareholder agreements for many decades. Repeated legislative and judicial reforms have been needed, however, to establish arbitration as a legitimate means of dispute resolution in the close corporation context. [The experience of the state of New York is illustrative].

[. . .]

[For example, a specific] close corporation arbitration problem that has vexed the New York courts is whether shareholder derivative claims may be arbitrated. A number of early New York cases suggested that arbitration of derivative suits violated public policy. Other cases found a more technical means of avoiding arbitration by focusing on the fact that the corporation, on whose behalf the derivative claim is brought, was not a party to the shareholder arbitration agreement.

Legal commentators quickly devised a means of solving the technical problem: have the corporation sign the arbitration agreement. As to the public policy argument, recent cases have refused to draw a distinction between close corporations and their shareholders and have thus permitted derivative suits to be arbitrated. These courts have found that derivative claims of managerial waste and misappropriation are, realistically, disputes among the shareholders, not between the corporation and the alleged wrongdoer. The public policy of litigating derivative claims has therefore now given way to the policy of encouraging arbitration.

[. . .]

[A]fter nearly seventy years of legal evolution, arbitration is now utilized in New York as a close corporation remedy for virtually every kind of corporate dispute. Indeed, detailed case administration statistics compiled by the American Arbitration Association reveal that between 1984 and August 1988 the AAA received over one thousand claims and counterclaims worth over $118,000,000 under its case administration category dealing with close corporation disputes. These claims include disputes regarding stock valuation and appraisal, allegations of breach of contract, mismanagement, misrepresentation, wrongful discharge, and breach of fiduciary duty.

The few exceptions to the present pro-arbitration policy that may remain in New York or elsewhere are now subject to a new challenge. As noted earlier, the Supreme Court has recently reinterpreted the FAA as preempting attempts by the states to preclude access to the arbitral forum. When parties can convince a court that their close corporation dispute involves interstate commerce, they may be able to bypass even express statutory restrictions on arbitration, such as the New York requirement that an arbitration clause appear in the charter. Not only do FAA standards facilitate enforcement of arbitration clauses, federal law also supports confirmation of corporate arbitration awards involving attorneys' fees, punitive and multiple damages, and other extraordinary relief that might be prohibited under state law.

[. . .]

Given the seeming advantages of arbitration and the Supreme Court's enthusiastic endorsement of this dispute resolution mechanism, what objection could there be to using arbitrators to settle the complaints that public shareholders bring against their corporation and its managers and directors? The answer to this question lies in the existing legal model of state control over the large corporation. Lawsuits brought by disgruntled shareholders against incumbent managers and directors occupy a prominent place in the current model of public corporate governance. This model would be profoundly altered by the use of arbitrators in place of judges to resolve public shareholder claims.

[. . .]

Assuming a charter arbitration provision would be subject to enforcement under the FAA, who among corporate stakeholders would be entitled to enforce the provision against whom? It would appear that arbitration charter provisions could be drafted to bind both the corporation and its shareholders in disputes among themselves. Such a provision would simply declare that all disputes between shareholders and the corporation or among the shareholders *inter se* regarding corporate activities are to be arbitrated. For such a provision to encompass derivative actions, the clause would have to be expanded to include suits brought by shareholders on behalf of the corporation.

Surprisingly, directors and officers who are likely to be defendants in some derivative actions have available to them a technical argument that they should not be bound by the arbitration provision. Directors and officers are, respectively, trustees and agents of the corporation and are sued as such for breaches of fiduciary duty. Whatever the contractual status of the charter, it has not been traditionally viewed as a contract between the shareholders and the corporation's management elite. Therefore, a director might argue that he should not be bound by the charter to arbitrate any more than a third party, such as a supplier, would be bound on a contract or tort claim brought against it by the corporation.

This argument is unpersuasive. Directors and officers are much more intimately associated with the corporation than outside suppliers, other contracting parties, or even lower-level employees of the corporation. As the individuals who govern the corporation, they should be bound by any dispute resolution system provided for in the charter just as they must honor any charter rules determining the number of seats on the board, voting requirements for removal of directors, or other basic governance matters.

The binding nature of the corporation's basic documents on officers and directors is well settled, although most of the law in this area has concerned the corporate bylaws rather than the charter. Indeed, as a precautionary measure, drafters of corporate arbitration clauses may wish to include reference to the duty of officers and directors to arbitrate shareholder derivative claims in the bylaws as well as the charter. In this way, the duty to arbitrate will be brought home to those who may find themselves defendants in such actions.

Another means of eliminating any dispute regarding the duty of directors and officers to arbitrate would be through the use of signed employment agreements between them and the corporation calling for arbitration or referencing the duty to arbitrate set forth in the charter and bylaws. With an explicit contract in hand, the shareholders suing on behalf of the corporation would have the strongest possible grounds for insisting on arbitration.

By the same token, directors, officers, and the corporation itself would have standing to demand that plaintiff shareholders abide by the charter arbitration agreement. Since the corporation is joined in a derivative action as a nominal defendant, it could easily move to compel arbitration of any derivative claim brought improperly by shareholders.

[...]

Scholars representing diverse points of view appear ready to accept arbitration as a means of resolving public shareholder disputes. Economist Daniel Fischel, while not advocating arbitration, has nevertheless expressed surprise that arbitration is not encountered in the public corporation setting. [...]

Professor John Coffee, the Reporter for the American Law Institute's Corporate Governance Project section on 'Remedies,' has identified numerous practical and legal objections to the arbitration of public shareholder disputes based on current law and policy, but he has nevertheless advocated that public corporations be permitted to adopt arbitration under certain conditions. He has proposed that arbitration be permitted so long as the process is adequately structured to protect shareholder and public interests. Such protection should be assured, according to Coffee, by requiring corporations to adopt model arbitration provisions drafted and monitored by neutral groups such as the ALI.

Other scholars favoring intrusive legal intervention in corporate affairs have not yet spoken on the issue of arbitration, but some are sure to criticize the arbitration alternative. Such critics are likely to raise a number of objections. Critics can be expected to echo the objections already discussed regarding sterilization of the board, the inadequacy of arbitration procedures to handle complex cases, and the possibility of collusive settlements if there is no oversight by a court.

On a practical level, critics may also argue that arbitration will result in prejudice to shareholders because courts are reluctant to grant injunctive relief in cases where arbitration has been stipulated. In cases where mergers and takeovers are at issue, injunctions may be crucial in preserving the corporate status quo pending a resolution on the merits of the controversy. There is also danger that corporations will manipulate the manner in which arbitrators are named and 'stack the deck' against shareholders to assure favorable results in arbitration. Finally, arbitrators may refuse to award legal fees to successful plaintiffs' lawyers and remove the incentive for bringing derivative suits in the first instance.

On a more fundamental level, critics may argue that arbitration threatens substantive shareholder rights and weakens the deterrent effects of fiduciary rules. Arbitration awards need not be based on or explained in terms of the law. Fiduciary norms may therefore be subordinated to general equitable principles in arbitration, a result that would lead to inconsistent application of existing legal rules and a reduction in the deterrent value of such rules. Arguably, shareholders would cease to have any meaningful legal rights under corporate law if the only decision makers to which they could apply for relief would be free to misapply the law.

* * *

Arbitration of internal corporate disputes is gaining traction in several systems, as part of the general trend favoring arbitration. Arnoldo Wald, a Brazilian lawyer, for example, has recently reported that "[t]he Brazilian Corporations Act (Law No 6404/76, as amended by Law No 10303/2011) allows for a company's by-laws to provide for arbitration to settle disputes between the company and its shareholders, and disputes between majority and minority shareholders (Article 109(3)) [. . .]. The companies which participate in the New Market (Novo Mercado) of BOVESPA are subject to the New Market Rules, which provide for arbitration in broader terms than Article 109(3) and expressly state that the company's senior managers [. . .] are also subject to arbitration in order to settle disputes concerning listing and sanctions regulations, listing agreements, etc. Further, the Arbitration Centre of BOVESPA has recently revised its arbitration rules." (*Current Problems in Brazilian Arbitration Involving Corporate Law*, 17 No. 1 IBA Arb. News 67 (2012)). Issues under Brazilian law are not profoundly different from issues discussed in other legal systems, for example concerning whether an arbitration clause in the bylaws also binds shareholders that did not vote in favor of it, and the problem of representation of minority shareholders in arbitrations concerning listed corporations, which might be treated as multiparty arbitration.

Under Italian law, arbitration of corporate disputes is allowed (and to some degree favored), but only in closely held corporations. Article 34 of Legislative decree No. 5 of 2003 reads as follows:

"1. A clause in the charters of non-listed and non-registered corporations can provide for the arbitrability of some or all controversies among shareholders or between shareholders and the corporation.

2. The clause sets forth the number and the rules for the appointment of the arbitrators conferring in any case the power to appoint all the arbitrators to a third party. If the third party

does not appoint the arbitrators, the appointment is made by the President of the tribunal where the corporation has its seat.

3. The clause binds the corporation and all shareholders, including the ones whose status as shareholders is disputed.

4. The charters can provide that the arbitration provision includes lawsuits in which the plaintiffs or defendants are the directors, the statutory auditors or the liquidators of the corporation. Such provision is binding upon these subjects as a consequence of their acceptance of the office. [. . .]

5. Amendments to the corporate charter introducing or eliminating an arbitration provision must be approved by a majority of two-thirds of the outstanding shares. Absent or dissenting shareholders can exercise, within ninety days, an appraisal right."

Although arbitration is also a common form of dispute resolution in Germany, it is not particularly common in German corporate law. One reason might be that the German statutes on closely held corporations (GmbH) and stock corporations (AG) do not explicitly deal with arbitration, therefore leading to uncertainty. However, since especially disputes concerning the validity of shareholders' meetings resolutions usually drag along for a long time in German courts, practitioners began to use arbitration as a form of dispute resolution in this area. Since this usually requires an agreement of the parties of the dispute, which is normally hard to reach once the dispute has arisen, the question came up whether a binding arbitration clause governing these disputes could be included in the corporate charter. Originally, the Federal Court of Justice was reluctant and held that such arbitration clauses are void (BGHZ 132, 278 = NJW 1996, 1753). More recently, however, joining a worldwide trend toward greater acceptance of arbitration, the Federal Court of Justice generally upheld these provisions as long as certain protections for shareholders are met (BGHZ 180, 221 = NJW 2009, 1962). Unfortunately, this decision concerns closely held corporations and it is not entirely clear if it also applies to stock corporations. The uncertainty is fostered by the fact that Sec. 23 subs. 5 of the German Stock Corporation Law provides that the charter can opt out of its provisions only if it is explicitly permitted (in other words, in this respect you might argue that everything that is not expressly permitted, is prohibited). Since the German Stock Corporation Law only refers to state courts, the majority of legal scholars conclude that arbitration clauses cannot be included in the charters of stock corporations. Nevertheless, it is generally accepted that a dispute concerning a shareholders' meeting resolution can be decided by an arbitration tribunal if all shareholders agree. Needless to say, based on this approach, arbitration would be impossible in a listed corporation considering the obvious fact that, given the high number of shareholders and the difficulty in identifying beneficial owners of shares, unanimous consent cannot be reached.

NOTES AND QUESTIONS

1.   What do you think are the reasons for greater skepticism, of both scholars and policy makers, for arbitration of corporate law disputes in publicly held corporations rather than in closely held corporations? Can you come up with a list of arguments?

2.   Consider however the intriguing case of Brazil briefly mentioned above. The Bovespa, the Brazilian Stock Exchange, requires corporations listing on the so-called "Level 2" or "Novo Mercado," two segments reserved for corporations that adopt best practices, to provide arbitration of disputes with shareholders through an arbitration panel sponsored by the Bovespa itself. It is quite controversial, in Brazil, if minority shareholders can still decide to have their case heard by a court, and whether they are bound by the arbitration procedure, but the procedure must be available for corporate disputes. In other words, you can argue that the Brazilian Stock Exchange has adopted an approach that is opposite to the one of the legislatures we have mentioned before: they favor arbitration in listed companies, and in fact make it almost necessary. The explanation might have to do with the perception that state courts are either inefficient, incompetent or corrupt. What do you think? Do you think that under certain circumstances arbitration can be preferable to courts also to protect small investors? One additional data that you might consider is that arbitration is the preferred dispute resolution mechanism used in case of breach of shareholders' agreement in Brazil. According to an empirical research by H. Masullo, *Shareholder Agreement in Publicly Traded Companies: A Comparison Between the U.S. and Brazil* (2015), available on *www.ssrn.com*, roughly 78% of Brazilian agreements are subject to arbitration. What do you think it means?

3.   In your opinion, are some (or all) of the arguments that we have considered before, in the two cases discussing the admissibility of forum selection clauses, relevant in the discussion on arbitration agreements too?

4.   What could be the problems of applying an arbitration clause included in the charter or bylaws of a corporation to derivative lawsuits brought against corporate directors?

5.   The Italian legislature allows arbitration agreements in closely held corporations, but only if approved with a supermajority (2/3), and in any case granting to dissenting and absent shareholders an appraisal right. What is the rationale of these provisions? Why so much concern for shareholders that do not explicitly approve arbitration? Can you make a comparison with what we discussed concerning the approval of extraordinary corporate transactions when we discussed mergers and sales of assets in Chapter 9?

6. One argument commonly used against the practicability of arbitration in the corporate context is the following: a typical arbitration clause provides that each party appoints an arbitrator, and the two party-appointed arbitrators jointly appoint the president of the arbitration tribunal. Also when the clause provides for a single arbitrator, the two parties are supposed to agree on the person to appoint. These provisions are generally designed for situations in which there are two parties. Corporate disputes, however, often involve multiple parties, for example three shareholders with different and conflicting positions, two directors, and the corporation itself. The critique, therefore, is that arbitration is ill-suited for these disputes. Can you imagine an answer to this objection? Or, better, can you imagine a system to avoid the problem indicated? What about having an independent third party, for example a highly respected judge or the dean of a law school, appoint the arbitrator or the arbitrators when the litigants are more than two? Have you noticed, in this respect, that another condition imposed by the Italian legislature is that the arbitrators must be appointed by a third party? Do you think this might be the reason for such a provision?

7. What about the possibility to obtain preliminary injunctions in arbitration? And the ability of an arbitral tribunal to subpoena witnesses? Are these instruments available in arbitral proceedings? And do you think they are particularly important in corporate disputes?

8. Based on our discussion, do you think it is admissible to include an arbitration clause in a shareholders' agreement applying to the disputes arising from the agreement? And in a merger agreement?

9. It is fairly common, in international joint-venture agreements, or in shareholders' agreements among parties from different countries, to provide for an arbitration clause. If your goal is to ensure a broad coverage of the arbitration clause, however, be aware that there might be clever ways to go around it. Imagine for a moment that you are assisting a Chinese corporation, Jang Inc., creating a joint venture with a Serbian corporation, Zbatin Inc. The joint venture will be established as a corporation incorporated in Serbia, Jatin Inc., in which Jang, your client, will have a 48% stake and Zbatin a 52% participation. As part of the agreement, Zbatin requires that Jang and Jatin execute a contract under which Jang will provide Jatin with certain materials. On behalf of Jang, you negotiate the contract and obtain the inclusion of an arbitration provision, because both you and your client do not want to have to litigate in a Serbian court. In case of a dispute concerning an alleged breach of this contract, however, Zbatin might argue, for example, that there was a tortious interference with contractual relationships by Jang, which damaged Jatin and/or Zbatin. In this way they might conclude that the arbitration provision, covering contractual disputes, would not apply, and that Serbian courts would have jurisdiction. What we want to warn you about here is that it is difficult to write an arbitration provision that covers any possible way in which the parties might present their claims. A common strategy to try to avoid an arbitration provision is to argue that the claim is not based on the contract,

but it is instead a tort. Sometimes this is possible. How would you protect your client against this risk?

10. In 2010, new rules were adopted in Delaware implementing a new statutory arbitration procedure that employs sitting chancellors as arbitrators in confidential proceedings before the Delaware Chancery Court. This procedure raises several questions: is it appropriate for judges to also act as arbitrators? Is it desirable to have confidential proceedings in front of adjudicators that also serve as judges? For a discussion of this fascinating issue, see Brian J.M. Quinn, *Arbitration and the Future of Delaware's Corporate Law Franchise*, 14 CARDOZO J. CONFLICT RESOL. 829 (2013).

* * *

In multinational corporate groups, one issue frequently litigated is if the forum of the parent corporation can adjudicate controversies concerning the subsidiaries and, vice versa, if the parent can be sued in the forum of the subsidiaries. Here we are not talking specifically of disputes concerning the internal affairs of a corporation, but more generally controversies concerning corporate activities, and in particular torts. There are several variations of this question, but consider, for example, if the courts of the forum where the subsidiary of a foreign parent corporation is located have jurisdiction over the parent for the acts of the subsidiary. This problem is often very important in international practice because it might happen that the parent corporation has deeper pockets than the subsidiaries, and also because the settlement value of the case might increase if the plaintiffs are able to sue the parent. Consider, for example, the situation of an investor alleging to be defrauded in France by the French wholly owned subsidiary of a Japanese corporation. Can the investor hold also the Japanese parent corporation liable? Can she sue it in France? The first question depends on substantive law issues, including possibly veil-piercing theories, and the second on connected jurisdictional principles.

Needless to say, there might be some specific statutory provisions concerning extraterritorial jurisdiction (so-called "long-arm" statutes), but what about general rules?

In the U.S., according to one source (Justin Kesselman, *Note. Multinational Corporate Jurisdiction & the Agency Test: Should the United States Be a Forum for the World's Disputes?* 47 NEW ENG. L. REV. 361 (2012)), "The vast majority of circuits apply the 'alter-ego' test, under which a parent company may be sued in a jurisdiction where its subsidiary sits if the subsidiary is a mere instrumentality of the parent, and failure to disregard their separate entities would result in fraud or injustice." Basically, this is a form of veil piercing for jurisdiction purposes. "A minority of circuits permit variations of the 'agency' test as an alternative, setting a much lower threshold for personal jurisdiction."

According to this test (which has been adopted, even if with minor variations, by the Second and Ninth Circuits, both very important courts for international law purposes since they cover respectively New York and California) "a court can assert jurisdiction over a foreign corporation when it affiliates itself with a resident representative entity 'that renders services on behalf of the foreign corporation that . . . are sufficiently important to the foreign entity that the corporation itself would perform equivalent services if no agent were available.' The defendant need not 'exercise[ ] direct control over its putative agent,' and thus '[a]lthough termed 'agency' by the courts . . . [i]t is manifestly not a common law agency relationship."

Also the opposite question is interesting: can the foreign subsidiary of a U.S. parent be sued in the U.S. for an alleged tort committed abroad? The Supreme Court has addressed this question in several cases; the following short excerpt offers an interesting and fairly recent perspective.

GOODYEAR DUNLOP V. BROWN
Supreme Court of the United States
131 S.Ct. 2846 (2011)

JUSTICE GINSBURG delivered the opinion of the Court.

This case concerns the jurisdiction of state courts over corporations organized and operating abroad. We address, in particular, this question: Are foreign subsidiaries of a United States parent corporation amenable to suit in state court on claims unrelated to any activity of the subsidiaries in the forum State?

A bus accident outside Paris that took the lives of two 13-year-old boys from North Carolina gave rise to the litigation we here consider. Attributing the accident to a defective tire manufactured in Turkey at the plant of a foreign subsidiary of The Goodyear Tire and Rubber Company (Goodyear USA), the boys' parents commenced an action for damages in a North Carolina state court; they named as defendants Goodyear USA, an Ohio corporation, and three of its subsidiaries, organized and operating, respectively, in Turkey, France, and Luxembourg. Goodyear USA, which had plants in North Carolina and regularly engaged in commercial activity there, did not contest the North Carolina court's jurisdiction over it; Goodyear USA's foreign subsidiaries, however, maintained that North Carolina lacked adjudicatory authority over them.

A state court's assertion of jurisdiction exposes defendants to the State's coercive power, and is therefore subject to review for compatibility with the Fourteenth Amendment's Due Process Clause. International Shoe Co. v. Washington, 326 U.S. 310 (1945) (assertion of jurisdiction over out-of-state corporation must comply with "traditional notions of fair play and substantial justice") [. . .]

A court may assert general jurisdiction over foreign (sister-state or foreign-country) corporations to hear any and all claims against them when their affiliations with the State are so "continuous and systematic" as to render them essentially at home in the forum State. [. . .] Specific jurisdiction, on the other hand, depends on an "affiliatio[n] between the forum and the underlying controversy," principally, activity or an occurrence that takes place in the forum State and is therefore subject to the State's regulation. [. . .] In contrast to general, all-purpose jurisdiction, specific jurisdiction is confined to adjudication of "issues deriving from, or connected with, the very controversy that establishes jurisdiction." [von Mehren & Trautman, *Jurisdiction to Adjudicate: A Suggested Analysis*, 79 Harv. L.Rev. 1121, 1136 (1966)].

Because the episode-in-suit, the bus accident, occurred in France, and the tire alleged to have caused the accident was manufactured and sold abroad, North Carolina courts lacked specific jurisdiction to adjudicate the controversy. The North Carolina Court of Appeals so acknowledged. Were the foreign subsidiaries nonetheless amenable to general jurisdiction in North Carolina courts? Confusing or blending general and specific jurisdictional inquiries, the North Carolina courts answered yes. Some of the tires made abroad by Goodyear's foreign subsidiaries, the North Carolina Court of Appeals stressed, had reached North Carolina through "the stream of commerce"; that connection, the Court of Appeals believed, gave North Carolina courts the handle needed for the exercise of general jurisdiction over the foreign corporations.

A connection so limited between the forum and the foreign corporation, we hold, is an inadequate basis for the exercise of general jurisdiction. Such a connection does not establish the "continuous and systematic" affiliation necessary to empower North Carolina courts to entertain claims unrelated to the foreign corporation's contacts with the State.

NOTES AND QUESTIONS

1. Based on what you have read, let's consider a more general question. Imagine a corporate group in which A, the holding corporation, is incorporated, has its real seat and does business in country X; and its subsidiary B is incorporated, has its real seat and does business in country Y. Now imagine two possible plaintiffs: Mr. C, claiming that he has been defrauded by A in X, and Ms. D, claiming that she has been defrauded by B in Y. Without knowing anything else (obviously the answer might depend on the countries, the precise underlying claim, where the conduct of the defendants occurred and where their effects were felt, etc.), do you think it might be easier for Mr. C to have the courts of X asserting jurisdiction also on B, or for Ms. D to have the courts of Y assert jurisdiction also on A? Why?

2.   We have mentioned before that veil piercing or agency principles might be used to establish jurisdiction over the parent of a subsidiary in the forum of the latter. We should also underline, however, that sometimes veil piercing or agency concepts can be the ground to sue in a court different from the one where the subsidiary is located. A typical example is the following: imagine that your client is a Texan suing in Texas a Texas corporation in state court, but is concerned that, for a number of reasons, the Texan state court might not be the best option for her, and she would prefer to sue in a federal court. If she can argue that the parent of the Texan corporation, for example a Delaware company with its headquarter in Massachusetts, is responsible for the alleged wrongdoing based on agency principles or veil-piercing, your client might be able to invoke diversity jurisdiction and go to federal court. You might remember this example: we mentioned a variation of this case in Chapter 3.

3.   If you are from a jurisdiction different from the U.S., or if you are familiar with a jurisdiction different from the U.S., how do you think in this jurisdiction the above-mentioned questions would be answered? For example, how would the issue decided by the U.S. Supreme Court in *Goodyear Dunlop v. Brown* be decided in your system or the system you are considering? (This question can also be assigned as a take-home).

ENFORCEMENT OF FOREIGN JUDGMENTS AND ARBITRAL AWARDS

Without the possibility of having a foreign judgment recognized and enforced where the losing party has assets, the judgment can obviously result in a mockery for the winning party. Interestingly enough, thanks to the 1958 New York Convention on the Recognition and Enforcement of Foreign Arbitral Awards, it is somehow easier and more likely to enforce an international arbitral award than the judgment of a foreign court. This is in fact often used as an argument for the superiority of arbitration in international disputes. As of 2014, roughly 150 countries had ratified the Convention, with most exceptions in Africa, and some non-signatories states in South America (Guyana and Suriname), in the Middle East (Yemen, Iraq), and in Asia (Papua New Guinea, Taiwan, and North Korea). No international agreement with a scope similar to the one of the New York Convention exists for the recognition and enforcement of foreign judgments, even if several bilateral, multilateral, or regional treaties have been signed (for example, think of the 1969 Brussels Convention in Europe, and the 2005 Hague Convention).

With respect to foreign judgments, to make a long story short, courts are generally willing to enforce them as long as the decision or its effects do not violate some principle of "public order" or "public policy" of the State of enforcement. The standard is fairly high, and generally violations are only relevant if they offend basic notions of justice. As you can imagine, in the area of corporate law, it is not very common—at least among countries that share a basic regulatory framework—that a judgment is so egregious from the perspective of the legal values of another country to be denied enforcement on public policy grounds.

Similarly, with respect to arbitration, the grounds for setting aside and not enforcing an arbitral award under the New York Convention are very narrow. Most of them concern the arbitral agreement and major procedural violations (incapacity of the parties or invalidity of the agreement, due process violations, decision not limited to the terms of the submission, composition of the arbitral tribunal not according with the agreement or the applicable law, non-finality of the award). In addition, enforcement is not possible if the award is contrary to the public policy of the country where enforcement is sought, but this is generally interpreted in the sense that the award must violate the most basic notions of morality and justice, a clearly extreme hypothesis.

It is, however, not entirely impossible, also in the area of corporate law, that a country might find a judgment or an arbitral award based on the substantive or procedural laws of another country profoundly contrary to its public policy principles. Examples can be decisions in class action litigation in countries that do not recognize collective redresses, and especially U.S.-style opt-out class actions; decisions awarding punitive damages in countries in which private parties are only entitled to compensatory damages; and also some substantive corporate law principles, for example—but this could be a stretch—piercing the corporate veil in legal systems in which piercing is impossible or allowed only on very narrow grounds.

The following Japanese case, although not dealing specifically with the internal affairs of a corporation, offers the occasion to discuss the public policy defense to the enforcement of a foreign judgment.

SUPREME COURT OF JAPAN, 11 JULY 1997

11 July 1997, 51 Saiko Saibansho Minji Hanreishu 2573

Facts

Northcon I, the plaintiff, is an Oregon partnership established to develop a facility for Maruman Integrated Circuits, Inc. (hereinafter, "MIC"), which is a California corporation. MIC was a subsidiary of Mansei Kogyo Co. (hereinafter, "Mansei Co."), a Japanese corporation. A dispute arose between Northcon I and MIC, and MIC filed an action in the Superior Court of the State of California against Northcon I. The present case relates to the counterclaim filed by Northcon I against Mansei Co., its CEO, Mr. Katayama, and other officers of Mansei Co. and MIC.

Section 3294 of the California Civil Code entitles plaintiff for payment of punitive damages in addition to actual damages for fraudulent actions by the defendant.

On May 19, 1982, the Superior Court of California rendered a judgment, ordering Mansei Co. and Katayama to pay $1,125,000 as punitive damages, in addition to $425,251 as compensatory damages and $40,104.71 as costs. On May 12, 1987, the Court of Appeals of California affirmed this judgment, which became irrevocable.

Northcon I filed this action in the Tokyo District Court against Mansei Co. and Katayama, seeking the enforcement of the Californian judgment. On February 18, 1991, the District Court granted permission to enforce the part of the judgment regarding compensatory damages, but refused to grant permission to enforce the part regarding punitive damages. Both sides appealed to the Tokyo High Court. The High Court affirmed the judgment of the District Court and dismissed both appeals.

Northcon I appealed to the Supreme Court.

Court's Decision

In an action for the enforcement of a foreign judgment under Article 24 of the Civil Execution Act, courts must determine whether the judgment for which enforcement is sought satisfies the conditions set forth in Article 200 of the Code of Civil Procedure [Article 118(iii) of the current Code of Civil Procedure]. In particular, pursuant to Article 200(iii) of the Code the foreign judgment must not violate the public policy of Japan. The mere fact that the rules or institutions upon which the foreign judgment is based are not adopted in Japan, in itself, does not constitute a breach of Japanese public policy. When a foreign judgment is incompatible with the fundamental principles or basic tenets of the Japanese legal system, however, it is against Japanese public policy under the above provision.

The law on punitive damage under the California Civil Code obviously intends to achieve retribution and deterrence by sentencing the perpetrator of a malicious act to pay more than the amount of actual damages. Thus, it has basically the same function of criminal sanctions such as fines in Japan. In contrast, tort law in Japan purports to compensate the victim and to restore the situation existing before the tort, by making the tortfeasor pay the amount of actual damages suffered by the victim (*see* Supreme Court of Japan, March 24, 1993, MINSHU Vol.47, No.4, 3039). Punishment of the tortfeasor or deterrence of future similar conducts (general deterrence) is not the objective, even if it can be a side effect of liability. This is essentially different from punitive damage, the primary purposes of which are punishment of the tortfeasor and general deterrence. In Japan, these objectives are left to criminal and administrative sanctions. Thus, punitive damages exceeding actual damages are incompatible with the fundamental principles or basic tenets of Japanese tort law.

The part of the foreign judgment in the present case ordering the appellee company to pay punitive damages in addition to the compensatory damages and costs, with a punitive purpose, may not be enforced, as it is against the public policy of Japan.

NOTES AND QUESTIONS

1. The Supreme Court of Japan clearly states that a mere difference between foreign law and Japanese law is not sufficient to make a foreign judgment unenforceable. The foreign decision must be "incompatible with the fundamental principles or basic tenets of the Japanese legal system." Which rules shall be considered "fundamental or basic" and which ones not, however, is often hard to determine. Now, at the end of this book, try to list possible "fundamental tenets" of corporate law in some of the jurisdictions we considered, or in a different one you are familiar with. Check out this list: free transferability of the shares, proportionality between equity investment and voting rights (one-share, one-vote), limited liability of shareholders, liability of directors for violations of their duties toward the corporation, appraisal rights for dissenting shareholders in case of merger, pre-emptive rights when new shares are issued, limits to the issuance of bonds, prohibition of insider trading. Is any of these a "fundamental" principle of corporate law, at least in some jurisdictions, so that a foreign decision that might offend it would not be enforced?

2. Judgments granting punitive damages are not so common in the context of corporate law. Some rules, however, could have a punitive effect. One example is the disgorgement of short-swing trade profits by insiders under Section 16(b) of the Securities and Exchange Act of 1934 in the U.S. (see Chapter 11). Interestingly enough, in this respect, even if Japan does not allow punitive damages and, as we have seen, considers judgments awarding them unenforceable, Japan has a similar rule in the Financial Instruments and Exchange Act: Article 164. The method for calculating the profits is the "first-in, first-out," however, which differs from the U.S. rule and generally makes the Japanese rule less punitive. Based on this admittedly limited information, do you think that a U.S. court decision for disgorgement of short-swing profits under Section 16(b) would be enforceable in Japan if the measure of "damages" would exceed what would be allowed under Japanese law? Put yourself in the shoes of a Japanese judge.

3. Discuss whether a U.S. judgment in a securities class action case would be enforceable in Japan, or in other jurisdictions that we have considered or that you are familiar with (for a brief comparative analysis of class actions, see Chapter 7). Why yes, or why not?

FINAL THOUGHTS

■ ■ ■

The father of one of the authors of this book (we will not disclose which one) is an engineer. As a young lawyer before, and law professor later, this author was often asked legal questions by his father. His answers would generally start with "It depends." The father was not very pleased. "The law," he would comment, "offers no certainties, it always depends. As an engineer, if I am asked if a bridge will collapse, I cannot say that it depends, I must give a straightforward answer."

Well, that is not entirely true. Also the fact that a bridge will not fall depends on certain variables: how strongly will the wind blow, what type of earthquake might hit the area, how well maintained the structure is, how much heavy traffic will drive over it. At best, an engineer can say that the bridge will not collapse *under certain* conditions, offer a confidence interval, which is a cool way to say that it depends. Not to sound like a rabid relativist, but even the so-called "hard sciences," especially after the twentieth century, have acquired the instruments to embrace complexity and uncertainty: think of chaos theory, just to mention one example. A professor of English literature, in an interesting little book that is actually better than its title might suggest, warns his readers: "If I sometimes speak [. . .] as if a certain statement is always true, a certain condition always obtains, I apologize. 'Always' and 'never' are not words that have much meaning in literary study" (Thomas C. Foster, *How to Read Literature Like a Professor*, HarperCollins, 2003). The same caveat applies—to some degree—to fields as diverse as engineering, astrophysics, heart surgery, ethology, philology, criminology, and certainly law.

But we can be sympathetic with the frustration of an engineer talking to a jurist. The problem is that the layperson would ask: "If Cain kills Abel, is he guilty of first degree murder and will he be sentenced to life in prison?" But the professional jurist, correctly, must reply: "It depends. It depends on his intentions, on whether he premeditated the murder, on whether he acted in self-defense, on how he obtained the weapon he used, on whether there were attenuating or aggravating circumstances. And as for the second part of the question, on the possible outcome of the trial, it also depends on the evidence gathered, on how it is presented, on whether there is a jury or not, and so on." (Well, in *that* case the Judge had pretty broad discovery powers, but was quite magnanimous. . .).

653

In many ways the important and difficult task, for a jurist—but also for other professionals—is not so much to find the "right answers," but to be able to formulate the right questions; to know what to look for and where to look for it is the real intellectual challenge. To find and effectively formulate the answers is not to be discounted, but is often easier. A vet must know that he has to look at your pet's pupils and check if they are dilated and how they react to light to rule out poisoning. A good question is a place to start, and if you do not have a place to start, you can hardly go anywhere.

When you add an international and comparative dimension to your legal studies or practice, questions multiply, and everything becomes even more relative. "It depends" becomes almost a *Leitmotif*. But that does not mean that, after a few well-thought "It depends," you cannot come up with a more precise, complete, useful, and sophisticated answer than the one you would have uttered without considering all the relevant variables.

With this book we hope to have given you some hints on how to formulate your questions, and how to find your answers. As we said since the beginning, we think that this exercise has not only an obvious pedagogical, cultural, and theoretical importance (think out of the box, understand better your own system, ponder the causes and effects of different legal rules . . .), but also a practical value. No one is an expert in many legal systems, and in any case not to work with a local counsel when you are dealing with a jurisdiction in which you are not licensed is not only unadvisable, but Professional Liability 101. However, to have an idea of the major comparative differences, or at least to be trained in the comparative methodology, helps you not to take anything for granted, and possibly ask the right questions to the local counsel you are working with.

More concretely, we have been on a long and challenging journey. A quest, we might say. It has started with a "motivational speech" and some methodological and background information (Chapter 1). We have then considered how you identify the applicable corporate laws, and how the interaction between different jurisdictions can contribute to shape corporate laws (Chapter 2). How corporations are born, what financial resources they need to grow, and how they take their decisions have been the next issues (Chapters 3, 4, and 5). As in all families, also in the corporate law family fights occur, and in this perspective we have talked about directors' liability (Chapter 6) and shareholders' litigation (Chapter 7). Chapter 8, on Shareholders' Agreements, discussed to what extent shareholders can modify the normal inner workings of the corporation with separate contracts among themselves. We have not shied away from occasionally spicy topics, such as marriages (i.e., mergers, Chapter 9), and other trysts, consensual and not (i.e., friendly and hostile takeovers, Chapter 10). One particular type of pathology, insider trading, has been examined in Chapter 11. And finally we have—even if just briefly—placed the corporation on the chessboard of international litigation, talking about jurisdiction, arbitration, and enforcement of judgments (Chapter 12).

In this quest, we have encountered specific rules, but we have also— sometimes implicitly—discussed broader concepts. Different regulatory techniques have been examined, for example ex ante statutory provisions versus ex post judge-made norms, and "rules" versus "standards." Often we have questioned what the economic, historical, and political causes and consequences of certain provisions have been or could be. We have sometimes called your attention to what an intelligent (cagey?) lawyer could do to better serve the interests of her client, to what an enlightened legislature might provide, to what a Solomonic adjudicator would decide. Hopefully the menu has been varied enough that most of you found something to his or her liking.

In literature, the archetype of the quest story requires certain fixed elements: a young person with a stated mission (Gilgamesh must go to the Cedar Forest to kill the ogre Humbaba); several hurdles along the way (slaying Humbaba and Gugalanna the Bull of Heaven, coping with the death of Enkidu); and a final revelation, generally unrelated to the quest and concerning the hero or heroine himself or herself, a revelation that gives him or her a more profound self-awareness and self-knowledge (Gilgamesh's acceptance of his mortality). Our hurdles have been tricky contractual provisions, abstruse codes, mysterious court's opinions, unclear economic effects. What knowledge, if any, you have acquired along the way is something that we leave for you to decide.

One final thing. To have an international and comparative perspective does not mean to operate in an "international" legal vacuum, in a jurist's no-man's-land, to forget that most legal systems are, by definition, national and local, to superficially overlook the details of a legal system in order to only consider broad, and inevitably vague, general concepts. On the contrary, it requires you to understand as deeply as possible one system (often, the one in which you receive your legal education and in which you operate), but to be able to derive from your knowledge a broader understanding of legal problems and rules that can be effectively used also to understand other systems, and to communicate effectively with jurists from other systems. We call this the "Bruce Springsteen principle." Bruce Springsteen has acquired international fame, and is able to get his message across in virtually all countries and cultures, singing of things that could hardly be more local, including the New Jersey Turnpike and Asbury Park. Audiences in Ghana, Uruguay, Latvia and Burma equally understand and appreciate his lyrics. "Local" does not mean "provincial," and "international" does not mean "superficial": It all depends on your perspective and on how you work.

Most (hopefully not all) the readers of this book have a legal career ahead of them. But whatever your career will be, one thing is certain: it will require extensive learning. We hope this book has provided a piece of that learning, and comparing what you have learned here with what you will need to learn in the future, we can say, as Winston Churchill did after the battle of El Alamein was won: "Now this is not the end. It is not even the beginning of the end. But it is, perhaps, the end of the beginning."

INDEX

References are to Pages

657